Early United States

HARCOURT BRACE SOCIAL STUDIES

Series Authors

Dr. Richard G. Boehm

Claudia Hoone

Dr. Thomas M. McGowan

Dr. Mabel C. McKinney-Browning

Dr. Ofelia B. Miramontes

Dr. Priscilla H. Porter

Series Consultants

Dr. Alma Flor Ada

Dr. Phillip Bacon

Dr. W. Dorsey Hammond

Dr. Asa Grant Hilliard, III

HARCOURT BRACE & COMPANY

Orlando Atlanta Austin Boston San Francisco Chicago Dallas
New York Toronto London

 Visit The Learning Site at http://www.hbschool.com

Copyright © 2000 by Harcourt Brace & Company

All rights reserved. No part of this publication may be reproduced or transmitted in any form or by any means, electronic or mechanical, including photocopy, recording, or any information storage and retrieval system, without permission in writing from the publisher.

Requests for permission to make copies of any part of the work should be mailed to the following address: School Permissions, Harcourt Brace & Company, 6277 Sea Harbor Drive, Orlando, Florida 32887-6777.

HARCOURT BRACE and Quill Design is a registered trademark of Harcourt Brace & Company.

Acknowledgments and other credits appear in the back of this book.

Printed in the United States of America

ISBN 0-15-309788-4

6 7 8 9 10   032   02   01   00

Contents

2

CHAPTER 3

Amerigo Vespucci

CHAPTER 4

Motecuhzoma

v

Juan Bautista de Anza

A British colonist

John Adams

Mercy Otis Warren

7

CHAPTER 13

Frederick Douglass

CHAPTER 14

Edwin Jennison

CHAPTER 15

Bella Schonbach

CHAPTER 16

Cinthya Guzman

For Your Reference

The Lincoln Memorial, Washington, D.C.

F.Y.I.

Time Lines

F.Y.I.

Charts, Graphs, Diagrams, and Tables

Atlas

Contents

Atlas

The World: Political

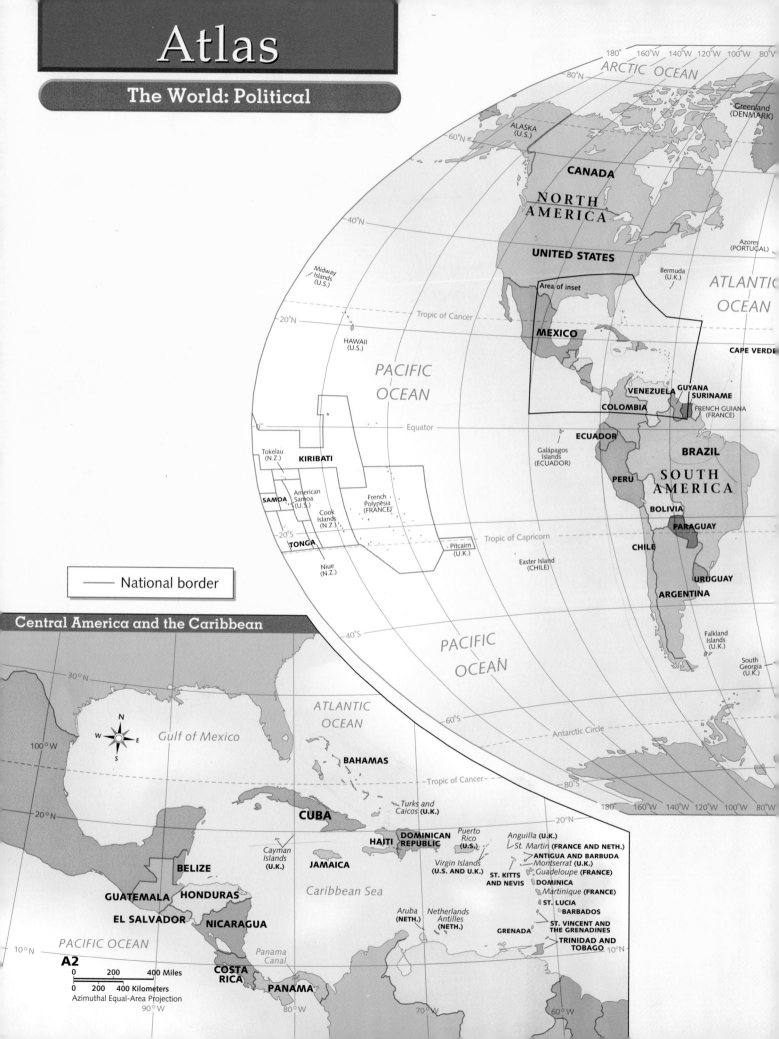

ARCTIC OCEAN

180° 160°W 140°W 120°W 100°W 80°

80°N

Greenland (DENMARK)

ALASKA (U.S.)

CANADA

NORTH AMERICA

40°N

UNITED STATES

Azores (PORTUGAL)

ATLANTIC OCEAN

Bermuda (U.K.)

Area of inset

20°N   Tropic of Cancer

MEXICO

CAPE VERDE

Midway Islands (U.S.)

HAWAII (U.S.)

PACIFIC OCEAN

VENEZUELA   GUYANA   SURINAME

COLOMBIA

FRENCH GUIANA (FRENCH)

Equator

ECUADOR

Galápagos Islands (ECUADOR)

BRAZIL

Tokelau (N.Z.)

KIRIBATI

SOUTH AMERICA

PERU

SAMOA

American Samoa (U.S.)

French Polynesia (FRANCE)

BOLIVIA

Cook Islands (N.Z.)

PARAGUAY

20°S

TONGA

Pitcairn (U.K.)

Tropic of Capricorn

CHILE

URUGUAY

Niue (N.Z.)

Easter Island (CHILE)

ARGENTINA

── National border

40°S

PACIFIC OCEAN

Falkland Islands (U.K.)

South Georgia (U.K.)

60°S

Antarctic Circle

80°S

180° 160°W 140°W 120°W 100°W 80°W

Central America and the Caribbean

30°N

ATLANTIC OCEAN

20°N

Gulf of Mexico

BAHAMAS

100°W

Tropic of Cancer

Turks and Caicos (U.K.)

20°N

CUBA

Cayman Islands (U.K.)

JAMAICA

HAITI

DOMINICAN REPUBLIC

Puerto Rico (U.S.)

Anguilla (U.K.)
St. Martin (FRANCE AND NETH.)
ANTIGUA AND BARBUDA
Montserrat (U.K.)
Guadeloupe (FRANCE)
DOMINICA
Martinique (FRANCE)
ST. LUCIA
BARBADOS
ST. VINCENT AND THE GRENADINES
TRINIDAD AND TOBAGO

Virgin Islands (U.S. AND U.K.)

ST. KITTS AND NEVIS

BELIZE

Caribbean Sea

GUATEMALA   HONDURAS

Aruba (NETH.)

Netherlands Antilles (NETH.)

EL SALVADOR

NICARAGUA

GRENADA

PACIFIC OCEAN

10°N

Panama Canal

10°N

A2

0   200   400 Miles

0   200   400 Kilometers

Azimuthal Equal-Area Projection

COSTA RICA

PANAMA

90°W   80°W   70°W   60°W

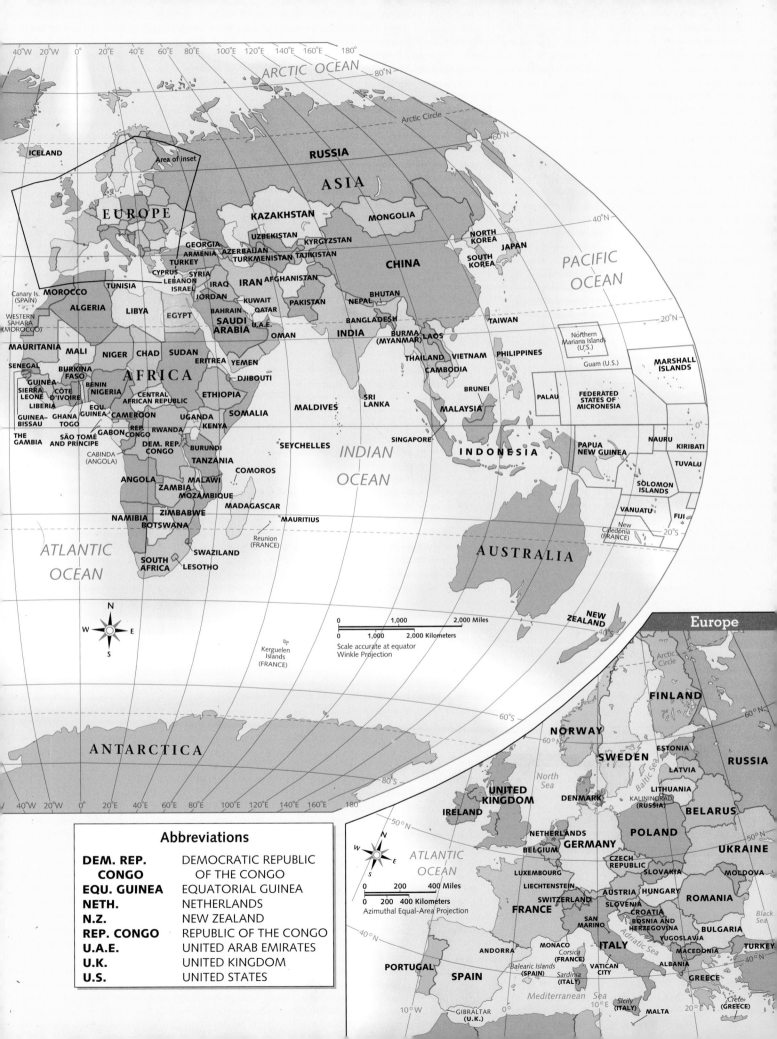

Atlas

The World: Physical

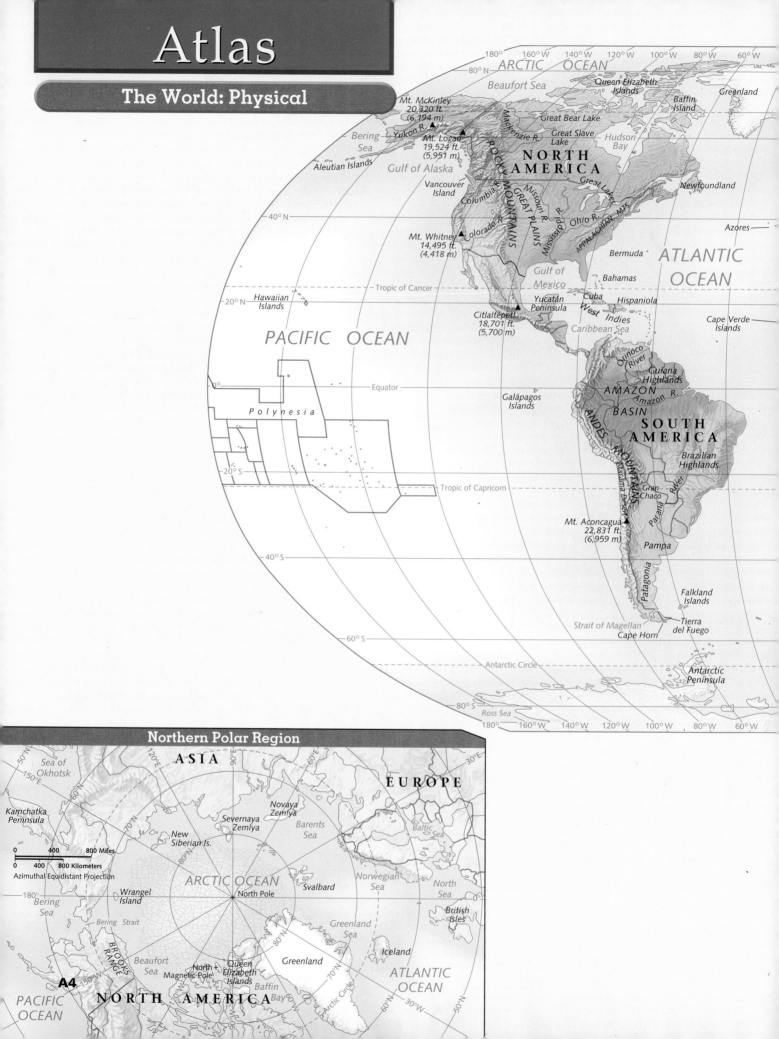

ARCTIC OCEAN
80° N
Beaufort Sea
Queen Elizabeth Islands
Greenland
Baffin Island
Great Bear Lake
Mackenzie R.
Great Slave Lake
Hudson Bay

Mt. McKinley 20,320 ft. (6,194 m)
Bering Sea
Yukon R.
Mt. Logan 19,524 ft. (5,951 m)
ROCKY MOUNTAINS
NORTH AMERICA
Aleutian Islands
Gulf of Alaska
Vancouver Island
Columbia R.
GREAT PLAINS
Missouri R.
Mississippi R.
Ohio R.
Great Lakes
APPALACHIAN MTS.
Newfoundland
Azores

40° N
Mt. Whitney 14,495 ft. (4,418 m)
Colorado R.
Bermuda
ATLANTIC OCEAN

Tropic of Cancer
20° N
Hawaiian Islands
Gulf of Mexico
Bahamas
Citlaltépetl 18,701 ft. (5,700 m)
Yucatán Peninsula
Cuba
West Indies
Hispaniola

PACIFIC OCEAN
Caribbean Sea
Cape Verde Islands
Galápagos Islands
Orinoco River
Guiana Highlands

Equator
0°
AMAZON
Amazon R.
Polynesia
BASIN
SOUTH AMERICA
ANDES MOUNTAINS
Brazilian Highlands

20° S
Gran Chaco
Atacama Desert
Paraná River

Tropic of Capricorn
Mt. Aconcagua 22,831 ft. (6,959 m)
Pampa

40° S
Patagonia
Falkland Islands

Strait of Magellan
Tierra del Fuego
Cape Horn

60° S
Antarctic Circle
Antarctic Peninsula

80° S
Ross Sea
180° 160° W 140° W 120° W 100° W 80° W 60° W

180° 160° W 140° W 120° W 100° W 80° W 60° W

Northern Polar Region

ASIA
EUROPE
Sea of Okhotsk
Kamchatka Peninsula
Novaya Zemlya
Severnaya Zemlya
Barents Sea
Baltic Sea
New Siberian Is.

0   400   800 Miles
0   400   800 Kilometers
Azimuthal Equidistant Projection

ARCTIC OCEAN
North Pole
Svalbard
Norwegian Sea
North Sea

Wrangel Island
Bering Sea
Bering Strait
Greenland Sea
British Isles

BROOKS RANGE
Beaufort Sea
North Magnetic Pole
Queen Elizabeth Islands
Greenland
Iceland
ATLANTIC OCEAN
Arctic Circle

A4
PACIFIC OCEAN
NORTH AMERICA
Baffin Bay

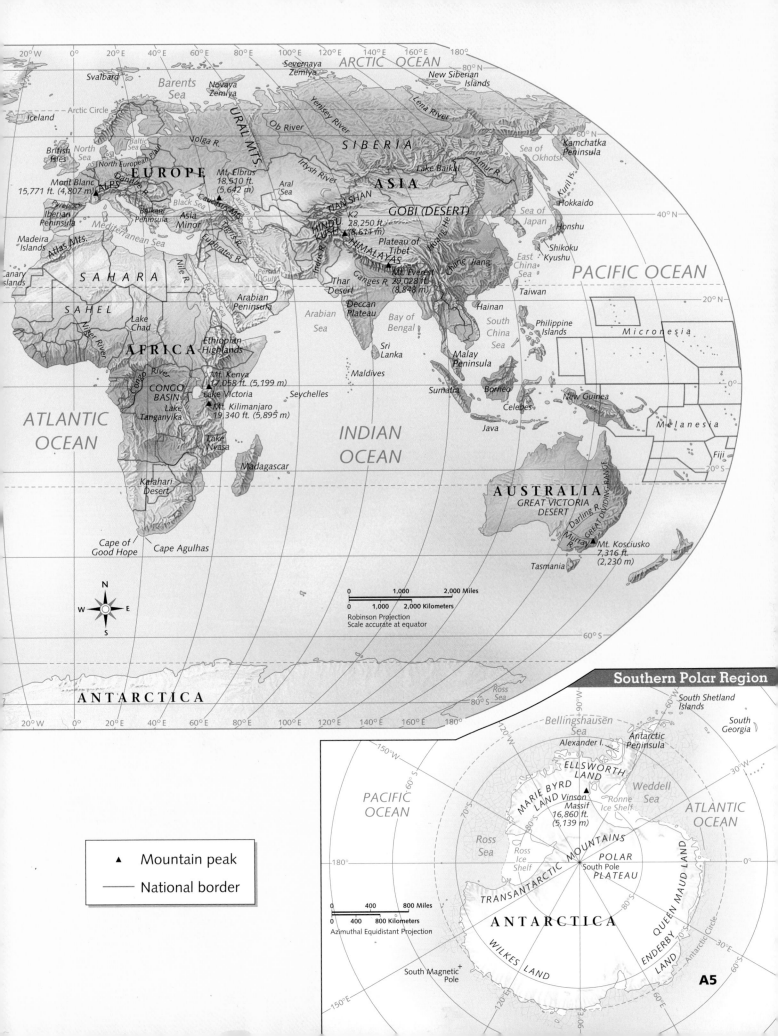

20°W 0° 20°E 40°E 60°E 80°E 100°E 120°E 140°E 160°E 180°

ARCTIC OCEAN

Svalbard
Barents Sea
Novaya Zemlya
Severnaya Zemlya
New Siberian Islands
80°N

Iceland
Arctic Circle
60°N

URAL MTS.
Volga R.
Yenisey River
Ob River
Irtysh River
Lena River
SIBERIA
Amur R.
Kamchatka Peninsula
Sea of Okhotsk

British Isles
North Sea
Baltic Sea
North European Plain
EUROPE
Mont Blanc 15,771 ft. (4,807 m)
ALPS
Danube R.
Caucasus Mts.
Mt. Elbrus 18,510 ft. (5,642 m)
Caspian Sea
Aral Sea
ASIA
Lake Baikal
Kuril Is.
Hokkaido
Sea of Japan
40°N

Pyrenees
Iberian Peninsula
Balkan Peninsula
Black Sea
Asia Minor
TIAN SHAN
K2 28,250 ft. (8,611 m)
HINDU KUSH
GOBI (DESERT)
Plateau of Tibet
Honshu
Shikoku
Kyushu

Madeira Islands
Atlas Mts.
Mediterranean Sea
Tigris R.
Euphrates R.
HIMALAYAS
Mt. Everest 29,028 ft. (8,848 m)
Chang Jiang
Huang He
East China Sea
Taiwan

Canary Islands
SAHARA
Nile R.
Persian Gulf
Arabian Peninsula
Indus R.
Thar Desert
Ganges R.
Deccan Plateau
PACIFIC OCEAN
20°N

SAHEL
Lake Chad
Arabian Sea
Bay of Bengal
South China Sea
Hainan
Philippine Islands
Micronesia

Niger River
AFRICA
Ethiopian Highlands
Mt. Kenya 17,058 ft. (5,199 m)
Lake Victoria
Sri Lanka
Maldives
Malay Peninsula

ATLANTIC OCEAN
Congo River
CONGO BASIN
Lake Tanganyika
Mt. Kilimanjaro 19,340 ft. (5,895 m)
Seychelles
Sumatra
Borneo
Celebes
New Guinea
Melanesia

Lake Nyasa
INDIAN OCEAN
Java
Fiji
20°S

Madagascar
AUSTRALIA
GREAT VICTORIA DESERT

Kalahari Desert
Darling R.
GREAT DIVIDING RANGE

Cape of Good Hope
Cape Agulhas
Murray R.
Mt. Kosciusko 7,316 ft. (2,230 m)

Tasmania

N
W E
S

0 1,000 2,000 Miles
0 1,000 2,000 Kilometers
Robinson Projection
Scale accurate at equator

60°S

Ross Sea
80°S

ANTARCTICA

20°W 0° 20°E 40°E 60°E 80°E 100°E 120°E 140°E 160°E 180°

▲ Mountain peak
— National border

Southern Polar Region

South Shetland Islands
South Georgia
Bellingshausen Sea
Alexander I.
Antarctic Peninsula
ELLSWORTH LAND
Weddell Sea

PACIFIC OCEAN
MARIE BYRD LAND
Vinson Massif 16,860 ft. (5,139 m)
Ronne Ice Shelf
ATLANTIC OCEAN

Ross Sea
Ross Ice Shelf
TRANSANTARCTIC MOUNTAINS
South Pole
POLAR PLATEAU
QUEEN MAUD LAND

180°
ANTARCTICA
ENDERBY LAND

WILKES LAND
Antarctic Circle

0 400 800 Miles
0 400 800 Kilometers
Azimuthal Equidistant Projection

South Magnetic Pole

A5

Atlas

Western Hemisphere: Physical

ARCTIC OCEAN

North Magnetic Pole +

Ellesmere Island

Queen Elizabeth Islands

Melville Island

Devon Island

Baffin Bay

Greenland

Viscount Melville Sound

Point Barrow

Beaufort Sea

Banks Island

Victoria Island

Brooks Range

Great Bear Lake

Foxe Basin

Baffin Island

Mt. McKinley 20,320 ft. (6,194 m)

Yukon River

Mackenzie Mts

Mackenzie River

Great Slave Lake

Hudson Strait

Arctic Circle

60° N

Alaska Range

Yukon Plateau

Liard R.

Peace River

CANADIAN

Hudson Bay

Labrador Sea

Cape Farewell

Davis Strait

Gulf of Alaska

Mt. Logan 19,524 ft. (5,951 m)

Coast Mountains

Athabasca R.

Saskatchewan River

Lake Athabasca

Lake Winnipeg

James Bay

SHIELD

Labrador

Alaska Peninsula

Kodiak Island

Queen Charlotte Islands

ROCKY

GREAT

NORTH AMERICA

Newfoundland

Gulf of St. Lawrence

Aleutian Islands

Vancouver Island

Cascade Range

MOUNTAINS

PLAINS

Great Lakes

St. Lawrence R.

Nova Scotia

Puget Sound

Coast Ranges

Snake R.

Black Hills

Missouri R.

Mississippi

Platte R.

INTERIOR PLAINS

Ohio R.

APPALACHIAN MTS.

Bay of Fundy

Cape Cod

Long Island

Sierra Nevada

Great Salt Lake

GREAT BASIN

Colorado R.

Arkansas

Ozark Plateau

R.

Cape Hatteras

Mt. Whitney 14,495 ft. (4,418 m)

Death Valley (lowest point in N.A.) -282 ft. (-86 m)

Sonoran Desert

Rio

Grande

COASTAL PLAIN

ATLANTIC OCEAN

30° N

Baja California

Sierra Madre Occidental

Sierra Madre Oriental

Gulf of Mexico

Bahamas

Tropic of Cancer

Hawaiian Islands

PACIFIC OCEAN

Gulf of California

Citlaltépetl 18,701 ft. (5,700 m)

Yucatán Peninsula

Cuba

Greater Antilles

Hispaniola

Puerto Rico

Lesser Antilles

Lake Nicaragua

Caribbean Sea

Line Islands

Isthmus of Panama

Lake Maracaibo

Orinoco R.

Guiana Highlands

Equator

Marquesas Islands

Galápagos Islands

Chimborazo 20,561 ft. (6,267 m)

Llanos

Río Negro

Amazon R.

Cape São Roque

ANDES

AMAZON

BASIN

Tapajós R.

Xingu River

Tocantins R.

São Francisco River

Cook Islands

Tuamotu Archipelago

Huascarán 22,205 ft. (6,768 m)

Lake Titicaca

Altiplano

Paraguay R.

Mato Grosso Plateau

Brazilian

Highlands

SOUTH

Society Islands

Atacama Desert

MOUNTAINS

AMERICA

Tropic of Capricorn

Gran Chaco

Paraná R.

Uruguay R.

Iguazú Falls

30° S

0   1,000   2,000 Miles

0   1,000   2,000 Kilometers

Miller Cylindrical Projection

Mt. Aconcagua 22,831 ft. (6,959 m)

Pampa

Rio de la Plata

▲ Mountain peak

▼ Point below sea level

— National border

≈ Waterfall

Patagonia

Valdés Peninsula (lowest point in S.A.) -131 ft. (-40 m)

N
W   E
S

A7
South Georgia

Falkland Islands

Strait of Magellan

Tierra del Fuego

Cape Horn

150° W   120° W   90° W   60° W   30° W

RUSSIA

Bering Sea

60°N

ALASKA
(AK)

180°

40°N

PACIFIC OCEAN

WASHINGTON
(WA)

OREGON
(OR)

NEVADA
(NV)

CALIFORNIA
(CA)

0   250   500 Miles
0   250   500 Kilometers
Modified Azimuthal Equal-Area Projection

National border
State border
⊛ National capital

N
W   E
S

Tropic of Cancer

160°W   HAWAII
(HI)
20°N

140°W   120°W

ICELAND

Greenland

Arctic Circle

40° W

60° N

CANADA

Hudson
Bay

40° W

MONTANA
(MT)

NORTH
DAKOTA
(ND)

MINNESOTA
(MN)

Lake Superior

MICHIGAN

Lake Huron

VERMONT
(VT)

MAINE
(ME)

IDAHO
(ID)

WYOMING
(WY)

SOUTH
DAKOTA
(SD)

WISCONSIN
(WI)

MICHIGAN
(MI)

Lake Michigan

Lake
Ontario

Lake Erie

NEW
YORK
(NY)

NEW HAMPSHIRE
(NH)

MASSACHUSETTS
(MA)

RHODE ISLAND (RI)

60° W

40° N

UTAH
(UT)

COLORADO
(CO)

NEBRASKA
(NE)

IOWA
(IA)

ILLINOIS
(IL)

INDIANA
(IN)

OHIO
(OH)

PENNSYLVANIA
(PA)

NEW
JERSEY
(NJ)

CONNECTICUT
(CT)

DELAWARE
(DE)

Washington,
D.C.

WEST
VIRGINIA
(WV)

MARYLAND
(MD)

ARIZONA
(AZ)

NEW MEXICO
(NM)

KANSAS
(KS)

MISSOURI
(MO)

KENTUCKY
(KY)

VIRGINIA
(VA)

OKLAHOMA
(OK)

ARKANSAS
(AR)

TENNESSEE
(TN)

NORTH
CAROLINA
(NC)

TEXAS
(TX)

MISSISSIPPI
(MS)

ALABAMA
(AL)

GEORGIA
(GA)

SOUTH
CAROLINA
(SC)

LOUISIANA
(LA)

ATLANTIC OCEAN

FLORIDA
(FL)

BAHAMAS

MEXICO

Gulf of Mexico

CUBA

DOMINICAN
REPUBLIC

20° N

A9 PUERTO
RICO (U.S.)

HAITI

100° W

80° W

20° N

Atlas

United States: Political

RUSSIA

ARCTIC OCEAN

70° N

120° W

ALASKA

Arctic Circle

170° E

Yukon River

CANADA

60° N

Fairbanks

Bering
Sea

Anchorage

Juneau

180°

PACIFIC
OCEAN

0   250   500 Miles
0   250   500 Kilometers

50° N

170° W   160° W   150° W   140° W   130° W

CANADA

120° W

110° W

CANADA

40° N

Seattle
★ Tacoma
Olympia   Spokane
WASHINGTON

Great Falls

Portland   Columbia River
★ Salem
Eugene
OREGON

Helena ★ **MONTANA**

Billings

IDAHO

★ Boise

Snake River

WYOMING

Pocatello

Casper

PACIFIC

OCEAN

130° W

30° N

Sacramento ★

San Francisco
Oakland
San Jose

Reno
NEVADA
Carson City

Great
Salt
Lake

Ogden
★ Salt Lake City
Provo

UTAH

Cheyenne

Denver

Colorado
Spring

COLORADO

Puebl

Fresno

CALIFORNIA
Bakersfield

Colorado River

Las
Vegas

Los Angeles
San Bernardino

Flagstaff

ARIZONA

Santa Fe ★

Albuquerque

San Diego

★ Phoenix

NEW MEXICO

Roswell

Tucson

El Paso

Rio Grande

	Northeast	⊛	National capital
	Southeast	★	State capital
	Middle West	•	Major city
	Southwest	—	National border
	West	—	State border

MEXICO

N
W   E
S

160° W   PACIFIC   155° W
OCEAN

Honolulu ★

HAWAII

20° N

Hilo

0   100   200 Miles
0   100   200 Kilometers

0   250   500 Miles
0   250   500 Kilometers
Albers Equal-Area Projection

20° N

120° W

110° W

A10

Atlas

United States: Physical

RUSSIA

ARCTIC OCEAN

170° E

180°

70° N

Bering Strait

Brooks Range

ALASKA

Seward Peninsula

Yukon River

Arctic Circle

60° N

CANADA

Mt. McKinley 20,320 ft. (6,194 m)

Alaska Range

Yukon River

St. Lawrence Island

Bering Sea

160° W

Gulf of Alaska

Kodiak Island

Aleutian Islands

50° N

170° W

160° W

150° W

140° W

130° W

CANADA

MEXICO

120° W

110° W

WA

Mt. Rainier 14,410 ft. (4,392 m)

Mt. St. Helens 8,364 ft. (2,549 m)

Columbia River

Mt. Hood 11,235 ft. (3,427 m)

OR

Columbia Plateau

ID

Salmon River Mountains

Snake River

Bitterroot Range

ROCKY

MT

Fort Peck Lake

Yellowstone River

Bighorn Mts.

Wind River Range

Teton Range

WY

Great Divide Basin

Cape Mendocino

Coast Ranges

Cascade Range

Coast Ranges

Sacramento River

San Joaquin Valley

Sierra Nevada

Pyramid Lake

Donner Pass

Lake Tahoe

NV

G R E A T

B A S I N

Great Salt Lake

Wasatch Range

Uinta Mts.

MOUNTAIN

Mt. Elbert 14,433 ft. (4,399 m)

Front Range

San Juan Mts.

CO

Sangre de Cristo Mts.

Mt. Whitney 14,495 ft. (4,418 m)

CA

Death Valley -282 ft. (-86 m)

Mojave Desert

Lake Mead

Lake Powell

Colorado River

Grand Canyon

C o l o r a d o

P l a t e a u

UT

PACIFIC OCEAN

Point Conception

Channel Islands

Salton Sea

Imperial Valley

Sonoran Desert

AZ

Baldy Peak 11,403 ft. (3,476 m)

NM

Guadalupe Peak 8,749 ft. (2,667 m)

Rio Grande

MEXICO

Legend

	Arid
	Evergreen forest
	Grassland
	Mixed forest
	Mountains
	Tundra
▬	National border
—	State border
▲	Mountain peak
△	Highest point
▽	Lowest point

Alaska inset scale

0 — 250 — 500 Miles
0 — 250 — 500 Kilometers

Hawaii inset

160° W

155° W

PACIFIC OCEAN

Kauai

Niihau

Oahu

Molokai

Lanai

Maui

HAWAII

Kahoolawe

Hawaii

Mauna Kea 13,796 ft. (4,205 m)

20° N

0 — 100 — 200 Miles
0 — 100 — 200 Kilometers

Main map scale

N
W — E
S

0 — 250 — 500 Miles
0 — 250 — 500 Kilometers

Albers Equal-Area Projection

40° N

30° N

130° W

120° W

20° N

110° W

100°W 90°W 80°W 70°W

50°N

CANADA

St. Lawrence River

ME
Moosehead Lake
Mt. Katahdin
5,267 ft.
(1,605 m)

Lake of the Woods

Upper Red Lake
Lower Red Lake
Leech Lake
Mille Lacs Lake

Isle Royale
Keweenaw Peninsula

Lake Superior

Mesabi Range

Lake Sakakawea

ND

MN

WI

Wisconsin River

Upper Peninsula

Lake Michigan

Lower Peninsula

Lake Huron

Lake Ontario

VT
NY
Adirondack Mountains
Finger Lakes
Green Mts.
White Mts.
Mt. Washington
6,288 ft.
(1,917 m)
NH
Cape Ann
MA
Cape Cod
Lake Champlain
Niagara Falls
Hudson R.
Connecticut R.
CT
RI

Lake Oahe

SD

IA

Lake Winnebago

MI
Lake St. Clair

Lake Erie

PA

Allegheny Mts.
APPALACHIAN MOUNTAINS

Long Island

40°N

Black Hills

Sand Hills

NE

North Platte R.
South Platte R.
Platte River

G R E A T   P L A I N S

I N T E R I O R
P L A I N S

IL
Illinois River
Wabash River
IN

OH

WV
Ohio River
VA
Potomac R.
MD
DE
Delaware Bay

Cape Charles
Chesapeake Bay

70°W

Smoky Hills

KS

Red Hills

Missouri River

MO
Lake of the Ozarks
Harry S. Truman Reservoir

CENTRAL PLAINS

Mississippi River

KY
Lake Barkley
Cumberland Gap
Cumberland R.
Mt. Mitchell
6,684 ft.
(2,037 m)

Roanoke R.
James R.
NC
Albemarle Sound

Cape Hatteras

P I E D M O N T

Ozark Plateau

Arkansas
River

Canadian
River

OK

Red River

Ouachita Mountains
Lake Texoma

AR

Cape Fear River

SC
Stone Mountain
Clark Hill Lake
Savannah River

Cape Fear

C O A S T A L   **P L A I N**

ATLANTIC OCEAN

Llano
Estacado

Sabine River

MS
Tombigbee R.
AL
Alabama R.
Chattahoochee R.
GA
Oconee R.
Altamaha R.
Okefenokee Swamp

30°N

TX
Edwards Plateau

Pecos River

Brazos River

Colorado River

Sam Rayburn Reservoir

Toledo Bend Reservoir

LA
Lake Maurepas
Lake Pontchartrain

Mississippi Delta

Mobile Bay

St. Johns River

Cape Canaveral

Galveston Bay

Gulf of Mexico

Tampa Bay
Lake Okeechobee

FL

Everglades

Cape Sable
Florida Keys
Straits of Florida

BAHAMAS

CUBA

100°W 90°W 80°W

United States: Population Density

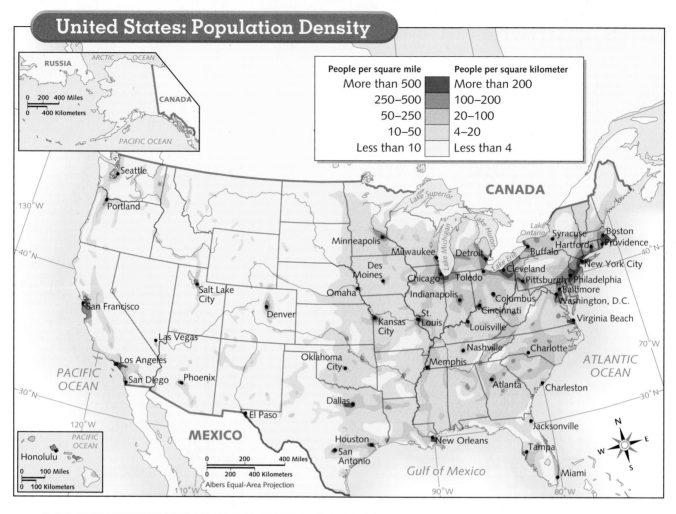

People per square mile
- More than 500
- 250–500
- 50–250
- 10–50
- Less than 10

People per square kilometer
- More than 200
- 100–200
- 20–100
- 4–20
- Less than 4

RUSSIA
ARCTIC OCEAN
CANADA
PACIFIC OCEAN
0 200 400 Miles
0 400 Kilometers

Seattle
Portland
130°W
40°N
San Francisco
PACIFIC OCEAN
Las Vegas
Los Angeles
San Diego
Phoenix
30°N
120°W
110°W
MEXICO

Salt Lake City
Denver

Minneapolis
Milwaukee
Des Moines
Chicago
Omaha
Kansas City
St. Louis
Oklahoma City
Dallas
El Paso
Houston
San Antonio
New Orleans
Memphis
Nashville
Indianapolis
Cincinnati
Louisville
Columbus
Toledo
Detroit
Cleveland
Pittsburgh
Buffalo

CANADA
Lake Superior
Lake Michigan
Lake Huron
Lake Ontario
Lake Erie
Syracuse
Boston
Hartford
Providence
New York City
Philadelphia
Baltimore
Washington, D.C.
Virginia Beach
Charlotte
Atlanta
Charleston
Jacksonville
Tampa
Miami
ATLANTIC OCEAN
70°W
80°W
90°W
30°N
40°N

Gulf of Mexico
Honolulu
PACIFIC OCEAN
0 100 Miles
0 100 Kilometers
0 200 400 Miles
0 200 400 Kilometers
Albers Equal-Area Projection

United States: Land Use and Resources

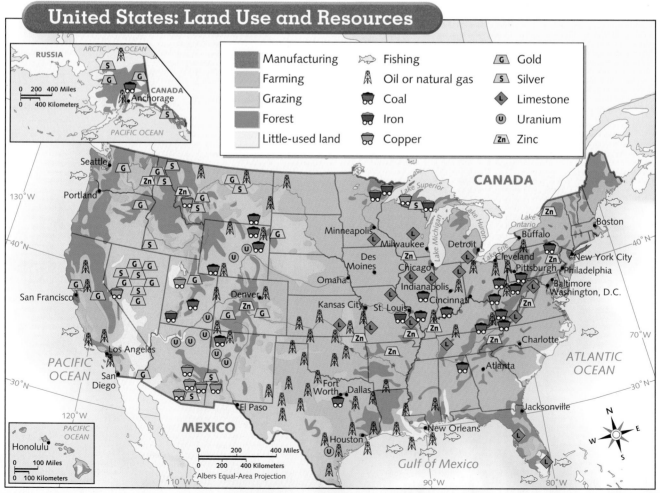

- Manufacturing
- Farming
- Grazing
- Forest
- Little-used land

- 🐟 Fishing
- Oil or natural gas
- Coal
- Iron
- Copper

- G Gold
- S Silver
- L Limestone
- U Uranium
- Zn Zinc

RUSSIA
ARCTIC OCEAN
CANADA
Anchorage
0 200 400 Miles
0 400 Kilometers
PACIFIC OCEAN

Seattle
Portland
130°W
40°N
San Francisco
Los Angeles
San Diego
PACIFIC OCEAN
30°N
120°W
110°W
MEXICO
El Paso

Denver
Kansas City
Minneapolis
Milwaukee
Des Moines
Chicago
Omaha
St. Louis
Indianapolis
Cincinnati
Fort Worth
Dallas
Houston
New Orleans

CANADA
Lake Superior
Lake Michigan
Lake Huron
Lake Ontario
Lake Erie
Detroit
Cleveland
Pittsburgh
Buffalo
Boston
New York City
Philadelphia
Baltimore
Washington, D.C.
Charlotte
Atlanta
Jacksonville
ATLANTIC OCEAN
70°W
80°W
90°W
30°N
40°N

Gulf of Mexico
Honolulu
PACIFIC OCEAN
0 100 Miles
0 100 Kilometers
0 200 400 Miles
0 200 400 Kilometers
Albers Equal-Area Projection

A14

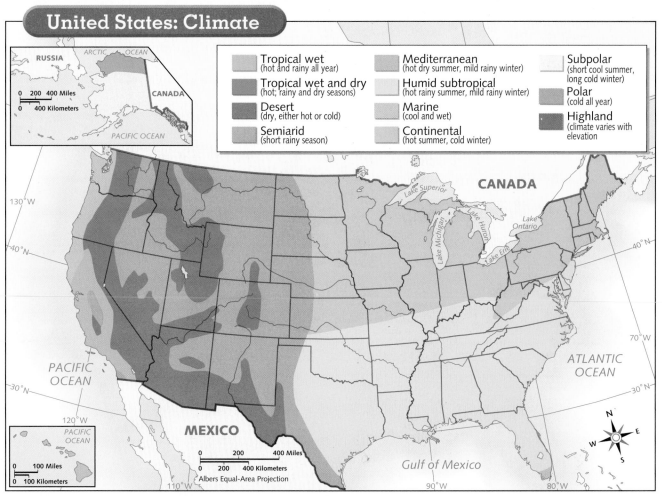

United States: Climate

RUSSIA · ARCTIC OCEAN · CANADA · PACIFIC OCEAN

Legend:
- **Tropical wet** (hot and rainy all year)
- **Tropical wet and dry** (hot; rainy and dry seasons)
- **Desert** (dry, either hot or cold)
- **Semiarid** (short rainy season)
- **Mediterranean** (hot dry summer, mild rainy winter)
- **Humid subtropical** (hot rainy summer, mild rainy winter)
- **Marine** (cool and wet)
- **Continental** (hot summer, cold winter)
- **Subpolar** (short cool summer, long cold winter)
- **Polar** (cold all year)
- **Highland** (climate varies with elevation)

CANADA · Lake Superior · Lake Michigan · Lake Huron · Lake Ontario · Lake Erie · PACIFIC OCEAN · ATLANTIC OCEAN · MEXICO · Gulf of Mexico

130°W · 120°W · 110°W · 90°W · 80°W · 70°W · 40°N · 30°N

0 200 400 Miles
0 400 Kilometers

0 100 Miles
0 100 Kilometers

0 200 400 Miles
0 200 400 Kilometers
Albers Equal-Area Projection

N E S W

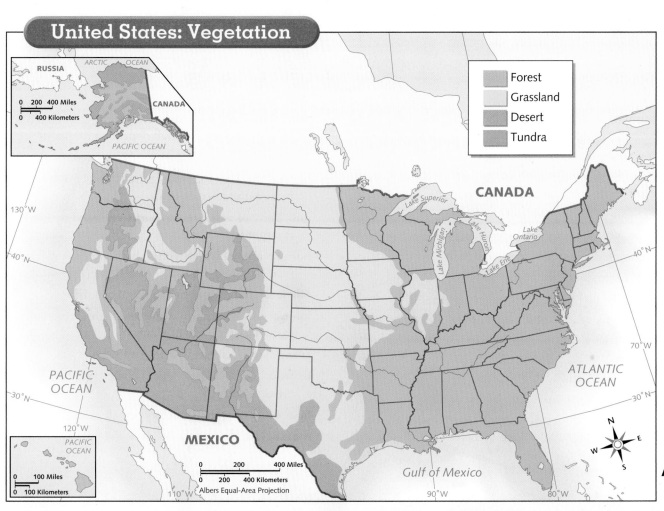

United States: Vegetation

RUSSIA · ARCTIC OCEAN · CANADA · PACIFIC OCEAN

Legend:
- **Forest**
- **Grassland**
- **Desert**
- **Tundra**

CANADA · Lake Superior · Lake Michigan · Lake Huron · Lake Ontario · Lake Erie · PACIFIC OCEAN · ATLANTIC OCEAN · MEXICO · Gulf of Mexico

130°W · 120°W · 110°W · 90°W · 80°W · 70°W · 40°N · 30°N

0 200 400 Miles
0 400 Kilometers

0 100 Miles
0 100 Kilometers

0 200 400 Miles
0 200 400 Kilometers
Albers Equal-Area Projection

N E S W

A15

Atlas

Geography Terms

Timberline

Sea level
Glacier
Slope
MOUNTAIN RANGE

Inlet
PLATEAU
VALLEY

Canyon
Fall line

Mesa
PLAIN

COASTAL PLAIN

Coast
Lake

Sea level
Mouth of river
Channel

Isthmus

Peninsula

Cape

OCEAN

---

basin bowl-shaped area of land surrounded by higher land

bay body of water that is part of a sea or ocean and is partly enclosed by land

bluff high, steep face of rock or earth

canyon deep, narrow valley with steep sides

cape point of land that extends into water

channel deepest part of a body of water

cliff high, steep face of rock or earth

coast land along a sea or ocean

coastal plain area of flat land along a sea or ocean

delta triangle-shaped area of land at the mouth of a river

desert dry land with few plants

dune hill of sand piled up by the wind

fall line area along which rivers form waterfalls or rapids as the rivers drop to lower land

floodplain flat land that is near the edges of a river and is formed by the silt deposited by floods

foothills hilly area at the base of a mountain

glacier large ice mass that moves slowly down a mountain or across land

gulf body of water that is partly enclosed by land but is larger than a bay

harbor area of water where ships can dock safely near land

hill land that rises above the land around it

inlet a narrow strip of water leading into the land from a larger body of water

island land that has water on all sides

isthmus narrow strip of land connecting two larger areas of land

lake body of water with land on all sides

marsh lowland with moist soil and tall grasses

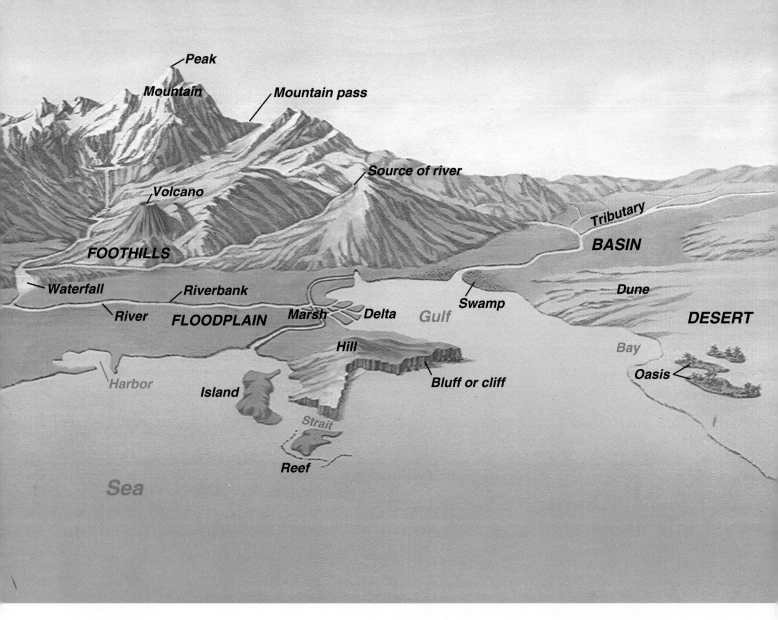

Peak

Mountain

Mountain pass

Source of river

Volcano

Tributary

BASIN

FOOTHILLS

Waterfall

Riverbank

Dune

River

FLOODPLAIN

Marsh

Delta

Gulf

Swamp

DESERT

Harbor

Hill

Bay

Island

Bluff or cliff

Oasis

Strait

Reef

Sea

mesa flat-topped mountain with steep sides

mountain highest kind of land

mountain pass gap between mountains

mountain range row of mountains

mouth of river place where a river empties into another body of water

oasis area of water and fertile land in a desert

ocean body of salt water larger than a sea

peak top of a mountain

peninsula land that is almost completely surrounded by water

plain flat land

plateau area of high, flat land with steep sides

reef ridge of sand, rock, or coral that lies at or near the surface of a sea or ocean

river large stream of water that flows across the land

riverbank land along a river

sea body of salt water smaller than an ocean

sea level the level that is even with the surface of an ocean or sea

slope side of a hill or mountain

source of river place where a river begins

strait narrow channel of water connecting two larger bodies of water

swamp area of low, wet land with trees

timberline line on a mountain above which it is too cold for trees to grow

tributary stream or river that empties into a larger river

valley low land between hills or mountains

volcano opening in the Earth, often raised, through which lava, rock, ashes, and gases are forced out

waterfall steep drop from a high place to a lower place in a stream or river

WHY STUDY SOCIAL STUDIES?

"Every one of you already holds the important office of citizen. Over time you will become more and more involved in your community. You will need to know more about what being a citizen means. Social studies will help you learn about citizenship. That is why social studies is important in your life."

The authors of
*Harcourt Brace
Social Studies*

The Themes of Social Studies

T hink about the many groups of which you are a part. Your family, your class, and your community are different kinds of groups, and you are a member of each one. You are also a member—or **citizen**—of your town or city, your state, and your country. Citizens work to improve the many groups they belong to and to make their world a better place.

To help you think, feel, and act as a citizen, *Harcourt Brace Social Studies* begins every lesson with a question. That question connects the lesson to one or more of five themes, or key topics, of social studies. Citizens need to understand these themes in order to make decisions. Each question also links you to the lesson's story, helping you see how the story relates to your own life. The lesson helps you learn about being a citizen by letting you see how people from many places and times have thought, felt, and acted. Each lesson will help you organize your thinking around one or more of the following five themes of social studies.

In this painting by Howard Chandler Christy, American leaders are shown in 1787 signing the Constitution, the plan of government for the United States. By taking part in government, these leaders were carrying out the office of citizen.

Commonality and Diversity

In some ways people everywhere are alike. We all have the same basic needs for things such as food, clothing, and shelter. We all laugh, get angry, and have our feelings hurt. These are examples of our commonality (kah•muh•NA•luh•tee), or what we all share. At the same time, we need to understand that each person is different from everyone else. We each have our own ways of thinking, feeling, and acting. That is our diversity (duh•VER•suh•tee). Learning about commonality and diversity can help you see that every person is unique and deserves understanding and respect.

All people are alike in some ways, but each person has different ways of thinking, feeling, and acting.

Conflict and Cooperation

Because people are different from one another, they sometimes have conflicts, or disagreements. People can often settle their conflicts by cooperating, or working together. In social studies you will learn about the disagreements people have had in the past and about many of the ways people have found to settle their disagreements. You will also learn ways to cooperate and to settle conflicts in your own life.

Continuity and Change

While some things change over time, other things stay the same. Many things have stayed the same for years and will probably stay the same in the future. This means that they have continuity (kahn•tuhn•OO•uh•tee). Understanding continuity and change can help you see how things in the world came to be as they are. You will learn how a past event, or something that has happened, may have helped shape your life. You will also learn how present events can help you make better decisions about the future.

Individualism and Interdependence

Citizens can act by themselves to make a difference in the world. Their actions as individuals (in•duh•VIJ•wuhlz) may be helpful or harmful to other citizens. Much of the time, however, people do not act alone. They depend on others for help, and others depend on them. People depend on one another in families, schools, religious groups, government groups, and other groups and organizations. Such interdependence (in•ter•dih•PEN•duhns) connects citizens with one another.

Interaction Within Different Environments

People's actions affect other people. People's actions also affect their environment (in•VY•ruhn•muhnt), or surroundings. This is true of their physical environment, their home environment, their school environment, and any other environments of which they may be a part. Their environments affect them, too. Understanding such interactions is important to understanding why things happened in the past and why things happen today.

Understanding interaction is important for understanding social studies. The subjects that make up social studies are all related. You will learn, for example, that history—the study of the past—is related to geography—the study of the Earth's surface and the way people use it. Civics and government, or the study of how people live together in a community, is related to economics, or the study of how people use resources. And all of these subjects are related to the study of culture. **Culture** is a people's way of life, including their customs, ideas, and practices. These subjects interact with one another to tell a story. Together they tell how people have lived over time and how they have made contributions as citizens. Understanding this story will help you learn how to hold the office of citizen.

When you take part in student government or other groups, you are also carrying out the office of citizen. Understanding each of the themes of social studies will help you make decisions as a citizen.

REVIEW *What are the five themes of social studies?*

21

Read Social Studies

1. Why Learn This Skill?

Social studies is made up of stories about people, places, and events. Sometimes you read these stories in library books. At other times you read them in textbooks like this one. Knowing how to read social studies can make it easier to study and do your homework. It can help you find important ideas and learn about people, places, and events.

2. Getting Started

Your book is divided into eight units. At the beginning of each unit, you will find several pages that will help you preview the unit and predict what it will be about.

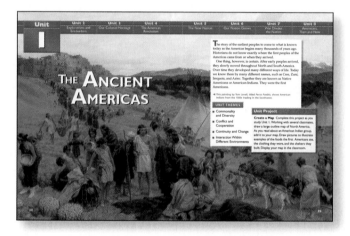

▲

Each unit begins with a short overview of the unit and a list of the social studies themes it teaches. You will also read about a project you can complete as you study the unit.

▲

The Unit Preview has a map that shows where some of the important events you will read about took place. It also has a time line that shows the order in which the events happened. There may be a story line that shows some of the people, places, or events.

▲

Each unit has at least one literature selection that helps you understand the time and place you are studying. The literature selection may be a story, or it may be a poem or a song.

3. The Parts of a Lesson

Each unit has two chapters, and each chapter is divided into lessons. The first two pages and the last two pages of a lesson are shown below.

The time line shows the period of time in which the events in the lesson took place.

This question helps you see how the lesson relates to life today.

This statement gives you the lesson's main idea. It tells you what to look for as you read the lesson.

These are the new terms you will learn in the lesson.

Each new vocabulary term is highlighted in yellow and defined.

Each lesson, like each chapter and each unit, ends with a review. A time line may show the order of some of the events in the lesson. The review questions and activities help you check your understanding and show what you know.

4. Understand the Process

You can follow these steps to read any lesson in this book.

1 Preview the whole lesson.
- Look at the title and the headings to find out what the lesson is about.
- Look at the pictures, the captions, and the questions to get an idea of what is most important in the lesson.
- Read the Focus question at the beginning of the lesson to see how the lesson relates to life today.
- Read the Main Idea statement to find out the main idea of the lesson.
- Look at the Vocabulary list to see what new terms you will learn.

2 Read the lesson to learn more about the main idea. As you read, you will come to a number of questions with the label **REVIEW**. Be sure to answer these questions before you continue reading the lesson.

3 When you finish reading the lesson, say in your own words what you have learned.

4 Look back over the lesson. Then answer the Lesson Review questions from memory. These questions will help you check your understanding of the lesson. The activity at the end of the review will help you show what you know.

5. Some Other Parts of Your Book

Your textbook has many other features to help you learn. Some of them are shown below.

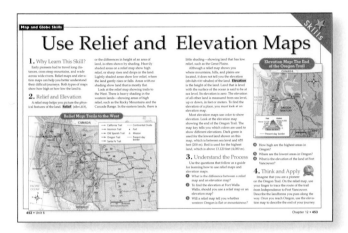

The feature called Making Social Studies Relevant helps you see how social studies is connected to your life and the lives of other people.

The skills lessons help you build basic study skills. They also help you build citizenship skills as you work with others.

The Counterpoints pages help you understand the different points of view people may have about certain issues.

At the back of your book is a section called *For Your Reference*. It includes the following reference tools.

- How to Gather and Report Information
- Almanac
- American Documents
- Biographical Dictionary
- Gazetteer
- Glossary
- Index

6. Think and Apply

Use the four steps in Understand the Process each time you read a lesson in *Harcourt Brace Social Studies*.

History

History helps you see the links between the past and the present. It also helps you understand how things that happen today can affect the future. History is about what happened last month and last year as well as in the ancient past.

As you read about the people, places, and events of the past, ask yourself the four questions below. They will help you think more like a historian, a person who studies the past.

- What happened?
- Who took part in it?
- How and why did it happen?
- When did it happen?

What Happened?

To find out what really happened in the past, you need proof. You can find proof by studying two kinds of sources—primary sources and secondary sources. Historians use these kinds of sources in writing history.

Primary sources are the records made by people who saw or took part in an event. They may have written down their thoughts in a journal. They may have told their story in a letter or a poem. They may have taken a photograph, made a film, or painted a picture. Each of these records is a primary source, giving the people of today a direct link to a past event.

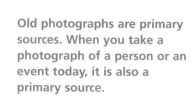

Old photographs are primary sources. When you take a photograph of a person or an event today, it is also a primary source.

A **secondary source** is not a direct link to an event. It is a record of the event written by someone who was not there at the time. A magazine article, newspaper story, or book written at a later time by someone who only heard or read about an event is a secondary source. A newspaper may include both primary sources and secondary sources.

When there are no written records of an event, historians gather proof through oral histories. An **oral history** can be either a primary or a secondary source, depending on the events a person describes. Oral histories tell the experiences of people who did not have a written language or who did not write down what happened. Oral histories can be recorded by writing down an interview with someone. Today they also can be recorded by making an audiotape or a videotape of the interview.

As you read this book, you will read many kinds of primary and secondary sources. The stories told in each lesson contain primary sources—the words and photographs of people in the past—as well as secondary sources written by historians. Maps, graphs, literature, pictures, and diagrams also help tell the stories you will read.

Newspapers help keep citizens aware of the events occurring all over the world. Newspapers and this textbook contain both primary and secondary sources.

You may gather information about the past through interviews.

Who Took Part in It?

To understand the stories of the past, you need to know something about the people who took part in the stories and about the times and places in which people lived. This will help you understand their actions and feelings. This understanding is called **historical empathy**.

By reading the words of people of the past, you can come to understand their **perspective**, or point of view. A person's perspective will depend on whether that person is old or young, man or woman, rich or poor. Perspective is also shaped by a person's culture and race. Your understanding of history will grow as you study the many perspectives of the people who took part in the stories. You will see that all people, even those living in other places and times, are a lot like you.

History lets you come face to face with people from the past.

How and Why Did It Happen?

Many events in history are linked to other events. To find the links between events, you will need to identify causes and effects. A **cause** is any action that makes something happen. What happens because of that action is an **effect**. Historians have found that most events have many causes and many effects.

To understand an event, you need to analyze its causes and effects. When you **analyze** something, you break it into its parts and look closely at how those parts connect with one another. Once you have analyzed an event, you can summarize it or draw a conclusion about how or why it happened.

When Did It Happen?

One way to tell or write a story of the past is to put the events in the order in which they happened. This presents the story's **chronology**, or time order. As you read this book, you will notice that it is organized by chronology. The events described at the beginning of the book happened before the events described at the end of the book.

You will see many time lines in this book. They will help you understand each story's chronology. A time line is a diagram that shows the events that took place during a certain period of time in the order in which they happened. Time lines may show a period of a month or a year. Others may show a period of 10 years, 100 years, or 1,000 years. Time lines can help you understand how one event may have led to another.

Time lines help you understand *when* in the past something happened.

REVIEW *What questions should you ask yourself when you read about the past?*

29

Work Together in Groups

1. Why Learn This Skill?

Many of the projects you do in social studies will be easier if you work with a partner or in a group. Each of you can work on part of the project. For a group project to succeed, each member needs to cooperate with the others. Knowing how to work together is an important skill for students and for all citizens.

2. Understand the Process

Suppose your group were asked to do a project, such as presenting a short play about everyday life long ago. You might find it helpful to follow a set of steps.

1 Organize and plan together.
- Set your goal as a group.
- Share your ideas.
- Cooperate with others to plan your work.
- Make sure everyone has a job.

2 Act on your plan together.
- Take responsibility for your work.
- Help one another.
- If there are conflicts, talk about them until they are settled.
- Show your group's finished work to the class.

3 Talk about your work.
- Discuss what you learned by working together.
- Discuss what could have been done differently to improve how your group worked together.

3. Think and Apply

Follow the steps above for working together as you take part in the activities in *Harcourt Brace Social Studies*.

These students are preparing for a class play about life in the American colonies.

Geography

The stories you will read in this book all have a setting. The setting of a story includes the place where it happens. Knowing about places is an important part of geography. **Geographers**, people whose work is to study geography, think about the following five topics or questions when they study a place.

- **Location**
  Where is it?
- **Place**
  What is it like there?
- **Human-environment interactions**
  How does this place affect the lives of people living there?
  How do people living there affect this place?
- **Movement**
  How and why do people, ideas, and goods move to and from this place?
- **Regions**
  How is this place like other places? How is it different?

Asking yourself these questions will help you understand the setting of a story. These five topics are so important that many people call them the five themes of geography.

Location

Everything on the Earth has its own location. To tell exactly where you live in your town or city, you can use the names and numbers of your home address. To find your **absolute location**, or exact location, on the Earth, you can use the numbers of your "global address." These numbers appear on a pattern of imaginary lines drawn on maps and globes. You will read more about these lines on pages 34–36 when you review how to read a map.

The location of a place can also be described in relation to the location of other places. You describe the **relative location** of a place when you say what it is near. You might say that the bus stop is on the corner by the gas station, or you might also say that the city of New Orleans is southeast of the city of St. Louis.

Place

Every location on the Earth has a place identity made up of unique features that make it different from all other locations. A place can be described by its **physical features**—landforms, bodies of water, climate, soil, plant and animal life, and other natural resources. Many places also have **human features**—buildings, bridges, farms, roads, and the people themselves. People's culture also helps form a place's identity.

The Golden Gate Bridge is a human feature that helps make the San Francisco skyline unique.

People are affected by the environment when floods cover the ground with muddy water.

Human-Environment Interactions

Humans and the environment interact, or behave in ways that affect each other. People interact with their environment in different ways. Sometimes they change it. They clear land to grow crops. They build cities and towns. Sometimes people pollute the environment. The environment can also cause people to change the way they act. People who live in cold places wear warm clothing. Sometimes things that happen in nature, such as hurricanes, tornadoes, and earthquakes, cause great changes in people's lives.

Movement

Each day, people in different parts of the country and different parts of the world interact with one another. People, products, and ideas move by transportation and communication. Geography helps you understand the causes and effects of this movement. It also helps you understand how people came to live where they do.

An air traffic controller helps track the movement of airplanes.

Regions

Areas on the Earth with features that make them different from other areas are called **regions**. A region can be described by the physical features, such as mountains or a dry climate, that exist there. A region can also be described by its human features, such as the language most of its people speak or the way they are governed. Sometimes a region is described by its political, cultural, or economic features.

Regions are sometimes divided into smaller regions that are easier to compare. Some geographers who study the Earth's surface and its people divide the United States into regions named for their relative locations—Northeast, Southeast, Middle West, Southwest, and West.

The states in each region are alike in many ways. They are all in the same part of the United States. They may have the same kind of landforms, climate, and natural resources. The people who live in those states often earn their living in the same ways. Dividing the 50 states into regions makes the geography of the United States easier to understand.

REVIEW *What are the five themes of geography?*

LEARNING FROM DIAGRAMS The 50 states are often grouped into five regions. The states in each region are all in the same part of the country.
■ *In which region of the United States is your state located?*

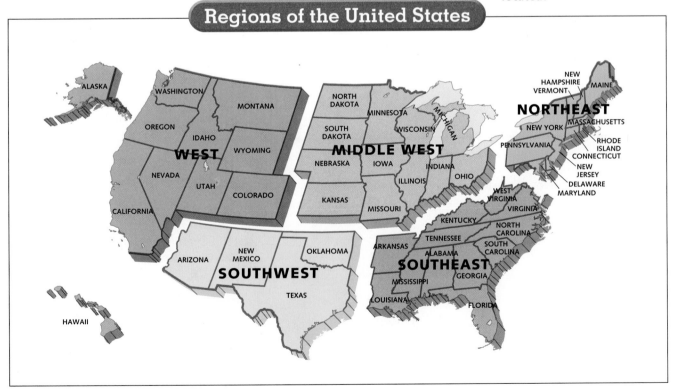

Regions of the United States

Read a Map

1. Why Learn This Skill?

To answer questions about the world around you, you need information. One way you can get this information is by studying maps. Maps tell you about the world by using one or more of the five themes of geography. Knowing how to read and understand maps is an important skill both for learning social studies and for taking action as a citizen.

2. The Parts of a Map

Maps are drawings that show the Earth or part of the Earth on a flat surface. To help you read maps, mapmakers add certain features to most maps they draw. These are a title, a map key, a compass rose, a locator, a map scale, and an inset map. Mapmakers may also put a grid of numbered lines on maps to help people locate places more easily.

The United States

National capital
State capital
National border
State border

The **map title** tells the subject of the map. What is the title of the map shown on page 34? A map title may also help you understand what kind of map it is. Physical maps show landforms and bodies of water. Sometimes, shading is used to help you see where the hills and mountains are located. Political maps show cities and national boundaries, or borders. Many of the maps in this book are historical maps that show the United States as it was in the past. Historical maps often have dates in their titles. When you look at any map, look for information in the title to find out what the map is about.

⊛ National capital

★ State capital

—— National border

—— State border

The **map key**, sometimes called a map legend, explains what the symbols on the map stand for. Symbols may be colors, patterns, lines, or other special marks, such as circles, triangles, or squares. According to the map key for the map on page 34, stars are used to show state capitals. What symbol is used to show the national capital?

The **compass rose**, or direction marker, shows the **cardinal directions**, or main directions—north, south, east, and west. A compass rose also helps you find the **intermediate directions**, which are between the cardinal directions. Intermediate directions are northeast, northwest, southeast, and southwest.

The **locator** is a small map or picture of a globe. It shows where the area shown on the main map is located in a state, in a country, on a continent, or in the world. The locator on the map of the United States on page 34 is a globe that shows the continent of North America. The United States is shown in red.

0		200		400 Miles
0	200		400 Kilometers	

The **map scale** compares a distance on a map to a distance in the real world. A map scale helps you find the real distance between places on a map. Each map in this book has a scale that shows both miles and kilometers.

Map scales are different, depending on the size of the area the map shows. Look at the map of the United States on page 34. On that map are two smaller maps—one of Alaska and one of Hawaii. A small map within a larger map is called an **inset map**. The boxes around Alaska and Hawaii show that they are inset maps. Inset maps have their own scales. Inset maps make it possible to show places in greater detail or to show places that are beyond the area shown on the main map.

The north-south and east-west lines on a map cross each other to form a pattern of squares called a **grid**. The east-west lines are **lines of latitude**. The north-south lines are **lines of longitude**. This grid helps you find the absolute location, or global address, of a place.

3. Understand the Process

Use the map of California on this page to answer the following questions.

1 What is the title of the map?

2 What three states share a border with California?

3 Find the map key. What symbol is used to show the state capital?

4 Find the compass rose. In which direction would you travel if you went from Bakersfield to Los Angeles?

5 Find the locator. How is the location of California shown?

6 Find the map scale. How long is the line that stands for 150 miles?

7 About how many miles is it from Redding to Sacramento?

8 Find the inset map. What is its title?

9 What line of latitude is closest to Stockton?

10 What line of longitude is closest to Monterey?

4. Think and Apply

Look again at the map of California. Find the different parts of the map, and discuss with a partner what information the map gives you about California.

California

San Francisco Area

- San Pablo Bay
- Vallejo
- Antioch
- Concord
- Berkeley
- Oakland
- San Francisco
- PACIFIC OCEAN
- San Francisco Bay
- Hayward
- Fremont
- Sunnyvale
- San Jose

0 5 10 Miles
0 5 10 Kilometers

OREGON

124°W 123°W 122°W 121°W 120°W 119°W 118°W 117°W 116°W 115°W 42°N

41°N
- Eureka
- Redding

40°N

39°N
- Sacramento ★

124°W
38°N
- San Francisco
- Oakland
- Stockton
- San Jose

37°N
- Monterey
- Fresno

36°N

PACIFIC OCEAN

35°N
0   75   150 Miles
0   75   150 Kilometers
Albers Equal-Area Projection

34°N
- Los Angeles
- Long Beach
- Palm Springs
- San Diego

NEVADA

N
W   E
S

38°N
37°N
36°N
35°N
34°N
33°N

ARIZONA

116°W 115°W
117°W
119°W 118°W

MEXICO

★ State capital
— National border
— State border

Civics and Government

Civics and government is the study of citizenship and the ways in which citizens govern themselves. A government is a system of leaders and laws that helps people live together in their community, state, or country. In the United States, citizens have an important part in making the government work. The laws that guide the actions of people are written and carried out by citizens.

In *Early United States* you will find out how the United States government works today. You will read about the people and events that shaped the government in the past. You will also learn about citizenship and the rights and responsibilities of citizens.

Economics

The **economy** of a country is the ways its people use its resources to meet their needs. The study of how people do this is called economics. In this book you will read about how people in the past made, bought, sold, and traded goods to get what they needed or wanted. You will learn how the economy of the United States came to be what it is today—an economy in which businesses are free to offer for sale many kinds of goods and services.

Culture

In this book you will learn about the people of the past who shaped the present. You will learn who these people were, what they looked like, and how they spoke and acted. You will explore their customs and beliefs and their ways of thinking and expressing ideas. You will look at their families and communities. All these things make up their culture. Each human group, or **society**, has a culture. This book will help you discover the many cultures that are part of our country's story, both past and present. You will also learn about our country's **heritage**, or culture that has come from the past and continues today.

REVIEW *What kinds of things do you learn when you study civics and government, economics, and culture?*

Unit

1

Unit 2
Explorations and
Encounters

Unit 3
Our Colonial Heritage

Unit 4
The American
Revolution

The Ancient Americas

The story of the earliest peoples to come to what is known today as the Americas begins many thousands of years ago. Historians do not know exactly where the first peoples of the Americas came from or when they arrived.

One thing, however, is certain. After early peoples arrived, they slowly moved throughout North and South America. Over time they developed many different ways of life. Today we know them by many different names, such as Cree, Zuni, Iroquois, and Aztec. Together they are known as Native Americans or American Indians. They were the first Americans.

◀ This painting by Tom Lovell, titled *Pecos Pueblo,* shows American Indians from the 1500s trading in the Southwest.

UNIT THEMES

- Commonality and Diversity
- Conflict and Cooperation
- Continuity and Change
- Interaction Within Different Environments

Unit Project

Create a Map Complete this project as you study Unit 1. Working with several classmates, draw a large outline map of North America. As you read about an American Indian group, add it to your map. Draw pictures to illustrate examples of the foods the first Americans ate, the clothing they wore, and the shelters they built. Display your map in the classroom.

ARCTIC OCEAN

Beaufort
Sea

Ellesmere
Island

Brooks Range

Bering
Sea

Yukon River

Victoria
Island

Alaska Range

Great
Bear
Lake

Aleutian Islands

Gulf of
Alaska

Mackenzie River

Great
Slave Lake

C A N A D I A N

Coast Mountains

R O C K Y

Lake
Winnipeg

Vancouver
Island

Columbia River

G R E A T   P L A I N S

M O U N T A I N S

Missouri River

Cascade Ranges

Coast Ranges

Mississippi
River

PACIFIC
OCEAN

GREAT
BASIN

Great
Salt
Lake

Sierra Nevada

Coast Ranges

Colorado River

Arkansas River

Sonoran
Desert

Rio Grande

Baja California

Gulf of California

Sierra Madre Occidental

Sierra Madre Oriental

Rio Balsas

0   500   1,000 Miles

0   500   1,000 Kilometers
Modified Azimuthal Equal-Area Projection

N
W   E
S

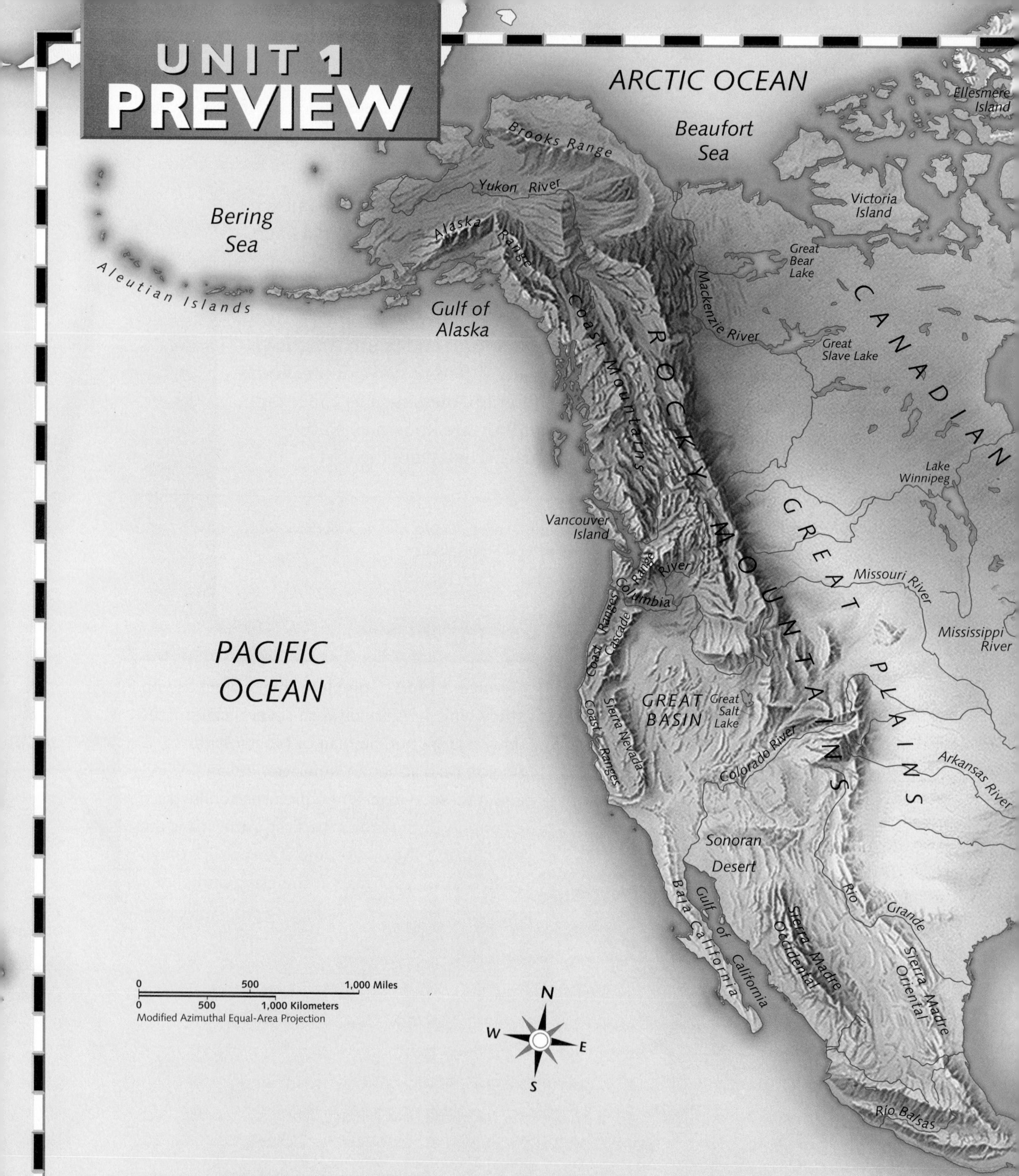

| 15,000 years ago | 12,500 years ago | 10,000 years ago | 7,500 years ago |

North America

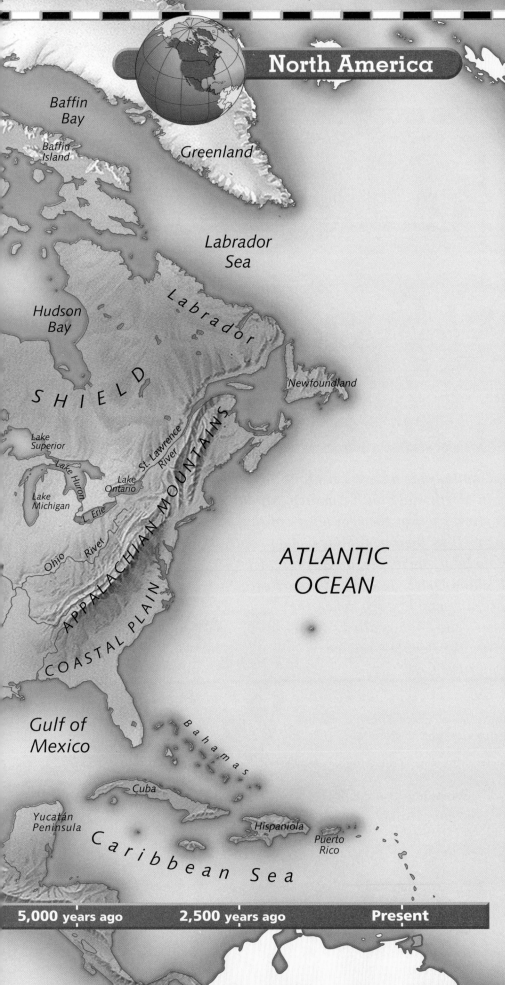

Baffin
Bay

Baffin
Island

Greenland

Labrador
Sea

Hudson
Bay

Labrador

S H I E L D

Newfoundland

Lake
Superior

St. Lawrence
River

Lake
Huron

Lake
Ontario

Lake
Michigan

L. Erie

APPALACHIAN MOUNTAINS

Ohio   River

COASTAL PLAIN

ATLANTIC
OCEAN

Gulf of
Mexico

Bahamas

Cuba

Yucatán
Peninsula

Hispaniola

Puerto
Rico

C a r i b b e a n   S e a

5,000 years ago   2,500 years ago   Present

Northwest Coast
PAGE 75

Southwest
PAGE 81

Great Plains
PAGE 86

Eastern Woodlands
PAGE 92

Middle America
PAGE 98

THE PEOPLE

Shall Continue

by Simon Ortiz

American Indians have a very long history in North and South America. Many of their stories tell of the beginnings of the Earth as well as their beginnings as a people. Read now how one writer, an Acoma poet named Simon Ortiz, describes the earliest years of American history, when the first Americans—who called themselves the People—settled throughout the land.

This Acoma pot from a pueblo in New Mexico was used to store food.

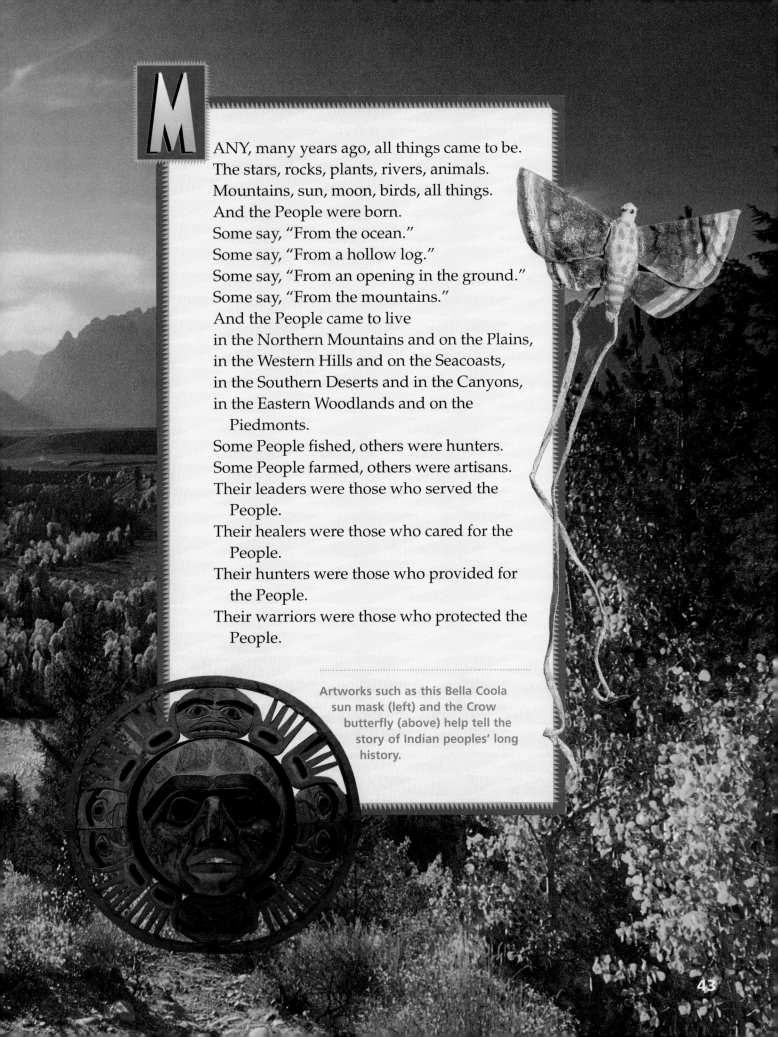

MANY, many years ago, all things came to be.
The stars, rocks, plants, rivers, animals.
Mountains, sun, moon, birds, all things.
And the People were born.
Some say, "From the ocean."
Some say, "From a hollow log."
Some say, "From an opening in the ground."
Some say, "From the mountains."
And the People came to live
in the Northern Mountains and on the Plains,
in the Western Hills and on the Seacoasts,
in the Southern Deserts and in the Canyons,
in the Eastern Woodlands and on the
    Piedmonts.
Some People fished, others were hunters.
Some People farmed, others were artisans.
Their leaders were those who served the
    People.
Their healers were those who cared for the
    People.
Their hunters were those who provided for
    the People.
Their warriors were those who protected the
    People.

Artworks such as this Bella Coola
sun mask (left) and the Crow
butterfly (above) help tell the
story of Indian peoples' long
history.

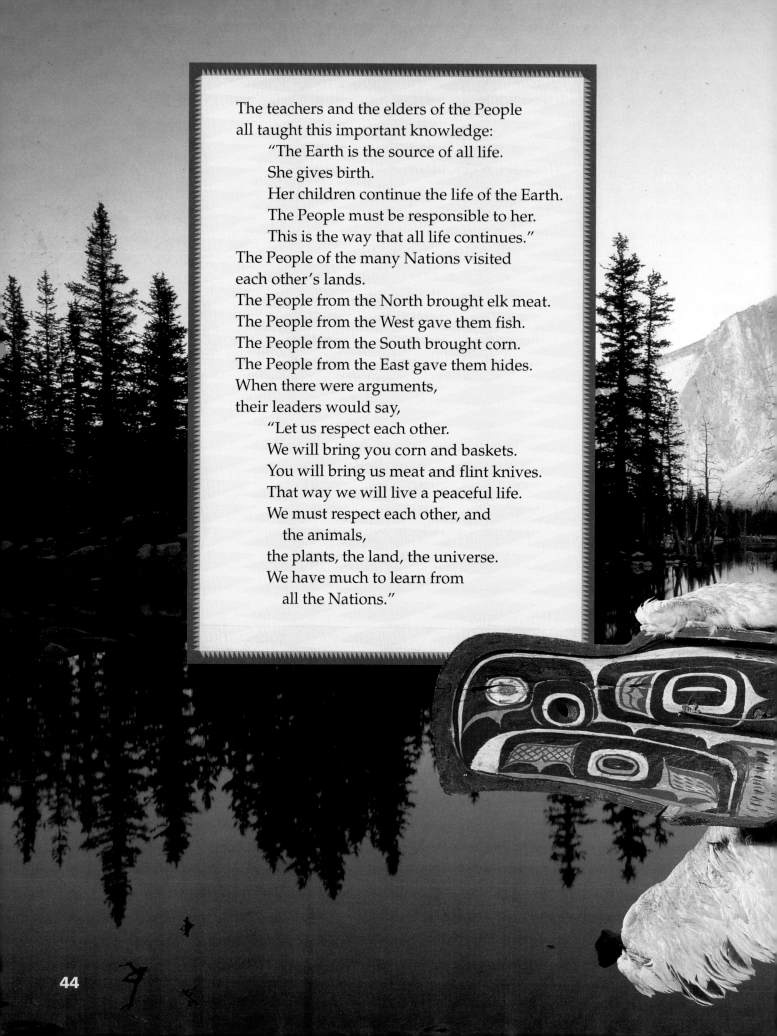

The teachers and the elders of the People
all taught this important knowledge:
    "The Earth is the source of all life.
    She gives birth.
    Her children continue the life of the Earth.
    The People must be responsible to her.
    This is the way that all life continues."
The People of the many Nations visited
each other's lands.
The People from the North brought elk meat.
The People from the West gave them fish.
The People from the South brought corn.
The People from the East gave them hides.
When there were arguments,
their leaders would say,
    "Let us respect each other.
    We will bring you corn and baskets.
    You will bring us meat and flint knives.
    That way we will live a peaceful life.
    We must respect each other, and
      the animals,
    the plants, the land, the universe.
    We have much to learn from
      all the Nations."

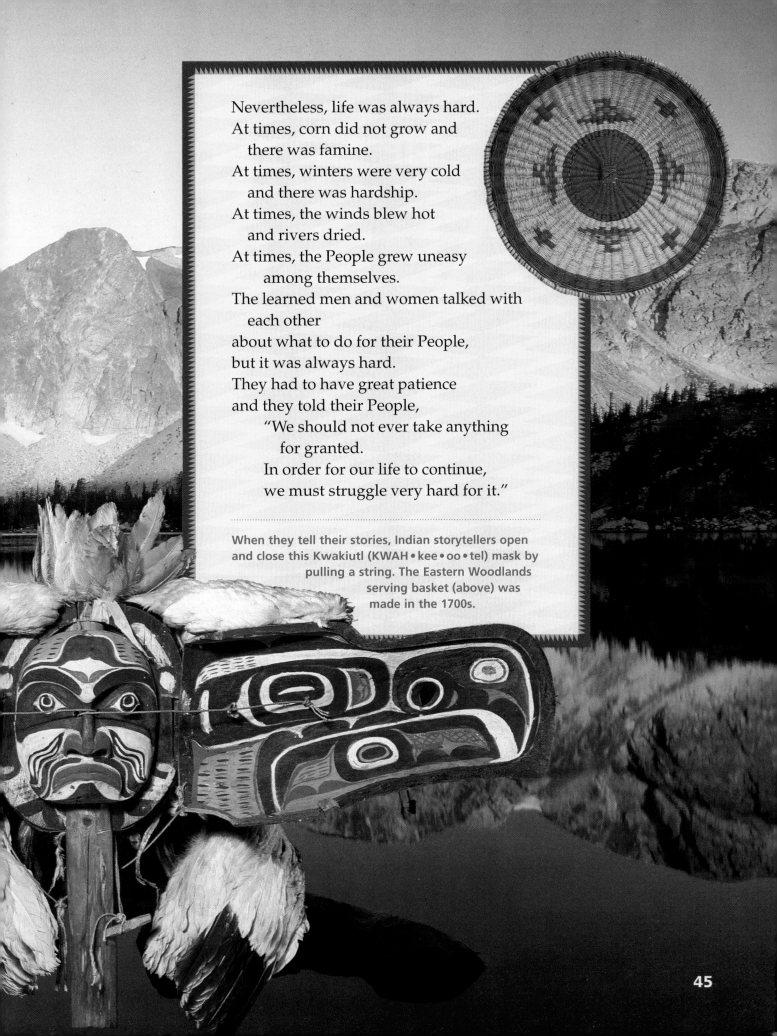

Nevertheless, life was always hard.
At times, corn did not grow and
   there was famine.
At times, winters were very cold
   and there was hardship.
At times, the winds blew hot
   and rivers dried.
At times, the People grew uneasy
     among themselves.
The learned men and women talked with
   each other
about what to do for their People,
but it was always hard.
They had to have great patience
and they told their People,
     "We should not ever take anything
       for granted.
     In order for our life to continue,
     we must struggle very hard for it."

When they tell their stories, Indian storytellers open and close this Kwakiutl (KWAH•kee•oo•tel) mask by pulling a string. The Eastern Woodlands serving basket (above) was made in the 1700s.

45

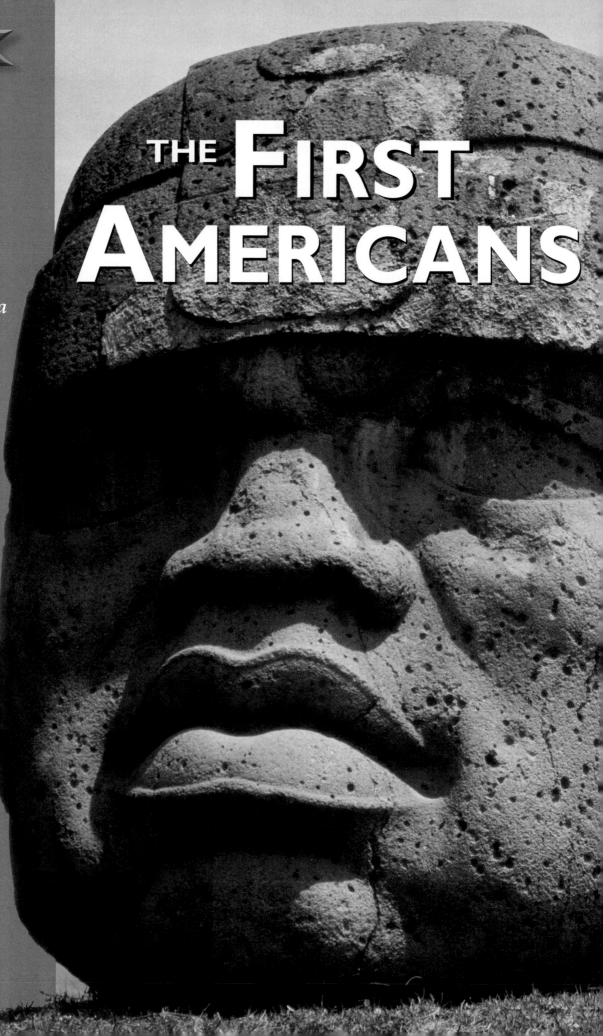

THE FIRST AMERICANS

"*My forebears have been in North America for many thousands of years. . . . [Their] resources were few, as we think of them from our vantage point in the twentieth century. . . .*"

N. Scott Momaday from *America in 1492*

An ancient stone head carved by the Olmec people

The Search for Early Peoples

LESSON

1

FOCUS

How does the environment affect the ways people today move from place to place?

Main Idea   As you read, think about how the environment affected the ways early peoples moved from place to place.

Vocabulary

migration
glacier
band
nomad
theory
culture
archaeologist
artifact
evidence
origin story

Humans have always been on the move. From the earliest times until today, people have wandered the Earth. Sometimes their journeys are fast-moving, exciting adventures. Other times their movements are so slow that they are hard to notice. It was in just this way—very, very slowly—that early peoples first moved from place to place.

Over the Land Bridge

At a number of times in its history, the Earth has had long periods of freezing cold. During these periods, known as the Ice Ages, people who lived anywhere but near the equator shivered through long, hard winters.

Life could not have been easy in those wintry times. Days, even weeks, were spent inside small shelters made of animal skins. Fires inside helped keep people warm while icy winds blew outside. The weather was warmer during the short summers, but melting ice turned the frozen ground into fields of mud.

Many groups of people, however, still set out into these lands. During hundreds of thousands of years, their ancestors had traveled from Africa into Europe and central and southern Asia. Now some people in this great **migration**, or movement, turned northward to the vast area of Asia known today as Siberia.

These early peoples did not travel alone. They followed huge Ice Age animals that they hunted for food. One such animal was the mammoth—a giant, hairy elephant. The hunters depended on these animals to survive. They ate the meat and used the fur, skins, and bones to make clothing, shelters, and tools.

An Ice Age mammoth

Chapter 1 • **47**

The last Ice Age started about 2 million years ago and ended about 10,000 years ago. At times it was so cold that huge sheets of ice called **glaciers** formed over much of the land. So much water was locked up in the glaciers that the oceans became shallower.

The Bering Strait, a narrow strip of water that today separates Siberia and Alaska, also became shallower. Over time, hundreds of miles of land that had been under water were uncovered. This strip of land connected Asia and North America. The land bridge that joined the two continents is known as Beringia (buh•RIN•gee•uh).

Most scientists believe that the first humans to find Beringia were bands of hunters from central Siberia. A **band** is a small group of people who work together to do activities. At that time, bands were probably made up of one or two families.

Many bands probably crossed into northwestern Siberia and Beringia. They probably traveled only a few miles in an entire lifetime. Wanderers like these hunters, who have no settled home, are called **nomads**.

Finally, after thousands of years, the hunters reached what is today Alaska. But there they—and the animals they followed—had to stop. Huge glaciers blocked their path. They could go no farther.

Then, about 12,000 years ago, the climate began changing. The Earth warmed up. Over many years, some of the glaciers started to melt. The oceans began to rise, once again covering Beringia. At the same time a narrow path opened between two melting glaciers that covered what is now Canada. It was as if one door behind the hunters closed as another door in front of them opened. Animals followed the path between the glaciers. Hunters followed the animals, slowly making their way farther and farther into the Americas. These hunters became the first Americans.

REVIEW *What was Beringia?*

Glaciers once covered much of the Earth's surface. Today glaciers are found only in the coldest parts of the world.

Early Migration Routes

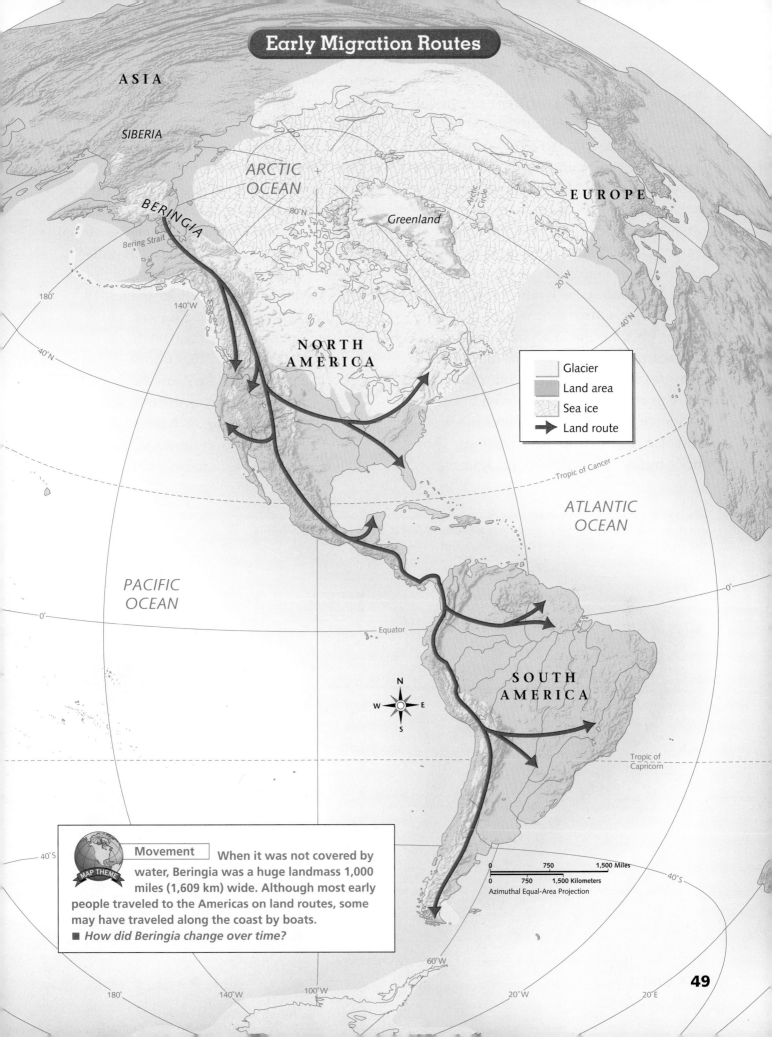

ASIA

SIBERIA

ARCTIC OCEAN

80°N

Greenland

Arctic Circle

EUROPE

BERINGIA

Bering Strait

180°

140°W

40°N

NORTH AMERICA

20°W

40°N

Legend

	Glacier
	Land area
	Sea ice
➤	Land route

Tropic of Cancer

ATLANTIC OCEAN

PACIFIC OCEAN

0°

0°

Equator

SOUTH AMERICA

N
W · E
S

Tropic of Capricorn

40°S

0   750   1,500 Miles
0   750   1,500 Kilometers
Azimuthal Equal-Area Projection

40°S

Movement When it was not covered by water, Beringia was a huge landmass 1,000 miles (1,609 km) wide. Although most early people traveled to the Americas on land routes, some may have traveled along the coast by boats.

■ *How did Beringia change over time?*

60°W

180°   140°W   100°W   20°W   20°E

49

New Discoveries

If this **theory** (THEE•uh•ree), or possible explanation, about the land bridge is correct, the first people arrived in the Americas about 12,000 years ago. But could they have been here earlier? Many scientists today say yes.

Once early peoples moved into the Americas, they settled all over both of the continents, in time reaching the southern tip of South America. Each native group developed its own **culture**, or way of life. Some groups lived in cities. Others were nomads who roamed the plains. Some made their clothing of furs and skins, while others made theirs of cotton. They lived in large wooden lodges, grass huts, tents made of animal skins, or steep cliff dwellings. They spoke thousands of different languages.

To build and develop such different cultures must have taken a great deal of time. Scientists now argue that it must have taken much longer than 12,000 years.

But how could people have arrived earlier? It turns out that Beringia may have been uncovered at another time during the last Ice Age—from 45,000 to 75,000 years ago. Asian hunters could have crossed then into North America on dry land. It is also possible that the first Americans did not cross the land bridge at all. Instead, they could have traveled along the coast of Beringia to the Americas by boat.

Scientists who study the cultures of people of long ago are known as **archaeologists** (ar•kee•AH•luh•jists). In recent years archaeologists have made discoveries that seem to support the "early arrival" theory. One of the most important

These two ancient tools (below) were found at Meadowcroft Rock Shelter (right). What do you think each tool could have been used for? Archaeologists also found this piece of bowl (bottom) that was made from a tortoise shell.

was at a dig, or an archaeological site, in the sandstone cliffs of southwestern Pennsylvania. In these cliffs, archaeologists discovered an Ice Age campsite they called the Meadowcroft Rock Shelter. At the campsite they found a number of **artifacts**, or objects that early people had made. These artifacts are 14,000 to 15,000 years old. A few are more than 19,000 years old.

There are other discoveries that also support the early arrival theory. In Monte Verde (MOHN•tay VAIR•day), Chile, archaeologists have uncovered stone tools, wooden digging sticks, and animal bones that are 13,000 years old. And in Brazil archaeologists have found stone chips that may have been made by early people. Some archaeologists believe that these artifacts are 30,000 years old.

The number of artifacts that have been found is growing. Some archaeologists, though, are still not convinced that people arrived in the Americas any earlier than 12,000 years ago. They believe that there is not enough **evidence**, or proof, to support the early arrival theory. Some so-called artifacts, they say, are not artifacts at all. What one archaeologist believes is a stone tool that has been shaped by humans could really be a stone that was shaped by nature—by wind or water.

Archaeologists today continue to search for more evidence from the past. Each new discovery brings new information about the first Americans. This information helps archaeologists figure out what life may have been like long ago.

REVIEW *What is the early arrival theory?*

These archaeologists (right) are searching for ancient objects at Meadowcroft Rock Shelter. White tags identify the different layers of earth. The rock shelter is the site of the Ice Age campsite.

Origin Stories

The Indian peoples themselves have many different stories about the origins of their lands and about their own beginnings long ago. These stories tell of the peoples' beliefs about the world and their place in it. Such stories are called **origin stories**.

Some origin stories are much like the story of creation in the Bible that tells how the world was made. The Blackfoot people, for example, tell a story of how Old Man the Creator made the animals and plants and formed the prairies and mountains. He made a woman and her child from clay and brought them to life.

Animals and natural surroundings such as mountains, rivers, rocks, and trees play an important part in many origin stories. The Huron (HYUR•ahn) people tell a story that says that in the beginning the Earth was covered with water. Dry land was

The Pueblo clay figure (above left) shows the importance of storytellers to their listeners. In some origin stories, animals like the elk (left) are able to talk to humans. The painting *Creation Legend* (above), by Tom Dorsey, shows that the turtle is included in the Onondagas' creation story.

This present-day storyteller describes stories about the past to his listener.

formed from a bit of soil taken from under the claws of a turtle. The turtle had picked up the soil after diving to the bottom of the ocean. Because of this story, some Indian people today still use the name Turtle Island for the Americas.

Even though no one knows exactly when the first people arrived in the Americas, many agree that it was thousands of years ago. It was so long ago that the descendants of the first Americans—the American Indians—have no memories of distant homelands. They do not tell stories of far-away places where their ancestors once lived. They tell stories of the Americas—the only home they have known.

REVIEW *Why are origin stories important to Indian peoples?*

LESSON I REVIEW

Check Understanding

❶ **Remember the Facts** In what ways did the Ice Ages change the Earth's environment?

❷ **Recall the Main Idea** How did the environment affect the ways early peoples moved from place to place?

Think Critically

❸ **Think More About It** What skills do you think would have been important to help the early people survive during the Ice Ages?

❹ **Explore Viewpoints** Why do some people believe that the first Americans arrived about 12,000 years ago? What evidence do others give to support the early arrival theory?

Show What You Know

Diorama Activity Make a diorama of an Ice Age scene that includes people or giant mammals. Write a caption describing the scene. Display your diorama and caption in the classroom.

How Long Have People

No one really knows how long people have lived in the Americas. For many years archaeologists agreed that the first people in the Americas arrived by crossing Beringia no more than 12,000 years ago. These people, called the Clovis (KLOH•vuhs) people, were named for the place in New Mexico where their stone artifacts were discovered. Many archaeologists now believe that people may have reached the Americas over 20,000 years ago.

Clovis points like this one are evidence that people lived in the Americas nearly 12,000 years ago.

The walls and ceiling of a cave at Pedra Furada, Brazil, are covered with paintings of animals. Archaeologists disagree about how old some of the artifacts found there really are.

Jacques Cinq-Mars

Jacques Cinq-Mars (ZHAHK SANK MAR) of the Archaeological Survey of Canada studied the Bluefish Caves in Canada's Yukon Territory. The caves are in an area that people from Siberia could have reached by crossing Beringia. Cinq-Mars said:

66 I found a bone flake in one of the caves, and two years later I found the mammoth bone from which the flake was chipped, both dating around 24,000 B.P. [before the present]. . . . It's good evidence for human presence . . . certainly at 25,000 B.P. 99

Lived in the Americas?

Vance Haynes

Many archaeologists still think that the Clovis people were the first to migrate to the Americas. Vance Haynes, a professor at the University of Arizona, studied evidence in layers of rock in the ground. The layers on top are the newest. Layers below are older. Haynes said:

66 I've spent a good part of a lifetime as a geologist, as well as an archaeologist, and from Clovis up I've seen one layer after another with artifacts, while from Clovis down there's nothing human. . . . Hardly a year goes by that there isn't a new site that's claimed to be old, but they all fall away . . . unless you're a believer. 99

Glenn Morris

Glenn Morris works for the American Indian Anti-Defamation Council in Colorado. He believes that the Indian peoples did not come to the Americas from Siberia or anywhere else. He believes they have *always* been in the Americas. Morris said:

66 The problem with the Bering Strait theory is that it is wrong, not only according to indigenous [native] peoples' creation stories and histories, it is also wrong according to a growing body of Western research. . . . Digs at Lewisville, Texas; San Diego, California; and Pedejo Cave, New Mexico, have revealed [uncovered] human remains at 38,000, 44,000, and 48,000 years old. . . . By contrast, the oldest human remains found in the Siberian region of northern Asia . . . are a mere 20,000 years old! Other scientific evidence . . . indicates that a migration did occur, but the footprints went in the other direction, from the Americas to Asia! 99

Compare Viewpoints

1. What evidence does Cinq-Mars have for his view? Why does Haynes disagree?

2. What evidence does Morris have for his view? How does his view differ from those of Cinq-Mars and Haynes?

3. A Yakima Indian once said, "I . . . did not come here. I was put here by the Creator." Which of the three views would this person most likely support?

Think and Apply

Historians and scientists often use physical evidence, such as artifacts, to support their views. However, people do not always agree on what the evidence means. Use newspapers or magazines to identify some disagreements today that are based on the meaning of physical evidence.

Compare Map

1. Why Learn This Skill?

Because the Earth is round and maps are flat, maps cannot represent the Earth's shape exactly. Only a globe, which is round, can do that. To show the round Earth on a flat sheet of paper, mapmakers must change the shape of the globe, splitting or stretching it to make it flat. As a result, every map has **distortions**, or areas that are not accurate.

Over the years, mapmakers have found different ways of showing the Earth on flat paper. These different views are called **projections**. All map projections have distortions, but different kinds of projections have different kinds of distortions. Identifying areas on a map that are distorted will help you understand how maps can best be used.

2. Understand the Process

Both Map A and Map B show the same area of the Earth, but they are different projections. Map A is an equal-area projection. Equal-area projections show the size of regions in correct relation to one another, but they distort, or change, their shapes. There are many kinds of equal-area projections. The azimuthal (a•zuh•MUH•thuhl) equal-area projection on Map A is one kind. Another is the Albers equal-area projection.

Map A: Western Hemisphere

160°E
North Pole
20°E
ARCTIC OCEAN
80°N
Greenland
0°
180°
60°N
160°W
140°W
20°W
40°N
40°N
NORTH AMERICA
ATLANTIC OCEAN
20°N
20°N
N
W E
S
0° Equator
0°
PACIFIC OCEAN
SOUTH AMERICA
20°S
20°S

0   1,000   2,000 Miles
0   1,000   2,000 Kilometers
Azimuthal Equal-Area Projection

40°S
40°S
140°W   120°W   100°W   80°W   60°W   40°W   20°W

Projections

Map B is a conformal projection. Notice that the lines of longitude are all an equal distance apart. On a globe, however, these lines get closer together as they approach the poles. Notice also that the lines of latitude that are closer to the poles are farther apart than those near the equator. But when you look at a globe, the lines of latitude are all equal distances apart. Conformal projections show directions correctly, but they distort sizes, especially of the places near the poles. The Miller cylindrical projection used on Map B is one example of a conformal projection. Another is the Mercator (mer•KAY•ter) projection.

Use Map A and Map B to answer the following questions.

1. On which parts of Map A and Map B do the shapes of the land areas appear to be the same?

2. On which map does Greenland appear to be larger? On which map is the size of Greenland more accurate?

3. On which map do the lines of longitude get closer together toward the poles?

4. On which map does the space between the lines of latitude get greater toward the poles?

3. Think and Apply

Look at the maps in the Atlas on pages A2–A15 to see other map projections. Write a paragraph about the advantages and disadvantages of using equal-area and conformal projections. Compare your ideas with those of your classmates.

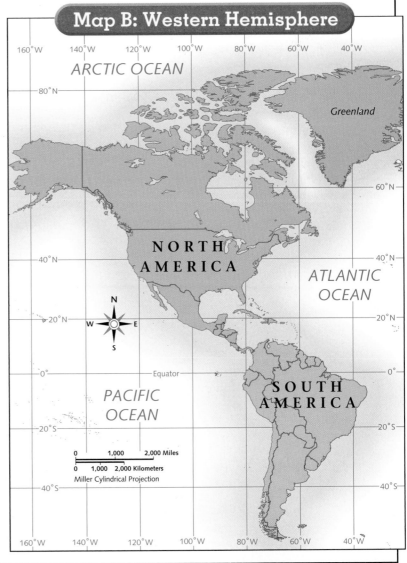

Map B: Western Hemisphere

ARCTIC OCEAN

Greenland

NORTH AMERICA

ATLANTIC OCEAN

PACIFIC OCEAN

Equator

SOUTH AMERICA

0   1,000   2,000 Miles
0 1,000 2,000 Kilometers
Miller Cylindrical Projection

FOCUS

What do people today do when their environment changes?

Main Idea Read to find out what the ancient Indians did when their environment changed.

Vocabulary

technology	religion
extinct	tribe
agriculture	surplus
maize	specialize

LEARNING FROM DIAGRAMS Due to the size and strength of the mammoths, ancient Indians often had to work together when hunting the giant animals. Each of the hunters in this picture is using an atlatl to bring down the mammoth. The atlatl allowed the hunter to throw a spear with deadly force while staying a safe distance away from the target.

■ *Why do you think it was important for hunters to work together?*

Ancient Indians

As early peoples made their way across the Americas, the climate of the Earth continued to change. Over thousands of years, it became drier and warmer. In some places, lakes slowly dried up. In other places, grassy meadows turned to sand. Without water and food, the huge Ice Age animals began to die out. Many of the first Americans had depended on these animals for food, clothing, and shelter. Now they had to find new ways to survive.

Giant-Mammal Hunters

Compared to the mighty mammoth, standing 14 feet (4.3 m) high at the shoulder and weighing about 5 tons, early hunters seemed small and weak. Their spears were little more than sharpened sticks made by sharpening and hardening the ends of long wooden poles. In time they learned to sharpen stones into spear points and tie them onto the wooden poles. Some hunters also made and used clubs and axes with stone blades. Yet the early hunters

1 the hunter rests the spear on the atlatl

2 the hunter sets the spear in motion

survived mainly by tracking the mammoths and other giant Ice Age mammals and killing them when they could.

The earliest native hunters were nomads who lived in small bands. As they trailed behind the giant animals, they gathered fruits, nuts, and roots for food. They lived in caves or in tents made from animal skins. Their tools and weapons were made mostly from sticks, animal horns, and bones. From time to time, different peoples invented new tools, such as the atlatl (AHT•lah•tuhl), or spear-thrower. They also found new ways of sharpening stones and of leading animals into a trap.

About 11,600 years ago, something very important happened. Someone found a way to make a spear point by a process called flaking. First, a piece of bone or stone was used to knock off flakes, or thin pieces, from flint or another type of stone. The flakes were knocked off until the stone formed a sharp point. The point was then fluted, or hollowed out, on one or both sides. This made it easier to fasten the point tightly to a spear.

TECHNOLOGY

The Atlatl

The atlatl, or spear-thrower, was an important weapon used by early hunters. Although archaeologists are not certain when it was invented, they do know that it was used in North America at least 10,000 years ago. Atlatls were spear holders 2 to 3 feet (61 to 91 cm) long and made of wood. The spear rested in a groove, against a base at the end of the atlatl. The hunter held on to the atlatl and then snapped it forward with a whiplike motion to send the spear toward its target. The motion of the atlatl made the spear travel with much greater speed and force than it would have had alone.

3 the spear is released from the atlatl

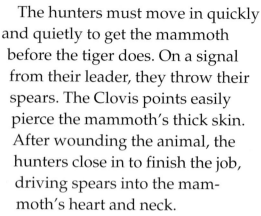

These delicate yet deadly spear points are called Clovis points. They are named after the town of Clovis, New Mexico, where they were first found. Archaeologists call the early Indians who made these spear points the Clovis people. Other artifacts of the Clovis people have been found in places from Alaska to the Andes Mountains.

Clovis points were one of the important improvements in technology for early peoples. **Technology** is the use of scientific knowledge or tools to make or do something. You may not think of sharpened stones as technology. But these spear points were just as important to the Clovis people as computers are to us today. Clovis points were razor-sharp, making them the best weapons early hunters had ever had.

Imagine one band of early people moving closely behind a large herd of mammoths they have been tracking for weeks. Finally the hunters see what they are looking for! In the shallow water of a small lake is a giant woolly mammoth taking a drink.

Looking over the area, the hunters quickly realize that they are not the only ones that are interested in the mammoth. A saber-toothed tiger, eager to sink its 8-inch (20.3 cm) teeth into the animal, is also watching, waiting to make its move.

Clovis points were 1.5 to 5 inches (3.8 to 12.7 cm) long and very sharp. These points were fastened tightly to spears so they could be used again and again.

60 • Unit 1

The hunters must move in quickly and quietly to get the mammoth before the tiger does. On a signal from their leader, they throw their spears. The Clovis points easily pierce the mammoth's thick skin. After wounding the animal, the hunters close in to finish the job, driving spears into the mammoth's heart and neck.

The band then sets to work. They waste little of the fallen animal. From this one kill, they get about 2 tons of meat—enough to feed the band for months. Much of the meat will be dried and saved for later. The giant mammoth's hide will be used to make clothing and shelters. Its bones will become tools and weapons.

Even so, the hunters cannot carry everything with them as they move on. Some of the kill must be left behind. This does not seem important to them. After all, there will always be another herd of mammoths or other animals just ahead.

Over the next thousand years, however, the giant mammals would become **extinct** (ik•STINGT), or die out. The drier climate was drying up lakes and rivers and killing the tall, lush grasses that the animals ate. By about 10,000 years ago, most of the animals weighing 100 pounds (45.4 kg) or more, such as mammoths, horses, camels, and saber-toothed tigers, were gone from the Americas.

REVIEW *Why were Clovis points so important to the early hunters?*

Food Gatherers

As the environment changed and the huge Ice Age animals became extinct, early peoples had to change their ways of life. Life no longer centered around the hunting of giant mammals. People began to fish and to hunt more of the smaller animals. They also began to gather and store more plants for food. These changes in the way people lived took place from about 9,000 years ago to 3,000 years ago.

Because they did not follow herds of large animals, food gatherers stayed in places a little longer than hunters did. In time they learned where certain plants grew best and at what time of year the plants became ripe. Their bands then traveled to these places each season to gather food.

As food gatherers collected more food than they could use at a time, they needed ways to store the extra food. They learned to make baskets that could be used as storage containers. The baskets were made from reeds, vines, or splints of wood. Some were woven so tight they could hold water. Later, people learned to make storage containers out of other materials, such as clay.

Picture one band of food gatherers, moving from their winter camp to their summer camp. After days of walking, they reach the marshy tidelands near the river where they will spend the summer. The people set up camp in the shelter of a large rock along a hillside. Then both the women and the men begin to prepare the food.

First, the women empty their willow baskets of the seeds and nuts they have gathered along the way. Then, they use flat stones to grind the food into flour. Next, they mix the flour with water and put the dough in a cooking basket. They put the basket on stones that have been heated in the fire and wait for the dough to cook.

While the women make the bread, the men skin the animals they have killed that day. They often hunt raccoons, deer, antelope, and otters, but today's meal will be rabbits. The men then heat up more stones in the fire and place the rabbits on a wooden rack to roast.

American Indians used these decoys about 3,000 years ago to hunt ducks. The decoys are made of reeds—water plants that grow along the shores of lakes and rivers.

After the meal the women check and repair the knives and baskets they will use to gather plants the next day. The men check and repair the spears and nets they will use to hunt and fish. Finally, they lie down in their shelters to sleep. At dawn they will be up again, ready to begin another day of hunting, gathering, and storing food.

To this day some Native Americans gather foods that grow wild in nature. Some Ojibwa (oh•jib•WAY), for example, gather wild rice that grows near the Great Lakes.

REVIEW *What changes did early peoples make when the giant Ice Age animals became extinct?*

Early Farmers

Over time some American Indians changed their way of life as food gatherers. They took the first steps toward a new technology that would change their lives forever. They began to plant seeds and grow some of their own food. This was the beginning of **agriculture**, or farming, in the Americas.

Indian peoples in Central America were among the first to develop agriculture in the Americas. Some of the earliest farmers lived in the Tehuacán (tay•wah•KAHN) Valley in central Mexico. There archaeologists have found evidence of farming that dates from 7,000 years ago to 4,700 years ago. The early farmers of the valley harvested at least 12 kinds of corn, as well as avocados, squash, pumpkins, and beans.

Corn, or **maize** (MAYZ), was the most important food grown in the Americas.

For thousands of years people ground corn into flour using a grinding stone (above). The pictures of corn (right) show some of the many varieties of corn that can be found in the Americas.

Maize gave early peoples more food than any other crop. For this reason, they thought of maize as a gift from their gods. This idea was part of the Native American peoples' **religion**, or beliefs about God or gods. The religion of many early peoples centered around a number of gods that helped to explain the many qualities found in nature. Among these were a sun god and a rain god.

For some Native American groups, growing their own food meant that they no longer had to move from camp to camp. They could settle in one place, build stronger homes, and form villages. With more food, people lived longer and their population grew. In time, people joined together to form tribes. A **tribe** is a group

Ears of corn appear on this carving of a god. The god is believed to bring good harvests. Early corn, or maize, was much smaller than the corn grown today.

made up of many bands of people with a shared culture and land.

Agriculture also meant that people no longer had to spend all their time searching for food. For once, they had a food **surplus**, or more than was needed. Now people could spend more time doing other things to help the tribe. Soon they began to **specialize**, or work on one job they could do well. Early people were no longer only hunters, gatherers, or farmers. Some members of the tribe specialized in making pots, weaving, or trading.

REVIEW *What changes did farming bring about in the lives of some ancient Indians?*

LESSON 2 REVIEW

Check Understanding

1 **Remember the Facts** Why did the giant Ice Age mammals become extinct?

2 **Recall the Main Idea** What did the ancient Indians do when their environment changed?

Think Critically

3 **Personally Speaking** Would you rather have lived as a hunter, a food gatherer, or a farmer? Explain your answer.

4 **Past to Present** List five changes in technology that are important to our lives today.

5 **Cause and Effect** What effect did Clovis points have on the lives of early Indians?

Show What You Know

Mural Activity Recall what you read about the ways of life of the hunters, food gatherers, and early farmers. Select one group and make a mural that shows how the group lived in the Americas. Give your mural a title and write a caption that provides additional information. Display completed murals and share them with your classmates.

Identify Patterns

1. Why Learn This Skill?

When you think about history, there are a great many events, and they took place over a very long time. An easy way to understand events in history is to look at a time line. Knowing how to read a time line can help you understand the order in which events happened in the past and the amount of time that passed between those events.

2. Using Time Lines

A **time line** is a diagram that shows events that took place during a certain period of time. It looks something like a ruler marked in dates instead of inches. Like inches marked on a ruler, the dates on a time line are equally spaced.

Not all time lines look the same or are read in the same way. Most time lines run horizontally, or across the page from left to right. But some run vertically, or from top to bottom. To be able to use time lines, it is important to know how to read both kinds.

Horizontal time lines, like the one shown below, are read from left to right. The earliest date is on the left end, and the most recent date is on the right end. The time line shown on page 65 is a vertical time line. It is read from top to bottom. The earliest date is at the top, and the most recent date is at the bottom.

Time lines can show events that took place during any period of time. Some time lines, for example, show events that took place over a **decade**, or a period of 10 years. Others show events that took place over a **century**, or a period of 100 years. A decade and a century are shown on the horizontal time line. Some time lines even show events that took place over a **millennium**, or a period of 1,000 years. A millennium is shown on the vertical time line.

The vertical time line also shows dates from the ancient past to today. Notice the letters *B.C.* and *A.D.* in the middle of the time

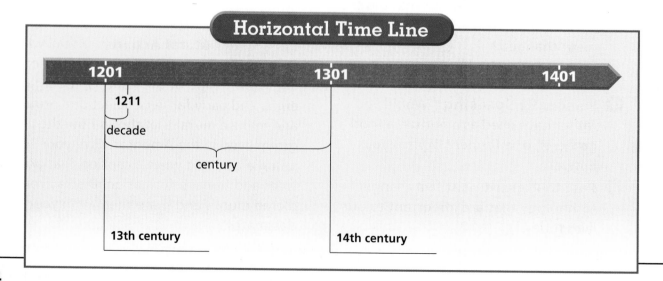

Horizontal Time Line

1201   1301   1401

1211

decade

century

13th century   14th century

on Time Lines

line. Many people today identify years by whether they took place before or after the birth of Jesus Christ. Years before the birth of Christ are labeled *B.C.* This stands for "before Christ." Years after the birth of Christ are labeled *A.D.* This stands for the Latin words *Anno Domini*, which mean "in the year of the Lord."

An event that happened in 100 B.C. took place 100 years before the birth of Christ. An event that happened in A.D. 100 took place 100 years after the birth of Christ. Because every year in modern times is A.D., the letters are usually not used.

You may also see the letters *B.C.E.* or *C.E.* with dates. The abbreviation *B.C.E.* stands for "before the Common Era." It is sometimes used instead of *B.C.* The abbreviation *C.E.*, which stands for "Common Era," is sometimes used in place of *A.D.*

3. Understand the Process

Use the horizontal time line on page 64 to answer the following questions.

1 How many centuries are shown on the time line?

2 Between which years did the 13th century take place?

Use the vertical time line on this page to answer the following questions.

3 How many millenniums are shown on the time line?

4 Which happened first, the year 1000 B.C. or the year A.D. 500?

4. Think and Apply

Make a time line that shows events in your life. Start with the year you were born. Add years in which something important happened. Display your time line.

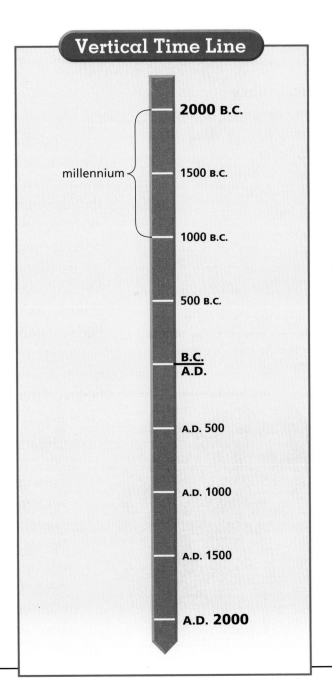

Vertical Time Line

- 2000 B.C.
- millennium ⎱ 1500 B.C.
- 1000 B.C.
- 500 B.C.
- B.C.
  A.D.
- A.D. 500
- A.D. 1000
- A.D. 1500
- A.D. 2000

FOCUS

How are the ways of life of people today different in different parts of the world?

Main Idea Read to learn about the different ways of life of early peoples living in different parts of the Americas.

Vocabulary

civilization   drought

temple   kiva

pyramid

cultural diffusion

earthwork

pueblo

adobe

mesa

This Olmec mask was found in a temple near what is today Mexico City. It is a little over 4 inches (10.2 cm) high.

Early Civilizations

With farming and settled life, American Indian cultures grew and changed. Over time, people in different cultures came to hold different beliefs, speak different languages, and live in different ways. Three of these early peoples were the Olmecs (AHL•meks), the Mound Builders, and the Anasazi (ah•nuh•SAH•zee).

The Olmecs

For hundreds of years the artifacts of a people called the Olmecs lay hidden beneath thick jungle growth. When the artifacts were finally found, archaeologists learned that the Olmecs had built one of the earliest civilizations in the Americas. A **civilization** is a culture that has developed forms of government, religion, and learning.

The Olmecs lived in the green river valleys along Mexico's east coast as early as 1500 B.C. So many later groups learned so much from the Olmec culture that it has become known as the "mother civilization" of the Americas.

Powerful priests governed the Olmecs, and many activities of daily life centered around religion. The Olmecs believed in many gods. One of the most important was the rain god. The Olmecs believed that the rain god appeared as a jaguar (JA•gwar), a large, spotted cat. To honor the gods, the Olmecs built great stone **temples**, or places of worship. Some temples were built on top of pyramids. A **pyramid** is a building with three or more sides shaped like triangles. The sides slant upward toward a point at the top. The Olmecs made the tops of their pyramids flat and built temples there.

Near the temples were paved roads that led to other buildings and a marketplace. Government leaders lived in this central area. Most other people lived in nearby villages. Huge stone faces looked out over the villages. Some

The Olmecs carved giant stone heads from basalt (buh•SAWLT), a kind of volcanic rock. They moved the statues from miles away by floating them down rivers on rafts.

stone faces weighed as much as 20 tons each. Olmec artists may have carved the faces to look like their rulers' faces.

Religious services held in the temples were important to the people. The priests standing before the crowds wore bright-red robes covered with jaguar skins. On their heads they wore bird feathers and flowers.

The Olmecs developed their own number system, writing system, and calendar. Their writing used pictures to stand for words or ideas. They also traded with people hundreds of miles away in present-day Mexico and Central America and along the coast of the Gulf of Mexico. Trade gave people a chance to meet and exchange ideas. In this way Olmec culture spread to other places. This process is called **cultural diffusion**.

No one knows how the Olmec civilization came to an end. We do know, however, that by A.D. 300 the Olmec civilization had been replaced by other civilizations. Yet Olmec ideas had spread through trade and lived on in other cultures.

REVIEW *Why is the Olmec culture called the "mother civilization" of the Americas?*

The Mound Builders

About the same time that the Olmec people were building a civilization in Central America, a people called the Adenas (uh•DEE•nuhz) were building a civilization in North America. The Adena people lived in the Ohio River valley from about 1000 B.C. to A.D. 200.

The Adena people were the first of several ancient civilizations known as Mound Builders. The Mound Builders lived in the eastern half of what is today the United States. The Mound Builders got their name because of the large mounds, or hills of earth, that they built. These mounds are called **earthworks**.

One of the most famous Adena earthworks, the Serpent Mound, is about 5 feet (1.5 m) high, 20 feet (6.1 m) across, and 1,330 feet (405.4 m) long. It does not look like much from the ground, but when you look at it from the air, you can see that it forms the shape of a snake.

Nobody knows why the Adena people built the snake-shaped mound. Perhaps it was built for religious purposes. Archaeologists do know that they also built many smaller mounds to bury the dead.

The most important people were given the fanciest mound burials. First, the Adenas covered the body of the person who had died with a kind of paint that was made of reddish-colored earth. Red was the color of blood and of life. The Adenas believed the red paint would allow the person's spirit to live on after death. Then they laid the body on a bed of bark strips set in the floor of a house.

To help the dead enjoy their life after death, people placed jewelry, clay pipes, beads, and other goods around the body. Then they went outside and set the house on fire. After the house had burned down, they covered the ashes with earth. Over time more people would be buried there and the mound would rise higher.

About 300 B.C. a second, larger mound-building civilization began to take shape in the middle of what is now the United States. This was the Hopewell civilization. The culture of the Hopewells grew to be the strongest in the region for nearly 500 years.

The Hopewells had great skill at arts and crafts. They made ceramic pots, woven mats, and figures carved from bone, wood, and metal. The Hopewells made spear points and knives from obsidian (uhb•SIH•dee•uhn), a hard, shiny black stone. They also wore clothing made of animal skins and jewelry made from copper and shells.

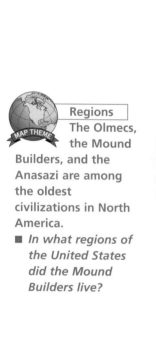

Regions
The Olmecs, the Mound Builders, and the Anasazi are among the oldest civilizations in North America.

■ In what regions of the United States did the Mound Builders live?

Ancient Cultures of North America

Olmecs, 1500 B.C.–A.D. 300
Mound Builders, 1000 B.C.–A.D. 1500
Anasazi, 100 B.C.–A.D. 1300
• Major settlement
— Present-day border

The Serpent Mound (above) is found in southern Ohio. Other Adena mounds are shaped like birds, tortoises, and people. A Hopewell artist made this eagle in flight (left) out of copper.

Like Olmec goods and ideas, Hopewell goods and ideas were spread far and wide through trade. This trade reached from the Atlantic Ocean to the Great Plains and from Lake Superior to the Gulf of Mexico. Hopewell traders were often away from home for weeks at a time, visiting trading centers hundreds of miles away.

The greatest mound-building civilization was that of the Mississippians. This civilization developed in the Mississippi River valley about A.D. 800. The Mississippians lived in hundreds of towns and several large cities. They built huge mounds, some nearly as big as a football field. Some of these high, box-shaped mounds had large temples built on top.

The largest Mississippian city was near where East St. Louis, Illinois, stands today. By A.D. 1200 as many as 40,000 people lived in this city, which was called Cahokia (kuh•HOH•kee•uh).

Picture the large city of Cahokia, dotted with 85 different mounds, as it looked one autumn morning. The powerful chief, who is both priest and ruler, has just come out of his house on the flat top of the huge main temple mound. He and the other priests are getting ready to greet the sun god and ask his blessing on the corn harvest.

Monk's Mound, where Cahokia's chief is standing, is 110 feet (33.5 m) high and covers 16 acres. It took more than 300 years to build. The people had to carry soil to the mound one basketful at a time.

Below Monk's Mound is the town square. It is already filling up with thousands of people gathering for worship. Later, the square will be used as a marketplace.

The chief looks past the square to the smaller mounds that have houses on top, where other important people live. Outside the large wooden fence around the city are the houses of the farmers, hunters, and workers. The people are hurrying toward the temple, and the chief's thoughts return to the religious service that is about to begin.

By about A.D. 1500 the great Mississippian civilization began to break down. War, hunger, or sickness may have played a part. Slowly, the Mississippian culture, the last of the great mound-building civilizations, ended.

REVIEW *Why did the Mound Builders construct earthworks?*

The Anasazi

From about 100 B.C. to A.D. 1300, another early civilization grew up in the dry lands of what is today the southwestern United States. This was the civilization of the Anasazi, or "Ancient People."

The Anasazi lived in groups of houses that Spanish people later described as **pueblos** (PWEH•blohs). *Pueblo* is the Spanish word for "town" or "village." Pueblos were multi-story and made of adobe (ah•DOH•bay) bricks or stone bricks. **Adobe** is a mixture of sand and straw that is dried into bricks. The Anasazi had to carry wood for roof beams from miles away, but adobe and stone were near at hand.

Most pueblos were built on top of **mesas** (MAY•sahz), or high, flat-topped hills. The buildings had few windows or doors on the lower levels. People moved from one level to another by using ladders.

One great Anasazi settlement was Pueblo Bonito, or "beautiful town." Pueblo Bonito was built beneath the towering rock walls of Chaco (CHAH•koh) Canyon, in what is today New Mexico. It was made

This Anasazi shelter (below) found in Colorado, was built around A.D. 1100. The pottery jar and pair of sandals (left) are artifacts of Anasazi life.

up of 800 rooms and housed more than 1,200 people. Nearly 5,000 people lived in smaller villages nearby. The villages were connected by paved roads, which also served as trade routes.

The Anasazi built some pueblos into the sides of high cliffs, far out of the reach of enemies. One pueblo at Mesa Verde (MAY•sah VAIR•day), in present-day Colorado, is known as the Cliff Palace. Rising three stories high, this pueblo village has 200 rooms. As many as 1,000 people may have lived there.

Even though their land was very dry, the Anasazi grew fields of corn, squash, and beans. They planted their seeds deep in the ground to get the most water out of the soil. They also dug holes and ditches to store water for use in drier times. In case a long dry spell, or **drought**, should come, they saved enough dried corn in clay jars to feed the people for up to two years.

Religion was an important part of Anasazi life. Religious services were held in special underground rooms called **kivas** (KEE•vuhs). Chiefs, their faces and bodies painted white, led the people in giving thanks to the Earth Mother, the sun god, and the rain god.

The Anasazi civilization changed by about A.D. 1300. Some archaeologists believe that a 22-year drought in the high mesa lands may have been the reason the Anasazi people left the great pueblos and moved into the valleys of rivers such as the Rio Grande. There they built smaller pueblos or joined other groups in small farming villages.

REVIEW *What materials did the Anasazi use to build pueblos?*

LESSON 3 REVIEW

Check Understanding

1 **Remember the Facts** List three of the earliest civilizations found in the Americas.

2 **Recall the Main Idea** What different ways of life did early peoples of the Americas develop?

Think Critically

3 **Think More About It** In what ways did the environment affect the lives of the Anasazi?

4 **Past to Present** How do ideas spread from one culture to another today?

Show What You Know

Art Activity Imagine that you have written a book about one of the civilizations described in this lesson. Now create a cover for your book. First, choose a title for the book. Then, draw a cover picture that shows the lives of the people you describe. Use your book cover in a bulletin board display.

REVIEW

CONNECT MAIN IDEAS

Use this organizer to show how the environment affected the lives of early people. Write three details to support each main idea. A copy of the organizer may be found on page 7 of the Activity Book.

The First Americans

Environment

The Search for Early Peoples

The environment affected the ways early peoples moved from place to place.

1. _____
2. _____
3. _____

Ancient Indians

The ancient Indians changed their ways of life as the environment changed.

1. _____
2. _____
3. _____

Early Civilizations

Early peoples living in different parts of the Americas had different ways of life.

1. _____
2. _____
3. _____

WRITE MORE ABOUT IT

Write a Letter Imagine that you are an archaeologist searching for evidence of the first Americans. Write a letter to a friend or family member that tells what it is like to work at a dig. Explain the kinds of artifacts or other evidence you hope to find.

Write a Menu Write a menu that lists the kinds of foods an Ice Age hunter might have eaten on a typical day. Then write a menu for a food gatherer and a menu for an early farmer. How are the three menus different? How are they alike?

USE VOCABULARY

Write the term that correctly matches each definition. Then use each term in a complete sentence.

adobe   band

agriculture   nomad

1 a small group of people who work together to do activities

2 a wanderer who has no settled home

3 farming

4 a mixture of sand and straw that can be dried into bricks

CHECK UNDERSTANDING

5 Why did Ice Age hunters move from place to place?

6 What is the name of the land bridge that once linked Asia and the Americas?

7 Why are artifacts from the Meadowcroft Rock Shelter important?

8 How did agriculture change the ways of life of early peoples?

9 What was the most important food crop grown by the first Americans? Why?

10 Why was the Olmec culture so important to the early history of the Americas?

11 What was the greatest mound-building civilization?

12 What was a kiva? What was it used for?

THINK CRITICALLY

13 **Cause and Effect** Why did the oceans become shallow during the last Ice Age?

14 **Personally Speaking** How does the environment affect your life today?

15 **Think More About It** The cultures of the Olmecs, the Mound Builders, and the Anasazi developed in very different ways. Explain how this fact could be used to support the early arrival theory.

APPLY SKILLS

Compare Map Projections Write the term that correctly matches each definition.

conformal   equal-area

16 a projection that shows the sizes of regions in correct relation to one another but distorts shapes

17 a projection that shows directions correctly but distorts sizes of places, especially near the poles

Identify Patterns on Time Lines Draw a time line, and label the year A.D. 2000 in the center. Now label the year one decade before A.D. 2000 and the year one decade after it. Label the year one century before A.D. 2000 and one century after it. Label the year one millennium before A.D. 2000 and one millennium after it.

READ MORE ABOUT IT

The Earliest Americans by Helen Roney Sattler. Clarion Books. This book traces the history of the earliest Americans until about A.D. 1492.

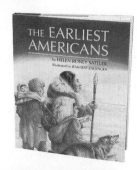

HARCOURT BRACE

Visit the Internet at **http://www.hbschool.com** for additional resources.

INDIANS OF NORTH AMERICA

"*May it be delightful my house;*
From my head may it be delightful;
To my feet may it be delightful;
Where I lie may it be delightful;
All above me may it be delightful;
All around me may it be delightful."

A Navajo house blessing

Dora Pino, a Navajo woman
of Magdalena, New Mexico

74

Northwest Coast

Over hundreds of years, as old Indian civilizations gave way to new cultures, different tribes with different ways of life slowly settled the continent. North America became a land of great **diversity**, or many differences, among its peoples. By the 1400s people from hundreds of different tribes lived in North America.

Often peoples living in the same area share some ways of life. Such an area is called a **cultural region**. People living in a place with cold weather, for example, wear heavy clothing. Many people living in a place with rich soil farm the land. Yet in North America, there were great differences even among the people of the same cultural region. Think about these differences as you read about the Indians of one cultural region—the Northwest Coast.

The Great Northwest

High in the mountains of the Cascade Range on the border of what are today the states of Washington and Oregon, the Columbia River passes through a narrow gap in the cliffs. For 15 miles (24.1 km) the river thunders through waterfalls and rapids. This area is known as The Dalles (DALZ). For hundreds of years, it was one of the greatest trading centers in North America.

People came to The Dalles from hundreds of miles away. Dozens of tribes, some speaking languages as different from each other as English is from Chinese, took part in the trading through the warm summer months.

FOCUS

How does living near an ocean affect the lives of people in coastal communities today?

Main Idea Read to find out how living near an ocean affected the lives of the Northwest Coast Indians.

Vocabulary

diversity
cultural region
dugout
pit house
clan
barter
potlatch
totem pole

This Makah artifact (right) of a carved figure in a shell is about 500 years old. The cedar chest (above right) may have been used to store fish oil. Cedar trees were an important resource to the Northwest Coast Indians.

The Dalles is part of the area known as the Northwest Coast. The Northwest Coast is a narrow strip of land that stretches 2,000 miles (3,219 km) along the Pacific Ocean from present-day southern Alaska to northern California.

The Northwest Coast Indians lived between the ocean and rugged mountain ranges, in a land of rivers and forests filled with fish and game. The growing season was short, and the climate was too wet for much agriculture. Growing their own food was difficult, so the Indians had to fish, hunt, and gather plants to survive. There were plenty of fish, deer, bears, and other animals. There was wood to build houses and make tools. If tribes could not get something by themselves, they could get it by trade.

It might seem surprising that trade was common in an area where travel was so hard. Because mountains made travel by land difficult, people traveled by water. The Columbia River was the "highway" of the Northwest, carrying people from place to place in wooden dugouts. **Dugouts** are boats made from large, hollowed-out logs.

REVIEW *What foods were available to the peoples of the Northwest?*

GEOGRAPHY

The Columbia River

The Columbia River flows 1,214 miles (1,953 km) from the Canadian Rocky Mountains in British Columbia to the Pacific Ocean at Astoria, Oregon. It is the second-longest river in the Western Hemisphere that flows into the Pacific Ocean.

The Columbia River was a major transportation route for the Indians of the Northwest Coast. It continued to be a major route for people in the Pacific Northwest until the Northern Pacific Railway was completed in 1883.

Dams and locks built in the 1930s made the river one of the world's greatest sources of hydroelectric power. Hydroelectric power is electricity made by using the energy of rushing water to turn machines in dams.

The Columbia River continues to be an important resource today.

Early Cultures of North America

ASIA

ARCTIC OCEAN

PACIFIC OCEAN

ATLANTIC OCEAN

Legend:
- Arctic
- Subarctic
- Northwest Coast
- Plateau
- California
- Great Basin
- Southwest
- Plains
- Eastern Woodlands
- Middle America
- Caribbean
- Present-day border

Hudson Bay

Gulf of Mexico

Caribbean Sea

Tropic of Cancer

SOUTH AMERICA

Culture names on map: INUPIAT, YUP'IK, ALEUT, ATHABASKAN, HAN, KASKA, TLINGIT, HAIDA, BELLA COOLA, NOOTKA, MAKAH, CHINOOK, YAKIMA, NEZ PERCÉ, KOOTENAI, BLACKFOOT, ASSINIBOINE, OJIBWA, CREE, CHIPEWYAN, NASKAPI, BEOTHUK, MICMAC, PENOBSCOT, ALGONKIN, OTTAWA, HURON, MASSACHUSET, IROQUOIS LEAGUE, CAYUGA, MOHAWK, ONEIDA, ONONDAGA, SENECA, ERIE, DELAWARE, POWHATAN, POMO, PAIUTE, SHOSHONE, UTE, CHEYENNE, CROW, MANDAN, SIOUX, PAWNEE, ARAPAHO, IOWA, SAUK, FOX, MIAMI, ILLINOIS, SHAWNEE, TUSCARORA, YOKUTS, CHUMASH, HOPI, NAVAJO, PUEBLO, ACOMA, ZUNI, APACHE, KIOWA, KAW, OSAGE, MISSOURI, QUAPAW, YUCHI, CHICKASAW, CHEROKEE, TOHO'NO-O-OTAM, COMANCHE, CADDO, CHOCTAW, NATCHEZ, YAQUI, COAHUILTEC, HUICHOL, TIMUCUA, CALUSA, CIBONEY, TAINO, ARAWAK, TOLTEC, AZTEC, MAYA, MIXTEC, ZAPOTEC, MOSQUITO, INUIT, CHIPPEWA, IROQUOIS, ASSINIBOINE, OJIBWA

Scale: 0 — 300 — 600 Miles / 0 — 300 — 600 Kilometers
Azimuthal Equal-Area Projection

Regions Many of our names for cities, states, rivers, and regions come from Indian languages.

■ *What connections do you see between the names of the Indian cultures on the map and the names of places today?*

Chinook pit houses were made of split wood. These houses usually had no windows and only one door (right). The picture (above) shows the inside of a Chinook house.

The Chinooks

The Chinooks (shuh•NUKS) were the best-known traders of the Northwest Coast. This Indian tribe lived near the coast, at the mouth of the Columbia River. Chinook villages were made up of rows of long wooden houses. The houses were built of wooden boards and had no windows. The Chinooks built each house partly over a hole dug in the earth so that some of its rooms were under the ground. Such a house is called a **pit house**.

Several families belonging to the same clan lived in each house. A **clan** is a group of families that are related to one another. Each clan was headed by its oldest member. Like many other tribes, the Chinooks traced their clans through the mother's line. In other words, the people of the clan had the same mother, grandmother, or great-grandmother. Children belonged to their mother's clan, not to their father's.

The Chinooks controlled the Columbia River from the coast all the way to The Dalles. They even made other peoples pay them for the right to travel the river. There were so many peoples speaking different languages that it became difficult to talk at The Dalles. To help solve the problem, the Chinooks developed a language for trading. It was made up of Chinook words and words borrowed from other languages. This language made it easier for different peoples to talk to each other and to **barter**, or exchange goods.

This Chinook statue of a mother and child was carved in the "X-ray" style, showing the bones of people and animals.

And what a lot of different goods there were! People traded dried fish, shells, furs, whale products, seal oil, cedar, dugouts, masks, jewelry, baskets, and copper. They also traded prisoners.

Wealth was very important to the people in the Northwest Coast area. Tribes often attacked one another to gain wealth and, in turn, respect. Prisoners, a sign of wealth, were frequently taken during the many wars. Only very important people could use prisoners as servants.

To show off the things they owned, the Chinooks and other tribes who lived along the coast held **potlatches**. These were special gatherings or celebrations with feasting and dancing. During a potlatch, the hosts gave away valuable gifts as a sign of their wealth. Members of some clans spent years preparing hundreds of gifts to be given away at the next potlatch.

REVIEW *What role did the Chinooks play in the Northwest Coast trade?*

The Makahs

The waters of the Northwest helped give the peoples who lived there plenty of food. Salmon and other fish, sea otters, and whales were in good supply. Most coastal tribes captured only beached whales, those that had become stranded on shore. The Makahs (mah•KAWZ), however, built canoes to hunt the whales at sea.

Makah whale hunters often spent months preparing for a whale hunt. They fasted and prayed to their gods to favor them. They made new wooden harpoons—long spears with sharp shell points. And they repaired their canoes and paddles. Made of wood, the canoes were 6 feet (1.8 m) wide and carried up to 60 people. They were built for the open ocean. However, they still could be tipped over by an angry whale.

Imagine one group of whale hunters setting out to sea. The chief harpooner leads the hunters. His father and grandfather

A chief harpooner prepares to throw his weapon at a whale. Whale hunting was important for the Makahs' survival.

held the same job before him. After several hours the Makah hunters spot a gray whale. They follow the animal for about 20 miles (32 km) out into the open ocean, slowly closing in. Along the way the chief harpooner shows his respect for the huge animal by singing a special song that promises to give the whale gifts if it allows itself to be killed.

Finally the chief harpooner sees his chance and throws his harpoon. The whale is hit! Sealskin floats tied to the harpoon line make it difficult for the whale to dive down into the water. Harpooners from other nearby canoes throw their weapons, too. When the whale dies, the hunters start towing it to shore.

After hours of paddling, the Makah hunters are glad to see their village. Wooden houses line the narrow beach between the water and the forest. Outside each house stands a tall wooden post called a **totem pole**. Each totem pole is beautifully carved with shapes of people and animals. The

Many Northwest Coast Indians placed carved totem poles outside their houses. Symbols on the pole often tell a family's history. This totem pole was made by a member of the Haida (HY·duh) tribe.

carvings show each family's history and importance. As the hunters draw near the village, the people on shore rush to greet them.

Little of the prized whale is wasted. The chief harpooner receives the best piece of blubber, or fat. The rest is stored for later. The people will eat the whale's meat and skin. They will make ropes and bags from different parts of the animal's body. They also will melt some of the fat for oil to burn as fuel.

REVIEW *How did Makah hunters prepare for a whale hunt?*

LESSON 1 REVIEW

Check Understanding

❶ **Remember the Facts** What resources were available on the Northwest Coast?

❷ **Recall the Main Idea** How did living near an ocean affect the lives of the Northwest Coast Indians?

Think Critically

❸ **Think More About It** How do you think people from different tribes learned the special trading language used at The Dalles?

❹ **Explore Viewpoints** Why were potlatches important to people of the Northwest Coast?

Show What You Know

Art Activity Draw a scene showing part of daily life for one of the tribes of the Northwest Coast. Work with your classmates to put all of your scenes together to form a bulletin board display. Label the display *Lifeways of the Northwest Coast Indians.*

Southwest

The Southwest is a mostly dry land of rocky mesas, deep canyons, steep cliffs, and beautiful mountains. Fierce heat during the day can be followed by sharp cold at night. Months can go by without a drop of rain. Then a sudden storm can bring so much rain that flash floods race through normally dry canyons.

It is difficult to survive in such a land. But the many peoples of the Southwest found ways not only to survive but to live well.

The Hopis

"Up the ladder and down the ladder." In the Southwest, these words meant "to enter a house." Like their Anasazi ancestors, many peoples of the Southwest lived in pueblos—adobe houses of many rooms built next to or on top of one another. To enter a house or to reach other levels, people climbed ladders. In time all of the tribes who lived in pueblos, peoples such as the Hopis (HOH•peez), the Zunis, and others, became known as the Pueblo peoples.

The name *Hopi* means "Peaceful One." The early Hopis lived in present-day northeastern Arizona, just as many Hopis do today. In early times most of their villages were built on top of high, flat mesas. Steep, narrow trails cut into the rocks led from the mesas down to the fields. There the men grew corn, beans, squash, and cotton. The climate was very dry, or **arid**, so the people used water from springs under the ground and from rain showers to water their crops.

While the men worked in the fields or hunted, the women ground corn into flour, using flat, smooth stones.

A Hopi dancer performs during a ceremony. The dance is not for show but is part of the Hopis' religion.

FOCUS
What steps do people take today to help themselves live in a dry environment?

Main Idea As you read, think about what the Indians of the Southwest did to help themselves live in a dry environment.

Vocabulary

arid   hogan
kachina   shaman
ceremony

Kachina Figures

Pueblo families taught their children the names and special powers of the kachinas by giving them kachina figures. Fathers and grandfathers carved and painted the wooden figures to look like the different kachinas. By studying the figures, children learned what the spirits stood for. Kachina figures were not for play. They were meant to be treasured and passed on to each child's own children.

Women spent hours each day grinding corn, often singing songs as they worked. Part of every home was filled with jars of corn and flour prepared by the women. A surplus of food meant survival during times of drought.

Like other Pueblo peoples, the Hopis believed in gods of the sun, rain, and earth. Spirits called **kachinas** (kuh•CHEE•nuhz) were also an important part of the Hopis' religion. These spirits remain important today. The Hopis believe that kachinas visit the world of living people once a year and enter the bodies of the kachina dancers. The dancers are Hopi men wearing painted masks and dressed to look like the kachinas. Kachina dancers take part in many Hopi **ceremonies**, or special services. Some of these ceremonies are held in kivas underground, and others are held in large meeting places outside.

REVIEW *Why was storing extra food important to the Hopis?*

Daily Life

Here is how Charlotte and David Yue describe the daily lives of the early Hopis and other Pueblo peoples in their book *The Pueblo*.

66 Pueblo families lived in one room, but most of their daily activities were out of doors. Their homes were used mainly for sleeping and for being sheltered from bad weather. The terrace was an outdoor kitchen and sitting room. The women went up and down ladders to outside ovens on the terrace or down on the ground. The outdoor drying racks had to be tended, and baskets and pottery were often worked on outside.

The workday began at the first light of dawn. Pueblo people hung up their bedding and everyone washed up. They worked first and ate later. The men would start off to the fields, and the women would sweep the floor and begin preparing the day's food.

LEARNING FROM ILLUSTRATIONS
Each Pueblo family lived together in a single room. Married couples lived with the wife's family. When one house became too crowded, part of the clan moved to a house nearby. More rooms were added to the pueblo when more space was needed.
■ *What are some of the activities being shown?*

Children learned by helping. Boys worked with their fathers and uncles. They would go together to the fields. Younger boys scared away crows or gathered up brush. When a boy was old enough, his father might let him work a plot by himself. Girls worked with their mothers and aunts, grinding beside them at the grinding stones. Even small children would be asked to bring some sticks of firewood. Grandfathers worked on their weaving and often taught the children, giving instruction in what was right and wrong and why. Or the wisdom of their years might entitle them to a ceremonial office or a place in the town council. Grandmothers might still do some of the pottery work. They also gave advice and helped take care of the children.

The men took leftover bread with them to eat in the fields, and the women might have some leftovers for a late morning meal. The workday ended in the late afternoon. The men returned from the fields, and the family sat on the floor and shared the main meal of the day. The evenings were spent talking, laughing, and visiting neighbors. At dark the blankets were again rolled out on the floor for sleeping. **99**

REVIEW *In what ways did Pueblo children help with the work of the household?*

The Navajos

Not all the people of the Southwest were Pueblo Indians. Some had different ways of life. Often, however, other tribes learned from the success of the Pueblos and took on some of their lifeways. This was true, for example, of the Navajos (NA•vuh•hohz).

The Navajos moved into the Southwest about A.D. 1100. They settled in an area known today as the Four Corners. This is the place where the corners of the states of Arizona, New Mexico, Utah, and Colorado meet. Many Navajo people still live in the Four Corners area today.

The early Navajos were nomads. They traveled with their clans and did not have a formal chief. They used brushwood, animal skins, and leaves to make new shelters in each place where they stopped to hunt and gather food. Imagine their wonder when they first saw the great pueblos of the Hopis, built high on the mesas and surrounded by fields of corn!

To the Navajos, Hopi villages were filled with treasures—treasures that the Navajos wanted. When items could not be traded, the Navajos sometimes attacked the Hopis and stole baskets, weaving looms, pottery, blankets, and farm tools. In time, however, the Navajos learned Hopi ways. Soon they, too, were growing crops and weaving cotton clothing, as the Hopis did.

The Navajos lived in houses called hogans. A **hogan** (HOH•gahn) is a cone-shaped house built by covering a log frame with mud or grass. Rather than building their hogans together to form villages, the Navajos built them in small, family-sized groups miles apart from one another.

The wood of Navajo hogans is held together by mud. A hogan is always built so that the doorway faces east.

The Navajos believed in gods they called the Holy People. Some gods, such as the Earth Mother, were kind. Others, such as the sun god, could cause crops to dry up and die. The Navajos believed that they needed to keep praising the gods so that the gods would not use their powers against the people.

As in other Indian cultures, Navajo ceremonies were led by a religious leader and healer called a **shaman** (SHAH•muhn). Shamans called upon the gods to give the people special favors.

Navajo shamans made beautiful sand-paintings, also called dry paintings, that were believed to hold healing powers. First, the shaman created a pattern of religious symbols on the ground, using colored sand. Then, the sick person sat or lay on the sand-painting while the shaman held a special ceremony believed to help him or her feel its healing powers. The painting was always rubbed away after the ceremony.

REVIEW *What lifeways did the Navajos learn from the Hopis?*

A Navajo shaman creates a sandpainting. The shaman uses charcoal, sandstone, gypsum, and ocher, ground up into powders. The powders give the shaman different colors for the painting.

LESSON 2 REVIEW

Check Understanding

1 Remember the Facts Why were tribes such as the Hopis known as the Pueblo peoples?

2 Recall the Main Idea What did the Indians of the Southwest do to help themselves live in their dry environment?

Think Critically

3 Past to Present In what ways do you think early pueblos were like present-day apartment buildings? In what ways do you think they were different?

4 Think More About It Why do you think the Navajos decided to end their nomadic way of life and learn Hopi ways?

Show What You Know

Model Activity Use several small boxes to build a three-dimensional model of a Pueblo village. Use toothpicks, straws, or other things to make ladders, and place the ladders in the model. Then write a paragraph that describes what life was like for the Pueblo people and display your village in the classroom.

FOCUS

How do people in your community use the resources in their environment?

Main Idea Read to learn how the Indians of the Great Plains used the resources in their environment.

Vocabulary

lodge
sod
tepee
travois

Great Plains

Imagine looking out over miles and miles of flat land and gently rolling hills. Tall green grasses move slowly in the breeze. The grassy lands of the Great Plains once fed the buffalo that were the region's most important resource.

At the time of the early Indians, millions of buffalo, or American bison, as scientists call them, roamed the land. These hairy, cowlike beasts moved in huge herds made up of thousands of animals. The herds were so large that they were said to blacken the horizon. These buffalo were an important resource to the Indians of the Great Plains.

The Mandans

Among the Indians of the northern Great Plains were the Mandans. They lived in forests along the Missouri River, in the western part of present-day North Dakota. In their villages the Mandans built circular houses called **lodges**. Each lodge was built over a shallow pit and covered with sod. **Sod** is earth, cut into blocks or mats, that is held together by

This copy of Karl Bodmer's painting, *Mih-Tutta-Hangkusch, a Mandan Village*, shows the boats the Mandans used. To make the boats, they stretched buffalo skins around a wooden frame.

Two hunters hiding under wolf skins crawl slowly toward a herd of buffalo.

the grass and its roots. Because Mandan houses were covered with earth, they are often called earth lodges.

Each round earth lodge was home to several families. Sometimes as many as 60 people, plus their dogs, lived in one lodge. Each family had its own bed or beds next to the outer wall. In the center of the lodge was a shared fireplace under a hole in the roof for letting out smoke. The lodge was warm, and it protected the people during the cold winters.

About twice a year the Mandan villages emptied, as men, women, and children took part in a great buffalo hunt. The people walked for several days from their villages in the river valley forest to the grassy hunting areas of the plains.

Imagine a Mandan hunting party coming upon a herd. The Mandans do not attack right away. First, the hunters meet to decide exactly what they will do. When each one knows his job, the group is ready.

At dawn the hunt begins. Wearing animal skins as disguises, the hunters creep into position around some of the buffalo. The men move quickly to surround a number of the huge beasts.

At a signal, the hunters shout all together. The frightened buffalo run, and the hunters drive them toward a steep cliff. The buffalo fall over the cliff and are killed.

Most of the women did not take part in the hunt. Their job was to skin the buffalo and prepare them for many uses. The Mandans ate some of the meat right away. The rest they dried and saved to eat when there were no buffalo to hunt. Dried meat,

Buffalo were one of the most important resources to the Indians of the Great Plains. This painted Mandan robe (left) was made from the whole skin of a buffalo. The triangles on the robe stand for the feathers of a war bonnet.

which people today call jerky, can be kept for many months.

The Mandans used every part of the buffalo they hunted. They made clothing, blankets, and moccasins from the skins. They carried water in bags made from the stomachs. They twisted the hair into cord. They made needles, arrowheads, and other tools from the bones. Some Mandans even used the horns of the buffalo to make bows.

The Mandans also farmed. The men of the tribe hunted, and the women grew the crops. Their farms were small, more like gardens. Their crops were mainly beans, corn, squash, and sunflowers.

The Mandans often traded their crops for goods that other tribes brought to them. Their villages became trade centers.

REVIEW *In what two ways did the Mandans get their food?*

The Kiowas, another tribe of the Plains, used buffalo skins to make much of their clothing, such as moccasins (right). The Mandan shield (far right) has an image of a turtle painted on it.

The Kiowas

The Kiowas (KY•uh•wahz) of the southern Great Plains did not farm or live in villages. They were nomads, always moving on the vast Plains. This region had no rich river valleys or forests. It was flat grassland. The roots of the short grass were so tough that it was impossible to break the soil with a digging stick. So instead of growing crops, the Kiowas followed the buffalo from place to place.

Although the Kiowas were nomads, they claimed certain areas. Their first known homeland was in what is now western Montana. Later they migrated eastward over the Rocky Mountains and onto the Great Plains.

The Kiowas followed the known routes of the buffalo herds. Like the Mandans, the Kiowas depended on the buffalo as the most important resource in their way of life. The Kiowas' houses, their clothing, their food, and even the fuel for their fires came from the buffalo. For fuel the Kiowas used dried buffalo droppings, called chips.

Because the Kiowas followed the buffalo herds, they built shelters that were easy to move. One kind was a cone-shaped tent called a **tepee** (TEE•pee). The Kiowas set wooden poles in a circle and tied them together at the top. Then they covered the poles with buffalo skins, leaving a hole at the top to let out the smoke from their fire. The Kiowas also used buffalo skins for their beds and blankets.

Like the Kiowas, the Apaches built shelters that could be easily moved. Dogs were used to help the Indians move from place to place.

Wood was hard to find because few trees grew on the Great Plains. The Kiowas made double use of their wooden tepee poles by turning them into a kind of carrier called a **travois** (truh•VOY). A travois was made up of two poles fastened to a harness on a dog. Goods were carried on a skin tied between the poles. Later the Kiowas used horses, which they called "big dogs," to drag the poles.

Among the Kiowas each person was equal in the group. No one person was born more important than anyone else. Any man could become chief by proving himself a good hunter and a good leader of people. He was chief because his people chose and trusted him.

Kiowas who did not follow the ways of the group were free to live on their own. Sometimes a leader and his followers would start a new village. In this way, one tribe often had many subgroups. Each subgroup was made up of families who worked together.

REVIEW *What kind of person did the Kiowas choose as chief?*

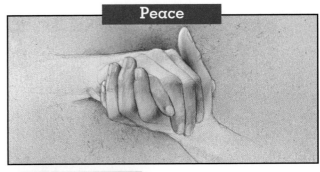
Peace

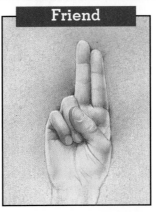
Friend

LEARNING FROM DIAGRAMS
The Plains Indians often communicated with one another through sign language.
■ *Why do you think the Indians crossed their arms to make the sign for trade?*

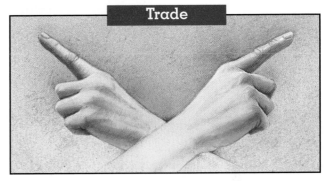
Trade

LESSON 3 REVIEW

Check Understanding

1 Remember the Facts In what kinds of shelters did the Mandans and the Kiowas live?

2 Recall the Main Idea How did the Mandans and the Kiowas use the resources that were found in their environment?

Think Critically

3 Think More About It Why do you think it was important to carefully plan a buffalo hunt?

4 Personally Speaking Why do you think it was important for a chief to be a good hunter?

Show What You Know

Poster Activity Make a poster that shows the many ways the Plains Indians used buffalo. At the top of the poster, draw a buffalo. Then fill your poster with pictures of items the Indians made from different parts of the buffalo. Share your poster with the class.

FOCUS

How does conflict affect the lives of people today?

Main Idea As you read, think about the ways conflict affected the lives of the peoples of the Eastern Woodlands.

Vocabulary

legend
Iroquois League
confederation
council
longhouse

Eastern Woodlands

With this prayer, the Haudenosaunee (hoh•dee•noh•SAW•nee), known later as the Iroquois (IR•uh•kwoy), gave thanks for the many resources of their land:

66 We return thanks to our mother, the earth, which sustains us. We return thanks to the rivers and streams, which supply us with water. We return thanks to all herbs, which furnish medicines for the cure of our diseases. We return thanks to the corn, and to her sisters, the beans and squashes, which give us life. We return thanks to the bushes and trees, which provide us with fruit. . . . 99

The Iroquois lived in what is today the eastern part of the United States. This cultural region was called the Eastern Woodlands. It got its name from the many forests that covered the land. The forests were so thick that in some places sunlight could barely reach the ground.

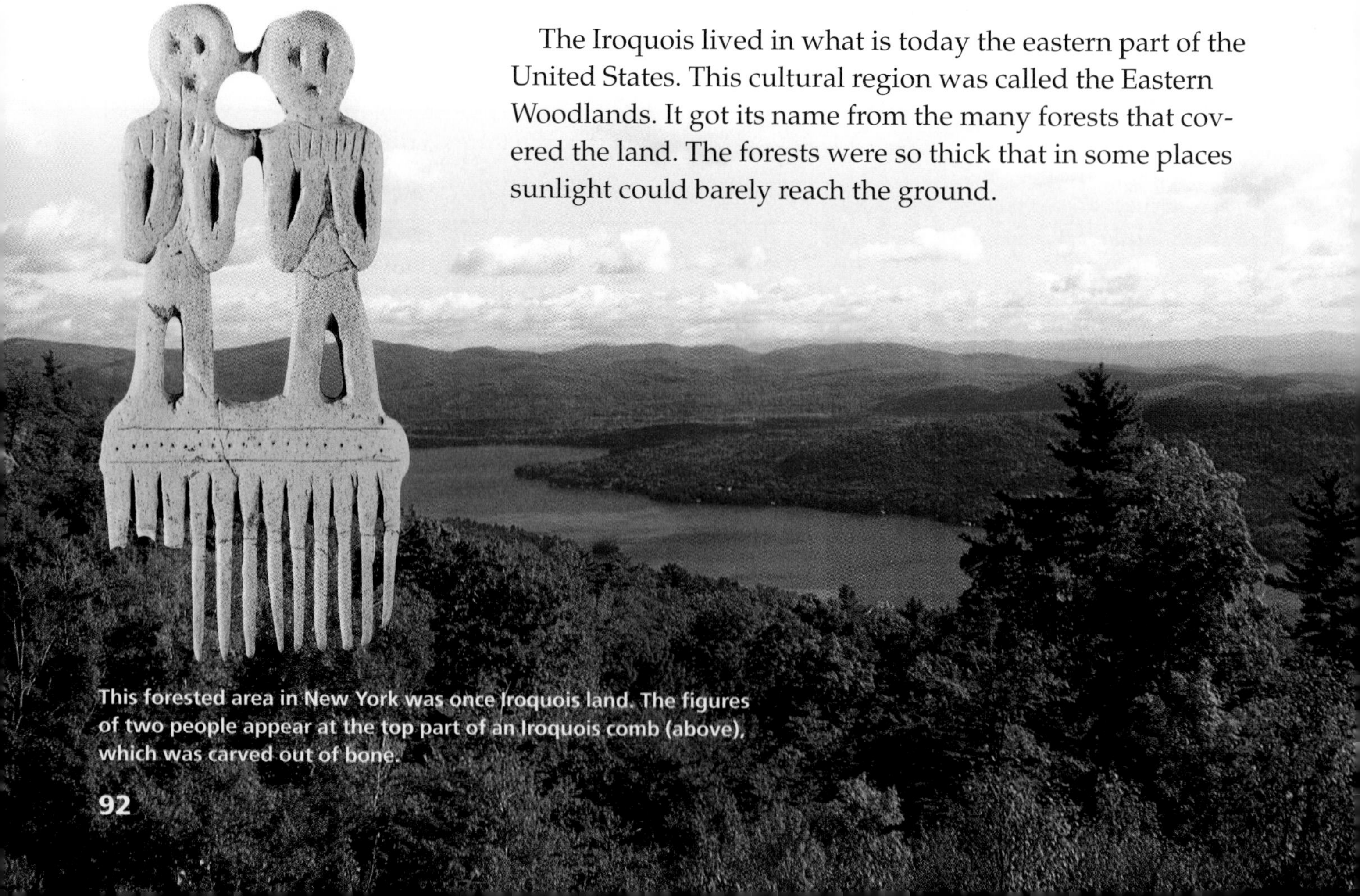

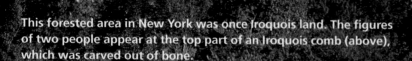

This forested area in New York was once Iroquois land. The figures of two people appear at the top part of an Iroquois comb (above), which was carved out of bone.

The Eastern Woodlands was a huge region of great diversity. It had rugged, snow-covered mountains in the north and hot, wet swamps in the south. It also was home to hundreds of different peoples. So many lived there, in fact, that some places became quite crowded, with different tribes often fighting each other for room.

The Iroquois

The Iroquois lived in the northeastern part of the woodlands. They were among the most powerful peoples of the region. The Iroquois were not one tribe but a group of tribes that lived near each other and spoke similar languages. These tribes were the Seneca (SEN•uh•kuh), Cayuga (ky•YOO•guh), Onondaga (ah•nuhn•DAHG•uh), Oneida (oh•NY•duh), and Mohawk.

For many years the Iroquois fought with each other and with the neighboring Algonkins (al•GON•kins). The fighting often began over land. Over the years farmers had cleared more and more forest land to raise crops to feed their people. This meant that hunters had to go farther away to find animals, often entering other tribes' lands. But the fighting that began over land continued out of revenge.

Think about this story of a Seneca woman who had lost her son in a battle with the Cayugas. Sad and angry, she asked the men of her clan to attack the Cayugas and pay them back for her son's death. The Seneca leaders agreed, and their warriors acted quickly. They attacked a Cayuga village, killing many people and taking others prisoner. One of the Cayuga men was given to the Seneca woman in place of her lost son. But now there was likely to be a return attack, and the fighting would go on.

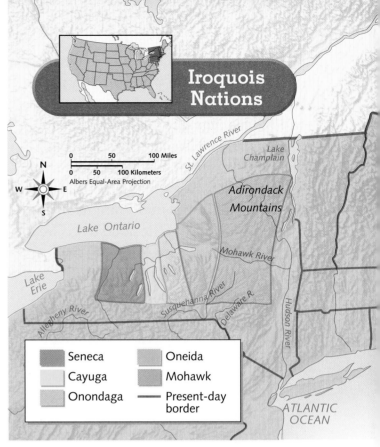

Iroquois Nations

Seneca
Cayuga
Onondaga
Oneida
Mohawk
Present-day border

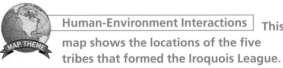

Human-Environment Interactions This map shows the locations of the five tribes that formed the Iroquois League.

■ *How did the locations of the tribes help make working together so important?*

Like many native peoples, the Iroquois often used **legends**, or stories handed down over time, to explain the past. One legend says that a holy man named Dekanawida (deh•kahn•uh•WIH•duh) was one of the first to speak out against all the fighting. He said that the Iroquois must come together "by taking hold of each other's hands so firmly and forming a circle so strong that if a tree should fall upon it, it could not shake nor break it, so that our people and grandchildren shall remain in the circle in security, peace, and happiness."

An Onondaga chief named Hiawatha (hy•uh•WAH•thuh) shared Dekanawida's hopes for peace. Hiawatha visited the Iroquois tribes, asking for an end to the fighting. Tired of war, they finally agreed.

They decided to work together in what became known as the **Iroquois League** (LEEG).

In 1570 the members of the Iroquois League agreed to form a **confederation** (kuhn•feh•duh•RAY•shuhn), or loose group of governments. Each tribe governed itself. But matters that were important to all, such as war and trade, were decided by a Great Council. A **council** is a group that makes laws.

Men from each of the five Iroquois tribes, together called the Five Nations, served on the Great Council. The oldest women of each tribe chose the council members. Each member had one vote. All had to agree before anything was done.

The Iroquois said that their confederation was like a big longhouse. A **longhouse** is a long wooden building in which several Iroquois families lived together. It was made of elm bark and had a large door at each end. Just as several families shared a longhouse, the five tribes shared the confederation. They thought of the confederation as a longhouse as big as their land, with the Mohawks guarding the eastern door and the Senecas guarding the western door.

REVIEW *What problems led the Iroquois to form a confederation?*

Longhouses (left) had no windows, only a door at each end and small holes in the roof. This computer-generated picture (below) shows the inside of a longhouse.

Green Corn Ceremony

Each year the Cherokees, like other tribes from the Southeast, held the Green Corn Ceremony. Some tribes, however, called it the Busk Ceremony. The ceremony was a multi-day festival during which the Indians celebrated the ripening of the first corn of the year. Some of the ways the Indians prepared for the ceremony were by making repairs to the buildings in the community and by cleaning their homes. Later, everyone gathered for feasting, the Green Corn Dance, and games. The Cherokee Indians of today continue to celebrate with this festival.

The *Creek Baskita Green Corn Dance* painted by Fred Beaver shows the Creeks celebrating the Green Corn Ceremony.

The Cherokees

Far to the south of the Iroquois lived another people of the Eastern Woodlands—the Cherokees (CHAIR•uh•keez). The Cherokees made their homes in the rich river valleys of the southern Appalachian Mountains. There they grew corn, beans, squash, pumpkins, sunflowers, and tobacco. They gathered wild plants from the forests. They also fished, and they hunted squirrels, rabbits, turkeys, bears, and deer.

Like other tribes of the Southeast, most Cherokee families had two houses. One was built to keep them warm in the winter, and the other was built to keep them cool in the summer. Winter houses were small, cone-shaped pit houses made of wooden poles covered with earth. Summer houses were larger, box-shaped houses with grass or clay walls and bark roofs. In both houses, several families of the same clan lived together.

Cherokee houses—often as many as 300 to 400—were built close together to form villages. At the center of each village was an open square with a temple built high on a flat-topped mound. There the shamans led ceremonies for the community. The most important was the Green Corn Ceremony, held at the end of the summer to give thanks for a good harvest. Shamans also led healing ceremonies. Like other Indian peoples, the Cherokees made many medicines from the plants of the forest.

Leaders, called chiefs, governed each village, telling the people what to do in day-to-day matters. But the villages were also part of a larger Cherokee confederation. From time to time, chiefs from as many as 100 villages came together to discuss important matters—especially matters of war. As in other places in the Eastern Woodlands, wars with neighboring tribes took place often. High wooden fences made

This painting by George Catlin shows the Choctaws, who, like the Cherokees, played Little War. To control the ball, each player carried two sticks like these (right).

of logs were built around each of the villages to keep out enemies.

In most villages the chief in charge of matters of war was also in charge of a game called Little War. It was something like today's game of lacrosse, but it had more players and fewer rules and was much rougher. The object of the game was to throw a small ball between two posts, using a special stick with a net on the end. People came from miles around to watch the game.

REVIEW *Why did the Cherokee chiefs meet as a confederation?*

LESSON 4 REVIEW

Check Understanding

1 Remember the Facts What caused the wars in the Eastern Woodlands?

2 Recall the Main Idea In what ways did conflict affect the lives of the peoples of the Eastern Woodlands?

Think Critically

3 Past to Present How was the Iroquois Confederation like governments today? How was it different?

4 Explore Viewpoints Why did the Iroquois feel that a confederation was like a longhouse?

5 Think More About It Why do you think the Cherokee chief who was in charge of matters of war was also in charge of a ball game?

Show What You Know

Simulation Activity Create a conversation between Hiawatha and members of an Iroquois tribe. In the conversation Hiawatha should try to get the people to join the confederation. With your classmates, put your conversations together to write a scene about the formation of the Iroquois League.

Identify Causes and Effects

1. Why Learn This Skill?

Any action that makes something else happen is a cause. What happens because of that action is an effect. To find the links between events in history, you will need to identify causes and effects. Knowing about causes and effects can also help you predict likely outcomes for your actions so that you can make more thoughtful decisions.

2. Understand the Process

Before the Iroquois League was formed, tribes often fought one another. Most of the time the fighting happened because of disagreements over land. The fighting that was first caused by conflicts over land often continued out of revenge.

The Iroquois leaders Dekanawida and Hiawatha feared that all the fighting would destroy their people. They talked to the tribes about peace and helped them end the fighting. The tribes began to work together to form the Iroquois League.

Follow the arrows on the chart on this page to help you understand the causes and the effects that led to the formation of the Iroquois League.

1. What first caused the fighting among the Iroquois tribes?
2. What effect of that fighting caused more fighting?
3. What caused Dekanawida and Hiawatha to work to end the fighting?
4. What was the effect of Dekanawida's and Hiawatha's work?

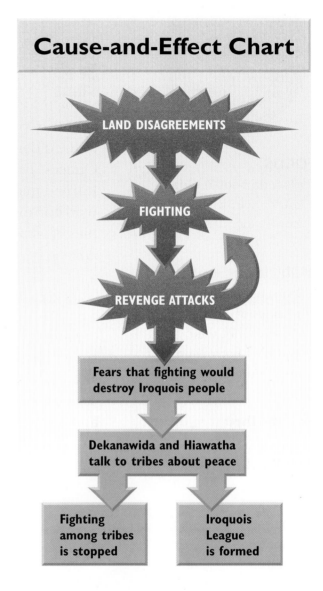

Cause-and-Effect Chart

LAND DISAGREEMENTS

FIGHTING

REVENGE ATTACKS

Fears that fighting would destroy Iroquois people

Dekanawida and Hiawatha talk to tribes about peace

Fighting among tribes is stopped

Iroquois League is formed

3. Think and Apply

Suppose that you are hurrying to school. It is raining, and there are wet leaves on the sidewalk. You slip on the leaves and fall, hurting your leg. As a result, you are late for school and miss an important test. Draw a cause-and-effect chart to show the causes and effects of your fall.

FOCUS

How do people today meet their needs by borrowing ideas from others?

Main Idea
Read to learn how Indian peoples of Middle America met their needs by borrowing ideas from other peoples.

Vocabulary

city-state
class
noble
slavery
empire
emperor
tribute

The plate (above) shows patterns of the Mayan culture. This clay figure (right) shows the dress worn by men of the Mayan upper classes.

Middle America

The cultural region of Middle America includes most of the present-day country of Mexico as well as several countries of Central America. This region was home to one of the oldest civilizations in the Americas—that of the Olmecs. The Indian peoples who came after the Olmecs learned much from this "mother civilization." Two groups who borrowed ideas from the Olmecs and from other peoples of Middle America were the Mayas (MY•uhz) and the Aztecs.

The Mayas

From far off, it looked as if the whole city were made of stone. There were temple pyramids reaching high into the sky. There was a round-topped building where priests studied the stars. There were palaces, towers, ball courts, and bridges, all connected by roads paved with stones. This was Tikal (tih•KAHL), one of the cities built by a people known as the Mayas.

Mayan civilization began to take shape about 500 B.C., during the time of the Olmecs. Building on what the Olmecs had done, the Mayas slowly created their own culture. In time Mayan culture took Olmec ways of life to even greater heights.

The Mayas built more than 100 stone cities in Middle America. Each city had its own ruler and its own government. For this reason, each was called a **city-state**. Tikal, in what is today the country of Guatemala, was the largest. Up to 100,000 people lived there.

Like the Olmecs and some other Indian peoples, the Mayas were divided into social **classes**. These are groups of people that are treated with different amounts of respect in their society. At the top were the all-powerful priests. Next were the **nobles**, or people from important families. The nobles ruled along with the priests. Below them were traders and craftspeople who worked with wood, stone, leather, gold, and clay. Near the bottom were the farmers, whose corn fed the other classes and made Mayan civilization possible. The only people treated with less respect than the farmers were the slaves.

The Mayas, like some other cultures, enslaved other people. **Slavery** is the practice of holding people against their will and making them carry out orders. Most Mayas who held slaves were nobles. They were thought of as slave owners. The enslaved people were thought of as the owner's property. Most slaves were people accused of crimes. Slavery was their punishment.

The priests and nobles lived in luxury in the cities. But everyday life for most Mayas, who lived in the countryside, meant hard work. Think about the members of one farm family, beginning their day when it is still dark outside. Rising first, the mother lights a fire in the family's small hut, which is made of mud. There are no windows and no furniture. The family eats and sleeps on mats laid on the ground. The mother prepares tortillas (tor•TEE•yahz), or thin corn pancakes. She bakes them over the fire for her husband and son. At dawn both will leave for the fields. It takes hard work to keep the jungle from taking over the land where they grow corn, beans, and squash.

At Mayan temples priests held religious ceremonies and studied the stars. Most temples looked like this one at Chichén Itzá (chih•CHEN it•SAH).

The Mayas and the Aztecs

Gulf of Mexico

PACIFIC OCEAN

- Tula
- Chapultepec
- Tenochtitlán
- Cholula
- Coxcatlán
- Monte Albán
- Yagul
- Palenque
- Bonampak
- Copán
- Tikal
- Uxmal
- Cozumel

Yucatán Peninsula

Río Balsas

Río Usumacinta

0   100   200 Miles
0 100 200 Kilometers
Azimuthal Equal-Area Projection

■ Maya civilization, A.D. 900
■ Aztec civilization, A.D. 1500

Regions The Mayas and the Aztecs lived in parts of what are today Mexico and Central America.

■ *Why do you think this cultural region is called Middle America?*

When father and son have left, the mother cares for her new baby and begins her own work. Today she will weave cloth and begin to make extra baskets to store corn. The harvest this season should be good. There should be enough corn to feed the family. They might even have some left over to trade at the market in the city.

Mayan markets were busy places. Traders from many miles around bought and sold honey, cotton cloth, cocoa, feathers, copper bells, gold dishes, pearls, salt, and dried fish. All of these goods were carried to and from the markets on the backs of slaves.

The Mayas believed in gods of the sun, rain, and many other qualities found in nature. Mayan priests led religious ceremonies and spent many hours studying the stars. From watching the movement of the stars and working out long mathematical

This is a Mayan figure of a woman weaving at a loom. The loom is fastened to a pole, probably a tree trunk.

problems, the Mayas made several different calendars. One of their calendars had 365 days, as our calendar does today. To help keep track of time, the Mayas used a way of counting that had the idea of zero—a very important idea in mathematics. And they recorded what they learned, using their own form of picture writing.

REVIEW *How was the Olmec civilization important to the Mayas?*

The Aztecs

Another culture that developed in Middle America was that of the Mexicas, a tribe later known as the Aztecs. For many years the Aztecs were nomads. Then, about A.D. 1200, they began to settle in the Valley of Mexico.

The Aztecs built their capital, Tenochtitlán (tay•nohch•teet•LAHN), on two islands in the middle of Lake Texcoco (tes•KOH•koh). Today Mexico City, the capital of Mexico, stands on this same spot. Legend says that the Aztec tribe built their capital where they saw a sign from the gods—an eagle with a snake in its mouth, sitting on a cactus. Today the eagle with the snake appears on the Mexican flag.

From their capital at Tenochtitlán, the Aztecs built a great civilization. By about A.D. 1500 the Aztecs' huge empire included 200,000 square miles (518,000 sq km) and more than 5 million people. An **empire** is a conquered land of many people and places governed by one ruler. That ruler is called an **emperor**.

Just as the Mayas had learned from the Olmecs, the Aztecs learned from the Mayas. The Aztecs also borrowed new ways of doing things from peoples they conquered. In this way, the Aztec Empire became one of the greatest of the time.

To have more land for farming, the Aztecs built small islands in Lake Texcoco. To do this, they tied large baskets to the lake's bottom and filled them with mud. Then they planted corn and other crops in the new soil. Canals and paved roads connected the many islands to the shore.

In the city's most important square were palaces with hundreds of rooms. There were also gardens and a large zoo. The palaces were the homes of the all-powerful Aztec emperor.

Near the emperor's palaces were huge warehouses piled high with tribute. **Tribute** is the name for payments a ruler demands from his or her people. Each year the people had to send goods such as cloth, jewelry, feathers, gold, and corn to Tenochtitlán. If they refused, the emperor would send Aztec soldiers to make them pay.

To protect their empire, the Aztecs had a large army. In wartime, an Aztec leader beat the drum on top of the war god's temple to call the Aztec army. The soldiers moved at once to

This drawing tells the story of the Aztecs' search for a place to build their capital. The name Tenochtitlán means "cactus rock." The blue lines in the drawing stand for the water of Lake Texcoco. The symbol of the eagle on the cactus can be seen today on the Mexican flag.

This is the lake city of Tenochtitlán, as painted by Mexican artist Diego Rivera. The city and nearby land were joined by bridges.

prepare for war and join their fighting groups in front of their clan's temple. In 24 hours the Aztec army would be 200,000 strong and ready to fight. Most Aztec soldiers wore special clothing. An Eagle Knight, for example, wore a wooden helmet shaped like an eagle's head. The soldier's quilted cotton armor was covered with eagle feathers.

In the very center of Tenochtitlán, white flat-topped pyramids rose toward the sky. On top of the pyramids stood the great stone temples that were built to honor the Aztecs' gods.

Past the temples was a large, open area where the daily market was held. Each morning canoes crowded the lake, bringing goods from all over the empire and from places outside of it. People quickly set up their stalls, eager to do business. More than 60,000 people—from the highest nobles to the lowest farmers—came to the market-place every day to exchange goods. At the same time they exchanged ideas, often adding new ways of life to Aztec culture.

REVIEW *From whom did the Aztecs learn many of their lifeways?*

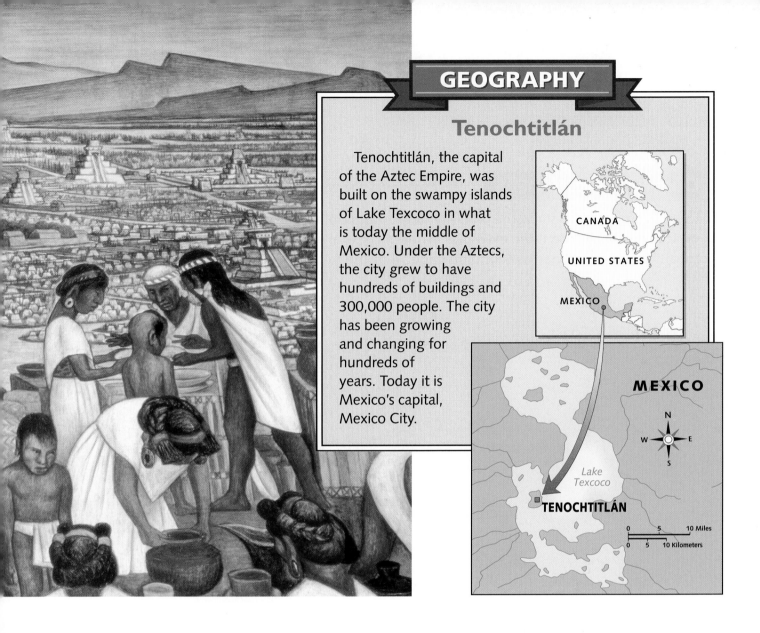

Tenochtitlán

Tenochtitlán, the capital of the Aztec Empire, was built on the swampy islands of Lake Texcoco in what is today the middle of Mexico. Under the Aztecs, the city grew to have hundreds of buildings and 300,000 people. The city has been growing and changing for hundreds of years. Today it is Mexico's capital, Mexico City.

CANADA

UNITED STATES

MEXICO

MEXICO

N
W   E
S

Lake
Texcoco

TENOCHTITLÁN

0   5   10 Miles
0   5   10 Kilometers

LESSON 5 REVIEW

Check Understanding

1 Remember the Facts Why was each city in the Mayan civilization called a city-state?

2 Recall the Main Idea How did the Indian peoples of Middle America meet their needs by borrowing ideas from other peoples?

Think Critically

3 Think More About It How was a Mayan priest's life different from the life of a Mayan farmer?

4 Cause and Effect How did the Aztecs change their environment when they built the city of Tenochtitlán?

Show What You Know

Art Activity Create a travel brochure inviting people today to visit the cities of either the Mayan or the Aztec civilization. Your brochure should include a map showing where the civilization was located, as well as a short introduction to the people's history. Present your brochure to the class.

REVIEW

CONNECT MAIN IDEAS

Use this organizer to show the diversity of the ways of life of the American Indians. Write three examples for each cultural region. A copy of the organizer may be found on page 14 of the Activity Book.

Northwest Coast

1. _____
   _____
2. _____
   _____
3. _____
   _____

Indians of North America

Diversity

Great Plains

1. _____
   _____
2. _____
   _____
3. _____
   _____

Southwest

1. _____
   _____
2. _____
   _____
3. _____
   _____

Middle America

1. _____
   _____
2. _____
   _____
3. _____
   _____

Eastern Woodlands

1. _____
   _____
2. _____
   _____
3. _____
   _____

WRITE MORE ABOUT IT

Write an Invitation Imagine that you are a wealthy Chinook getting ready to hold a potlatch. Write an invitation to a friend, describing your plans for the feast.

Write a Story Write a story entitled *A Day in the Life of an American Indian Family.* Include the conversations of friends and family members in your story.

USE VOCABULARY

Write a term from this list to complete each of the sentences that follow.

barter	shaman
clan	slavery
council	travois

1. A _____ is a group of families that are related to one another.

2. At The Dalles, Indians from many different Northwest Coast tribes met to _____ , or exchange goods.

3. A religious leader and healer called a _____ led many Navajo ceremonies.

4. A _____ is a kind of carrier used by the Kiowas to transport goods.

5. A _____ is a group that makes laws.

6. _____ is the practice of holding people against their will and making them carry out orders.

CHECK UNDERSTANDING

7. Why were dugouts especially important to the Indians of the Northwest Coast?

8. What do the carvings on totem poles show?

9. How did Pueblo people prepare for times of drought?

10. What are kachina figures used for?

11. In what ways did the tribes of the Great Plains use the buffalo they hunted?

12. What was the Iroquois League? What was its purpose?

13. What group was in the highest class in Mayan society? What group was in the lowest class?

THINK CRITICALLY

14. **Past to Present** Many Indian clans traced their families through the mother's line. How is that different from the way many people today trace their families?

15. **Think More About It** How were the lifeways of the Makahs and the Kiowas similar, even though they lived in different cultural regions?

16. **Cause and Effect** How did the environment affect the ways the Hopis, Mandans, and Cherokees built their homes?

APPLY SKILLS

Identify Causes and Effects
Think again about the busy trading center at The Dalles. Draw a cause-and-effect chart similar to the chart on page 97. The chart should trace the development of the special trading language that was used at The Dalles. Show the causes that led the Indians to make up the language, and show its effects.

READ MORE ABOUT IT

Potlatch: A Tsimshian Celebration by Diane Hoyt-Goldsmith. Holiday House. Text and photographs are used to describe the tradition of the potlatch which is held by the Tsimshian Indians to celebrate their heritage.

Visit the Internet at **http://www.hbschool.com** for additional resources.

A MULTICULTURAL Country

If a huge quilt could show you what life was like in the Americas in the late 1400s, it would have hundreds of different patches. Their different colors and designs would stand for the many different Indian cultures.

The United States is still a patchwork of many cultures—American Indian, Hispanic, European, African, Asian, Pacific Island, Alaska Native, and others. The people from these many backgrounds are united by being Americans. Yet they also have kept alive their own cultural traditions. This has made the United States a multicultural country—a country of many cultures.

Many people believe that our country's diversity of cultures adds to the richness of American life. Most Americans experience this diversity every day. You hear it in the languages people speak and in the music they play. You see it on signs and in the ways people dress. You taste it in the foods they make. You feel it at times of special celebration.

Think and Apply

BUILDING CITIZENSHIP

Think about the many ways people express their culture. Design a colorful patch that shows a part of your cultural heritage. Then combine your patch with those of your classmates to create a quilt that shows the cultures in your classroom community.

HARCOURT BRACE

Visit the Internet at **http://www.hbschool.com** for additional resources.

CNN Turner Le@rning

Check your media center or classroom video library for the Making Social Studies Relevant videotape of this feature.

UNIT 1 REVIEW

VISUAL SUMMARY

Summarize the Main Ideas
Study the pictures and captions to help you review what you read about in Unit 1.

Illustrate a Scene
Choose one of the Indian peoples described in Unit 1 but not shown here. Draw a picture that shows a scene of daily life for the group you chose. Then write a paragraph that explains the scene. Tell where the scene should be placed on the visual summary.

1 One of the greatest trading centers in North America was located in the Northwest Coast. People from dozens of tribes came in dugout canoes to barter at The Dalles.

3 Many of the peoples of the Southwest lived in pueblos. Drying and storing surplus food helped the people survive during times of drought.

5 The Aztec capital of Tenochtitlán was one of the largest cities of Middle America. The city center had palaces, warehouses, temple pyramids, and a huge market.

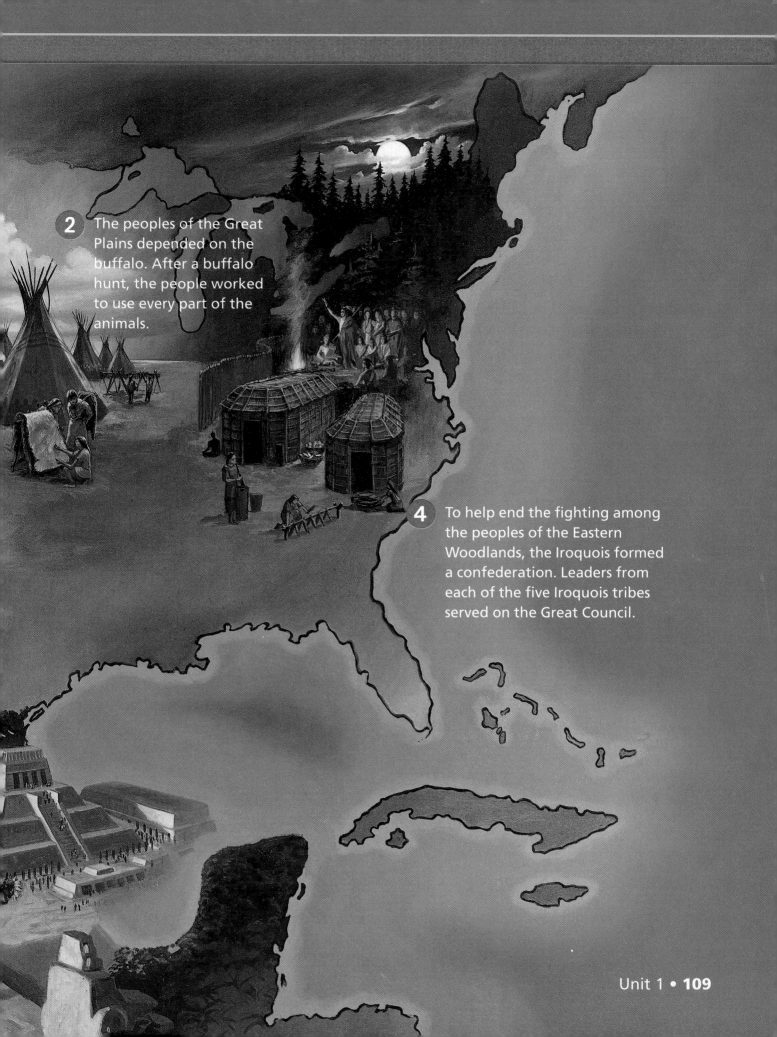

2 The peoples of the Great Plains depended on the buffalo. After a buffalo hunt, the people worked to use every part of the animals.

4 To help end the fighting among the peoples of the Eastern Woodlands, the Iroquois formed a confederation. Leaders from each of the five Iroquois tribes served on the Great Council.

UNIT 1
REVIEW

USE VOCABULARY

Use each term in a sentence that will help explain its meaning.

1 culture   **3** earthworks

2 dugouts   **4** maize

CHECK UNDERSTANDING

5 What is cultural diffusion?

6 What was the religious leader called who led the Navajo ceremonies?

7 In what ways did the Indians of the Great Plains depend on the buffalo?

8 What problems led the Iroquois to form a confederation?

THINK CRITICALLY

9 **Think More About It** What changes in technology brought changes to the lives of early Americans?

10 **Past to Present** Give three examples that show that North America in ancient times was a land of great diversity. Give three examples that show that North America today is a land of great diversity.

APPLY SKILLS

Compare Map Projections Map A is an azimuthal equal-area projection. Map B is an orthographic projection. Use the maps to answer the following questions.

11 On which map does the United States look larger?

12 On which map can you more clearly see the North Pole?

13 Which map shows parts of both the Eastern and the Western Hemispheres?

14 What are the advantages and disadvantages of each map?

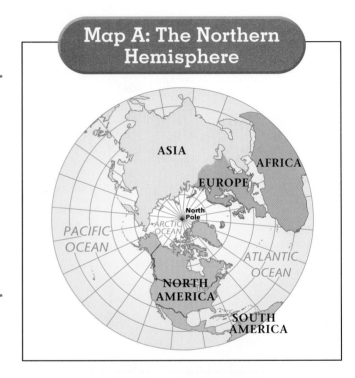

Map A: The Northern Hemisphere

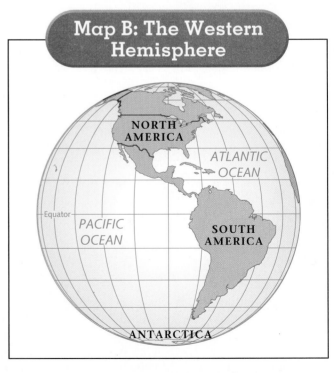

Map B: The Western Hemisphere

REMEMBER

- Share your ideas.
- Cooperate with others to plan your work.
- Take responsibility for your work.
- Help one another.
- Show your group's work to the class.
- Discuss what you learned by working together.

Unit Project Wrap-Up

Create a Map Work with several of your classmates to finish the Unit Project that was described on page 39. First, make sure that your map includes an American Indian group from each of the five cultural regions— the Northwest, the Southwest, the Great Plains, the Eastern Woodlands, and Middle America. Work together to write captions that explain how each Indian group governed itself and met its needs. Display the maps and captions in the classroom or hallway.

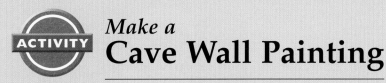

ACTIVITY *Make a* **Cave Wall Painting**

Imagine that you and your classmates are Clovis people. You want to draw pictures of a mammoth hunt on a cave wall so your children will learn from your experiences. Tape large pieces of paper to your classroom wall. Form several groups, with each group responsible for a different part of the hunt. Using paint, colored chalk, or markers, draw scenes of the hunt. One scene should show the weapons that were used, including Clovis points and the atlatl. Another scene should show the many ways the people used the mammoth.

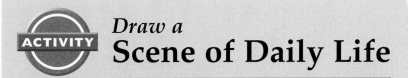

ACTIVITY *Draw a* **Scene of Daily Life**

To show how the environment helps shape the way people live, draw a scene of the daily life of an Indian group. Use your textbook and other reference materials to get ideas. Give your scene a title, and add it to a classroom display.

Unit 1
The Ancient Americas

Unit 2

Unit 3
Our Colonial Heritage

Unit 4
The American Revolution

EXPLORATIONS AND ENCOUNTERS

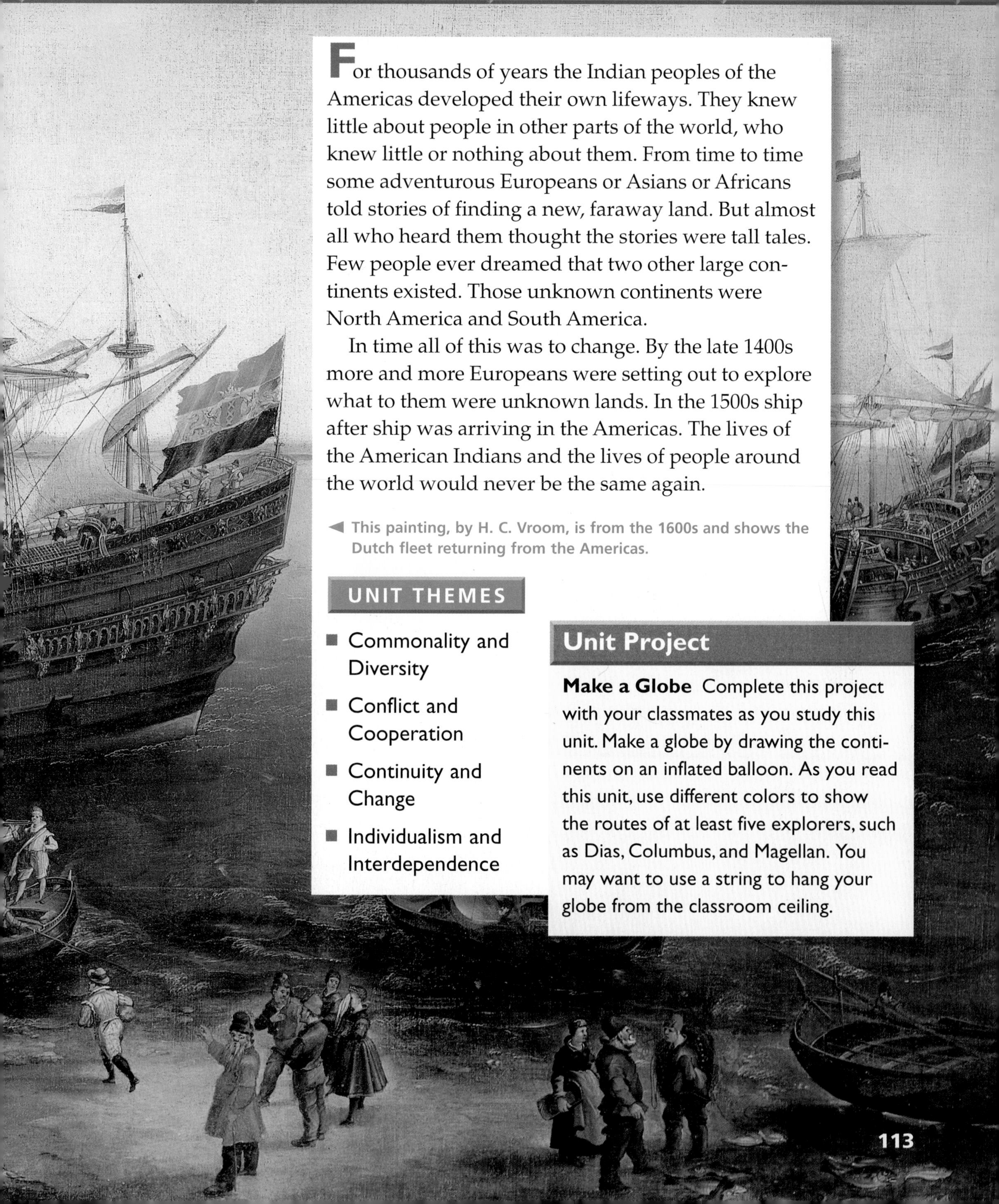

For thousands of years the Indian peoples of the Americas developed their own lifeways. They knew little about people in other parts of the world, who knew little or nothing about them. From time to time some adventurous Europeans or Asians or Africans told stories of finding a new, faraway land. But almost all who heard them thought the stories were tall tales. Few people ever dreamed that two other large continents existed. Those unknown continents were North America and South America.

In time all of this was to change. By the late 1400s more and more Europeans were setting out to explore what to them were unknown lands. In the 1500s ship after ship was arriving in the Americas. The lives of the American Indians and the lives of people around the world would never be the same again.

◄ This painting, by H. C. Vroom, is from the 1600s and shows the Dutch fleet returning from the Americas.

UNIT THEMES

- Commonality and Diversity

- Conflict and Cooperation

- Continuity and Change

- Individualism and Interdependence

Unit Project

Make a Globe Complete this project with your classmates as you study this unit. Make a globe by drawing the continents on an inflated balloon. As you read this unit, use different colors to show the routes of at least five explorers, such as Dias, Columbus, and Magellan. You may want to use a string to hang your globe from the classroom ceiling.

NORTH
AMERICA

Cahokia

Tenochtitlán

SOUTH
AMERICA

Cuzco

PACIFIC
OCEAN

ATLANTIC
OCEAN

N
W · E
S

0   1,000   2,000 Miles
0   1,000   2,000 Kilometers
Miller Cylindrical Projection

1400   1500

1492
Columbus Lands in
America
PAGE 130

1519
Cortés Arrives at
Tenochtitlán
PAGE 149

Major Cities of the 1400s

● Major city

ARCTIC OCEAN

ASIA

EUROPE

Moscow

London

Venice

Khanbalik (Beijing)

Lisbon

Constantinople

Damascus

Baghdad

Herāt

Jerusalem

Lhasa

Alexandria

Delhi

Mecca

Canton

Timbuktu

Goa

AFRICA

Calicut

Benin

Mombasa

INDIAN OCEAN

ATLANTIC OCEAN

AUSTRALIA

Great Zimbabwe

1600

1700

1600
The French Continue to Trade for Furs
PAGE 166

1607
The English Settle Jamestown
PAGE 173

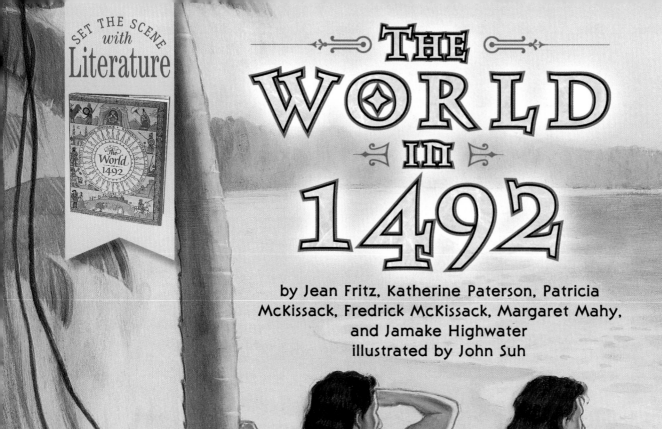

THE WORLD IN 1492

by Jean Fritz, Katherine Paterson, Patricia
McKissack, Fredrick McKissack, Margaret Mahy,
and Jamake Highwater
illustrated by John Suh

The Tainos (TY•nohz) lived on the islands of the Caribbean Sea. Because they lived so close to the water, they were expert sailors. They traveled in large dugout canoes to trade with the tribes of Middle and South America. They also traded with North American peoples along the Florida coast.

The Tainos grew corn, cotton, sweet potatoes, peanuts, tobacco, and other crops in the warm climate. They also hunted small animals and birds, and they fished. They lived in houses made from palm trees and slept in swinging beds called hammocks.

Read now about the first meeting between the Tainos and the strange people who landed on their shores. As you read, think about what the Tainos thought of these newcomers.

On that morning of October 12, 1492, a miraculous sight is seen by the people of a little island, now called High Cay, that lies just off the coast of San Salvador in the Caribbean Sea. There in the twilight, as they climb from their hammocks and come out of their palm-leaf-covered houses, they see three moving islands that gradually make

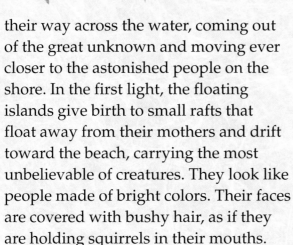

their way across the water, coming out of the great unknown and moving ever closer to the astonished people on the shore. In the first light, the floating islands give birth to small rafts that float away from their mothers and drift toward the beach, carrying the most unbelievable of creatures. They look like people made of bright colors. Their faces are covered with bushy hair, as if they are holding squirrels in their mouths.

Despite the strangeness of these creatures, the people are delighted and astounded to see them, and they run toward the water to greet them. At close range, the people realize that the strangers from the sea look like real men, except they have very pale faces covered with bunches of curly hair. They are terribly ugly and have a dreadful smell of spoiled milk. Yet they seem harmless, despite the strange gray and black weapons they carry. The people smile happily when the strangers admire their spears made of reeds and the lovely little ornaments of gold they wear on their ears and nostrils. The people cannot understand why the yellow metal is so fascinating to them.

To make them happy, they bring their strange guests many gifts—green parrots and bundles of precious cotton—in return for which they are given beautiful colored beads and small bells that make a delightful sound. These strangers, who completely hide themselves behind clothing, seem ill at ease with the nakedness of the people of the island, who do not cover their handsome bodies except for lavish painted designs of black, white, and red.

Then a man with a scarlet chest steps forward and tries to talk to the people, though he does not know how to speak properly and can only make strange noises and wave his arms in the air. Despite this strange behavior, the people smile at him respectfully. Hoping to teach him how to speak, they gesture across the landscape, and they tell the scarlet man that their island is called Guanahani. He seems to understand. Then the man points to himself and repeatedly tells the people his name. At this the people of the island begin to laugh. For this stranger has a most peculiar name!
Christopher Columbus.

THE AGE OF EXPLORATION

"I have found a continent, more full of people and animals than our Europe or Asia or Africa."

Amerigo Vespucci, 1503

This portrait of the Italian explorer Amerigo Vespucci was painted by Cristofano dell' Altissimo in the sixteenth century.

A Legendary Land

A.D. 500   **A.D. 1000**   **A.D. 1500**

The Tainos welcomed Christopher Columbus to the island of Guanahani (gwahn•uh•HAH•nee) in 1492. Like most other Europeans of the time, Columbus knew little about Asia and Africa. He knew nothing about the Americas. Columbus thought he had sailed to Asia. He never knew that he had reached an unknown land.

Stories of an Unknown Land

For a very long time, people had told stories about an unknown land in the ocean between Europe and Asia. The Irish said that a monk named Brendan had sailed to this land in the A.D. 500s. The Chinese told a story about Huishen, a Buddhist monk. He was said to have sailed to this unknown land at about the same time.

No one knows if these stories are true. Sailors from many different places, blown off course by stormy winds, may have been landing on the coast of the Americas for hundreds of years. So many stories were told that it became hard to know what was fact and what was not.

Only one report of an early landing has been proved true. The landing was made by a people known as the Vikings, who lived in an area in northern Europe that is today the countries of Norway, Sweden, and Denmark. From these lands the Vikings sailed west and built settlements in Iceland and Greenland.

The earliest stories about Vikings visiting an unknown land are found in Viking sagas (SAH•guhz). A **saga** is an adventure story that tells about the brave deeds of people of long ago. A story called the *Greenlanders' Saga* tells of the travels of the Vikings from

FOCUS
In what ways do we learn today about the world around us?

Main Idea As you read, think about ways early Europeans learned about the world around them.

Vocabulary

saga   exploration
knoll   cartographer
encounter

Vikings wore bronze helmets like this one to protect themselves and to frighten their enemies. The pin (above) was worn by a Viking over 1,200 years ago.

settlements in Greenland to the Americas. Archaeologists have since found evidence proving that much of the *Greenlanders' Saga* is true.

REVIEW *Who were the first Europeans known to have landed in the Americas?*

The Greenlanders' Saga

About the year A.D. 1000, a Viking named Leif Eriksson (LAYV AIR•ik•suhn) hired a crew and set sail from Greenland, heading west. Eriksson was looking for a land he had heard about since he was a boy. It was a land "not mountainous, well-timbered, and with small knolls upon it." A **knoll** is a small, round hill.

The land Eriksson reached was part of what is now Canada. Moving south along the coast, Eriksson soon found a place to spend the winter. The sailors went ashore and built temporary houses of mud and grass. They called the settlement *Vinland*, or "vine land," for the many grapevines that grew there.

Eriksson and his crew soon returned to Greenland. During the next several years, the Vikings sailed many times to Vinland. They used it as a base for fishing and hunting.

Leif's brother Thorvald led one trip to Vinland. When the Vikings arrived, they saw what looked like three knolls on the beach. They walked up to them and, instead, found nine people sleeping under boats. The Vikings attacked them. Later, during that same trip, boats filled with people came to Vinland and attacked the Vikings. Thorvald was wounded and later died.

Soon after this **encounter**, or meeting, the Vikings ended their trips to North America. The stories of their adventures, however, were kept alive over the years in the *Greenlanders' Saga*.

REVIEW *What and where was Vinland?*

Viking longships could travel on rough, open seas. This longship is about 75 feet (23 m) long and could carry up to 35 people.

Route of Leif Eriksson

Arctic Circle
GREENLAND
HELLULAND (BAFFIN ISLAND)
80°W
40°
ATLANTIC OCEAN
MARKLAND (LABRADOR)
NORTH AMERICA
50°N
VINLAND (NEWFOUNDLAND)
N W E S
70°W
60°W
50°W

0   200   400 Miles
0   200   400 Kilometers
Orthographic Projection

→ Leif Eriksson, about A.D.1000

Place Eriksson went to places he named Helluland, or "land of flat rocks," and Markland, or "forest land," before settling in Vinland.
■ *What names are used today for these places?*

Viking settlements were made up mainly of one-room houses. Most permanent houses were made of wood or stone.

Europeans and Exploration

Nearly five hundred years passed before the Europeans returned to the Americas. During these years most Europeans did not want to travel to unknown places. They believed the world outside the place they lived was very dangerous. They thought horrible sea monsters waited beneath the ocean, ready to swallow ships whole. They thought the sun was so hot in some places that it made the sea boil.

Another problem was that the Europeans had square-sailed ships that were slow and could sail only with the wind. This would have made a long ocean trip very hard. Even worse, there were not many maps. Those that could be found were so different from one another that no one knew which were correct.

In any case few European rulers were willing to spend their time or money on sailing trips past their borders. Until the 1400s, Europe did not have strong central governments. Instead, it was made up of many small kingdoms and villages. Each was ruled by a noble. These nobles spent too much time fighting each other to care about **exploration**, or searching the unknown.

REVIEW *What kept Europeans from searching for unknown lands?*

The Known World

In 1492, the year the Tainos greeted Christopher Columbus, a group of people in Germany paid Martin Behaim (BAY•hym) an amount equal to $75 to make a new kind of map. The map was in the shape of a ball. It was the first globe ever made in Europe.

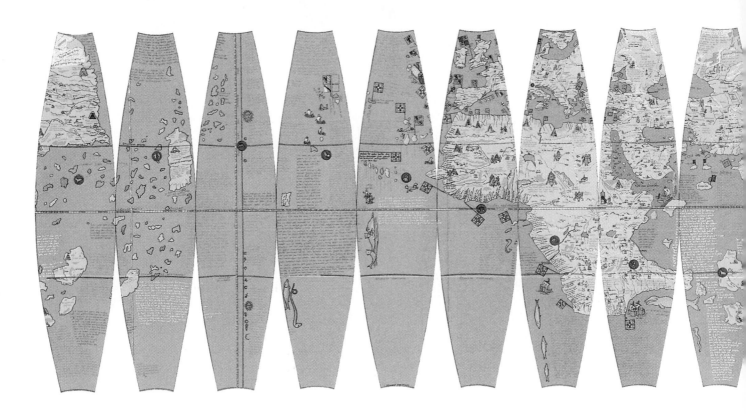

Muslim Mapmakers

Around the 700s the Muslims controlled lands that reached east to the Indus River, west to what is now Spain and Portugal, and south to the Sahara. Over time the Muslims established many trade routes over land and across the Indian Ocean. Years of travel and trade made the Muslims expert geographers. Using the study of stars and the journals of travelers, Muslim mapmakers began to draw highly accurate maps. Many of these maps were used by European explorers.

Al-Idrisi's map shows the known world in 1154. The Arabian peninsula is shown in the center.

Behaim called it his "Earth apple." He made it from pieces of leather stitched together.

Behaim's globe showed what he and other European **cartographers**, or makers of maps, thought the Earth was like. Behaim wanted his globe to show the Earth as it really was, but he did not have the facts. Behaim's globe showed the Earth much smaller than it really is. This made it seem as if sailing west from Europe to Asia would be easy. The globe made the trip look as if it would be only about 3,000 miles (4,828 km) long. Today's globes show that the trip is about 10,000 miles (16,093 km) long. More importantly, North and South America block the way. Behaim had no idea that these two continents were there. He did not know about Australia or Antarctica, either. His globe also showed Africa too small and the wrong shape.

Behaim knew a lot more than other Europeans of his time, though. Some Europeans had heard about the riches in Asia. But few knew about China's cities,

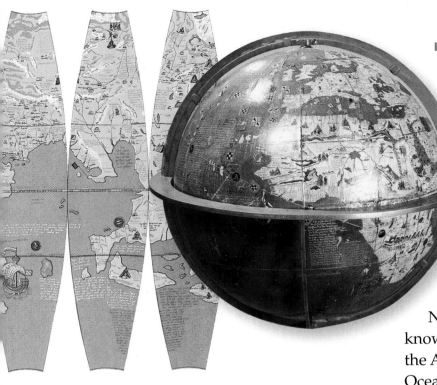

African city of Timbuktu (tim•buk•TOO) was a center of learning where people studied subjects from mathematics to medicine. And most Europeans knew nothing of the Chinooks, Hopis, Mandans, Cherokees, Mayas, or other Indian cultures of North and South America. They did not know that two other continents lay across the Atlantic Ocean. Even the Atlantic Ocean, which the Europeans called the Ocean Sea or the Green Sea of Darkness, was largely unknown.

highways, and art. Most Europeans had never heard of the great African empires, such as Mali (MAH•lee) and Songhay (SAHNG•hy). They had no idea that the

REVIEW *What was incorrect on Martin Behaim's globe?*

LESSON 1 REVIEW

A.D. 500	A.D. 1000	A.D. 1500
A.D. 500s Brendan sails to new lands	**About A.D. 1000** Leif Eriksson sets sail from Greenland	**A.D. 1492** Columbus sails to the Americas

Check Understanding

1 Remember the Facts What did most Europeans know about the Americas in the late 1400s?

2 Recall the Main Idea In what ways did early Europeans learn about the world around them?

Think Critically

3 Personally Speaking Why do you think the Vikings stopped traveling to Vinland?

4 Think More About It Why do you think that Europeans explained the unknown with ideas about monsters living in the seas?

Show What You Know

Mapping Activity Without looking at a map, draw the world and label the continents and oceans. Compare your drawing with the World Map in the Atlas on pages A2–A3. What areas are unknown to you?

FOCUS

What conditions might lead people to explore the unknown today?

Main Idea As you read, think about the conditions that led Europeans to begin exploring the unknown in the 1400s.

Vocabulary

monarch
Renaissance
compass
navigation

Background to European Exploration

| 1200 | 1350 | 1500 |

Marco Polo liked to tell stories. He often told of adventures to faraway places. Europeans called these places Cathay and the Indies. Marco Polo had been to Cathay, as China was then called. He had also traveled to the Indies, the islands off the China coast. He told of meeting Kublai Khan (KOO•bluh KAHN), China's ruler, and seeing amazing things—white bears, black stones that burned, and a place where night lasted all winter and day lasted all summer.

People laughed and called him Marco Millions because he told so many tales. Few Europeans had ever been to Asia, so they could not prove he was wrong. They just thought that the stories he told could not be true. But many were.

Marco Polo

In 1271 Marco Polo left his home in Venice, Italy, to go to Asia with his father and uncle. Niccolò and Maffeo Polo were traders who had first heard of the riches of this far-off land from fellow traders. Marco was just 17 years old when they set out.

Four years later, after riding on horses and camels and walking thousands of miles through mountains and deserts, the Polos reached China. There they saw the palace of Kublai Khan. They described it as having walls "all covered with gold and silver and decorated with pictures of dragons and birds and horsemen and . . . scenes of battle." One hall was so big that "a meal might well be served there for more than 6,000 men."

Marco Polo (right) gave fantastic descriptions of Asia. Many of Polo's stories were about what is today Beijing, China. The drawing (above) appears in an atlas made in 1375. The three people shown are Marco Polo, his father, and his uncle.

The Polos went on to other places in Asia, such as India and Persia. Marco never reached Japan, but he described it from stories he had heard. In Japan, he said, there was so much gold that whole palaces were built of it.

Twenty-four years after leaving Venice, Marco Polo returned home with his pockets full of jewels. In time someone wrote down his stories. But it would be nearly 200 years before *The Travels of Marco Polo* appeared as a printed book. When it did, Europeans read it in amazement. Wanting to share in this great wealth, more and more traders took the long land route from Europe to Asia.

REVIEW *What information did Marco Polo bring back to Europe?*

Kublai Khan, the ruler of China during Marco Polo's visit

Trade Routes to the East

For hundreds of years Europeans carried on a busy trade with people from Asia. The goods Europeans wanted most were gold, jewels, silk, perfumes, and especially spices. In the days before refrigerators, Europeans prized spices such as pepper, cloves, cinnamon, and nutmeg. They used these spices to make their food taste better and to hide the bad taste of spoiled meat.

For most European traders, however, travel to Asia and back was too hard and took too much time. So instead of going to the Far East, as they then called Asia, most

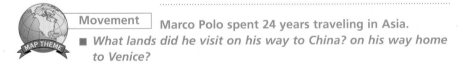

Movement — Marco Polo spent 24 years traveling in Asia.
■ *What lands did he visit on his way to China? on his way home to Venice?*

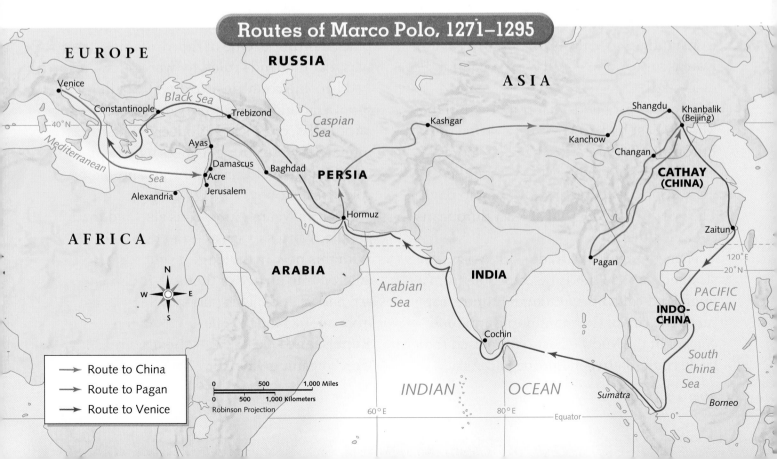

Routes of Marco Polo, 1271–1295

EUROPE
RUSSIA
ASIA

Venice
Constantinople
Black Sea
Trebizond
Caspian Sea
Kashgar
Shangdu
Khanbalik (Beijing)
40°N
Ayas
Kanchow
Damascus
Baghdad
Changan
Acre
PERSIA
CATHAY (CHINA)
Jerusalem
Alexandria
Mediterranean Sea
Hormuz
Zaitun
AFRICA
120°E
ARABIA
Arabian Sea
INDIA
20°N
INDO-CHINA
Pagan
PACIFIC OCEAN
Cochin
South China Sea
Sumatra
Borneo
INDIAN OCEAN
Equator

→ Route to China
→ Route to Pagan
→ Route to Venice

0   500   1,000 Miles
0   500   1,000 Kilometers
Robinson Projection
60°E
80°E

Silk and spices were valuable goods to the Europeans. The spices shown here are pictured both whole and ground. From left to right are cinnamon, pepper, nutmeg, and cloves.

Europeans traveled only part of the way. They went to cities in North Africa and Southwest Asia, which the Europeans called the Middle East. The cities they went to included Alexandria (a•lig•ZAN•dree•uh), Constantinople (kahn•stant•uhn•OH•puhl), Damascus (duh•MAS•kuhs), and Baghdad (BAG•dad). European traders exchanged their goods for goods that traders from the Middle East had gotten in Asia. Then the Europeans made the journey back home, where they sold the Asian goods at the highest prices people were willing to pay. The goods cost a lot. But at least Europeans could get them.

Then suddenly the trade with Asia stopped. In 1453 the Turks, a people from a huge land called the Ottoman Empire, captured the city of Constantinople and took control of the Middle East. This closed the trade routes between Europe and Asia.

There would be no more spices or gold or silk unless someone found another way to get to these treasures.

REVIEW *Why was trade with Asia so important to Europeans?*

Changes in Europe

By the time the city of Constantinople was captured, many changes had taken place in Europe. One of the most important was that the lands ruled by warring nobles had become countries. Portugal, Spain, France, and England were now ruled by **monarchs**, or kings and queens. Most monarchs were strong leaders who kept close watch over their countries and their countries' money.

Over the years, Europeans also had made great advances in science and technology. With this new knowledge, Europeans entered into an age of thought, learning, art, and science. This period, which lasted from about 1400 to 1600, is called the **Renaissance** (REH•nuh•sahns), a French word meaning "rebirth." During this period, people were more eager to try new things and explore unknown lands. They had learned how to build faster ships. They had made a new kind of sail that allowed ships to sail against the wind. They also had made a better compass. A **compass** is an instrument used to find direction. It has a needle that always points north.

All of these changes helped set the stage for European exploration. With Constantinople closed to most traders, Europeans now had a good reason to set out into the unknown to find a new route to Asia and were better able to do so.

REVIEW *What major changes set the stage for European exploration?*

Portugal Leads the Way

Portugal took the lead in the search to find the first water route to Asia. Portugal's monarch, King John, decided to spend as much money as was needed to reach that goal. The trade with Asia was important to him and his people, and they did not want to lose it. King John asked Henry, a prince of Portugal, to direct his country's search.

Prince Henry set up the first European school for training sailors in navigation (na•vuh•GAY•shuhn). **Navigation** is the study of how to plan and control the course of a ship. Because the rewards of being the

TECHNOLOGY

The Compass and the Astrolabe

In the 1100s Chinese and European sailors discovered how to make and use a compass. The early compasses were just pieces of magnetic iron floating on straw or cork in a bowl of water. The magnetic iron always pointed north and south, following the direction of the Earth's magnetic field. By the 1400s sailors were using a magnetic needle and had found other ways to make the compass more accurate. The astrolabe (AS•truh•layb) was used by sailors in the early 1400s. By finding the position of the sun and other known stars, sailors were able to determine their location.

The astrolabe was used by positioning the central rod so that it lined up with the sun or the North Star.

The compass (left) and the astrolabe (above) helped sailors determine their position and direction.

first to find a water route to Asia would be great, lessons taught at Prince Henry's school were kept secret. Anyone caught taking a map or chart from the school was sentenced to death.

Prince Henry later became known in the English-speaking world as Prince Henry the Navigator. He organized more than 50 voyages of exploration, but he did not go on any of them. For this reason he is sometimes called "the explorer who stayed at home."

Prince Henry thought that the most direct way to reach Asia by sea was to go south around Africa and then sail east. Under his direction dozens of Portuguese ships made their way down Africa's west coast. There they found new markets, where they could trade European goods for nuts, fruit, gold, and slaves.

Africans and others, such as Native Americans, had been taking prisoners of war as slaves for hundreds of years. Often people sold these slaves to others. European traders quickly saw that they could make money by buying slaves in Africa and taking them to Europe to be sold as servants.

Prince Henry (above) led Portugal's search for a water route to Asia. During the late 1400s Europeans used a kind of ship called the caravel (right) for exploration. With three masts and a lateen, or triangular sail, the caravel could sail against the wind.

By the time of Prince Henry's death in 1460, the Portuguese traders were buying about 800 slaves from African traders each year.

At the same time, the search for a water route to Asia went on. Finally, in 1488, Bartholomeu Dias (DEE•ahsh) became the first to sail all the way around the southern tip of Africa—around what is today called the Cape of Good Hope. But fierce storms battered the ship. The sailors grew hungry, sick, and frightened. Dias wanted to sail on to India, but his sailors made him return to Portugal.

Almost ten years later Vasco da Gama (dah GAH•mah) sailed around the Cape of Good Hope to India. Soon afterward he sailed back to Portugal with his ship full of spices. Da Gama had finally found a sea route to Asia, showing the way for future explorations.

REVIEW *How did Portugal lead the way in finding a water route to Asia?*

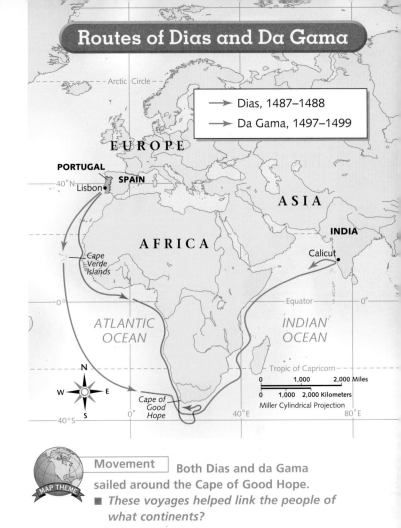

Routes of Dias and Da Gama

→ Dias, 1487–1488
→ Da Gama, 1497–1499

EUROPE
PORTUGAL
Lisbon — 40°N SPAIN
ASIA
Arctic Circle
AFRICA
INDIA
Calicut
Cape Verde Islands
Equator — 0°
ATLANTIC OCEAN
INDIAN OCEAN
Tropic of Capricorn
Cape of Good Hope
0 1,000 2,000 Miles
0 1,000 2,000 Kilometers
Miller Cylindrical Projection
40°S 0° 40°E 80°E

Movement Both Dias and da Gama sailed around the Cape of Good Hope.
■ *These voyages helped link the people of what continents?*

LESSON 2 REVIEW

1200 — 1350 — 1500

1271
• Marco Polo travels to Asia

1453
• The Turks capture Constantinople

1488
• Dias sails around Africa

1497
• Da Gama sails for India

Check Understanding

1 Remember the Facts How did the capture of Constantinople affect the Europeans?

2 Recall the Main Idea What conditions led Europeans to begin exploring the unknown in the 1400s?

Think Critically

3 Cause and Effect What effects did Marco Polo's travels have on Europeans?

4 Think More About It Why were strong monarchs important to European exploration?

Show What You Know

Chart Activity Make a chart with four rows and two columns. Draw a picture of a different spice in each of the four rows of the first column. In the next column, identify the spice and some of its uses. Present your chart to the class.

I, COLUMBUS

MY JOURNAL

1492 - 1493

edited by Peter Roop and Connie Roop

Christopher Columbus had been a sailor almost all his life. Born and raised in Italy, he had sailed all over the known world—to England and the Canary Islands, across the Mediterranean Sea, and along the coast of Africa. He had read **The Travels of Marco Polo** again and again. He was fascinated by the stories he had heard of the wealth of Asia—especially the Indies.

The painting (above) by Peter F. Rothermel, titled *Columbus Before the Queen,* was painted in 1842. Queen Isabella's scepter (right) was decorated with dolphins to illustrate Spain's sea power.

Christopher Columbus was the captain of the *Santa María*. Replicas of the *Niña*, *Pinta*, and *Santa María* (front) were built in Spain.

For years Columbus had asked Spain's monarchs, King Ferdinand and Queen Isabella, to support his plan to reach Asia by sailing west instead of going around Africa. Columbus believed that sailing west was a quicker, more direct route.

Spain's king and queen, however, were more concerned about life at home. They believed that true unity would come to Spain only if it were a completely Catholic country. For this reason, they drove out the Muslims living in Spain. By 1492 the monarchs had claimed all the land that the Muslims once ruled. That same year they forced the Jews to leave Spain. Spain was then united under one religion and one government.

In 1492 Columbus once again asked King Ferdinand and Queen Isabella to support his voyage of exploration. He promised them great wealth and new lands. Columbus also said that he would take the Catholic faith to the people of Asia. This time, the king and queen agreed to support his voyage.

On August 3, 1492, Columbus set forth with 89 sailors and three ships—the **Niña** (NEEN•yuh), the **Pinta** (PEEN•tuh), and the **Santa María**. After two months at sea, Columbus made the following entries in his log, or ship's journal. As you read his entries, think about the challenges people face when they are exploring the unknown.

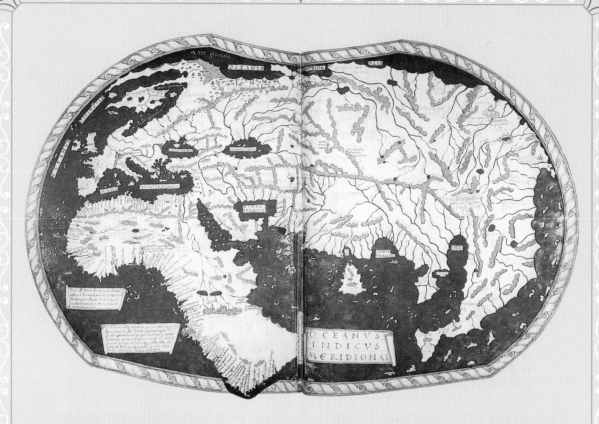

This map, made in 1489, represents the world view of the time. Many people, like Columbus, believed that the only land west of Europe was Asia.

Wednesday, 10 October, 1492.

Between day and night I made one hundred seventy-seven miles. I told the crew one hundred thirty-two miles, but they could stand it no longer. They grumbled and complained of the long voyage. I told them that, for better or worse, they had to complete the voyage. I cheered them on, telling them of the honors and rewards they would receive. I told them it was useless to complain. I had started to find the Indies and would continue until I had.

Thursday, 11 October, 1492.

I sailed to the west-southwest. The crew of the *Pinta* spotted reeds and a small board. A stick was found that looks man-made, perhaps carved with an iron tool. These made the crew breathe easier; in fact, the men have even become cheerful. A special thanksgiving was offered to God for giving us renewed hope through the many signs of land.

About ten o'clock at night I saw a light to the west. It looked like a wax candle bobbing up and down.

It had the same appearance as a light or torch belonging to fishermen or travellers who raised and lowered it. I am the first to admit I was so eager to find land that I did not trust my own senses so I called Gutierrez and asked him to watch for the light. After a few moments, he too saw it. I then summoned Rodrigo Sanchez. He saw nothing, nor did any other member of the crew. It was such an uncertain thing I did not feel it was adequate proof of land. Then, at two hours after midnight, the *Pinta* fired a cannon, my signal for the sighting of land.

I now believe the light I saw was truly land. When we caught up with the *Pinta*, I learned Rodrigo de Triana, a seaman, was the first man to sight land. I lay-to till daylight. The land is about six miles to the west.

Martín Pinzón (top) was captain of the *Pinta*. His brother, Vincente Pinzón (bottom), was captain of the *Niña*.

Friday, 12 October, 1492.

At dawn we saw naked people. I went ashore in the ship's boat, armed, followed by Martin Pinzon, captain of the *Pinta*, and his brother Vincente Pinzon, captain of the *Niña*. I unfurled the royal banner and the captains brought the flags. After a prayer of thanksgiving, I ordered the captains to witness I was taking possession of this island for the King and Queen. To this island I gave the name San Salvador, in honor of our Blessed Lord. No sooner had we finished taking possession of the island than people came to the beach.

The people call this island Guanahani. Their speech is very fluent, although I do not understand any of it. They are a friendly people who bear no arms except for small spears. They have no iron. I showed one my sword, and through ignorance he grabbed it by the blade and cut himself.

In the painting (above), titled *Landing of Columbus on the Island of Guanahani*, Columbus claims the new land for the king and queen of Spain. Columbus (left) tried to develop a friendship with the natives of Guanahani.

I want the natives to develop a friendly attitude toward us because I know they are a people who can be converted to our Holy Faith more by love than by force. I think they can easily be made Christians, for they seem to have no religion. I will take six of them to Your Highnesses when I depart, in order that they may learn our language.

I gave some red caps to some and glass beads to others. They took great pleasure in this and became so friendly it was a marvel. They traded and gave everything they had with good will, but it seems to me that they have very little and are poor in everything. I warned my men to take nothing from the people without giving something in exchange.

This afternoon the people came swimming to our ships and in boats made from one log. They brought parrots, balls of cotton thread, spears, and many other things. We swapped them little glass beads and hawks' bells.

Saturday, 13 October, 1492.

I have tried very hard to find out if there is gold here. I have seen a few natives wear a little piece of gold hanging from a hole made in the nose. By signs, if I interpret them correctly, I learned by going south I can find a king who possesses great containers of gold. I tried to find some natives to take me, but none want to make the journey.

This island is large and very flat. It is green, with many trees. There is a very large lagoon in the middle of the island. There are no mountains. It is a pleasure to gaze upon this place because it is all so green, and the weather is delightful.

In order not to lose time I want to set sail to see if I can find Japan.

One of the rewards Columbus received when he returned to Spain was a personal coat of arms. Notice the pictures of anchors and islands on his coat of arms.

LITERATURE REVIEW

1 What challenges did Columbus face on his journey of exploration?

2 What did Columbus first think about the people of Guanahani? Compare this view with the Tainos' view of Columbus, which you read about at the beginning of this unit on pages 116–117.

3 Suppose that you are a sailor on one of Columbus's ships. Write a journal entry for the day you finally see land and encounter new people.

Use Latitude

1. Why Learn This Skill?

The numbers of your global address tell where your town is located on the Earth. The numbers in a global address stand for lines of latitude and lines of longitude. You can use these lines to describe the absolute location of any place.

2. Lines on a Map

Mapmakers use a system of imaginary lines to form a grid on maps and globes. The lines that run east and west are the lines of latitude. They are also called **parallels** (PAIR•uh•lelz) because they are parallel, or always the same distance from each other. Parallel lines never meet.

Lines of latitude are measured in degrees north and south of the equator, which is labeled 0°, or *zero degrees*. The parallels north of the equator are marked *N* for *north latitude*. This means they are in the Northern Hemisphere. The parallels south of the equator are marked *S* for *south latitude*. This means they are in the Southern Hemisphere. The greater the number of degrees marking a parallel, the farther north or south of the equator it is.

The lines that run north and south on a map or globe are the lines of longitude, or **meridians**. Each meridian runs from the North Pole to the South Pole. Unlike parallels, which never meet, meridians meet at the poles. Meridians are farthest apart at the equator.

Meridians are numbered in much the same way that parallels are numbered. The meridian marked 0° is called the **prime meridian**. It runs north and south through Greenwich, near the city of London in Britain. Lines of longitude to the west of the prime meridian are marked *W* for *west longitude*. They are in the Western Hemisphere. The meridians to the east of the prime meridian are marked *E* for *east longitude*. They are in the Eastern Hemisphere.

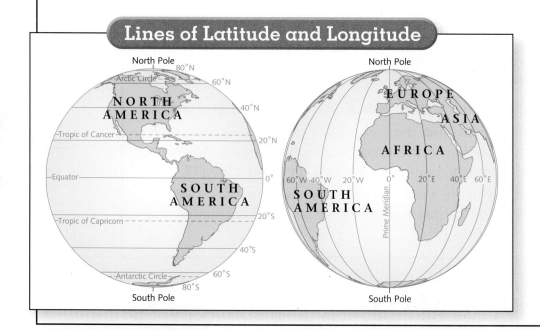

Lines of Latitude and Longitude

and Longitude

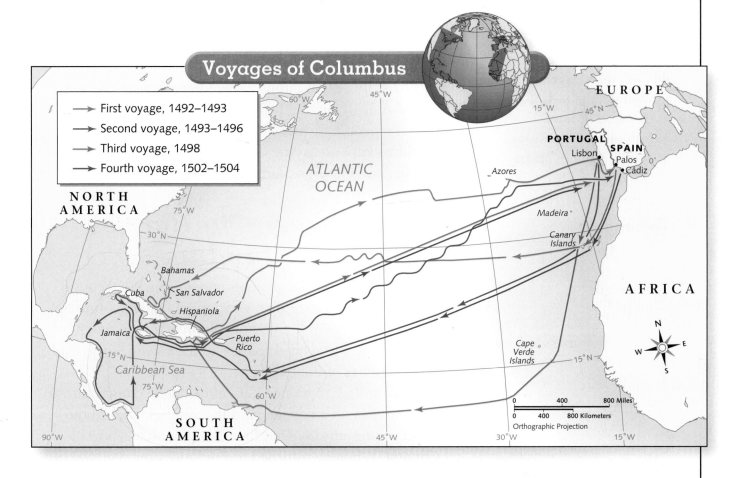

Voyages of Columbus

→ First voyage, 1492–1493
→ Second voyage, 1493–1496
→ Third voyage, 1498
→ Fourth voyage, 1502–1504

ATLANTIC OCEAN

NORTH AMERICA

EUROPE

PORTUGAL SPAIN
Lisbon Palos
Cádiz

Azores

Madeira

Canary Islands

AFRICA

Bahamas
Cuba San Salvador
Hispaniola
Jamaica Puerto Rico

Caribbean Sea

Cape Verde Islands

SOUTH AMERICA

0   400   800 Miles
0   400   800 Kilometers
Orthographic Projection

60°W 45°W 15°W 45°N
75°W 30°N
15°N 75°W 60°W 45°W 30°W 15°W
90°W

3. Understand the Process

The map above shows the four voyages of Christopher Columbus to the Americas. The lines of latitude and longitude make it possible to describe absolute location.

Near the left side of the map, find 30°N. At the top or bottom, find 15°W. Use your fingers to trace these lines to the point where they cross. The Canary Islands are not far from this point. So you can say that the Canary Islands are near 30°N, 15°W. Now use the map to answer these questions.

❶ What line of latitude is closest to Hispaniola?

❷ What islands are near 15°N, 30°W?

❸ Which location is farther north— 45°N, 60°W or 30°N, 90°W?

4. Think and Apply

Use latitude and longitude to tell where you live. Write a paragraph to describe how you found your location. Have a classmate find your location on a map.

FOCUS

In what ways can new facts change the way we think about events that happened in the past?

Main Idea In what ways did the facts gathered by later explorers change what people thought about the voyages of Columbus?

Vocabulary

conclusion
isthmus
expedition
scurvy

Early Voyages of Exploration

1495	1510	1525

Christopher Columbus never knew that he had not reached Asia. Believing he had reached the Indies, he called the people he met Indians. Until his death in 1506, Columbus kept on saying that he had found a new water route to Asia. Other explorers, however, proved him wrong.

Vespucci Challenges Columbus

News of Columbus's voyages spread quickly through Europe. The news stirred an excitement for adventure not felt since the days of Marco Polo. Soon every monarch in Europe wanted to send ships across the Ocean Sea to find the great riches of the Indies.

In 1497 an Italian named Giovanni Caboto sailed across the Ocean Sea on a voyage paid for by England. Caboto landed in present-day Newfoundland, which is part of Canada. When he returned to England, however, Caboto told everyone that he had found Cathay, the land of the great Kublai Khan. The English made Caboto a hero. They even gave him an English name, John Cabot.

But not everyone in Europe really believed that Columbus had found the Indies or that Caboto had landed in what is now called China. Amerigo Vespucci (uh•MAIR•ih•goh veh•SPOO•chee) from the Italian city-state of Florence was one of those who did not believe it. In 1499, under orders from the king of Spain, Vespucci sailed to a place south of where Columbus had landed. Two years later the king of Portugal sent Vespucci on another voyage. This time he sailed down the coast of South America from present-day Venezuela to present-day Argentina.

Explorers used an astrolabe to help them navigate their ships.

Martin Waldseemüller's map shows Ptolemy (top left) and Vespucci (top right). The Americas are shown (far left) as a long piece of land.

On these voyages Vespucci looked for signs that he had reached Asia, as Columbus believed this land to be. Like Columbus, Vespucci had read books by Marco Polo and others who had visited Asia. Yet Vespucci saw nothing that fit what Marco Polo and the others had seen. He saw no cities of gold and marble. He saw no people wearing jewels and cloth of gold.

Something else did not make sense to Vespucci. Years earlier he had studied the work of Claudius Ptolemy (TAH•luh•mee), an astronomer in ancient Egypt. From Ptolemy's work, Vespucci had learned that the Earth was larger and Asia was smaller than most people had thought. If Asia were as far east as Columbus claimed, it would have to cover half the Earth. Vespucci knew that could not be true.

Vespucci also thought about the distance he had traveled. Most sailors of the time could judge how far north or south they had sailed by using instruments such as the cross-staff. The cross-staff was a pole with measurements on it and a sliding crosspiece. Sailors still had trouble, however, measuring how far east or west they had sailed. Vespucci had found a new way of measuring distances east and west. Using his new way, Vespucci figured he had sailed 6,500 miles (10,460 km) from Europe. This figure was more than three times as far as Columbus thought he had sailed.

Based on all the information he now had, Vespucci formed a conclusion. A **conclusion** is a decision or an idea reached by thoughtful study. Vespucci concluded that he and Columbus and Caboto had not sailed to Asia. He concluded that the land they had found had to be another continent—the "new world" that some Europeans thought might be there.

Soon a German cartographer named Martin Waldseemüller (VAHLT•zay•mool•er) drew a map that included the new continent. He decided to name the new land for Amerigo Vespucci. In 1507 *America* appeared on a map for the first time.

REVIEW *What conclusion did Vespucci form?*

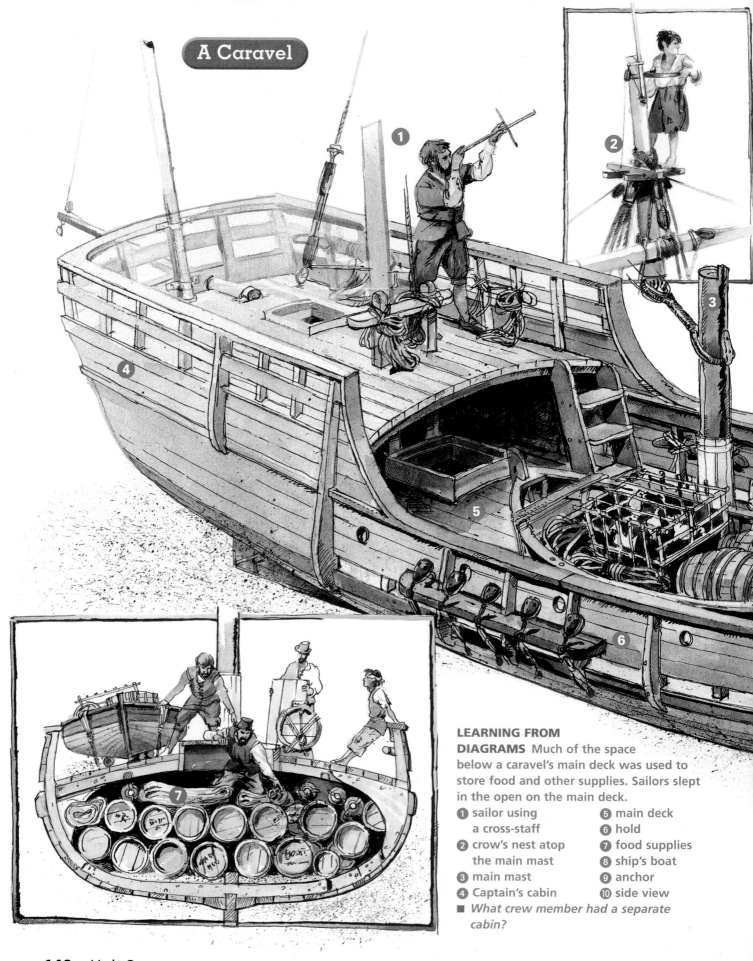

A Caravel

LEARNING FROM DIAGRAMS Much of the space below a caravel's main deck was used to store food and other supplies. Sailors slept in the open on the main deck.

1. sailor using a cross-staff
2. crow's nest atop the main mast
3. main mast
4. Captain's cabin
5. main deck
6. hold
7. food supplies
8. ship's boat
9. anchor
10. side view

■ *What crew member had a separate cabin?*

Balboa Reaches the Pacific

On September 27, 1513, a group of explorers climbed up a mountain. It was on the west coast of what today is called the Isthmus of Panama. An **isthmus** (IS•muhs) is a narrow strip of land that connects two larger land areas. The Isthmus of Panama connects the continents we know today as North America and South America. The group of explorers, made up of Spanish and African soldiers and Native American guides, had landed on the east coast and walked west until they reached the mountain.

Moving ahead of the rest, Vasco Núñez de Balboa (NOON•yes day bahl•BOH•ah) quickly climbed the last few feet to the mountain peak. Before him lay a huge blue sea. Falling to his knees, Balboa said that the sea—what would later be called the Pacific Ocean—belonged to Spain. A few days later Balboa and the others reached the ocean and explored the coast.

Christopher Columbus had believed that Asia stretched from near the eastern edge of Europe all the way around the world. He

Panama Canal

Balboa crossed the Isthmus of Panama and found the Pacific Ocean in 1513. It was another 400 years before a canal was built that connected the Atlantic and Pacific oceans. The Panama Canal, which cuts through the Isthmus of Panama, reduces the shipping distance between the lands in the North Atlantic Ocean and the lands in the North Pacific Ocean by 7,000 miles (11,265 km). The canal, which opened in 1914 after 10 years of construction, was a difficult challenge. As many as 43,000 people worked to build the canal. The builders cut through mountains and flooded a valley to make the canal.

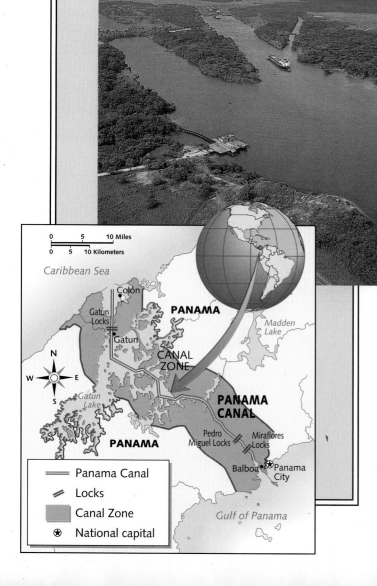

thought that if he sailed west from Europe across a very narrow Atlantic Ocean, he would reach it. Now Balboa had come upon a huge ocean on the western side of what Columbus had said was Asia. This proved that Vespucci was right. This also proved that Columbus was wrong. Columbus had not reached Asia but had reached a new continent instead.

REVIEW *What body of water did Balboa reach in 1513?*

Magellan's Crew Sails Around the World

On a September day in 1519, loud cannons boomed as five ships and about 250 sailors set sail from Spain into the Atlantic Ocean. Ferdinand Magellan (muh•JEH•luhn), a Portuguese explorer, led the fleet. Magellan had convinced the king of Spain to pay for his expedition (ek•spuh•DIH•shuhn). An **expedition** is a journey taken for a special reason. The reason for Magellan's expedition was to find a way to reach Asia by sailing west around the Americas.

Magellan sailed to what is now Brazil and then south along South America's eastern coast. For months he sailed up rivers into the middle of the continent, hoping to find a river that would go all the way to the ocean on the other side. But he never did, and each time he had to sail the rivers back to the coast. As the ships fought their way through huge, pounding waves and against howling winds, one ship and many of its crew were lost.

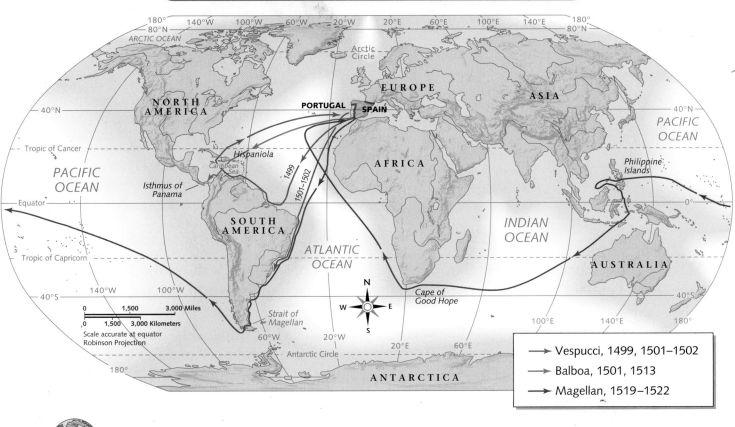

Vespucci, 1499, 1501–1502
Balboa, 1501, 1513
Magellan, 1519–1522

Movement Vespucci, Balboa, and Magellan all went to places that Europeans had never seen before.
■ *Which explorer's voyage do you think was most important? Why?*

Finally, in the fall of 1520, three of Magellan's ships sailed through what is now called the Strait of Magellan, near the southern tip of South America. The sailors found themselves in the same ocean that Balboa had seen. Magellan named it *Pacific*, which means "peaceful," because it seemed so still and quiet compared with the Atlantic Ocean.

For more than three months, the ships sailed across the Pacific Ocean. As the months passed, the small amount of food that was left quickly spoiled. There was no place to stop for fresh food. Antonio Pigafetta (pee•gah•FET•ah), a sailor traveling with Magellan, wrote in his journal,

66 We ate biscuit which was no longer biscuit, but powder of biscuit swarming with worms, for they had eaten the good. We drank yellow water that had been putrid for many days. 99

When the food was gone, the sailors ate rats, sawdust, and leather. Some died of hunger. Others died of **scurvy**, a sickness caused by not getting enough vitamin C, which is found in fruit and vegetables. As the bodies of dead sailors were thrown into the ocean, sharks followed the ships.

In March 1521 the ships reached what are today called the Philippine Islands.

Magellan (left), like most other explorers of his time, made mistakes in figuring distances. He and other explorers often found places by accident. This map (far left), drawn in 1545, shows Magellan's voyage around the world.

Magellan and his crew stayed in the Philippines for several weeks. Then, on April 27, while taking part in a battle between the people of one of the islands, Magellan was killed. In September 1522, the 18 sailors who were left finally returned to Spain.

One of Magellan's ships, the *Victoria*, had sailed around the world. What Columbus had dreamed of was true. Europeans could reach Asia by sailing west. But first they had to go around the Americas.

REVIEW *Where did Magellan's crew sail?*

LESSON 4 REVIEW

1495	1510	1525
1499 • Vespucci sails to South America	**1513** • Balboa claims the Pacific Ocean	**1522** • Magellan's crew returns to Spain

Check Understanding

1 Remember the Facts For whom was America named?

2 Recall the Main Idea In what ways did the facts gathered by Vespucci, Balboa, and Magellan change what people thought about the place where Columbus landed?

Think Critically

3 Think More About It How do you think the findings of Vespucci, Balboa, and Magellan affected the Europeans' goal of finding a new route to Asia?

4 Cause and Effect In what ways did food supplies affect early expeditions?

Show What You Know

Mobile Activity You are responsible for ordering the supplies for a voyage like Magellan's. The ship will be on the ocean for a month, with no refrigeration. Find pictures in magazines of foods and other supplies you would take aboard. Cut out the pictures and paste them on cutouts of a sailing ship. Make a mobile with your pictures. Hang your mobile in the classroom.

Form a Logical Conclusion

1. Why Learn This Skill?

A logical conclusion is a decision or an idea that is thought out carefully, based on the evidence. To form a logical conclusion, you must be able to separate facts from opinions. A **fact** is a statement that can be proved true. An **opinion** is a statement that tells what a person believes, and cannot be proved true. To form a logical conclusion, you also must be able to put new facts together with those you already know. This will help you see why events happened in the past and in your life today.

You have read that Christopher Columbus formed the conclusion that he had landed in Asia. However, when

Amerigo Vespucci looked at the facts and gathered new information, he formed a different conclusion. Think about the explorers' conclusions as you answer the following questions.

1. Why did Columbus form the conclusion that he had landed in Asia?
2. What evidence did Vespucci have that supported Columbus's conclusion? What evidence did not support Columbus's conclusion?
3. What conclusion did Vespucci form about where Columbus had landed?

2. Understand the Process

There are many ways to form a conclusion. One way is to follow these steps.

- Form a question about the subject or the situation.
- Think about what you already know that might help you answer the question.
- Gather new evidence that might help you answer the question.
- Form a conclusion based on the strongest evidence.

3. Think and Apply

Write a list of clues that would lead to a certain place in your school. Read the clues one by one to a partner. Can your partner form a conclusion about where the mystery place is, based on only one or two clues? Why is it important to have as many facts as possible before reaching a conclusion?

Amerigo Vespucci, using an astrolabe

REVIEW

About 1000
• Leif Eriksson sets
  sail from Greenland

CONNECT MAIN IDEAS

Use this organizer to show how new information helped Europeans gain knowledge and explore the unknown. Write three details for each lesson. A copy of the organizer may be found on page 21 of the Activity Book.

The Age of Exploration

A Legendary Land

1. _____
2. _____
3. _____

New Information

Background to European Exploration

1. _____
2. _____
3. _____

New Information

Early Voyages of Exploration

1. _____
2. _____
3. _____

New Information

I, Columbus: My Journal 1492–1493

1. _____
2. _____
3. _____

WRITE MORE ABOUT IT

Write a Report Imagine that you are a Viking who has traveled with your family to Vinland. You are living in a base camp for the summer, hunting and fishing. Write a short report about your adventures.

Write an Advertisement Imagine that you are a ship's captain on one of the explorations discussed in this chapter. Write an advertisement calling for sailors. Include places you plan to explore in your advertisement.

1453
• The Turks capture Constantinople

1492
• Columbus sails to the Americas

1522
• Magellan's crew returns to Spain

USE VOCABULARY

Write a term from this list to complete each of the sentences that follow.

cartographer   encounter

compass   isthmus

conclusion   navigation

1 An _____ is a meeting.

2 A _____ is a person who makes maps.

3 A _____ is an instrument used to find direction.

4 _____ is the planning and directing of a ship's course.

5 A _____ is a decision or idea reached by thoughtful study.

6 An _____ is a narrow strip of land that connects two larger land areas.

CHECK UNDERSTANDING

7 Who was Leif Eriksson?

8 How did Marco Polo's reports about his travels affect people living in Europe?

9 What goods from Asia did Europeans want to buy?

10 What did Columbus hope to find when he began his expedition in 1492?

11 What conclusion did Vespucci draw about the lands that he, Columbus, and Caboto had reached?

12 What continents does the Isthmus of Panama connect?

13 What did Magellan's crew accomplish?

THINK CRITICALLY

14 **Cause and Effect** How did the capture of Constantinople affect trade between Europe and Asia?

15 **Past to Present** What unknown places might people be interested in exploring today?

APPLY SKILLS

Use Latitude and Longitude Look at the map on page 143. Next, use the lines of latitude and longitude to describe the following locations: the Cape of Good Hope, the Strait of Magellan, and the part of South America that Vespucci first reached in 1499.

Form a Logical Conclusion Use encyclopedias or other books from the library to find information about the Viking settlement in Vinland. What evidence supports the historians' conclusion that the Vikings were the first Europeans to visit North America?

READ MORE ABOUT IT

Accidental Explorers: Surprises and Side Trips in the History of Discovery by Rebecca Stefoff. Oxford. A look at the many important discoveries made by chance.

HARCOURT BRACE

Visit the Internet at **http://www.hbschool.com** for additional resources.

CHAPTER

4

ENCOUNTERS IN THE AMERICAS

". . . We have discovered a land rich in gold, pearls, and other things. . . . There are in the city many large and beautiful houses . . . and many rich citizens. . . . And also very pleasant gardens. . . ."

Hernando Cortés

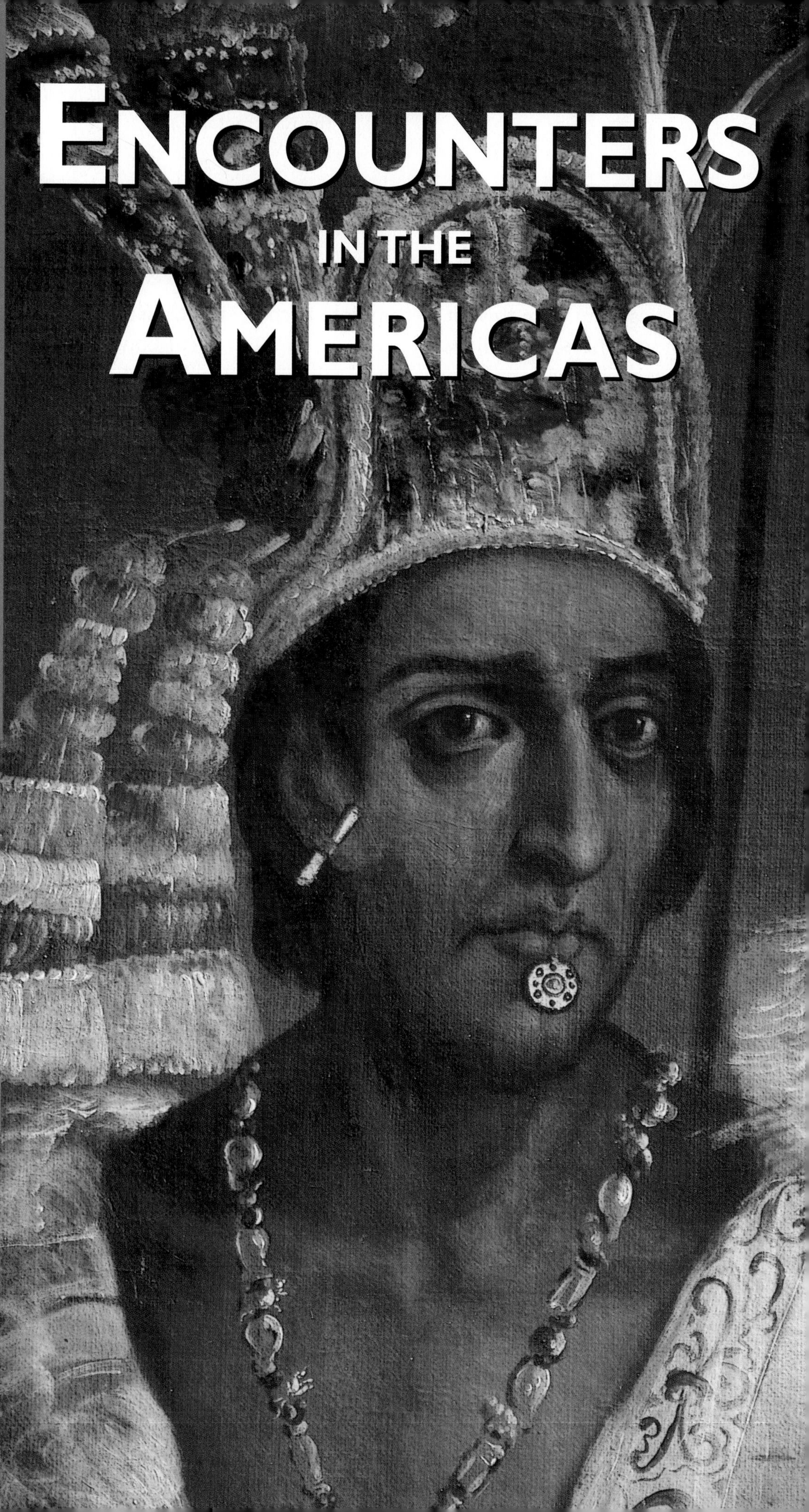

A European artist painted this portrait of Motecuhzoma.

Conquest
of the Aztecs and Incas

1515	1525	1535

After Columbus, others from Spain—Balboa and Magellan among them—went on to explore the Americas. Driven by their desire for gold and other riches, they pushed deep into North and South America. This was new land to the Spanish. But it was home to the people already living there.

Fall of the Aztecs

The year was 1519, and the Aztec king Motecuhzoma (maw•tay•kwah•SOH•mah) stood at his palace at Tenochtitlán, looking out at the night sky. The king watched for signs that would tell him what was to happen.

In the last two years, some odd things had taken place in the Aztec capital. The Earth had shaken. The lake had flooded the city. Comets had been seen in the sky. Aztec priests had studied these natural wonders and decided they were signs that the Aztec Empire was coming to an end.

Then one day people came to the palace bringing news of another strange happening. Men who had white skin and black beards and who rode deer without antlers were coming toward Tenochtitlán. The news startled the king. The Aztec people believed

FOCUS
What might cause people of different cultures to fight with one another today?

Main Idea Read to learn what led to fighting between the Spanish and the Aztecs and between the Spanish and the Incas during the 1500s.

Vocabulary
conquistador
civil war

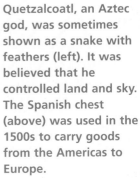

Quetzalcoatl, an Aztec god, was sometimes shown as a snake with feathers (left). It was believed that he controlled land and sky. The Spanish chest (above) was used in the 1500s to carry goods from the Americas to Europe.

Chapter 4 • **149**

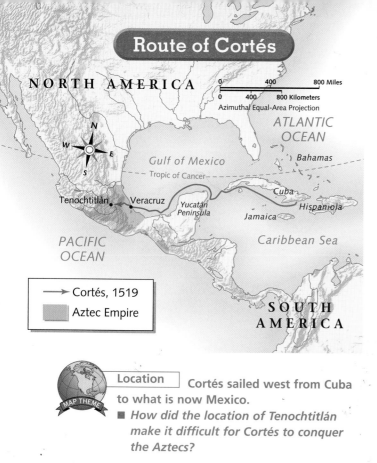

NORTH AMERICA

ATLANTIC OCEAN

Gulf of Mexico

Tropic of Cancer

Bahamas

Tenochtitlán • Veracruz

Yucatán Peninsula

Cuba

Hispaniola

Jamaica

PACIFIC OCEAN

Caribbean Sea

SOUTH AMERICA

→ Cortés, 1519

■ Aztec Empire

Location Cortés sailed west from Cuba to what is now Mexico.
■ *How did the location of Tenochtitlán make it difficult for Cortés to conquer the Aztecs?*

that the light-skinned god Quetzalcoatl (keht•zahl•koo•WAH•tahl) would one day return to rule his people. Could it be that this god of old was coming back?

The person the Aztec Indians thought might be Quetzalcoatl was the explorer Hernando Cortés (kawr•TEZ). He had been sent by the Spanish govern-ment to look for gold. With Cortés were more than 500 soldiers, 14 cannons, 16 horses, and several dogs. The horses were the first in the Americas for thousands of years.

This painting shows Motecuhzoma (left) meeting with Cortés (right) in Tenochtitlán. Malintzin (next to Cortés) helped translate for the Spanish explorers.

Cortés had heard stories about the great wealth of the Aztec Empire. Before setting out, he told his soldiers,

❝ We are waging a just and good war which will bring us fame. Almighty God, in whose name it will be waged, will give us victory. I offer you great rewards, although they will be wrapped about with great hardships. If you do not abandon me, as I shall not abandon you, I shall make you the richest men who ever crossed the seas. ❞

In the spring of 1519, Cortés landed on the east coast of Mexico. He defeated the Indians there, then set out for Tenochtitlán. The journey covered 200 miles (322 km)— from the tropical coast, through snowy mountains, and into the Valley of Mexico.

After marching for 83 days, Cortés and his soldiers, joined by large numbers of the

Tenochtitlan.

Aztecs' Indian enemies, finally reached Tenochtitlán. Thinking that Cortés might be Quetzalcoatl, Motecuhzoma welcomed him, offering housing and gifts of gold. When the Spanish soldiers saw the gold, they were overjoyed.

Cortés took Motecuhzoma prisoner. Within two years the Aztec ruler was dead and his capital city was in ruins. Spanish weapons and European diseases, which were new to the Indians, had nearly destroyed the Aztec civilization. By 1521 Cortés had conquered the Aztecs.

Conquering the Aztecs won for Cortés both wealth and glory. He and his soldiers were now able to capture the Aztecs' treasures. Among the Europeans, the soldiers soon became known as **conquistadors** (kahn•KEES•tah•doors). This word in Spanish means "conquerors."

Spain now ruled Mexico. On the ashes of the Aztec capital, the Spanish built Mexico City. Mexico City became the capital of Spain's new empire in the Americas.

REVIEW *How did the Spanish acquire Mexico for their empire?*

Route of Pizarro

Movement Pizarro traveled south from Panama to the Inca capital of Cuzco (KOOS•koh). Along the way he found stone-paved roads built by the Incas.

■ *Why do you think these roads were important to the Incas?*

Fall of the Incas

Other conquistadors soon followed Cortés to the Americas. Sixty-year-old Francisco Pizarro (pee•ZAR•oh) was one of them. Pizarro had heard stories of an Indian people whose empire was far richer and more powerful than that of the Aztecs. These people were called the Incas.

In 1531 Pizarro and a group of 180 Spanish and African soldiers sailed from Panama and landed on the west coast of South America. For the next two years, they wandered about the Andes Mountains, stealing gold and riches from the Indian peoples they found. Then one day they came across a large Inca camp. One of Pizarro's soldiers described the camp as "beautiful." There were so many tents

This statue, made of silver and gold, represents an Inca noble. Shells were used to decorate the statue.

Chapter 4 • **151**

that the sight filled the Spanish with fear. The soldier said,

> 66 We never thought the Indians could occupy such a proud position, nor so many tents, so well set up. It filled all of us . . . with confusion and fear. But we dared not show it. 99

The Spanish would soon learn that the empire of the Incas was even larger and more powerful than they had heard. The empire covered 3,000 miles (4,828 km) of the western coast of South America, including parts of the present-day countries of Peru, Ecuador, Bolivia, Argentina, and Chile. The empire also included more than 9 million people. A network of roads and stations connected the towns, and all the people paid taxes to the Inca ruler. Some paid in potatoes or corn, while others paid in gold.

When Pizarro and his soldiers arrived, the Inca Empire was not at peace. It was being torn in two by a civil war. A **civil war** is a war between people of the same country. The war was being fought between the followers of two brothers, Atahuallpa (ah•tah•WAHL•pah) and Huascar (WAHS•kar). Both said they had the right to the throne. The war finally ended when Atahuallpa killed his brother and became emperor. But the fighting had weakened the empire.

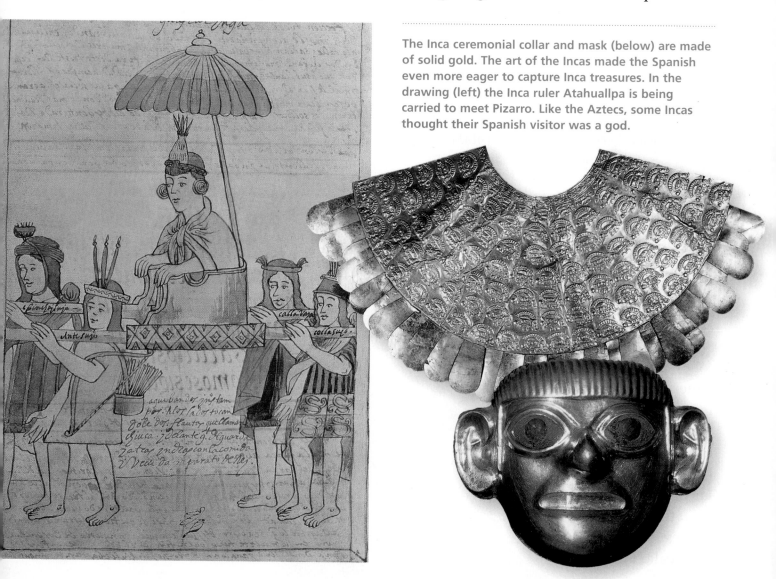

The Inca ceremonial collar and mask (below) are made of solid gold. The art of the Incas made the Spanish even more eager to capture Inca treasures. In the drawing (left) the Inca ruler Atahuallpa is being carried to meet Pizarro. Like the Aztecs, some Incas thought their Spanish visitor was a god.

Offering friendship to the new emperor, Pizarro invited Atahuallpa to the Spanish camp. The emperor arrived the next day with several thousand of his people. They carried him on a golden throne lined with parakeet feathers. Around his neck he wore a necklace of giant green emeralds. He wore gold ornaments in his hair.

Pizarro's priest asked Atahuallpa to give up his own religion and accept Christianity. He also asked him to accept the king of Spain as his master.

When Atahuallpa refused, Pizarro took the emperor prisoner. To buy his freedom, Atahuallpa promised Pizarro

This maize plant, made of silver, shows that maize was an important food to the Incas. This artifact is about 500 years old.

enough silver and gold to fill a whole room. Atahuallpa's people provided the riches, but Pizarro had him killed anyway.

After Atahuallpa's death in 1533, the Spanish conquered the Inca Empire and made slaves of its people. Inca weapons were no match for Spanish guns and crossbows. For the Spanish, the conquest brought riches and power. But for the Incas, the encounter ended a civilization.

REVIEW *Why did Pizarro order that Atahuallpa be taken prisoner?*

LESSON I REVIEW

1515 — 1519 • Cortés lands in Mexico — 1525 — 1533 • Pizarro conquers the Incas — 1535

Check Understanding

1 **Remember the Facts** What was the goal of Cortés and Pizarro?

2 **Recall the Main Idea** What was the major reason for the fighting between the Spanish and the Aztecs and between the Spanish and the Incas?

Think Critically

3 **Explore Viewpoints** Compare the viewpoints of Pizarro and Atahuallpa about who should control land in the Americas. List the reasons each leader might have given to support his ideas.

4 **Past to Present** Why do some countries today try to conquer other countries? Compare and contrast these reasons with the reasons the Spanish conquistadors had for conquering the Aztecs and the Incas.

Show What You Know

Journal-Writing Activity
Imagine that you are a soldier traveling with Cortés or Pizarro. Write a journal entry that describes what you see as you arrive in the Aztec or Inca Empire. Share your entry with a friend.

The Search for Gold and Riches

FOCUS

What are some reasons people take actions that involve risk and danger?

Main Idea As you read, think about why the Spanish risked the unknown to explore North America in the 1500s.

Vocabulary

grant
mainland
rumor
claim
desertion

1510	1530	1550

Eager to add to their growing empire, Spain's rulers wanted the conquistadors to explore the lands north of Mexico. The Spanish king offered **grants**, or gifts of money, to explorers who would lead expeditions into the northern continent. Believing that North America held riches far greater than the treasures already taken in Middle America and South America, many were quick to set out.

The Spanish Move into Florida

One of the Spanish explorers who received a grant was Juan Ponce de León (PAHN•say day lay•OHN). Ponce de León had sailed with Columbus on his second voyage. He lived for a time on the island of Hispaniola (ees•pah•NYOH•lah), which today is made up of the countries of Haiti and the Dominican Republic. He later explored and conquered what has become Puerto Rico. As the governor there, he had heard about a fountain whose waters were said to make old people young again. This "Fountain of Youth" was on an island to the north called Bimini (BIH•muh•nee). Ponce de León decided to find it.

He sailed north but did not find Bimini. Instead, in April 1513 he landed on the **mainland**, or the main part of the continent, near what is now the city of St. Augustine. He named the mainland *La Florida*, the Spanish word for "filled with flowers." When he tried to start a settlement in Florida, the Calusa Indians, who lived there, attacked. Ponce de León was wounded, and he died. Though he did not discover a fountain of youth, he was the first Spaniard to set foot in what is today the United States.

REVIEW *What was Ponce de León searching for?*

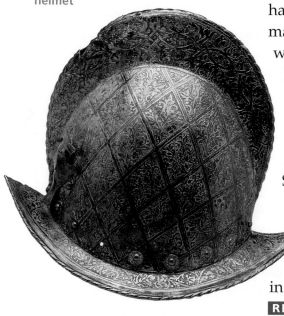

A sixteenth-century Spanish helmet

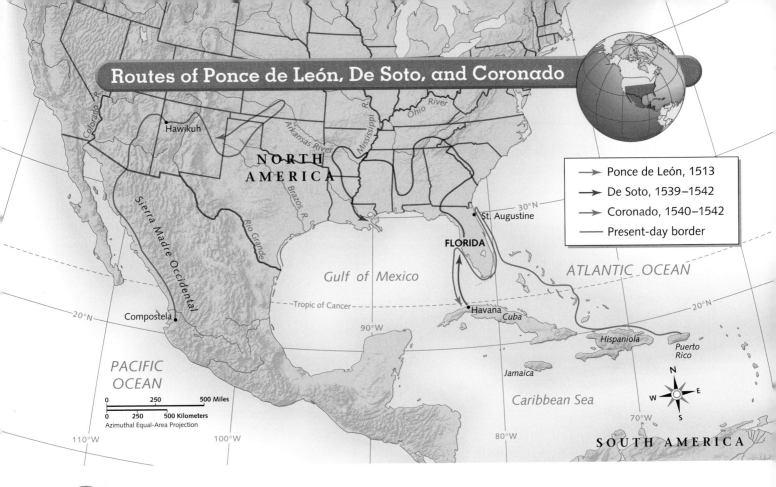

Routes of Ponce de León, De Soto, and Coronado

→	Ponce de León, 1513
→	De Soto, 1539–1542
→	Coronado, 1540–1542
—	Present-day border

Regions The Spanish explored large areas of North America.

■ *How do the regions touched by the routes of Ponce de León, de Soto, and Coronado reflect the Spanish culture today?*

The Seven Cities of Gold

Stories about treasure sparked more expeditions into the lands north of Mexico. These stories were only **rumors**—stories without proof. But many people believed them. One of the most exciting was about seven cities believed to be built all of gold.

In 1536 four ragged men arrived in Mexico City. They were Álvar Núñez Cabeza de Vaca (kah•BAY•sah day VAH•kuh), two other Spaniards, and a North African named Estéban (ehs•TAY•bahn). They had lived through a shipwreck off the coast of what is today Texas. During their long journey to Mexico, they had heard from the people they met along the way about seven cities rich in gold, silver, and jewels.

The four men told their story to Spanish leaders in Mexico City, who listened carefully. In 1539 the leaders sent Estéban and a priest named Marcos de Niza (day NEE•sah) to see if the rumor was true. During the expedition Estéban was killed by Zuni Indians who believed he had been sent by an enemy tribe. But Niza returned safely, saying he had seen a golden city.

After hearing Niza's report, Francisco Vásquez de Coronado (kawr•oh•NAH•doh) and more than 1,000 soldiers set out in 1540 to find the seven cities. They moved north out of Mexico and through the present-day states of Arizona, New Mexico, Texas, and

Portuguese Exploration

In the early days of European exploration, Portugal and Spain disagreed about the ownership of the unexplored lands in the Americas. In 1493 Pope Alexander VI tried to settle the conflict. The Pope drew an imaginary line of demarcation, a line that marks a boundary, that ran north and south, dividing the world as he knew it. Portugal had the right to all lands east of the line and Spain got all lands west of the line. A year later both Portugal and

Spain signed the Treaty of Tordesillas (tawr•duh•SEE•yuhs). This treaty moved the Line of Demarcation farther west, allowing Portuguese explorer Pedro Cabral (kah•BRAHL) to claim Brazil for Portugal when his fleet accidentally sailed there in 1500. The Portuguese eventually set up successful colonies in Brazil based on the farming of sugarcane, cotton, and tobacco.

Pedro Cabral's ship

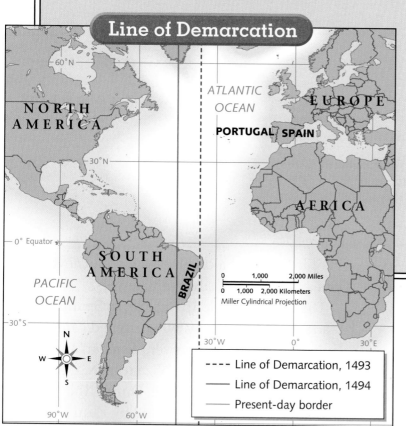

Line of Demarcation

- - - - Line of Demarcation, 1493
———— Line of Demarcation, 1494
———— Present-day border

Location At the time the Line of Demarcation was declared, people were not aware of all of the land found in the Western Hemisphere.

■ *According to the Line of Demarcation, which country could declare ownership of North America?*

Oklahoma into Kansas. They marched through the Zuni village of Hawikuh (hah•wee•KOO) and other Pueblo towns, but nowhere did they find any trace of the Seven Cities of Gold. Bitter and disappointed, Coronado began the long trip home. The route he took would later become the Santa Fe Trail.

In June 1542 Coronado arrived back in Mexico with only 100 of his soldiers. Some had died. Others had run away. Coronado had not found the Seven Cities of Gold. But he had **claimed** many new lands for Spain, declaring that Spain owned them.

REVIEW *What were the results of Coronado's expedition?*

De Soto Moves Ahead

About the same time that Coronado started his expedition, the king of Spain gave Hernando de Soto (day SOH•toh) a grant for an expedition to the northern continent. De Soto put together an army of 600 soldiers and sailed to the west coast of Florida. They landed in May 1539. The conquistadors moved north and reached what is now Georgia by winter. Finding no gold there, they traveled on through parts of present-day South Carolina and North Carolina, into the Smoky Mountains of Tennessee, and south into Alabama.

De Soto encountered many Indian peoples during his expedition. These encounters often ended in death for many people. One of the worst battles took place in Alabama. There the Spanish encountered some descendants of the Mississippian Mound Builders, the Mobile people, who were led by Tascalusa (tuhs•kah•LOO•sah). People who saw the battle later wrote that the number of Indians killed ranged from 2,500 to 11,000. They had fought, as a Spanish soldier later wrote, "with the desire to die" rather than be defeated. The Spanish lost only 20 men, but most of their supplies were destroyed in the fighting.

By this time de Soto's army was in poor condition. It had been reduced in size by deaths and **desertions**, in which soldiers ran away from their duties. Yet de Soto and what remained of his army marched on, reaching the banks of the Mississippi River in May 1541. They were the first Europeans

LEARNING FROM PICTURES The bells (right) were brought by de Soto to trade with the Indians. De Soto and his men (below) also brought horses to the Americas.
■ *What might Native Americans have thought when they first saw people riding horses?*

to see the great river. The Spanish army hurried to build rafts to cross it so they could continue their search for gold on the other side. In Arkansas and Louisiana the soldiers faced more fights with the Indians they encountered.

For three years the Spanish searched for gold without finding any. Then, in 1542, de Soto died of fever. "Many of his men did not mourn his passing," one soldier noted, "for he was a stern man." The soldiers buried their leader in the Mississippi River to hide his death from the Indians. Then the Spanish army finally made their way back to Mexico.

Though he found no gold, de Soto claimed much of the land he explored for Spain. The Spanish now claimed all of what is today the southeastern United States.

REVIEW *What lands did de Soto claim for Spain?*

Spanish Conquistadors

EXPLORER	DATES OF EXPLORATION	AREA EXPLORED
Juan Ponce de León	1513	Puerto Rico and Florida
Hernando Cortés	1519–1536	Eastern and central Mexico and California
Francisco Pizarro	1531–1535	The western coast of South America
Hernando de Soto	1539–1542	Southeastern North America and the Mississippi River
Francisco Vásquez de Coronado	1540–1542	Southwestern North America

LEARNING FROM TABLES This table lists several Spanish conquistadors who explored North America during the early 1500s.
■ *What lands did each conquistador explore?*

LESSON 2 REVIEW

Timeline:
1510 — 1530 — 1550

- **1513** • Ponce de León lands in Florida
- **1539** • De Soto explores the Southeast
- **1540** • Coronado explores the Southwest

Check Understanding

1 Remember the Facts Describe what took place when the Spanish explorers encountered different Indian peoples during their travels.

2 Recall the Main Idea Why did the Spanish risk the unknown to explore North America in the 1500s?

Think Critically

3 Personally Speaking How would you react if strangers arrived to explore your community?

4 Think More About It In their battle with the Mobiles, what do you think gave the Spanish an advantage?

Show What You Know

Table Activity Make a table of Spanish explorers and the Indian peoples they encountered. Start with the table on this page. Use reference books or databases to add the names of the Indian tribes each explorer met. Add other conquistadors to your table and display it in the classroom.

New People in America

The conquistadors changed the history of Spain in the Americas. Up to the time of the Spanish conquests, very few Spanish people had settled in the Americas. Most were either soldiers or missionaries. **Missionaries** are people who teach their religion to others. Spanish soldiers searched for gold. Spanish missionaries taught Christianity to the native peoples.

In time, other people came to the Americas to live. Some came for the wealth they had heard about. Others were made to come as slaves.

Building New Spain

The Spanish government rewarded many of the conquistadors by giving them large areas of conquered land. Most of the land was in Mexico, which the Spaniards called New Spain. It became one of Spain's colonies in the Americas. A **colony** is a settlement ruled by another country. People who live in a colony are called settlers, or **colonists**.

Many colonists worked in gold mines and silver mines. Others set up **plantations**, or huge farms, to grow sugarcane, tobacco, coffee, cocoa, cotton, and other crops to be sold in Spain. The colonists brought with them oxen and plows to work the land and horses to ride. They brought cattle and sheep, fruit trees, grain, and vegetable seeds. Soon the Spanish built new cities, and tens of thousands more colonists came to these cities to live.

The Spanish colonists needed many workers to grow their crops, to mine their gold and

FOCUS
What brings people to a new place to live?

Main Idea As you read, think about what brought the Spanish and the Africans to the Americas to live.

Vocabulary
missionary
colony
colonist
plantation

Cotton (right) was one of the many crops grown in New Spain. Spanish coins like the doubloon (above right) were made of pure gold from mines in South America.

159

silver, and to build and take care of their new cities. So they made the Indian peoples their slaves. They put the enslaved people to work on the plantations and in the mines. The Indians had to work day and night with little food or rest. They had no freedom.

The Indians fought against being enslaved. Thousands of Indians had already died fighting the Spanish. Now thousands more died from hunger, overwork, and disease. The Indians had never had the diseases the settlers brought from Europe, such as measles, influenza, smallpox, and scarlet fever. Because of this, their bodies could not fight these diseases. Sometimes whole tribes became ill and died.

Not all of the Spanish colonists believed that the Indians should be enslaved. A friar named Bartolomé de Las Casas (bar•toh•luh•MAY day lahs KAH•sahs), like other Spanish settlers, was given land. He was also given the right to have Indians work on his land as slaves. However, Las Casas spent many years of his life trying to help the Indians. He spoke out so strongly that in 1542 the king of Spain, Charles I, agreed to pass laws to protect the native peoples. These laws, however, were not always carried out.

As the number of Indian workers fell sharply, the Spanish colonists who had depended on slaves faced a problem. Who would work on the plantations and in the mines?

REVIEW *Who did much of the work building New Spain?*

Bartolomé de Las Casas (right) was among the first Europeans to call for an end to Indian slavery. He often spoke out against cruelty toward Indian peoples in the colonies. Under Spanish rule, Indians were forced to mine gold and silver as slaves (below).

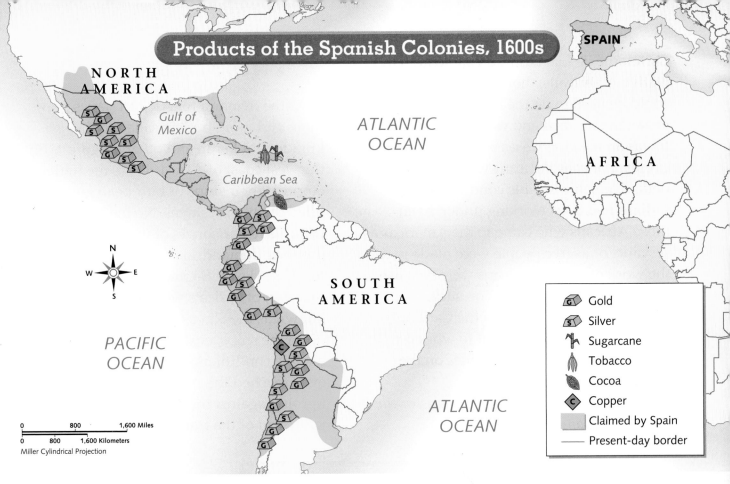

Products of the Spanish Colonies, 1600s

Legend:
- **G** Gold
- **S** Silver
- Sugarcane
- Tobacco
- Cocoa
- **C** Copper
- Claimed by Spain
- Present-day border

0   800   1,600 Miles
0   800   1,600 Kilometers
Miller Cylindrical Projection

Movement Many of the products produced in New Spain were sent back to Europe.
■ *Which products do you think were the most important to the Spanish?*

Demand for Labor

For many years people in Europe had been trading goods for slaves with several West African kingdoms. People in the kingdom of Benin (buh•NEEN), for example, carried on a large trade in slaves. They also traded ivory and gold for goods such as tools and guns.

Slavery had been practiced in Africa for a very long time. Most slaves were people taken as prisoners in war. In some parts of Africa slaves could rise to positions of honor and trust. After a time, they could be given their freedom.

At first, enslaved people were treated almost the same in Europe as in Africa. They often worked as house servants. Few owners thought of making slaves do hard work on farms or in mines. Some slaves in Europe became free after a time and worked at jobs they chose. Some even joined European expeditions and armies in the Americas. West African soldiers were with Cortés in Mexico and Pizarro in South America. And 30 Africans were with Balboa when he first saw the Pacific Ocean.

Little by little, however, life for Africans in Europe and in the Americas began to change. One of the most important reasons for this change was that there were not enough workers in the Americas.

As more and more Indians died from disease and overwork, Spanish colonists looked for other workers. In time they turned to Africans held as slaves. Even

Bartolomé de Las Casas, trying to help the Native Americans, thought that Africans could be used to do the hard work of growing the crops and working in mines. It was an idea Las Casas came to regret deeply. For soon Africans were working under the same terrible conditions as the Indians had been working under. Even those Africans who came to the Americas as servants or as free people were made to do the work of slaves. Africans were first used as slaves in large numbers on sugarcane and tobacco plantations on the Caribbean islands. Later they were put to work on the plantations and in the mines on the mainland.

REVIEW *Why did life for Africans in the Americas change?*

The Slave Trade

As the demand for African slaves grew, more and more traders sailed to the kingdom of Benin and other kingdoms on the west coast of Africa. There the traders emptied their ships of European goods and filled them with slaves. No longer were most slaves prisoners of war. To meet the growing demand, slave traders took people to sell as slaves. So many slaves were traded that part of Africa's west coast became known as the Slave Coast.

On the ships, enslaved people faced terrible conditions. Many died before they even reached the Americas. Some died fighting against the chains and the cruel treatment of the traders. Other Africans

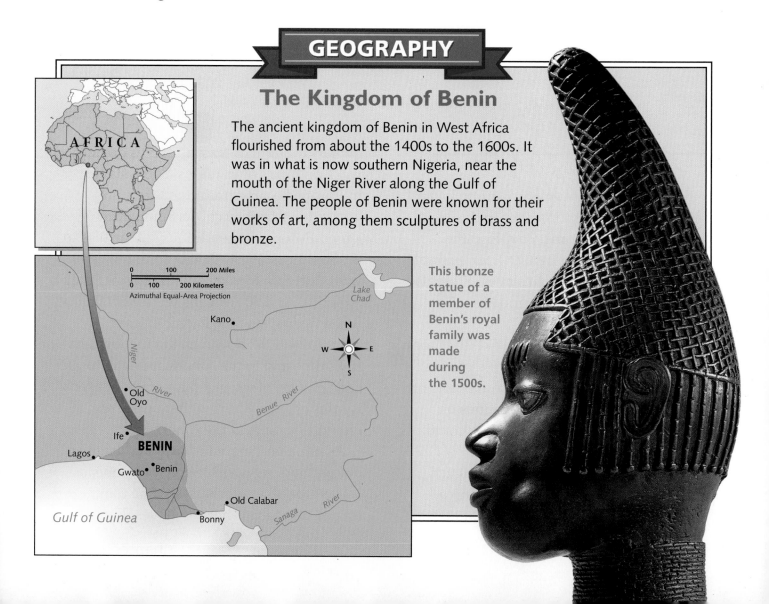

GEOGRAPHY

The Kingdom of Benin

The ancient kingdom of Benin in West Africa flourished from about the 1400s to the 1600s. It was in what is now southern Nigeria, near the mouth of the Niger River along the Gulf of Guinea. The people of Benin were known for their works of art, among them sculptures of brass and bronze.

AFRICA

0   100   200 Miles
0   100   200 Kilometers
Azimuthal Equal-Area Projection

Lake Chad

Kano

Niger

Old Oyo

River

Benue River

Ife

BENIN

Lagos

Gwato • Benin

Old Calabar

Sanaga River

Gulf of Guinea

Bonny

This bronze statue of a member of Benin's royal family was made during the 1500s.

This painting (right) by Lieutenant Francis Meinell, a British naval officer, was painted in 1846. The painting shows the conditions on slave ships. This ship, the *Abanez*, was Spanish. The diagram of a slave ship (below) shows the close conditions the enslaved people were transported in.

died of diseases that quickly passed from person to person on the crowded ships. Still others jumped into the ocean to escape living as slaves.

For those who survived the journey, life in the Americas was difficult. Slaves worked long hours in the fields and in the mines. Their work helped raise money for the Spanish government—money that for a time made Spain the most powerful country in Europe.

REVIEW *How did the slave traders meet the growing demand for African slaves?*

LESSON 3 REVIEW

Check Understanding

1 **Remember the Facts** How did the Spanish get workers to help build New Spain?

2 **Recall the Main Idea** What brought Spanish people to the Americas? What brought African people?

Think Critically

3 **Think More About It** Did the Spanish treat the Indians and the Africans fairly? Give reasons for your answer.

4 **Cause and Effect** What effects did European diseases have on the Native Americans?

Show What You Know

Chart Activity Draw a chart that shows the job descriptions of missionaries, colonists, Indians, and Africans. Use your textbook along with other reference materials to complete your chart. Then share your chart with a classmate.

Use a Map to

1. Why Learn This Skill?

Some information is easiest to understand when it is shown in a drawing. One way to show how people, products, and ideas get from one place to another is to use a map. Maps often use arrows to show such movement. Learning to read these maps will help you understand the exchange of products between Europe and the Americas.

2. Columbian Exchange

As people continued to explore and cross the Atlantic Ocean, plants, animals, and people were brought from one continent to another. This movement is what historians call the **Columbian Exchange**. Its name was taken from Christopher Columbus,

Tomatoes were taken from the Western Hemisphere.

Bananas came from the Eastern Hemisphere.

since he was one of the first explorers to transfer items across the Atlantic Ocean. The exchange of foods helped people all over the world plant new crops and increase their food supply.

3. Directions on a Map

To use a map to describe movement, you first need to understand direction. A direction marker called a compass rose is found on most maps. The compass rose shows the cardinal directions and the intermediate directions.

The compass rose on the map on page 165 is located near the center of the map. The compass rose shows the arrow with the N for north pointing toward the top of the map. This means that south is toward the bottom of the map, east is toward the right, and west is toward the left.

The north arrow on a compass rose points to what is called true north. This is the direction of the North Pole. On some maps the compass rose may be placed so that the north arrow is not pointing straight up toward the top of the map.

The map of the Columbian Exchange on page 165 shows some of the foods that were brought to and from the Americas. The route arrows show the direction in which they traveled across the Atlantic Ocean. The arrows do not stand for the exact routes taken. They only show the general direction.

Show Movement

4. Understand the Process

Now that you know about the use of the compass rose and route arrows in showing movement on a map, trace each arrow on the map below from beginning to end with your finger. Use the compass rose to find out the direction in which the arrows are pointing. Then use the map to answer the following questions.

1 In what general direction did products move from Europe, Africa, and Asia to the Americas?

2 In what general direction did products move from the Western Hemisphere?

3 What foods did the explorers bring with them as they traveled to the Americas?

4 What foods did the explorers bring with them as they traveled from the Americas?

5 Why do you think people traveling to the Americas would also have taken plants and animals with them?

5. Think and Apply

Use the library and the Internet to research some of the foods that are grown in your community or state. Find out if the food items are sent to other states or countries. Then write a paragraph that discusses where each food item is sent and in what direction it travels. Share your paragraph with a classmate.

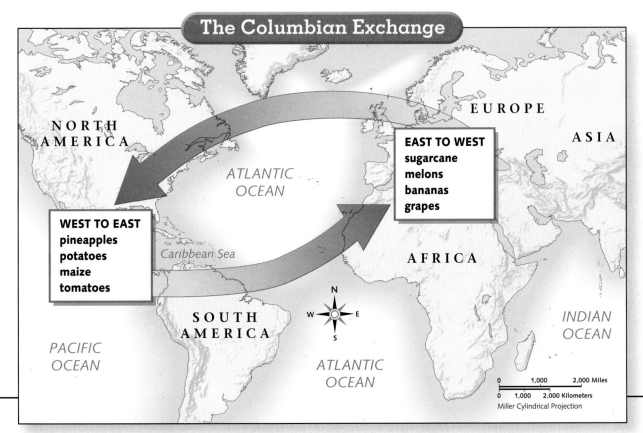

The Columbian Exchange

NORTH AMERICA

EUROPE

ASIA

ATLANTIC OCEAN

EAST TO WEST
sugarcane
melons
bananas
grapes

WEST TO EAST
pineapples
potatoes
maize
tomatoes

Caribbean Sea

AFRICA

SOUTH AMERICA

INDIAN OCEAN

PACIFIC OCEAN

ATLANTIC OCEAN

N W E S

0   1,000   2,000 Miles
0 1,000 2,000 Kilometers
Miller Cylindrical Projection

165

LESSON 4

FOCUS

How can trade between cultures have both advantages and disadvantages?

Main Idea
Read to learn how the fur trade had both advantages and disadvantages for Europeans and Native Americans in North America.

Vocabulary

Northwest Passage
trade network
agent

Encounters with the French and Dutch

1600	1615	1630

While the Spanish were growing rich and powerful from their colonies in Middle and South America, the French and the Dutch were making their own claims in North America. They found good fishing waters along the northeast coast, and they began to trade with the Native Americans. In time the trade brought the French and the Dutch new wealth. This was because they traded for a good that became nearly as valuable as gold—fur.

The French in North America

When French fishers set up camps on shore to dry their fish, they began to barter for animal furs with Indians who lived nearby. The Indians traded beaver furs and other furs for European goods. The furs the Europeans wanted most were beaver furs, which they made into hats. The goods the Indians wanted most were iron tools, pots, pans, and guns.

Jacques Cartier (left), a French explorer, sailed up the St. Lawrence River (below) searching for a passage through North America to Asia.

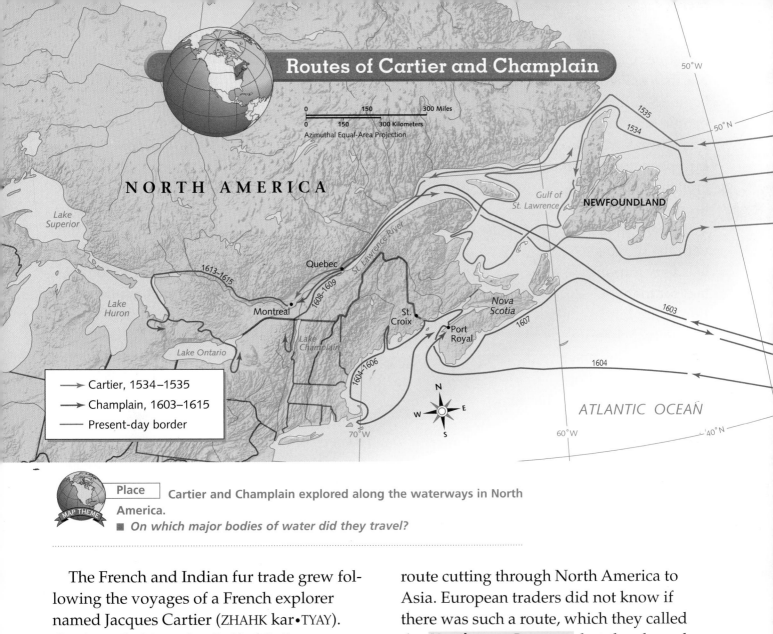

Routes of Cartier and Champlain

NORTH AMERICA

Lake Superior

Lake Huron

Lake Ontario

Quebec

1613–1615

1608–1609

St. Lawrence River

Montreal

Lake Champlain

1604–1606

St. Croix

Port Royal

1607

Nova Scotia

Gulf of St. Lawrence

NEWFOUNDLAND

1535

1534

1603

1604

ATLANTIC OCEAN

50°W

50°N

70°W

60°W

40°N

0   150   300 Miles
0   150   300 Kilometers
Azimuthal Equal-Area Projection

N   E   W   S

→ Cartier, 1534–1535
→ Champlain, 1603–1615
— Present-day border

Place Cartier and Champlain explored along the waterways in North America.
■ *On which major bodies of water did they travel?*

The French and Indian fur trade grew following the voyages of a French explorer named Jacques Cartier (ZHAHK kar•TYAY). Cartier sailed into the Gulf of St. Lawrence in 1534. The next year he sailed up the St. Lawrence River. Cartier thought that by sailing up the river, he might find a water route cutting through North America to Asia. European traders did not know if there was such a route, which they called the **Northwest Passage**, but they hoped so. Finding the Northwest Passage would mean finding a much faster way to reach Asia.

Jacques Cartier did not find the Northwest Passage, but he did begin to trade with an Indian people known as the Hurons. The Hurons were as eager for European goods as the French were eager for furs.

By 1600 trade with the Indians was very important for many Europeans, and for the French more than most. The business people in France competed with each other to control the trade. The French monarch, King Henry IV, wanted to build colonies in North America. He said that any business in France that wanted to trade with the Indians in North America would first have to start a colony there.

French business people jumped at the chance for riches. Several of them formed a company to start a colony in America. The company sent a cartographer there to map the places where beavers were found. The person they sent was Samuel de Champlain (sham•PLAYN). Champlain made his first trip to North America in 1603. At the time no Europeans had settled along the east coast north of the Spanish settlements in Florida.

Champlain spent three months exploring the forests of what is now eastern Canada, which he called New France. When Champlain returned to Europe, his reports about the wonderful country across the ocean made many more people want to go to New France. Champlain himself went again, this time as the king's geographer.

Samuel de Champlain founded the first settlement and trading post in New France.

For the next five years, he explored the lands along the St. Lawrence River and in what is today Nova Scotia and the state of New York. The search for a place to build a settlement took Champlain back to the St. Lawrence River. There he chose a place that the Hurons called *kebec*, meaning "the place where the river narrows." In 1608 Kebec became Quebec, the first important French settlement in the Americas. Three years later Champlain founded a trading post at Montreal, where an Indian village called Hochelaga (hahsh•uh•LAG•uh) had once stood.

REVIEW *Why was Samuel de Champlain sent to North America?*

The Struggle for the Fur Trade

The fur trade brought wealth to the French and to their Huron trading partners. Huron traders learned how to use a **trade network**, or system of trading, among the American Indian tribes in eastern Canada. At first the network was good for all the groups that took part in it.

The Hurons acted as **agents**—that is, they did business for other Indian groups. The Hurons traded food for beaver furs with these groups. Then they took the furs to Quebec or Montreal to trade with the French for European goods. The Hurons took home guns, kettles, and metal tools. They then returned to the other Indian tribes to trade some of these goods for more beaver furs.

The Huron trade network lasted until the mid-1600s, when the Iroquois began to trade in the same way as the Hurons. The Iroquois at the time were trading partners with the Dutch. The Dutch had begun building settlements after 1609, when explorer Henry Hudson claimed the land along what is now the Hudson River. The capital of the Dutch colony of New Netherland was New Amsterdam, at the

mouth of the Hudson River, where New York City is today. Founded in 1625, New Amsterdam quickly became a center for trade in North America and also for trade with countries around the world.

The Hurons and the Iroquois soon argued over trade with the French and the Dutch. The two Indian groups began to fight for control of the fur trade. Control of the trade would give the winner power over other Indian peoples.

This painting by Paul Kane shows that in order to survive, many fur trappers lived with Indian tribes (below) and learned their ways of life. Indian snowshoes (right) helped people walk on deep snow.

Trading posts (above) were places to live, as well as places for trading with Indians. The French traded iron goods such as pots (right) for beaver furs.

The fighting made both the Hurons and the Iroquois weaker and weaker. The Europeans did nothing to stop the fighting and sometimes they even tried to keep it going. In time the Europeans were able to take away the warring Indians' land with all its furs.

The trade and the wars that went with it changed the lifeways of many Indians of the Eastern Woodlands. The more they wanted European goods, the less they lived in their traditional ways. They changed the ways in which they farmed, hunted, cooked, and even dressed. Many stopped using the skills that had helped them live in the woodlands. Instead, they spent their time hunting for furs and fighting each other over the trade with the Europeans.

REVIEW *How was the fighting between Indian groups good for the Europeans?*

LESSON 4 REVIEW

1600	1615	1630

1608
• The French found Quebec

1625
• The Dutch found New Amsterdam

Check Understanding

1 Remember the Facts What groups took part in the fur trade?

2 Recall the Main Idea What were the advantages and disadvantages of the fur trade for the Europeans? for the Native Americans?

Think Critically

3 Past to Present How is trade today both an advantage and a disadvantage for some people?

4 Cause and Effect How did the market for furs in Europe affect the lives of people living in North America?

Show What You Know

Diagram Activity Create a diagram that shows how the Hurons acted as agents in the fur trade. Your diagram should show who the Hurons traded with and what goods they exchanged. Compare your diagram with those of your classmates.

The English in the Americas

1585   1605   1625

LESSON 5

FOCUS
In what ways is cooperation better than conflict?

Main Idea Read to find out how cooperation helped the English colonists at Jamestown and Plymouth.

Vocabulary
armada
profit
pilgrim
compact
Mayflower Compact
interpreter

By the 1600s English people, too, were coming to the Americas. Some came looking for wealth, as many of the Spanish, the French, and the Dutch did. Others came hoping to start a new and better life. Many were nobles and adventurers who had heard rumors of great riches. But most were just ordinary people—men and women, young and old. There were skilled workers, such as carpenters, tailors, and blacksmiths. There were farmers who wanted cheap or free land. And there were people who wanted the freedom to follow their own religion.

The Mystery of Roanoke

English explorers had been sailing across the Atlantic Ocean since the mid-1500s. Sometimes they explored the eastern coast of North America. Other times they attacked Spanish treasure ships carrying gold and other riches from the Americas to Spain. England's most famous explorer was Francis Drake. During an expedition in 1577, Drake attacked a Spanish ship, stole its treasure, and sailed around the world to escape Spanish warships.

England's monarch, Queen Elizabeth I, encouraged exploration. In 1584 the queen said that Sir Walter Raleigh (RAH•lee), an English noble, could set up England's first colony in North America. In July 1585 Raleigh's colonists landed on an island just off the coast of what is today North Carolina. The Hatteras Indians called the island

Queen Elizabeth I of England encouraged people to build colonies in North America.

171

The painting by John White, a leader of the colony at Roanoke Island, is one of the first drawings made by Europeans showing Native Americans.

Roanoke (ROH•uh•nohk). The English called their colony Virginia. In less than a year, however, the colony had failed. The colonists did not know how to survive in their new environment. When Francis Drake visited the colony in 1586, he found the colonists starving and took them back to England.

In July 1587 Raleigh sent a second group to settle Roanoke Island. Raleigh had chosen John White to lead the new colony. In August, after White had helped the colonists get settled, he went back to England for supplies. At this time England needed all its ships for a war with Spain, so White could not get back to the people he had left on Roanoke Island.

Three years later, after England had defeated Spain's **armada**, or fleet of warships, John White returned to Roanoke—only to find everyone gone. All that remained were some books with their covers torn off, maps ruined by rain, and weapons covered with rust. White found

the letters *CRO* carved on a nearby tree and the word *CROATOAN* carved on a wooden post. White and the people who were with him fired shots into the air. They searched but found nothing. They shouted but no one answered.

Nothing was ever found of the people of Roanoke Island. Many people believe they went to live with the Croatoan Indians, who later became known as the Lumbee Indians. Many Lumbee Indians today still have the last names of people from the "lost colony."

REVIEW *What happened to the English colony on Roanoke Island?*

GEOGRAPHY

Roanoke Island

Roanoke Island is off the coast of North Carolina, south of Albemarle (AL•buh•marl) Sound, between the Outer Banks and the mainland. The island is in what is now Dare County. The county was named for John White's granddaughter, Virginia Dare. Virginia was born August 18, 1587. She was the first child born of English parents in North America. The baby vanished with the other settlers of the Lost Colony.

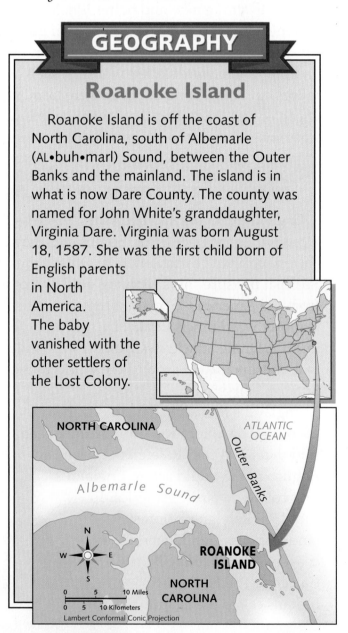

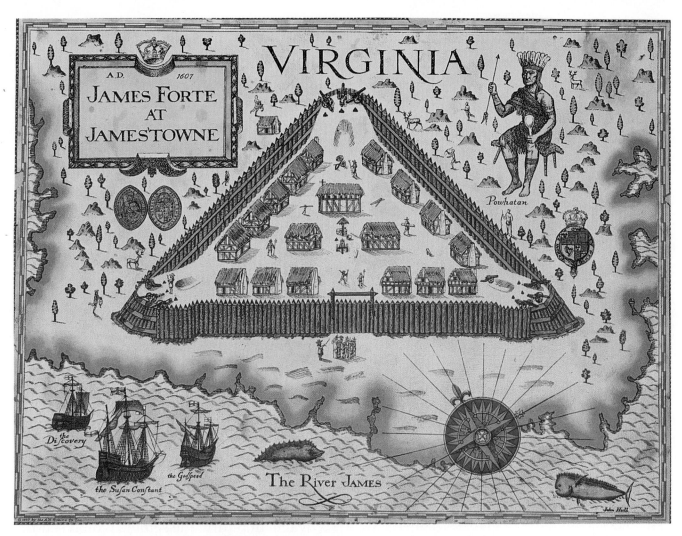

Captain John Smith led the colony of Jamestown and kept its settlers from starving. The colony was located near the Indian Confederation that was led by Chief Powhatan. Chief Powhatan is shown in the upper right corner of the map.

Success at Jamestown

On May 24, 1607, three English ships sailed into the deep bay now called the Chesapeake. The ships and the 105 men and boys aboard had been sent to North America by the English business people who formed the Virginia Company of London. The company planned to build a trading post and colony in North America to make a profit. A **profit** is the money left over after everything has been paid for. Despite the company's plans, however, most of the colonists came looking for gold.

The three ships sailed up a river that the men named the James, to honor King James I of England. They landed on a peninsula and decided to start a settlement there. However, the place they built Jamestown, as they called the settlement, turned out to be a poor choice. The men dug wells, but the water was bad. The land was wet and full of disease-carrying mosquitoes. The way the colonists behaved toward the Indians who lived nearby—taking Indian lands and destroying their crops—also put them in danger of attack.

By the end of the first year, about half of the colonists had died. One colonist later

Captain John Smith maintained peace with the nearby Algonquian Indians.

wrote, "Our men were destroyed with cruel diseases, . . . burning fevers, and by wars." They had come to the Americas to get rich. No one had bothered to plant or gather food for the winter. Many colonists starved.

Life in the colony changed when Captain John Smith became its leader. He probably saved Jamestown from becoming another lost colony. Smith's first act was to make one unbreakable rule: Anyone who did not work did not eat. Soon the colonists were planting gardens, building shelters, and putting up fences to protect the settlement from attack.

More than 30 tribes of Eastern Woodlands Indians lived in Virginia during this time. Most were members of a confederation led by Chief Powhatan (pow•uh•TAN). One day Captain Smith was captured by the Indians. A legend says that the chief's daughter, Pocahontas (poh•kuh•HAHN•tuhs), saved his life. Because of this act Captain Smith

made peace with Chief Powhatan. Whether or not this story is true, it is known that fighting continued between the settlers and the Indians of the Eastern Woodlands.

Despite Jamestown's many troubles, the colony survived and, in time, did well. Five years after the first colonists had sailed up the James River, they found the "gold" that would make the colony rich. It was tobacco. Selling tobacco was the beginning of a profitable business for the Virginia colonists.

REVIEW *Why did colonists go to Jamestown?*

The Founding of Plymouth Colony

On a cold day late in 1620, a ship called the *Mayflower* set sail from England for the Americas. The 101 colonists on board had agreed to work for the Virginia Company. The company's owners would pay for the voyage. In return, the settlers would send them furs, fish, and lumber.

Among the colonists on board was a group of families going to the Americas for

In 1620 the *Mayflower* landed on the coast of Massachusetts.

The Mayflower Compact

In the name of God, Amen. We, whose names are under-written, the Loyal Subjects of our dread Sovereign Lord, *King James*, by the Grace of God, of *Great Britain, France* and *Ireland*, King, *Defender of the Faith*, etc.

Having undertaken for the Glory of God, and Advancement of the Christian Faith, and the Honour of our King and Country, a voyage to plant the first colony in the northern Parts of Virginia; do by these Presents, solemnly and mutually in the Presence of God and one of another, convenant and com-bine ourselves together into a civil Body Politick, for our better Ordering and Preservation, and Furtherance of the Ends afore-said; And by Virtue hereof to enact, constitute, and frame, such just and equal Laws, Ordinances, Acts, Constitutions and Offices, from time to time, as shall be thought most meet and convenient for the General good of the Colony; unto which we promise all due Submission and Obedience.

In Witness whereof we have hereunto subscribed our names at *Cape Cod* the eleventh of *November*, in the Reign of our Sovereign Lord, King *James* of *England, France* and *Ireland,* the eighteenth, and of *Scotland* the fifty-fourth. *Anno Domini, 1620.*

a special reason. They were Separatists, or people who had separated from the Church of England. At the time, everyone in England had to belong to this church. Those who refused to belong to the Church of England were not safe. So these Separatists decided to go to the Americas, where they hoped to find the freedom to follow their own religion. In time they became known as Pilgrims. A **pilgrim** is a person who makes a journey for a religious reason.

The colonists had planned to settle in the lands governed by the Virginia Company. But the *Mayflower* was blown off course by storms and reached the coast of what is today Massachusetts. The settlers were not sure where they were, but they knew that they were not in the lands of the Virginia Company. To keep order, the 41 men aboard the *Mayflower* signed an agreement, or **compact**. They agreed to make laws for the good of the colony and to obey those laws. Women were expected to follow the laws even though they were not asked to sign the compact. This agreement became known as the **Mayflower Compact**. It is the first example of self-rule by colonists in the Americas.

Thanksgiving Day

In the fall of 1621, the Pilgrims gathered their first harvest. William Bradford, governor of Plymouth Colony, decided they should have a celebration so that the people could "rejoice together" to give thanks to God. He invited the neighboring Wampanoag Indians to join the Pilgrims for a festival that lasted for three days. This is what many people today think of as the first Thanksgiving. Thanksgiving celebrations, however, have been held in the Americas for thousands of years. During celebrations such as the Green Corn Ceremony, Indian peoples gave thanks for a good harvest. Some people think the first European Thanksgiving in the Americas took place in 1598, when Spanish settlers gave thanks for safely reaching the Rio Grande. Thanksgiving became a national holiday in 1863, when President Abraham Lincoln declared the last Thursday in November as "a day of thanksgiving and praise to our beneficent Father."

This painting, titled *The First Thanksgiving*, was painted by Jennie A. Brownscombe. The Pilgrims' Thanksgiving feast included turkeys, fish, clams, oysters, and lobsters.

On December 21, 1620, the Pilgrims landed at a place they called Plymouth, near present-day Cape Cod. The first winter was hard. The weather was cold, there was not enough food, and many settlers became ill. About half of them died.

Help came in the spring. A Native American walked into their village one day and said, "Welcome, Englishmen." The Indian was a Wampanoag (wahm•puh•NOH•ag) named Samoset. He had learned English from sailors who fished along the coast. Several days later Samoset returned to the settlement with an Indian who spoke English better than he did. This Indian was Tisquantum, or Squanto. Tisquantum had been kidnapped years before and sold as a slave in Spain. He had escaped and spent several years in England before returning to his own land.

Tisquantum stayed with the Pilgrims and became their **interpreter**. He translated the Indians' language and explained their lifeways. He showed the Pilgrims where to fish and how to plant squash, pumpkins, and corn. He helped the Pilgrims survive.

For a time the Pilgrims lived in peace with the Wampanoags, who were led by their chief, Massasoit (ma•suh•SOYT). However, as more English colonists came to settle in Massachusetts, things changed. The new people were not friendly toward the Indians and settled on more and more of their lands. This caused many quarrels between the Wampanoags and the English colonists that became fights and grew into terrible wars.

During these wars the Wampanoags and other tribes were forced off their lands. Soon very few Native Americans lived along the eastern coast.

REVIEW *How did the Indians help the Pilgrims survive in their colony?*

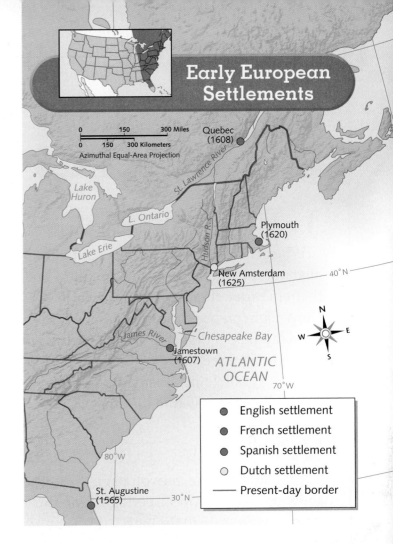

Early European Settlements

- ● English settlement
- ● French settlement
- ● Spanish settlement
- ○ Dutch settlement
- — Present-day border

Location Several European countries had established American colonies by 1625.
■ *Why were all the earliest European settlements located near water?*

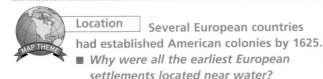

LESSON 5 REVIEW

1585	1605	1625
1587 • The English found a second colony at Roanoke	**1607** • The English settle Jamestown	**1620** • The Pilgrims land at Plymouth

Check Understanding

1 Remember the Facts How was life different for the English colonists in Roanoke, Jamestown, and Plymouth?

2 Recall the Main Idea How did cooperation help the settlers at Jamestown and Plymouth?

Think Critically

3 Think More About It Why did the Pilgrims think it was important to write the Mayflower Compact?

4 Personally Speaking Would you rather have been a Jamestown colonist or a Pilgrim at Plymouth? Explain.

Show What You Know

Questioning Activity Prepare a list of questions you might ask people who wanted to join you in starting a colony. As you write the questions, think about the personal qualities of people you would want to have as your colonists.

Read Parallel

1. Why Learn This Skill?

When there are many events happening at about the same time, it is difficult to put them in order. It even can be difficult to show them on one time line. Parallel time lines can help. Parallel time lines are two or more time lines that show the same period of time. Parallel time lines can also show events that happened in different places.

2. Understand the Process

The parallel time lines on pages 178–179 show dates of European settlement in the Americas from 1520 through 1645. Time Line A shows dates for the English settlements in the Americas. The French and Dutch settlements in the Americas are shown on Time Line B. Time Line C shows the Spanish settlements. You can use these time lines to compare when different events happened. Use the time lines to answer the following questions.

1. Which English settlement was built first, Jamestown or Plymouth? In what year was each settlement built?

2. How many settlements did the English build on Roanoke Island?

3. Who founded a settlement in the Americas first, the French or the Dutch?

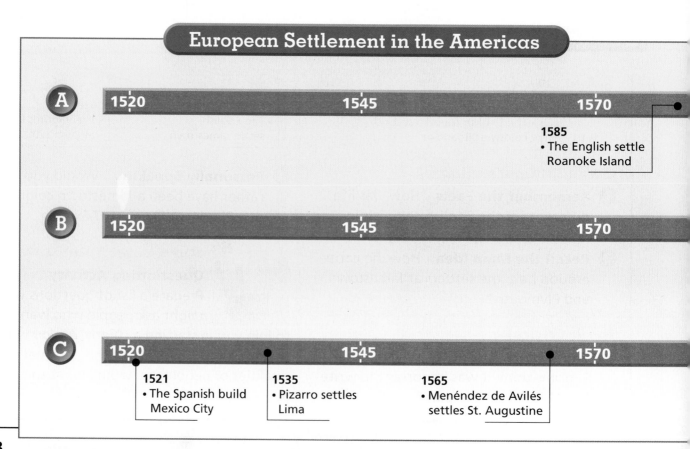

European Settlement in the Americas

A 1520   1545   1570

1585
• The English settle Roanoke Island

B 1520   1545   1570

C 1520   1545   1570

1521
• The Spanish build Mexico City

1535
• Pizarro settles Lima

1565
• Menéndez de Avilés settles St. Augustine

Time Lines

4 When was the first French settlement built in the Americas? Where was the settlement located?

5 When was the first Dutch settlement built in the Americas? Where was the settlement located?

6 In what year did the Spanish settle St. Augustine? Who founded the settlement?

7 Was St. Augustine settled before or after Lima?

8 Which European country was the first to build a settlement in the Americas? When was the settlement founded? Where was the settlement located?

9 How many years passed between the building of Mexico City and the first English settlement?

10 How many French settlements were in the Americas by the time the Pilgrims landed at Plymouth? How many Spanish settlements were there?

3. Think and Apply

Create a parallel time line comparing important events in your life with those of classmates. Make sure that you have a time line and a title for each person. Write three questions for another classmate to answer using your parallel time lines.

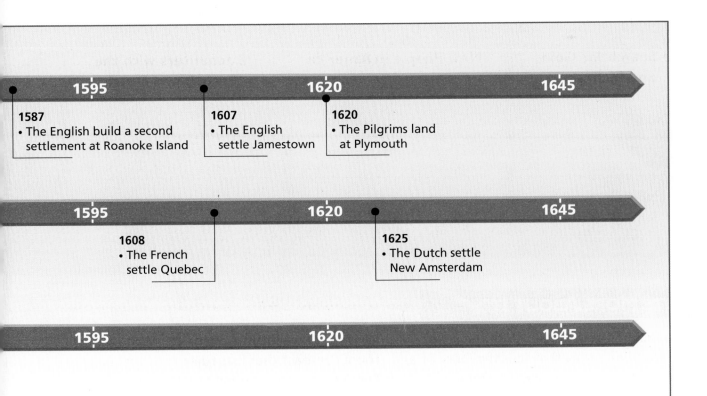

1595   1620   1645

1587
• The English build a second settlement at Roanoke Island

1607
• The English settle Jamestown

1620
• The Pilgrims land at Plymouth

1595   1620   1645

1608
• The French settle Quebec

1625
• The Dutch settle New Amsterdam

1595   1620   1645

1510		1540

1519
• Cortés lands in Mexico

1533
• Pizarro conquers the Incas

1540
• Coronado explores the Southwest

CONNECT MAIN IDEAS

Use this organizer to show how the chapter's main ideas are connected. Write the main idea of each lesson. A copy of the organizer may be found on page 29 of the Activity Book.

Encounters in the Americas

Indians

Europeans   Africans

Conquest of the Aztecs and Incas

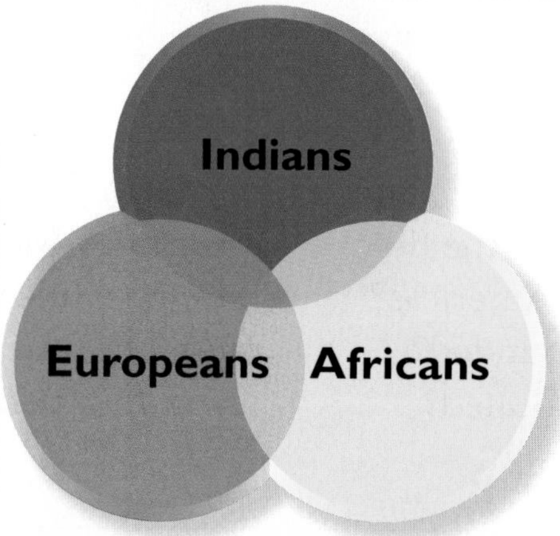

_____

_____

_____

The English in the Americas

_____

_____

_____

The Search for Gold and Riches

_____

_____

_____

New People in America

_____

_____

_____

Encounters with the French and Dutch

_____

_____

_____

WRITE MORE ABOUT IT

Write a Script for a Play   Write the script for one scene of a play that tells the story of a European settlement in America. Share your script with a classmate.

Write a Classroom Compact   Write a classroom compact that lists rules for your class. Explain how this compact will be good for members of your class.

1587
• The English found a second colony at Roanoke

1607
• The English settle Jamestown

1620
• Pilgrims land at Plymouth

1625
• The Dutch found New Amsterdam

USE VOCABULARY

For each group of terms, write a sentence or two that explains how the terms are related.

1. conquistador, claim

2. colony, colonist, plantation

3. trade network, agent

4. pilgrim, Mayflower Compact

CHECK UNDERSTANDING

5. Why did Motecuhzoma welcome Cortés to the Aztec Empire?

6. How did Pizarro conquer the Incas?

7. Who was the first Spaniard to set foot in what is today the United States?

8. What was Coronado searching for on his journey across what is today the southwestern United States? Did he find what he was looking for?

9. Who were the first Europeans to see the Mississippi River?

10. Why did Spanish missionaries come to the Americas?

11. What was the Northwest Passage?

12. How did the Hurons run their trade network?

13. Why did the Virginia Company want to build a colony in North America?

THINK CRITICALLY

14. **Think More About It** Why do you think some soldiers exploring the Americas deserted their expeditions?

15. **Explore Viewpoints** How might an Indian have viewed the fighting over control of the fur trade? How might a European settler have viewed it?

APPLY SKILLS

Read Parallel Time Lines Use the time lines on pages 178–179 to answer the questions.

16. How many years after the Pilgrims landed at Plymouth did the Dutch settle New Amsterdam?

17. Did the French settle Quebec before or after Pizarro settled Lima?

Use a Map to Show Movement
Draw a map of your community. Show your school in the center of the map, and show the neighborhoods where some of your classmates live. Make sure to draw a compass rose on your map. Then draw arrows from the neighborhoods to the school. Write a sentence that tells in which direction most of the students travel to get from home to school.

READ MORE ABOUT IT

Stranded at Plimoth Plantation, 1626 by Gary Bowen. HarperCollins. Journal entries tell of one boy's first few months in the Americas.

HARCOURT BRACE

Visit the Internet at
http://www.hbschool.com
for additional resources.

THE GREAT EXCHANGE CONTINUES

Christopher Columbus's first encounter with the Tainos began a worldwide exchange of plants, animals, people, and ideas that we call the Columbian Exchange or the Great Exchange. In many ways the Great Exchange has never stopped. Products, people, and ideas continue to move all over the world. Today, however, the exchange takes place faster than ever before.

With modern transportation, people and products can reach any location in the world in less than a day. Telephones, fax machines, television, and computers —especially the World Wide Web—have made it possible for people to communicate within minutes or even seconds. The World Wide Web is a network of computers that helps people exchange information from across the country and around the world. News that took months to cross the ocean five centuries ago as the Great Exchange began now takes almost no time at all!

UNIT 2 REVIEW

VISUAL SUMMARY

Summarize the Main Ideas
Study the pictures and captions to help you review the events you read about in Unit 2.

Write a Diary Entry
Imagine that you are living during the time of an event shown in this visual summary. Write a diary entry that explains what is taking place. Share your work with a classmate.

1 Viking explorers were the first Europeans known to land in the Americas, arriving about A.D. 1000.

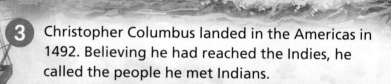

3 Christopher Columbus landed in the Americas in 1492. Believing he had reached the Indies, he called the people he met Indians.

5 The demand for workers in the Americas led many colonists to enslave Indians and then Africans.

184 • Unit 2

2 New maps, faster ships, and other advances in technology helped set the stage for European exploration in the late 1400s.

4 Aztec king Motecuhzoma welcomed Hernando Cortés. The Aztecs, like the Incas, were conquered by Spanish conquistadors.

6 By 1600 trade with Indian peoples in the Americas was very important to many Europeans. The fur trade brought wealth to French and Huron traders.

7 Jamestown was settled in 1607. It was the first lasting English settlement in North America.

USE VOCABULARY

Write the term that correctly matches each definition.

cartographer   expedition

colony   Mayflower Compact

1 a maker of maps

2 a journey taken for a special reason

3 a settlement ruled by another country

4 the first written plan for self-rule by colonists in the Americas

CHECK UNDERSTANDING

5 What was Vinland?

6 What changes in technology helped set the stage for European exploration?

7 What empire did Cortés conquer? What empire did Pizarro conquer?

8 Why were Africans brought to the Spanish colonies?

9 In what ways did the fur trade change the lives of many Indians of the Eastern Woodlands?

10 Why did the Pilgrims come to the Americas?

THINK CRITICALLY

11 **Cause and Effect** How did the European demand for spices, silk, and other Asian goods lead to the exploration of the Americas?

12 **Personally Speaking** Do you think the voyages of Columbus were more important than the voyages of other explorers? Why or why not?

13 **Think More About It** Why do you think John Smith started a "no work, no food" policy in the Jamestown colony?

APPLY SKILLS

Use Latitude and Longitude Use the map below to answer the questions.

14 Does the map show an area in the Northern Hemisphere or the Southern Hemisphere? in the Eastern Hemisphere or the Western Hemisphere? How can you tell?

15 Who traveled farther south, Ponce de León or de Soto?

16 What island is located near 20°N, 70°W?

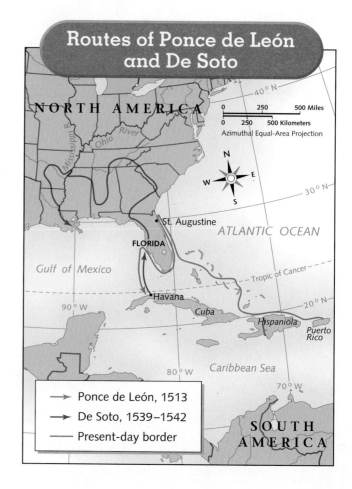

Routes of Ponce de León and De Soto

→ Ponce de León, 1513
→ De Soto, 1539–1542
— Present-day border

REMEMBER

- Share your ideas.
- Cooperate with others to plan your work.
- Take responsibility for your work.
- Help one another.
- Show your group's work to the class.
- Discuss what you learned by working together.

ACTIVITY

Write a Short Play

Work with other members of your group to write a short play about what you think happened to the settlers of the second colony on Roanoke Island. Include Sir Walter Raleigh and John White as characters. Be sure to explain in your play why you think the settlers carved the word *CROATOAN* on a post.

Unit Project Wrap-Up

Make a Globe With several classmates, finish the Unit Project that was described on page 113. Work together to write a short essay comparing two explorers who sailed for different countries. You may want to list the country each explorer sailed for, the reasons for each expedition, the hardships that each explorer faced, and the results of each expedition. Share your globes and essay with the rest of your classmates.

ACTIVITY

Draw a Ship

Work together to find out more about one of these ships: the *Santa María*, the *Golden Hind*, or the *Mayflower*. Draw a picture of the ship on a large sheet of paper. Then write a report that gives information about the ship and its history.

187

OUR COLONIAL HERITAGE

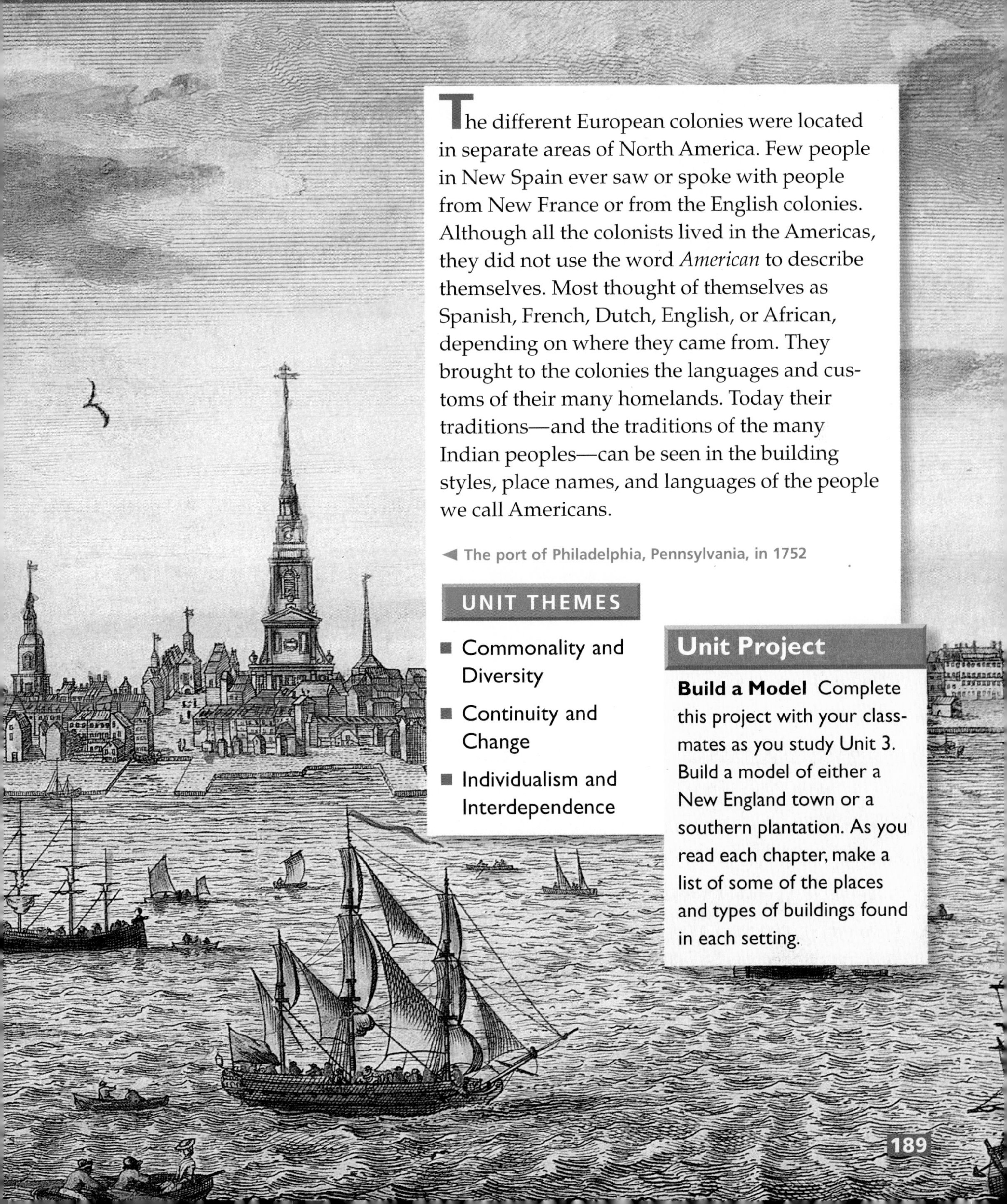

The different European colonies were located in separate areas of North America. Few people in New Spain ever saw or spoke with people from New France or from the English colonies. Although all the colonists lived in the Americas, they did not use the word *American* to describe themselves. Most thought of themselves as Spanish, French, Dutch, English, or African, depending on where they came from. They brought to the colonies the languages and customs of their many homelands. Today their traditions—and the traditions of the many Indian peoples—can be seen in the building styles, place names, and languages of the people we call Americans.

◄ The port of Philadelphia, Pennsylvania, in 1752

UNIT THEMES

- Commonality and Diversity

- Continuity and Change

- Individualism and Interdependence

Unit Project

Build a Model Complete this project with your classmates as you study Unit 3. Build a model of either a New England town or a southern plantation. As you read each chapter, make a list of some of the places and types of buildings found in each setting.

189

PACIFIC
OCEAN

Gulf of
Alaska

Yukon River

Mackenzie River

Great Bear
Lake

Great
Slave Lake

River

Athabasca River

Lake
Winnipeg

Columbia

Snake R.

Missouri

River

Platte River

Colorado River

LOUISIANA

Arkansas R.

Santa Fe

Tucson

El Paso
del Norte

Rio

Grande

NEW SPAIN

Gulf of California

Mexico
City

Rio Balsas

	Spanish
	British
	French
	Russian
●	Major city
—	Present-day border

0   500   1,000 Miles
0   500   1,000 Kilometers
Modified Azimuthal Equal-Area Projection

1500   1550   1600

MID-1500s
El Camino Real Is Started
PAGE 198

1600s
Plantations Grow Tobacco
PAGE 218

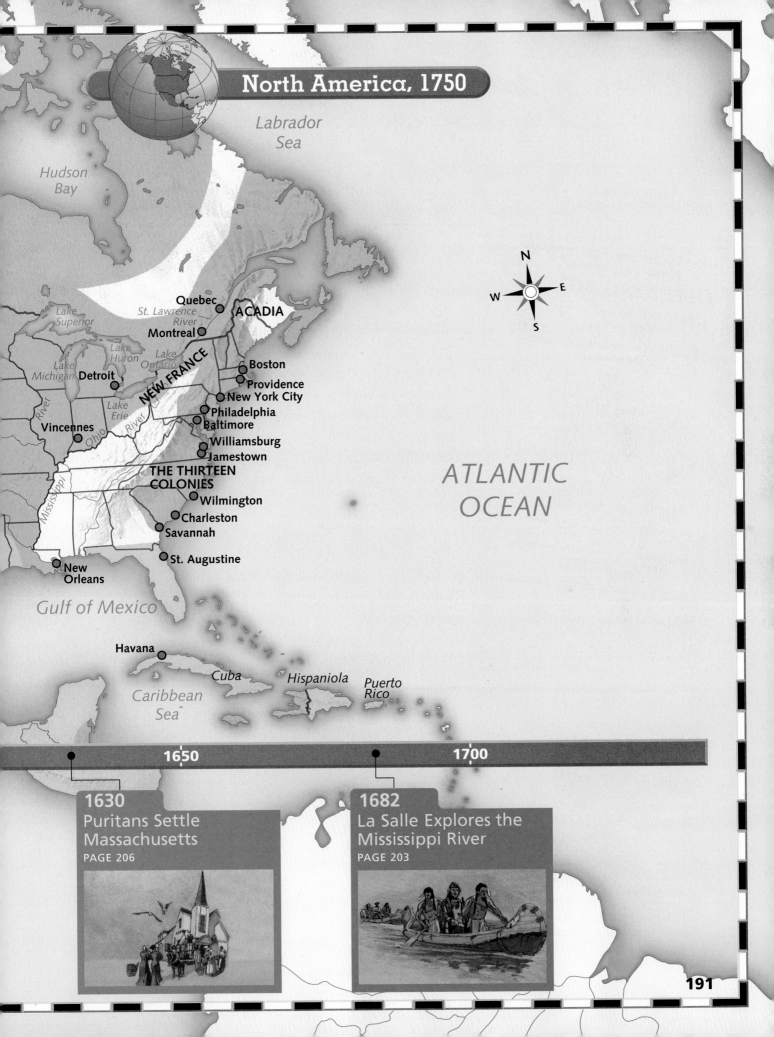

North America, 1750

Labrador Sea

Hudson Bay

Lake Superior

Lake Michigan

Lake Huron

Lake Ontario

Lake Erie

Detroit

Vincennes

Mississippi River

Ohio River

Quebec

St. Lawrence River

ACADIA

Montreal

NEW FRANCE

Boston

Providence

New York City

Philadelphia

Baltimore

Williamsburg

Jamestown

THE THIRTEEN COLONIES

Wilmington

Charleston

Savannah

St. Augustine

New Orleans

Gulf of Mexico

Havana

Cuba

Hispaniola

Puerto Rico

Caribbean Sea

ATLANTIC OCEAN

N
W E
S

1650   1700

1630
Puritans Settle Massachusetts
PAGE 206

1682
La Salle Explores the Mississippi River
PAGE 203

GOING TO THE
Colonies

NOVA BRITANNIA.
OFFERING MOST
Excellent fruites by Planting in
VIRGINIA.

Exciting all such as be well affected
to further the same.

LONDON
Printed for SAMVEL MACHAM, and are to besold at
his Shop in Pauls Church-yard, at the
Signe of the Bul-head.
1609.

Companies seeking the wealth of the Americas promised colonists good land and riches.

Few Europeans going to North America as colonists knew what to expect when they arrived. To help them prepare for the experience, one group in England published the following list of things to take when moving to North America. The list was based on the experiences of other colonists. It shows what many colonists brought from Europe to begin their new lives in North America.

PROPORTION OF PROVISIONS NEEDFUL FOR SUCH AS INTEND TO PLANT themselves in New England, for one whole year.
Collected by the Adventurers, with the advice of the Planters.

Victual
Meal, one Hogshead.
Malt, one Hogshead.
Beef, one hundred weight.
Pork pickled, 100. or Bacon, 74 pound.
Peas, two bushels.
Greates, one bushel.
Butter, two dozen.
Cheese, half a hundred.
Vinegar, two gallons.
Aquavita, one gallon.
Mustard seed, two quarts.
Salt to save fish, half a hogshead.

Men used razors like this one to trim or shave their beards.

Apparel

Shoes, six pair.
Boots for men, one pair.
Leather to mend shoes, four pound.
Irish stockings, four pair.
Shirts, six.
Handkerchiefs, twelve.
One Sea Cape or Gown, of coarse cloth.
Other apparel, as their purses will afford.

Tooles, which may also serve a family of four or five persons.
One English Spade.
One steele Shovel. Two Hatchets.
Axes 3. one broad axe, and 2. felling axes.
One Wood hook.
Hoes 3. one broad of nine inches, and two narrow of five or six inches.
One Wimble, with six piercer bits.
One Hammer.
Other tools as men's several occupations require, as Hand saws, Whip saws, Thwart saws, Augers, Chisels, Frowes, Grind stones, etc.

For Building

Nails of all sorts.
Locks for Door and Chests.
Gimmows for Chests.
Hooks and twists for doors.

Hats made of beaver fur were passed down from older to younger family members. These eyeglasses belonged to Peter Browne, a passenger on the *Mayflower*.

Arms

One Musket, Rest, and Bandeliere.
Powder, ten pound.
Shot, sixteen.
Match, six pound.
One Sword.
One Belt.
One Pistol. With a mold.

For Fishing

Twelve Cod hooks.
Two Lines for fishing.
One Mackerel line, and twelve hooks.
28 pound of Lead for bullets and fishing lead.

Printed at London for Fylke Clifton in 1630

This cradle was used by a baby named Peregrine White. The baby was born on the *Mayflower*. Tools like this saw (right) were brought to help build homes in North America.

EUROPEANS
SETTLE THROUGHOUT
NORTH AMERICA

"In my travels I saw very good sites and beautiful country . . . And I think that if it could be well settled like Europe there would not be anything more beautiful in all the world . . ."

Friar Pedro Font, during an expedition through California in 1776

Juan Bautista de Anza, a Spanish explorer

The Spanish Borderlands

1500   1540   1580

The Spanish conquistadors who explored the Americas found what they were looking for—gold and silver. Mining for these treasures became the most important money-making activity in Spain's American colonies. To protect its gold and silver mines from the other European countries that were building colonies in North America, the Spanish created a buffer. A **buffer** is an area of land that serves as a barrier. The buffer north of New Spain protected it from New France, New Netherland, and the English colonies. It came to be known as the Spanish **borderlands**. The borderlands stretched across what are today northern Mexico and the southern United States from Florida to California.

Presidios

Spanish soldiers led the way into the borderlands. Once the soldiers found a good place to settle, their first duty was to build a fort, called a **presidio** (pray•SEE•dee•oh), and shelters for the settlers. The largest and most important presidio in the borderlands was named St. Augustine. It was located on the Atlantic coast of Florida on a bay first explored by Juan Ponce de León in 1513.

Pedro Menéndez de Avilés (meh•NEN•dehs day ah•vee•LAYS) and 1,500 soldiers and settlers reached the location of present-day St. Augustine in 1565. St. Augustine became the first **permanent**, or long-lasting, European settlement in what is now the United States. It was founded 42 years before the

FOCUS
Why might a government today decide to expand its lands?

Main Idea As you read, look for reasons the Spanish government decided to expand its lands in North America.

Vocabulary
buffer
borderlands
presidio
permanent
scarce
hacienda
self-sufficient
mission

This glass bottle from St. Augustine is over 400 years old. The mission bell (above) is from the San Juan Bautista Mission in California.

English landed at Jam~ll
before the French ~adio in
Once the Span~ction.
St. Augustine~to~the Indian
wooden ho~ing walls of
which th~. It took 25
Fearfu~kah•STEE•yoh)
raid~io was called,
st~ect Spanish set-

~living in the bor-
~t that the settlement
~reat promise. In a

letter to the Spanish king, he wrote that
Florida could

> 66 bring enormous profits from vine-
> yards, sugar, cattle, ship stores,
> pearls, timber, silk, wheat, and
> endless supplies of fruit. 99

St. Augustine never lived up to the hopes
of becoming a source of wealth for Spain.
But it became important for another reason.
It served as Spain's military headquarters in
North America. It was one of a line of hun-
dreds of presidios stretching from Florida to
California that protected the settlers.

REVIEW *Why did Spain build presidios
across the borderlands?*

GEOGRAPHY

St. Augustine

St. Augustine is located in northeastern Florida, near
the Atlantic Ocean. Spain built the city and ruled it for
more than 200 years. During that time its settlers lived
through many invasions and attacks. In 1763 the
English gained control of St. Augustine. Spain again
ruled the settlement from 1783 until 1821, when
Florida became part of the United States.

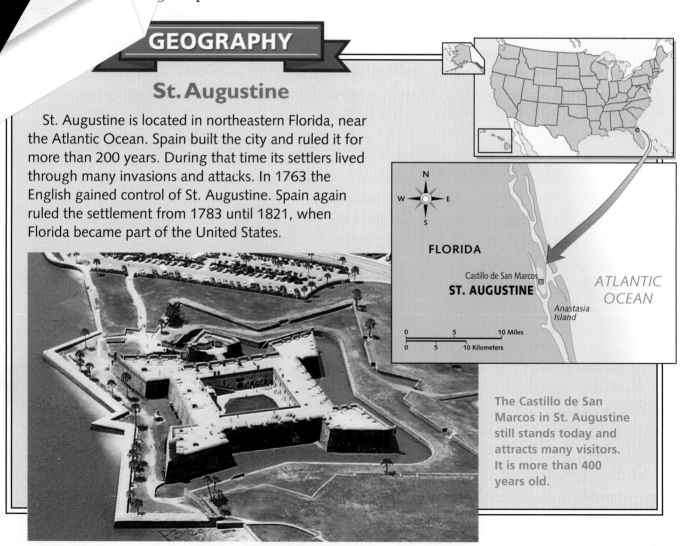

FLORIDA

Castillo de San Marcos
ST. AUGUSTINE

Anastasia Island

ATLANTIC OCEAN

0   5   10 Miles
0   5   10 Kilometers

The Castillo de San
Marcos in St. Augustine
still stands today and
attracts many visitors.
It is more than 400
years old.

The Spanish were the first cowhands in North America.

Ranches and Haciendas

The Spanish realized that gold and silver were **scarce**, or not plentiful, in the border-lands. They also knew that in many places the land was so hot and dry "that even the cactus pads appeared to be toasted." But settlers moved there anyway. Most made money by raising livestock and selling the hides and animal fats to markets in the colonies and in Spain. They often traded with Indian tribes for things they needed. They traded with the Pueblos, for example, for corn, pottery, and cotton cloth.

Some ranchers in the borderlands of northern Mexico built large estates called **haciendas** (ah•see•EN•dahs), where they raised cattle and sheep by the thousands. In what are now Texas and California, cattle were the most important kind of livestock.

In the drier climate of what is now New Mexico, settlers raised sheep.

Ranchers on the haciendas raised their own livestock, grew their own crops, and made most of what they needed to live. These **self-sufficient**, or self-supporting, communities developed far from the markets of Mexico City and other large cities.

As they settled throughout the border-lands, the Spanish—and the animals they brought with them—changed life for many of the Indians living there. Horses, long extinct in the Americas, once again roamed the land. The Plains Indians learned to tame horses and use them for transportation, which helped them in hunting and in war-fare. In the Southwest, the Navajos learned to raise sheep. They began weaving sheep's wool into colorful clothing and blankets.

REVIEW *How did the horse change the Indians' way of life?*

Missions

Spain's main interests in settling the borderlands were to protect its empire and expand its economy. But the Spanish king also wanted to "bring the people of that land to our Holy Catholic faith." So the Spanish government sent missionaries to the borderlands to persuade the Indians to become Catholics as well as loyal Spanish subjects.

The first successful missionaries in the Spanish borderlands were the Franciscans, a group of Catholic religious workers. The Franciscans built **missions**, or small religious communities, in what are now the states of Georgia, Florida, Texas, New Mexico, Arizona, and California. Their first mission was Nombre de Dios (NOHM•bray day DEE•ohs), or "Name of God." It was the oldest Spanish mission in the United States. Nombre de Dios was built near St. Augustine in 1565 and was the first in a chain of Spanish missions that would link the Atlantic and Pacific coasts of North America. Father Junípero Serra helped build a string of 21 missions in California, each "one day's journey" from the next.

When missionaries came to the Spanish borderlands, they usually brought with them livestock, fruit trees, and seeds for crops. The missions they built included churches and ranch and farm buildings. Some missions were built near Indian villages. In other places Indians settled around the missions.

The Spanish and the Indians learned from one another. The Indians taught the Spanish how to build adobe houses and how to use herbs as medicines. The Spanish taught the Indians how to guide a plow instead of using a stick and hoe in the Indian way. The Indians also learned to use other tools and machines the missionaries brought from Spain.

The coming of the Spanish missions changed the way many Indians lived and worked. It also changed something more important to the Indians—the way they worshipped. While many Indians kept to their traditional religions, others became Catholics.

A Spanish Mission

LEARNING FROM DIAGRAMS The Spanish built missions to spread Christianity.

❶ olive trees
❷ vineyard
❸ tannery
❹ orchards
❺ river
❻ Indian village
❼ vegetable garden
❽ washbasin
❾ ranch-workers' quarters
❿ workshops
⓫ candlemaking
⓬ weaving
⓭ storerooms
⓮ patio
⓯ well
⓰ priests' quarters
⓱ church

■ *In what ways were missions self-sufficient?*

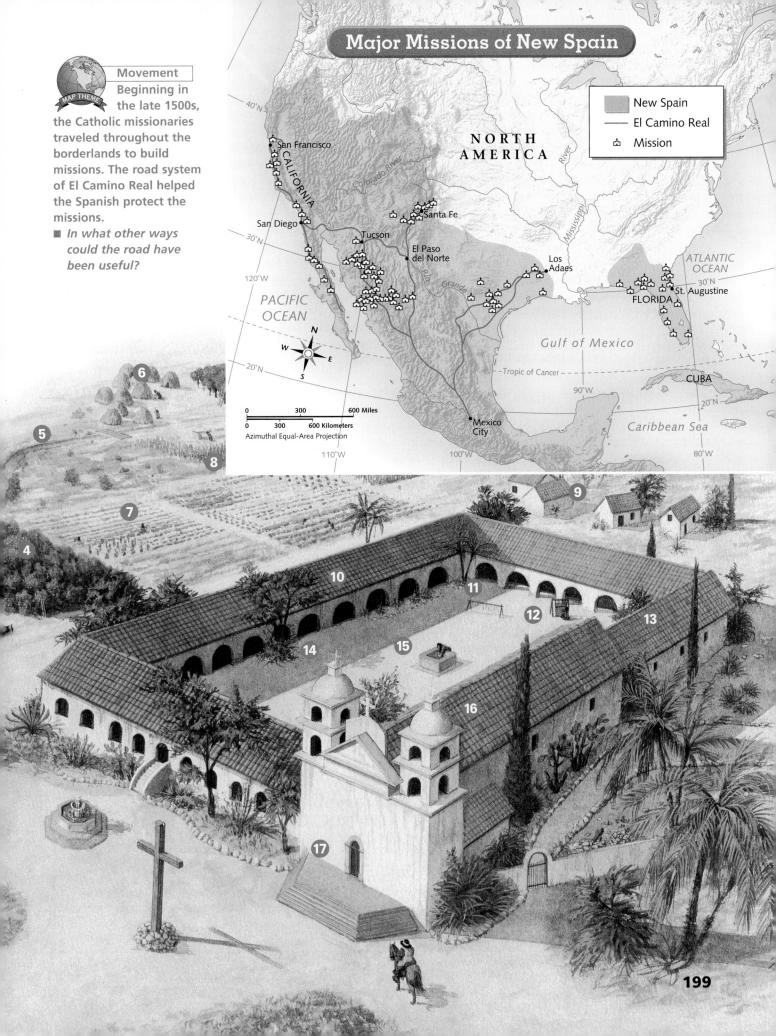

Movement
Beginning in the late 1500s, the Catholic missionaries traveled throughout the borderlands to build missions. The road system of El Camino Real helped the Spanish protect the missions.

■ *In what other ways could the road have been useful?*

Map Labels:

New Spain
El Camino Real
Mission

NORTH AMERICA

San Francisco
CALIFORNIA
San Diego
Tucson
Santa Fe
El Paso del Norte
Colorado River
Rio Grande
Los Adaes
Mississippi River
ATLANTIC OCEAN
St. Augustine
FLORIDA
PACIFIC OCEAN
Gulf of Mexico
Tropic of Cancer
CUBA
Caribbean Sea
Mexico City

120°W, 110°W, 100°W, 90°W, 80°W
40°N, 30°N, 20°N

0   300   600 Miles
0   300   600 Kilometers
Azimuthal Equal-Area Projection

199

At first some of the American Indians welcomed living at the missions. Like the missionaries, they were learning new ways. And the Spanish missionaries and soldiers protected them from their enemies. But problems soon developed. Many Indians had to give up their religious traditions and had to work on mission farms and ranches against their will. Many missionaries also used cruel treatment to control the Indians.

Some Indians fought back. They killed missionaries and destroyed churches and other mission buildings. To protect its missions, the Spanish government built roads linking them with nearby presidios.

This bowl was found at a Spanish mission. It shows a feathered serpent—a traditional Indian design.

El Camino Real (ray•AHL), or "The Royal Road," was started in the middle 1500s. The first section stretched for more than 600 miles (966 km) from San Diego to Sonoma in what is today California.

The government of New Spain, and later the Mexican government, continued to build missions in the borderlands until the 1830s. Many cities in the southwestern United States—such as San Antonio, Texas, and San Diego, California—began as missions.

REVIEW *Why did the Spanish government send missionaries to the borderlands?*

LESSON 1 REVIEW

1500	1540	1580

1513
• Juan Ponce de León explores the coast of Florida

1565
• The Spanish settle St. Augustine

Check Understanding

1 **Remember the Facts**   What is the oldest Franciscan mission in the United States?

2 **Recall the Main Idea**   Why did the Spanish government decide to expand its lands in North America?

Think Critically

3 **Think More About It**   What effects did the Spanish have on the Indians living in the borderlands? What effects did the Indians have on the Spanish?

4 **Explore Viewpoints**   How might a Spanish missionary and an Indian mission worker each describe the benefits and problems of living at a mission?

Show What You Know
Letter-Writing Activity
Suppose that you are a soldier sent by the Spanish government to a fort in the borderlands. Write a letter to your family in Spain telling what you have learned about the presidios, haciendas, and missions you visited.

The Growth of New France

1670   1700   1730

FOCUS
What steps do governments take today to protect their interests?

Main Idea   Read to find out what steps the French government took to protect its interests in New France.

Vocabulary
royal colony
portage
tributary
proprietary colony
proprietor

In New Spain the Spanish grew wealthy from silver and gold. In New France the French grew wealthy from the fur trade. But unlike the Spanish, most French people were not interested in settling North America. From 1608 to 1763 the French built only two towns in New France—Quebec and Montreal. They also built some small towns across Canada and along the Mississippi River.

A Slow-Growing Empire

The French had been fishing along the eastern coast of North America since the 1500s. In time they moved inland and established a trade in animal furs with the Hurons. The fur trade led to the founding of Quebec in 1608. But by 1625 its population had grown to only about 60 people.

In the early 1600s, civil wars kept many people from leaving France. Later, under the rule of King Louis XIV, peaceful times returned. The French now had even less reason to leave home.

Meanwhile, English and Dutch colonists began settling the coastal region south of New France. It was not long before conflicts over the fur trade broke out among the French, the English, and the Dutch, as well as the Iroquois and the Hurons. In time, the Iroquois defeated the Hurons, who were the main trading partners of the French. By the 1660s the French fur trade was nearly destroyed, and the French hold in North America was crumbling.

Hoping to rebuild the French empire in North America, Louis XIV declared New France to be a **royal colony**. The king, rather than business people, would now rule the colony. The king appointed officials to live in New France and help

King Louis XIV of France hoped to rebuild New France.

201

him govern. The head of these officials was called the governor-general.

In 1672 King Louis XIV appointed Count de Frontenac (FRAHN•tuh•nak) governor-general of New France. The count's hot temper and stern ways often got him into trouble with the king. His friendly ways with the Indian peoples, however, helped the colony prosper, or do well.

Frontenac encouraged exploration of the West. But the way west was not easy. French ships could not travel very far inland before coming to water that was too shallow or dangerous for sailing. To travel the rivers, the French learned from their American Indian trading partners how to build and use birchbark canoes. These boats could navigate shallow rivers. They also were light enough to be carried around waterfalls and rapids or overland between rivers. The French called this method of transportation **portage** (PAWR•tij).

The Indian peoples often talked with the French traders about a great river, larger

Europeans used birchbark canoes to explore waterways.

than all the others. The Algonkins (al•GON•kins) called it the Mississippi, which means "Big River." Ever since the days of Jacques Cartier, the French had hoped to find a Northwest Passage through North America to Asia. Frontenac believed that the Mississippi River just might be the route they were looking for.

REVIEW *Why did King Louis XIV declare New France a royal colony?*

Exploring the Mississippi

In 1673 Governor-General de Frontenac sent an expedition to explore the rivers and lakes that he hoped would lead French traders to the Mississippi River and then to Asia. The members of the expedition were Jacques Marquette (ZHAHK mar•KET), a Catholic missionary who knew several

The expeditions of Marquette and Joliet and of La Salle gave France claim to the Mississippi River, the longest river in North America.

Indian languages; Louis Joliet (loo•EE zhohl•YAY), a fur trader; and five others.

The seven explorers set out in two birch-bark canoes from northern Lake Michigan. They crossed the huge lake, entered the Fox River, and then traveled overland to the Wisconsin River. At the mouth of the Wisconsin, they saw the Mississippi River for the first time. The explorers followed the big river but soon realized that it could not be the Northwest Passage because the river flowed south.

When the explorers reached the Arkansas River, they met American Indians who told them that Europeans lived farther south along the river. The explorers feared that the Europeans might be Spanish or English, so they turned back. In four months Marquette and Joliet had traveled about 2,500 miles (4,023 km). Their expedition opened the Mississippi River to trade and settlement by the French. In time, they built trading posts that grew into towns and cities with such French names as St. Louis, Des Moines, and Louisville.

REVIEW *What did Marquette and Joliet find on their expedition?*

Founding Louisiana

After the Marquette and Joliet expedition, another French explorer set out to find the mouth of the Mississippi. This explorer was René-Robert Cavelier (ka•vuhl•YAY), known as Sieur de La Salle, or "Sir" La Salle (luh SAL). La Salle and an expedition of 20 French people and about

Routes of Marquette and Joliet and La Salle

Movement Marquette, Joliet, and La Salle traveled on waterways in the interior of North America.

■ *How far south did Marquette and Joliet travel? How far south did La Salle travel?*

30 Indians paddled south from the mouth of the Illinois River on February 6, 1682. Two months later the expedition reached the mouth of the Mississippi River. With shouts of "Long live the king!" the explorers fired their guns and claimed the entire Mississippi River valley, including all of its **tributaries**, or branch rivers, for France.

The region La Salle claimed was much larger than he could have imagined. It

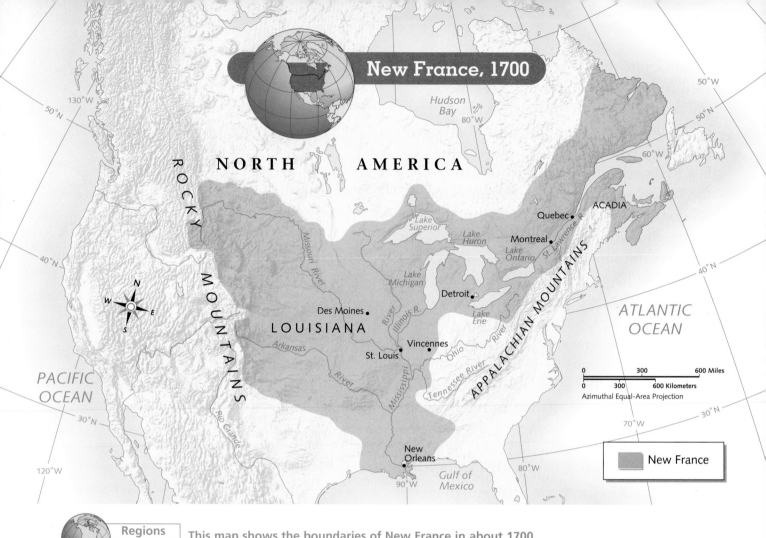

New France, 1700

NORTH AMERICA

ROCKY MOUNTAINS

APPALACHIAN MOUNTAINS

LOUISIANA

Hudson Bay

Lake Superior
Lake Huron
Lake Michigan
Lake Ontario
Lake Erie

Quebec
Montreal
St. Lawrence
ACADIA

Detroit

Des Moines
St. Louis
Vincennes

Missouri River
Illinois R.
Ohio River
Tennessee River
Arkansas River
Mississippi
Rio Grande

New Orleans

PACIFIC OCEAN

ATLANTIC OCEAN

Gulf of Mexico

New France

0   300   600 Miles
0   300   600 Kilometers
Azimuthal Equal-Area Projection

Regions This map shows the boundaries of New France in about 1700.
■ *French lands stretched across what major river valleys of North America?*

extended from the Appalachians in the east to the Rocky Mountains in the west and from the Great Lakes in the north to the Gulf of Mexico in the south. La Salle named the area Louisiana, to honor King Louis XIV.

La Salle tried to establish a settlement in this region. However, hardships led to disagreements, and he was killed by one of the settlers. The settlement failed.

In 1698 the French king sent another expedition to Louisiana to find La Salle's river and try again to start a settlement. The leaders of this new expedition were Pierre Le Moyne (luh MWAHN), known as Sieur d'Iberville (dee•ber•VEEL), and his brother Jean Baptiste (ZHAHN ba•TEEST), known as Sieur de Bienville (byan•VEEL).

In 1699 Iberville and Bienville reached the northern coast of the Gulf of Mexico. Their ships entered the mouth of a great river and sailed upstream. The brothers were not sure they were on the Mississippi until they met Mongoulacha (mahn•goo•LAY•chah), a Taensa (TYN•suh) Indian leader. He was wearing a French-made coat and carrying a letter addressed to La Salle. Mongoulacha told the Europeans his coat was a gift from Henri de Tonti (ahn•REE duh TOHN•tee). Tonti had stayed in Louisiana after traveling with La Salle several years earlier. Mongoulacha said that Tonti asked him to give the letter to a white man who would come from the sea. The explorers had found La Salle's river.

The brothers soon began to build settlements along the river and, in time, settlers began to arrive. The settlers faced terrible hardships, and many died.

In 1712 the French king made Louisiana a **proprietary colony**. This meant that the king gave ownership to one person, and allowed that person to rule. In 1717 John Law, a Scottish banker, became Louisiana's **proprietor**, or owner. Law formed a company to build plantations and towns. He brought in thousands of settlers. Finally Louisiana began to grow. In 1722 the town of New Orleans became Louisiana's capital.

Despite Law's efforts, however, the colony needed workers—especially on the plantations. Many planters began to bring in enslaved Africans to do the work. The French government soon passed laws called the Code Noir (KOHD NWAR), or "Black Code." These laws restricted the ways in which the Africans in Louisiana could live.

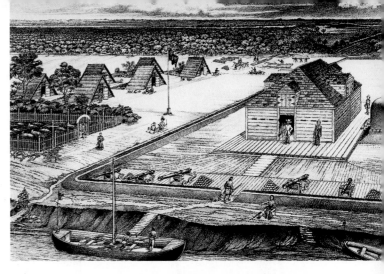

This drawing of a French fort shows Iberville standing in a doorway, Bienville sitting on the riverbank, and Tonti walking from the riverbank into the fort.

Like the rest of New France, Louisiana failed to attract enough people for it to prosper. By 1763 there were only 80,000 French colonists in the area from Canada to Louisiana. By the same year, and in a much smaller area, there were more than 1,500,000 English colonists in North America.

REVIEW *What lands did La Salle claim?*

LESSON 2 REVIEW

1670	1700	1730

1682
• La Salle claims the Mississippi River valley for France

1712
• Louisiana becomes a proprietary colony

Check Understanding

1 **Remember the Facts** Which explorers opened the Mississippi to French trade and settlement?

2 **Recall the Main Idea** What steps did the French government take to protect its interests in New France?

Think Critically

3 **Think More About It** How did the environment affect the settlement of New France?

4 **Cause and Effect** What were the effects of the shortage of workers in Louisiana?

Show What You Know

Newspaper Headline Activity Write three newspaper headlines about French exploration in North America and the settlement of the Louisiana colony. Compare your headlines with those of your classmates.

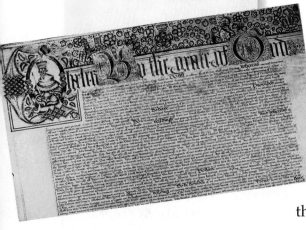

The charter of the Massachusetts Bay colony (above) was granted in 1629. Hornbooks (top) were used in the colony to teach children to read.

The New England Colonies

1620	1660	1700

Less than ten years after the Pilgrims founded their colony at Plymouth in 1620, another group of religious settlers founded an English colony in North America. Like the Pilgrims, these settlers disagreed with many practices of the Church of England. Unlike the Pilgrims, however, they did not separate from the church. They simply wanted to change some of the religious practices—they wanted to make the religion more "pure." For this reason they were called **Puritans**. The Puritans decided to set up a community in North America where they could live by their Christian ideas. They founded their colony in the region that English explorers first called New England.

Massachusetts Bay Colony

In 1628 a group of English Puritans formed the New England Company. That year King Charles I granted the company a charter that allowed the Puritans to settle the Massachusetts Bay area of New England. A **charter** is a document that gives a person or group of people official approval to take a certain action. John Endecott led the first group of Puritans in building a settlement he named Salem. The following year, the king granted a new charter that changed the name of the company to the Massachusetts Bay Company.

In 1630 John Winthrop became the new leader of the Puritans. He brought a second and much larger group of Puritans to settle Massachusetts Bay. More than 1,000 people arrived in 15 ships. Once the colony was set up,

Winthrop became its governor. He led the colony for many of the next 20 years.

The Puritans built many settlements in the region. Most were small villages built around the Puritans' chief town, Boston. They hoped that their communities would be models for Christian living. Winthrop told his followers,

> 66 For we must consider that we shall be a City upon a hill. The eyes of all people are upon us. . . . 99

At the center of each Puritan village was a meetinghouse. There the men of the village met to make the laws and settle the problems of the community.

The Puritans wanted every person to be able to read the Bible. They passed a law requiring parents to teach their children to read. Some parents paid other people to teach their children. Most children learned only reading because teachers charged extra for writing and arithmetic lessons.

Another law was passed stating that every village of 50 families or more must have a school, where children would learn reading, writing, and arithmetic. Puritan schools were the first community schools in the English colonies. In villages with fewer than 50 families, Puritan children often

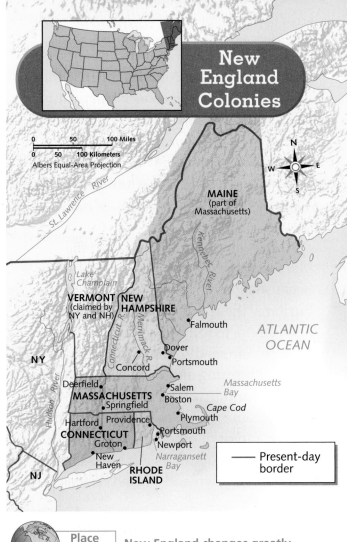

New England Colonies

0   50   100 Miles
0   50   100 Kilometers
Albers Equal-Area Projection

MAINE (part of Massachusetts)

St. Lawrence River

Kennebec River

Lake Champlain

VERMONT (claimed by NY and NH)

NEW HAMPSHIRE

Merrimack R.

Falmouth

Dover

Portsmouth

ATLANTIC OCEAN

NY

Connecticut R.

Concord

Deerfield

MASSACHUSETTS

Springfield

Salem

Boston

Massachusetts Bay

Cape Cod

Hudson River

Hartford

Providence

Plymouth

CONNECTICUT

Portsmouth

Groton

Newport

New Haven

RHODE ISLAND

Narragansett Bay

NJ

—— Present-day border

Place New England changes greatly with the seasons.

■ *Which season do you think was hardest for the settlers, considering the climate?*

attended schools run by women in their homes.

Schools were open all year. There was no summer vacation. The Puritans thought a vacation was a waste of "God's precious time." They believed that working hard was a way to please God. Most children, however, actually went to school for only 10 or 12 weeks. At other times they were needed to work at home or in the fields.

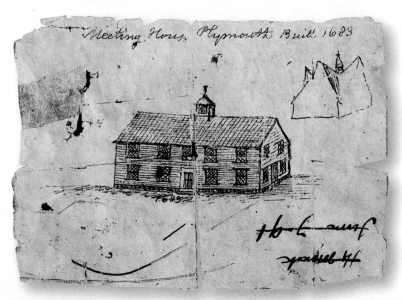

This drawing shows the Plymouth colony meetinghouse in 1683. The bell above the roof was rung to call people to meetings.

The Puritans also founded the first college in the English colonies. In 1636 they built Harvard College, now Harvard University, in Cambridge, Massachusetts, near Boston. They named the school for John Harvard, who had given it more than 400 books. There were so few books in the colonies that this gift was as valuable as money.

At the center of Puritan life in the Massachusetts Bay colony was religion. Because religion was so important to the Puritans, the colony's leaders expected newcomers to follow the Puritans' beliefs. If the newcomers did, the leaders gave them land for farming and a voice in governing their community. If they did not, they were not welcomed. The leaders sent them back to England or to other colonies in North America. Some settlers left Massachusetts Bay on their own and started new settlements nearby.

REVIEW *Who was the first governor of the Massachusetts Bay colony?*

New England Grows

In 1636 the settlers who lived along the Connecticut River joined to form the Connecticut colony. One of the settlers was a minister—the Reverend Thomas Hooker. Hooker had left Massachusetts Bay because he did not like the way the colony's Puritan leaders controlled the lives of the colonists.

Hooker thought that a colony's government should be based on what its people wanted, not just on what its leaders wanted. There were other settlers who agreed with Hooker. In 1639 the Connecticut colony adopted Hooker's beliefs in the form of the **Fundamental Orders**. This was the first written system of government in North America. The Fundamental Orders allowed Connecticut's male colonists to elect their

This picture by William Burgis shows Harvard College almost 100 years after it was founded. Harvard College later became Harvard University.

government leaders. They were the first colonists in North America to do so.

Roger Williams was another colonist who did not like the way the Puritan leaders governed. Williams spoke out time after time, asking for more freedom. He also said that the Indians, not the king or the Puritan leaders, should have the power to grant lands to the settlers. Because of Williams's views, Puritan leaders voted to expel him. This meant that he was no longer allowed to live in the Massachusetts Bay colony.

Roger Williams traveled south to Narraganset (nair•uh•GAN•suht) Bay. There he and his followers received food and protection from the Narraganset Indians. In 1636 he bought land from the Indians and founded the settlement of Providence, in present-day Rhode Island.

Not long after Roger Williams left Massachusetts Bay, the Puritans faced other challenges to their leadership. One such attack came from a colonist named Anne Marbury Hutchinson. Hutchinson began to question the authority of the Puritan ministers and their religious teachings. Because of this, the Puritan leaders said she was "a woman not fit for our society." They forced her to leave, too.

With her family and many followers, Anne Hutchinson founded a settlement on an island near Providence. This settlement and three others were united under a single charter to form the Rhode Island colony.

Some settlers decided to move out of Massachusetts

This portrait of a Puritan mother and her baby was painted around 1674.

Bay for reasons other than to find political or religious freedom. They left the rocky fields of the Massachusetts Bay colony for more fertile land and greater economic opportunity.

Settlers started the town of Strawberry Banke, now known as Portsmouth, New Hampshire, for business reasons. The area had plenty of trees, which the settlers cut down and shipped as lumber back to England. By 1680 the town of Strawberry Banke had been granted a charter under the name of the New Hampshire colony.

REVIEW *For what reasons did people leave the Massachusetts Bay colony?*

Anne Hutchinson was forced to leave Massachusetts Bay.

King Philip's War

Metacomet, the Wampanoag chief, was known as King Philip by the settlers.

As settlers moved beyond the Massachusetts Bay colony, they tried to keep the peace with the many Indian groups. In the Connecticut Valley, however, settlers fought with the Pequots (PEE•kwahts), who tried to keep them from taking over Indian land. With the help of soldiers from Massachusetts Bay, the Connecticut settlers defeated the Pequots.

The source of most disagreements between the Indians and the settlers was land ownership. The Indians felt that no one could own land. When Indians "sold" land to the settlers, they thought they were only sharing the use of it. The English, however, expected the Indians to leave.

In 1675 bad feelings between the Indians and the settlers became an all-out war. The settlers called it King Philip's War. Metacomet, known as King Philip by the English, was the leader of the Wampanoags who decided to fight to keep their lands. Metacomet was also the son of Massasoit, who years earlier had helped the Pilgrims.

The war began when the Indians attacked and destroyed many colonial villages. In return, the English settlers destroyed the Indians' crops. Without food, the Indians lost their will to fight. The settlers then took their lands.

REVIEW *What was the cause of King Philip's War?*

LESSON 3 REVIEW

1620		1660		1700

1628
• Puritans settle Massachusetts Bay

1636
• Colonists settle Connecticut and Rhode Island

1680
• The New Hampshire colony is chartered

Check Understanding

❶ **Remember the Facts** Which leaders or groups of people started colonies in New England?

❷ **Recall the Main Idea** Why did New England colonists set up different colonies?

Think Critically

❸ **Think More About It** How was a Puritan school like your school? How was a Puritan school different from your school?

❹ **Personally Speaking** How do you think disagreements over land ownership could have been settled and King Philip's War avoided?

Show What You Know

Planning Activity Suppose that you are going to a New England colony to live. First, select a colony. Then list the ten most important items you would take with you and why. Compare your list with those of your classmates.

The Middle Colonies

1620   1660   1700

FOCUS
In what ways do people from different cultures contribute to communities today?

Main Idea Read to find out how people from different cultures contributed to life in the middle colonies.

Vocabulary
influence
refuge
immigrant
frontier

When the first settlers of the middle colonies arrived, most of the land was covered with hardwood trees. Since the soil was less rocky and more fertile than that of New England, the land would be good for farming. The climate was also better for growing crops. The summers were longer, and the amount of rain each year was just right.

One colonial farmer used poetry to describe his feelings about the land of the middle colonies.

66 The fields, most beautiful, yield such crops of wheat,
And other things most excellent to eat, . . . 99

The colonies of New York, New Jersey, Delaware, and Pennsylvania produced so much wheat that they were called the "breadbasket" colonies. These colonies were alike in another important way. The people living in them came from different countries and were of different religions.

New Netherland and New Sweden

Not long after the English began setting up colonies in North America, the Dutch began to build settlements in their own colony, called New Netherland. They built their colony along the Hudson River, in parts of what are today New York and northern New Jersey. The Dutch had settled that area because explorer Henry Hudson had claimed that land for their country, Holland, in 1609.

The Dutch, along with settlers from French-speaking Belgium, founded the city of New Amsterdam in 1625. New Amsterdam did well under the leadership of its governor, Peter Stuyvesant (STY•vuh•suhnt).

Peter Stuyvesant was the last Dutch leader of New Amsterdam. He lost his leg during a battle in the West Indies.

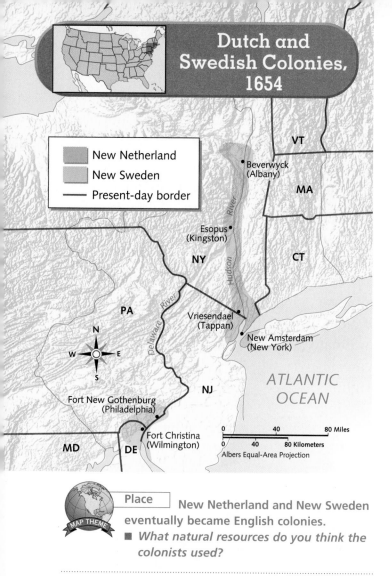

Dutch and Swedish Colonies, 1654

New Netherland
New Sweden
— Present-day border

VT

• Beverwyck
(Albany)

MA

Esopus •
(Kingston)

NY

Hudson River

CT

PA

Delaware River

Vriesendael
(Tappan) •

• New Amsterdam
(New York)

ATLANTIC
OCEAN

Fort New Gothenburg
(Philadelphia) •

NJ

0   40   80 Miles
0   40   80 Kilometers
Albers Equal-Area Projection

Fort Christina
(Wilmington)

MD   DE

Place New Netherland and New Sweden eventually became English colonies.

■ *What natural resources do you think the colonists used?*

Stuyvesant was a powerful and stubborn governor, who ruled the Dutch colony as he chose. There were often serious disagreements between Stuyvesant and the citizens of New Amsterdam. The citizens disliked his strong-handed rule and wanted more voice in government. Stuyvesant would not allow it, however.

Soon Stuyvesant expanded New Netherland into what is now New Jersey. Then he traveled south into what is now Delaware, taking over the small colony of New Sweden in 1655. This Swedish colony had been founded in 1638. It was chiefly a string of trading posts built around Fort Christina, where Wilmington, Delaware, stands today.

There were few people in New Sweden and New Netherland, compared to the colonies in New England. Knowing this, the king of England declared war on Holland. The king told his brother, the Duke of York, that he could have the Dutch colonies. In 1664 the Duke of York sailed into the harbor of New Amsterdam. Stuyvesant tried to get the citizens to fight the English, but they refused. Stuyvesant had to give up the colony. The English seized both New Sweden and New Netherland. The land was then split up and given its present-day names of New York and New Jersey. The city of New York grew from the Dutch capital of New Amsterdam.

REVIEW *Why were the English able to take over New Netherland so easily?*

A Dutch cottage in New York

Colonial New York City

In colonial times transportation was often slow and difficult. At that time the only way to travel was by boat, by horseback, or on foot. The journey from one colony to another could take days. The first colonial roads started as trails through the countryside. Later, the trails were widened for those traveling by horseback and in carriages.

In October 1704 a colonist named Sarah Knight made a journey by horseback to New York City from Boston. When she reached New York City, she wrote in her diary that the city was a "pleasant" place. She noted that it was located on a river with a "fine harbour for shipping." She found New York City different from Boston in many ways.

The Dutch had been the first European settlers of New York, but a mixture of people from other countries had also settled there. In addition to the English, there were free Africans, French people, and Jews from many European countries. New York was

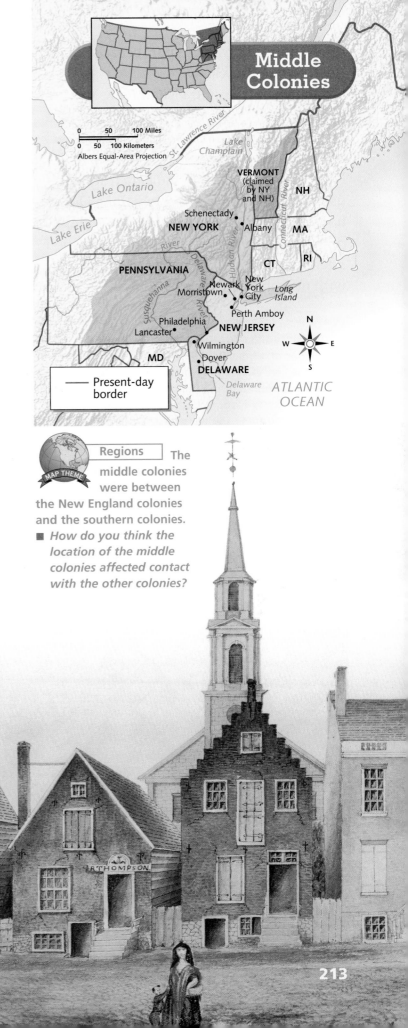

Middle Colonies

Regions The middle colonies were between the New England colonies and the southern colonies.
■ *How do you think the location of the middle colonies affected contact with the other colonies?*

LEARNING FROM PICTURES This painting by James Eights shows that more than 100 years after the English took over, the Dutch influence was still strong in many parts of New York.
■ *What are some examples of the Dutch influence?*

different from Boston in part because of this mixture of cultures.

When Sarah Knight visited New York, the Dutch influence was still strong. **Influence** is the ability people or things have to affect other people or things. Many houses in New York were built in the Dutch style, using bricks of different colors. Like Dutch houses, they often had a stoop—a wide, high doorstep. Family members spent their free time there talking with each other and with neighbors passing by.

The door of the house also made it easy to be friendly to neighbors. It was made in two parts. The top part could be open while the bottom part stayed closed. This kept dogs and pigs from wandering into the house.

The New York skyline in colonial days also showed a Dutch influence. Large windmills stood on the highest hills. The sails captured the wind's power to turn the mills that ground grain into flour.

REVIEW *How did the Dutch influence colonial New York City?*

LEARNING FROM DIAGRAMS Ships docked at the port of New York City to pick up cargoes of wheat flour. The flour was brought to other colonies and to people across the sea. ❶ Wheat is harvested. ❷ Sails catch the wind that powers the mill. ❸ Wheat is poured into a hopper to be ground. ❹ Flour slides down a chute and is put into sacks. ❺ Flour is ready to be taken to market.
■ *Why do you think the windmills face different directions?*

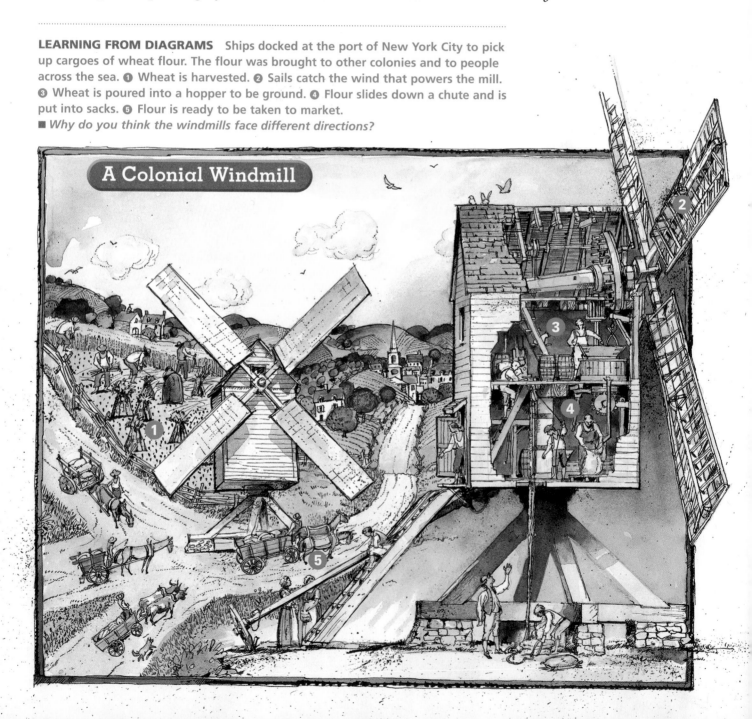

A Colonial Windmill

Pennsylvania

While the Dutch had been settling New York and northern New Jersey, Swedish colonists had settled Delaware and southern New Jersey. The Swedish colonists also set up trading posts in what is now Pennsylvania. In 1681, after the English had taken control of New Sweden, the English king gave William Penn a charter that made him proprietor of Pennsylvania.

Penn was a member of the Society of Friends, a religious group also known as the Quakers. Quakers believe that all people are equal and are basically good. They feel that violence is always wrong, so they refuse to carry guns or to fight. They also believe in solving all problems peacefully.

English Quakers often were treated unfairly because of their beliefs. William Penn wanted to create a **refuge**, or safe place, where people could worship as they

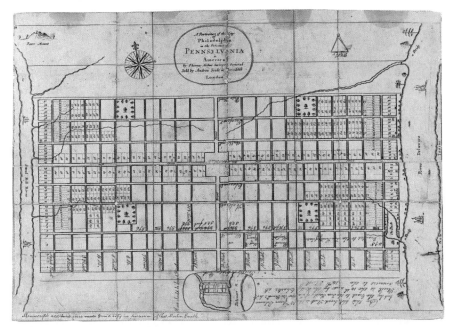

This map of Philadelphia was drawn by William Penn. He planned this settlement with straight streets.

pleased. Quakers and other settlers who wanted religious freedom soon came to Pennsylvania, a name that means "Penn's Woods."

Before coming to Pennsylvania, William Penn had planned the government of his colony. He wrote a document called the Frame of Government, which allowed

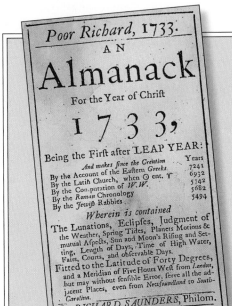

BIOGRAPHY

Benjamin Franklin, 1706–1790

Ben Franklin was 12 years old when he learned to be a printer. In his spare time he read books and worked at improving his own writing skills. As an adult, Franklin owned a print shop in Philadelphia, where he published many of his own books. His best-known books are his *Autobiography*, or story of his life, and *Poor Richard's Almanack*. Many of the sayings in his almanac are about the value of hard work and saving money. Some well-known examples are "Early to bed and early to rise, makes a man healthy, wealthy, and wise," "God helps them that help themselves," and "Little strokes fell great oaks."

freedom of speech, freedom of worship, and trial by jury. In England and other European countries, people rarely had these freedoms. There was also a group, or council, of men appointed to make the laws for the colony. Penn called this council the General Assembly.

Penn also planned the settlements in Pennsylvania. One of them, the town of Philadelphia, was laid out like a checkerboard, with straight streets that formed squares. Philadelphia's location was excellent for shipping and trading since it was located on the Delaware River. The town became the colony's main port for receiving not only goods but also immigrants. **Immigrants** are people who come to live in a country after leaving their home country.

People who liked Penn's ideas of freedom came to Pennsylvania and the other middle colonies from all over Europe. These immigrants included Irish Catholics, German Lutherans, and Jews from many countries. These immigrants helped Pennsylvania prosper as a colony. Some were skilled workers—bakers, carpenters, shoemakers, tailors, butchers, and blacksmiths. They set up shops in Philadelphia and in smaller towns. Other immigrants started small farms nearby. They raised fruits, vegetables, and wheat, which they sold in the colony's city and towns.

Scotch-Irish settlers also came to Pennsylvania. These were people from Scotland who had settled in northern Ireland in the 1600s. The Scotch-Irish were among the first to settle the **frontier**, the land beyond the settlements.

REVIEW *How did immigrants help Pennsylvania prosper?*

This painting by Edward Hicks shows William Penn signing a treaty with the Indians.

Relations with Indians

William Penn was always fair in his dealings with the American Indians. Indian leaders respected Penn and felt he was a friend. Penn had said,

> 66 Let them have justice, and you win them. 99

Although Penn had a friendship with the Indians, problems came up. As more European settlers arrived, they took lands from the Indian tribes. The Scotch-Irish, who settled the frontier, often fought with the Indians. They paid no attention to the agreements that Penn and the Quakers had made with the Indians.

When the Indians fought for their land by attacking frontier settlements, the settlers demanded military protection and help from the Quakers of Philadelphia. The

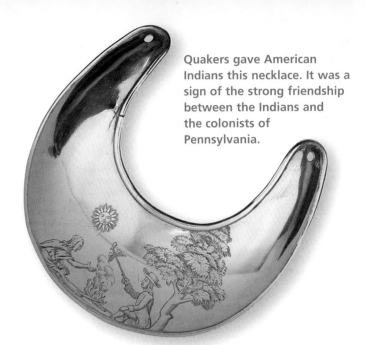

Quakers gave American Indians this necklace. It was a sign of the strong friendship between the Indians and the colonists of Pennsylvania.

Quakers, most of whom did not live on the frontier, told them they must solve the problem peacefully. They refused to provide military help. This made the settlers on the frontier very angry with the Quakers.

REVIEW *How did relations with the Indians change as more settlers arrived?*

LESSON 4 REVIEW

1620	1660	1700
1625 • The Dutch found New Amsterdam	**1655** • Stuyvesant takes over New Sweden	**1681** • William Penn founds Pennsylvania

Check Understanding

1 Remember the Facts From what countries did people come to settle in the middle colonies?

2 Recall the Main Idea How did people from different cultures contribute to life in the middle colonies?

Think Critically

3 Past to Present Which leader, Penn or Stuyvesant, led his colony most like a leader in the United States today?

4 Cause and Effect How did the environment of the middle colonies affect how the settlers made a living?

Show What You Know

Writing Activity Imagine that it is the 1600s and you are an immigrant who has just arrived in the middle colonies. Use the information in this lesson to write a diary entry about what you might see and do. Share your entry with a classmate.

FOCUS

How might a crop or a product be important to a state or country today?

Main Idea As you read, look for reasons why selling crops was important to the people in the southern colonies.

Vocabulary

cash crop
House of Burgesses
naval stores
indigo
debtor

The Southern Colonies

| 1600 | 1675 | 1750 |

Virginia was the first permanent English colony in North America. In 1607 the king granted it a charter allowing settlement of the Chesapeake Bay region. By the 1730s the English had settled the remaining southern colonies. With its 13 colonies, the English controlled much of the Atlantic coast of North America from present-day Maine to present-day Georgia.

Virginia

Virginia began with the settlement of Jamestown in the southern Chesapeake Bay region. In 1607 the Virginia Company of London started Jamestown as a trading post. Five years later, a settler named John Rolfe brought tobacco plants from the Caribbean region to the colony. Some colonists began growing tobacco as a **cash crop**—a crop that people raise to sell to others rather than to use themselves. The Virginia Company sold its tobacco all over Europe and made huge profits.

By 1619 Virginia had more than 1,000 settlers. The first women arrived that year, as did the first Africans. The first Africans came as free workers paid to work in the tobacco fields. As more workers were needed, more Africans were brought to Virginia. But instead of paying these workers, plantation owners made them slaves. By the middle 1660s, all Africans coming to the colonies were made slaves. In 1661 the Virginia colonial assembly made it legal to enslave Africans.

Virginia's assembly first met in 1619 to make laws for the colony. It was called the **House of Burgesses**. A burgess is a representative who speaks for other people. The Virginia House of Burgesses was made up of wealthy landowners who grew and sold tobacco. It was the first assembly of lawmakers in the English colonies.

For a time tobacco was the main reason for the growth of the Virginia colony and the success of the Virginia Company. At first James I, who was the king of England at the time, objected to the sale of tobacco. He thought using it was

> 66 a custom loathsome to the eye, hateful to the nose, harmful to the brain, [and] dangerous to the lungs. 99

In 1624 the Virginia Company went out of business because of poor management. The king was quick to take back its charter and make Virginia a royal colony. This allowed him to rule Virginia and to keep its tobacco profits for himself.

REVIEW *What cash crop caused the growth of the Virginia Company?*

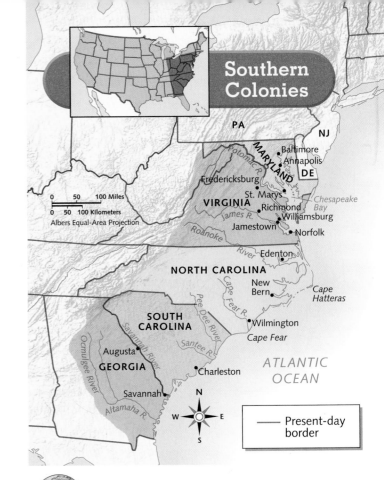

Southern Colonies

Place Some southern landowners built huge farms like those in New Spain.
■ *Why do you think most of the settlements in the southern colonies were located in Virginia?*

The marketplace at Jamestown, the first English settlement in North America

Thirteen British Colonies

New England colonies
Middle colonies
Southern colonies
—— Present-day border

MAINE
(part of Massachusetts)

St. Lawrence River

VERMONT
(claimed by NY and NH)

Lake Champlain

NEW HAMPSHIRE

NEW YORK

Lake Ontario

Connecticut River

MASSACHUSETTS

RHODE ISLAND

CONNECTICUT

Hudson River

Lake Erie

PENNSYLVANIA

Delaware River

Susquehanna R.

APPALACHIAN MOUNTAINS

NEW JERSEY

Ohio River

MARYLAND

Potomac River

DELAWARE

Chesapeake Bay

VIRGINIA

Roanoke River

NORTH CAROLINA

SOUTH CAROLINA

Savannah River

GEORGIA

ATLANTIC OCEAN

N
W   E
S

0   100   200 Miles
0   100   200 Kilometers
Azimuthal Equal-Area Projection

Maryland

Tobacco became an important cash crop for the Maryland colony also. Maryland was founded by the Calverts, a family of wealthy English business people. The Calverts wanted to build a colony in North America not only to make money but also to provide a refuge for Catholics. Like English Quakers at the time, the Catholics in England could not worship as they wanted. The government allowed only one form of worship—that of the Church of England.

In 1632 King Charles I chartered the northern Chesapeake Bay region as a proprietary colony. He made Cecilius Calvert, the second Lord Baltimore, its proprietor. One year later the first colonists left England. "I have sent a hopeful colony to Maryland," Calvert wrote. Calvert had named his colony for Queen Henrietta Maria, the king's wife.

From the beginning, Maryland's proprietors welcomed settlers of many religions. In 1649 Maryland passed the first law to guarantee some people religious freedom in North America. The law allowed all Christians to worship as they pleased. Sometimes, however, people with different religious beliefs had trouble getting along with one another. In time, disagreements based on religious differences affected life in all 13 English colonies.

REVIEW *Why did the Calverts start a colony in Maryland?*

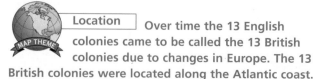

Location   Over time the 13 English colonies came to be called the 13 British colonies due to changes in Europe. The 13 British colonies were located along the Atlantic coast.

■ *Why do you think some people think of Maryland as a middle colony while others consider it a southern colony?*

St. Marys

St. Marys was Maryland's first European settlement and the first capital of Maryland. It is located not far from the mouth of the Potomac River. The settlers at St. Marys prospered because of the mild climate and the rich soil and by learning from the experiences of other colonists. The settlers did not suffer through a period of starvation and did not fight wars with the Indians. With the Jamestown colony nearby, the colonists also had a place to seek supplies or help.

The Carolinas

The southern colonies of Virginia and Maryland continued to grow during the 1600s. Then in 1663 King Charles II, the son of King Charles I, granted a charter for another colony in the region. The new colony was south of Virginia, in the lands between Virginia and Spanish Florida. The charter divided the colony, known as Carolina, among eight proprietors.

Even before the charter was granted, colonists from Virginia had been building villages and farming in the northern part of Carolina. After 1663, colonists from England and the Caribbean, as well as French Protestants called Huguenots (HYOO•guh•nahts), came to settle there.

But the colonists could not survive just by owning land. They needed a cash crop. At first they tried tobacco, silk, grapes, and cotton. They had more success raising cattle and hunting animals for their fur. Only when they "found out the true way of raising and husking rice" did the colony begin to prosper. The colonists also produced **naval stores**, which were products made from pine tar that were used in building and repairing ships.

In 1712 the northern two-thirds of the chartered area was divided into two colonies, North Carolina and South Carolina. North Carolina continued to develop as a colony of small farms. In South Carolina, landowners created huge farms in the style of the Spanish plantations of New Spain.

The main cash crop on many of South Carolina's plantations was rice. On land where rice would not grow, landowners found they could grow indigo. **Indigo** is a plant from which a blue dye is made.

Indigo became an important cash crop after Eliza Lucas, the 17-year-old daughter of a planter, experimented with the

The indigo plant supplied cloth manufacturers in England with dye and helped the southern colonies prosper.

This engraving from the 18th century shows how the workers pass fresh water through a series of tubs or barrels to extract the dye from the indigo plant.

plant in the 1740s. Lucas was in charge of three South Carolina plantations owned by her father. Using seeds from the Caribbean, she spent several years growing different kinds of indigo. In 1743 samples of the dye made from her plants were found to be of excellent quality. Lucas gave indigo seeds to her neighbors and friends. Within a few years South Carolina plantation owners were selling a million pounds of indigo a year.

The plantations of South Carolina required many workers. Many landowners filled this need by buying enslaved Africans. The coastal settlement of Charles Towne, later Charleston, South Carolina, became the most important seaport, social center, and slave market in the southern colonies.

REVIEW *What cash crops grew successfully in the Carolinas?*

Georgia

The southern one-third of what had originally been Carolina was not settled by English colonists until 1733. A year earlier King George II had given James Oglethorpe a charter to settle Georgia, a colony named for the king. In 1733 Oglethorpe and a group of 114 settlers set up the new colony at Savannah, which was located at the mouth of the Savannah River.

with the work of these small farms. Oglethorpe hoped that debtors would better themselves through hard work instead of spending time in prison. Few people were interested in Oglethorpe's offer, though, and his plan failed.

In the beginning, Georgia's charter did not allow traders to bring enslaved Africans to the colony. As a result, there were no plantations. After 1750, when Georgia law was changed to allow slavery, plantations quickly began to develop.

REVIEW *Who were the first people to settle in Georgia?*

Indian Wars

As in New England and the middle colonies, Indians and English settlers in the southern colonies were generally friendly to each other at first. As more and more settlers pushed into Indian lands, however, friendly relations turned to disagreements and then to war.

Oglethorpe had the idea of bringing over **debtors**, people who had been in prison for owing money, to settle the colony. Oglethorpe offered each settler 50 acres of land plus a bonus of 50 acres for every debtor the settler brought along to help

This 1734 engraving (below left) of Savannah, Georgia, was used to attract settlers to the colony. Present-day Savannah has the same rectangular street plan. James Oglethorpe (below right) founded Georgia.

After Chief Powhatan died, the Indian confederation he led stopped being helpful to the settlers. The Indians did not like losing their fishing and hunting lands to the Virginia settlers. In 1622 they attacked the settlements and killed more than 340 people. Having lost nearly one-third of the Virginia settlement, the English started a war against the Indians. The Indians were defeated and the settlers took over their land.

Nearly 100 years later, another war between the Indians and the English settlers was fought in the Carolina colony. Angry over losing their land, the Tuscaroras (tuhs•kuh•RAWR•uhz) attacked the colonial towns of Bath and New Bern in 1711. The Indians hoped this would stop further English settlement. Instead, the attacks

After Chief Powhatan's death the Indian confederation stopped helping the Virginia settlers.

started the Tuscarora War. In this war many of the farms and settlements in the colony were destroyed, and many settlers and Indians were killed.

The war in the Carolina colony lasted for nearly three years. In 1713 the English settlers finally defeated the Tuscaroras in a battle in which many Indians were killed or captured. Many of the Indians who survived were later made to leave the colony. The English settlers continued to build more farms and towns on the Indians' land. The settlers also built new towns along the Atlantic coast.

REVIEW *What caused the first war between the Indians and the English settlers?*

LESSON 5 REVIEW

1600			1675		1750

1607
• Jamestown is settled

1632
• The Maryland colony is chartered

1663
• The Carolina colony is chartered

1733
• James Oglethorpe establishes the Georgia colony

Check Understanding

1 Remember the Facts What were the important cash crops grown in the southern colonies?

2 Recall the Main Idea Why was selling crops for a profit important to the people in the southern colonies?

Think Critically

3 Think More About It Why do you think King James I allowed Virginia's settlers to continue to grow tobacco?

4 Cause and Effect What might have happened if rice and indigo had not grown well in the South Carolina colony?

Show What You Know

Research Activity Find out what kinds of cash crops are grown today in the states that were once the southern colonies. Use an encyclopedia and other research tools. Share your findings with your classmates.

Classify Information

1. Why Learn This Skill?

Imagine looking through a drawer full of clothes. The socks and shirts are all together in a jumble. It is hard to find things.

The same problem can happen with information. Like clothing, information is easier to find if it is **classified**, or sorted.

When you read about the English colonies in the Americas, you were given a lot of information. You learned about where the colonies were built and when they were founded and settled. This and other information can be classified by using a table.

2. Understand the Process

The tables below classify information about the 13 colonies in two different ways.

1 In Table A, the colonies are classified according to when they were founded. Which colony was founded first? Was Maryland founded before or after Massachusetts?

2 Table B gives the same information as Table A, but the information is classified differently. In Table B, the colonies are classified according to their location. Name the four New England colonies. Was New York a middle colony or a southern colony?

3. Think and Apply

Make your own table to show information about why each English colony was founded and how the colonists made a living.

Table A: The 13 Colonies

DATE FOUNDED	COLONY	LOCATION
1607	Virginia	Southern colony
1629	Massachusetts	New England colony
1632	Maryland	Southern colony
1636	Connecticut	New England colony
1638	Delaware	Middle colony
1647	Rhode Island	New England colony
1663	North Carolina	Southern colony
1664	New Jersey	Middle colony
1664	New York	Middle colony
1680	New Hampshire	New England colony
1681	Pennsylvania	Middle colony
1712	South Carolina	Southern colony
1733	Georgia	Southern colony

Table B: The 13 Colonies

LOCATION	COLONY	DATE FOUNDED
New England colony	Massachusetts	1629
New England colony	Connecticut	1636
New England colony	Rhode Island	1647
New England colony	New Hampshire	1680
Middle colony	Delaware	1638
Middle colony	New Jersey	1664
Middle colony	New York	1664
Middle colony	Pennsylvania	1681
Southern colony	Virginia	1607
Southern colony	Maryland	1632
Southern colony	North Carolina	1663
Southern colony	South Carolina	1712
Southern colony	Georgia	1733

1560

1565
• The Spanish
  settle
  St. Augustine

1600

1607
• Virginia colonists
  build Jamestown

1628
• Puritans settle
  Massachusetts

CONNECT MAIN IDEAS

Use this organizer to show how the chapter's main ideas are connected. Write three examples to support each main idea. A copy of the organizer may be found on page 37 of the Activity Book.

The Spanish Borderlands

The Spanish government decided to expand its land in North America.

1. _____
2. _____
3. _____

The Growth of New France

The French government took steps to protect its interests in New France.

1. _____
2. _____
3. _____

Europeans Settle Throughout North America

The New England Colonies

New England colonists set up different colonies.

1. _____
2. _____
3. _____

The Middle Colonies

People from different cultures contributed to life in the middle colonies.

1. _____
2. _____
3. _____

The Southern Colonies

Selling crops was important to the people in the southern colonies.

1. _____
2. _____
3. _____

WRITE MORE ABOUT IT

Write a Travelogue It has been more than 300 years since Marquette and Joliet explored the Mississippi River. Use a map of the United States, your textbook, and other reference materials to describe the route these French explorers followed.

Write "Who Am I?" Questions Choose three of the people who helped build the English colonies. For each person, write a question that gives clues about his or her identity and ends with "Who Am I?" Exchange your questions with those of a classmate.

1640		1680			1720		1760

1636
• Colonists settle Connecticut and Rhode Island

1680
• New Hampshire colony is chartered

1681
• Penn founds Pennsylvania

1712
• Carolina is divided into North Carolina and South Carolina

1733
• Georgia colony is established

USE VOCABULARY

Write the term that correctly matches each definition.

buffer	**mission**
charter	**proprietary colony**
immigrant	**refuge**
indigo	**royal colony**

1 an area of land that serves as a barrier

2 a small religious community

3 a colony ruled by a king

4 a colony owned and ruled by one person who is not the king

5 a document giving a person or group of people the official approval to take a certain action

6 a safe place

7 a person who comes to live in a country from another country

8 a plant from which a blue dye is made

CHECK UNDERSTANDING

9 What was the first permanent European settlement in North America?

10 How did conflicts over the fur trade change the way New France was ruled?

11 Who were the Puritans, and where did they first settle?

12 What were the Fundamental Orders?

13 What city grew from the Dutch capital of New Amsterdam?

14 What cash crop was important to the early English colonies? Why?

THINK CRITICALLY

15 **Explore Viewpoints** What reasons did the Spanish king give for wanting to build missions in the borderlands? How might the Indians have viewed those reasons?

16 **Past to Present** Why do many large cities in the Middle West region of the United States have French names?

APPLY SKILLS

Classify Information The following figures give the estimated population for each of the 13 English colonies in 1750. Use this information to make a table that shows which colonies had more than 100,000 people and which ones had fewer than 100,000 people.

Connecticut 111,280	New York 76,696
Delaware 28,704	North Carolina . . . 72,984
Georgia 5,200	Pennsylvania 119,666
Maryland 141,073	Rhode Island 33,226
Massachusetts 188,000	South Carolina . . . 64,000
New Hampshire . . . 27,505	Virginia 231,033
New Jersey 71,393	

READ MORE ABOUT IT

Jacques Marquette and Louis Jolliet by Zachary Kent. Childrens Press. This book, from The World's Great Explorers series, tells about the exploration of the Mississippi River.

HARCOURT BRACE

Visit the Internet at **http://www.hbschool.com** for additional resources.

LIFE IN THE BRITISH COLONIES

"Such a medley! Such a mixed multitude of all classes and complexions."

Charles Woodmason, a minister, describing the people of a Carolina settlement in the 1760s

John Singleton Copley painted this portrait of a British colonist in the 1770s.

Life in Towns and Cities

FOCUS
What different kinds of towns and cities are found in the United States today?

Main Idea As you read, think about the different kinds of towns and cities found in the British colonies.

Vocabulary
town meeting
common
militia
farm produce
import
Conestoga
county seat
county
export
triangular trade route
apprentice

During the late 1600s and early 1700s, more and more immigrants traveled to the Americas. England, which later became part of Britain, had settled 13 colonies along the Atlantic coast of North America. In time, some of the early settlements grew into towns and cities. Life in the towns and cities varied from place to place.

New England Towns

Many settlers in the New England colonies lived in towns where, as one settler wrote, "every man . . . lives in a tidy warm house, has plenty of good food and fuel, with whole clothes from head to foot, [made by] his family." Most New England towns were self-sufficient communities in which the people grew or made most of what they needed.

The earliest New England towns were built on a narrow road. Each of the town's families had a house on this lane. Families had their own gardens and pens for cows, sheep, chickens, or pigs. In the fields near the town, the people grew crops to sell to others and to use for themselves.

A meetinghouse stood at the center of most New England towns. In many places people came to the meetinghouse several times a week to worship together. The meetinghouse was also used for town meetings. At a **town meeting** male landowners could take part in government.

Two of the most important town workers were the herder and the constable. The herder was the person who took care of the animals on the town's **common**, an open area where livestock grazed. The constable was a police officer who made sure people obeyed the town's laws. Another important worker was the leader of the town's **militia**, or volunteer army. Men and boys gathered on the common to train.

REVIEW *What was the meetinghouse used for?*

This picture, titled *Colonial Days*, was painted by E. L. Henry.

A New England Town

230

Market Towns

Another kind of town developed in many places, especially in the middle colonies. This was the market town. Farmers traveled to market towns to trade their **farm produce**—grains, fruits, and vegetables—for goods and services.

In most market towns a general store sold **imports**, or goods brought into the colonies from other countries. The imports included tea, sugar, spices, cloth, shoes, stockings, and buttons. Near the general store was the shop of a cobbler, who made and repaired shoes. There was often a blacksmith's shop, where iron was made into horseshoes, hinges, and nails. Most market towns also had a gristmill, where grain was ground into flour and meal, and a sawmill, where logs were sawed into lumber.

Market towns often had more than one church. A Lutheran church might be a block away from a Quaker meetinghouse or just down the street from a Methodist church.

To carry their produce to the market towns, many Pennsylvania farmers used big covered wagons called **Conestogas**. Conestogas were much larger than regular wagons. When a visitor from Europe first

The Conestoga wagon had a canvas cover for protection and a curved floor to hold cargo steady.

saw them, he called them "huge moving houses."

When market towns grew along rivers, farmers carried their produce to the towns by boat instead of by wagon. It was easier and cheaper to ship heavy goods by water. After unloading their produce, farmers returned home, their boats filled with goods from the general store.

REVIEW *What kinds of goods were bought and sold in market towns?*

County Seats

In the colonies that depended on cash crops, especially the southern colonies, there were few towns. But several times a year, plantation families would pack their bags, dress in their finest clothes, and travel to the **county seat**. This was the main town for each **county**, or large part of a colony. People went to church, held dances, and traded crops for goods at the county seat. Some plantation owners bought and sold slaves there. Along with a church and a general store, most county seats had a courthouse and a jail.

LEARNING FROM DIAGRAMS The most important building in most New England towns was the meetinghouse. There also was a general store and shops for skilled workers. People who were punished were sometimes made to stand in the stocks on the common.

❶ houses
❷ fields
❸ mill
❹ school
❺ meetinghouse
❻ minister's house
❼ general store
❽ shops
❾ pasture
❿ common
⓫ well
⓬ cobbler
⓭ cooper
⓮ stocks
⓯ blacksmith
⓰ garden

■ *What else was the town common used for?*

White men who owned land and other property met at the county seat to make laws and vote for government leaders. This meant, however, that women, Africans, and American Indians had no voice in how the colony was run.

REVIEW *Why was the county seat important for people living on plantations?*

Cities

By the middle of the 1700s, several towns along the Atlantic coast had grown into cities. Among these were New York City, Philadelphia, and Charleston. They all had good harbors, and they grew because of trade. Ships arrived at these cities, carrying new settlers and imported goods. After a few weeks in port, the ships sailed away loaded with **exports**, or goods to be sold in other countries. Exports from the colonies included raw materials such as furs, lumber, and dried fish, as well as cash crops.

Many ships followed a direct trade route between Britain and the 13 colonies. This was because the British government wanted the colonies to send their exports only to Britain or to other British colonies. The government also wanted the colonists to buy manufactured goods only from Britain.

Some ships followed what came to be known as **triangular trade routes**. These routes linked Britain, the British colonies, and Africa as the three points of a great triangle on the Atlantic Ocean. Traders carried manufactured goods from Britain and

Movement Some traders followed triangular routes between Britain, Africa, and the British colonies.
■ *What was traded at each point of the triangular trade route?*

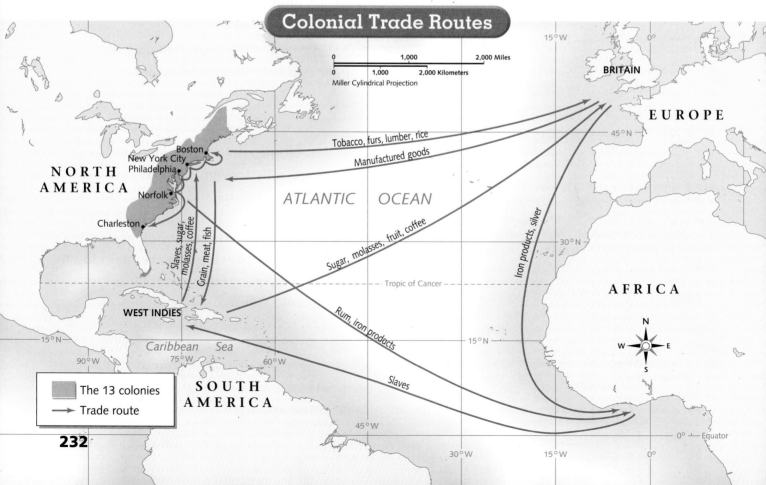

Colonial Trade Routes

This harbor scene shows the city of Charleston, South Carolina, in the 1730s. Charleston was one of the busiest port cities in colonial America.

raw materials from the 13 colonies and the West Indies. They carried enslaved people from Africa. Their trip across the Atlantic Ocean is called the Middle Passage.

Most coastal cities grew because of trade. However, people in the cities also worked in other kinds of businesses. Many people made their living from the sea—by fishing, whaling, or shipbuilding. Others sold goods that they made by using special skills. There were hatmakers, tailors, printers, and many other skilled workers. Young people learned such jobs by becoming **apprentices**. A child would move in with the family of a skilled worker and help in the family's business for several years.

REVIEW *Why were the first colonial cities located along the Atlantic coast?*

LESSON 1 REVIEW

Check Understanding

1 Remember the Facts In colonial times, where were the different kinds of towns and cities located?

2 Recall the Main Idea In what ways were colonial towns different from one another? How were the towns different from the cities?

Think Critically

3 Think More About It What needs of the colonists did towns and cities meet?

4 Past to Present Town meetings are still held in many towns in the New England states today. Why do you think this tradition continues?

Show What You Know

Diorama Activity Work with a group of classmates to make a diorama. Create a scene showing everyday life in a colonial city. Write a paragraph describing the scene and display your diorama in the classroom.

Read a Circle Graph

1. Why Learn This Skill?

Suppose you are writing a report on the British colonies. You want to show in a simple, clear way that the population of the colonies was made up of people from many different places. One way to show the information is by making a graph. Graphs make it easier to see and compare information.

2. Circle Graph

One kind of graph is a circle graph. A circle graph is often called a pie graph because it is round and is divided into pieces, or parts, like a pie. A circle graph compares amounts and makes it easy to see how much each part is in relation to the whole.

The circle graph on this page shows the population of the British colonies in 1775.

The graph's parts are the many different ethnic groups that made up the population.

You will see that a percent, shown by the symbol % in the graph, is given in each part of the graph. Suppose you cut a giant pie into 100 pieces. Those 100 pieces together equal the whole pie, or 100 percent of it. Fifty pieces would be one-half of the pie, or 50 percent of it. Ten pieces would be one-tenth of the pie, or 10 percent of it.

3. Understand the Process

Find *English* on the graph. The English made up about 49 percent of the population of the British colonies in 1775. That "slice" is almost 50 percent, or one-half, of the "pie."

Like other graphs, a circle graph can help you make comparisons. You can compare the parts to one another or to the whole.

Use the circle graph to answer the following questions.

❶ What percent of the population did the Germans make up?

❷ What percent of the population was made up of Swedish colonists?

❸ Were there more Scottish and Swedish colonists or German and French colonists?

4. Think and Apply

Use information from the circle graph to write a paragraph about the different ethnic groups of the British colonies. Compare the sizes of the different groups.

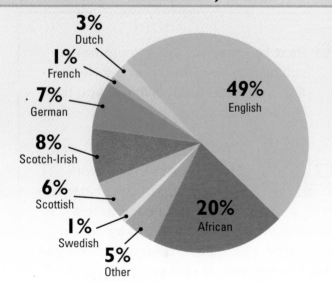

**Population of
the 13 Colonies, 1775**

3% Dutch
1% French
7% German
8% Scotch-Irish
6% Scottish
1% Swedish
5% Other
49% English
20% African

Life on Plantations

FOCUS

How do societies today separate people into different groups?

Main Idea Read to learn about the ways that plantation life separated people into different groups.

Vocabulary

broker

indentured servant

auction

As towns and cities grew in many of the British colonies, plantations also grew—especially in the southern colonies. Settlements in Virginia, Maryland, the Carolinas, and Georgia became successful because the plantations there were able to grow more and more cash crops. Plantation owners were known as planters. Many planters bought as much land as they could. With bigger plantations, they could grow more crops to sell.

Plantations needed many hands to do the work. Most planters hired farm workers as well as servants to help out. Before long they added other workers—enslaved Africans. Over time slaves had a major impact on life in the southern colonies.

A Southern Plantation

From the time the Jamestown settlers began growing tobacco, plantations became important to the economy of the South. Planters soon learned to grow other cash crops as well, such as rice and indigo, and plantations spread to other southern colonies.

The earliest plantations were usually built along waterways. The main building was the planter's house. Servants and slaves lived in small buildings nearby. Because of the danger of fire, kitchens were in a separate building. There were sheds for storing crops and barns for livestock. There also might be a carpenter's shop, a blacksmith's shop, and a laundry. If the plantation was on a river, it most likely had its own dock. Plantations that were not on a waterway were connected by roads to another planter's dock.

Money was rarely used in the plantation economy. Instead, crops were used to trade. Crop buyers would travel up and down southern waterways, their boats filled

Rice was an important cash crop in the southern colonies.

with British-made goods such as shoes, lace, thread, farm tools, and dishes. The planters traded tobacco, rice, and indigo for these goods.

Owners of the largest plantations most often sold their crops through a British broker. A **broker** is a person who is paid to buy and sell for someone else. Planters sent their crops to Britain with a list of things they wanted the broker to buy for them. The broker then sold the crops, bought what the planter wanted, and sent the goods back to the colonies.

REVIEW *What was used instead of money in the plantation economy?*

Servants and Slaves

On small plantations, everyone in the planter's family worked. As plantations grew, planters added more workers. In time, the main job of the planter's family was to help watch over the work of others—both servants and slaves.

Many of the earliest workers in the Americas came as indentured servants. An **indentured servant** was a person who agreed to work for another person without pay for a certain length of time. Many indentured servants were Europeans who had wanted to move to the colonies but had no money. A planter or other business owner paid for the trip, and the person agreed to work without pay for anywhere from two to seven years. Once this time was over, the indentured servant was free.

A Southern Plantation

LEARNING FROM DIAGRAMS

Like a Spanish hacienda, a plantation was mostly self-sufficient. Planters grew food, and skilled workers produced many needed goods. Goods that could not be made on a plantation were brought in through trade.

1. brickmaker
2. cattle pen
3. slave cabins
4. overseer's house
5. stable
6. tobacco barn
7. tobacco fields
8. garden
9. carpenter
10. smokehouse
11. kitchen
12. main house
13. office
14. laundry
15. warehouse
16. dock

■ *Why were many plantations built near waterways?*

Not all of the indentured servants came willingly to the British colonies. Some were sent by British courts to work in the colonies as punishment to pay for their crimes. Other indentured servants were people who had been kidnapped and then sold in the colonies.

Among the first indentured servants to be sold in the British colonies were kidnapped Africans. By the middle 1600s, however, traders were bringing thousands of Africans to the British colonies not as indentured servants but as slaves. Unlike indentured servants, slaves were not given their freedom after a certain length of time. They were enslaved for life. In time, laws were passed saying that the children of enslaved people were slaves, too.

Olaudah Equiano (OHL•uh•dah ek•wee•AHN•oh) was 11 years old when he was taken from his village in Africa. He described what happened this way:

> ❝ One day, when all our people were gone out to the fields to work, and only I and my dear sister were left to mind the house, two men and a woman got over our walls. In a moment they seized us both, and without giving us time to cry out, they stopped our mouths and ran off with us into the nearest woods. ❞

Equiano was soon parted from his sister and sold at an **auction**, or public sale. Like other enslaved Africans, he had no choices about his future.

REVIEW *What kinds of workers were there on plantations?*

Advertisements for enslaved people (right) were given out before auctions. Slaves who were sick were often forced to hide their illnesses long enough to be sold. Iron shackles (bottom right) were sometimes used to prevent slaves from escaping. Olaudah Equiano (far right) was freed from slavery and later wrote a book about his life.

Charlestown, July 24th, 1769.

TO BE SOLD,
On THURSDAY the third Day
of AUGUST next,
A CARGO
OF
NINETY-FOUR
PRIME, HEALTHY
NEGROES,
CONSISTING OF
Thirty-nine MEN, Fifteen BOYS,
Twenty-four WOMEN, and
Sixteen GIRLS.
JUST ARRIVED,
In the Brigantine DEMBIA, Fran-
cis Bare, Master, from SIERRA-
LEON, by
DAVID & JOHN DEAS.

Most plantation owners and their families lived in large houses filled with expensive furnishings. Many had ballrooms, music rooms, and libraries. The home of plantation owner William Byrd had the largest private library in all of the colonies. It had about 4,000 books.

Plantation Duties

Plantations in the southern colonies were often far from one another and far from any towns. Weeks or months could go by without visitors and without news about the latest happenings. For this reason visitors were always welcome.

Although slaves did most of the work, planters had many responsibilities. A planter had to see that the crops were planted, harvested, stored, and shipped. Careful records had to be kept in order to run the plantation as a successful business.

One of the most famous early Virginia planters was William Byrd II. We know much about him because he kept a diary.

Byrd's diary shows how difficult life on plantations could be. Many of his diary entries are about sickness and death. Some are about financial worries. More than once Byrd learned that the ships carrying his cash crops to Britain had sunk at sea. Even his neighbors gave him problems.

66 In the evening I took a walk about the plantation and found that some of my good neighbors had dug down the bank of my ditch to let their hogs into my pasture, for which I was out of humor. 99

A planter's wife had the same responsibilities as other colonial women caring for a household. She had to clothe and feed her family. Her household—family, servants, and slaves—sometimes numbered in the hundreds. It was up to her to see that all these people had food, clothing, and medical care.

There were few schools in the southern colonies because people lived so far apart. Large plantations had their own small schools for children to learn basic reading and writing. Planters often hired teachers from Europe for their children. When they were about 12 or 13 years old, the young people might attend special town schools. After that, boys often went to college either in Britain or in the colonies. By age 12 or 13, girls stopped going to school. Planters' daughters were supposed to learn only basic skills and "to read and sew with their needle."

Many of the furnishings in plantation homes were imported from Europe, such as this mirror.

There were no schools for servants or for the African slaves on the plantations. Laws in the colonies did not allow slaves to learn to read and write. By the age of 10, most young Africans were working alongside the adults.

Enslaved people were expected to spend their days working. At any time, they could be whipped for falling behind in their work. But at night, when their work was finished, the Africans often told stories and sang songs about their homeland. The Africans found ways to keep their heritage alive.

REVIEW *Why were there so few schools in the southern colonies?*

LESSON 2 REVIEW

Check Understanding

1 Remember the Facts   Describe life on a typical plantation in the southern colonies.

2 Recall the Main Idea   In what ways were people on southern plantations separated into different groups?

Think Critically

3 Think More About It   Describe the differences between being an indentured servant and being a slave.

4 Explore Viewpoints   How do you think Olaudah Equiano and William Byrd each viewed life on the plantations?

Show What You Know

Diary Activity   Suppose that you are living on a plantation in colonial times. Take on a role, and write an entry in a diary to show what a day on the plantation is like. Share your entry with a classmate.

Life on the Frontier

The history of the British colonies, like the history of all of the United States, is the story of people on the move. People left settled areas along the Atlantic coast and pushed farther inland to claim what they saw as open land. Settlers hoped to make a piece of this frontier land into a farm, where they could build a house and raise a family. They felt that moving to the frontier would give them a chance for a better life.

The Great Wagon Road

In the early 1700s most of the cities, towns, plantations, and farms in the British colonies were located in the Coastal Plain region of the present-day United States. Few colonists had settled in the **backcountry**, which is the land between the Coastal Plain and the Appalachian Mountains. People called this region the frontier or the backcountry because it was beyond, or "in back of," the settled area.

The lack of roads and the waterfalls in the rivers along the Fall Line made travel to the backcountry difficult. A **fall line** is a place where the land drops sharply, causing rivers to form waterfalls. Settlers who went into the back-country had to carry their boats and supplies around the waterfalls.

By the middle 1700s large numbers of German and Scotch-Irish immigrants had begun moving from Pennsylvania into the backcountry of western Virginia and the Carolinas. To get there, the settlers followed an old Indian trail. As more settlers used the trail, it became wider, until finally wagons could travel on it. It became known as the Great Wagon Road.

From Pennsylvania the Great Wagon Road passed through the Shenandoah Valley of Virginia and along

FOCUS

How do people today meet the challenges in their lives?

Main Idea As you read, look for ways the settlers met the challenges of living on the frontier.

Vocabulary

backcountry
fall line
loft
coureur de bois

Making dolls like this one from corn husks was a craft that settlers learned from American Indians. The wooden bucket (above) was used by settlers on the frontier.

the eastern side of the Blue Ridge Mountains. The land there was hilly, and travel on the road was difficult. "[In places] it was so slippery the horses could not keep their footing but fell . . . to their knees," wrote one traveler. However, the Great Wagon Road was the only way to get wagons loaded with household goods to the backcountry.

Among the thousands of people who followed the Great Wagon Road from Pennsylvania was a young man named Daniel Boone. Later Boone would make new roads that took settlers even farther west. Boone's roads led through the Appalachian Mountains into what is now Kentucky and Tennessee.

REVIEW *Why was the Great Wagon Road important to the settlement of the backcountry?*

Living in the Backcountry

Most of the people who settled the backcountry, including the Boone family, lived simply. Their homes were no more than log huts with chimneys made of sticks and mud. Most houses had one room with a dirt floor and no windows. Light came through the open door in the daytime and from the fireplace at night. Families burned wood in the fireplace to cook their food and to keep their homes warm.

As time went on, families made their homes more comfortable. Some added windows. Others covered their dirt floors with wooden boards.

LEARNING FROM DIAGRAMS Life was hard and often lonely for early settlers in the backcountry. Families had to work together to provide all the items they might need.

❶ candlemaking
❷ farming
❸ cleared land
❹ chopping wood
❺ mud used to fill cracks
❻ fire used for cooking and warmth
❼ sewing
❽ children's loft
❾ butter churn
❿ corn-husk doll
■ *In what ways is this frontier family self-sufficient?*

At night the adults in a family spread their blankets over piles of dry leaves on the floor. The children slept in the **loft**, a part of the house between the ceiling and the roof. To get up to the loft, they climbed a ladder, which was often just wooden pegs driven into the wall.

A settler named Oliver Johnson remembered sleeping in a loft when he was a child growing up on the frontier. He wrote,

66 If you slept in the loft, you pulled your head under the covers during a storm. When you got up in the mornin[g], you [would] shake the snow off the covers, grab your shirt and britches [pants] and hop down the ladder to the fireplace, where it was good and warm. 99

Frontier Life

4

5

6

7

8

9

10

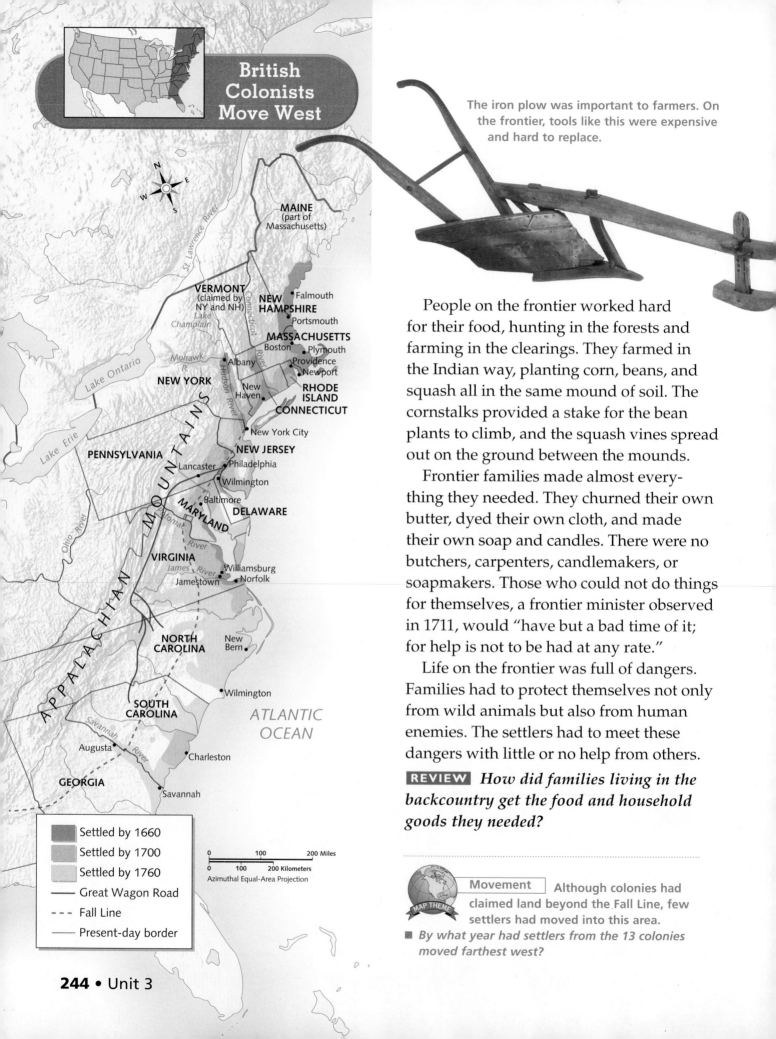

British Colonists Move West

The iron plow was important to farmers. On the frontier, tools like this were expensive and hard to replace.

MAINE
(part of Massachusetts)

VERMONT
(claimed by NY and NH)

NEW HAMPSHIRE
Falmouth
Portsmouth

Lake Champlain

MASSACHUSETTS
Boston
Plymouth
Providence
Newport

Albany

Mohawk R.

Lake Ontario

NEW YORK

Hudson River

New Haven

RHODE ISLAND

CONNECTICUT

New York City

Lake Erie

NEW JERSEY

PENNSYLVANIA
Lancaster
Philadelphia
Wilmington

APPALACHIAN MOUNTAINS

Baltimore

MARYLAND

DELAWARE

Ohio River

Potomac River

VIRGINIA
James River
Williamsburg
Jamestown
Norfolk

NORTH CAROLINA
New Bern

Wilmington

SOUTH CAROLINA

Savannah River

ATLANTIC OCEAN

Augusta
Charleston

GEORGIA
Savannah

Settled by 1660
Settled by 1700
Settled by 1760
Great Wagon Road
Fall Line
Present-day border

0   100   200 Miles
0   100   200 Kilometers
Azimuthal Equal-Area Projection

People on the frontier worked hard for their food, hunting in the forests and farming in the clearings. They farmed in the Indian way, planting corn, beans, and squash all in the same mound of soil. The cornstalks provided a stake for the bean plants to climb, and the squash vines spread out on the ground between the mounds.

Frontier families made almost everything they needed. They churned their own butter, dyed their own cloth, and made their own soap and candles. There were no butchers, carpenters, candlemakers, or soapmakers. Those who could not do things for themselves, a frontier minister observed in 1711, would "have but a bad time of it; for help is not to be had at any rate."

Life on the frontier was full of dangers. Families had to protect themselves not only from wild animals but also from human enemies. The settlers had to meet these dangers with little or no help from others.

REVIEW *How did families living in the backcountry get the food and household goods they needed?*

Movement Although colonies had claimed land beyond the Fall Line, few settlers had moved into this area.
- *By what year had settlers from the 13 colonies moved farthest west?*

The Ohio River Valley

Always wanting more land, people on the frontier moved farther and farther west. By the middle 1700s, British fur traders had crossed the Appalachian Mountains into the Ohio River valley. They moved into land claimed by several British colonies as well as by France.

France claimed the huge region but had settled very little of it. The French **coureurs de bois** (koo•RUR duh BWAH), or "runners of the woods," traded with American Indians for furs. The furs were bought by trading companies who sold them in Europe at a profit. Many coureurs de bois had good relations with the Indians of the area.

British fur traders moved into the Ohio River

The beaver was hunted for its valuable fur.

valley to take the fur trade away from the French. To do this, the British offered the Indians more goods for fewer furs. The tribes had to decide whether they would trade with the British or the French. The French had been friends to the Indians for many years. But the British gave the Indians more of the goods they wanted at a lower price. In time the French lost many of their Indian trading partners to the British.

In 1753 British settlers began arriving in the Ohio River valley. Even though there were only a few British colonists who settled west of the Appalachian Mountains, the French were upset. They built a line of forts in what is now western Pennsylvania to protect their lands from the British. It was not long before the bad feelings between the British and the French turned into a war on the frontier.

REVIEW *Why did the British and the French want to settle the Ohio River valley?*

LESSON 3 REVIEW

Check Understanding

1 Recall the Facts Why did the French lose many of their Indian trading partners to the British?

2 Remember the Main Idea In what ways did the settlers meet the challenges of living on the frontier?

Think Critically

3 Think More About It What skills did the settlers need to survive on the frontier? Which skills do you think they learned from the Indians?

4 Personally Speaking If you had been a settler in frontier days, do you think you would have enjoyed life in the backcountry? Why or why not?

Show What You Know

Writing Activity Imagine that you are a settler who has moved to the frontier in the early 1700s. Write a journal entry in which you describe your journey to the backcountry and the building of your new home. Share your journal entry with a classmate.

Use a Product Map to

1. Why Learn This Skill?

Symbols provide people with information every day. Map symbols also provide information. They tell you such things as what cities are state capitals or where state borders are located.

Product maps can help give you a general picture of a place. Symbols for products tell you where certain products are made or grown. This can help you understand more about the kinds of work people in those places do and the economic activities of a place.

This general picture of a place can help you make generalizations. A **generalization** is a statement based on facts. It is used to summarize groups of facts and show relationships between them. A generalization tells what is true most of the time. It may contain words such as *often, many, most, generally,* or *usually.*

2. Map Symbols

Notice that this map of colonial products has two map keys. The key in the lower right part of the map uses colors as symbols. The one in the upper left part of the map uses pictures.

The map key that uses colors shows the division of the British colonies into three regions. These regions are identified as the New England colonies, the middle colonies, and the southern colonies. The colonies within each region are shown in the same

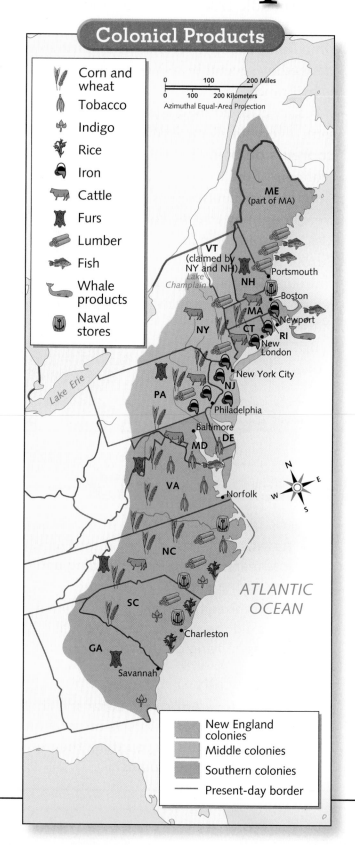

Colonial Products

Key (upper left):
- Corn and wheat
- Tobacco
- Indigo
- Rice
- Iron
- Cattle
- Furs
- Lumber
- Fish
- Whale products
- Naval stores

0   100   200 Miles
0 100   200 Kilometers
Azimuthal Equal-Area Projection

Key (lower right):
- New England colonies
- Middle colonies
- Southern colonies
- Present-day border

Make Generalizations

The New England Colonies		The Middle Colonies		The Southern Colonies	
Connecticut	New Hampshire	Delaware	New York	Georgia	South Carolina
Massachusetts	Rhode Island	New Jersey	Pennsylvania	Maryland	Virginia
				North Carolina	

color. This map key also tells you that the borders shown on the map are those of the present-day states, not those of the colonies.

In the other map key, pictures stand for the important goods produced in the colonies. These goods were important not only because they were sold in the colonies, but also because they were exported for sale in Britain. The map shows only some of the most important goods that were produced in the colonies.

Some of the map symbols stand for certain products and raw materials, such as tobacco, indigo, iron, and lumber. Others stand for groups of products. Whale products, for example, include the oils used for making lamp fuel and candles.

3. Understand the Process

Now that you know more about the symbols in the map keys, you can use these questions as a guide for making generalizations about the colonial economy.

1 What color is used to show the New England colonies? the middle colonies? the southern colonies?

2 What products appear most often on the map in the New England colonies?

3 What generalization can you make about the kinds of work most people did in the New England colonies?

4 What generalization can you make about the economy of the New England colonies?

5 What generalization can you make about the kinds of work most people did in the middle colonies?

6 What generalization can you make about the economy of the middle colonies?

7 What generalization can you make about the economy of the southern colonies?

8 What generalization can you make about the economy of the 13 colonies?

4. Think and Apply

Draw a product map of your state. Use an encyclopedia, atlas, or almanac to gather the information you will need. Use colors to show the different regions of your state, and then use pictures to show the products that are important there. Label the cities and nearby states. Have a friend use your map to make some generalizations about the economy of your state.

REVIEW

CONNECT MAIN IDEAS

Use this organizer to compare the ways of life of the early colonists. Write three examples for each place. A copy of the organizer may be found on page 43 of the Activity Book.

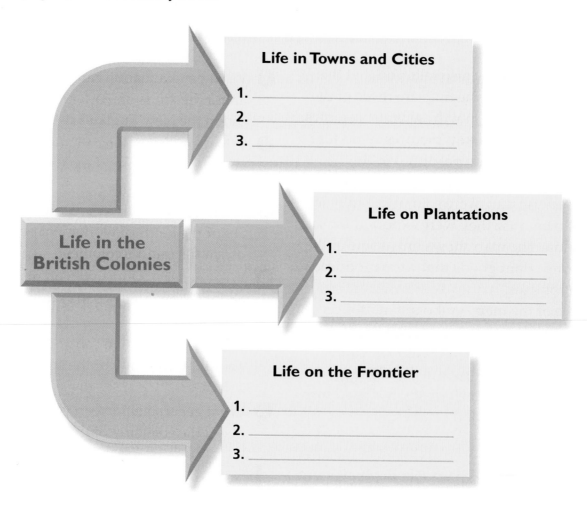

Life in the British Colonies

Life in Towns and Cities
1. _____
2. _____
3. _____

Life on Plantations
1. _____
2. _____
3. _____

Life on the Frontier
1. _____
2. _____
3. _____

WRITE MORE ABOUT IT

Write a Description The people who lived in market towns depended on one another for different goods and products. Imagine that you are visiting a colonial market town for the first time. Describe the sights, sounds, and smells around you.

Write a Conversation Write a conversation that might have taken place between two settlers who lived in the backcountry. The two settlers should discuss the work they did during the day and their hopes for their families in the future.

USE VOCABULARY

For each pair of terms, write a sentence or two that explains how the terms are related.

1. town meeting, common
2. import, export
3. county seat, county
4. apprentice, indentured servant
5. backcountry, fall line

CHECK UNDERSTANDING

6. What were the purposes of the meetinghouse in most New England towns?
7. What kinds of goods did general stores sell?
8. Who made the laws and voted for government leaders in the colonies?
9. What were the triangular trade routes?
10. What effect did trade have on coastal cities?
11. How did planters get their indentured servants?
12. How were indentured servants different from slaves?
13. What was the main job of the planter's family?
14. Why did the British move into the Ohio River valley?

THINK CRITICALLY

15. **Past to Present** People in New England gathered at the meetinghouse for town meetings. Where do you think town meetings are held today?
16. **Explore Viewpoints** How would living on a plantation have been different from living in or near a town?

17. **Cause and Effect** What effect did the triangular trade routes have on the people of the British colonies?
18. **Think More About It** How were southern waterways important to plantation life?
19. **Personally Speaking** Would you have been willing to become an indentured servant in order to move to the colonies? Explain your answer.

APPLY SKILLS

Read a Circle Graph Use the circle graph on page 234 to answer these questions.

20. Who made up the second-largest group of people in the 13 colonies?
21. Were there more German or more French settlers in the 13 colonies?

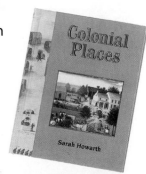

Use a Product Map to Make Generalizations Use the map on page 246 to list the major products of the southern colonies. Then write a generalization about which products were related to the rise of slavery.

READ MORE ABOUT IT

Colonial Places by Sarah Howarth. Millbrook. Through art and text, the author discusses the importance of 13 places around which life occurred in a colonial community.

Visit the Internet at
http://www.hbschool.com
for additional resources.

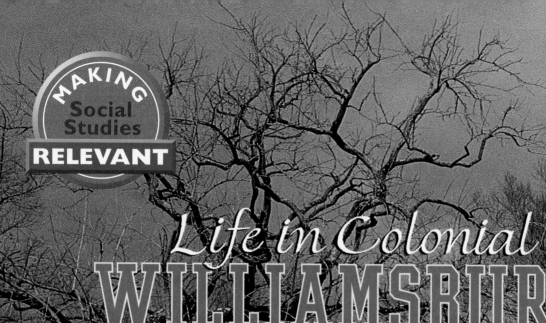

Life in Colonial WILLIAMSBURG

Many students think of history as something that happened to other people in other times. It may not seem real to them. It might even seem like a fantasy. At a living history museum, however, history comes alive. You can see it. You can hear it. You can smell it. You can even act it out.

Colonial Williamsburg is the restored capital of eighteenth-century Virginia. On a visit there you can experience the sights, sounds, and smells of colonial life in the 1700s. You can see the homes and other buildings. You can talk with the shop owners and the crafts people. You can smell food cooking at the inn. You can also try activities such as churning butter, dipping candles, and playing colonial games.

History is more than just names and dates. It is the story of people just like you who lived in another time.

Dressed in colonial-style clothing, this woman makes a basket as people did over 200 years ago.

Think and Apply

Imagine that you are making a living history museum to show life in your town or city today. What kinds of displays and exhibits would be in your museum? How would you help visitors make history come alive? Share your ideas with the class.

HARCOURT BRACE

Visit the Internet at **http://www.hbschool.com** for additional resources.

CNN Turner Le@rning

Check your media center or classroom video library for the Making Social Studies Relevant videotape of this feature.

Before the capital of Virginia was moved from Williamsburg to Richmond in 1780, Virginia governors lived in the Governor's Palace (background). Lenses for glasses were prepared by hand in the colonies (above). In colonial times weavers at large looms (right) made fabric by using linen and wool yarns.

UNIT 3 REVIEW

Summarize the Main Ideas
Study the pictures and captions to help you review the events you read about in Unit 3.

Write a Story
Imagine that you are one of the people in a picture on this visual summary. Write a story about yourself. Tell who you are and where you came from or where you are going. Describe where you live. Tell about a problem you had. How did the problem get solved?

1 The Spanish built many missions in their borderlands.

2 The French grew wealthy by trading with Indian peoples for furs.

5 Roads such as El Camino Real connected the Spanish missions with haciendas and presidios.

7 In the borderlands north of Mexico, Spanish settlers raised large herds of livestock.

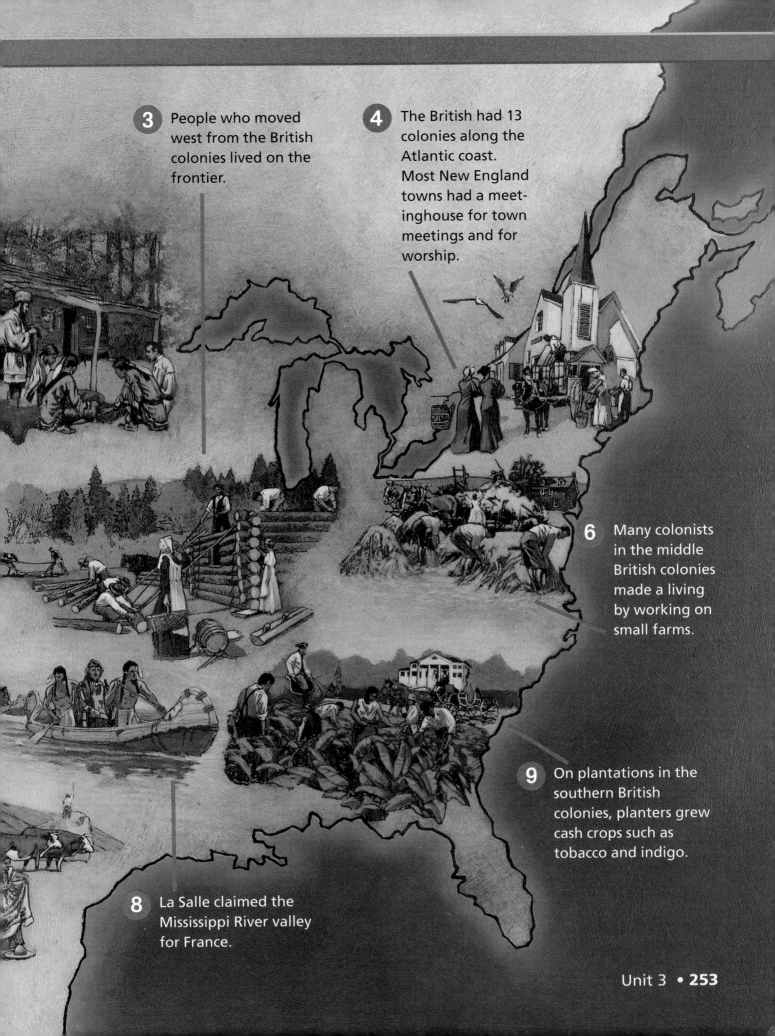

3 People who moved west from the British colonies lived on the frontier.

4 The British had 13 colonies along the Atlantic coast. Most New England towns had a meetinghouse for town meetings and for worship.

6 Many colonists in the middle British colonies made a living by working on small farms.

9 On plantations in the southern British colonies, planters grew cash crops such as tobacco and indigo.

8 La Salle claimed the Mississippi River valley for France.

USE VOCABULARY

Use each term in a sentence that will help explain its meaning.

1. presidio
2. permanent
3. tributary
4. charter
5. debtor
6. militia
7. broker
8. auction

CHECK UNDERSTANDING

9. What was the most important money-making activity in Spain's American colonies?

10. Why did the Spanish government build roads linking Spanish missions to presidios?

11. What convinced Iberville and Bienville that they had found La Salle's river?

12. What attracted European immigrants to the middle colonies?

13. What different groups of people worked on southern plantations? What work did each group do?

14. What route did many people follow as they traveled to the backcountry?

THINK CRITICALLY

15. **Cause and Effect** How did the beliefs of the Puritans lead to the founding of other colonies in New England?

16. **Past to Present** Describe how religious freedom affects people in the United States today.

17. **Personally Speaking** Would you rather have been a planter or a planter's broker? Explain your answer.

APPLY SKILLS

Use a Product Map to Make Generalizations The map below shows some important colonial industries. What generalizations can you make about New England's economy?

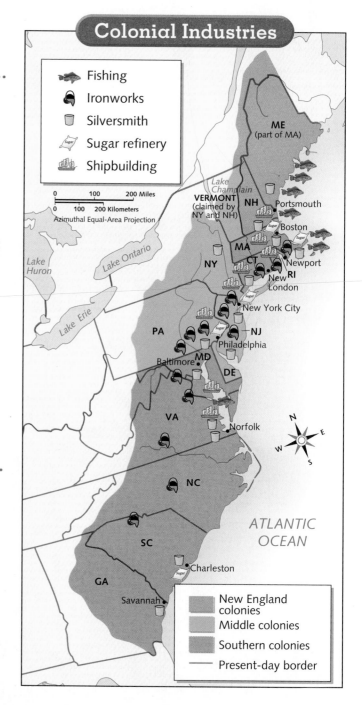

Colonial Industries

Fishing
Ironworks
Silversmith
Sugar refinery
Shipbuilding

0   100   200 Miles
0   100   200 Kilometers
Azimuthal Equal-Area Projection

Lake Huron
Lake Ontario
Lake Erie
Lake Champlain

ME (part of MA)
VERMONT (claimed by NY and NH)
NH
Portsmouth
Boston
MA
CT
Newport
NY
RI
New London
New York City
PA
NJ
Philadelphia
Baltimore
MD
DE
VA
Norfolk
NC
SC
Charleston
GA
Savannah

ATLANTIC OCEAN

New England colonies
Middle colonies
Southern colonies
Present-day border

REMEMBER

- Share your ideas.
- Cooperate with others to plan your work.
- Take responsibility for your work.
- Help one another.
- Show your group's work to the class.
- Discuss what you learned by working together.

Draw a Product Map

Work in a group to draw an outline map of the 13 British colonies on a large sheet of paper. Maps in your textbook and in encyclopedias can help you. Label the colonies and their largest cities. Also label large bodies of water. Then draw symbols to show each colony's major products. Point out places and products as you present the map to the class.

Plan a Presentation

Enslaved Africans found ways to keep their traditions alive. Some told stories and sang songs they remembered from Africa. Work in a group, using reference books, to find a traditional African story or song. As a group, decide how you will present the story or song to your classmates and invited guests. You may want to perform a story as a play or do a dramatic reading of it. You may want to sing a song as a group or invite the whole class to take part.

Make a Poster

You have learned about the ways in which Spanish settlers changed the lives of Indians in the borderlands. Work in a group to make a poster that shows at least three of these ways. Display the poster in your classroom.

Unit Project Wrap-Up

Build a Model Work in a group to finish the Unit Project on page 189. Use small boxes, construction paper, and other materials to build your model. The town should have a common, a general store, a blacksmith's shop, a mill, a meetinghouse, and a school. The plantation should include the planter's house, a kitchen, barns, buildings for servants and slaves, and fields.

255

THE AMERICAN REVOLUTION

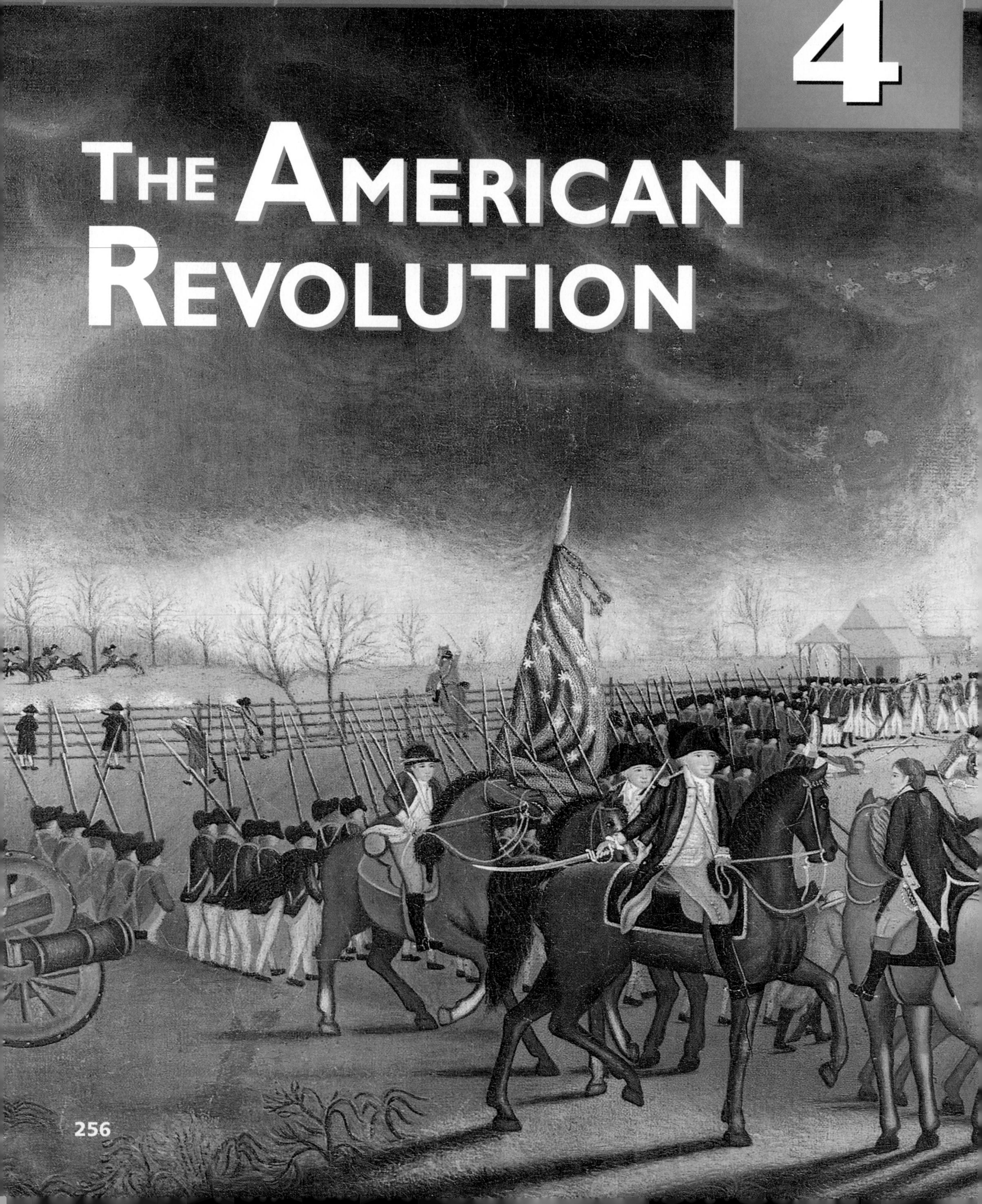

The colonists who moved to North America continued to be citizens of the European lands they came from. Over the years many British colonists grew unhappy with British rule. They had little voice in a government that was thousands of miles away. In time the British colonies in North America decided to break away from their homeland. They won their freedom, but only after a long and bitter fight.

◀ The Battle of Princeton, 1777

UNIT THEMES

■ Conflict and Cooperation

■ Continuity and Change

■ Individualism and Interdependence

■ Interaction Within Different Environments

Unit Project

Create a Book Complete this project as you study Unit 4. With your classmates, you will create a book about the American Revolution. As you read, make a list of the key events, people, and places you learn about. Your list will help you decide which items to include in your book.

257

CANADA

YAKIMA

Columbia River

CHINOOK

NEZ
PERCE

Missouri River

KIOWA

CROW

MANDAN

SIOUX

CHEYENNE

PACIFIC
OCEAN

Snake River

MODOC

PAIUTE

Great Salt
Lake

Platte River

POMO

San Francisco O

MIWOK

UTE

PAWNEE

ARAPAHO

YOKUTS

PAIUTE

Colorado River

HOPI   NAVAJO

O Santa Fe

The 13 colonies

Major British colonial town

Major Spanish colonial town

Major French colonial town

SIOUX Name of Indian tribe

Present-day national border

CAHUILLA

O San Diego

APACHE   COMANCHE

O Tucson

PIMA

0   200   400 Miles
0   200   400 Kilometers
Albers Equal-Area Projection

MEXICO

Rio Grande

1765   1770   1775

1765
The Stamp Act

PAGE 273

1773
Boston Tea Party

PAGE 280

1775
The American
Revolution Begins

PAGE 289

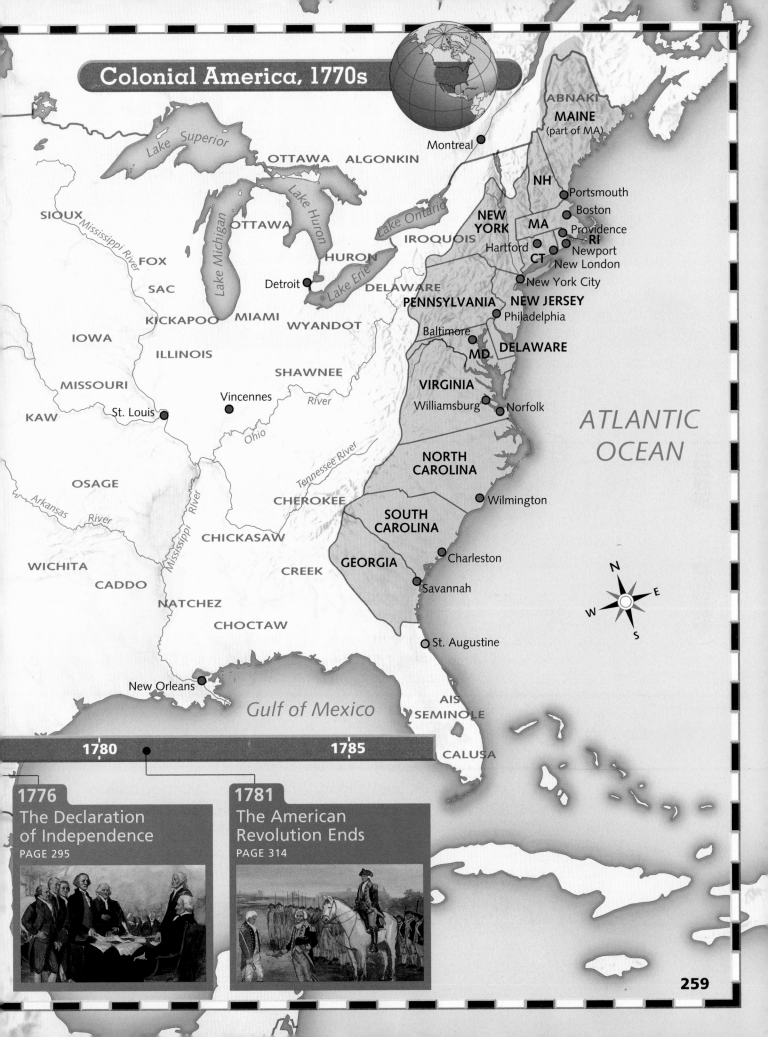

Colonial America, 1770s

ABNAKI

MAINE
(part of MA)

OTTAWA   ALGONKIN

Montreal

Lake Superior

SIOUX   Mississippi River

FOX

SAC

OTTAWA

Lake Michigan   Lake Huron

HURON

Lake Erie   Detroit

KICKAPOO   MIAMI

IOWA

ILLINOIS   WYANDOT

MISSOURI

SHAWNEE

Vincennes   River

KAW   St. Louis

Ohio

OSAGE

Arkansas   River

CHEROKEE

Tennessee River

Mississippi River

WICHITA

CADDO

CHICKASAW

NATCHEZ

CHOCTAW   CREEK

New Orleans

Gulf of Mexico

Lake Ontario

IROQUOIS

DELAWARE

PENNSYLVANIA

Baltimore

MD

VIRGINIA

Williamsburg   Norfolk

NORTH CAROLINA

SOUTH CAROLINA

GEORGIA   Charleston

Savannah

St. Augustine

AIS
SEMINOLE

CALUSA

NH   Portsmouth
Boston

NEW YORK   **MA**   Providence
RI
Hartford   Newport
CT   New London
New York City

NEW JERSEY

Philadelphia

DELAWARE

Wilmington

ATLANTIC OCEAN

N
W   E
S

1780 ──────●────── 1785

1776
The Declaration of Independence
PAGE 295

1781
The American Revolution Ends
PAGE 314

G·U·N·S
for
GENERAL
WASHINGTON

by Seymour Reit
illustrated by Paul Bachem

Crack! Crack! Crack!

The sound of musket fire cut through the stillness of the sleeping camp. Colonial soldiers, bleary-eyed, tumbled out of their shelters with their weapons ready and raced toward the palisade.[1] One of these men was a trooper named William Knox, who had been hoping to see action. Excited, he joined the others on the firing line and peered into the gray mist.

The news spread quickly among the waiting men. Hidden by morning fog, a British patrol had slipped across Mill Creek in an attempt to probe the rebel defenses. But an alert sentinel had spotted them in the marshes and opened fire. Others had joined in and the redcoats, giving up, had raced to their barge and escaped. The immediate crisis was over.

With shrugs and yawns, the soldiers trudged back to their warm beds. But Will Knox was too keyed up to go back to sleep. Unloading his musket, he walked across the drill grounds and climbed a rise called Prospect Hill. From here he could see his beloved Boston, locked in the hands of

[1]**palisade:** fence of wooden stakes

the enemy to the southeast. The city was only a few miles away, but it could well have been a thousand; the British had thrown a tight blockade around the city, and nobody could get in or out.

On this frosty morning in October of 1775, a sharp wind was blowing, but William was warmly dressed. Some weeks earlier a regiment of Pennsylvania frontiersmen had come marching into camp. Tough, hardy men, they wore long homespun shirts of butternut brown, fringed leather tunics, leggins, and Indian-style moccasins. Will had traded his best hunting knife, plus half a pound of sugar, for a long shirt and tunic. He'd also fancied one of the fine coonskin caps worn by the Pennsylvania men, but those were scarce, so he had to make do with an ordinary militia tricorn.[2]

Now, sitting with his back against a log rampart,[3] the trooper studied the sweeping view. From where he sat the city looked like an island; it was entirely surrounded by water, except for a narrow causeway called Boston Neck. This strip of land was fortified and guarded by British redcoats. The rest of the area, lying in Boston Harbor, was patrolled by the powerful frigates[4] of the Royal Navy.

Will had just turned nineteen and had joined the Continental Army after the fighting at Lexington and Concord. He'd been born in Boston on Sea Street and had lived there with his parents, brothers, and sisters. When Will was only three, his father had gone off to the West Indies to seek his fortune. He died while away and Will's older brother, Henry, became the head of the little family. Henry Knox was now twenty-five and a trusted officer on General Washington's staff. In Will's admiring eyes, Henry was a true hero—at least, William felt, he *would* be a hero if there were only something to be heroic *about*.

Many people at the time of the American Revolution believed that it was heroic to fight for their freedom. In this unit you will read the story of the American Revolution. You will learn about the causes of the war and about the colonists who, like Will and Henry Knox, fought to win their freedom from the British government.

[2]**tricorn:** three-cornered hat
[3]**rampart:** protective barrier
[4]**frigate:** kind of warship

DIFFERENCES DIVIDE
BRITAIN
AND ITS
COLONIES

"The Revolution was effected before the war commenced. The Revolution was in the minds and hearts of the people . . ."

John Adams, colonial leader from Massachusetts

Government in the Colonies

1

| 1750 | 1760 | 1770 |

During colonial times, Spain, France, and Britain were ruled in different ways. So, too, were their colonies. New Spain and New France were ruled by monarchs in Europe. Sometimes the king or queen asked advisers to help make laws. More often the monarch ruled alone. In the 13 British colonies, however, the government ruled in a different way.

British Rule

The British monarch made some of the laws. Some British citizens also took part in deciding what laws were made. The people in Britain elected leaders to speak for them in the part of the government called **Parliament**. The members of Parliament passed the laws for all British people.

The monarch and Parliament governed not only Britain but also the British colonies in North America. But the people living in the colonies were not allowed to vote in British elections. So, unlike other British citizens, the colonists could not elect lawmakers to speak and act for them in Parliament.

Some of the American colonists thought they should have **self-government**. That is, they thought they should be able to make their own laws. The colonists felt that people in Britain did not understand life in the colonies. After all, the colonies were more than 3,000 miles (4,828 km) from London, Britain's capital city. What worked for Britain did not always work for the colonies, where ways of life were different.

As the colonies developed in the 1600s and 1700s, the monarch and Parliament let the colonists make some of the laws that affected them. Government in the British colonies became more like a **democracy**, a government in which the

FOCUS

Why might people today become unhappy with their government?

Main Idea As you read, look for reasons the British colonists became unhappy with British rule.

Vocabulary

Parliament
self-government
democracy
legislature
ally
tax
authority

Hudson Bay

NEW FRANCE

NORTH AMERICA

CIFIC OCEAN

LOUISIANA

ATLANTIC OCEAN

BRITISH COLONIES

50°W

30°N

30°N

FLORIDA

NEW SPAIN

Gulf of Mexico

10°N

110°W

Caribbean Sea

80°W

British
French
Spanish
Russian
Disputed

0   600   1,200 Miles
0   600   1,200 Kilometers
Azimuthal Equal-Area Projection

Regions This map shows the lands in North America that were claimed by Europeans in 1750. Notice that the British claimed much of the Atlantic coast.

■ *What advantages did the British gain by having control of the coast?*

people take part. But Parliament was quick to remind the colonists that they were still British subjects. Parliament had to approve the laws the colonists made. And the colonists still had to follow the laws made by Parliament.

The British colonists welcomed the chance for some self-government. In New England, towns had been making laws from

the beginning. Soon every colony began making its own laws. People serving in **legislatures**, which were like small, local Parliaments, made most of the decisions. The first of these colonial legislatures was known as the House of Burgesses. It was established in the Virginia colony in 1619.

The 13 colonial legislatures were made up of wealthy male property owners. People were elected to the legislatures by the property owners in each colony. The legislatures made laws for ruling their own colonies and set up local militias for protection.

Besides its legislature, each colony had a governor. The king chose the governor of a royal colony. In proprietary colonies, the proprietor named the governor. The governor made sure that the laws the colonial legislatures made were ones the British government would agree to. The governor also made sure that the colonists obeyed the laws that were passed by the monarch and Parliament.

REVIEW *How were laws made for governing the British colonies?*

The French and Indian War

British colonists lived under this system of government for many years. Then, little by little, things began to change. In 1753 the French in Canada began building forts on lands in the Ohio River valley claimed by both France and Britain. The British colonists viewed this move as an attack.

In the fighting that followed, the French and the British colonists were helped by their Indian **allies**, or friends in war. The British colonists, however, could not fight off the French and their Indian allies with just the help of their own Indian allies.

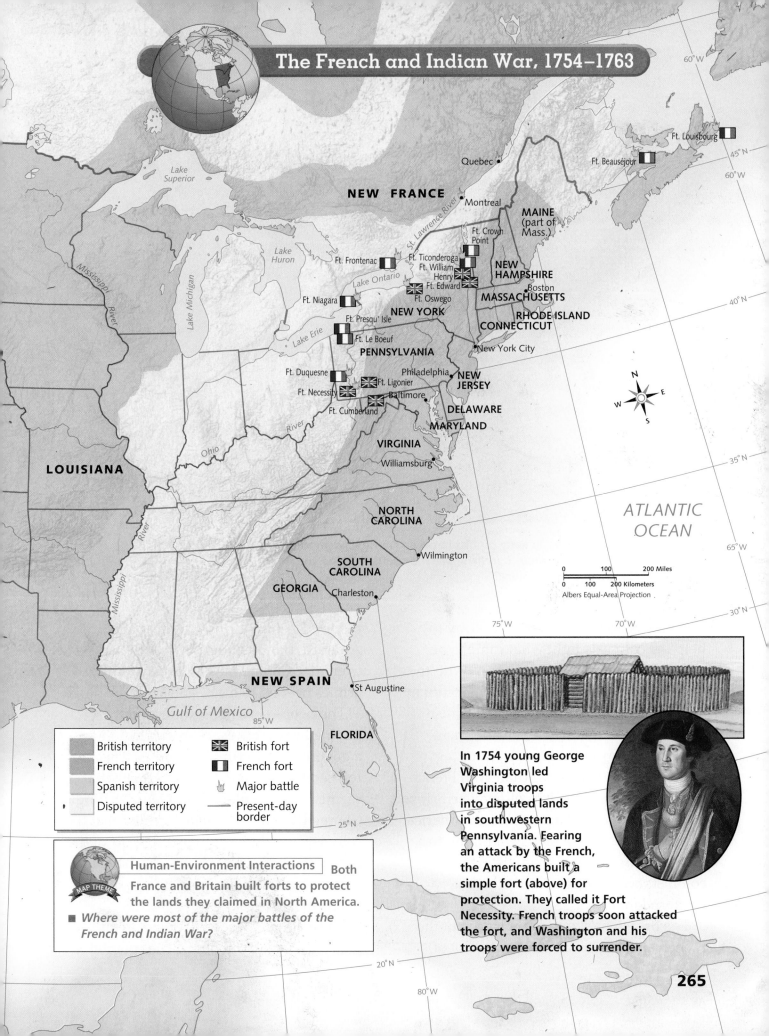

The French and Indian War, 1754–1763

Ft. Louisbourg

Ft. Beauséjour

Quebec

NEW FRANCE

Montreal

MAINE (part of Mass.)

Ft. Crown Point

Ft. Frontenac

Ft. Ticonderoga

Ft. William Henry

Ft. Edward

Ft. Oswego

NEW HAMPSHIRE

Boston

MASSACHUSETTS

RHODE ISLAND

CONNECTICUT

Ft. Niagara

NEW YORK

Ft. Presqu' Isle

Ft. Le Boeuf

New York City

PENNSYLVANIA

Ft. Duquesne

Philadelphia

NEW JERSEY

Ft. Ligonier

Ft. Necessity

Baltimore

DELAWARE

Ft. Cumberland

MARYLAND

VIRGINIA

Williamsburg

Lake Superior

Lake Huron

Lake Michigan

Lake Ontario

Lake Erie

St. Lawrence River

Mississippi River

Ohio River

LOUISIANA

NORTH CAROLINA

ATLANTIC OCEAN

SOUTH CAROLINA

GEORGIA

Charleston

Wilmington

NEW SPAIN

St Augustine

Gulf of Mexico

FLORIDA

	British territory		British fort
	French territory		French fort
	Spanish territory		Major battle
	Disputed territory		Present-day border

Human-Environment Interactions Both France and Britain built forts to protect the lands they claimed in North America.

■ *Where were most of the major battles of the French and Indian War?*

In 1754 young George Washington led Virginia troops into disputed lands in southwestern Pennsylvania. Fearing an attack by the French, the Americans built a simple fort (above) for protection. They called it Fort Necessity. French troops soon attacked the fort, and Washington and his troops were forced to surrender.

This scene from 1704 shows an early conflict between France's Indian allies and American colonists in the town of Deerfield, Massachusetts. Why do you think the Indians fought on different sides?

The British government sent its army to help the colonists fight what came to be called the French and Indian War. With the help of the British army and of their Indian allies, especially the Iroquois, the British colonists defeated the French and their Indian allies in 1763.

After the French and Indian War, French Canada became a British colony. The British also gained French lands in North America between the Appalachian Mountains and the Mississippi River. Many British colonists were eager to settle these new western lands.

The British had won more land, but the French and Indian War had cost a lot of money. Keeping British soldiers in North America to protect the newly won land cost even more. Someone had to pay for the armies needed to make and keep the peace.

The people in Britain were already paying heavy **taxes**, or money paid to a government to run the country. They refused to pay more to take care of what seemed to be a colonial problem. So King George III and Parliament decided that the colonists would have to pay for part of the cost of the war. They would also have to pay for the cost of keeping British soldiers in North America.

The colonists agreed to this plan, but many were angry about it. The colonial legislatures had been making their own tax laws. Now Parliament was telling them what taxes they had to pay. Then the British king took steps that angered the colonists even more.

First, he gave an order stating that the colonists were to stop settling the western lands just won from France. Settlers already living in the area were to leave immediately. This order, called the Proclamation of 1763, reserved these western lands for the Native Americans as their "hunting grounds." The king hoped this order would prevent more wars between the colonists and the Indians. But the colonists became furious.

Then, to make matters worse, the king gave his colonial governors greater **authority**, or control, over the colonies. The

This horn, used to carry gunpowder, was given to a British officer during the French and Indian War. It is engraved with a map showing some of the areas where the heaviest fighting took place.

colonists were allowed to keep their legislatures. However, the governor could order the legislatures to change any laws he did not like.

The colonists did not expect these changes. They had hoped to gain more authority to govern themselves. Now they were reminded that they had to obey laws made in London. The colonists felt that the king knew little or nothing about their lives in North America. What could they do?

REVIEW *How did the lives of the British colonists change after the French and Indian War?*

LESSON 1 REVIEW

1750	1760	1770

1754
• The French and Indian War begins

1763
• The French and Indian War ends
• Proclamation of 1763

Check Understanding

1 Remember the Facts What were the causes of the French and Indian War?

2 Recall the Main Idea Why did the colonists become unhappy with British rule?

Think Critically

3 Think More About It Why do you think only wealthy male property owners were allowed to serve in the colonial legislatures?

4 Explore Viewpoints Explain how each of the following people might have felt about the Proclamation of 1763: a member of Parliament, a colonist, and a Native American.

Show What You Know

Speech Activity Plan a speech in favor of colonial self-government to give to the British Parliament. Present your speech to the class.

Use a Historical

1. Why Learn This Skill?

A historical map gives information about a place as it was in the past. It can show where past events took place. It can also show what features cities and countries had at a particular time. Knowing how to use a historical map can help you gather information about the past.

2. Understand the Process

Many atlases and history books contain historical maps. The title of a historical map usually tells you the subject of the map and the time period the map shows. The map on page 269 shows North America in 1763, at the end of the French and Indian War.

Colors are important map symbols. Sometimes colors help you tell water from land on a map. Colors on a map can also show the area claimed by a city, state, or nation. Look at the map key to learn what each color stands for. Then use these questions to guide you in gathering information.

1 What color is the land controlled by the British in 1763? by the French? by the Spanish?

2 What land did the Russians control in North America in 1763?

3 Which country controlled more land in North America in 1763, Britain or France?

4 Which European country claimed Florida in 1763?

This historical map shows North America in 1760. The map was drawn by John Blair, a member of a British scientific society.

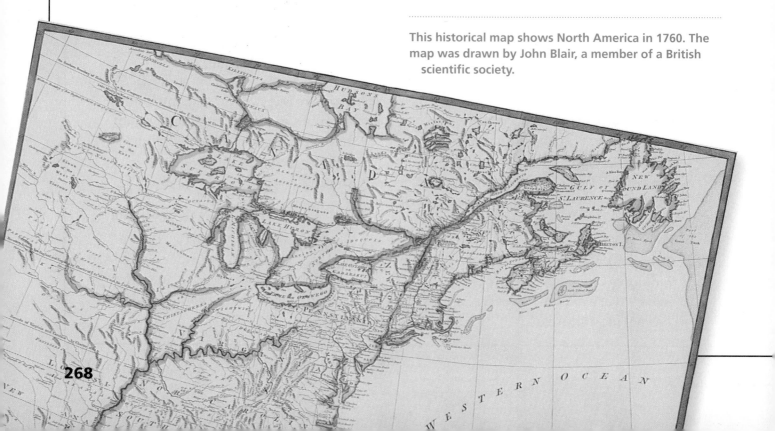

Map

One of the symbols in the map key has a pattern of diagonal stripes, called **hatch lines**. Hatch lines are often used on historical maps to indicate land that was claimed by two or more countries.

Hatch lines may also be used to show land that had a special purpose. The map key on this page tells you that land shown by hatch lines was controlled by the British—that is why one of the colors of the hatch lines is the same as the color used for the British. It also tells you that the British reserved this land for another group—the Native Americans.

In 1763 King George III of Britain drew an imaginary line through North America called the Proclamation Line of 1763. Find the line on the map. The map shows that the Proclamation Line of 1763 served as the border between the land of the 13 colonies and the land that the British reserved for the Native Americans. The British king gave an order stating that the colonists had to stop settling on lands west of this line.

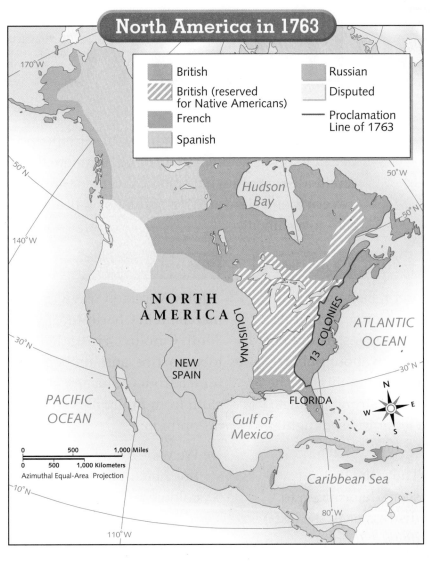

North America in 1763

- British
- British (reserved for Native Americans)
- French
- Spanish
- Russian
- Disputed
- —— Proclamation Line of 1763

170°W
50°N
140°W
30°N
10°N
110°W
Hudson Bay
NORTH AMERICA
LOUISIANA
NEW SPAIN
PACIFIC OCEAN
13 COLONIES
ATLANTIC OCEAN
FLORIDA
Gulf of Mexico
Caribbean Sea
50°W
50°N
30°N
80°W

0   500   1,000 Miles
0   500   1,000 Kilometers
Azimuthal Equal-Area Projection

N E S W

3. Think and Apply

Look at the historical map on page 264 showing North America in 1750. Then write a paragraph that describes what the map shows. What time period is shown? What special symbols are used to show information? How was the United States different then from the way it is today? Share your paragraph with a classmate, and use it to explain why historical maps are useful.

Self-Government

After the French and Indian War, Britain and the colonies began to disagree on matters of government. People had different ideas about what colonies were for and who should govern them. Here are five opinions on British rule and colonial self-government.

Joseph Fish

Joseph Fish was a minister in Connecticut. Like most colonists, he did not talk much about public affairs. But in this case he had very strong feelings. In a letter to his daughter Mary, he wrote:

> "They [the British] seem determined to distress us to the last degree, if not to destroy us, unless we submit to the yoke of slavery they have prepared for us."

John Appleton

John Appleton was a merchant in Charleston, South Carolina. He traded tobacco, rice, and lumber for tea from China and cloth from India. This was his opinion:

> "We were doing fine here in the colonies when they [the king and Parliament] left us alone. Now I find taxes on everything I bring into the colonies to sell. It is bound to hurt business."

British Leader

In a letter to a friend, a member of Parliament told how he felt about the colonies. Here is part of his letter:

> "Certainly, you don't think we are going to let all these colonies make whatever rules they want. English authority must be obeyed wherever the English flag flies."

The idea of self-government was important to many families living in the colonies.

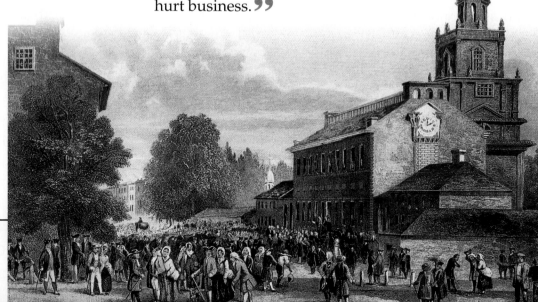

or British Rule?

Parliament

A committee of Parliament wrote a report on the purpose of the colonies. Part of the report said:

❝We must remind all members of Parliament that colonies were set up for the good of England, not for the good of the colonists. These settlements can provide us with many needed things—tobacco, lumber, whale oil, fish, grain, and furs. And, they also provide England with a place to sell our manufactured goods.❞

Prime Minister

In a speech to the members of Parliament, Prime Minister George Grenville explained why new rules were being made for the colonies. Here is part of what he said:

❝So it is only right and just that the colonists help to pay for the protection we are giving them. Clearly, Parliament and the King have authority over the colonies. It is in the name of that authority that we suggest new rules which will make the colonists pay taxes to the English government.❞

Compare Viewpoints

1. What views about government did each person or group hold?
2. Why do you think each person or group held those views?

Think and Apply

People often hold different views about issues because of their jobs or backgrounds or the place where they live. Choose an issue about which the people in your class or community have different ideas. Find out what people think about the issue.

Many people in Britain had strong opinions about colonial rule.

FOCUS

How do individuals and groups today work to make changes in their government?

Main Idea   Read to learn how individuals and groups in the British colonies worked to make changes in their government.

Vocabulary

tariff	repeal
Loyalist	massacre
representation	
treason	
public opinion	
petition	
liberty	
boycott	
congress	

Barrels like this one were used to ship goods during colonial times. King George III appears on the British coin shown above.

Quarrels and Conflicts

1760	1765	1770

The people in the 13 British colonies had to buy many goods they could not grow or make themselves. They bought sugar, molasses, paper, glass, lead, paint, and tea from Britain, the British colonies in the Caribbean, and other countries. To pay for these goods, the colonists sold furs, fish, wood, tobacco, rice, wheat, corn, cattle, and other products to the British and people in other countries. Quarrels over these imports and exports were among the first to come between the colonists and the British king and Parliament.

New Taxes for the Colonists

When Parliament decided that the colonists should help pay the cost of the French and Indian War, it also decided how the payment would be made. In 1764 Parliament passed a law that came to be known as the Sugar Act. This law said the colonists must pay a tax on many goods coming to the colonies from other places. When colonists bought a pound of sugar, for example, they had to pay an extra amount in addition to the item's price. The extra money they paid was a **tariff**, a tax on goods brought into a country.

This tariff angered the colonists. But what bothered them most was that they had had no part in making this tax law. The king and Parliament had taxed the colonists without their consent.

Two of the first colonists to speak out against the new taxes were Mercy Otis Warren and her brother, James Otis, of

Massachusetts. She called the British "greedy," while he called the tariff "unjust" and "a burden."

But not all the colonists agreed with Warren and Otis. Some held the British view. These people were called **Loyalists** or Tories. Loyalist Martin Howard of Rhode Island felt that the colonists should be more grateful to the king and Parliament than they were. After all, he and other Loyalists argued, without British help, France or even Spain might have ruled the colonists. As Howard said,

> 66 Yet for a moment I wish that those unworthy subjects of Britain could feel the iron rod of a Spanish inquisitor or a French tax agent. This would indeed be a punishment suited to their ungrateful feelings. 99

REVIEW *What did the colonists think of the new taxes on sugar and other goods?*

The Stamp Act

Less than a year after the Sugar Act went into effect, Parliament made another tax law. This one angered the colonists even more than the first had. It was called the Stamp Act. Almost everything written or printed on paper in the colonies—from newspapers to playing cards—had to have a special stamp on it to show that a tax had been paid.

In the case of the Stamp Act, as with the other tariffs, the money was not the issue that the colonists minded most. What really bothered them was that they had not agreed to the taxes. They had no **representation** in Parliament—no one acting or speaking for them.

Under the Stamp Act, colonists had to pay for stamps (left) to be attached to printed goods of all kinds. The tax money collected for the stamps was sent to the British government. Some colonists made cartoon stamps (above) to show how they felt about the Stamp Act.

James Otis asked his fellow colonists not to buy paper goods that had been stamped. He told a crowd in Boston that they should refuse to pay the taxes. Colonists began repeating Otis's words,

66 no taxation without representation. 99

Other colonists also dared to speak out against the Stamp Act. In Virginia, Patrick Henry told the members of the House of Burgesses that they alone should decide what taxes were placed. Henry said that Parliament did not represent the colonies. The colonies had their own legislatures to represent them.

Some Loyalist Virginia lawmakers shouted "Treason!" By accusing Patrick Henry of **treason**, they were saying that he was working against the government. Henry answered,

66 If this be treason, make the most of it! 99

What James Otis and Patrick Henry had said about the Stamp Act influenced **public opinion**, or what people thought, in the colonies. The Virginia legislature listened to Patrick Henry. It voted against paying any new taxes the monarch or Parliament made unless the colonists agreed to them. More and more people decided not to buy goods that had been stamped. Everywhere people repeated the words *no taxation without representation.*

REVIEW *Why were many colonists angry at the British government about the Stamp Act?*

Crowds often gathered to hear Patrick Henry's fiery speeches. Henry, shown here arguing a court case, was a lawyer and a member of the House of Burgesses.

People Protest in Different Ways

Word of the colonists' anger over the Stamp Act soon reached King George III and the British Parliament. Some members of Parliament said that James Otis and Patrick Henry should be thrown in prison for speaking out against the government. But no harm came to the two men.

Some colonists wrote letters to Parliament about the law. Others held public meetings and sent long **petitions**—requests for action signed by many people—asking King George III to change the Stamp Act. But the king paid little attention to the colonists.

Throughout the 13 colonies, people met in groups to talk and act against the new taxes. In the Massachusetts colony they called themselves the Sons of Liberty and the Daughters of Liberty. *Liberty* was the word heard over and over again. To most colonists, **liberty** meant the freedom to make their own laws.

Members of these groups told other colonists that they should stop buying stamped goods. They even asked the people to **boycott**, or refuse to buy, any British goods. In Boston the Daughters of Liberty knitted, wove cloth, and spun thread so that colonists could boycott British-made cloth. People sang this song:

❝ Young ladies in town, and those
　　that live 'round,
　Wear none but your own country
　　linen,
　Of economy [saving money] boast,
　　let your pride be the most,
　To show clothes of your own make
　　and spinning. ❞

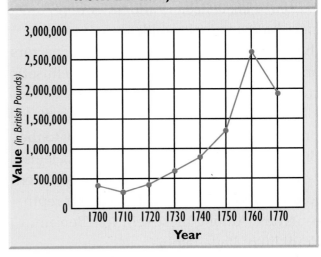

Colonial Imports
from Britain, 1700–1770

LEARNING FROM GRAPHS This graph shows the value of the goods imported from Britain to the 13 colonies between 1700 and 1770. The values are shown in British pounds, the money used in both Britain and the colonies.

■ *In which year did colonial imports increase the most?*

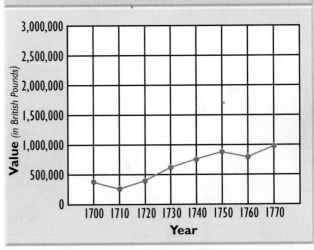

Colonial Exports
to Britain, 1700–1770

LEARNING FROM GRAPHS This graph shows the value of the goods exported from the 13 colonies to Britain between 1700 and 1770.

■ *Why do you think that in most years the colonists imported more goods than they exported?*

Some of the Sons of Liberty protested in more violent ways. They attacked the homes of tax collectors and other royal officials, breaking their windows and stealing their property. They beat some tax collectors and chased several out of the Massachusetts colony.

Other colonists tried peaceful ways of protest. They decided to talk directly to the British lawmakers. The Pennsylvania legislature sent representatives to ask Parliament to think about the colonists' wish for representation. Among those sent was Benjamin Franklin of Philadelphia.

Over the course of 50 years Franklin had helped change Philadelphia from a simple colonial town to one of the best-planned cities in North America. He had organized the volunteer fire department, started Philadelphia's first hospital, and directed street lighting and paving projects. He also had organized the town watch, a group of volunteers that protected Philadelphia's citizens. Benjamin Franklin was his city's and his colony's most respected scientist, business leader, and citizen.

Franklin warned the British lawmakers that the colonists would fight if Parliament sent the British army to make them pay the new taxes. He said,

> 66 The seeds of liberty are universally sown there [in Pennsylvania], and nothing can eradicate [destroy] them. 99

But British leaders did not listen to Franklin's warning.

REVIEW *In what different ways did colonists act against the new taxes?*

Benjamin Franklin was an inventor and a scientist as well as a colonial leader. Among his inventions were the lightning rod and bifocal reading glasses (above).

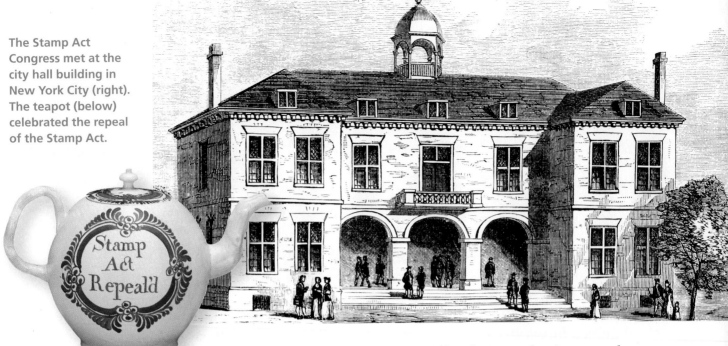

The Stamp Act Congress met at the city hall building in New York City (right). The teapot (below) celebrated the repeal of the Stamp Act.

The Stamp Act Congress

Benjamin Franklin, James Otis, and other colonial leaders had long thought that the colonies should work together instead of acting separately. In 1765 people who felt this way held a meeting in New York City called the Stamp Act Congress. A **congress** is a meeting of representatives who have the authority to make decisions. Nine colonies sent representatives to the Stamp Act Congress. They discussed the problems that the new tax laws had caused. The congress decided to ask people in all the colonies to refuse to buy stamped goods.

When Parliament heard about the Stamp Act Congress and the anger of the colonists, it **repealed** the Stamp Act. This meant that the Stamp Act was no longer a law. Although Parliament repealed this law, in 1767 it added some new ones, called the Townshend Acts. These laws affected trade in the colonies. By passing these new laws, the British government meant to show that it still could make laws for the colonists.

To show clearly its authority over the colonists, Parliament sent more soldiers to North America. By 1770 there were more than 9,000 British soldiers in the 13 colonies. The colonists were told that the soldiers were there to protect the far-off western lands won in the French and Indian War. But the soldiers were living in the cities along the coast!

Having British soldiers in their cities angered many of the colonists. The soldiers seemed like a police force that the colonists did not need. Sometimes this anger led to rock throwing and name calling. The colonists called the British soldiers "redcoats" and "bloodybacks," making fun of their red uniforms. The British soldiers paid them back by destroying colonial property and doing other damage—by riding their horses through churches and other buildings, for example.

As the anger between the British soldiers and the colonists grew stronger, fights broke out more and more often. Some of the worst fighting took place in Boston on March 5, 1770. In the evening a crowd gathered near several British soldiers. Some colonists in the crowd shouted insults at the soldiers and

This engraving (far left) by Paul Revere shows his view of the Boston Massacre. Crispus Attucks (left) and four others were killed. The drawing below appeared on protest posters and contained the initials of the five people who were killed.

began to throw rocks and snowballs. As the crowd moved forward, the soldiers opened fire. Three colonists were killed, and two died later. Among the dead was a 47-year-old runaway slave named Crispus Attucks (AT•uhks). Attucks had led the charge against the soldiers. He was the first person to be killed for American independence.

The events of that day have become known as the Boston Massacre. A **massacre** is the killing of a number of people who cannot defend themselves. After the Boston Massacre took place, an uneasy calm settled over the people in the 13 colonies.

REVIEW *What was the purpose of the Stamp Act Congress?*

LESSON 2 REVIEW

1760	1765	1770
1764 • The Sugar Act	1765 • The Stamp Act Congress	1770 • The Boston Massacre

Check Understanding

1 **Remember the Facts** Why did the Sugar Act anger the colonists?

2 **Recall the Main Idea** How did the colonists work to make changes in the British government?

Think Critically

3 **Past to Present** How do you think people would feel today if they were taxed without representation?

4 **Think More About It** Why do you think the British government wanted to show its authority over the colonies?

5 **Cause and Effect** Why did the British want to make new tax laws for the colonies? What happened when they did?

Show What You Know

Writing Activity Imagine that you are a reporter who has just interviewed a colonist protesting British rule. Write a newspaper article that describes this person's opinion on British taxation or the representation the colonists have. In the article tell whether or not you share the same opinion.

Colonists Unite

1770	1775

In the months following the Boston Massacre, King George III received report after report of continued fighting and boycotts in the 13 British colonies. Petitions, too, poured in to the king from the colonists. When the king chose not to act on them, the colonists decided to act on their own.

The Committees of Correspondence

The Stamp Act Congress had shown that the colonists could work together. But when their representatives were not meeting, it was not as easy for them to work together or even to communicate from day to day. This was because news traveled slowly. It could take weeks for people in one colony to find out what was happening in the other colonies.

Samuel Adams of Massachusetts found an answer to this problem. Adams was one of his colony's leaders. He had spoken out many times against British rule. Adams's answer was to set up a Committee of Correspondence in Boston. Then he got cities and towns in other colonies to do the same.

These **Committees of Correspondence** corresponded with, or wrote letters to, one another. Writers told what was being done in their colonies to protest the latest British laws. The letters were then delivered by riders on horseback. In this way anything that happened in one colony quickly became known in all the others.

REVIEW *Why were the Committees of Correspondence set up?*

FOCUS
What brings people together in difficult times?

Main Idea
As you read, think about what brought the colonists together as they protested British rule.

Vocabulary
Committee of
  Correspondence
consequence
blockade
quarter
Continental Congress
right
Minuteman
Patriot

Quill pens (left) used during colonial times were made from feathers. Legend says that the chest above washed ashore the morning after the Boston Tea Party.

Samuel Adams of Massachusetts led many colonists in protesting British rule. He helped form the Sons of Liberty and organized the Committees of Correspondence.

The Boston Tea Party

In 1773 Lord North, the Prime Minister of Britain, worked with Parliament to pass another new law. This law allowed a British company to sell tea in the colonies for a very low price. This would hurt colonial merchants and the colonists would still have to pay a tax on tea!

People in the colonies soon decided to boycott British tea. In Pennsylvania and New York, colonists did not allow ships carrying British tea to enter their ports. In Massachusetts, however, ships' captains refused to be turned away. Angry colonists showed their feelings in what later became known as the Boston Tea Party.

British ships carrying tea arrived in Boston Harbor in December 1773. Late one night, members of the Sons of Liberty, disguised as Mohawk Indians, boarded the ships, broke open all the chests of tea, and dumped the tea into the harbor. As they threw the tea overboard, they sang:

> **❝** Rally, Mohawks! bring out your axes,
> And tell King George we'll pay no taxes. **❞**

The colonists knew that their actions would have very serious **consequences** (KAHN•suh•kwens•ihz), or results. After hearing about the Boston Tea Party, Parliament decided to punish the colony of Massachusetts. A law was passed saying that no ship carrying colonial goods could leave Boston Harbor until the colonists had paid for all the tea that was destroyed. To enforce the new law, Parliament ordered the Royal Navy to blockade Boston Harbor. To **blockade** is to use warships to prevent other ships from entering or leaving a harbor. The British government wanted to show the colonists that they had to obey its laws.

To further prove its authority, the British government ordered the colonists to **quarter** British soldiers, or pay for their housing. The colonists had to feed the soldiers and give them a place to sleep. The king also made General Thomas Gage the new colonial governor of Massachusetts. Gage was head of the British army in North America. In response to the new laws, colonists shouted, "Intolerable Acts!"

People acted against the tax on tea in other colonies, too. In Edenton, North Carolina, a colonist named Penelope Barker led 51 women in a "tea party" of their own. They agreed to do everything they could to help with the tea boycott. They declared that they could not "be indifferent to whatever affected the peace and happiness of the

This painting shows one artist's idea of what happened at the Boston Tea Party. One colonist remembered, "In about three hours from the time we went on board, we had thus broken and thrown overboard every tea chest to be found."

country." The Edenton Tea Party has been called by one historian "the earliest known instance of political activity on the part of women in the American colonies."

REVIEW *Why did colonists hold the Boston and Edenton tea parties?*

The Continental Congress

Many of the colonists believed that the British government would do anything, even use its army, to make them obey the laws. So the Committees of Correspondence called a meeting of representatives of all the colonies to decide what to do. The meeting took place in Philadelphia in September 1774. Because it was the first meeting of its kind on the North American continent, the colonists called it the **Continental Congress**. Representatives from 12 of the colonies came to the meeting.

Members of the Continental Congress agreed to stop all trade with Britain. The Congress also said that the colonies would no longer obey British laws when the laws took away their liberty as citizens. The colonists told Parliament, "We are *for the present* only resolved to pursue . . . peaceable measures."

The Congress agreed that if the demands for colonial **rights**, or freedoms, were not met, they would meet again in May 1775 to decide what to do next.

In Virginia the House of Burgesses suggested that colonists start preparing for war. Others strongly opposed the idea. In March of 1775, Patrick Henry gave the most famous speech of his career. Americans have long remembered its last words:

> 66 I know not what course others may take; but as for me, give me liberty or give me death! 99

REVIEW *Why did the Continental Congress meet?*

Lexington and Concord

Dawes
Revere
British

Concord

Boston

1
2
3
3
3
3
4
6
7
8

N

Lexington

Charlestown

Fighting at Lexington and Concord

By the end of the Continental Congress, anger against the British government had turned Massachusetts into an armed camp. Members of the colony's militia companies became **Minutemen**, fighters who could be ready in a minute to defend Massachusetts. The British, too, kept their soldiers and their weapons ready.

The colonists who were against the British now called themselves **Patriots**. In April 1775 British General Thomas Gage, the new governor of Massachusetts, heard that the Patriots were storing weapons in the town of Concord near Boston. Gage also heard that John Hancock and Samuel Adams, two leaders of the Sons of Liberty, were staying nearby, in the village of Lexington. The general sent 700 British soldiers to find the weapons and arrest the Patriot leaders.

But Paul Revere and William Dawes, members of the Sons of Liberty, rode out the night of April 18 to warn Hancock and Adams that the British were on their way. When the British arrived in Lexington on April 19, they found Minutemen waiting for them. The Minutemen were of all ages. Many owned property, but some were workingmen. At least five were Africans. Several of these were slaves. Shots were fired, and eight of the Minutemen were killed. Several others were wounded.

The British marched on to Concord, but the weapons they expected to find had been moved. As they marched back to Boston, they were shot at by Minutemen from the woods and fields beside the road. British losses for the day were 73 killed and

Paul Revere
1735–1818

Paul Revere was one of the few people in Boston to own a horse. He kept one because he liked to spend his free time galloping through the countryside. Revere was a silversmith. As a Son of Liberty, Revere often carried messages from the Boston Committee of Correspondence to committees in other towns. In 1773 he rode to Philadelphia with news of the Boston Tea Party. But his most famous ride was the one he made to Lexington on the night of April 18, 1775, carrying the news "the British are coming!"

174 wounded. Of the 4,000 Minutemen at Lexington and Concord, 93 were killed or wounded in the fighting.

To honor the event, poet Ralph Waldo Emerson wrote a poem called the "Concord Hymn," which begins,

66 By the rude bridge that arched the flood,
Their flag to April's breeze unfurled,
Here once the embattled farmers stood,
And fired the shot heard round the world. 99

The shots fired at Lexington and Concord marked the beginning of a long, bitter war between Britain and its American colonies.

REVIEW *Why did the British go to Lexington and Concord?*

LESSON 3 REVIEW

1770 ———————————————— 1775

1773
• The Boston Tea Party

1774
• The Continental Congress meets

1775
• Fighting at Lexington and Concord

Check Understanding

1 Remember the Facts   How did the Committees of Correspondence help bring the colonies together?

2 Recall the Main Idea   What brought the colonists together as they protested British rule?

Think Critically

3 Explore Viewpoints   Describe how people in each of these groups might have viewed the Boston Tea Party: Parliament, Loyalists, Patriots.

4 Personally Speaking   Do you think the Minutemen had any advantages over the British soldiers? Explain your answer.

Show What You Know
Letter-Writing Activity
Imagine that it is the spring of 1775, and you are a member of the Committee of Correspondence in Boston. Write a letter to a member of the committee in Philadelphia, telling what is taking place in your city.

Make Economic Choices

1. Why Learn This Skill?

When you buy something, you are making an economic choice. Sometimes, making an economic choice is difficult. In order to buy or do one thing, you have to give up buying or doing something else. This is called a **trade-off**. What you give up is the **opportunity cost** of what you get. Knowing about trade-offs and opportunity costs can help you make thoughtful economic choices.

2. Understand the Process

The colonists had to make many economic choices. Their economic choices, however, were made even more difficult by the continuing protests against British rule. You have read that in 1773 Lord North and Parliament passed a new law that affected the tea trade in the colonies.

Imagine that you are a colonist living in Annapolis, Maryland, in 1774. Should you buy British tea? Or should you buy the local tea, sassafras?

❶ Think about the trade-offs. To do this, you must balance the advantages and disadvantages of your choices. British tea tastes much better than sassafras, but you would have to pay a tax. And by buying British tea, you would not be taking part in the boycott. Sassafras tea does not cost as much, but it tastes spicy. Buying sassafras tea, however, would show that you support the boycott.

A colonist in Boston reads a notice about the tea tax.

❷ Think about the opportunity costs. You do not have enough money to buy both teas, so you have to give up one. If you buy the British tea, you give up extra money to pay the tax. You also give up taking part in the boycott. If you buy the sassafras, you give up the good taste of the British tea. What choice would you make?

3. Think and Apply

Imagine that you have $25. You may want to buy two compact discs or take three friends out for pizza. You do not have to spend all your money on one choice. You can choose some of one choice and some of another. Explain to a partner the trade-offs and opportunity costs of your choices.

CHAPTER 7

REVIEW

1750   1755

1754
• The French
  and Indian
  War begins

CONNECT MAIN IDEAS

Use this organizer to show how the chapter's main ideas are connected. Write three details to support each main idea. A copy of the organizer may be found on page 49 of the Activity Book.

Britain Rules the Colonies

Differences Divide Britain and Its Colonies

Britain and the Colonies Go to War

Government in the Colonies

The British colonists became unhappy with British rule.

1. _____
2. _____
3. _____

Quarrels and Conflicts

Individuals and groups in the British colonies worked to make changes in their government.

1. _____
2. _____
3. _____

Colonists Unite

The colonists came together as they protested British rule.

1. _____
2. _____
3. _____

WRITE MORE ABOUT IT

Write a Persuasive Letter Imagine that you are living in one of the British colonies in 1770. Write a letter in which you try to persuade a member of Parliament to help American colonists gain self-government.

Write a Report Choose one of the colonists you read about in this chapter. Then write a report on his or her life. Explain the person's role in the events leading to the American Revolution.

1763
• The French and Indian War ends

1765
• The Stamp Act Congress

1767
• The Townshend Acts

1770
• The Boston Massacre

1773
• The Boston Tea Party

1775
• Fighting at Lexington and Concord

USE VOCABULARY

For each group of terms, write a sentence or two that explains how the terms are related.

1. tax, tariff
2. Parliament, congress
3. Loyalist, Patriot
4. self-government, democracy
5. boycott, petition

CHECK UNDERSTANDING

6. How were laws made in the British colonies?

7. What was the purpose of the Proclamation of 1763? How did most colonists react to it?

8. Why were some colonists unhappy with the Sugar Act?

9. Why was the Stamp Act repealed?

10. What was the purpose of the Committees of Correspondence?

11. Why did the Intolerable Acts make the colonists so angry?

12. Who were the Minutemen?

13. What was the effect of the fighting at Lexington and Concord?

THINK CRITICALLY

14. **Personally Speaking** Do you think it was the colonists' responsibility to help pay for the French and Indian War? Explain your answer.

15. **Explore Viewpoints** What do you think members of Parliament thought about the idea of taxation without representation?

16. **Cause and Effect** What were some of the causes and effects of the Boston Tea Party?

17. **Think More About It** How do you think the Committees of Correspondence affected decisions made by colonial leaders?

APPLY SKILLS

Use a Historical Map Compare the map on page 265 with a present-day political map of the United States. What states have been formed from the land between the Appalachian Mountains and the Mississippi River?

Make Economic Choices Imagine that you need to choose between buying a video game or a pair of soccer shoes. How would you make this economic choice? Identify the trade-offs and opportunity costs.

READ MORE ABOUT IT

The Boston Tea Party by Laurie A. O'Neill. Millbrook Press. Diaries, letters, and biographies bring to life the Boston Tea Party.

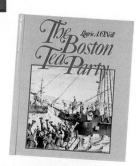

HARCOURT BRACE

Visit the Internet at **http://www.hbschool.com** for additional resources.

THE WAR FOR INDEPENDENCE

"In Freedom we're born, and like Sons of the brave, Will never surrender, . . ."

Mercy Otis Warren, American writer

At War with the Homeland

| January 1775 | December 1775 |

FOCUS
What might give one side an advantage over the other in a war today?

Main Idea   As you read, think about what gave the British army an advantage over the Continental army as the war began.

Vocabulary
olive branch
Continental
mercenary
enlist

The Committees of Correspondence quickly spread the news of the fighting at Lexington and Concord. A second Continental Congress was called, and it met in Philadelphia in May 1775. Some of the most important colonial leaders went to the meeting to decide what to do now that a battle had been fought. Pennsylvania sent Benjamin Franklin. Massachusetts sent John Hancock, Samuel Adams, and John Adams. Virginia sent George Washington and the fiery Patrick Henry.

The Second Continental Congress

The Second Continental Congress moved carefully. The Patriots sent a letter called the Olive Branch Petition to King George III, telling him of their desire for peace and asking him to repeal the Intolerable Acts. An **olive branch** has stood for peace since ancient times. But in case the king refused to repeal the laws, the Second Continental Congress decided to form a colonial army.

The Congress asked all the colonies to send soldiers to Massachusetts. It chose George Washington of Virginia to lead this new Continental army. Washington, who had fought in the French and Indian War, came to the meeting in uniform to show that he would like to be the army's general. It was Washington's understanding of soldiers and war that caused the Congress to choose him instead of such leaders as Artemas Ward, Charles Lee, or John Hancock.

The Patriots sent the king the Olive Branch Petition to ask him to repeal unfair laws.

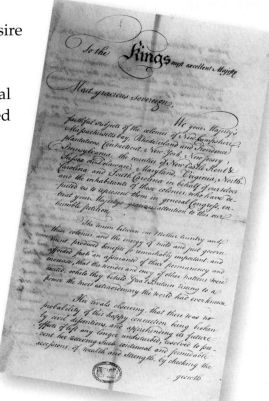

Philadelphia

Philadelphia calls itself "The Most Historic City in America"—and with good reason. It first earned its place in history in 1774, when the First Continental Congress met in Carpenters' Hall, in the city's center. Over the next 30 years, many of the most important events in American history took place in Philadelphia.

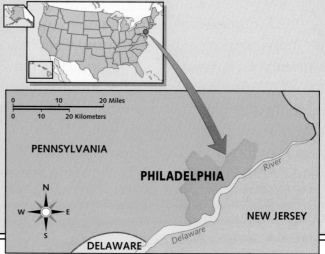

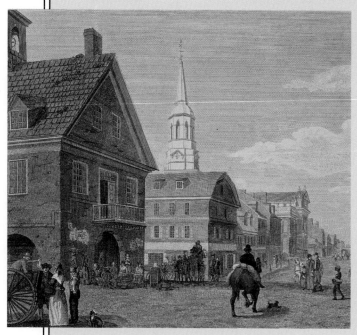

This scene of colonial Philadelphia shows the intersection of Second and Market.

The Second Continental Congress asked each colony to give money to support the new army. The money was needed to pay full-time soldiers and to buy guns, bullets, food, and uniforms. The Congress also voted to print its own paper money, which came to be known as Continental currency.

In everything it did, the Congress wanted to believe the words of Patrick Henry,

> 66 The distinctions between Virginians, Pennsylvanians, New Yorkers are no more. I am not a Virginian but an American. 99

The Second Continental Congress came to stand for the new unity of the 13 colonies.

REVIEW *Why did colonial leaders call a second meeting of the Continental Congress?*

The Continental Army

George Washington left Philadelphia right away to take charge of his army, which had already fought its first major battle. The Battle of Bunker Hill, which took place in Boston on June 17, 1775, was among the fiercest battles of the whole war. It was so fierce that to save bullets, the colonists were ordered, "Don't fire until you see the whites of their eyes." The colonists drove the British back twice before running out of bullets.

George Washington arrived in Massachusetts to meet his army less than three weeks after this battle. The 14,500 soldiers, mostly from the northern colonies, wore no uniforms—only their ordinary clothes. Those who had guns carried flintlock muskets, which could not be used to shoot very far. Many of the soldiers had no guns at all. Instead, they carried spears and axes.

Some of Washington's soldiers had fought on the frontier and in the French and Indian War. The soldiers had learned to fight the way the Native Americans did—in irregular lines and from hiding places. They did not fight the way a European army would—side by side in straight lines. In fact, they had never fought as an army. Washington made rules for his soldiers and trained them. Slowly, Washington created the beginning of an army whose soldiers were proud to be called **Continentals**. The Continentals made up the first colonial army.

With little money and not much training, the Continentals went to war against the most powerful army in the world. Later, an officer would report,

66 It is incredible that soldiers composed of men of every age, even children of fifteen, of whites and blacks, almost naked, unpaid, and rather poorly fed, can march so well and withstand fire so steadfastly. 99

REVIEW *What was the Continental army like when Washington took charge?*

The artist and soldier Charles Willson Peale painted this portrait of George Washington at the Battle of Trenton. The poster below called for young men to join Washington's Continental army to defend the American colonies from enemies.

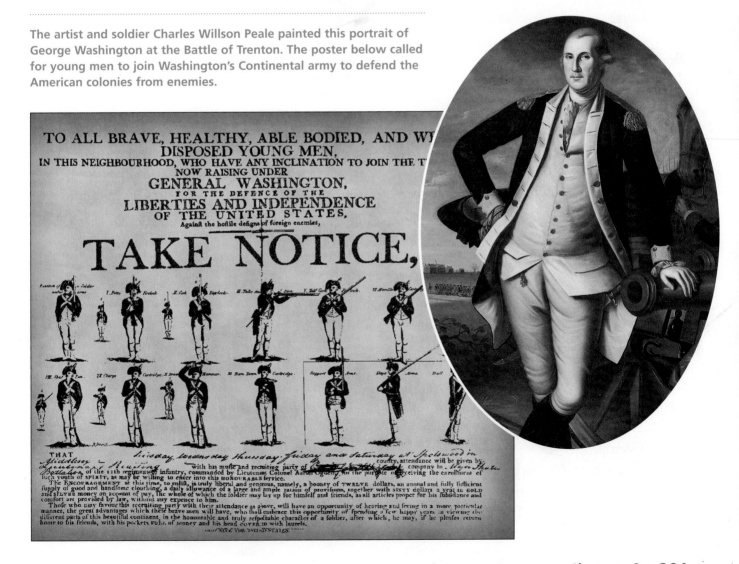

This scene at the Battle of Bunker Hill in 1775 was painted by Howard Pyle. Although the British eventually took the hill, their way of marching in straight lines during an attack caused more than 1,000 British soldiers to be killed or wounded.

The British Advantage

Unlike George Washington's army of mostly first-time soldiers, the British army was made up of professional soldiers. They had the best training, the most experienced officers, and the newest weapons. They also had help. The British used **mercenaries** (MUHR•suhn•air•eez), or hired soldiers, to fight on their side. Some of these soldiers were Hessians, from the Hesse region of Germany. The British also had Native American allies. Many tribes hated the colonists because settlers had taken over Indian lands.

But the British had problems, too. It was difficult to fight a war that was 3,000 miles (4,828 km) from home. They had trouble getting supplies across the Atlantic Ocean.

In the early days of the war, the British army used their greater numbers and experience as fighters as an advantage over the Continental army. While the British had 50,000 soldiers, General Washington usually had no more than 10,000 soldiers in his army at any one time.

Most of the Americans **enlisted** in, or joined, the army for one year at a time. They might stay that long or longer, or they might not. When harvesttime came, some of the Continentals would go home to their farms. If they did not get their pay as soldiers, they would not stay in the army. General Washington did his best to keep his army together to defend the American colonies from the British.

REVIEW *How was the British army different from the army trained by General Washington?*

On the night of June 16, 1775, Continental soldiers in Boston prepared for what came to be known as the Battle of Bunker Hill. Taking the high ground was an important plan in defending the city.

LESSON I REVIEW

January 1775	• •	December 1775

May 1775
• Second Continental Congress

June 1775
• Battle of Bunker Hill

Check Understanding

1 **Remember the Facts** What actions did the Second Continental Congress take?

2 **Recall the Main Idea** What gave the British army an advantage over the Continental army as the war began?

Think Critically

3 **Personally Speaking** What do you think might have happened if the British king had accepted the Olive Branch Petition?

4 **Think More About It** Washington overcame many problems in leading his soldiers against the British army. What qualities should a good leader have?

Show What You Know

Simulation Activity Role-play a conversation in which you tell a partner why he or she should join the Continental army. Try to make each side of the conversation as real as you can. Discuss your conversation with classmates.

Read a Political Cartoon

1. Why Learn This Skill?

Cartoons that express opinions about politics or about government are called **political cartoons**. Political cartoons are most often found in newspapers and magazines. Knowing how to read a political cartoon will help you understand its humor and its meaning.

2. Study an American Political Cartoon

Benjamin Franklin drew the cartoon shown below. It may have been the first American political cartoon. It appeared in the *Pennsylvania Gazette* in 1754. Franklin was representing the Pennsylvania colony at the Albany Congress in New York. At this meeting he presented a "Plan of Union" for the colonies. He hoped his cartoon would make colonial leaders want to unite.

The snake in the cartoon stands for most of the colonies. Each piece of the snake represents one of the colonies. The saying "Join, or Die" was based on an old tale about snakes. According to this story, a snake that was cut into pieces would come to life again if it was put back together before sunset. Benjamin Franklin wanted the pieces of the snake—the colonies—to come together to survive.

3. Understand the Process

In his cartoon, Benjamin Franklin used the snake as a symbol. Symbols are a good way to show ideas that are sometimes hard to draw in a picture—ideas such as unity among the colonies. The use of symbols can make the message of a political cartoon easier to understand.

Animals are often used as symbols for ideas in political cartoons. The eagle is often used to represent the idea of freedom. The dove stands for the idea of peace. The hawk stands for war. The snail is used as a symbol of slowness.

4. Think and Apply

Begin a collection of political cartoons. Cut political cartoons out of old newspapers or magazines. Then write short captions to help explain the meaning of each cartoon. Make up a political cartoon of your own to add to the collection.

Franklin hoped this cartoon would help unite the colonies. It represents all the colonies except Delaware and Georgia.

The Decision for Independence

June 1776	July 1776	August 1776

LESSON 2

FOCUS

Why is it important for leaders today to explain the reasons for their decisions?

Main Idea Read to learn why it was important for colonial leaders to explain their decision to break free from British rule.

Vocabulary

revolution
independence
allegiance
declaration
grievance

Although they were already at war, many colonists still believed that their problems with the British government could be settled without more fighting. They hoped the king and Parliament would let them take part in making the laws. By 1776 that thinking began to change, and the colonists prepared for a longer war.

The First Steps

One of the Patriots who did the most to change public opinion in the colonies was Thomas Paine. In January 1776 Paine published a pamphlet he called *Common Sense*. In it he attacked King George III as a bully and questioned the idea of one person having all the authority to rule. Paine felt that people should rule themselves. He called for a sudden, complete change of government—a **revolution** (reh•vuh•LOO•shuhn). The colonies should cut their ties with the British government, he said, and set up their own government.

People throughout the colonies talked about *Common Sense*. After nearly a year of war, the idea of **independence**, or freedom to govern on their own, sounded good to many colonists. It also sounded good to many members of the Second Continental Congress. The time to act had come.

On June 7, 1776, Richard Henry Lee of Virginia gave a speech to Congress. He said that

> 66 these United Colonies are, and of Right ought to be Free and Independent States. 99

In Britain, Thomas Paine lost his job as a tax collector after asking for a raise. Benjamin Franklin, who was in London at the time, suggested that Paine go to America.

He went on to say that the colonies no longer owed **allegiance** (uh•LEE•juhnts), or loyalty, to the king.

The Congress waited almost a month before voting on the idea of cutting ties with the British government. Not all of the colonies were ready for independence. They needed more time before taking such a dangerous step. The leaders of the Congress hoped that a month's wait would help all 13 colonies decide in favor of independence. In the meantime, they formed a committee to draw up a **declaration**, or official statement, of independence.

The members of the committee were Benjamin Franklin of Pennsylvania, John Adams of Massachusetts, Robert R. Livingston of New York, Roger Sherman of Connecticut, and Thomas Jefferson of Virginia. Each member added ideas about what the Declaration should say. But Jefferson did most of the writing.

Only 33 years old, Thomas Jefferson was a leader of the Patriots in Virginia. He was a lawyer, he had studied government, and he had already written about colonial problems with British rule. Two years before, he had written *A Summary View of the Rights of*

A Declaration by the Representatives of the U
OF AMERICA, in General Congress assembled.
When in the course of human events it becomes
dissolve the political bands which have connected them with
-sume among the powers of the earth the separate and equa
which the laws of nature & of nature's god entitle the
to the opinions of mankind requires that they should
which impel them to the separation.
We hold these truths to be self-evident;
created equal
that they are endowed by
inherent & inalienable rights; that among these are
life, liberty, & the pursuit of happiness; that to secu
-vernments are instituted among men, deriving their ju
the consent of the governed; that whenever any form of
becomes destructive of these ends, it is the right of the people to alter
or to abolish it, & to institute new government, laying it's foundation on
such principles & organising it's powers in such form, as to them sh
seem most likely to effect their safety & happiness.
prudence indeed
will dictate that governments long established should not be changed for
light & transient causes: and accordingly all experience hath shewn that
mankind are more disposed to suffer while evils are sufferable, than to
right themselves by abolishing the forms to which they are accustomed. but
when a long train of abuses & usurpations [begun at a d

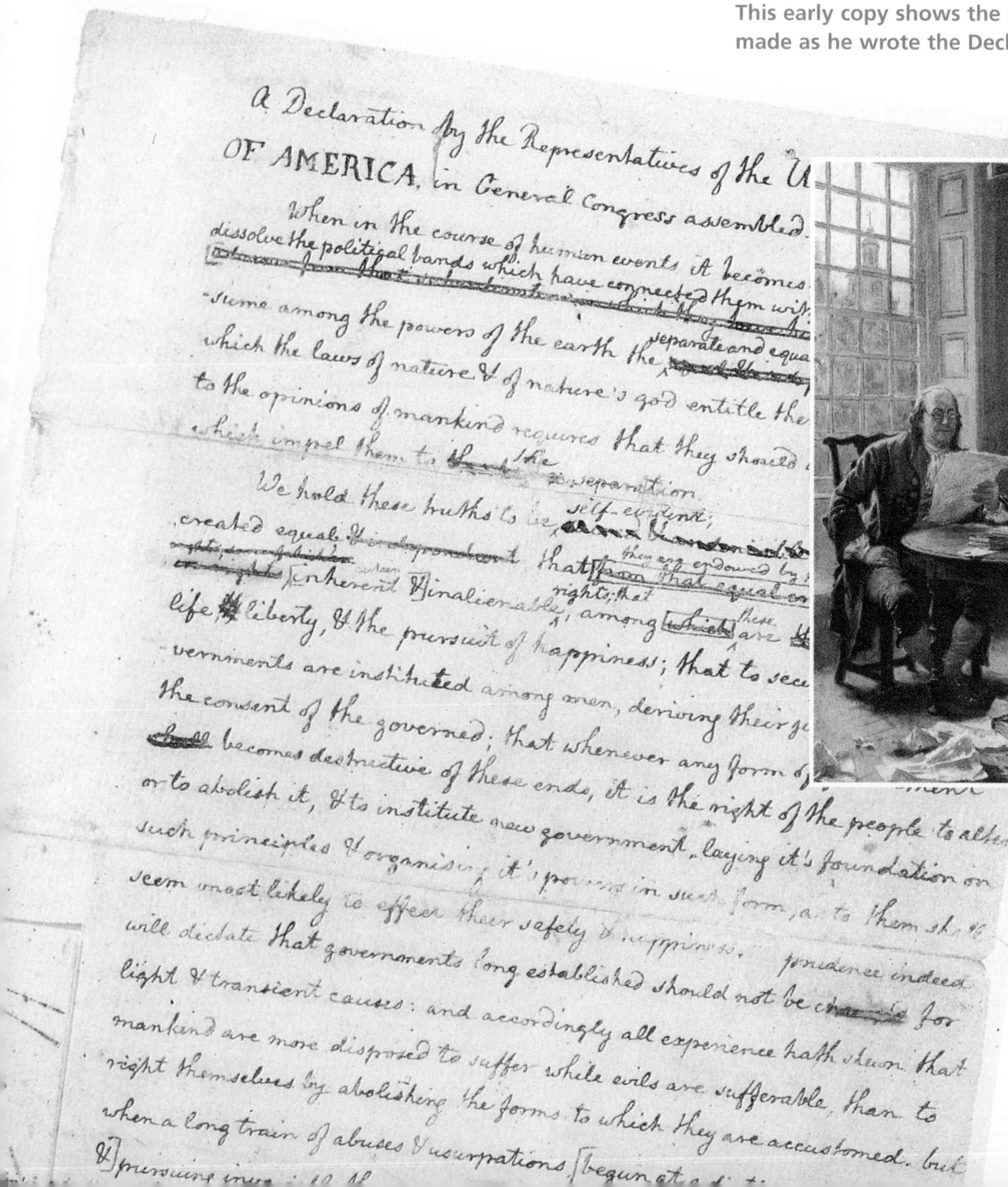

This early copy shows the many changes Jefferson made as he wrote the Declaration of Independence.

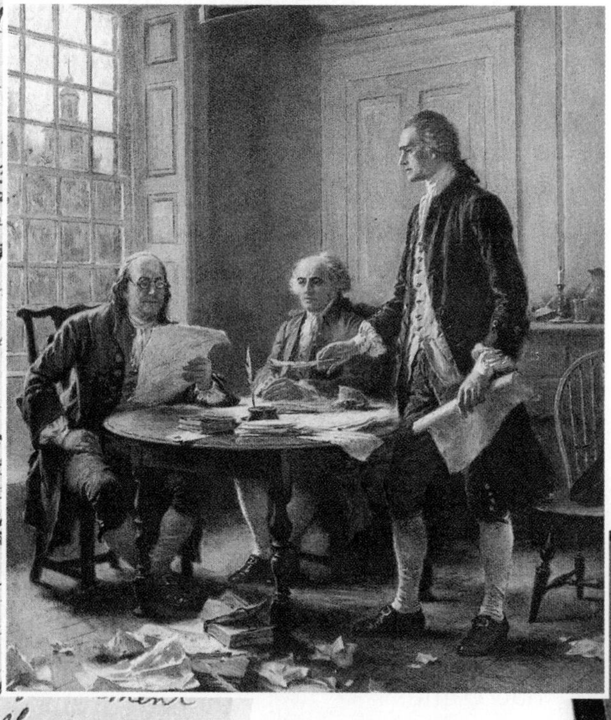

Benjamin Franklin, John Adams, and Thomas Jefferson included in the Declaration the idea that a government gets its power from the consent of the people.

British America, in which he had listed for the First Continental Congress the changes the colonies wanted in their government. When the Declaration committee was selected, Jefferson began work at once. Every evening for the next 17 days, Jefferson wrote—and rewrote—the document that would become the Declaration of Independence.

REVIEW *Why did Congress wait before voting on independence?*

Writing the Declaration

Thomas Jefferson wanted his words to help the colonists win their war for freedom. He wrote very carefully. He had to state the facts so that people would agree that the cause for independence was right and that it was worth fighting for.

Jefferson planned the Declaration in several parts. In the introduction, he stated why the Declaration was needed. He said that sometimes a group of people must cut themselves off from the country they once belonged to. They find they have no choice but to form a new nation with the same authority as other independent countries. Jefferson said that when people do this, they must have good reasons. And, he said, they must explain their reasons so there is no doubt about why such a step is taken.

In the second part of the Declaration, Jefferson listed the colonists' main ideas about government. The words he wrote in 1776 are among the most famous in American history. Jefferson said:

> **"** We hold these truths to be self-evident, that all men are created equal, that they are endowed [provided] by their Creator with certain unalienable Rights, that among these are Life, Liberty and the pursuit of Happiness. **"**

Jefferson's travel desk holds the first draft of the Declaration of Independence.

John Trumbull's painting of the signing of the Declaration of Independence shows 48 members of the Second Continental Congress. The delegates met in Pennsylvania's State House, known today as Independence Hall. Those who signed the Declaration did so knowing that they were risking their lives and property.

In the third and longest part of the Declaration, Jefferson listed the colonists' **grievances** (GREE•vuhns•ez), or complaints, about the unfair practices of the king and Parliament. He also listed the ways the colonists had tried to settle their differences with the British government peacefully. But, he noted, the king had refused to listen to the colonists. Such a king, Jefferson wrote, was "unfit to be the ruler of a free people."

Then, in the last part of the Declaration, Jefferson wrote that for all of the reasons he had described, the 13 colonies were no longer a part of Britain.

66 We, therefore, . . . in the Name, and by Authority of the good People of these Colonies, solemnly publish and declare, That these United Colonies are, and of Right ought to be Free and Independent States. . . . 99

When he finished writing, Jefferson gave the Declaration to Congress, and on June 28 it was read aloud. Then the members returned to Richard Henry Lee's idea of cutting ties with Britain. On the morning of July 2, 1776, Lee's idea was approved. The Congress spent the next two days talking about the Declaration. After several small changes were made, it was approved on July 4, 1776. The 13 colonies had declared independence.

REVIEW ***What did Jefferson describe in the longest part of the Declaration of Independence?***

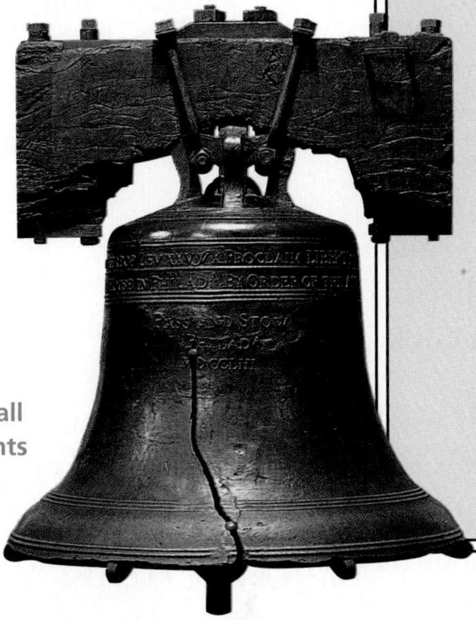

On July 8, 1776, Patriots rang the Liberty Bell in Philadelphia's State House to celebrate the adoption of the Declaration of Independence. The bell was rung each year after that until it cracked in 1835. The words written on the bell, "Proclaim Liberty throughout all the land unto all the inhabitants thereof," are from the Bible.

HERITAGE

Independence Day

On July 4, 1776, the Second Continental Congress approved the Declaration of Independence. After the vote, the president of the Congress, John Hancock, signed his name to the document in large, bold writing. John Adams, writing home to his wife, Abigail, said that the event should be remembered with shows, games, sports, guns, bells, bonfires, and fireworks "from this time forward for evermore." Americans have celebrated the Fourth of July, or Independence Day, as a national holiday ever since.

LESSON 2 REVIEW

June 1776 — July 1776 — August 1776

- **June 7, 1776** • Lee speaks in favor of independence
- **June 28, 1776** • The Declaration of Independence is read to Congress
- **July 4, 1776** • The Declaration of Independence is approved

Check Understanding

1. **Remember the Facts** What was the purpose of each part of the Declaration of Independence?
2. **Recall the Main Idea** Why was it important for colonial leaders to explain their decision to break free from British rule?

Think Critically

3. **Think More About It** Why do you think that Thomas Jefferson was asked to write the Declaration of Independence?
4. **Personally Speaking** What do you think Thomas Jefferson meant when he wrote "all men are created equal"?
5. **Past to Present** Why do you think the Declaration is still important today?

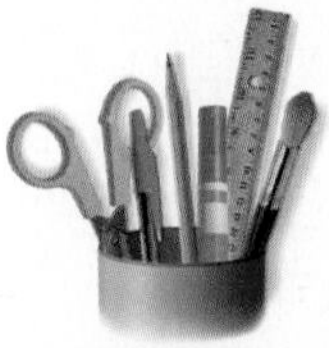

Show What You Know

Art Activity With a partner, create an advertisement for Thomas Paine's pamphlet *Common Sense*. Include in your advertisement at least one of the ideas the colonists will read about. Share your advertisements with the class.

Learn from Pictures

1. Why Learn This Skill?

Artists and photographers create pictures to share their feelings and ideas. A picture often can tell you more about a subject than words can. By studying a picture carefully, you can learn a variety of information about a subject. It is important that you learn to read a picture like you would read a book.

2. Understand the Process

The painting by John McRae on this page shows how some colonists reacted after the Declaration of Independence was approved and signed. Study this painting carefully and answer the questions below.

1 What part of the painting did you look at first? Why?

2 What do you think is happening in the painting?

3 Are the colonists in the picture happy that the Declaration was signed? How can you tell?

4 How do the people in the painting relate to one another? Does the painting show conflict or cooperation between the people?

5 How do you think John McRae feels about the scene he painted?

3. Think and Apply

Look at three other paintings from this unit. While looking at each painting, describe how each communicates different feelings and ideas. Share your descriptions with your classmates.

Americans Take Sides

LESSON
3

FOCUS
How do people's experiences affect the decisions they make?

Main Idea As you read, think about how people's experiences affected their decision to take sides in the American Revolution.

Vocabulary
neutral
pacifist
movement
encroach
regiment

After the Declaration of Independence was signed, people had to decide if they would support the rebelling colonies or the British king. Some chose to be **neutral** (NOO•truhl), taking neither side. Those who were neutral were willing to accept the outcome of the revolution, whichever way it went.

About a third of the colonists were Loyalists, and another third were Patriots. The last third chose to remain neutral. Friends, neighbors, and families were sometimes torn apart by the need to choose sides. The fighting became as much a civil war as it was a war with the British.

Churches and the War

Many factors affected people's views on independence. One was religion. "There is a time to pray and a time to fight," Peter Muhlenberg, a young Lutheran minister, told his followers. Then, before their eyes, he tore off his church robes to show the uniform of a Patriot militia officer. His father, the colonies' Lutheran leader, was shocked—he himself was a Loyalist. The Lutherans, like the people of other church groups, were divided between Patriots and Loyalists.

Taking sides was especially hard for Anglican Church members. The British king was the head of the Anglican Church, as the Church of England was called in the colonies. Many Anglicans in the northern and middle colonies supported the king, while many of those in the southern colonies worked for independence.

Most Congregationalists, members of the largest church group in the colonies, worked for independence, as did many

Button molds were used to make metal buttons for Continental army uniforms.

This illustration by Howard Pyle shows colonists in Boston watching a battle from their rooftops. Some of the churches influenced the colonists when the time came to choose sides during the war.

northern Presbyterians and Baptists. Many southern Presbyterians, however, were Loyalists.

Members of the Society of Friends, also called Quakers, would not fight in the war for independence. Quakers are against all wars, because they believe that violence for any reason is wrong. These **pacifists**, or believers in peaceful settlement of differences, published pamphlets calling for an end to the war. Loyalists and Patriots both saw pacifists as their enemies.

REVIEW *How did some people's religious beliefs affect the way they felt about independence?*

Women and the War

Many women in the colonies took part in the **movement**, or effort by many people, to gain freedom. When Patriot leaders asked the colonists to boycott British-made goods, women in Boston and other colonial towns banded together to make their own goods. Many women worked for independence in other ways.

Some women formed groups to raise money for the war and collect clothing for the soldiers. In Lancaster, Pennsylvania, women formed a group that was called the

Unmarried Ladies of America. Its members promised that they would never give their hand in marriage to any gentleman until he had first proved himself a Patriot.

Women also took part in the fighting. Like some women, Mary Ludwig Hays traveled with her husband after he joined the Continental army. When her husband fell during the Battle of Monmouth, Hays took over the firing of his cannon. Mary Slocumb rode through thick forests at night to join her husband and other members of the North Carolina militia. She fought with them in the Battle of Moores Creek Bridge.

In Boston, Phillis Wheatley wrote poems that were praised by George Washington.

She used her mind to champion the independence movement. So did Mercy Otis Warren. She wrote a play that made fun of the British and supported the Patriots.

Patriot Abigail Adams wanted to be sure that independence would be good for women as well as men. She wrote to her husband, John:

> 66 If particular care and attention are not paid to the ladies we are determined to foment [start] a rebellion and will not hold ourselves bound to obey any laws in which we have no voice or representation. 99

Mary Ludwig Hays (below) earned the name Molly Pitcher by bringing water to the troops during the long, hot Battle of Monmouth, fought in June 1778. Nancy Hart (right) also supported the Patriots.

Phillis Wheatley
1753?–1784

When she was only five or six years old, a young African girl, probably born in the country of Senegal, was kidnapped and enslaved. She was taken to Boston and sold to John Wheatley in 1761. Unlike many other slave owners, Wheatley educated the young girl and then freed her. Phillis Wheatley, who took the last name of her owner, was one of the earliest American poets.

Not all women were Patriots. There were Loyalist women in every colony. Some of them fought for the British. Many others brought the British food and supplies.

REVIEW *How did women on both sides take part in the Revolution?*

Native Americans and the War

An Oneida chief is said to have told a Patriot,

❝ We have heard of the unhappy differences and great contention betwixt [between] you and Old England. We cannot meddle in this dispute between two brothers. . . . Should the great king of England apply to us for aid, we shall decline him; if the colonies apply to us, we shall refuse. ❞

Over the years Native Americans had grown angry with both the American colonists and the British. Settlers from both sides continued to **encroach** on traditional Indian lands, moving onto them without

asking. By 1776 the land between the Appalachian Mountains and the Mississippi River was being taken over by Europeans, despite the Proclamation of 1763, which did not allow settlement there.

Yet many Native Americans had come to depend on Europeans as trading partners. For this reason the Patriots hoped that the Indians would at least stay out of the war, even if they would not fight for them. The British, however, promised to give the Indians guns and other European goods if they agreed to help the British army. Many tribes in the Ohio River valley, so often at war with each other, made peace in order "to assist His Majesty's troops." Other tribes, however, were divided. In the Hudson River valley, some of the Iroquois fought for the Patriots. Others decided to fight for the British.

Most Indians, however, stayed out of the fighting. When asked to take sides, one Cherokee chief is said to have told both the colonists and the British that the Great Spirit "has given you many advantages, but he has not created us to be your slaves. We are a separate people!"

REVIEW *What view did most Indians take about the fighting?*

Africans and the War

The Battle of Bunker Hill in Boston, Massachusetts.

At the start of the war, free Africans were as quick to take sides as many of their European neighbors. Peter Salem was among at least five Africans who fought at Concord with the Minutemen. A few weeks later he and other Africans, both free and enslaved, fought at the Battle of Bunker Hill in Boston, Massachusetts. About 5,000 Africans fought in the Continental army during the Revolutionary War.

Enslaved Africans who enlisted in the Continental army were promised freedom after the war as a reward. Many were so filled with ideas of freedom and liberty that they changed their names. Among the names listed in army records are Cuff Freedom, Dick Freedom, Ned Freedom, Peter Freeman, Cuff Liberty, Jeffrey Liberty, and Pomp Liberty.

The royal governor of Virginia, John Murray, Earl of Dunmore, also promised to give enslaved Africans their freedom if they ran away from their owners and were "able and willing to bear arms" for the British government. In a few weeks nearly 300 runaway slaves were enlisted in the Ethiopian Regiment of the British army. A **regiment** is a troop of soldiers. These soldiers wore uniforms that had patches reading *Liberty to Slaves*.

REVIEW *What promise caused some enslaved Africans to take sides?*

LESSON 3 REVIEW

Check Understanding

1 Remember the Facts Why was the American Revolution as much a civil war as it was a war with Britain?

2 Recall the Main Idea How did people's experiences affect their decision to take sides in the American Revolution?

Think Critically

3 Explore Viewpoints Imagine that you are a Native American or an African during the American Revolution. List the reasons you might have to choose one side over the other.

4 Past to Present How might people who are pacifists view conflicts that sometimes take place around the world today?

Show What You Know

Chart Activity Draw a chart showing the colonial groups that worked for independence and the groups that remained loyal to the British king and Parliament. Do some research to find out why each group chose the side it did. Include this information on your chart. Share your findings with your classmates.

SAMUEL'S
CHOICE

by RICHARD BERLETH
illustrated by BILL MAUGHAN

Taking the side of the Patriots was a difficult decision for many people, but especially difficult for enslaved Africans. The Declaration of Independence stated that "all men are created equal." Yet many Patriot leaders owned slaves. Even if the Patriots won their freedom from Britain, enslaved people knew that they probably would not win freedom from slavery.

Read now about the choice made by a 14-year-old boy named Samuel Abraham, who was held as a slave in Brooklyn, New York. Samuel, his friend Sana, and other slaves worked on the farm of a Loyalist named Isaac van Ditmas.

In the summer of 1776, General George Washington and the Continental army were forced to retreat from Brooklyn as the British approached. In the fighting that followed, Samuel chose to help the Patriots, carrying dozens of Patriots to safety in his boat. One of the people he helped was Major Mordecai Gist.

When I tied the boat to the dock below the Heights, Major Gist clapped his hands on my shoulders and looked me in the eyes. "Samuel," he said, "out in that creek you did more than many a free man for your country. I'd take it as a privilege if you'd consent to be my orderly and march beside me. And General Washington may need handy boatmen like you soon enough."

The next day it rained and rained. A thick sea fog covered the land. I looked everywhere for Sana. Many soldiers crowded into the camp, but they could tell me nothing. Alone and frightened, I mended the holes in my sail, pushing the big needle through the canvas, drawing it back again. Then, I heard voices nearby.

Major Gist stood there with an officer in a fine blue uniform. They asked me how deep the water was at this point between Brooklyn and Manhattan. They wanted to know if a British ship could sail between the two places. I told them that most ships could. Only the fog was keeping the British

men-of-war from trapping Washington's army on Long Island.

The officer in the blue uniform thanked me. He and Major Gist walked away, looking thoughtful.

The next day the heavy rains continued. I spread the sail over the boat and slept snug and dry. Then I heard the voice I missed more than any in the world calling, "Samuel, Samuel Abraham!" Sana had found me! It was not a dream. "You chose, Samuel," she said. "You did it right. You chose our new country." From under her cloak she took a hot, steaming loaf wrapped in a napkin—her freedom bread, the sweetest I ever tasted. While we ate, she told me that Toby and Nathaniel were safe.

But this new country was in danger. Major Gist came to me again and explained that every boat was needed to carry Washington's army from Brooklyn to Manhattan. The army had to retreat that night. I was going to help save the army with Farmer Isaac's boat. Wouldn't he be surprised?

On the night that General Washington's army left Brooklyn, the worst storm I'd ever seen blew

in from the Northeast. The wind howled. It drove the rain, stinging, into our eyes. It shook buildings and knocked down chimneys. And it whipped the water at Brooklyn Ferry into a sea of foam.

Down from the Heights in file marched Washington's army. The men entered the boats Major Gist and others had gathered at the ferry landing.

"What we need is a rope to cling to," someone said in the dark. "A rope stretching from here to Manhattan to guide us against the wind and current."

"There's rope here in the shipyard," a soldier

remembered. "Buoys to float the rope across, too. But who can cross this flood in the dark?"

"Can you do it, Samuel?" Major Gist asked. "Can you get across with the rope?"

"I can do it, Major," I shouted, the wind tearing the words out of my mouth. But I wasn't sure. Even if the rope were fed out from shore slowly, the sail might split or the rope might tear down the mast. But the British ships were sure to force their way between Brooklyn and Manhattan. I had to try.

When the rope was ready, I tied it to the foot of the mast. Sana jumped into the boat. I shouted at her to stay behind, but she wouldn't move. There was no time to lose. I shoved off into the swirling current.

My only hope was to let the shore current carry me out into midstream, and then, as the wind and tide thrust the boat toward the other shore, raise the sail and race for the Manhattan landing.

Fighting the rudder, I heard Sana's voice in my ear. "Will we make it, Samuel?" Water crashed over the side. Sana was bailing as fast as she could. "I can't swim, Samuel!" she cried into the wind. We were halfway across to Manhattan, and the boat was filling with sea. The gale was spinning us around. The rope was pulling us backward. I heaved at the sail, praying the mending wouldn't tear. Then, as the sail filled, the boom swung around with a crack, and we were darting forward at last.

On the Manhattan landing, by lantern

light, we could see people waiting. Over the roar of the storm, we heard them cheering us on. But Isaac's boat was sinking. The rope was tearing the mast out of the bottom. With a terrible crash, the mast broke and was carried over the side. A second later the bow smashed into the side of a wharf, and I found myself in the water swimming with one arm, clinging to Sana with the other.

We stumbled ashore on Manhattan Island, where kind people wrapped us in blankets. They were smiling—the rope was across! The boats full of Washington's soldiers would follow. We had done it, together.

All through the night Washington's men followed that rope, boat after boat, across the water. In the stormy darkness, every soldier escaped from Long Island.

And so the fight for freedom would go on. It would take many long years before we would beat the British king, but never again did I wonder what freedom was, or what it cost. It was people pulling together. It was strong hands helping. It was one person caring about another.

And where was Washington? Many times that night Sana and I hoped to see him.

"Why, Samuel," Major Gist told us later, "he was that officer in the blue coat who asked you how deep the water was between Brooklyn and Manhattan. Last night the general arrested a farmer in Brooklyn for helping the British. That farmer, Isaac van Ditmas, turned all of his property over to the Army of the Continental Congress in exchange for his freedom. It seems now that you and Sana have no master."

From that day forward, we and Isaac's other slaves were to be citizens of a new nation.

LITERATURE REVIEW

1 How did Samuel help the Continental army?

2 Why do you think Samuel chose to help the Patriots?

3 Write a conversation that could have taken place as Samuel and other slaves on Isaac's farm decided what to do when they learned they no longer had a master.

FOCUS

How do people meet difficult challenges today?

Main Idea As you read, look for ways the colonists met the challenges of their war for independence.

Vocabulary

siege

treaty

negotiate

The American flag in 1777 is shown above. The Badge of Merit (below) was designed by George Washington and given to soldiers who showed special bravery. Today this award is known as the Purple Heart.

Victory and Independence

| 1775 | 1780 | 1785 |

After General Washington's retreat following the Battle of Long Island, Continental troops moved into New Jersey. There they won important battles at Trenton and Princeton. But victory was still far from certain. In December 1777 Washington set up headquarters at Valley Forge, Pennsylvania, near Philadelphia. That winter his ragged army was almost destroyed by cold and hunger. By Washington's own count, 2,898 of his men had no boots. Many were ill, and many died. The Patriots had declared their independence, but would their army be strong enough to win it?

Help for the Continental Army

The Patriots got some help from soldiers of other countries. Among them were two Polish officers, Casimir Pulaski (puh•LAS•kee) and Thaddeus Kosciuszko (kawsh•CHUSH•koh). Later Kosciuszko returned to Poland to lead a revolution there. Among others who came from Europe were the German soldiers Johann de Kalb and Friedrich von Steuben (vahn SHTOY•buhn). The Marquis de Lafayette (lah•fee•ET), a 20-year-old French noble, also came to fight along with the Americans.

At Valley Forge during the winter of 1777, von Steuben reported to Washington and took on the job of drilling the Continental army so that the soldiers would be ready to move quickly. By the spring of 1778 the soldiers had been trained and were marching well.

In the meantime, the Continental Congress had sent Benjamin Franklin to Paris to ask the French to join the war.

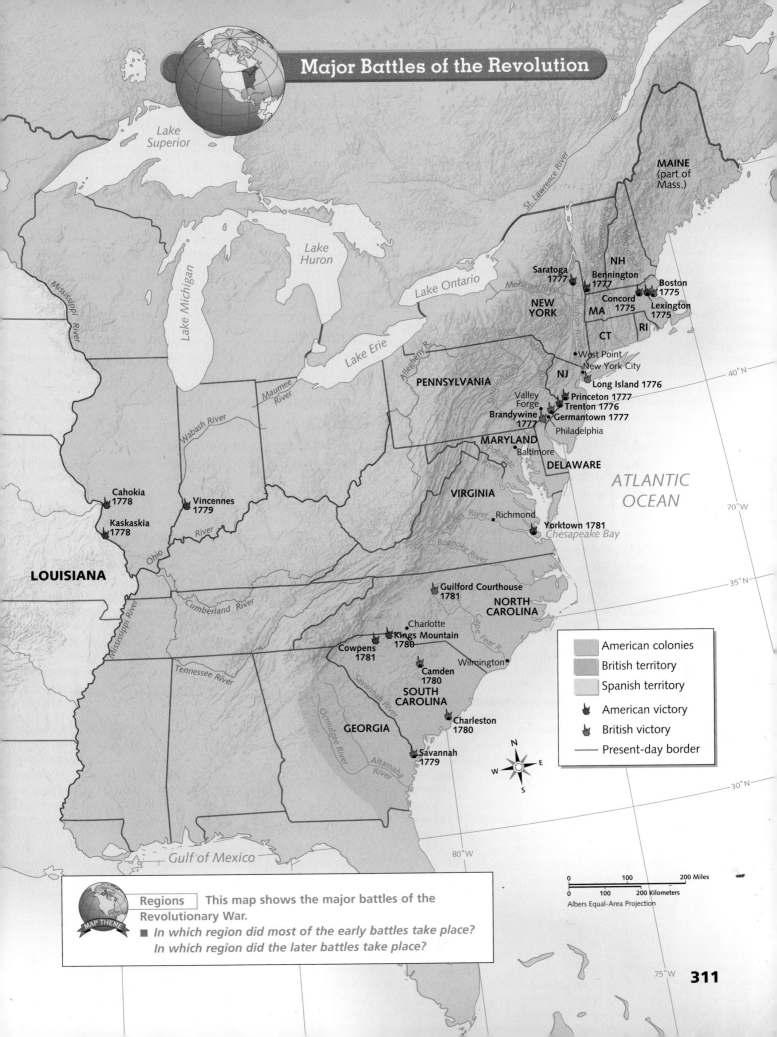

Major Battles of the Revolution

Lake Superior

Lake Huron

Lake Michigan

Lake Ontario

Lake Erie

MAINE
(part of
Mass.)

St. Lawrence River

Mohawk River

Saratoga
1777

NH

Bennington
1777

Boston
1775

Concord
1775

Lexington
1775

NEW
YORK

MA

CT

RI

Hudson River

West Point

New York City

Allegheny R.

PENNSYLVANIA

Susquehanna River

Delaware River

NJ

Long Island 1776

Princeton 1777

Valley
Forge

Trenton 1776

Brandywine
1777

Germantown 1777

Philadelphia

Maumee River

Wabash River

MARYLAND

Potomac River

Baltimore

DELAWARE

ATLANTIC
OCEAN

Cahokia
1778

Vincennes
1779

VIRGINIA

Richmond

Kaskaskia
1778

Ohio River

Mississippi River

James River

Yorktown 1781

Chesapeake Bay

LOUISIANA

Cumberland River

Roanoke River

Guilford Courthouse
1781

NORTH
CAROLINA

Tennessee River

Charlotte

Kings Mountain
1780

Cape Fear R.

Cowpens
1781

Wilmington

Camden
1780

Savannah River

SOUTH
CAROLINA

Charleston
1780

GEORGIA

Ocmulgee River

Altamaha River

Savannah
1779

N
W   E
S

Gulf of Mexico

40° N

70° W

35° N

30° N

80° W

75° W

Legend:
- American colonies
- British territory
- Spanish territory
- American victory
- British victory
- Present-day border

200 Miles
0   100   200 Kilometers
0   100
Albers Equal-Area Projection

Regions   This map shows the major battles of the
Revolutionary War.

■ *In which region did most of the early battles take place?
In which region did the later battles take place?*

The French were eager to see the American colonies win the war and weaken their longtime enemy, the British. But the French felt that the colonists did not have much of a chance of winning.

Franklin talked with the French leaders for months. Then came news of the colonists' great victory at Saratoga in New York. More than 5,000 British soldiers under General John Burgoyne (buhr•GOYN) had moved south from Canada, hoping to cut the colonies in two. Instead, on October 17, 1777, the British lost to American soldiers led by General Horatio Gates, commander of the Continental army in New York.

The colonists' victory at Saratoga showed the French that the colonists stood a chance of winning the war. The French sent guns, ships, and soldiers. With the help of the French, the Continental soldiers fought more battles, including the siege of Savannah in 1779. A **siege** is a long-lasting attack. At the siege of Savannah, more than 800 Haitians, 80 of them slaves, fought alongside the French and Continental soldiers. Haiti was a French colony in the Caribbean.

After the victory at Saratoga, other countries helped the colonists, too. In 1779 Bernardo de Gálvez (GAHL•ves), the Spanish governor of Louisiana, sent guns, food, and money to the Patriots. Later he led his own soldiers in capturing British forts in what are now the states of Mississippi, Alabama, and Florida. Spanish-born Jorge Farragut (HAWR•hay FAIR•uh•guht) fought in the Continental army and also the navy.

REVIEW *Why did the French decide to help the Patriots in their war for independence?*

General Friedrich von Steuben helped train Continental soldiers at Valley Forge. After learning how to march and move together on the battlefield, soldiers were able to attack and retreat faster.

Francis Marion, known as the Swamp Fox, led Continental soldiers through southern swamps as they defended the South against the British.

American Heroes

During the war the Patriots cheered news of the deeds of many brave military leaders. Their acts of courage helped convince Americans that they could win the war.

John Paul Jones, a navy commander, battled larger and better-equipped British ships. In one famous battle in the North Sea near England, the British demanded Jones's surrender. He replied, "I have not yet begun to fight." This has become a famous Navy saying in the United States.

In New York City, General Washington asked a young man named Nathan Hale to spy on the British. Hale dressed as a Dutch schoolteacher and obtained the information the general needed. As he returned to the American side, however, the British captured him. According to tradition, Hale told the British soldiers before they executed him, "I only regret that I have but one life to lose for my country."

In the mountains of the Northeast, Ethan Allen led the Green Mountain Boys. Allen and his soldiers from what is now Vermont won one of the first American victories in the war. In capturing Fort Ticonderoga, Allen is said to have demanded that the British surrender "in the name of the great Jehovah [God] and the Continental Congress."

In the Ohio River valley, George Rogers Clark helped protect the frontier claimed by many American settlers. He said, "If a country is not worth protecting, it is not worth claiming." Leading a small army, he marched through the West, defending settlers from attacks by the British and their Indian allies.

From bases in the swamps of South Carolina, Francis Marion led daring lightning-quick raids against the British. They called Marion the Swamp Fox because they could never catch him and his men.

Thousands of soldiers fought on the American side in the Revolution. They did so with courage and skill. "We fight, get beat, rise, and fight again," General Nathanael Greene wrote. General Greene commanded the Continental army in the southern colonies.

REVIEW *Name five Patriot military leaders other than General Washington.*

Victory at Yorktown

When the British government learned that the French were helping the Americans, British army leaders moved their attack from the northern colonies to the southern. The British hoped that the greater Loyalist support in the South would help defeat the Patriots once and for all. With the help of Loyalists, the British army captured Charleston, South Carolina, in 1780.

Pushing north from South Carolina, the British then charged through North Carolina and into Virginia.

During 1781 the fighting centered in Virginia. For several weeks Benedict Arnold, a former Continental army officer, attacked colonial towns in Virginia for the British. Arnold was a traitor—he acted against his country. Earlier, he had given the British the plans to the American fort at West Point, New York, in exchange for money and a high rank in the British army.

LEARNING FROM DIAGRAMS The American and French troops surround the British at Yorktown.
- ❶ French soldiers
- ❷ British soldiers
- ❸ American soldiers
- ❹ French navy
- ❺ Chesapeake Bay

■ *Why were the British at a disadvantage in the Battle of Yorktown?*

Battle of Yorktown

By late summer of 1781, British General Charles Cornwallis had set up at Yorktown, a small Virginia town on Chesapeake Bay, where it was easy for British ships to land supplies. The French and the Continentals moved quickly to defeat the British at Yorktown. The French soldiers joined the Continentals near New York City, and together the two armies marched to Virginia and surrounded Yorktown. At the same time, the French navy took control of Chesapeake Bay. Now the British navy could not get supplies to the British army at Yorktown. The British army was trapped.

In late September Cornwallis sent word to his commander in the North. "If you cannot relieve me very soon," he said, "you must be prepared to hear the worst."

The worst happened. Surrounded and under siege for two weeks from both land and sea, Cornwallis had to give up. A person who was there wrote, "At two o'clock in the evening Oct. 19th, 1781, the British army, led by General O'Hara,

In John Trumbull's painting (right) of the surrender at Yorktown, American General Benjamin Lincoln (center, on the white horse) receives the surrender from an aide to British General Cornwallis. George Washington is in front of the American flag.

marched out of its lines, with colors cased [flags folded] and drums beating a British march." When the French and American soldiers heard the drums, they stopped their fire. The British and Hessian soldiers then marched out of Yorktown and laid down their weapons in a field.

Though fighting dragged on in some places for more than two years, it was clear that victory had been decided at Yorktown in 1781. The Patriots had won after a long and hard fight.

REVIEW *How did the French help the Americans win the Battle of Yorktown?*

The Treaty of Paris

The Battle of Yorktown did not end the Revolutionary War. The Treaty of Paris did that. A **treaty** is an agreement between countries.

Work on the treaty began in April 1782 when the British sent Richard Oswald, a wealthy merchant, to Paris to talk with Benjamin Franklin. Franklin gave Oswald the American terms—that is, what the Americans wanted in the treaty. One of the terms was that the British monarch and Parliament had to accept American independence and remove British soldiers from American soil. Franklin told Oswald that Americans might feel better toward the British if Parliament paid those whose towns had been destroyed in the war.

In return, the British asked that Loyalists who chose to remain in the United States be treated fairly. Many Loyalists had fled to Nova Scotia and other parts of Canada, and to the Bahamas. Those who returned to Britain were sorry they did. Most could not find jobs and soon became very poor. Instead of being grateful for their support, the British government ignored them.

The British and Americans **negotiated**, or talked with one another to work out an agreement. After more than a year of such talks, the Treaty of Paris was signed by British and American representatives on September 3, 1783.

The Treaty of Paris named the United States of America as a new nation and described its borders. The United States would reach to Florida on the south. The northern border would be an imaginary line

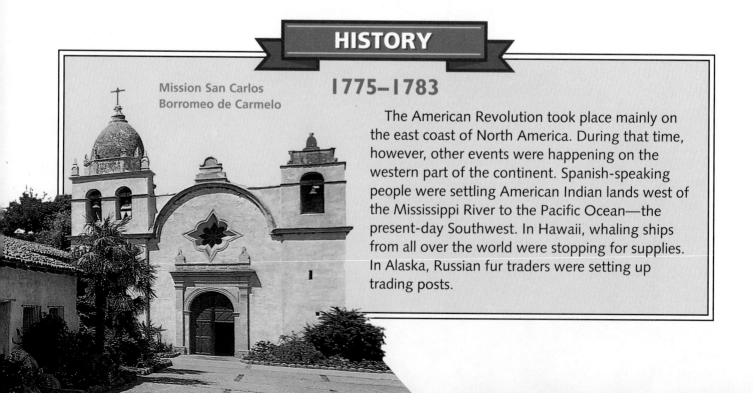

HISTORY

Mission San Carlos Borromeo de Carmelo

1775–1783

The American Revolution took place mainly on the east coast of North America. During that time, however, other events were happening on the western part of the continent. Spanish-speaking people were settling American Indian lands west of the Mississippi River to the Pacific Ocean—the present-day Southwest. In Hawaii, whaling ships from all over the world were stopping for supplies. In Alaska, Russian fur traders were setting up trading posts.

through the Great Lakes. The Mississippi River formed the western border. The fact that much of the land between the Appalachian Mountains and the Mississippi River was the home of many different American Indian tribes was of little or no interest to the leaders who signed the treaty.

The Treaty of Paris was just as much a victory as winning at Yorktown had been. Independence was now a fact. But the Americans faced many problems. They had formed a new country, yet the 3 million people in the 13 new states were far from united.

REVIEW *What were the effects of the Treaty of Paris?*

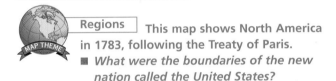

Regions This map shows North America in 1783, following the Treaty of Paris.
■ *What were the boundaries of the new nation called the United States?*

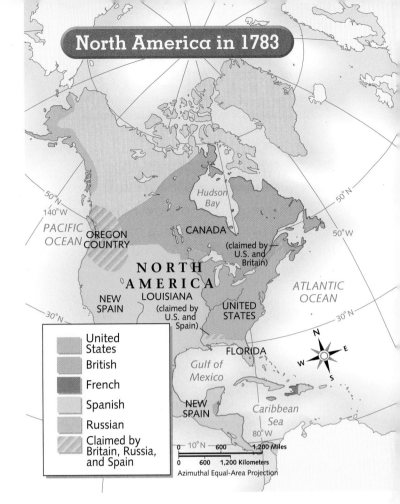

North America in 1783

United States
British
French
Spanish
Russian
Claimed by Britain, Russia, and Spain

PACIFIC OCEAN
OREGON COUNTRY
CANADA (claimed by U.S. and Britain)
NORTH AMERICA
NEW SPAIN
LOUISIANA (claimed by U.S. and Spain)
UNITED STATES
ATLANTIC OCEAN
FLORIDA
Gulf of Mexico
NEW SPAIN
Caribbean Sea
Hudson Bay

0   600   1,200 Miles
0   600   1,200 Kilometers
Azimuthal Equal-Area Projection

LESSON 5 REVIEW

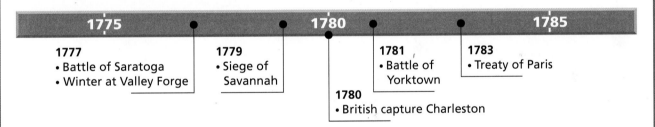

1775   1780   1785

1777
• Battle of Saratoga
• Winter at Valley Forge

1779
• Siege of Savannah

1780
• British capture Charleston

1781
• Battle of Yorktown

1783
• Treaty of Paris

Check Understanding

1 **Remember the Facts** How was help from Europeans important to the colonists in winning the war?

2 **Recall the Main Idea** How did the colonists meet the challenges of their war for independence?

Think Critically

3 **Think More About It** Why do you think the colonists did not give up when it looked as if they would not win the war?

4 **Past to Present** What can Americans today learn from the Patriots?

Show What You Know

Music Activity Think about the pride the colonists must have felt when they heard the news that the Americans had won the war. Then write a patriotic song about one of the key events, people, or places from the American Revolution. Use a familiar melody to sing your song as you share it with your classmates.

1775

1775
• Second Continental Congress

1776
• The Declaration of Independence

1777
• Battle of Saratoga
• Winter at Valley Forge

CONNECT MAIN IDEAS

Use this organizer to show how the chapter's main ideas are connected. Write the main idea of each lesson. A copy of the organizer may be found on page 57 of the Activity Book.

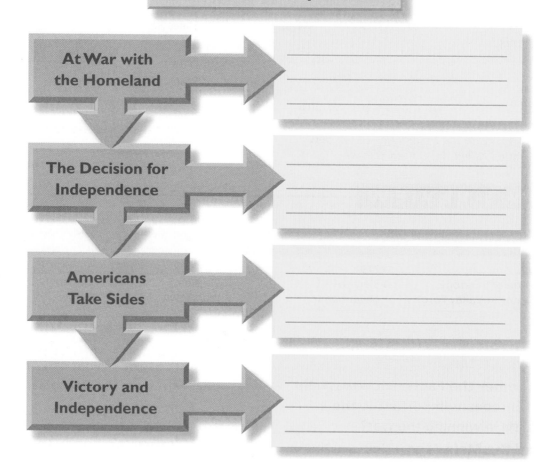

The War for Independence

At War with the Homeland

The Decision for Independence

Americans Take Sides

Victory and Independence

WRITE MORE ABOUT IT

Write a Pamphlet Take the role of a Loyalist or a Patriot. Write a short pamphlet that explains your point of view about British rule. Explain why you have chosen your side.

Write a Newspaper Article Imagine that you are a reporter who witnessed the British surrender at Yorktown. Write a newspaper article describing what you saw.

USE VOCABULARY

Use each term in a sentence that helps explain its meaning.

1. allegiance
2. declaration
3. enlist
4. grievance
5. negotiate
6. neutral
7. olive branch
8. pacifist

CHECK UNDERSTANDING

9. How did the Second Continental Congress try to make peace with Britain?

10. What did the Declaration of Independence tell the world?

11. How did people who did not fight in the war show their support for independence?

12. How was help from other countries important to the American victory?

13. What was the important result of the Battle of Saratoga?

14. Put these events in the proper order: the Treaty of Paris, the Declaration of Independence, Valley Forge, the Battle of Bunker Hill, and the Battle of Yorktown.

THINK CRITICALLY

15. **Think More About It** Many leaders of the Revolution, such as George Washington and Thomas Jefferson, were successful and wealthy. Why would they risk everything they had to take part in a revolution?

16. **Cause and Effect** How did the military training of Continental soldiers affect the war?

17. **Personally Speaking** Imagine that you are a delegate to the Second Continental Congress. Do you think you would sign the Declaration of Independence? Explain your answer.

18. **Past to Present** How do American citizens today let their government know about their grievances?

APPLY SKILLS

Read a Political Cartoon Look through newspapers and magazines for a political cartoon about a subject that interests you. Cut out the cartoon and paste it to a sheet of paper. Below the cartoon, write a brief paragraph that explains its meaning.

Learn from Pictures Look for a photograph or painting that you like. You can use books, magazines, or newspapers to find a picture. Describe what you learn from looking at the picture and what feelings or ideas the artist is trying to share.

READ MORE ABOUT IT

If You Were There in 1776 by Barbara Brenner. Macmillan. This book tells about how daily life during the late eighteenth century shaped the ideas in the Declaration of Independence.

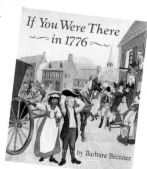

If You Were There in 1776
by Barbara Brenner

HARCOURT BRACE

Visit the Internet at
http://www.hbschool.com
for additional resources.

Tiananmen

In 1776 the American Patriots struggled for freedom. Today people in some parts of the world are doing the same. In April 1989, college students in China wanted their country to be more like a democracy. The college students gathered at Tiananmen (TYAHN•AHN•MEN) Square in the center of Beijing (BAY•JING), the capital city, to express their views.

Thousands of people, young and old, came to the square every day to show their support for the students. One group made its own Statue of Liberty out of plastic foam. Other people made posters. One poster quoted the Declaration of Independence, calling for "life, liberty and the pursuit of happiness" for all Chinese people. Another recalled Patrick Henry's famous words, "give me liberty or give me death."

The demonstration in Tiananmen Square ended violently on June 4, 1989. That

morning, hundreds of Chinese soldiers poured into the square, killing many of the demonstrators.

Shen Tong, a Beijing University student speaking at an Independence Day celebration in Boston on July 4, 1989, compared the Tiananmen Square massacre with the Boston Massacre. "People died," Shen said of the Boston Massacre, "but it sparked the American struggle for independence. I do not believe that the Tiananmen Square massacre was the end of the democracy movement in China. It was the beginning." Today many people in China continue the struggle for freedom.

Beijing

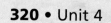

Square

Think and Apply

Think about what happened at Tiananmen Square. Find examples of people struggling today for freedom or independence. Select the example that interests you the most. Use a Venn diagram to compare and contrast the present-day struggles and events with those of the American Revolution. Share your findings with a classmate.

HARCOURT BRACE

Visit the Internet at **http://www.hbschool.com** for additional resources.

CNN
Turner Le@rning

Check your media center or classroom video library for the Making Social Studies Relevant videotape of this feature.

VISUAL SUMMARY

Summarize the Main Ideas
Study the pictures and captions shown in this visual summary to help you review Unit 4.

Show More of the Story
Draw pictures and write captions that describe more about the American Revolution. Label the pictures, and tell where they should go on the visual summary.

1 The colonists were forced to pay taxes to Britain. They especially hated the tax law called the Stamp Act.

4 Minutemen faced British soldiers at Lexington and Concord in April 1775. This was the start of the War for Independence.

6 Support from the colonists helped the soldiers in the Continental army face many hardships.

3 Paul Revere and William Dawes went on a night ride to warn of approaching British soldiers.

2 At the Boston Tea Party, colonists dumped tea from British ships into Boston Harbor.

5 On July 4, 1776, the Declaration of Independence was approved by members of the Continental Congress.

7 The American victory at Yorktown forced the British to surrender. In 1783 the Treaty of Paris named the United States as a new nation.

USE VOCABULARY

Write the term that matches each definition.

| Continental | tax |
| self-government | treaty |

1. making one's own laws
2. money paid to a government for running it
3. an agreement between countries
4. a soldier in George Washington's army

CHECK UNDERSTANDING

5. What actions by the British king angered the colonists?

6. Why did some enslaved Africans join the British side, while others fought on the side of the colonies?

7. How did the actions of Thomas Paine, Crispus Attucks, and Paul Revere affect the outcome of the American Revolution?

8. What battle made the French believe the colonists could really defeat the British?

THINK CRITICALLY

9. **Past to Present** What does the Declaration of Independence mean to Americans today?

10. **Explore Viewpoints** People in the British colonies were divided in their views about self-government and independence. What were these different views? Why did people hold them?

11. **Personally Speaking** What person who took part in the American Revolution do you admire most? Why?

APPLY SKILLS

Use a Historical Map The Treaty of Paris described the borders of the new country. However, there remained disputes over land between former colonies and between the United States and Britain. Use the map below to answer the questions.

12. What year does this map show?

13. How are disputed lands shown on the map?

14. Which two former colonies claimed the same land in 1784?

15. Describe the location of the land claimed by both the United States and Britain.

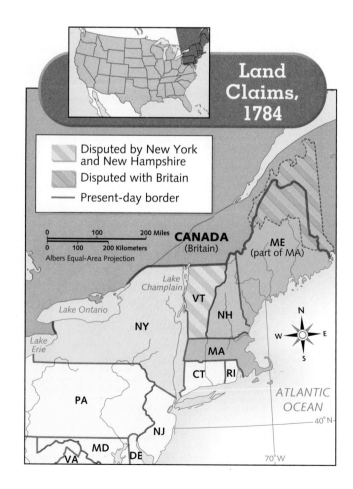

Land Claims, 1784

Disputed by New York and New Hampshire
Disputed with Britain
Present-day border

0 100 200 Miles
0 100 200 Kilometers
Albers Equal-Area Projection

CANADA (Britain)
ME (part of MA)
Lake Champlain
VT
Lake Ontario
NH
NY
Lake Erie
MA
CT RI
ATLANTIC OCEAN
40°N
PA
NJ
MD
DE
VA
70°W

N W E S

REMEMBER

- Share your ideas.
- Cooperate with others to plan your work.
- Take responsibility for your work.
- Help one another.
- Show your group's work to the class.
- Discuss what you learned by working together.

ACTIVITY Present a
Dramatic Reading

After the Declaration of Independence was signed in 1776, copies of it were sent to all the colonies. In many towns the Declaration was read aloud at public meetings. The readers showed the importance of the document by adding drama to their reading. Your class should work in four groups, each responsible for preparing a dramatic reading of one part of the Declaration of Independence. Each group member should help read his or her group's part.

ACTIVITY Make a
Time Line

Work with three or four classmates. Make a time line showing the important events of the American Revolution. Begin with the Stamp Act, and end with the signing of the Treaty of Paris. Be sure to label the date of each key event on the time line.

ACTIVITY Make a
Model

Imagine that you are taking part in a Fourth of July celebration. With three or four of your classmates, build a model for a parade float that shows an important event of the American Revolution. Display your model in the classroom.

Unit Project Wrap-Up

Create a Book Work with classmates to finish the Unit Project that was described on page 257. Choose a few items from your lists to include in a book about the American Revolution. Then write a description of each item. Work together to illustrate your book with either drawings or pictures cut out of magazines. Write captions describing the illustrations, and give your book a title. Invite students from other classes for a reading.

THE NEW NATION

When the American people won their independence from Britain, they had to decide what kind of government they should form. Should the former colonies have a single government? Should the colonies become 13 separate states with no central government? One thing was certain. The newly independent country had to give its people some authority over the new government.

◄ *Signing the Constitution*, a painting by Howard Chandler Christy

UNIT THEMES

- Conflict and Cooperation

- Individualism and Interdependence

Unit Project

Draw a Poster Complete this project as you study Unit 5. As you read, write a list of details about each event described in the unit. Choose one of the events to illustrate on a poster. Use your list to remind you of details you may add to your drawing. Give your poster a title, and share it with your classmates.

CANADA

ROCKY MOUNTAINS

GREAT PLAINS

OREGON COUNTRY

Columbia River

Snake River

Missouri

Platte River

PACIFIC OCEAN

GREAT BASIN

LOUISIANA

Colorado River

Arkansas

River

San Francisco ○

Mojave Desert

NEW SPAIN

● Santa Fe

Los Angeles ●

San Diego ●

El Paso del Norte ●

Rio Grande

San Antonio ●

Laredo ●

United States

British

Spanish

Claimed by Britain, Spain and Russia

● City or settlement

1786   1788

JAN. 1787
Shays's Rebellion

PAGE 334

MAY 1787
Delegates Meet in Philadelphia
PAGE 339

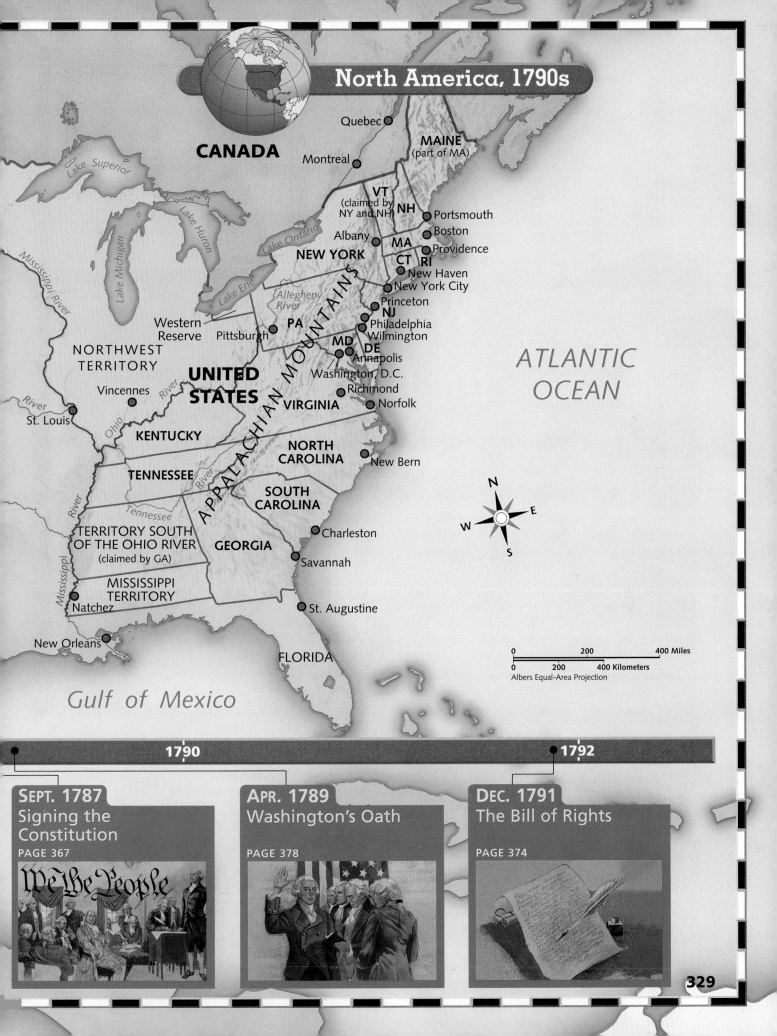

North America, 1790s

CANADA

Quebec

Montreal

MAINE
(part of MA)

Lake Superior

Lake Michigan

Lake Huron

Lake Ontario

Lake Erie

VT
(claimed by
NY and NH)

NH

Portsmouth

Boston

Albany

MA

Providence

NEW YORK

CT

RI

New Haven

Allegheny
River

New York City

Princeton

NJ

Mississippi River

Western
Reserve

PA

Philadelphia

Pittsburgh

Wilmington

MD

DE

APPALACHIAN MOUNTAINS

NORTHWEST
TERRITORY

Annapolis

Washington, D.C.

UNITED
STATES

Richmond

Vincennes

Ohio River

VIRGINIA

Norfolk

ATLANTIC
OCEAN

St. Louis

KENTUCKY

TENNESSEE

River

Tennessee River

NORTH
CAROLINA

New Bern

N

SOUTH
CAROLINA

W E

TERRITORY SOUTH
OF THE OHIO RIVER
(claimed by GA)

GEORGIA

Charleston

S

Savannah

Mississippi

MISSISSIPPI
TERRITORY

Natchez

St. Augustine

New Orleans

FLORIDA

0   200   400 Miles

0   200   400 Kilometers

Albers Equal-Area Projection

Gulf of Mexico

1790   **1792**

SEPT. 1787
Signing the
Constitution
PAGE 367

APR. 1789
Washington's Oath
PAGE 378

DEC. 1791
The Bill of Rights
PAGE 374

We the People

Shh!

We're Writing
the Constitution

by Jean Fritz
pictures by Tomie dePaola

The job of turning the 13 former British colonies into a single country was not easy. The biggest problem was getting people to think of themselves as citizens of a new country—the United States of America. Until this time most people thought of themselves as citizens of their states rather than of one country.

After the Revolutionary War most people in America were glad that they were no longer British. Still, they were not ready to call themselves Americans. The last thing they wanted was to become a nation. They were citizens of their own separate states, just as they had always been: each state different, each state proud of its own character, each state quick to poke fun at other states. To Southerners, New Englanders might be

"no-account Yankees." To New Englanders, Pennsylvanians might be "lousy Buckskins." But to everyone the states themselves were all important. "Sovereign states," they called them. They loved the sound of "sovereign" because it meant that they were their own bosses.

George Washington, however, scoffed at the idea of "sovereign states." He knew that the states could not be truly independent for long and survive. Ever since the Declaration of Independence had been signed, people had referred to the country as the United States of America. It was about time, he thought, for them to act and feel united.

Once during the war Washington had decided it would be a good idea if his troops swore allegiance to the United States. As a start, he lined up some troops from New Jersey and asked them to take such an oath. They looked at Washington as if he'd taken leave of his senses. How could they do that? they cried. New Jersey was their country!

So Washington dropped the idea. In time, he hoped, the states would see that they needed to become one nation, united under a strong central government.

But that time would be long in coming.

9 CONSTITUTION

"In the new code of laws, which I suppose it will be necessary for you to make, I desire you would remember the ladies, and be more generous and favorable to them than [were] your ancestors."

Abigail Adams,
in a letter to her
husband, John,
March 31, 1776

The Articles of Confederation

1780   1784   1788

LESSON 1

FOCUS
What problems might be caused by a weak government?

Main Idea
As you read, look for problems that were caused by the weaknesses of the United States government under the Articles of Confederation.

Vocabulary
constitution   territory
republic   township
ambassador   ordinance
inflation

Before the war with Britain had ended, the Continental Congress decided to set up a national government for the 13 former colonies. The newly independent states had already started to write their own **constitutions**, or plans of government. But leaders believed that the country also needed a national government with its own constitution. Then all 13 states could act together as one nation.

"A Firm League of Friendship"

Most people did not want a powerful national government for the country. After all, they had just fought a war to get rid of one. They were afraid that a strong national government would make laws for their states just as the British king and Parliament had made laws for the colonies. Now that they had finally won their independence, they did not want to give it away to a national government.

In 1781 the states accepted the plan for a central government approved by the Continental Congress. The plan, written mostly by representative John Dickinson, united the states in a confederation. The confederation would be something like the Iroquois League, which brought together different Indian tribes. The Confederation of the United States of America would bring together 13 independent states in "a firm league of friendship." This first plan of government for the new country was called the Articles of Confederation.

Some people thought that a single leader, such as George Washington, should run the country. Instead, the Articles of Confederation created a

John Dickinson headed the committee that wrote the first draft of the Articles of Confederation.

333

republic, a form of government in which people elect representatives to run the country. Under the Articles, voters of each state elected leaders who, in turn, chose representatives. These representatives met in a Congress, or national legislature. Each state, no matter what size or population, could send up to 7 delegates to Congress. Each state, however, had only one vote. Congress could do only certain things. Most important, it could declare war, make treaties, and settle serious disagreements between states.

For Congress to make a law or decide on important questions, at least 9 of the 13 states had to agree. However, the states seldom agreed on anything. Each wanted its own way. No state wanted to be under the control of the other states.

No state wanted to be under the rule of one person, either. That is why the Articles did not allow a single leader to control the government. The states were afraid of giving one person too much authority. That person might become like a monarch. So a committee of representatives kept the government running when Congress was not meeting. This committee was made up of one representative from each state.

The Articles also did not plan for a national court system. Congress acted as a court for settling disagreements between states. But most often the states did not obey Congress anyway. People who had disagreements with their state governments had no national court where they could settle their differences.

REVIEW *What could Congress do under the Articles of Confederation?*

Problems from the Start

Under the Articles of Confederation, the national government did not work well. It was, as George Washington called it, "a half-starved, limping government."

Often there were not enough representatives present to allow Congress to meet. Even when there were, the legislature had no place of its own to hold meetings. Congress met sometimes in Philadelphia and sometimes in Annapolis, Maryland. It also met in Princeton or in Trenton, New Jersey. Most Americans did not know where or when Congress was meeting. Foreign **ambassadors**, representatives from one country to another, did not know either. When the first Dutch ambassador arrived in the United States, he spent ten days looking for Congress. He finally found it in Princeton, where it had been chased by soldiers demanding their pay for fighting in the Revolutionary War.

Even when Congress met, however, it could do only what the Articles of Confederation allowed. The Articles did not allow Congress to raise a national army without the states' permission. State leaders were afraid the national government would use such an army to make them obey national laws. This rule let the states keep their authority, but it also meant there would be no army to defend the nation if Spanish troops

This staff was used to list the members of the League of the Haudenosaunee, a confederation of five Iroquois tribes. The pegs in the staff stood for each tribe's representatives. How was the early government of the United States like the Iroquois League?

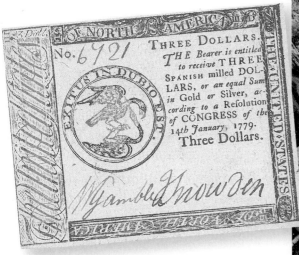

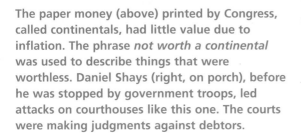

The paper money (above) printed by Congress, called continentals, had little value due to inflation. The phrase *not worth a continental* was used to describe things that were worthless. Daniel Shays (right, on porch), before he was stopped by government troops, led attacks on courthouses like this one. The courts were making judgments against debtors.

should attack from Florida or British troops should attack from Canada.

The Articles did not allow Congress to make laws about trade or about taxes. To get the money needed to run the national government, Congress had to ask each state to pay its share. But Congress did not have the authority to make the states pay what they owed. For three years Congress did not even have enough money to pay its members!

Congress did have the authority to print and to coin money. But when it tried to pay its debts from the war, it printed too much and caused terrible inflation. When there is **inflation**, more and more money is needed to buy the same goods. During this time, for example, goods that used to cost two cents would cost twenty dollars.

Many people, such as soldiers who had not been paid, soon had money problems.

Most of these people were farmers. They already had to pay state taxes—taxes they thought were too high. But they also had to buy tools and seeds for planting. Many had to go into debt or borrow money. Some states made debtors pay back what they owed right away. If they did not, the state could take away their land or send them to prison. Many farmers protested to their state governments. Some protests, such as Shays's Rebellion, became violent.

In the fall of 1786, Daniel Shays, a former captain in the Continental army, and about 1,200 other poor farmers joined to show their anger toward their state, Massachusetts. In January 1787 they attacked a building used for storing weapons in the western part of the state. The weapons belonged to the national government, not to Massachusetts, but Shays and the protesters did not care. "That crowd [the members of Congress] is too weak to act!" said Shays. But the governor of Massachusetts was not. He called out the state militia to end the rebellion. Four protesters died in the fighting.

Shays's Rebellion was quickly put down, but it showed that people were not happy with their government. Under the Articles of Confederation, Congress could do little to help them. Congress did not even have the money or the authority to defend national property—like the weapons in western Massachusetts. Many people feared that unrest would spread to other states.

REVIEW *What problems did people face under the Articles of Confederation?*

The Western Lands

Under the Articles of Confederation, Congress did make some important decisions on how to divide and govern the country's western lands. These lands stretched from the Appalachian Mountains to the Mississippi River.

After the French and Indian War, Britain had refused to allow new settlement west of the Proclamation Line of 1763, near the Appalachian Mountains. This land was reserved for the Indians. Once the new United States was independent, however, it opened the frontier to settlement. Settlers

Regions This map shows the system used to divide the Northwest Territory into townships and sections.

■ *In what ways do you think this system could be useful?*

The Northwest Territory, 1785

0   100   200 Miles
0   100   200 Kilometers
Albers Equal-Area Projection

CANADA (Britain)

Lake Superior
Lake Huron
Lake Michigan
Lake Ontario
Lake Erie

MINNESOTA
WISCONSIN
MICHIGAN
IOWA
ILLINOIS
INDIANA
OHIO
MISSOURI
KENTUCKY
WEST VIRGINIA
VIRGINIA
PENNSYLVANIA
NEW YORK
NJ
MD
DE

Mississippi River
Missouri River
Ohio River

ATLANTIC OCEAN

Northwest Territory
Present-day border
Present-day names of states are used.

Sections in One Township

36	30	24	18	12	6
35	29	23	17	11	5
34	28	22	16	10	4
33	27	21	15	9	3
32	26	20	14	8	2
31	25	19	13	7	1

1 mile
6 miles

N W E S

poured into the Ohio River valley. The land north of the river was called the Northwest Territory. A **territory** is land that belongs to a national government but is not a state.

In 1785 Congress set up a system to survey, or measure, the western lands. The land was divided into squares called **townships**. Each side of a township measured 6 miles (9.7 km). Each township, in turn, was divided into 36 squares, or sections. This system of surveying by townships and sections can still be seen in parts of the United States.

In 1787 Congress passed the Northwest Ordinance. The **ordinance**, or set of laws, established governments in the Northwest Territory and described the steps by which

George Washington was once a surveyor. He owned this bronze compass.

new states would be formed from the lands. The Northwest Ordinance also had other provisions. It did not allow people to keep slaves in the Northwest Territory. It said that Native Americans should be treated fairly. And it encouraged townships to help build schools.

The Northwest Ordinance was a good plan for the growth of the United States. It showed what could be done when members of Congress worked together. But since this did not happen often, many people thought that Congress was not important.

REVIEW *What did the Northwest Ordinance accomplish?*

LESSON I REVIEW

1780	1784	1788

1781
• The Articles of Confederation are approved

1787
• Shays's Rebellion
• The Northwest Ordinance is passed

Check Understanding

1 **Remember the Facts** What was the first plan for governing the 13 states after the Revolutionary War?

2 **Recall the Main Idea** What problems were caused by the weaknesses of the United States government under the Articles of Confederation?

Think Critically

3 **Think More About It** Why were the former colonists afraid of a strong national government?

4 **Explore Viewpoints** What do you think the Indians living in the western lands would have said about the Northwest Ordinance? Explain your answer.

Show What You Know

Speech Activity With a partner, plan a speech explaining how the 13 former colonies could solve the problems of the Articles of Confederation. Take turns delivering the speech to the class.

FOCUS

How can people cooperate to make changes in their nation?

Main Idea Read to learn how American leaders worked together to change the government of the United States.

Vocabulary

convention
delegate
Preamble

A New Plan of Government

| 1785 | 1786 | 1787 | 1788 |

Just after the Revolutionary War, the former colonists had been afraid of a national government that was too strong. Now the people had a government that was too weak to work well. The confederation was really 13 separate and independent states rather than one nation. The country was not really united. The British, in fact, called it the "Disunited States."

"A Rope of Sand"

James Madison was a member of Congress under the Articles of Confederation. In 1779 Madison had been elected to represent Virginia. Jemmy, as his friends called him, was 29 years old and the youngest member of Congress. He was to spend most of his life in public service.

Madison became a student of government. He read everything he could find about early and more recent ways of governing.

Madison was worried about the weaknesses of the Articles of Confederation. Congress had little authority over the states. Madison said he was afraid that Congress had become "a rope of sand."

Such leaders as George Washington, Thomas Jefferson, and John Adams agreed with Madison. Once, while traveling in Britain, John Adams had been asked, "Do you represent one nation or thirteen?" Madison and the other leaders began to argue for a stronger national government. Only a strong national government could keep the confederation from breaking apart, Madison said.

This United States flag was made in 1781. How is today's flag different?

James Madison (above) and Alexander Hamilton (right) called a meeting to give the states a chance to discuss their problems.

Others did not agree. Patrick Henry of Virginia was one of many who supported the Articles of Confederation. These leaders were afraid of a strong national government. A rope of sand, they said, was better than a rod of iron.

REVIEW *Why did Madison call Congress "a rope of sand"?*

Agreeing to Work Together

The states argued among themselves over such things as borders and trade. Maryland and Virginia fought over who had control of the Potomac River, which ran between them. Both states wanted to control the middle of the river because it was a good shipping lane. New York and New Hampshire still argued over who owned the region that is now Vermont.

The states argued about money, too. Each state printed its own paper money in addition to the money printed by the national government. States fought over whose money would be used when people from one state bought goods in another state. Some states even placed a tax on goods brought in from other states.

Things became so difficult that a **convention**, or an important meeting, was held in Annapolis, Maryland, in September 1786. Alexander Hamilton of New York and James Madison of Virginia called the meeting to give the states a chance to talk out their problems. However, representatives from only five states—New York, New Jersey, Pennsylvania, Delaware, and Virginia—attended. The representatives, or **delegates**, talked for days before deciding that the country needed a stronger national government. This meant that the Articles of Confederation had to be changed.

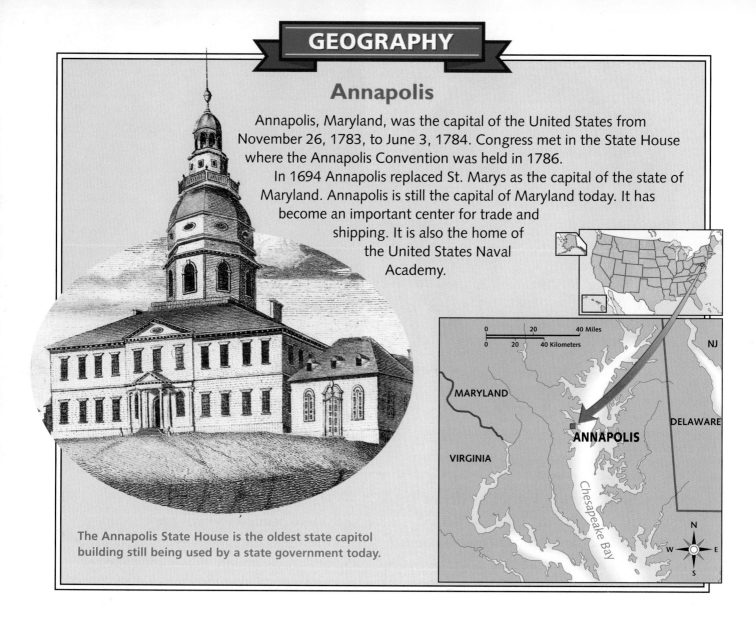

Annapolis

Annapolis, Maryland, was the capital of the United States from November 26, 1783, to June 3, 1784. Congress met in the State House where the Annapolis Convention was held in 1786.

In 1694 Annapolis replaced St. Marys as the capital of the state of Maryland. Annapolis is still the capital of Maryland today. It has become an important center for trade and shipping. It is also the home of the United States Naval Academy.

The Annapolis State House is the oldest state capitol building still being used by a state government today.

Led by Hamilton and Madison, the delegates to the Annapolis Convention sent a letter to Congress asking it to call a second convention. Delegates from all the states could meet at the convention to discuss their problems and decide whether changing the Articles might help solve them.

At first Congress did not want to call a convention, but after Shays's Rebellion it agreed to do so. Each state was asked to send delegates to a convention to be held in Philadelphia in the spring of 1787. Only Rhode Island refused the invitation.

The delegates to the convention began to gather in Philadelphia in May 1787. When Thomas Jefferson saw the list of those attending, he wrote to John Adams, "It really is an assembly of demigods [heroes]."

One of the first to arrive was George Washington of Virginia. In 1787 Washington was 55 years old and the most honored hero of the American Revolution. The first thing the delegates did was elect Washington president of the convention.

The most colorful arrival was made by Benjamin Franklin, then 81 years old and governor of Pennsylvania. Unable to walk far or to ride in a bumpy carriage, Franklin arrived in a Chinese sedan chair carried by prisoners from the Philadelphia jail.

In all, 55 delegates from 12 states met in the Pennsylvania State House. The delegates were mostly lawyers, planters, business people, and judges. Some had signed the Declaration of Independence, and almost all were members of Congress. Most shared the desire to do what was best for their state and their country.

Some famous people were not delegates. Thomas Jefferson, who had written the Declaration of Independence, was in Paris as ambassador to France. John Adams was in London as ambassador to Britain. His cousin Samuel Adams was in ill health, and John Hancock was too busy as governor of Massachusetts to attend. Patrick Henry refused to take part because he did not believe that a stronger national government was a good idea.

REVIEW *Why did Congress call for a convention of the states?*

The Convention Begins

From the beginning the delegates agreed to have a secret meeting. They believed this would help them make the best decisions. Windows were covered and sealed shut. Guards watched the doors and hallways.

As the meeting was called to order, many of the delegates offered ideas that they thought would make the Articles of Confederation better. But they soon saw that there was no way to simply fix up the old plan of government. Only a new plan—a new constitution—would do. They agreed to unite the nation under a strong central government instead of through "a firm league of friendship."

Delegates met at the Pennsylvania State House, known today as Independence Hall, to discuss a new plan of government.

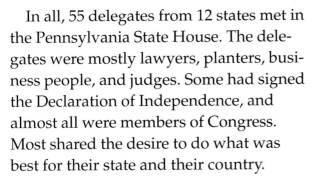

341

The delegates to this Constitutional Convention wrote the new rules of government with great care. They called these new rules the Constitution of the United States of America. Gouverneur (guh•vuh•NIR) Morris of Pennsylvania spent long hours working out each sentence. The delegates gave Morris the job of writing down all the ideas that had been approved during the convention.

In the **Preamble**, or introduction to the Constitution, Morris began with the words *We the people of the United States. . . .* He had originally written *We the people of the States of New Hampshire, Massachusetts, . . .* But Morris changed the words because he wanted the American people to know that the Constitution would make them citizens of a nation first and citizens of separate states second. This change also helped link

Delegates at the Constitutional Convention (bottom) decided on the new rules of government that were written down in the Constitution (below).

the Constitution with the idea in the Declaration of Independence that says a government should get its power from the consent of the people.

Morris went on to explain in the Preamble that the purpose of the Constitution was to create a better plan of government. This government would work toward justice and peace. It would allow the nation to defend itself against enemies. And it would promote the country's well-being.

Morris also wrote in the Preamble that the Constitution would provide "the blessings of liberty" for the American people. These words let the citizens of the new nation know that the Constitution would make sure that they remain a free people.

REVIEW *What was the purpose of the Constitution?*

Gouverneur Morris had been a member of the Continental Congress. He was responsible for the final wording of the Constitution.

LESSON 2 REVIEW

1785	1786	1787	1788

1786
• The Annapolis Convention

1787
• The Constitutional Convention
• The Constitution is written

Check Understanding

1 Remember the Facts Why did Gouverneur Morris change the opening of the Preamble?

2 Recall the Main Idea In what ways did American leaders work together to change the government of the United States?

Think Critically

3 Personally Speaking Would you have wanted to go to the Constitutional Convention? Explain your answer.

4 Cause and Effect What caused some states to argue among themselves?

5 Explore Viewpoints How might Patrick Henry have felt about the way Gouverneur Morris wrote the Constitution's Preamble?

Show What You Know

Research Activity Use the Internet, encyclopedias, and biographies to gather information about a convention delegate. Write a report and share it with the class.

Figure Travel Time

1. Why Learn This Skill?

When planning any trip, it is important to know the travel time, or how long the trip will take to complete. Travel time can be affected by many things, including the weather or the speed limit, if you are traveling by car. But the two most important things that affect travel time are the distance you will travel and the method of transportation you will use. As you know, traveling by airplane is faster than traveling by car.

2. Understand the Process

In the 1700s, travel was much slower and more difficult than it is today. Imagine that you are a delegate planning your trip to the Constitutional Convention in Philadelphia, Pennsylvania. You will start your trip from Charleston, South Carolina, traveling in a horse-drawn carriage. The roads are bad north of New Bern, North Carolina, so you will continue from New Bern to Annapolis, Maryland, on horseback. To save money, you will travel from Annapolis to Philadelphia on foot. How long will it take you to get from Charleston to Philadelphia? You will need to figure out the distance between the cities to answer this question. You will also need to know the travel time for the different forms of transportation used.

The map on this page shows some of the routes to the Constitutional Convention in Philadelphia. The map scale can help you figure out the distances on these routes. The map scale shows distance in both miles and

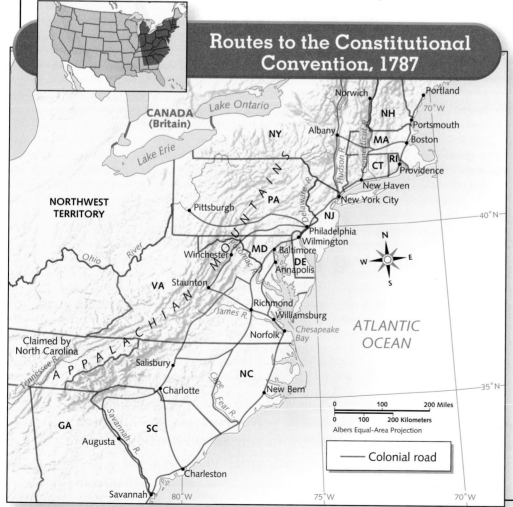

Routes to the Constitutional Convention, 1787

CANADA (Britain)
Lake Ontario
Lake Erie
NORTHWEST TERRITORY
NY
Albany
Norwich
Portland
NH
Portsmouth
MA
Boston
RI
Providence
CT
New Haven
New York City
PA
Pittsburgh
NJ
Philadelphia
Wilmington
MD
Baltimore
Winchester
DE
Annapolis
Ohio River
VA
Staunton
Richmond
Williamsburg
James R.
Norfolk
Chesapeake Bay
ATLANTIC OCEAN
Claimed by North Carolina
Salisbury
Tennessee R.
Charlotte
NC
New Bern
Cape Fear R.
GA
SC
Augusta
Savannah R.
Charleston
Savannah

70°W
40°N
35°N
80°W
75°W
70°W

N
W E
S

0   100   200 Miles
0   100   200 Kilometers
Albers Equal-Area Projection

—— Colonial road

and Distance

kilometers. In this skills lesson, you will use only miles to measure distance.

Use a ruler to measure the map scale. What length on the ruler equals 200 miles? To measure a curving route, you can use a string. Hold the string on the map, and use a pencil or pen to make a mark on the string at the starting point. Then lay the string along the route. Make another mark on the string at the ending point. Place the string against the map scale. You can measure the distance by making a mark at every length of 200 miles.

The chart on this page shows travel time for different forms of transportation. A horse-drawn carriage was used to travel from Charleston to New Bern. Carriages could go about 110 miles a day. To figure out how many days it took to get from Charleston to New Bern, divide the number of miles by the travel time. The total number of miles between Charleston and New Bern is about 225. If you divide that number by 110, you get 2 with a remainder of 5. So it took about 2 days to get from Charleston to New Bern.

Next, figure out the travel time from New Bern to Annapolis by horseback. Then, figure out how long it would take to walk from Annapolis to Philadelphia. Add all three travel times together to get the total time it would take to get from Charleston to Philadelphia.

Now use the map and the chart to answer the questions that follow.

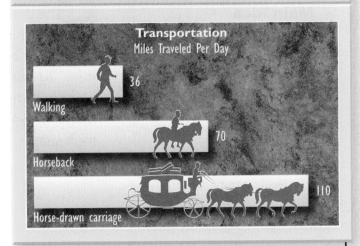

Travel Time

① About how many miles is it from Pittsburgh to Philadelphia?

② How long might it have taken a delegate traveling in a horse-drawn carriage to get from Pittsburgh to Philadelphia?

③ How long might it have taken a delegate to travel on horseback from New York City to Philadelphia?

④ How long might it have taken a delegate to walk from Wilmington, Delaware, to Philadelphia?

3. Think and Apply

Measure the distance between two cities on a present-day highway map, using the map scale. Find the shortest highway distance between the two cities. Then, using a travel rate of 55 miles per hour, figure out how long it would take to travel by car between those two cities.

FOCUS

How can people with different ideas reach agreement?

Main Idea   Read to learn how delegates to the Constitutional Convention reached agreement on a new plan of government.

Vocabulary

compromise   debate
federal system   Union
bill

Debates and Compromises

The delegates to the Constitutional Convention often did not agree with one another. The Constitution came into being only because the delegates were willing to compromise. To **compromise** means to give up some of what you want in order to reach an agreement. As compromises were made, decisions were written down and the Constitution took shape.

A Federal System of Government

The convention delegates first talked about the relationship between the states and the new national government. Only a few of the delegates agreed with George Read of Delaware, who thought that the states should be done away with altogether. Even those who wanted a strong national government said that getting rid of the states would be going too far.

But the delegates knew that the Articles of Confederation—with strong state governments and a weak national government—must be changed. So they agreed to create a **federal system** in which the authority to govern would be shared. The states would keep some authority, give away some authority, and share some authority with the national, or federal, government.

The states would keep authority over their own affairs. They would set up schools and local governments, for example. They would make laws for businesses and set rules for state and local elections. The national government would keep all authority over matters that affected the country as a whole.

The sketch above shows the original design for the Great Seal of the United States. The Great Seal (right) is still used on important government documents today.

The Federal System of Government

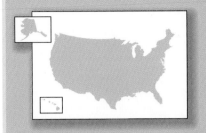

POWERS OF THE NATIONAL GOVERNMENT

Control trade between states and with foreign countries
Create an army and a navy
Print and coin money
Admit new states
Declare war and make peace
Make laws for immigration and citizenship

SHARED POWERS

Collect taxes
Set up court systems
Charter banks
Borrow money
Make laws to provide for public health and welfare

POWERS OF THE STATE GOVERNMENT

Set up public schools
Set up local governments
Conduct elections
Control trade within the state
Make laws for marriage and divorce
Set qualifications for voting

LEARNING FROM DIAGRAMS Under a federal system, some powers are given to the national government, some are given to the states, and others are shared.
■ *Which level of government can print money?*

The states would no longer print money, raise armies and navies, or make treaties with other countries, for example. Under the Articles of Confederation, each state had done these things as if it were a separate country.

The states would share authority with the national government, too. Both state and national governments would be able to set up their own court system and raise money by taxing citizens, for example.

The states and the national government might not always agree, however. In that case the national government would have authority over the state governments. The delegates made it clear that under this new federal system, the Constitution would be "the supreme law of the land."

REVIEW *How is a federal system of government different from a confederation?*

The Great Compromise

One of the first important disagreements among the delegates to the Constitutional Convention was about how each state would be represented in Congress, the new national legislature. Most delegates agreed that the Congress should have two parts, or houses. But they disagreed about how representatives should be chosen.

Edmund Randolph and the other Virginia delegates, including James Madison, thought the number of representatives a state would have in Congress should be based on the number of people living in that state. Under this plan, called the Virginia Plan, more people in a state would mean more representatives and more votes in Congress. This plan would help the large

Edmund Randolph (right) wrote the Virginia Plan, which called for representation to be based on population.

states, such as Virginia, Pennsylvania, and New York, which had large populations.

"Not fair!" shouted delegates from the small states. William Paterson of New Jersey said he "had rather submit to a monarch, to a despot [strict ruler], than to such a fate." Paterson offered his own plan for representation, called the New Jersey Plan. Under the New Jersey Plan, the new Congress would have one house rather than two. Each state would have one vote. This plan would help the small states by giving them the same amount of representation as the large states.

The delegates argued for weeks about representation. Which plan would be more fair? The larger states wanted the Virginia Plan. The smaller states wanted the New Jersey Plan. Neither side would give in. "We are now at a full stop," said Roger Sherman of Connecticut.

As president of the convention, George Washington chose a committee with one member from each state to work out a compromise. Roger Sherman, a member of the committee, offered a new plan, based on the idea of a two-house Congress. In one house, representation would be based on the number of people in each state, as in the Virginia Plan. In the other house, each state would have an equal vote, as in the New Jersey Plan. Either house could present a **bill**, or an idea for a new law. But the other house would have to agree to it before it could become a law.

Large-state delegates on the committee did not like Sherman's plan because they felt it gave too much authority to the small states. So the committee added another idea. The house in which representation was based on the number of people in each state would have the authority to tax. Bills having to do with money could come only from this house. The house in which each state had an equal vote could then agree to the bill or not.

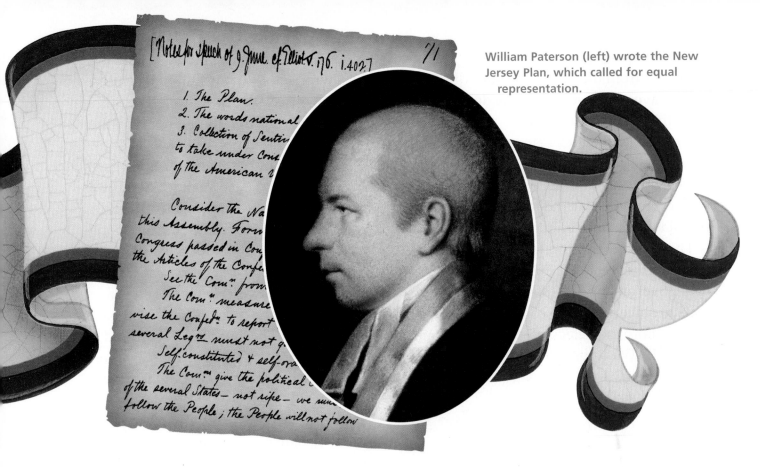

The committee presented its compromise plan to the whole convention. The delegates **debated**, or argued, the good and bad points of the compromise. At first, supporters of the Virginia and New Jersey plans held firm. But they came to understand that if they did not compromise, they would not have a new government. Because Sherman's compromise kept the plan for the Constitution alive, some people called it the Great Compromise of the convention.

REVIEW *What was the Great Compromise?*

The Three-fifths Compromise

More compromises were made before the convention was over. One had to do with a problem that had long divided the northern and southern states—slavery. Delegates from the two regions argued about whether enslaved Africans should be counted in determining how many representatives a state should have.

At the time of the convention, nearly 4 million people lived in the United States. Almost 2 million lived in the southern states. Of that number, about 667,000 were slaves.

Because the northern states had fewer enslaved Africans than the southern states had, the northern states did not want slaves to be counted for representation. After all, the delegates argued, slaves were not citizens under the Articles of Confederation, and they would not become citizens under the Constitution. Delegates from the southern states wanted slaves to be counted. That way the southern states could count more people and get more representatives, and therefore more votes, in Congress.

The delegates also debated how much each state should pay in taxes to support the national government. They agreed that each state's share should be based on the number of people in the state. For taxes, the delegates from the southern states did not want slaves counted, while the delegates from the northern states did.

Once again, the delegates reached a compromise. Three-fifths of the total number of slaves would be counted when figuring both representation and taxes. For every five slaves, a state could count three.

The delegates agreed to the Three-fifths Compromise to move closer to forming a new government. But there were still problems to solve and more compromises to make before the delegates' work was done.

REVIEW *What was the Three-fifths Compromise?*

Slavery and the Constitution

The delegates did not find it easy to compromise on every subject they debated. The subject of slavery nearly broke up the convention—and the United States of America.

Some of the delegates believed that slavery was wrong and that it should be ended. Others, especially those from the southern states, believed that the economy in their region depended on slavery.

More than one-fourth of the delegates owned slaves. These men decided not to use the word *slave* in the Constitution. Instead, they described enslaved people as "such persons" or "all other persons." The words *person held to service or labor* came closest to describing slaves. But even though the delegates did not use the word *slave*, they could not get around the problem of slavery. If the Constitution was to stand for liberty, how could it allow slavery?

The subject of slavery came up most often in the debate over the authority of Congress to control trade with other countries. Some delegates from both northern and southern states did not want Congress to have the authority to end the slave trade. But other delegates from both regions wanted the slave trade stopped.

George Mason of Virginia, an owner of more than 200 slaves, tried to end the trade of enslaved people. "I hold it essential," said Mason, "that the general government should have power to prevent the increase of slavery." He believed that over time all slaves should be set free.

John Rutledge of South Carolina did not agree. Plantation owners in his state and other southern states depended on enslaved workers to grow their cash crops. The slave problem was so important to Rutledge that he questioned "whether the

George Washington met with his advisers to discuss many issues related to the new government of the United States of America.

Enslaved people working on this South Carolina plantation lived in small shacks near the fields. Arguments over slavery nearly brought the Constitutional Convention to a halt.

Southern states shall or shall not be parties to the Union" if the slave trade were stopped.

Fearing that the southern states would break away from the **Union**—the United States of America—the delegates compromised. They gave Congress the authority to make laws controlling trade. But Congress could not stop the slave trade for at least 20 years. In the meantime, the delegates at the convention took no steps to end slavery in the states.

REVIEW *What compromise did the delegates reach on the slave trade?*

LESSON 3 REVIEW

Check Understanding

1 **Remember the Facts**   What debates almost ended the Constitutional Convention?

2 **Recall the Main Idea**   How did the delegates at the Constitutional Convention reach agreement on a new plan of government?

Think Critically

3 **Personally Speaking**   Why do you think it is important that government leaders today use compromise to reach agreements?

4 **Cause and Effect**   How might the southern states have been affected if the Constitution had put an end to the slave trade?

Show What You Know

Simulation Activity   With a partner, role-play a debate between delegates at the Constitutional Convention. One delegate should represent a large state and the other should represent a small state. Tell what you think of the Virginia Plan and the New Jersey Plan.

Compromise to Resolve Conflicts

1. Why Learn This Skill?

There are many ways to handle a disagreement. You can walk away and let the strong feelings fade over time. You can talk about it. You can also compromise. Knowing how to compromise gives you another way to resolve, or handle, conflicts.

2. Understand the Process

Many people believe that if the delegates to the Constitutional Convention had not been willing to compromise, the Constitution would never have been written. You have read that one of the most serious disagreements at the convention was over representation in the new legislature. Roger Sherman helped resolve this disagreement by suggesting what later became known as the Great Compromise.

Roger Sherman

Both sides got some of what they wanted, but both sides also had to give up other things they wanted.

To resolve a conflict through compromise, you can follow steps like the ones below.

1. Before you begin to talk with the person you disagree with, be aware that you may have to give up some things you would like.

2. Tell the other person what you want.

3. Decide which of the things you want are most important to you.

4. Present a plan for a possible compromise. Let the other person present his or her plan.

5. Talk about any differences in the two plans.

6. Present another plan for a compromise, this time giving up one of the things that is not most important to you. Continue talking until the two of you agree on a compromise plan.

7. If either of you becomes angry, take a break and calm down before you go on talking.

8. If there are many people on each side of the disagreement, each side should choose one or two people to do most of the talking.

3. Think and Apply

With your classmates, choose an issue that you do not all agree on. Form sides to discuss the issue, using the steps in Understand the Process.

A Government of Three Branches

FOCUS
How can people make sure that no branch of the government holds too much authority?

Main Idea   As you read, look for ways the delegates made sure that no branch of the United States government would have too much authority.

Vocabulary

legislative branch
executive branch
judicial branch
separation of powers
majority
census
electoral college
veto
impeach
justice
override
unconstitutional
checks and balances

Under the Articles of Confederation, Congress made the laws, approved the laws, and acted as a court to settle disagreements between the states. But having only one branch of government had created problems. So the delegates to the Constitutional Convention decided there would be three branches of government instead of one. Each would have its own authority. A **legislative branch** would make the laws. An **executive branch** would carry out the laws. A **judicial branch** would settle differences about the meaning of the laws. Once the delegates agreed to this **separation of powers**, or division of the national government, they had to decide how the three branches would work together.

The Legislative Branch

Like the Congress under the Articles of Confederation, the Congress under the Constitution would make laws. But the new Congress was to have more authority than the old one. The new Congress, for example, could make laws to raise taxes, control trade with other countries, print and coin money, raise an army and a navy, and declare war.

The new Congress would have two houses, the House of Representatives and the Senate. Either house could propose most bills. For a bill to become a law, the **majority**, or the greater part, of each house would have to vote for it.

The number of members each state sent to the House of Representatives would depend on the state's population. A **census**, or population count, would be taken every ten years to determine the number of people in each state. Today the number of members in the House of Representatives is limited to 435. In the

This early gavel, used in the Senate to open and close meetings, had no handle.

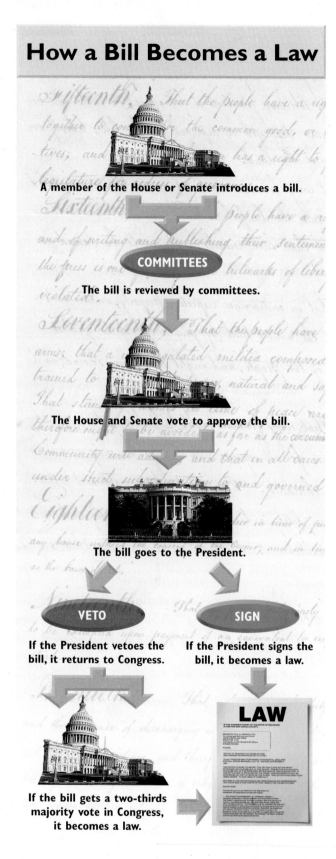

How a Bill Becomes a Law

A member of the House or Senate introduces a bill.

COMMITTEES

The bill is reviewed by committees.

The House and Senate vote to approve the bill.

The bill goes to the President.

VETO

If the President vetoes the bill, it returns to Congress.

SIGN

If the President signs the bill, it becomes a law.

LAW

If the bill gets a two-thirds majority vote in Congress, it becomes a law.

LEARNING FROM DIAGRAMS Under the Constitution, a bill must follow the steps shown in this diagram to become a law.

■ *When does the President receive the bill?*

Senate, each state has two senators, as originally planned.

James Madison thought that the members of both houses of Congress should be elected by the voters of each state. Other delegates, however, disagreed. Many felt that most people were not educated enough or informed enough to have a say in government. After a long debate, a compromise was worked out. The delegates agreed that citizens should vote directly for members of the House of Representatives. Senators would be elected by their state legislatures. Today, however, citizens vote directly for members of both houses of Congress, as Madison wanted.

The delegates also decided on other rules for Congress that are still in effect today. Members of the House of Representatives serve for two years. Senators serve for six years. To qualify, members of the House of Representatives must be at least 25 years old, must have been citizens of the United States for at least seven years, and must live in the state they represent. Senators must be at least 30 years old, must have been citizens of the United States for nine years, and must live in the state they represent.

REVIEW *What are the duties of Congress?*

The Executive Branch

Once Congress makes the laws, it is the job of the executive branch to carry them out. In doing so, the executive branch runs the day-to-day business of government.

The delegates had many long debates about the executive branch. One of the most heated debates was about whether it should be headed by one person or by a group of people. James Wilson of Pennsylvania felt that one person should be the chief executive, or leader. He thought that a single executive would govern more effectively than a committee. Even though some delegates feared that a single executive would be too much like a monarch, most agreed with Wilson. They decided on a single chief executive, called the President. The President serves for four years.

It was also Wilson's idea to have citizens vote for electors, who, in turn, would vote for the President. This group of electors is called the **electoral college**.

The delegates also had long debates about how much authority the President should have. Many thought the President should be able to **veto**, or reject, bills passed by Congress.

George Mason of Virginia disagreed. Such authority, he thought, was too much like that held by a king or queen. But most of the other delegates were willing to take a chance on a strong executive. The delegates counted on the other branches to keep the executive branch under control.

The debates went on and on, but finally the executive branch began to take shape. It was decided that the President would represent the nation in dealing with other countries and would head the nation's military forces. To run for President, a person

The scales of justice stand for fair treatment.

must be at least 35 years old and must have been born in the United States. The President's chief responsibility would be to "take care that the laws be faithfully executed." If these duties were not carried out, Congress could **impeach** the President. This means it could accuse the President of wrongdoing. The President could then be tried and removed from office if found guilty.

REVIEW *What are the duties of the President?*

The Judicial Branch

Once laws are made and carried out, someone must decide if they are working fairly. This is the job of the judicial branch, or court system. The states had always had their own courts. But the delegates to the Constitutional Convention agreed on the need for a national, or federal, court system. The courts in this system would decide cases having to do with national laws, treaties, or the Constitution. They would also decide cases between states and between citizens of different states.

The delegates did not plan the judicial branch in great detail. They made the most decisions about the highest court in the United States—which they called the Supreme Court.

Edmund Randolph wanted Congress to choose the **justices**, or judges, for the

Supreme Court. James Wilson wanted the President to have this authority. A compromise was worked out. The President would name the justices, and the Senate would vote on them. It was decided that a justice would stay in office for life. In this way justices could reach decisions fairly without worrying about losing their jobs.

No decision was made at the Constitutional Convention as to how many justices would be on the Supreme Court. Congress decided on that number later. At first there were six justices on the court. Today there are nine.

REVIEW *What are the duties of the judicial branch?*

LEARNING FROM DIAGRAMS This diagram shows the checks and balances among the three branches of government.
■ *How can the President check the authority of Congress? How can Congress check the authority of the Supreme Court?*

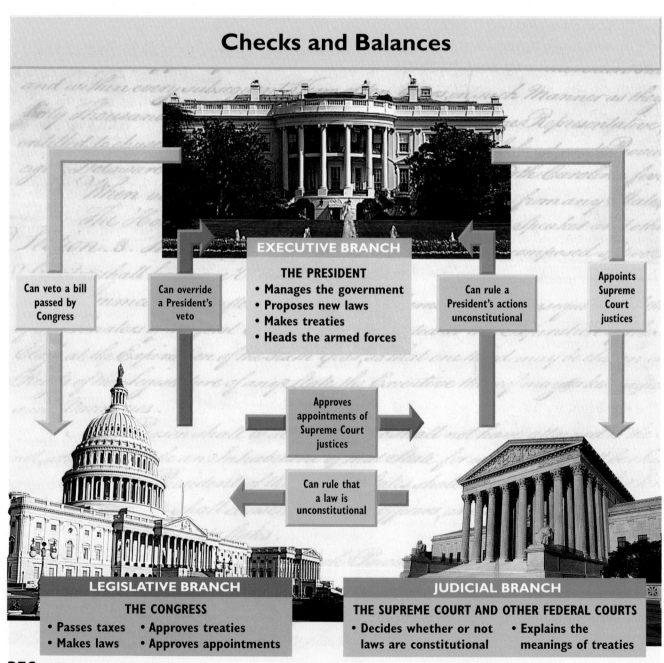

Checks and Balances

EXECUTIVE BRANCH

THE PRESIDENT
- **Manages the government**
- **Proposes new laws**
- **Makes treaties**
- **Heads the armed forces**

Can veto a bill passed by Congress

Can override a President's veto

Can rule a President's actions unconstitutional

Appoints Supreme Court justices

Approves appointments of Supreme Court justices

Can rule that a law is unconstitutional

LEGISLATIVE BRANCH

THE CONGRESS
- **Passes taxes**
- **Makes laws**
- **Approves treaties**
- **Approves appointments**

JUDICIAL BRANCH

THE SUPREME COURT AND OTHER FEDERAL COURTS
- **Decides whether or not laws are constitutional**
- **Explains the meanings of treaties**

The delegates at the Constitutional Convention decided to set up checks and balances so each branch of government would not have too much authority.

How the Branches Work Together

None of the delegates wanted any one branch of government to have too much authority. So they gave each branch some ways to check, or limit, the authority of the others.

Congress, for example, can check the authority of the President by overriding the President's veto. To **override** a veto means to vote to cancel it. The Supreme Court can check the authority of Congress by ruling that a law is **unconstitutional**, or does not follow the Constitution. The President can check the authority of the Supreme Court by choosing its justices.

The delegates set up these checks to keep a balance of authority among the three branches. The **checks and balances** keep any one branch from using its authority wrongly. They help all three branches work together as equal partners.

REVIEW *What is the purpose of checks and balances among the three branches of the United States government?*

LESSON 4 REVIEW

Check Understanding

1 **Remember the Facts** What are the duties of each branch of the national government?

2 **Recall the Main Idea** How did the delegates to the Constitutional Convention make sure that no branch of the government would have too much authority?

Think Critically

3 **Cause and Effect** What might happen if one branch of the government became too powerful?

4 **Think More About It** How do the separation of powers and the system of checks and balances help the national government work well?

Show What You Know

Diagram Activity Show your understanding of the separation of powers and the checks and balances by making a diagram. Your diagram should list the duties of each branch of government and show how each branch balances the authority of another. Share your work with a classmate.

LESSON 5

LEARN HISTORY *through* Literature

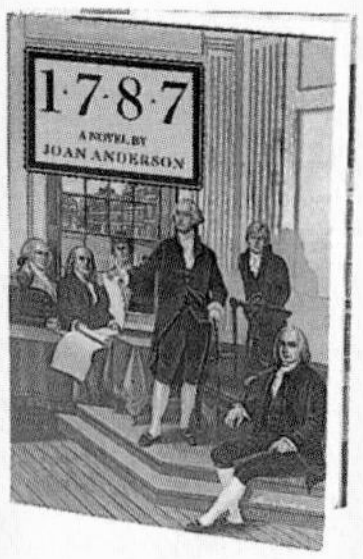

1787

by Joan Anderson

illustrated by Teresa Fasolino

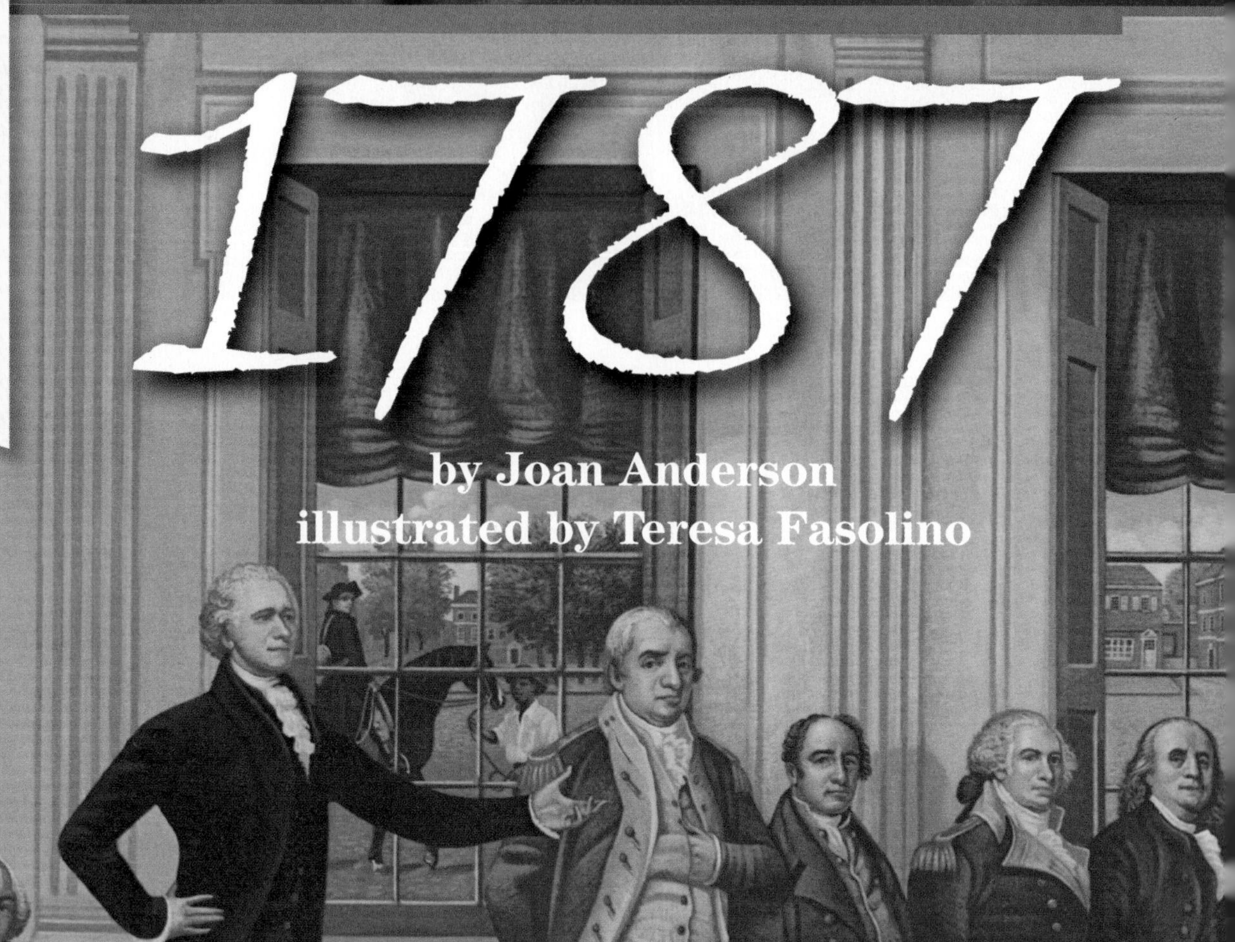

During the hot and humid summer of 1787, the 55 delegates to the Constitutional Convention worked at writing a new plan of government. In the seven parts, or Articles, of their plan, they described the duties of each branch of government and the relations among the states. They also wrote rules for making changes to the Constitution. Finally the time came for the delegates to sign their names to show they agreed with what had been written.

Read now about the last day of the convention in this story of historical fiction. Jared Mifflin, the boy who tells the story, is James Madison's helper. As Jared listens to the delegates debate, he wonders if the Constitution will ever be signed.

*WE, THE PEOPLE
OF THE UNITED STATES,*
*in order to form
a more perfect Union,
Establish Justice,
insure domestic Tranquillity,
provide for the common defense,
promote the general Welfare,
and secure the
Blessings of Liberty
to ourselves and our Posterity,
do ordain and establish
this Constitution for the
United States of America . . .*

As Secretary Jackson continued to read, Jared stood in the back of the East Room gazing upon the delegates, none of whom moved a hair as they listened to the words they had labored so hard to formulate[1] into a sturdy document. *Another hour or so, and the whole thing will be over,* Jared thought, a tinge of sadness stirring his soul as he realized his unique experience was coming to an end.

The windows of the East Room had finally been opened, allowing an unfamiliar cool breeze to descend upon the delegates at this, their last official meeting. . . .

---

[1] **formulate:** state in an exact way

"And so, let it be Done," General Jackson began the final phrase that now was familiar to Jared because he had read and reread Uncle Thomas's first draft, ". . . in convention by the unanimous[2] consent of the states present, the seventeenth day of September in the year of our Lord, One Thousand Seven Hundred and Eighty Seven and of the Independence of the United States of America the Twelfth. In witness whereof we have hereunto subscribed[3] our names."

Jared gazed about the room, wondering what would happen next. He focused on General Washington, assuming that he would make the next move. There were some stirrings from the Virginians. *They're probably thinking up last-minute suggestions,*

Jared surmised.[4] Suddenly, George Mason asked for the floor. Everyone was sitting on the edge of their chairs.

"Gentlemen," he said in a strong, bold tone, "after much soul-searching I must inform you that since this Constitution does not yet contain a Bill of Rights I cannot, in all good conscience, subscribe to the document that lays waiting."

Jared was stunned. Mr. Mason's attendance during the summer had been almost perfect, and he'd sat on many committees. How could he not sign? No sooner had he taken his seat than Virginia's Governor Randolph rose—to agree with George Mason. "I will gladly present this Constitution to the legislature in Virginia but cannot, at this time, find it in my heart to put name to paper."

---

[2]**unanimous:** in complete agreement
[3]**subscribed:** signed below

[4]**surmised:** guessed

Now the room was full of rumblings. Governor Randolph had been one of the early arrivals and the first to speak at the opening of the Convention. He was the one who presented the Virginia Plan, Jared recalled—the paper on which the new Constitution drew some of its ideas! The various states were now huddled together in discussion and General Washington had to bang the gavel several times to bring order to the room. *How many others would follow suit?* Jared wondered.

"I must inform my colleagues that I, too, will not sign this Constitution in its present form," Elbridge Gerry of Massachusetts announced from his seat at the back of the room.

Here we go, Jared thought. *Divisiveness spreading once again from state to state.*

"Mr. President," the voice of Alexander Hamilton rose from the other side of the room. "May I speak?"

Washington nodded, not a trace of emotion on his stoic[5] face.

Jared turned to look at Mr. Hamilton, the man responsible for calling the

HAMILTON

meeting at Annapolis, where the writing of a Constitution was first discussed. More than anyone else, it seemed that Alexander Hamilton cared about nationhood. He had written numerous articles and papers advocating[6] a strong federal government. Ironically he'd had to endure a delegation that completely disagreed with him throughout this Convention.

"I must express my deepest anxiety that every member should sign," he said with an urgency in his voice. "If a few characters of consequence refuse to sign, their actions could do infinite mischief by kindling latent sparks which lurk under the general enthusiasm for this Constitution." He sat down, but did not take his eyes off Governor Randolph, to whom he was obviously delivering these brief but firmly stated remarks.

There was momentary silence. Jared wished that General Washington would rise and simply commence the signing. Instead, yet another delegate took the floor. *Oh no*, Jared thought, *another Massachusetts man. Will he also dissent?*

---

[5]**stoic:** calm

[6]**advocating:** speaking for

Nathaniel Gorham instead moved that the stipulation for representation in the House be changed from one representative per forty thousand citizens to one per thirty thousand. *How could they change anything now?* Jared wondered, as he gazed over at the beautifully printed pieces of parchment that were spread out on the table. *With this latest diversion, the Convention will surely trail on for days*, he sighed. Knowing how meticulously[7] these men had worked over this document, clause by clause, article by article, Jared resigned himself to the delay and took a seat on the stool provided for him by the door.

Rufus King seconded the motion, and Jared got set to watch yet another debate on representation. But instead, General Washington rose from his seat to make a statement. "Being the presiding member," he informed the group, "I know I am not at liberty to comment one way or another and have not done so until this moment. However, I must agree with my colleagues," he continued. "It has always appeared to me that an

WASHINGTON

exceptional plan would be to have one representative for every thirty thousand citizens, and it would give me much satisfaction to see it adopted." That did it. Everyone agreed to vote with the man considered to be the foremost of all Americans. With the representation issue finally put to rest and no one else jumping up with final objections, Dr. Franklin asked for the floor.

Finally! Jared said to himself. *Not many men here are going to disagree with Benjamin Franklin, no matter what he says.*

"Due to a weakened voice, gentlemen," he began, "I have asked my friend James Wilson to read you my sentiments on this momentous day." He nodded for Wilson to begin:

"Mr. President, I confess that there are several parts of this Constitution which I do not at present approve, but I am not sure I shall ever approve them. For having lived a long time, I have experienced many instances of being obliged by better information or fuller consideration to change opinions even on important subjects which I once thought right, but found to be otherwise.

---

[7]**meticulously:** very carefully

It is, therefore, that the older I grow, the more apt I am to doubt my own judgment, and to pay more respect to the judgment of others.

In these sentiments, sir, I agree to this Constitution with all its faults, if they are such. . . . I doubt, too, whether any other convention we can obtain, may be able to make a better Constitution.

For when you assemble a number of men to have the advantage of their joint wisdom, you inevitably assemble with those men all their prejudices, their passions, their errors of opinion, their local interest, and their selfish views. From such an assembly can a perfect production be expected?

It, therefore, astonishes me, sir, to find this system approaching so near to perfection as it does; and I think it will astonish our enemies. . . .

Thus I consent, sir. I cannot help expressing a wish that every member of the Convention who may still have objections to it, would with me, on this occasion, doubt a little of his own infallibility,[8] and to make manifest our unanimity, put his name to this instrument."

FRANKLIN

When Franklin's speech was over, the signing began. George Washington was first to write on the cream-colored parchment. Delegates from each state followed. In the end, all but 16 of the 55 delegates signed the new United States Constitution on September 17, 1787. Mason, Randolph, and Gerry did not sign. The 13 others had already left the convention and returned home.

As Benjamin Franklin left the convention hall, he was asked by the wife of Philadelphia's mayor what kind of government the new nation would have. "A republic," he told her, "if you can keep it." Franklin's words were meant for all the people of the United States.

_____

[8]**infallibility:** inability to make a mistake

LITERATURE REVIEW

1. Why did the delegates decide to stop debating and sign the Constitution?
2. Why do you think Benjamin Franklin believed that a "perfect" Constitution was not possible?
3. Write a short scene about the closing of the Constitutional Convention. With classmates, act out your scene for the class.

1780   1782

1781
• The Articles of
  Confederation
  are approved

CONNECT MAIN IDEAS

Use this organizer to show how the chapter's main ideas are connected. Write the main idea of each lesson, and list the three branches of government. A copy of the organizer may be found on page 65 of the Activity Book.

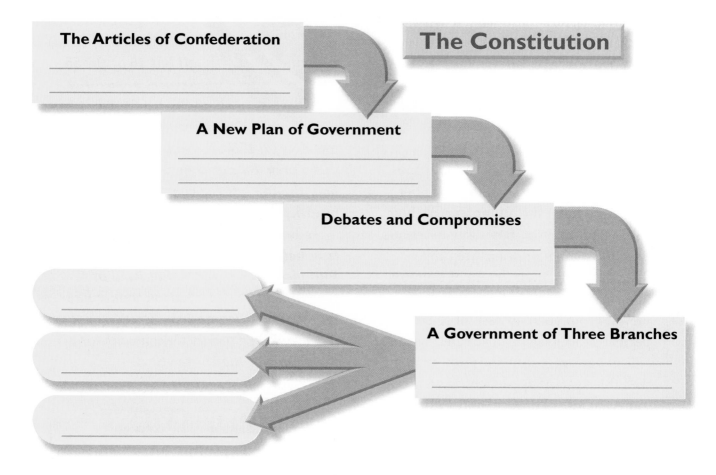

The Articles of Confederation
_____
_____

The Constitution

A New Plan of Government
_____
_____

Debates and Compromises
_____
_____

_____

_____

_____

A Government of Three Branches
_____
_____

WRITE MORE ABOUT IT

Write a Persuasive Letter Imagine that you are living during the time delegates were meeting to discuss the Articles of Confederation. Write a letter telling why you think the Articles of Confederation should or should not be changed.

Report a News Event Suppose that you are a newspaper reporter who has been asked to cover the Constitutional Convention. Write a short newspaper article in which you explain the Great Compromise. Be sure to tell how it will affect the outcome of the convention.

1786
• The Annapolis
  Convention is held

1787
• The Constitutional
  Convention is held
• The Constitution is written

USE VOCABULARY

Write one or two sentences for each pair of terms to explain how the terms are related.

1. territory, township

2. convention, delegate

3. compromise, debate

4. veto, override

CHECK UNDERSTANDING

5. How was the United States under the Articles of Confederation like the Iroquois League?

6. What powers did Congress have under the Articles of Confederation? What powers did it not have?

7. When and where was the Constitutional Convention held?

8. How is authority shared in a federal system?

9. What were the differences between the New Jersey Plan and the Virginia Plan?

10. What are the three branches of the United States government? Describe the duties of each branch.

11. How are justices on the Supreme Court chosen? How long do they serve?

THINK CRITICALLY

12. **Explore Viewpoints** Most delegates to the Constitutional Convention thought the chief executive should be paid. Benjamin Franklin thought the President should serve without pay. Which view would you have supported? Why?

13. **Think More About It** How did the Three-fifths Compromise settle one of the disagreements between the northern and southern states?

APPLY SKILLS

Figure Travel Time and Distance
Use the map on page 344 and the chart on page 345 to answer these questions.

14. How many days might it have taken to travel on horseback from Charleston to Philadelphia?

15. How many days might it have taken to walk from New York City to Philadelphia?

16. How many days might it have taken to get from Boston to Philadelphia by carriage?

Compromise to Resolve Conflicts
Think of something that you and a friend disagree about. Then list the steps that you might follow to resolve your conflict.

READ MORE ABOUT IT

The Great Little Madison by Jean Fritz. G. P. Putnam's Sons. This biography, which traces the life of James Madison, tells how he grew from a sickly child to become the fourth President of the United States.

Visit the Internet at
http://www.hbschool.com
for additional resources.

10

A New GOVERNMENT BEGINS

"The basis of our political systems is the right of the people to make and to alter their constitutions of government."

George Washington, in his farewell speech as President, 1796

A portrait of George Washington by Gilbert Stuart

Approving the Constitution

| 1786 | 1788 | 1790 |

LESSON
1

FOCUS
What would make the people of a country want to support its plan of government?

Main Idea As you read, think about what made the people of the United States want to support the Constitution.

Vocabulary
ratify
Federalist
Anti-Federalist

James Madison had taken careful notes all through the Constitutional Convention. The day his fellow delegates signed their approval for the new plan of government, Madison wrote in his notebook,

66 Whilst the last members were signing it Doctor Franklin looking towards the President's Chair, at the back of which a rising sun happened to be painted, observed to a few members near him, that Painters had found it difficult to distinguish in their art a rising from a setting sun. I have, said he, often and often in the course of the Session . . . looked at that behind the President without being able to tell whether it was rising or setting: But now at length I have the happiness to know that it is a rising and not a setting Sun. 99

Despite Franklin's words, the new plan of government that he and the other delegates had approved was not yet the law of the land. According to Article VII of the Constitution, 9 of the 13 states had to **ratify**, or agree to, the Constitution before it would become law.

State Ratifying Conventions

Once the delegates signed the Constitution on September 17, 1787, George Washington ordered it sent to Congress. Congress, in turn, sent copies to the states. To decide about the new plan of government, the states held their own

This ink stand was used by the signers of the Declaration of Independence and of the Constitution.

367

The chair that was used during the Constitutional Convention (left) is still on display inside Independence Hall in Philadelphia. The top part of the chair (above) shows the "rising sun."

the new national government was too strong. Samuel Adams told delegates in Massachusetts that he did not like the way the Preamble began with *We the People*. He thought it should say *We the States*.

There was one point, however, on which the delegates to just about every state convention agreed. They felt the Constitution needed to list the things the government could *not* do. This would protect the rights of the states and the people.

The state delegates wanted to protect freedoms such as the right to tell the government if it was doing something wrong. They remembered that Patrick Henry and James Otis had almost been sent to prison for speaking out against the British government. The delegates did not want the new national government to have the authority to do the same.

The delegates to the state ratifying conventions said they would be more willing to agree to the Constitution if a list of rights was added to it. So supporters of the Constitution promised that after it was ratified, a bill of rights would be added.

REVIEW *Why were many delegates not willing at first to agree to the new Constitution?*

ratifying conventions. In each state, the people elected delegates to go to the state convention and vote for or against the Constitution.

At the state conventions, debate began all over again. Some delegates, such as Patrick Henry in Virginia and George Clinton in New York, told their conventions that

This political cartoon celebrated the ratification of the Constitution by 11 of the 13 states. It expressed the hope that North Carolina and Rhode Island would also ratify the Constitution.

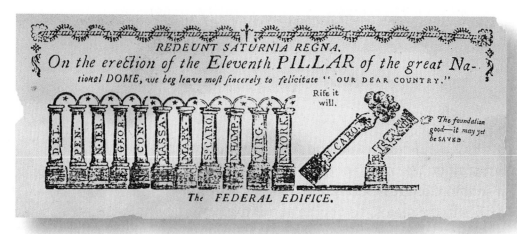

REDEUNT SATURNIA REGNA.

On the erection of the Eleventh PILLAR of the great National DOME, we beg leave most sincerely to felicitate "OUR DEAR COUNTRY."

Rise it will.

The foundation good—it may yet be SAVED

The FEDERAL EDIFICE.

Ratification of the Constitution

United States

1787 Year of ratification

Present-day border

0   100   200 Miles
0   100   200 Kilometers
Albers Equal-Area Projection

CANADA
(Britain)

Lake Ontario

Lake Erie

MAINE
(part of MA)

(claimed by NY and NH)

NEW HAMPSHIRE
1788

MASSACHUSETTS
1788

NEW YORK
1788

RHODE ISLAND
1790

CONNECTICUT
1788

PENNSYLVANIA
1787

NEW JERSEY
1787

DELAWARE
1787

MARYLAND
1788

VIRGINIA
1788

NORTH CAROLINA
1789

SOUTH CAROLINA
1788

ATLANTIC OCEAN

GEORGIA
1788

FLORIDA
(Spain)

Gulf of Mexico

The Vote

The first state to call for a vote on the Constitution was Delaware. On December 7, 1787, all the state delegates voted to ratify. Later that month, delegates in Pennsylvania and New Jersey also voted to ratify. In January 1788, delegates in Georgia and Connecticut voted to ratify. But several states still had not voted. Among those were New York and Virginia. People wondered how the new government could possibly work if the country's largest states voted against it.

From January to June 1788, people who were for the new Constitution and people who were against it both tried to get the

STATE	DATE	VOTES FOR	VOTES AGAINST
Delaware	December 7, 1787	30	0
Pennsylvania	December 12, 1787	46	23
New Jersey	December 18, 1787	38	0
Georgia	January 2, 1788	26	0
Connecticut	January 9, 1788	128	40
Massachusetts	February 6, 1788	187	168
Maryland	April 28, 1788	63	11
South Carolina	May 23, 1788	149	73
New Hampshire	June 21, 1788	57	47
Virginia	June 25, 1788	89	79
New York	July 26, 1788	30	27
North Carolina	November 21, 1789	194	77
Rhode Island	May 29, 1790	34	32

Place The map and table show when the Constitution was ratified in each of the 13 states. The table also lists the number of votes for and against the ratification.

■ *Which states ratified the Constitution in 1787? What state was the last to ratify the Constitution? In which state was the vote closest to being a tie?*

Chapter 10 • **369**

support of people in the states that had not yet voted. Those who wanted the Constitution came to be called **Federalists**. Those who did not want it became known as **Anti-Federalists**. Federalists wanted the plan's strong national government. Anti-Federalists did not want a strong national government unless a bill of rights was added to the plan.

In New York, Federalists and Anti-Federalists used the newspapers to tell how they felt and why. Alexander Hamilton, James Madison, and John Jay wrote letters to the newspapers, defending the Constitution. These letters were later published as a book called *The Federalist*.

Those who could read followed the debate in the newspapers. Others heard the arguments at community meetings and even at church services. Some people saw the new Constitution as the work of "lawyers, and men of learning, and moneyed men that talk so finely . . . to make us poor, illiterate people swallow down the pill." But others thought that having a government with three branches and a Congress with two houses was a good idea. They also liked the promise of a bill of rights.

No one was sure how all the arguing would affect the ratifying conventions. In Massachusetts, however, the promise of a bill of rights changed the minds of some very important people. Samuel Adams and John Hancock went to the ratifying convention as firm Anti-Federalists. They returned home as Federalists. Massachusetts easily ratified the Constitution in February 1788.

The banner (bottom right) was carried by members of the Society of Pewterers in a parade held to celebrate New York's ratification of the Constitution. Pewterers made plates and other items out of a metal called pewter. Alexander Hamilton wrote most of the letters published in *The Federalist* (bottom left). Many people believe that this book provides the best description of the ideas behind the Constitution.

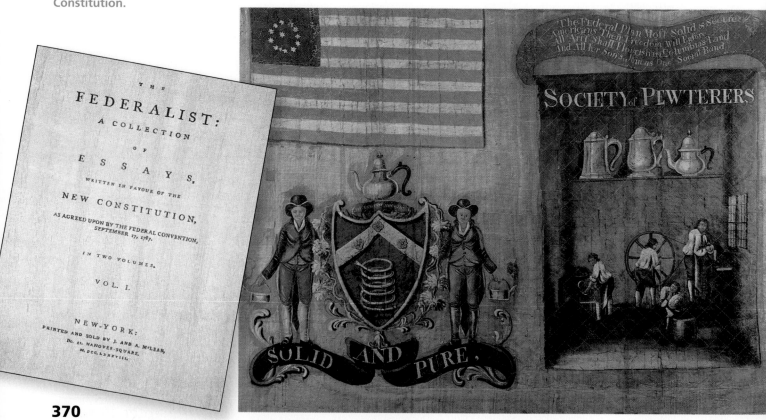

1789

The new government of the United States went to work early in 1789. That same year, in France, another change in government began. The French Revolution was a long, terrible conflict that took many lives. But when the revolution was over, the French had overthrown their monarchy.

In many ways what was important to the Americans during the American Revolution was also important to the French. The leaders of the French Revolution believed in democratic ideas such as liberty. Even the colors of the French Revolution were red, white, and blue, like those of the United States flag.

The present-day French flag also shares the same colors with the United States flag.

Maryland and South Carolina soon followed Massachusetts. Then, on June 21, 1788, New Hampshire became the ninth state to ratify. That was enough for the Constitution to become law. That summer, Virginia and New York voted for the Constitution. By early 1789 the new government was at work. North Carolina ratified later that year. The last state to ratify the Constitution, Rhode Island, finally gave its approval in 1790.

REVIEW *What was* **The Federalist?**

LESSON I REVIEW

1786 — 1788 — 1790

1787
• Delegates sign the Constitution

1788
• New Hampshire ratifies the Constitution

1789
• Government under the Constitution begins

Check Understanding

1 **Remember the Facts** Who were the Federalists and the Anti-Federalists?

2 **Recall the Main Idea** What made the people of the United States want to support the Constitution?

Think Critically

3 **Think More About It** Why do you think winning ratification in large states such as New York was so important?

4 **Cause and Effect** What effect did the promise of a bill of rights have on the debate over ratification?

Show What You Know

Cartoon Activity Choose one side in the debate over the ratification of the Constitution. Draw a political cartoon showing your point of view. Ask a family member or a classmate to interpret your political cartoon.

For or Against a

James Madison

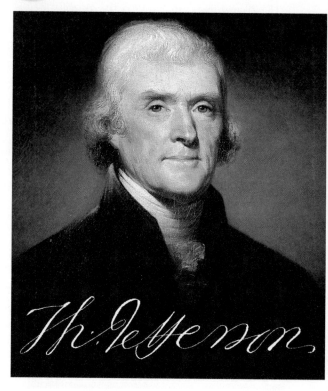

Thomas Jefferson

James Madison and Thomas Jefferson liked and respected one another. Both men were important leaders who were born and grew up in Virginia. Both served in Virginia's legislature. Jefferson took part in writing the Declaration of Independence, and Madison helped write the Constitution. But Jefferson and Madison disagreed about many things, such as the need for a bill of rights to be added to the Constitution.

Shortly after the Constitutional Convention ended, Madison sent Jefferson a copy of the Constitution along with a long letter about the convention. Jefferson wrote back, explaining why he felt a bill of rights was needed. At first, Madison saw little need for a bill of rights and felt that any changes to the Constitution would just prolong the debate and threaten ratification. Read the following parts of Jefferson's and Madison's letters.

Bill of Rights?

Jefferson to Madison—December 20, 1787

66 Let me add that a bill of rights is what the people are entitled to against every government on earth, general or particular, and what no just government should refuse . . . 99

Madison to Jefferson—April 22, 1788

66 Should this [the demand for a bill of rights] be carried in the affirmative, . . . I think the Constitution, and the Union will be both endangered. 99

Jefferson to Madison—July 31, 1788

66 I hope therefore a bill of rights will be formed to guard the peoples against the federal government, as they are already guarded against their state governments in most instances. 99

Madison to Jefferson—October 17, 1788

66 I have never thought the omission [of a bill of rights] a material defect, nor been anxious to supply it even by subsequent amendment . . . A bill of rights will be good ground for an appeal to the sense of the community. . . . 99

Jefferson to Madison—March 15, 1789

66 I am much pleased with the prospect that a declaration of rights will be added: and hope it will be done in that way which will not endanger the whole frame of the government, or any essential part of it. 99

Compare Viewpoints

1. What viewpoint about the Bill of Rights did Jefferson hold?

2. What viewpoint about the Bill of Rights did Madison hold at first?

3. How did Madison's viewpoint change over time?

Think and Apply

People often change their views about things over time. You have read that James Madison changed his view about the need for a bill of rights. Can you think of times when you changed your views on a subject? What caused you to change your views? Was it talks with friends, some new information you learned, or something else?

FOCUS

Why do citizens have responsibilities to their nation as well as individual rights?

Main Idea   Read to learn about individual rights that come from the Constitution and about American citizens' responsibilities.

Vocabulary

amendment
Bill of Rights
due process of law
human rights
jury
patriotism

Rights and Responsibilities

As promised, not long after the states had ratified the United States Constitution, it was changed. Ten **amendments**, or changes, were added to protect the rights of the people. These ten amendments, called the **Bill of Rights**, describe freedoms that the government cannot take away and list actions that the government is not allowed to take.

The Bill of Rights was modeled after the Magna Carta. The Magna Carta was a charter granted by the King of England in the year 1215 that listed the rights of the royal class. The British Bill of Rights was also modeled after the Magna Carta. But the British monarch and Parliament could ignore it or change it any time they wanted. The American Bill of Rights became part of the Constitution in 1791. There is only one way it can be changed—by another amendment.

The Bill of Rights

The First Amendment in the Bill of Rights is perhaps the most famous because the freedoms it guarantees are so much a part of our daily lives. The First Amendment says that people have the freedom to follow any religion they want, or no religion at all. It protects freedom of speech and freedom of the press. It also says that people can hold meetings to discuss problems and that they can ask the government to hear their complaints.

The Second Amendment protects people's right to carry arms, or weapons. It says, "A well-regulated militia being necessary to the security of a free State, the right of the people to keep and bear arms shall not be infringed."

The coin (top left) is one of the first silver dollars made by the new government of the United States. The First Amendment allowed people to hold town meetings like this one (left).

The painting (above) shows Benjamin Franklin in a print shop looking at a freshly printed page. During the late 1700s, the printing press (right) was the main tool for spreading news and opinions.

■ *Why do you think the Bill of Rights includes freedom of the press?*

The Third Amendment says that the government cannot force citizens to pay for quartering, or housing, soldiers. Before the Revolutionary War, many colonists had to spend their own money to house and feed British soldiers. Under the Fourth Amendment, the government cannot order that a person's home be searched or property taken away without there being a good reason.

The Fifth through Eighth Amendments have to do with **due process of law**. This means people have the right to a fair public trial. They do not have to speak against themselves. They have the right to have a lawyer speak for them in court. They cannot be put on trial twice for the same crime or be given "cruel or unusual" punishment.

The Ninth Amendment says that people have many other rights that are not listed in

LEARNING FROM TIME LINES This time line lists the key events of the nation's early history, leading toward the ratification of the Constitution and the addition of the Bill of Rights.

■ *How many years were the Articles of Confederation in effect as the nation's plan of government?*

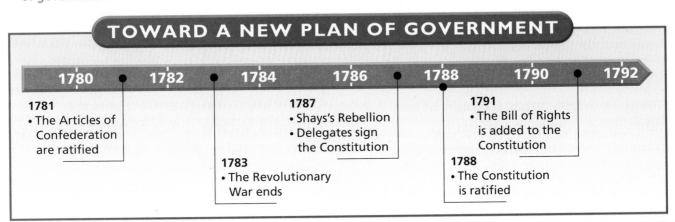

TOWARD A NEW PLAN OF GOVERNMENT

1780　1782　1784　1786　1788　1790　1792

1781
• The Articles of Confederation are ratified

1783
• The Revolutionary War ends

1787
• Shays's Rebellion
• Delegates sign the Constitution

1788
• The Constitution is ratified

1791
• The Bill of Rights is added to the Constitution

The Seventh Amendment gives people accused of crimes the right to a trial by jury. American citizens must be willing to be members of juries when asked.

detail in the Constitution. Among these are **human rights**—the freedoms that all people should have. The Declaration of Independence calls them "unalienable rights" and lists them as

❝ Life, Liberty, and the pursuit of Happiness. ❞

As a final protection for citizens, the Tenth Amendment says that the national government can do only those things listed in the Constitution. All other authority belongs to the states or to the people.

REVIEW *Why is the Bill of Rights an important part of the Constitution?*

Citizens' Responsibilities

With the first ten amendments, the American people made it clear that their rights were important. Government must protect these rights. But the people also have a role to play. Certain responsibilities go along with the rights of citizens. For the United States to remain free and strong, its citizens have to take an active part in its government.

The responsibilities of citizens are not written in the Constitution. They are implied, or suggested. The Constitution says, for example, that the laws of the United States are the highest laws in the nation. This implies that citizens should respect and obey the laws. The Constitution gives citizens the right to elect representatives to govern them. This implies that citizens should take part in government by voting in elections.

The Constitution gives Congress the authority to raise an army. This means that citizens should be ready to defend the country. The Constitution says that every person charged with a crime will be judged by a **jury**—a group of citizens who decide a case in court. So citizens must be willing to be members of juries when asked. The Constitution also gives Congress the authority to raise money to run the country. Citizens must be willing to pay taxes if the country is to run smoothly.

REVIEW *Why should citizens take an active part in government?*

"A Virtuous Citizenry"

The writers of the Constitution were not sure their new government would last. They looked to other countries and other times in history. No other nation had a government quite like the one described by the Constitution. No other people had the kinds of freedoms that American citizens now enjoyed. But would the people be able to keep their government going and protect their freedoms over time?

This would depend on having good citizens, or as the writers of the Constitution described them—"a virtuous citizenry." Past republics, like that of ancient Rome, broke up when the people grew greedy and selfish. To stay strong, the American people had to keep alive the spirit that had given the country its independence and its Constitution. The writers of the Constitution felt that a love of country is important because it helps keep this spirit alive. But **patriotism**, or love of country, is more than simply waving the American flag at special times. Americans have to be virtuous citizens all the time.

REVIEW *Why is love of country important?*

The bald eagle became the symbol of the United States in 1782. It represents the freedom of the American people and the strength of our nation as a whole. The rights listed in the Constitution guarantee the American people certain freedoms. To keep these freedoms, the American people must share responsibilities to help the nation remain free and strong.

LESSON 2 REVIEW

Check Understanding

1 Remember the Facts What important freedoms are protected by the Bill of Rights?

2 Recall the Main Idea What are the main rights and responsibilities of American citizens?

Think Critically

3 Think More About It Can American citizens have rights without responsibilities? Why or why not?

4 Personally Speaking What do you think is the most important right described in the Bill of Rights? Explain your answer.

Show What You Know

Art Activity Make a collage by cutting out drawings, photographs, and cartoons that show one or more of the rights listed in the Bill of Rights today. Share your collage with the class.

FOCUS

Why must a nation's leaders be willing to work together for government to work well?

Main Idea As you read, look for ways the nation's leaders worked together to make the new plan of government work.

Vocabulary

Cabinet
political party
campaign

This pitcher from 1789 marks the election of George Washington as President. The special button (top) was worn to honor him.

Putting the New Government to Work

1788	1793	1798

In early 1789, elections were held for the first time under the new government. Property-owning male citizens all over the United States elected members of the House of Representatives. Legislatures of the 13 states each chose two senators. The electoral college chose the nation's first President.

New Leaders

Fourteen years after Congress had chosen George Washington to lead the Continental army, the electoral college elected him as the nation's first President. John Adams, the runner-up to Washington in the voting, became the first Vice President. His job was to help President Washington with his duties.

On April 30, 1789, George Washington stood on the balcony of Federal Hall in New York City, where the new Congress was to meet for the first time. There he recited the President's oath of office:

“ I do solemnly swear (or affirm) that I will faithfully execute the office of President of the United States, and will to the best of my ability preserve, protect, and defend the Constitution of the United States. ”

The new President and the first Congress helped the government make a good start. Congress decided on the number of justices who would serve on the Supreme Court. The President named John Jay as the first chief justice.

Washington rode from Virginia to New York to take the oath of office. This painting shows children giving him flowers as he passes through Trenton, New Jersey.

Washington chose new leaders, too, for important jobs in the executive branch. These were the secretaries, or heads, of the departments of state, the treasury, and war. These departments would carry out the main responsibilities of the executive branch.

President Washington asked Thomas Jefferson to help him deal with other countries. He made Jefferson the nation's first secretary of state. Jefferson worked to set up ties with the leading world powers of that day—Spain, France, and the former enemy of the United States, Britain.

Alexander Hamilton was given the important job of secretary of the treasury. The national government badly needed money. Hamilton worked with Congress to set up a new banking system and pass new tax laws. He also ordered the printing and coining of money.

Washington chose Henry Knox, who had been a general in the Revolutionary War, as secretary of war. Knox had helped the Continental army defeat the British at the Battle of Yorktown. Knox began building a national army of 1,000 soldiers to defend the nation's western border.

Edmund Randolph became the President's legal adviser, now called the Attorney General. He told the President what the Constitution and the nation's other laws would and would not allow him to do.

Jefferson, Hamilton, Knox, and Randolph together were known as the **Cabinet**, a group of the President's most important advisers. Every President since Washington has relied on a Cabinet for help in carrying out the duties of the executive branch. Under later Presidents, the number of Cabinet members grew as the executive branch took on more responsibilities.

REVIEW *How did George Washington divide the responsibilities of the executive branch?*

New Disagreements

Almost as soon as the new government got started, President Washington's two top advisers began to quarrel. Thomas Jefferson and Alexander Hamilton disagreed on almost every problem facing the new nation.

One of the main disagreements between the two leaders had to do with the authority of the states and the national government. Jefferson worked for the rights of the states. He did not trust a strong national government. Hamilton liked a strong national government and did not trust the states to act on their own.

Jefferson and Hamilton also disagreed about what some parts of the Constitution meant. Jefferson said the national government had only the authority described in the Constitution. He said that all other authority belonged to the states. Hamilton said that the Constitution allowed the national government far greater authority over many more areas than those it listed. He felt that the government should be active in all parts of American life.

This print from 1789 celebrates George Washington and the 13 states of the new nation. Thirteen of the circles surrounding Washington show the coats of arms of the 13 states. The top circle is the Great Seal.

HERITAGE

Presidents' Day

George Washington's birthday was first celebrated as a holiday in the late 1700s. Washington was born on February 22, 1732, according to the calendar we use today. However, by the calendar used during Washington's time, he was born on February 11. For this reason the holiday was celebrated on different days by different people.

Another great President, Abraham Lincoln, was born on February 12, 1809. His birthday is also celebrated. Starting in the 1970s some states combined the birthday celebrations for Washington and Lincoln on a holiday called Presidents' Day. This day is the third Monday of February each year.

Pins like this one were worn to celebrate Washington becoming President.

There were other differences. Jefferson wanted Americans across the country to spread out and live on farms. "When we get piled upon one another in large cities," Jefferson argued, "we shall become corrupt." Hamilton wanted the United States to be a nation of cities. He thought the national government should build ports and factories.

Jefferson thought the United States should have close ties with France. After all, France had been an ally of the United States in the Revolutionary War. Hamilton wanted the United States to become friendlier with Britain to make use of Britain's trading network, which covered much of the world.

REVIEW *What were the main disagreements between Jefferson and Hamilton?*

Alexander Hamilton (left) and Thomas Jefferson (right) disagreed over how much authority they believed the Constitution gave to the national government. Hamilton favored a strong national government. Jefferson supported the power of the states.

The First Political Parties

Representatives and senators in Congress began to take sides in the Jefferson-Hamilton quarrel. They even started voting together as groups. These groups formed the nation's first **political parties**. Party members tried to get others to agree with their ideas and chose leaders who shared the party's point of view.

Hamilton's followers formed what became known as the Federalist party. The party's members were some of the same people who had supported the Constitution during the state ratifying conventions. John Adams, John Jay, and Henry Knox all became members of the Federalist party.

Many Anti-Federalists took Jefferson's side in the quarrel. Patrick Henry, George Clinton, and others formed the Democratic-Republican party. They were sometimes called simply Republicans. Jefferson's Republican party was not today's Republican party, which was formed much later. In fact, it was the beginning of the present-day Democratic party.

Most often Federalists and Republicans had to compromise so that laws could get passed. In one compromise, they agreed that a national capital would be built as a permanent home for the new government. But the capital would not be part of any one state. Maryland and Virginia would both give up some of their land to create the District of Columbia (D.C.). George Washington himself chose the location for the capital city that came to carry his name.

REVIEW *What were the main differences between Federalists and Republicans?*

The District of Columbia

President Washington selected a place for the capital city a few miles up the Potomac River from his plantation, Mount Vernon. Two former clockmakers, Andrew Ellicott and Benjamin Banneker, surveyed the land. An engineer, Pierre Charles L'Enfant, planned the buildings and the streets. L'Enfant's plan for the capital city called for wide streets reaching out from two main centers. In these centers stand the offices of the President and Congress today.

Benjamin Banneker, a free African, taught himself mathematics and astronomy. In addition to helping survey the land for the nation's capital, he made scientific calculations for his own almanacs.

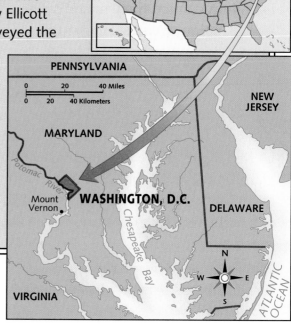

A Peaceful Change in Leadership

In 1792 the electoral college chose George Washington as President, just as it had done in 1789. Many people hoped Washington would remain President even longer than eight years. They said two 4-year terms were not enough—the country needed his leadership. In 1796, however, Washington turned down the chance to run again and went home to Mount Vernon, his plantation in Virginia. In leaving after two terms, Washington set an example that many other Presidents would follow. Later the Constitution would be changed so that no President could serve more than two terms in office.

But by 1796 the growth of political parties had changed the way the electoral college chose the President. Instead of making its own list of people to choose from, the electoral college was given lists made by each

party's leaders. The electoral college chose from these lists when it voted for the President.

When George Washington left office, the Federalist party backed John Adams, Washington's Vice President. Thomas Jefferson was the Republicans' choice.

As they had done with their quarrel over the Constitution, the Federalists and the Republicans took their fight to the people through the newspapers. This fight was less polite, though. Instead of arguing about problems, the political parties called one another names.

LEARNING FROM DIAGRAMS The streets of Washington, D.C., today reflect the original plan laid out by Pierre Charles L'Enfant.
■ *Which street names shown in the diagram have historical importance? What do you think they were named after?*

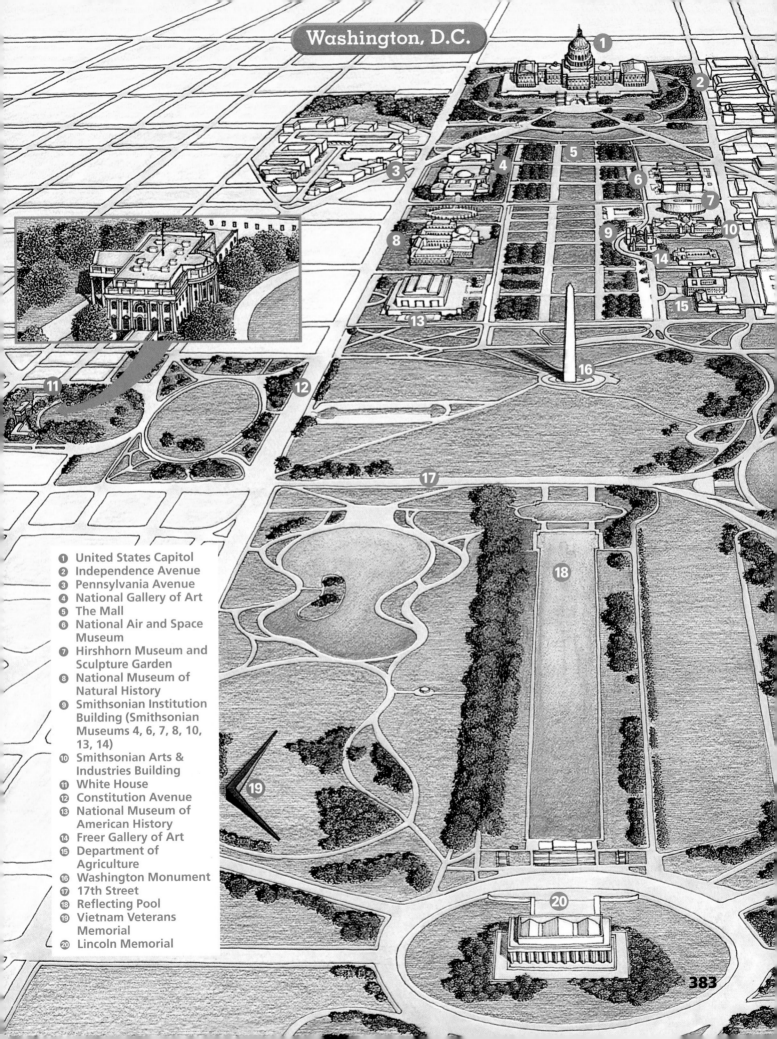

Washington, D.C.

1. United States Capitol
2. Independence Avenue
3. Pennsylvania Avenue
4. National Gallery of Art
5. The Mall
6. National Air and Space Museum
7. Hirshhorn Museum and Sculpture Garden
8. National Museum of Natural History
9. Smithsonian Institution Building (Smithsonian Museums 4, 6, 7, 8, 10, 13, 14)
10. Smithsonian Arts & Industries Building
11. White House
12. Constitution Avenue
13. National Museum of American History
14. Freer Gallery of Art
15. Department of Agriculture
16. Washington Monument
17. 17th Street
18. Reflecting Pool
19. Vietnam Veterans Memorial
20. Lincoln Memorial

The **campaign**, or race for office, was bitter. Yet the election was peaceful. In the end John Adams won by three electoral votes over Jefferson, who became the Vice President.

On March 4, 1797, John Adams took the President's oath of office in Philadelphia's Congress Hall, next door to the more famous Independence Hall. This was an important day in history. It marked one of the first times in the history of the world that a nation had changed leaders by means of a peaceful election.

John Adams started his term as President in Philadelphia, where Congress met. By the end of his term, in November 1800, the government had moved to the District of

Columbia. When John Adams and his family moved to the new capital city, they lived in a special house built for the President. It has had several names, among them the President's House, the Executive Mansion, and the White House—the name by which it is known today.

Abigail Adams, the President's wife, was impressed by her new home. She wrote to her daughter in Massachusetts that the house was "built for ages to come." Could the same be said for the nation's new government and its Constitution?

REVIEW *What was important about the way John Adams became President?*

LESSON 3 REVIEW

1788		1793		1798

1789
• George Washington becomes first President of the United States

1792
• George Washington serves a second term as President

1797
• John Adams becomes second President

Check Understanding

1 Remember the Facts What caused political parties to form? How did they change the way the electoral college chose the President?

2 Recall the Main Idea How did the nation's early leaders work together to make the new plan of government work?

Think Critically

3 Past to Present Why is the President's Cabinet larger today than in Washington's time?

4 Personally Speaking If you had been a member of the electoral college in 1796, which leader would you have chosen as President? Explain your answer.

Show What You Know

Newspaper Activity
Imagine a problem George Washington is facing as the first President of the United States. Then write a newspaper article comparing how Alexander Hamilton and Thomas Jefferson might feel about the problem.

Learn from a Document

1. Why Learn This Skill?

You have already studied many documents that are important to American history, such as the Mayflower Compact and the Declaration of Independence. In the study of history, a document is any photograph, recording, or written or printed paper that gives information. Maps, letters, drawings, and journals are all documents. So are some kinds of money, such as the paper money shown below.

Historical documents are primary sources that give information about the past. They tell us information that many books cannot tell us. Knowing how to gather information from a historical document can help you learn more about life in the past.

2. Understand the Process

In 1790 Secretary of the Treasury Alexander Hamilton asked Congress to set up the Bank of the United States. The bank would be a safe place to store the money the government collected in taxes. It would also loan money to merchants and manufacturers. One way the bank would loan money would be by printing paper money called banknotes.

In 1798 the Bank of the United States printed the banknote shown below. This is an important document because it gives information about the time in which it was printed.

Sometimes you have to look hard to find information on a document. Study the document by using these questions as a guide:

1. How do you know this banknote was printed by the Bank of the United States?

2. What tells you how much the banknote was worth?

3. The name of the holder and the date the money was given to the holder have been written by hand on the banknote. What might this tell you about how this banknote was used?

3. Think and Apply

With a partner, compare the 1798 banknote with a dollar bill of today. What can you learn from each one? Share your observations with classmates.

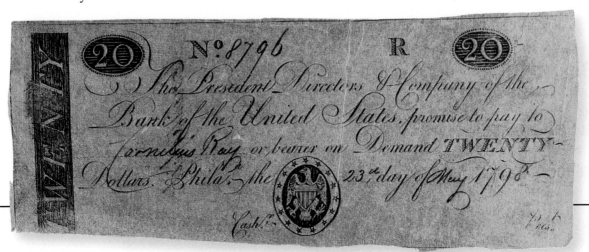

CHAPTER 10
REVIEW

1785

1787
• Delegates sign
the Constitution

CONNECT MAIN IDEAS

Use this organizer to show how the chapter's main ideas are connected. Write a sentence or two describing how each idea shown below helped to build a new government. A copy of the organizer may be found on page 70 of the Activity Book.

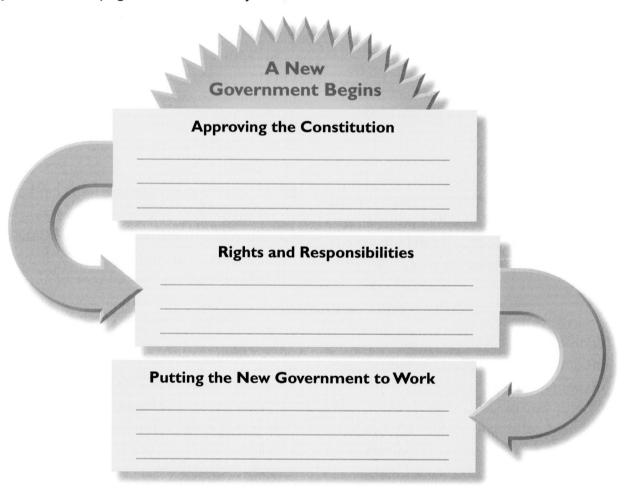

A New Government Begins

Approving the Constitution

_____
_____
_____

Rights and Responsibilities

_____
_____
_____

Putting the New Government to Work

_____
_____
_____

WRITE MORE ABOUT IT

Write a Persuasive Letter   Suppose that you are either an Anti-Federalist or a Federalist. Write a letter describing your views about the ratification of the Constitution. Tell in the letter why you think a bill of rights should or should not be added.

Write an Explanation   Imagine that you are an adviser to President Washington. He asks you to explain the differences that divide Thomas Jefferson and Alexander Hamilton. Write what you will tell the President about the leaders' disagreements.

1790	1795	1800

1789
• Government under the new Constitution begins
• George Washington becomes the first President of the United States

1797
• John Adams becomes the second President of the United States

USE VOCABULARY

For each group of underlined words, write the term from the list below that has the same meaning.

amendments	jury
Cabinet	patriotism
campaign	ratify

1 Nine of the 13 states had to <u>agree to</u> the Constitution before it would become law.

2 Ten <u>changes</u> were added to the Constitution.

3 A person charged with a crime is judged by a <u>group of citizens who decide a case in court</u>.

4 The writers of the Constitution felt that <u>love of country</u> was very important.

5 President Washington relied on a <u>group of the President's most important advisers</u>.

6 The <u>race for office</u> between Adams and Jefferson was bitter.

CHECK UNDERSTANDING

7 What collection of letters defended the Constitution?

8 What rights are granted under the First Amendment in the Bill of Rights?

9 What leaders were members of the first Cabinet? What office did each member hold?

10 What were the first two political parties?

11 Who was the second President of the United States? Who was his Vice President?

THINK CRITICALLY

12 **Cause and Effect** What promise helped persuade states to ratify the Constitution?

13 **Personally Speaking** The First Amendment protects freedom of speech and freedom of the press. Can you think of any examples in which these rights should be limited? Explain your answer.

APPLY SKILLS

Learn from a Document Use the banner on page 370 to answer these questions.

14 Who carried this banner?

15 Why do you think they chose to include the American flag on their banner?

16 What do the words *solid* and *pure* on the banner tell you?

17 What does the banner tell you about the work of a pewterer?

READ MORE ABOUT IT

A More Perfect Union: The Story of Our Constitution by Betsy and Giulio Maestro. Mulberry. This book presents an account of how the Constitution of the United States was drafted and ratified.

Visit the Internet at **http://www.hbschool.com** for additional resources.

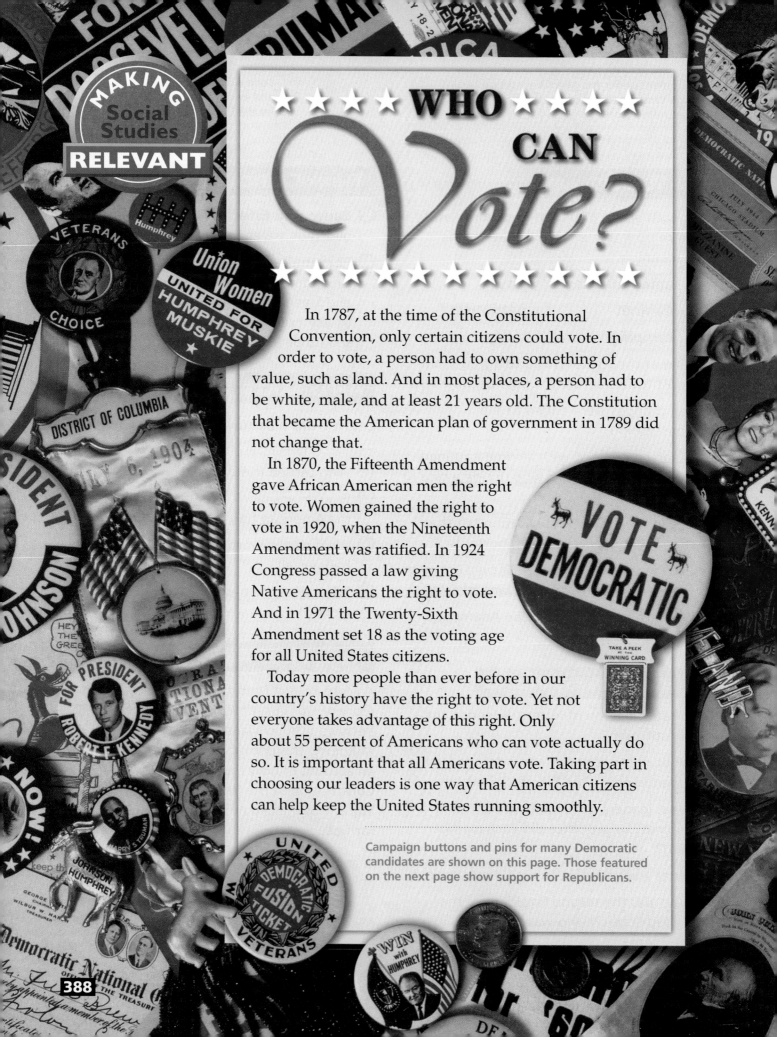

★★★★ WHO ★★★★ CAN *Vote?*

In 1787, at the time of the Constitutional Convention, only certain citizens could vote. In order to vote, a person had to own something of value, such as land. And in most places, a person had to be white, male, and at least 21 years old. The Constitution that became the American plan of government in 1789 did not change that.

In 1870, the Fifteenth Amendment gave African American men the right to vote. Women gained the right to vote in 1920, when the Nineteenth Amendment was ratified. In 1924 Congress passed a law giving Native Americans the right to vote. And in 1971 the Twenty-Sixth Amendment set 18 as the voting age for all United States citizens.

Today more people than ever before in our country's history have the right to vote. Yet not everyone takes advantage of this right. Only about 55 percent of Americans who can vote actually do so. It is important that all Americans vote. Taking part in choosing our leaders is one way that American citizens can help keep the United States running smoothly.

Campaign buttons and pins for many Democratic candidates are shown on this page. Those featured on the next page show support for Republicans.

Think and Apply

Think about the reasons why it is important for American citizens to vote. Then write a persuasive letter that explains why citizens need to take part in government by voting. Share your letter with the class.

BUILDING CITIZENSHIP

HARCOURT BRACE

Visit the Internet at
http://www.hbschool.com
for additional resources.

CNN
Turner Le@rning

Check your media center or classroom video library for the Making Social Studies Relevant videotape of this feature.

VISUAL SUMMARY

Summarize the Main Ideas
Study the pictures and captions to help you review the events you read about in Unit 5.

Write a Journal
Imagine that you are a delegate to the Constitutional Convention. Write several journal entries that tell what you think about the events shown in this visual summary.

1 Under the Articles of Confederation, the national government had little authority. In the late 1780s Daniel Shays led a rebellion in Massachusetts.

4 On September 17, 1787, the United States Constitution was signed at the convention. It was later ratified by all 13 states.

5 The Constitution says that the President is the head of the executive branch. George Washington, the first President, took the oath of office on April 30, 1789.

3 The delegates met at the Pennsylvania State House. They decided that a new plan of government was needed and described it in the Constitution.

2 Delegates from the states went to a convention in Philadelphia to discuss their problems.

6 Many people wanted the Constitution to protect their rights. Ten amendments were added to the Constitution—they form the Bill of Rights.

USE VOCABULARY

Write the term that correctly matches each definition.

ambassador	human rights
census	majority

1 a representative from one country to another country

2 the greater part

3 a population count

4 the freedoms that all people should have

CHECK UNDERSTANDING

5 What problems caused the delegates to the Constitutional Convention to disagree? How were the problems settled?

6 What was considered by many people to be a major problem with the Constitution after it was written? How was that problem finally solved?

7 How were Thomas Jefferson's and Alexander Hamilton's views about the role of government different?

THINK CRITICALLY

8 **Explore Viewpoints** James Madison said he was afraid Congress had become "a rope of sand" under the Articles of Confederation. Others, like Patrick Henry, argued that a rope of sand was better than a rod of iron. What did these two leaders mean?

9 **Think More About It** Imagine that you are a member of the House of Representatives and have just written a new bill. Describe the process your bill will take on its way to becoming a law.

APPLY SKILLS

Figure Travel Time and Distance
The map below shows George Washington's route from his home, Mount Vernon, to New York City, where he took the oath of office as the first President. Washington rode his horse on the journey. Use the map to answer the questions, figuring that Washington traveled about 70 miles a day.

10 How long would it have taken George Washington to ride from Mount Vernon, in Virginia, to Wilmington, Delaware?

11 How long would it have taken George Washington to ride from Philadelphia to New York City?

12 How long would Washington's entire journey from Mount Vernon to New York City have taken?

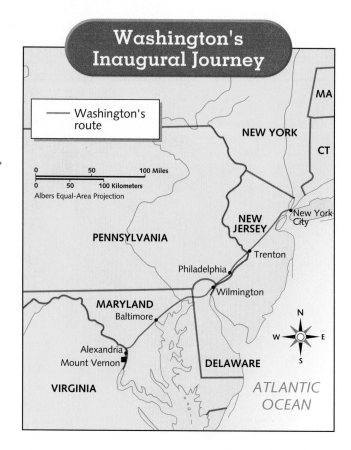

Washington's Inaugural Journey

— Washington's route

0   50   100 Miles
0   50   100 Kilometers
Albers Equal-Area Projection

MA
NEW YORK
CT
NEW JERSEY
New York City
PENNSYLVANIA
Trenton
Philadelphia
Wilmington
MARYLAND
Baltimore
Alexandria
Mount Vernon
DELAWARE
VIRGINIA
ATLANTIC OCEAN

N
W   E
S

REMEMBER

- Share your ideas.
- Cooperate with others to plan your work.
- Take responsibility for your work.
- Help one another.
- Show your group's work to the class.
- Discuss what you learned by working together.

ACTIVITY

Make a Book

Work in a group to write and design a book about the Bill of Rights. Your book should summarize each of the amendments in the Bill of Rights and explain how each is important to people today. To illustrate your book, draw pictures or cut out pictures from magazines and newspapers. Give your book a title, and display it where others in your school can read it.

ACTIVITY

Write and Perform a Class Play

Write and perform a play about the conflicts and cooperation that led to the ratification of the Constitution. As a class, decide on the people and events you want to include in your play. Give your play a title. Then form small groups. Each group will write one scene. Decide on roles and other responsibilities, such as making costumes and sets, and have at least one rehearsal. Then perform the play for invited guests from your school or community.

ACTIVITY

Draw a Map

Work in a group to draw a map that shows the United States at the time the Constitution was ratified. Include the 13 states, the state capitals, and the Northwest Territory. Color each state to show the year it ratified the Constitution. Use blue for 1787, red for 1788, yellow for 1789, and green for 1790. Make a key for your map. Then use the map to help explain to your classmates how the Constitution was ratified.

Unit Project Wrap-Up

Draw a Poster Work with several classmates to display your posters. Arrange the posters to show the order in which the events happened. Each group member should choose one of the events shown and write a short report. Use encyclopedias, biographies, and the Internet to find additional information. Present your posters and reports to the class.

OUR NATION GROWS

The United States grew rapidly in the 50 years after the War for Independence. As more people came to live in the new country, many began to leave the 13 states to find more land. At first, the settlers went only as far as the Appalachian Mountains. Later they traveled to the Mississippi River. By the 1840s they had crossed the continent and were building new settlements on the Pacific coast and in the Southwest.

During those same 50 years, the United States became more important among the countries of the world. The young nation fought another war with Britain and showed itself to be a leader among the countries in the Americas. While the United States built a strong industrial economy, more and more of its people demanded their rights as citizens.

◀ This scene of pioneers moving west was painted by Albert Bierstadt in 1867.

UNIT THEMES

- Conflict and Cooperation
- Continuity and Change
- Individualism and Interdependence
- Interaction Within Different Environments

Unit Project

Make a Diorama Complete this project as you study Unit 6. Make a diorama that shows pioneer life on the frontier. As you read, sketch pictures that illustrate the lives of the pioneers. Use your sketches to help you plan what you are going to show in your diorama.

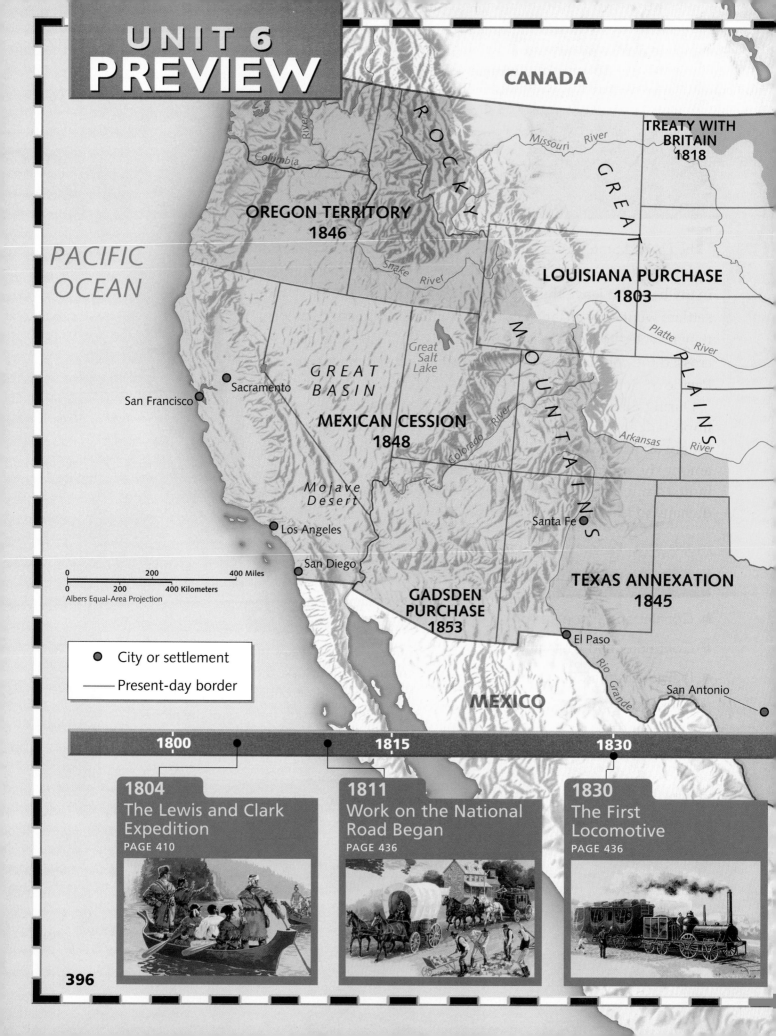

CANADA

TREATY WITH BRITAIN
1818

OREGON TERRITORY
1846

PACIFIC OCEAN

LOUISIANA PURCHASE
1803

Columbia River

Missouri River

ROCKY

Snake River

GREAT

MOUNTAINS

PLAINS

Platte River

Great Salt Lake

GREAT BASIN

Sacramento

San Francisco

Colorado River

MEXICAN CESSION
1848

Arkansas River

Mojave Desert

Los Angeles

San Diego

Santa Fe

TEXAS ANNEXATION
1845

GADSDEN PURCHASE
1853

El Paso

Río Grande

● City or settlement
— Present-day border

MEXICO

San Antonio

0   200   400 Miles
0   200   400 Kilometers
Albers Equal-Area Projection

1800   1815   1830

1804
The Lewis and Clark Expedition
PAGE 410

1811
Work on the National Road Began
PAGE 436

1830
The First Locomotive
PAGE 436

The United States, 1783–1853

TREATY WITH BRITAIN 1842

CANADA

Lake Superior

Lake Michigan

Lake Huron

Lake Erie

Lake Ontario

Mississippi River

Milwaukee

Chicago

Detroit

Cleveland

Pittsburgh

Allegheny River

Buffalo

Troy
Albany

Portland
Portsmouth
Boston
Providence
Hartford

New York City

Philadelphia
Wilmington
Baltimore
Annapolis
Washington, D.C.

Indianapolis

UNITED STATES
1783

Ohio River

Louisville

Richmond

Norfolk

Missouri River

St. Louis

APPALACHIAN MOUNTAINS

Nashville

Tennessee River

New Bern

Wilmington

ATLANTIC OCEAN

Atlanta

Charleston

Birmingham

Savannah

Dallas

Mississippi River

Natchez

1810   1813

1812

Houston

New Orleans

Jacksonville
St. Augustine

FLORIDA
1819

Gulf of Mexico

N
W   E
S

1845   1860

MID-1800s
Abolitionist Movement

PAGE 455

CASSIE'S JOURNEY

by Brett Harvey
illustrated by Ed Martinez

The people who settled the West came from many different places. Most came from the first 13 states, but some came from as far away as Europe and Asia. Almost everyone had read about the American West in newspapers, magazines, books, or letters. Many had heard about it in songs.

The West promised a new life to people like Cassie and her family, whom you will meet in this story. But getting to the West to enjoy its benefits was not easy. People traveling in wagon trains faced long, hard journeys. Sometimes food ran out, or water or firewood could not be found. People moving to the West faced these problems and more.

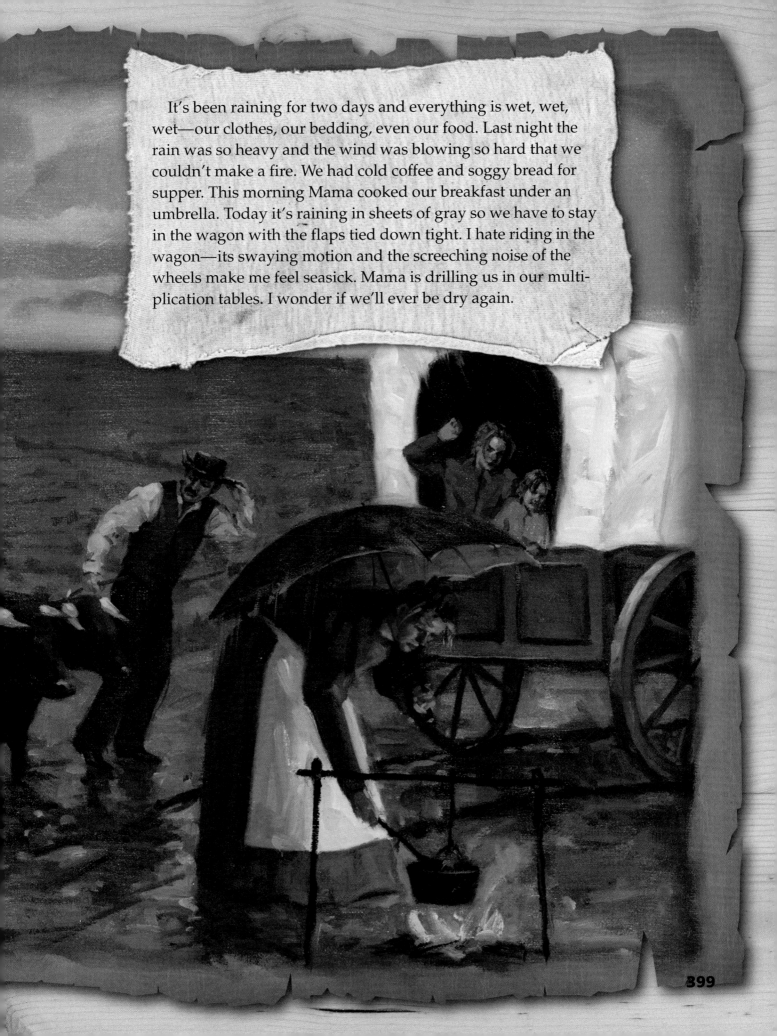

It's been raining for two days and everything is wet, wet, wet—our clothes, our bedding, even our food. Last night the rain was so heavy and the wind was blowing so hard that we couldn't make a fire. We had cold coffee and soggy bread for supper. This morning Mama cooked our breakfast under an umbrella. Today it's raining in sheets of gray so we have to stay in the wagon with the flaps tied down tight. I hate riding in the wagon—its swaying motion and the screeching noise of the wheels make me feel seasick. Mama is drilling us in our multiplication tables. I wonder if we'll ever be dry again.

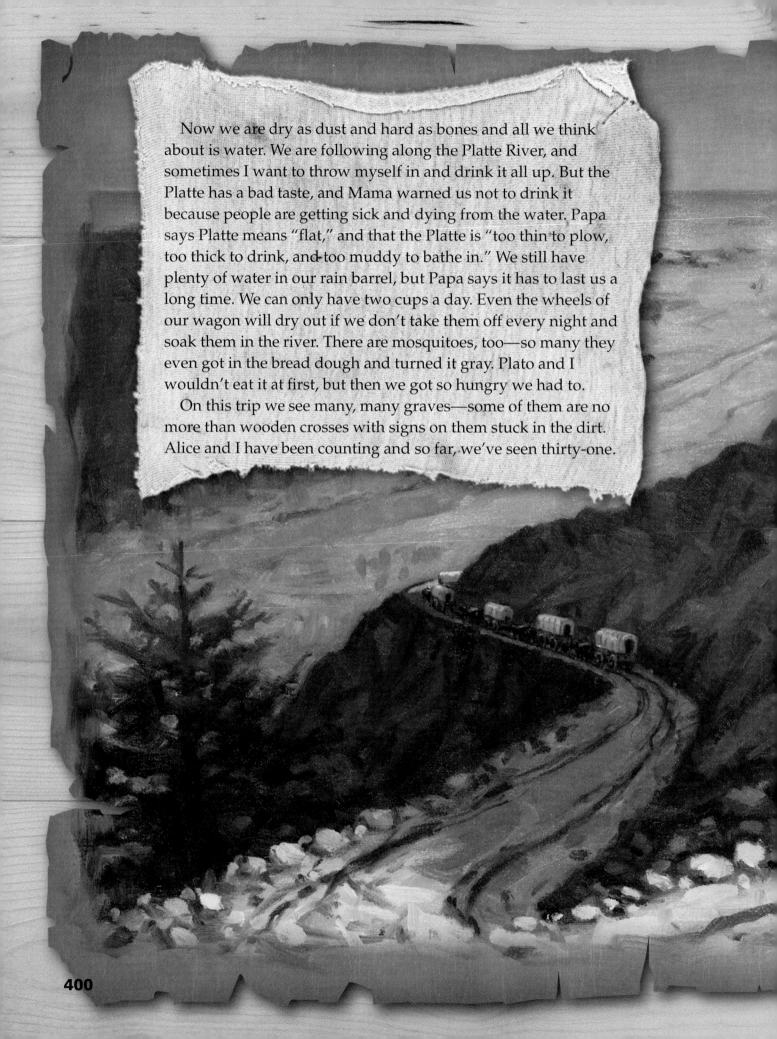

Now we are dry as dust and hard as bones and all we think about is water. We are following along the Platte River, and sometimes I want to throw myself in and drink it all up. But the Platte has a bad taste, and Mama warned us not to drink it because people are getting sick and dying from the water. Papa says Platte means "flat," and that the Platte is "too thin to plow, too thick to drink, and too muddy to bathe in." We still have plenty of water in our rain barrel, but Papa says it has to last us a long time. We can only have two cups a day. Even the wheels of our wagon will dry out if we don't take them off every night and soak them in the river. There are mosquitoes, too—so many they even got in the bread dough and turned it gray. Plato and I wouldn't eat it at first, but then we got so hungry we had to.

On this trip we see many, many graves—some of them are no more than wooden crosses with signs on them stuck in the dirt. Alice and I have been counting and so far, we've seen thirty-one.

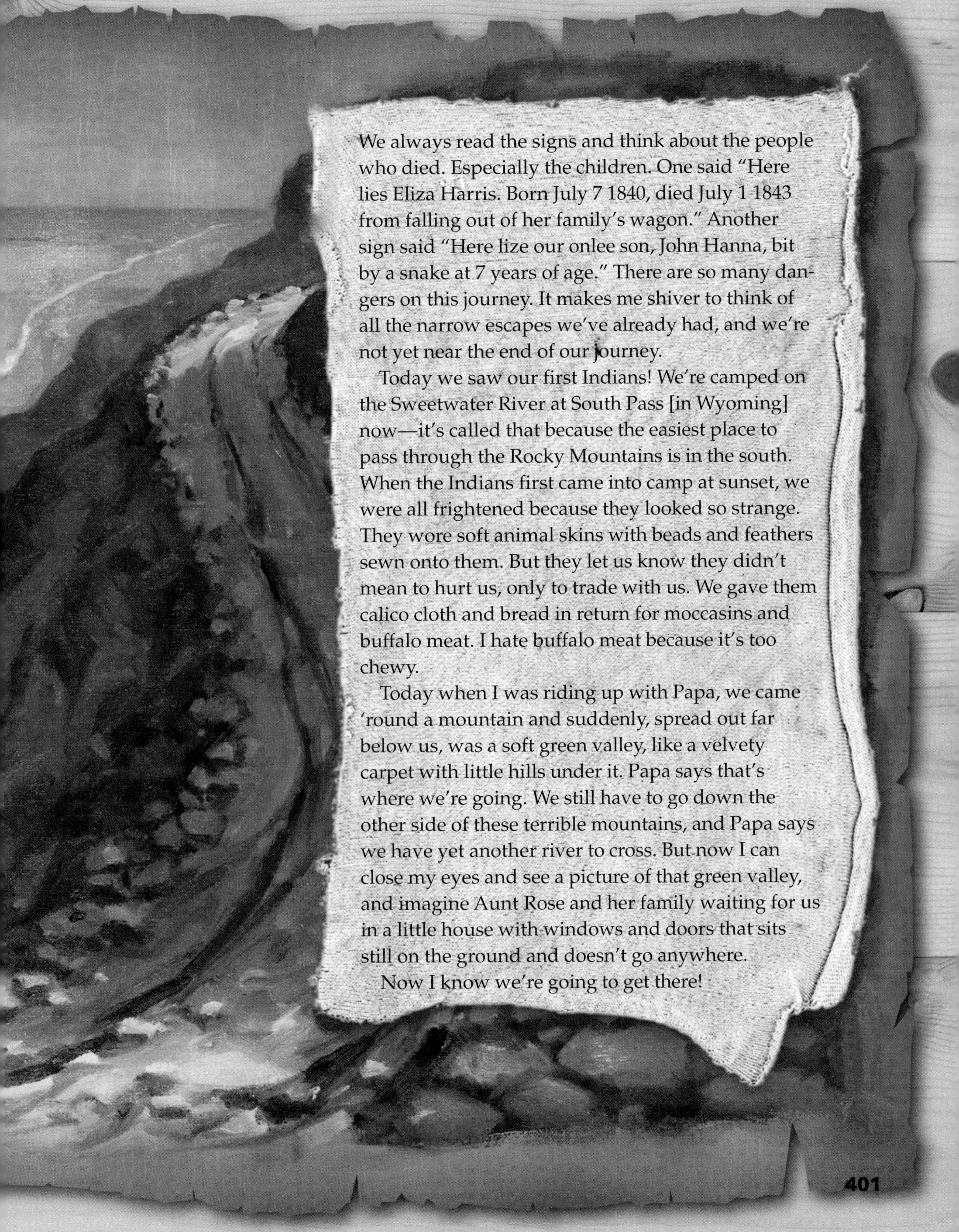

We always read the signs and think about the people who died. Especially the children. One said "Here lies Eliza Harris. Born July 7 1840, died July 1 1843 from falling out of her family's wagon." Another sign said "Here lize our onlee son, John Hanna, bit by a snake at 7 years of age." There are so many dangers on this journey. It makes me shiver to think of all the narrow escapes we've already had, and we're not yet near the end of our journey.

Today we saw our first Indians! We're camped on the Sweetwater River at South Pass [in Wyoming] now—it's called that because the easiest place to pass through the Rocky Mountains is in the south. When the Indians first came into camp at sunset, we were all frightened because they looked so strange. They wore soft animal skins with beads and feathers sewn onto them. But they let us know they didn't mean to hurt us, only to trade with us. We gave them calico cloth and bread in return for moccasins and buffalo meat. I hate buffalo meat because it's too chewy.

Today when I was riding up with Papa, we came 'round a mountain and suddenly, spread out far below us, was a soft green valley, like a velvety carpet with little hills under it. Papa says that's where we're going. We still have to go down the other side of these terrible mountains, and Papa says we have yet another river to cross. But now I can close my eyes and see a picture of that green valley, and imagine Aunt Rose and her family waiting for us in a little house with windows and doors that sits still on the ground and doesn't go anywhere.

Now I know we're going to get there!

ON THE MOVE

"The ax has cut the forest down, The laboring ox has smoothed all clear, Apples now grow where pine trees stood, And slow cows graze instead of deer."

From the poem "The Wilderness Is Tamed" by Elizabeth Coatsworth

Clara Brown, a pioneer woman

Across the Appalachians

| 1775 | 1800 | 1825 |

I n 1783 the Treaty of Paris, which ended the War for Independence, set the Mississippi River as the new nation's western border. When people talked about the West in those days, they meant all of the land between the Appalachian Mountains and the Mississippi River. This was the American frontier.

Daniel Boone

Even before the Treaty of Paris, American pioneers were pushing the frontier west. A **pioneer** is a person who first settles a new place. Daniel Boone was one of the earliest and best-known American pioneers to go west across the Appalachians.

Boone was born in Pennsylvania. He was 16 years old when his family moved to the Yadkin Valley of North Carolina. Boone came to love living in the woods and hunting.

During the French and Indian War, Boone served in the army. There he met John Finley, a fur trader. Boone later remembered the stories Finley told about a wonderful land west of the Appalachian Mountains. There, Finley said, green forests and meadows stretched for miles.

After the war Boone tried to find this land, now known as Kentucky. But he could not find a way over the mountains. He looked for the Warrior's Path, an Indian trail Finley had described that crossed the mountains, but he could not find it.

Soon after Boone returned home, a peddler, or seller, came to the door of the Boone house in North Carolina. The peddler was John Finley! With Finley's help, Boone again tried to find

FOCUS
What problems might a person face in moving to a new place today?

Main Idea As you read, look for some of the problems the early settlers faced when they crossed the Appalachian Mountains.

Vocabulary
pioneer

The hunting bag above was used by pioneer leader Daniel Boone (left).

403

Daniel Boone leads pioneers through the Cumberland Gap in this painting by George Caleb Bingham. Bingham was a young boy when his family moved to the frontier lands in the early 1800s. His paintings help people see what life was like for early pioneers.

Kentucky. This time he found the Warrior's Path and followed it across the Appalachian Mountains through what was called the Cumberland Gap. Boone later told a friend what he had seen on the other side.

66 Thousands of Buffalo roamed the Kentucky hills and the land looked as if it never would become poor. **99**

Both the Cherokees and Shawnees lived in settlements throughout Kentucky. Several times the Shawnees captured Boone during his visits there. Each time they let him go with a warning not to come back. But Boone did not listen. He returned again and again to Kentucky to explore and to hunt. Stories of Boone's adventures and Kentucky's rich land soon spread, making people want to settle there.

REVIEW *What did Daniel Boone find when he reached Kentucky?*

Human-Environment Interactions
This map shows the different routes people used to travel to Kentucky.

■ *What route did Boone follow through the Appalachian Mountains?*

Routes to Kentucky

OHIO

WEST VIRGINIA

Ohio River

Elk River
Kanawha R.
Gauley R.

KENTUCKY

Harrodsburg
Boonesborough

Kentucky River

Cumberland River

N
W   E
S

Cumberland Gap

Block House

VIRGINIA

TENNESSEE

Tennessee River

APPALACHIAN MOUNTAINS

Yadkin River

Salisbury

NORTH CAROLINA

| 0 | 50 | 100 Miles |
| 0 | 50 | 100 Kilometers |
Azimuthal Equal-Area Projection

SOUTH CAROLINA

——— Warrior's Path   ——— Wilderness Road
——— Boone's Trail   ——— Present-day border

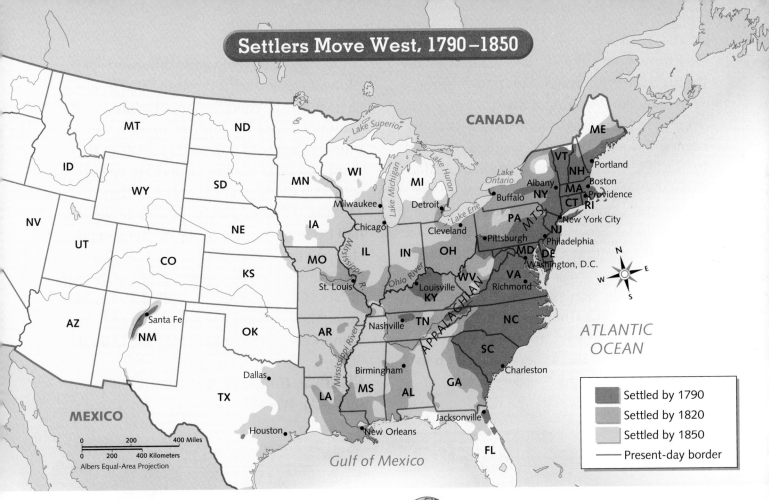

Settlers Move West, 1790–1850

Settled by 1790
Settled by 1820
Settled by 1850
Present-day border

Albers Equal-Area Projection

Regions This map shows the westward settlement of American pioneers at different times.

■ *What areas did pioneers settle from 1790 to 1820?*

Settling Kentucky

As word spread about Kentucky, several families tried to make their way over the mountains. But the Cherokees and Shawnees did not want to give up their land. They fought the pioneers, who had to turn back. Finally, in 1774, the Virginia militia fought a battle with the Indians and won. Virginia leaders made Indian leaders sign a treaty giving up their lands in Kentucky.

As soon as the treaty was signed, a land developer hired Daniel Boone to clear a road to Kentucky. In March 1775 Boone led a group through the Cumberland Gap. Cutting down trees and bushes to make way for wagons, the workers cleared a path through the wilderness. This path became known as the Wilderness Road.

Once in Kentucky, Boone built a fort and named it Boonesborough. He then returned to North Carolina to lead a group of settlers to Kentucky. In August he set out with his family and some neighbors for the new land. It was a slow, hard trip over the mountains. Getting a cow to walk 300 miles (483 km) was not easy. Sometimes wild animals scared the horses so that they ran off in all directions. The Cherokees and Shawnees made surprise attacks, hoping to scare off the pioneers. But the settlers pushed on to Boonesborough, joining others at Kentucky's first pioneer settlement.

Over the next few years, thousands of pioneers took the Wilderness Road to the rich valleys beyond the Appalachian Mountains. Many more settlements were built in Kentucky and in Tennessee to the south. By 1800, American and European settlers had moved as far west as the Mississippi River. Kentucky and Tennessee had become states. Farmers in these states shipped their crops and animals on flatboats down the Mississippi River to the port of New Orleans, then controlled by Spain. From New Orleans the goods went by ship to markets on the east coast of the United States.

REVIEW *How did Daniel Boone help settle the West?*

HISTORY

Log Cabins

Most pioneers in Kentucky lived in log cabins because such homes were quick and easy to build. First, a number of straight trees, all about the same size around, were chosen. Then the trees were cut down and trimmed to the right length. The logs were pulled by horses or dragged by hand to where the cabin was to be built. Notches were cut at the ends so that the logs would fit together. Next, the logs were lifted into place. The spaces between the logs were "chinked," or filled with mud, clay, or moss. Finally, a roof and a fireplace were added. Following this plan, two people could build a cabin in about two weeks.

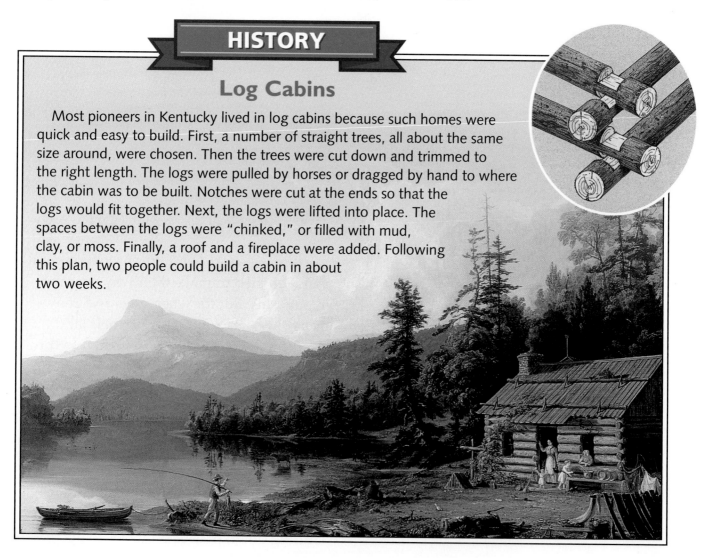

Pioneer Life

Life on the western frontier was hard for pioneer families. After they bought their land from a land developer, they had to clear thick forest in order to build their homes and farms. Most pioneers had little food to last until their first crops were ready. One pioneer told how poor his family was when they first settled in Kentucky.

> My Wife and I had neither spoon, dish, knife, or any thing to do with when we began life.

Pioneer families had to become self-sufficient very quickly, or they did not survive on the frontier. They built their own homes, grew their own food, and made their own clothes and tools. They bartered with the Indians, who traded furs, tobacco, cotton, and corn for cloth and other goods.

As pioneers continued moving onto Indian lands, many banded together in forts

This patriotic quilt shows people holding American flags. Pioneer families made quilts like this to help them keep warm during the winter.

to protect themselves. In some settlements they built their log houses close together with a high log fence all around.

REVIEW *How did pioneer families become self-sufficient?*

LESSON I REVIEW

1775 ——————— 1800 ——————— 1825

1775
• Daniel Boone settles Kentucky

1800
• Settlers move as far west as the Mississippi River

Check Understanding

1 Remember the Facts   Why did pioneers push west into the frontier?

2 Recall the Main Idea   What problems did the early settlers face as they crossed the Appalachian Mountains?

Think Critically

3 Cause and Effect   How did Daniel Boone's Wilderness Road help the settlement of Kentucky and the West?

4 Think More About It   Do you think the Indians and the pioneers could have lived peacefully together in Kentucky?

Show What You Know

Poster Activity   It is 1775, and you own a general store in North Carolina. Create a poster with pictures of some of the supplies you think a pioneer would need to take west. Display your poster in the classroom.

The Louisiana Purchase

| 1800 | 1803 | 1806 |

In time some of the pioneers who had settled between the Appalachians and the Mississippi began to look beyond the mighty river. Spain and France claimed these rich lands, although it was mostly Indian peoples who lived there. In one of the largest land sales in history, the United States bought part of this region from France in 1803. The way was now open for settlers to move even farther west.

The Incredible Purchase

Shortly before noon on March 4, 1801, Thomas Jefferson walked through the muddy streets of Washington, D.C., to the Capitol building. The writer of the Declaration of Independence was about to become the third President of the young nation. His simple clothes seemed right for the new capital, which was only half built.

After he took the President's oath of office, Jefferson spoke of his hopes for the country. He called the United States "a rising nation, spread over a wide and fruitful land." He knew, however, that the country faced a big problem. Spain had closed the port of New Orleans to western farmers, hoping to stop the United States frontier from moving farther west.

Spain had taken over all of Louisiana, including New Orleans, after France lost the French and Indian War. The French had given this huge area to Spain to keep the British from getting control of it. In 1802 President Jefferson learned that Spain had secretly given

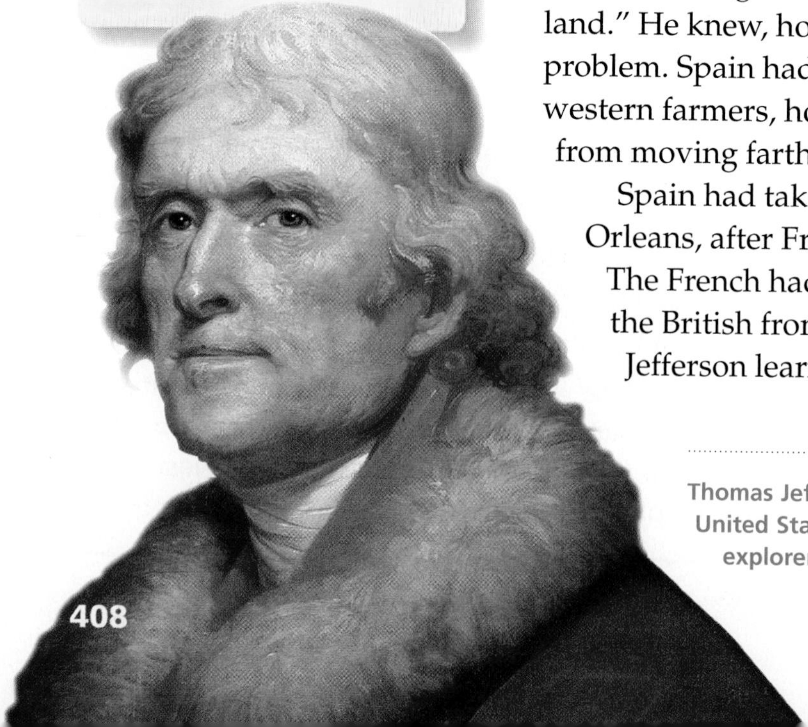

FOCUS

What might people today learn from the examples set by people in the past?

Main Idea As you read, look for things that American pioneers learned from the explorers who traveled west before them.

Vocabulary

purchase
pathfinder

Thomas Jefferson (left) became the third President of the United States. The compass (above left) was used by the explorer William Clark.

408

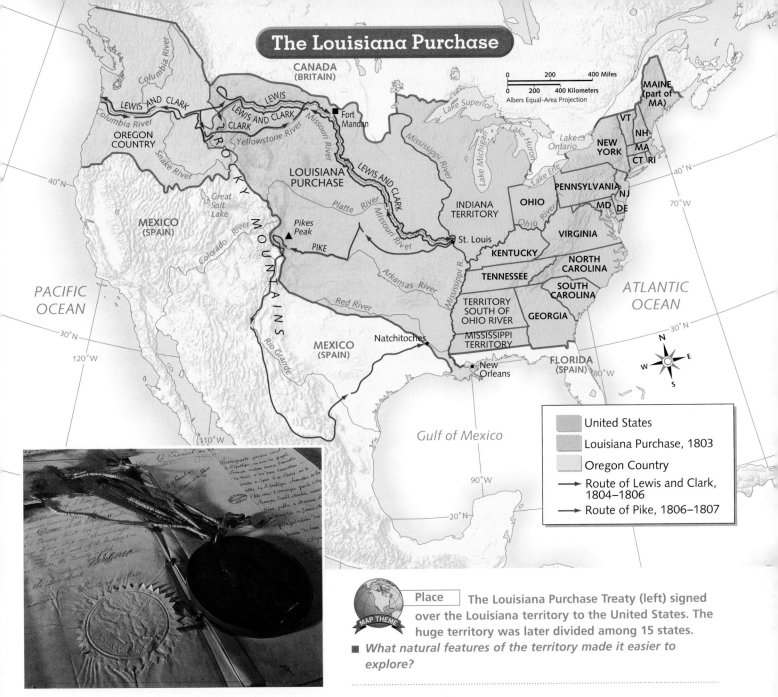

The Louisiana Purchase

CANADA
(BRITAIN)

0   200   400 Miles
0   200   400 Kilometers
Albers Equal-Area Projection

MAINE
(part of MA)

Columbia River

LEWIS AND CLARK

LEWIS

LEWIS AND CLARK

CLARK

Fort Mandan

Columbia River

OREGON COUNTRY

Yellowstone River

Missouri River

Lake Superior

VT
NH
NEW YORK
MA
CT RI

Snake River

ROCKY MOUNTAINS

LOUISIANA PURCHASE

LEWIS AND CLARK

Mississippi River

Lake Michigan

Lake Huron

Lake Ontario

Lake Erie

40°N

70°W

MEXICO
(SPAIN)

Great Salt Lake

Platte River

Missouri River

INDIANA TERRITORY

OHIO

PENNSYLVANIA
NJ
MD DE

Pikes Peak

PIKE

St. Louis

Ohio River

Colorado River

KENTUCKY

VIRGINIA

PACIFIC OCEAN

Arkansas River

TENNESSEE

NORTH CAROLINA

SOUTH CAROLINA

ATLANTIC OCEAN

120°W

Red River

TERRITORY SOUTH OF OHIO RIVER

GEORGIA

30°N

30°N

110°W

Rio Grande

MEXICO
(SPAIN)

Natchitoches

MISSISSIPPI TERRITORY

New Orleans

FLORIDA
(SPAIN)

80°W

Gulf of Mexico

90°W

20°N

N
W   E
S

Legend:
- United States
- Louisiana Purchase, 1803
- Oregon Country
- → Route of Lewis and Clark, 1804–1806
- → Route of Pike, 1806–1807

Place The Louisiana Purchase Treaty (left) signed over the Louisiana territory to the United States. The huge territory was later divided among 15 states.

■ *What natural features of the territory made it easier to explore?*

Louisiana back to France. Now, Jefferson thought, was the time to act.

Jefferson had two representatives ask the French leader, Napoleon Bonaparte (nuh•POH•lee•uhn BOH•nuh•part), to sell part of Louisiana, including New Orleans, to the United States. Jefferson was willing to offer $10 million. But Bonaparte had other problems on his mind. France was preparing for war with Britain. And people in the French colony of St. Domingue (SEN daw•MENG) in the Caribbean had rebelled

against France. Needing money to pay for two wars, Bonaparte offered to sell *all* of Louisiana to the United States. To the surprise of the Americans, the price was $15 million—for more than 800,000 square miles (2,071,840 sq km)!

On April 30, 1803, the United States agreed to **purchase**, or to buy, the huge territory, reaching from the Mississippi River west to the Rocky Mountains and from New Orleans north to Canada. The territory became known as the Louisiana Purchase.

Toussaint-Louverture
1743–1803

In 1791 Pierre Dominique Toussaint-Louverture (TOO•san LOO•ver•tur) helped lead a slave revolt in St. Domingue. Peace returned only after France agreed to end slavery in its colonies. An experienced soldier, Toussaint held several military positions on the island and soon became its most important leader. In 1802 the French tried to take back St. Domingue, and Toussaint was arrested. He died in prison, but the French could not defeat the rebels. On January 1, 1804, St. Domingue became the independent country of Haiti.

With it the United States doubled in size and became one of the largest countries in the world.

REVIEW *How did the Louisiana Purchase change the United States?*

The Lewis and Clark Expedition

Few people in the United States knew much about the lands of the Louisiana Purchase. It was an area that Americans had never explored. President Jefferson asked Meriwether Lewis to lead an expedition to learn all he could about the new land. Lewis was to be a **pathfinder**, someone who finds a way through an unknown region.

Lewis had been an army officer in the wilderness of the Northwest Territory. He

chose William Clark, a good friend, to help him lead the expedition. Clark was an excellent cartographer. Lewis and Clark put together a group of about 30 men, most of them frontier soldiers. One member of the group was York, William Clark's African slave. York contributed to the mission through his skill in hunting and fishing.

The leaders called their group the Corps of Discovery. On a spring morning in May 1804, the group left St. Louis and traveled up the Missouri River. The pathfinders spent the summer and fall pushing deep into the Louisiana Purchase. When they reached present-day North Dakota, they built a winter camp near a Mandan village.

While there, Lewis and Clark hired a French fur trader to translate some Indian languages for them. The fur trader was married to a Shoshone (shoh•SHOH•nee) woman who was named Sacagawea (sak•uh•juh•WEE•uh). Sacagawea agreed to serve as translator when the Corps of Discovery reached the land of the Shoshones.

In the spring of 1805, the Lewis and Clark expedition again moved up the Missouri River by boat. But they would need horses to cross the Rocky Mountains. They put their hope in Sacagawea and the Shoshones. "If we do not find them or some other nation who have horses, I fear the successful issue of our voyage will be very doubtful," Lewis wrote in his journal.

At last the expedition reached the lands of the Shoshones. Sacagawea's brother, Cameahwait (kah•MEE•ah•wayt), was now the chief. He gave the expedition horses, and the pathfinders continued their journey over the Rockies.

Once over the mountains, they built more boats. They went down the Snake River to

Sacagawea (above right) uses sign language to communicate with the Chinooks during the Lewis and Clark expedition. This page from William Clark's journal (below) shows a drawing he made during the journey.

the Columbia River and on to the Pacific Ocean. In November 1805, after traveling for more than a year and more than 3,000 miles (4,828 km), Clark wrote in his journal,

66 Great joy in camp. We are in view of the . . . great Pacific Octean which we have been so long anxious to see, and the roreing or noise made by the waves brakeing on the rockey shores (as I may suppose) may be heard distinctly. 99

The Corps of Discovery returned to St. Louis in September 1806. Lewis and Clark brought back seeds, plants, and even living animals. Among these were many birds. Lewis and Clark were able to report much about the land and its people. The expedition also brought back maps showing the major rivers and mountains. Clark had carefully mapped important passes through the Rockies. In later years these maps helped pioneers find their way to the Pacific coast.

REVIEW *What did Lewis and Clark learn from their expedition?*

Journey to the Southwest

A few weeks before Lewis and Clark returned to St. Louis, another expedition set out from Missouri to explore the southwestern part of the Louisiana Purchase. A small group of pathfinders led by Captain Zebulon Pike followed the Arkansas River through the middle part of the new lands.

By the winter of 1806, Pike had reached a great prairie in present-day Kansas. He saw with wonder that the prairie was covered with thousands of buffalo.

As the expedition traveled farther west, Pike saw what he described as a "blue mountain" in the distance. Today that blue mountain is called Pikes Peak, for the explorer. It is part of the Rocky Mountain range.

Pike's expedition followed the mountains south. The explorers built a small fort beside what Pike thought was the Red River. It was really the northern part of the

Rio Grande. The expedition had wandered out of the Louisiana Purchase and onto Spanish land!

Spanish soldiers soon arrived and took Pike and the other explorers to Santa Fe, the capital of the Spanish colony of New Mexico. The explorers were put in jail for being on Spanish land. In Santa Fe the Spanish governor asked Pike if the United States was getting ready to invade the Spanish lands. Pike said no, but in fact the expedition did lead to an "invasion" of another kind.

Zebulon Pike became a general in the War of 1812 and was killed in battle.

When he was set free several months later, Pike described the route to the Spanish lands. He reported that the people of Santa Fe needed manufactured goods. Soon American traders were heading for New Mexico as part of a great economic invasion.

REVIEW *How did Pike help start an economic invasion of the West?*

Pikes Peak (left) was named after Zebulon Pike, who tried to climb to the top but failed.

LESSON 2 REVIEW

1800 ● 1803 ● 1806

1801
• Thomas Jefferson becomes President

1803
• The Louisiana Purchase

1804
• Lewis and Clark expedition begins

Check Understanding

1 Remember the Facts What were the boundaries of the Louisiana Purchase?

2 Recall the Main Idea What did American pioneers learn from those who traveled west before them?

Think Critically

3 Think More About It Why do you think President Jefferson thought it was important for Lewis and Clark to explore the Louisiana Purchase?

4 Explore Viewpoints Why did the Spanish fear Pike's entry into their lands? What might Pike have thought of their viewpoint?

Show What You Know
Simulation Activity
Imagine that you are planning an expedition into an unknown land. List the things you hope to learn during your travels. Share your list with a classmate.

413

FOCUS

What do you think make people feel proud of their country?

Main Idea Read to learn how the War of 1812 helped make Americans proud of their country.

Vocabulary

impressment
nationalism
annex
doctrine

A Second War with Britain

1805	1815	1825

The exciting stories of pathfinders such as Meriwether Lewis, William Clark, and Zebulon Pike made many people want to move to the West. But American Indians still fought with American pioneers, trying to turn them back. In the Northwest Territory, the British helped the Indians by selling them guns. Before long, trouble in the Northwest Territory helped push the United States into a second war with Britain.

Tecumseh and the Prophet

As more and more pioneers moved to the Northwest Territory, many Indians grew angry that so much of their land was being lost. The leader of these Indians was a Shawnee named Tecumseh (tuh•KUHM•suh). Tecumseh dreamed of forming a strong Indian confederation. He went from one tribe to another with his brother, Tenskwatawa (ten•SKWAHT•uh•wah), whom people called the Prophet, talking about his plan. Tecumseh called on the tribes to stop fighting each other and to unite against the Americans settling their land.

Prophetstown was the Shawnee town where Tecumseh had his headquarters. It was just below the mouth of the Tippecanoe River, near where Lafayette, Indiana, is today.

In 1809, by signing the Treaty of Fort Wayne, a group of Indian tribes agreed to sell 3 million acres of land to the United States government. Upon hearing the news, Tecumseh cried,

66 Sell a country! Why not sell the air, the clouds, and the great sea? 99

The Prophet was a well-known religious leader of the Shawnee people.

Tecumseh said that no one tribe had the right to sell land. He warned the Americans that the Indians would fight if they were made to give up any more of their land. The Indians led by Tecumseh were eager for battle, but Tecumseh would not let them fight unless they were attacked first.

In 1811 Tecumseh decided to talk with the Creeks and other Indian tribes living in Kentucky and Tennessee about his plan for a confederation. Before he left, he told the Prophet to keep the peace until he returned.

REVIEW *What plan did Tecumseh have for the Indian tribes?*

Battle of Tippecanoe

William Henry Harrison was governor of the Indiana Territory in 1811. Knowing that Tecumseh was away from Prophetstown, Harrison sent 1,000 soldiers to the Shawnee town. They camped nearby on the night of November 6, 1811. The Prophet feared that the soldiers would soon attack, so he ordered the Indians to attack first. The morning of November 7, the terrible Battle of Tippecanoe took place.

Neither side clearly won the battle. The Americans destroyed Prophetstown, but

The Shawnee chief Tecumseh (right) wanted the United States to stop forcing Indians from their homelands. A computer drawing (below) shows what Prophetstown may have looked like before it was attacked.

415

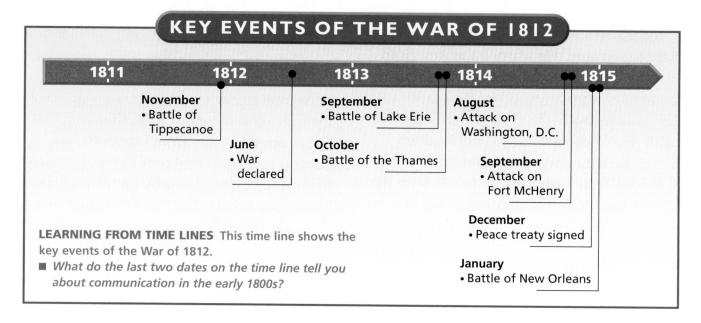

KEY EVENTS OF THE WAR OF 1812

1811   1812   1813   1814   1815

November
• Battle of Tippecanoe

June
• War declared

September
• Battle of Lake Erie

October
• Battle of the Thames

August
• Attack on Washington, D.C.

September
• Attack on Fort McHenry

December
• Peace treaty signed

January
• Battle of New Orleans

LEARNING FROM TIME LINES This time line shows the key events of the War of 1812.

■ *What do the last two dates on the time line tell you about communication in the early 1800s?*

Indians went through the Northwest Territory, attacking settlers.

Many people blamed the Indian attacks on Britain. They said the British were giving guns to the Indians and talking against American settlers. People in the Northwest Territory thought the answer was simple—take over Canada and drive the British out of North America.

REVIEW *What were the results of the Battle of Tippecanoe?*

War Fever

People in the South, too, were angry with Britain. To stop Americans from trading with the French and other Europeans, the British stopped American ships at sea. They even took sailors off American ships and put them to work on British ships. Taking workers this way is called **impressment**.

People in the West and the South called upon the United States government to declare war on Britain. Those who spoke up the most were known as War Hawks. The War Hawks blamed the British in Canada for encouraging the Indians to fight against settlers in the West. They blamed the British government for stopping trade in the South.

Eager for more land, the War Hawks even hoped to take Canada from Britain.

Not everyone wanted war, however. Northern merchants had made a lot of money trading with the British. They did not want a war that would end their trade. Yet the desire for war was so great all over the rest of the country that Congress voted to declare war on Britain in 1812. It seemed as if a "war fever" had swept the nation.

REVIEW *Which regions of the United States wanted war with Britain? Which did not?*

The War of 1812

As the fighting began, Britain had the strongest navy in the world. Yet the small United States Navy, with only 16 ships, won an important battle on Lake Erie that became a turning point in the war. Ships commanded by American Captain Oliver Hazard Perry defeated the British on September 10, 1813. After the battle, Perry sent a message to General William Henry Harrison, saying "We have met the enemy and they are ours."

Perry's victory allowed Harrison to lead 3,500 soldiers across Lake Erie into Canada.

Major Battles of the War of 1812

Lake Superior

CANADA (BRITAIN)

St. Lawrence River

Montreal

MAINE (part of Massachusetts)

Hampden

INDIANA TERRITORY

Châteauguay 1813

La Colle Mill 1814

Chrysler's Farm 1813

VERMONT

Plattsburgh (Battle of Lake Champlain) 1814

Lake Champlain

NEW HAMPSHIRE

Fort Mackinac 1812

Lake Huron

York (Toronto) 1813

Sackets Harbor (raid) 1813

Portsmouth

ILLINOIS TERRITORY

Lake Michigan

MICHIGAN TERRITORY

Lake Ontario

Oswego (raid) 1814

Boston

Stoney Creek 1813

Lundy's Lane 1814

Albany

MASSACHUSETTS

Mississippi River

The Thames 1813

Buffalo

The Chippewa 1814

NEW YORK

Hartford

RHODE ISLAND

Frenchtown 1813

Lake Erie

Erie

CONNECTICUT

Fort Dearborn (Chicago) 1812

Put-in-Bay 1813

PENNSYLVANIA

New York City

NEW JERSEY

Battle of Tippecanoe 1811

OHIO

Ohio River

Philadelphia

Fort McHenry (Baltimore) 1814

Battle of Godly Wood 1814

INDIANA TERRITORY

DELAWARE

Battle of Bladensburg 1814

Washington, D.C. 1814

MARYLAND

VIRGINIA

River

KENTUCKY

Ohio

Norfolk

NORTH CAROLINA

ATLANTIC OCEAN

TENNESSEE

Mississippi River

SOUTH CAROLINA

MISSISSIPPI TERRITORY

GEORGIA

Charleston

Horseshoe Bend 1814

Vicksburg

Savannah

N

W   E

S

Mobile

Pensacola

FLORIDA (SPAIN)

100   200 Miles

0   100   200 Kilometers

Albers Equal-Area Projection

New Orleans 1815

Fort Bowyer 1814

LOUISIANA

Gulf of Mexico

Regions Both sides won major battles during the War of 1812.
■ *How many battles were fought near the Great Lakes?*

MAP THEME

American victory

British victory

British blockade

At the Battle of the Thames (TEMZ) on October 5, 1813, the American forces led by Harrison defeated the British and their Indian allies. Among the dead was Tecumseh, who was fighting on the British side.

Tecumseh's plan for a strong Indian confederation died with him. From that time on, settlers in the Northwest Territory were free from attacks by Indians.

REVIEW *What was a turning point in the War of 1812?*

British Raids

In August 1814, British troops marched on Washington, D.C.—a city of only 8,000 people. As the cracking of rifles and the booming of cannons filled the air, President James Madison rode to the battle 7 miles (11.3 km) away. First Lady Dolley Madison stayed behind, racing through the White House to save what she could from the British soldiers. She narrowly escaped. When the British arrived, they set fire to the White House, the Capitol, and other buildings.

With Washington in flames, the British sailed up Chesapeake Bay to Baltimore. But Baltimore was protected by Fort McHenry. Although British ships bombed the fort for hours, the Americans refused to surrender.

Unable to defeat the American forces at Baltimore, the British sailed south to New Orleans. But American soldiers under General Andrew Jackson were waiting there for them.

During a battle off the coast of Nova Scotia, British cannonballs could not break through the hard oak sides of the American warship *Constitution.* Legend says that a crew member yelled, "Her sides are made of iron!" After that, the victorious *Constitution* was nicknamed Old Ironsides.

During the war the British burned several buildings in Washington, D.C.—the White House, the Capitol, the Treasury, and some private homes. Dolley Madison (right) was able to save just a few things from the White House before she was forced to flee from British troops.

Earlier that year, with the aid of the Cherokees, General Andrew Jackson had defeated the Creek Indians at the Battle of Horseshoe Bend. The Creeks had sided with the British. By doing so, they hoped to keep Americans off their land.

When word came to Jackson that the British might attack New Orleans, his troops hurried to defend the city. There they withstood an assault by more than 5,000 British soldiers. For ten days the British laid siege to New Orleans. Fierce fighting from Jackson's soldiers finally made the British leave the city. Americans would later learn that the Battle of New Orleans had not been necessary. On December 24, 1814—two weeks before the battle—the British and Americans had signed a peace treaty in Europe. Word that the war was over had not reached New Orleans in time.

REVIEW *What were the results of British attacks on American cities?*

The Era of Good Feelings

Neither side was clearly the winner in the War of 1812. However, Americans were proud that the United States had proved itself equal to a great European nation. A wave of **nationalism**, or pride in the country, swept the land. People began to feel for the first time that they were Americans, not Virginians, New Yorkers, or Ohioans. For this reason the years from 1817 to 1825 have been called the Era of Good Feelings.

National pride could be seen in the government's strong dealings with other countries. President James Monroe set a new border between the United States and British Canada. He also convinced Spain to give up claims in West Florida, which had been **annexed**, or added on, earlier, and to give East Florida to the United States.

Birth of the Monroe Doctrine, a painting by Clyde DeLand, shows President Monroe (standing) discussing his doctrine with members of his Cabinet.

President Monroe knew that if the United States wanted to keep growing, it had to stop the growth of the Spanish, French, and British colonies in the Americas. He also was concerned about Russian claims in North America. So on December 2, 1823, he announced a **doctrine**, or government plan of action, that came to be called the Monroe Doctrine. The Monroe Doctrine declared that the United States was willing to go to war to stop European countries from expanding their American empires.

REVIEW *How did the War of 1812 affect the United States and its people?*

LESSON 3 REVIEW

1805	1815	1825

1809
• Indian tribes sign the Treaty of Fort Wayne

1812
• The War of 1812 begins

1823
• The Monroe Doctrine is announced

Check Understanding

1 Remember the Facts   What did Tecumseh hope to accomplish by talking to other Indian tribes?

2 Recall the Main Idea   How did the War of 1812 help make Americans proud of their country?

Think Critically

3 Explore Viewpoints   Why did people from the North, the South, and the West feel differently about going to war with Britain?

4 Past to Present   Many Americans who took part in the War of 1812 became national heroes. Who are some heroes of today? What actions helped them become known as heroes?

Show What You Know

Research Activity   Use the Internet or encyclopedias to find out more about the navy's battles in the War of 1812. Draw a picture and write a report about one battle. Present your findings to the class.

Predict a Likely Outcome

1. Why Learn This Skill?

People often make **predictions**. This means that they look at the way things are and decide what they think will most likely happen next. People use information and past experiences to predict a probable, or likely, outcome.

2. Understand the Process

During the War of 1812, the British lost the Battle of the Thames. The Indian leader Tecumseh died during the battle, and Indian attacks on settlers in the Northwest Territory soon ended. Use this information to predict what probably happened next in the westward movement of settlers. Follow these steps:

1. Think about what you already know about the loss of Indian lands as settlers moved west during colonial times and during the early years of the United States. Look for patterns in the events that took place.

2. Review the new information you learned about Tecumseh and the War of 1812.

3. Make a prediction about the westward movement of settlers following the war.

4. As you read or gather more information, ask yourself whether you still think your prediction is correct.

5. If necessary, go through the steps again to form a new prediction.

After going through these steps, you should have been able to predict that pioneers would continue to move west, building settlements on Indian lands.

3. Think and Apply

In 1823 the Monroe Doctrine was announced. Follow the steps listed above to predict how the Monroe Doctrine would affect the growth of the United States. As you read the next chapter, see whether the new information you learn supports your prediction.

This painting, by German American artist Emanuel G. Leutze, shows one person's view of the westward movement of settlers.

By the Dawn's Early Light

The Story of The Star-Spangled Banner

by Steven Kroll

illustrated by Dan Andreasen

While the British prepared to attack Baltimore during the War of 1812, an American doctor named William Beanes was held prisoner on the warship H.M.S. Tonnant. With the permission of President Madison, Beanes's friend, Francis Scott Key, along with Colonel John S. Skinner, went to the ship to ask that Beanes be set free. Key explained to the British commanders that Beanes had cared for many wounded British soldiers during the Battle of Bladensburg. Major General Sir Robert Ross agreed to free Beanes but said the three men would not be set free until after the British had attacked Fort McHenry.

Read now about the frightening days early in September 1814 when the British fleet approached Baltimore. Key and Skinner have just been taken to see Dr. Beanes and have told him what is happening. As you read, think about how Francis Scott Key chose to describe his experiences.

"And we must sit and watch while our country is attacked?" Beanes exclaimed.

"I'm afraid so," Colonel Skinner replied.

The three Americans were put up on the frigate *Surprise*, and for three days the British fleet crept up Chesapeake Bay.

Meanwhile, Baltimore was getting ready. Though inexperienced, the militia was on call. The city was ringed by trenches and ramparts[1] built by citizens. At star-shaped Fort McHenry, out on Whetstone Point overlooking the Patapsco River, a thousand troops were under the command of Major George Armistead. They had thrown up barriers outside the moat, placed sandbags around the powder magazine,[2] and sunk many small ships and barges in the north channel of the river to slow enemy progress. They had also stationed a half-dozen small gunboats between the sunken hulls and the city.

There was a bold, new flag flying over the fort. Forty-two by thirty feet, fifteen stars and fifteen stripes, it was the work of Mary Pickersgill and her daughter, Caroline.

On Saturday, September 10th, the British fleet anchored off North Point at the mouth of the Patapsco River. Francis, Colonel Skinner, and Dr. Beanes were hustled from the *Surprise* back to their own small boat. Admiral Cochrane had decided to take personal command of the bombardment. He wanted the smaller, faster frigate as his flagship.

Sunday morning, Baltimore's church bells called the militia to arms. Monday, boats filled with British soldiers in scarlet uniforms began leaving for shore. Francis watched grimly. Things did not look good for the Americans.

With the troops underway on land, the fleet began moving upriver. As the ships came within view of Fort McHenry, the Stars and Stripes were waving overhead.

Later that afternoon, word came from shore. The Americans had retreated to positions outside the city. General Ross had been killed.

---

[1] **rampart:** protective barrier
[2] **powder magazine:** storage area for gunpowder

A silence seemed to fall over the fleet, but preparations continued. Francis, Dr. Beanes, and Colonel Skinner spent a restless night as sixteen smaller British ships moved into the shallower water closer to the fort.

At dawn the bombardment began. The noise was so great and the smell of burning powder so strong that the three hostages were forced to take refuge in their cabin. When the response from the fort seemed to die away for a moment, it became clear that the Americans' thirty-six-pound shells were not reaching the ships. But then the heavy shelling and rocketing began again and went on hour after hour.

At dusk Francis crawled out onto the deck. "Can you see the flag?" Dr. Beanes called after him.

Francis squinted through the smoke and the din and the glow of the setting sun. "The flag is flying," he replied.

Soon after, it began to rain.

Thunder and lightning joined the booming of the guns. Very late that night, Francis struggled out on deck again. Though he could not know it, at that moment the British were trying to land a thousand men at Ferry Branch. An American sentry discovered them and Fort McHenry began to fire. As the barges fled, every available American gun pursued them.

The rainy night sky was suddenly lit up, and in that moment Francis could see the flag again. It was soaked now and drooping from its staff, but it was there, still there.

By dawn the rain had stopped and the fight was over. Peering through the clouds, Francis, Dr. Beanes, and Colonel Skinner strained to see what flag was flying over the fort. Had the British triumphed in the night? But no, there it was, unfurling in the breeze, the Stars and Stripes!

All his life, Francis had written poetry. He reached into his pocket and found an old letter. With the tune to the song, "To Anacreon[3] in Heaven" in mind, he scribbled *O say can you see* and then *by the dawn's early light.*

He wrote a few more lines, crossed out a few, but there wasn't much time.

---

[3]**Anacreon:** a Greek poet

Already redcoats were leaving for the ships. The fleet was abandoning the assault!

The sails of the little cartel boat[4] were returned to the members of its American crew. By afternoon, Francis, Dr. Beanes, and Colonel Skinner were back in Baltimore.

Cheering crowds were everywhere. The three men went straight to the Indian Queen Hotel on Baltimore Street, rested and had supper, but later that night, Francis finished the four stanzas[5] of his poem.

The next day he went to visit his brother-in-law, Judge Joseph Nicholson, who had been at Fort McHenry. Judge Nicholson loved the new poem. "Let's get it printed," he insisted.

The judge rushed over to the *Baltimore American*, but the printers weren't back from defending the fort. A young apprentice, Samuel Sands, agreed to set the verses in type and run off the handbills. Because Francis hadn't thought of a title, Judge Nicholson came up with "The Defense of Fort McHenry," but it wasn't long before everyone was singing what had come to be known as "The Star-Spangled Banner."

---

[4]**cartel boat:** cargo boat
[5]**stanza:** section of a poem

Words by
Francis Scott Key
(1779-1843)

The Star-Spangled Banner

Music by
J. Stafford Smith
(1750-1836)

Oh— say can you see by the dawn's ear - ly light What so proud - ly we hail'd at the twi - light's last gleam - ing whose broad stripes and bright stars through the per - il - ous fight O'er the ram - parts we watch'd were so gal - lant - ly stream - ing? And the rock - ets' red glare the bombs burst - ing in air, Gave proof through the night that our flag was still there. Oh, say does that— star - span - gled ban - ner - yet— wave— O'er the land— of the free and the home of the brave?

LITERATURE REVIEW

1 How did Francis Scott Key describe his experiences during the Battle of Baltimore?

2 How did ordinary citizens help Baltimore survive the British bombing?

3 Imagine that you were part of the Baltimore militia during the British bombing. Write a letter to a friend, telling how you feel about Francis Scott Key's poem.

CHAPTER 11
REVIEW
1775   1785

1775
• Daniel Boone
  settles Kentucky

CONNECT MAIN IDEAS

Use this organizer to show how the chapter's main ideas are connected. Write one or two sentences to tell about each person or pair of people or to summarize each event or idea. A copy of the organizer may be found on page 76 of the Activity Book.

On the Move

Across the Appalachians

Daniel Boone _____

_____

Settling Kentucky _____

_____

Pioneer Life _____

_____

_____

The Louisiana Purchase

The Purchase _____

_____

Lewis and Clark _____

_____

Zebulon Pike _____

_____

A Second War with Britain

Tecumseh and the Prophet _____

_____

The War of 1812 _____

_____

The Era of Good Feelings

_____

WRITE MORE ABOUT IT

Express an Opinion Suppose that President Jefferson has asked for your opinion on whether or not the United States should purchase the Louisiana Territory. Write what you would tell him.

Write a Newspaper Article Imagine that you are a writer for a Baltimore newspaper. Write a headline and a short article about Francis Scott Key and the exciting events at Fort McHenry.

1795	1805	1815	1825

1801
• Thomas Jefferson becomes the third President

1804
• Lewis and Clark expedition begins

1812
• The War of 1812 begins

1823
• The Monroe Doctrine is announced

USE VOCABULARY

Use the terms from the list to complete the paragraphs that follow. Use each term once.

annex	**pathfinders**
impressment	**pioneers**
nationalism	**purchase**

When the American Revolution ended, __**1**__ settled the western frontier. Then, in 1803, the United States decided to __**2**__ land west of the Mississippi River. __**3**__ soon found ways through this unknown region.

The United States found itself at war with Britain. Americans were upset over the __**4**__ of sailors. Although neither side was clearly the winner, a wave of __**5**__ swept the land. The United States decided to __**6**__ Spanish West Florida.

CHECK UNDERSTANDING

7 What was the Wilderness Road?

8 Why did pioneers often band together in forts?

9 What did Spain hope to do by closing the port of New Orleans to western farmers?

10 What did Lewis and Clark accomplish? How did Sacagawea help them?

11 Why did many Americans blame the British for Indian attacks on settlers?

12 Why were many northern merchants against the idea of declaring war on Britain?

13 What was the Era of Good Feelings?

14 Who was Francis Scott Key?

THINK CRITICALLY

15 **Think More About It** What do you think Tecumseh meant when he said that no one had the right to sell land?

16 **Personally Speaking** Why do you think so many pioneers chose to risk their lives to settle in Kentucky and Tennessee? Would you have made the same choice? Explain.

17 **Explore Viewpoints** How do you think Americans viewed the Monroe Doctrine? How do you think Europeans viewed the Monroe Doctrine?

APPLY SKILLS

Predict a Likely Outcome Think about the events that usually take place in school on each day of the week. Predict the events that are likely to take place next week. What steps might you follow to make these predictions?

READ MORE ABOUT IT

A Pioneer Sampler: The Daily Life of a Pioneer Family in 1840 by Barbara Greenwood. Houghton Mifflin. This book tells about daily pioneer life and contains many activities for readers to enjoy.

Visit the Internet at **http://www.hbschool.com** for additional resources.

CHAPTER

12 THE WAY WEST

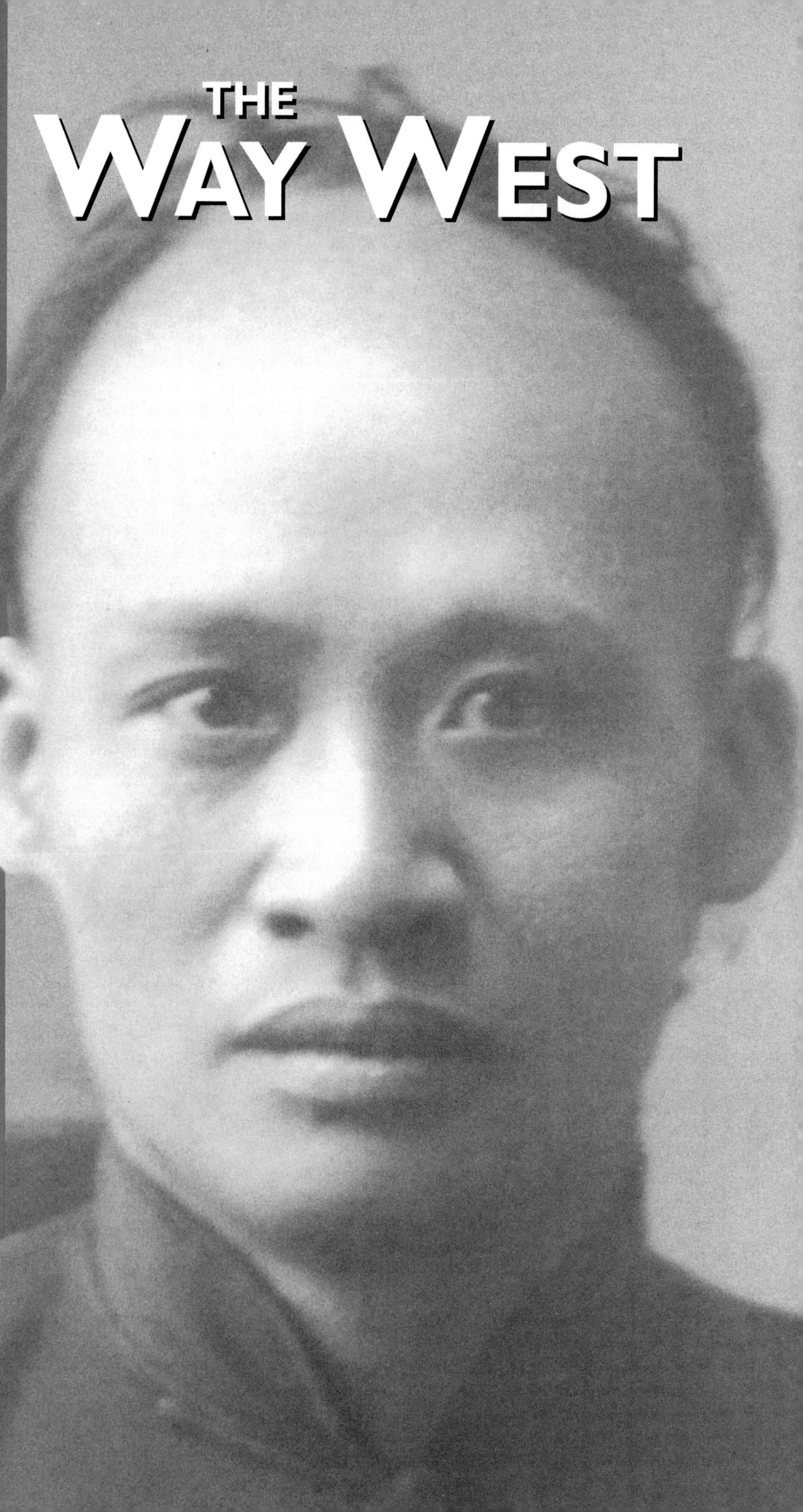

"Truly these are mountains of gold!"

Fatt Hing Chin, a Chinese miner, describing the land in California in the 1850s

A Chinese miner

The Industrial Revolution

1780	1800	1820	1840

Before the War of 1812, the economy of the United States had been growing. This growth increased after the war. New inventions changed the way goods were made. People began using machines instead of hand tools. New transportation routes were built. This **Industrial Revolution** brought great changes in the way people lived, worked, and traveled.

Industry Comes to the United States

In a factory in Britain, a young worker named Samuel Slater carefully studied the new spinning machine until he could remember exactly how each iron gear and wooden spool worked. This invention made large textile mills possible. **Textile mills** are factories where fibers such as cotton and wool are woven into cloth, or textiles. In 1789 Britain was the only country in the world that had this technology.

The British kept new inventions, such as those in the British textile mills, closely guarded secrets. Anyone caught leaving Britain with machine designs was put in jail. Samuel Slater was about to break British law.

Slater took his knowledge to the United States. Remembering each part he had studied, he made a spinning machine for a business person named Moses Brown. In 1790 Brown and Slater built a textile mill at Pawtucket, Rhode Island. It was America's first factory. Samuel Slater had brought the Industrial Revolution to the United States.

REVIEW *What technology did Samuel Slater bring to the United States?*

FOCUS
How might a new technology change a person's life today?

Main Idea As you read, look for ways new technology changed life in the United States in the 1800s.

Vocabulary
Industrial Revolution
textile mill
mass production
interchangeable part
transport
canal
locomotive

Born in Britain, Samuel Slater (left) came to the United States in 1789. The decorative box (above) shows a scene on the Erie Canal.

431

Samuel Slater built America's first cotton mill (above). The machines in the mill, such as this wooden spinning machine (right), ran on waterpower and made yarn quickly at low cost.

Mass Production Starts

Another idea changed American manufacturing forever. An inventor named Eli Whitney thought of a new way of manufacturing that could produce large amounts of goods at one time. His idea came to be called **mass production**.

Before this time, one craftworker made each product from start to finish. Muskets, for example, were made by hand, one at a time. Because each craftworker had his or her own way of making parts and putting them together, no two muskets were exactly the same. To repair a broken musket, a craftworker had to make a new part to fit it.

Whitney thought of a way workers could make more muskets. He built machines that made many identical copies of each part. Such **interchangeable parts** could be used to make or repair any musket. Whitney also made machines to put the parts together very quickly.

Mass production made it possible to use untrained workers in factories. No longer were craftworkers needed to make most products. Anyone could put together machine-made parts. Using interchangeable parts, factory workers could manufacture more goods much more quickly than craftworkers could.

REVIEW *How did the idea of mass production change manufacturing?*

The Lowell System

From 1810 to 1812 Francis Cabot Lowell of Massachusetts visited textile mills and factories in Britain. As Samuel Slater had done earlier, Lowell studied the way the machines worked. He took care to remember the way the separate spinning, dyeing, and weaving mills were planned.

When Lowell returned to the United States, he started his own textile mill at Waltham, Massachusetts. He put spinning, dyeing, and weaving together under one roof. This was a change from having a different factory for each step. In Lowell's textile mill raw cotton went into the factory and finished cloth came out. Nothing like that had ever been done before. Other manufacturers began following Lowell's lead as they built factories.

Young women and children came to work in Lowell's textile mills. When a girl named Harriet Hanson was ten years old, she began work as a "doffer." From five o'clock in the morning until seven in the evening, Harriet changed spools of thread on the spinning machines. She "wanted to earn money like the other little girls."

The hours were long, but Harriet did not think the work was hard. She had time to read, sew, and sometimes play. She enjoyed living in a boardinghouse where meals and rooms were provided for workers.

Lowell took care to set up good living conditions for his workers. Other manufacturers did not show the same care. As the demand for many manufactured goods grew, more factories—and more factory workers—were needed. Many workers, both young and old, soon were working long hours in dangerous conditions.

By the 1840s thousands of immigrants were coming to the United States each year to take jobs in the new factories. The populations of manufacturing cities like New York, Boston, Philadelphia, and Baltimore grew quickly. Almost half of the immigrants were from Ireland. Others came from Germany, Poland, and other parts of northern and central Europe.

REVIEW *Why were immigrants coming to the United States in the mid-1800s?*

Bells rang to tell Lowell's workers (right) when it was meal time and when it was time to start work. The picture (below) shows a young girl packing cotton into containers.

The Erie Canal

The new factories turned out many products. But factory owners had a problem. How could they **transport**, or carry, their products from the factories to their customers, many of whom lived in the West? The people in the West, too, needed to transport their farm products to the cities in the East.

To help solve this problem, the New York legislature voted in 1817 to build a **canal**, or human-made waterway. The Erie Canal would link Buffalo on Lake Erie with Troy on the Hudson River. It would be 363 miles (584 km) long—the longest canal in the world.

Most of the Erie Canal was dug by hand by some 3,000 Irish immigrants. The Irish came to the United States from Europe to get jobs working on the Big Ditch, as they called the Erie Canal. The workers were paid 80 cents a day and were given meals and housing. These wages were three times what the immigrants could earn in Ireland. The high wages acted like a magnet to attract thousands of Europeans to the United States.

When the Erie Canal was finished in 1825, it opened a transportation route to the heart of the young nation. The opening of this route helped make New York City the leading trade city in the United States.

REVIEW *Why was the Erie Canal built?*

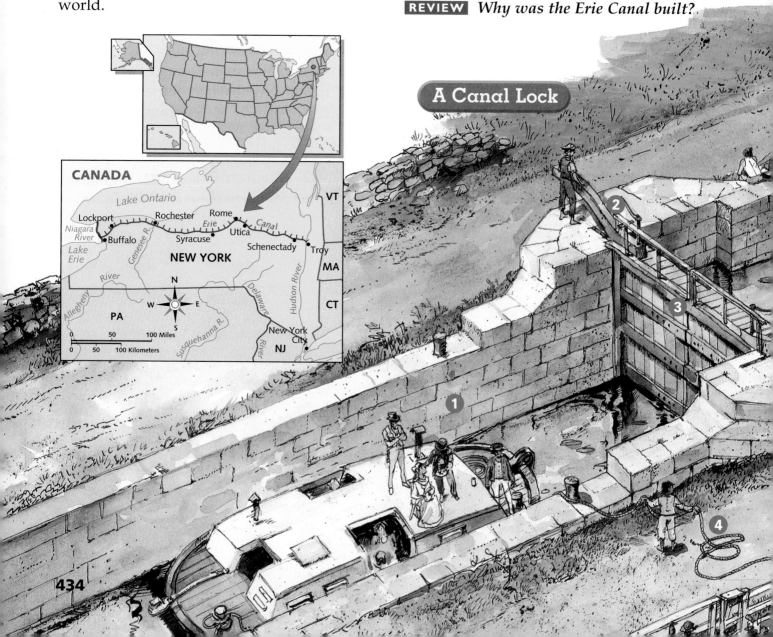

A Canal Lock

Locks

Boats on the Erie Canal must go "uphill" or "downhill" because Lake Erie is 572 feet (174 m) higher than the Hudson River. They do this by using locks. A lock is a short part of a canal, with a gate at each end. A boat enters the lock, both gates are shut, and the water level is raised or lowered. When it matches the level of the next part of the canal, the gate at that end opens and the boat goes on its way. A lock is like an elevator for canal boats!

Ships continue to pass through locks on the Erie Canal.

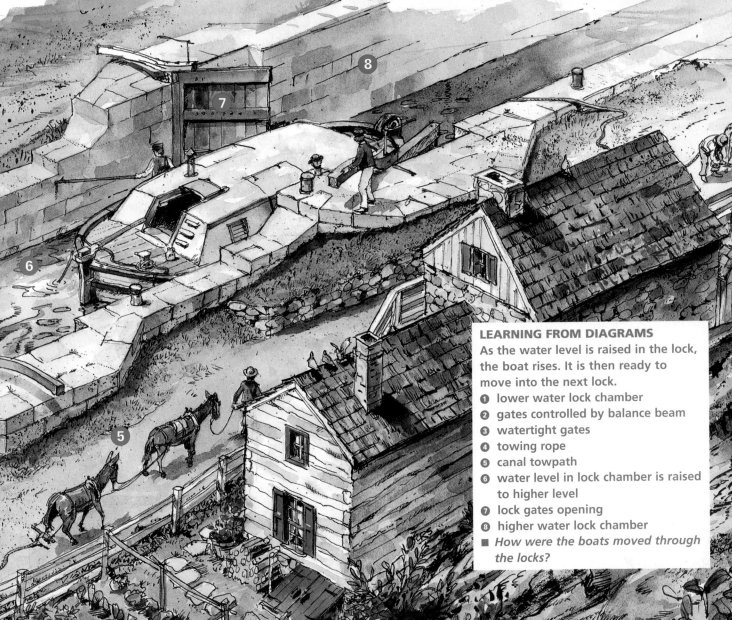

LEARNING FROM DIAGRAMS

As the water level is raised in the lock, the boat rises. It is then ready to move into the next lock.

1. lower water lock chamber
2. gates controlled by balance beam
3. watertight gates
4. towing rope
5. canal towpath
6. water level in lock chamber is raised to higher level
7. lock gates opening
8. higher water lock chamber

■ *How were the boats moved through the locks?*

The National Road made traveling west easier for settlers. Inns along the road gave settlers a place to eat and rest during their journey.

The National Road

During the early years of the nation, Americans lacked a good system of roads. Most roads were just dirt paths that were full of tree stumps and holes. The roads turned into rivers of mud when it rained.

Just before Ohio became a state in 1803, Congress voted to build a road from the Atlantic coast to Ohio. The road would be used to transport goods and help settlers travel to the new state. This route became known as the National Road.

Work on the National Road began on November 20, 1811. The road was built using the best technology of the day. It was wide and level, and it was paved with stones and tar. At first it stretched from Maryland to Pennsylvania. It was opened for traffic in 1818, when it reached what would become West Virginia. It then passed through Ohio and Indiana and finally ended in Vandalia, Illinois, in 1841. The National Road became the land route that linked the East with the West.

REVIEW *Why was the National Road built?*

Steamboats and Railroads

At about the same time that the National Road and the Erie Canal were being built, Americans were inventing new forms of travel. Steamboats took the place of flat-bottom barges as the main form of river transportation. Railroads changed the way people and goods moved on land.

In 1807 Robert Fulton amazed watchers when his steamboat, the *Clermont*, chugged

Movement These maps show major transportation links that had been built in the United States by 1850.

■ *Why do you think few links had been built west of the Mississippi River?*

up the Hudson River. The steamboat used a steam engine, which had been invented in Britain in the 1700s. In 1811 the *New Orleans* made the first steamboat voyage from Pittsburgh to New Orleans. By the 1820s great paddle-wheel steamboats could be seen on most large rivers and lakes in the United States. Trips that once took months by flatboat now took only a few days.

Railroads had a slower start. At first many people had fears about traveling by train. Some did not think the trains would stay on the tracks. Some thought that fast speeds would cause human blood to boil!

One of the first **locomotives**, or railroad engines, made in the United States was the *Tom Thumb*. A manufacturer named Peter Cooper built it in 1830 for the Baltimore and Ohio Railroad. The company had been

The *Clermont* was one of the first boats to use steam power successfully.

Transportation in the East, 1850

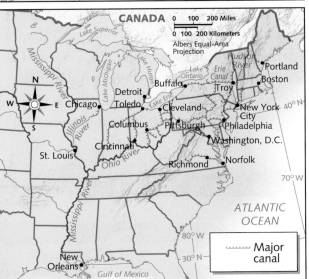

437

The *Tom Thumb* was made famous in a race with a horse. The locomotive was small, but powerful for its day. The first locomotives went about 10 miles (16.1 km) per hour.

using railroad cars pulled by horses for its 13-mile (21-km) service between Baltimore and Ellicott's Mills, Maryland. To prove a steam engine could pull a heavy load faster than a horse, Cooper raced his *Tom Thumb* against a railroad car pulled by a horse. The locomotive broke down before the finish line and lost the race. Even so, it was clear that the steam locomotive had better pulling power than a horse.

The number of railroads grew quickly after 1830. By 1850 about 9,000 miles (14,484 km) of track crossed the nation, mostly near the Atlantic coast. Railroads made it easier to move raw materials and manufactured goods to all regions of the country. As the railroads grew, so did manufacturing in the United States.

REVIEW *What inventions improved transportation in the early 1800s?*

LESSON I REVIEW

1780		1800		1820			1840

1790
• First American factory is built

1811
• Work on the National Road begins

1825
• Erie Canal is finished

1830
• American railroads begin to use steam locomotives

Check Understanding

1 **Remember the Facts**   Who brought the Industrial Revolution to the United States?

2 **Recall the Main Idea**   How did new technology change the way people lived in the United States in the 1800s?

Think Critically

3 **Cause and Effect**   How did more factories lead to better transportation?

4 **Past to Present**   What kinds of transportation connect the regions of the United States today?

Show What You Know

Writing Activity   Imagine that you work at a Lowell textile mill or another early factory. Write a letter to a friend, telling what you like and do not like about factory work. Share your letter with a classmate.

The Age of Jackson

| 1825 | 1830 | 1835 | 1840 |

LESSON 2

FOCUS
What problems might divide people living in a country today?

Main Idea Read to learn about the problems that divided the American people in the early 1800s.

Vocabulary
sectionalism
states' rights
secede
ruling

On July 4, 1826, the United States was 50 years old. Americans everywhere celebrated with parades, speeches, and parties. Many hoped that the two old patriots John Adams and Thomas Jefferson would live to see the celebration. Both men did live to greet that Fourth of July, but they both died before sunset. In Philadelphia the Liberty Bell tolled at their passing. The deep sound of the bell marked the end of an age that had brought the American people independence and a new nation. But as the old age ended, a new age dawned with new leaders and new challenges for the United States.

"Old Hickory"

On March 4, 1829, Andrew Jackson took the oath of office as the seventh President of the United States. The Union he was about to lead had grown from the original 13 states to 24 states. Vermont, Maine, Kentucky, and Tennessee had become states. The states of Ohio, Illinois, and Indiana had been carved from the Northwest Territory. The states of Louisiana and Missouri had been formed from the Louisiana Purchase. Alabama became a state after the Creeks were forced off their land. Mississippi and the Territory of Florida had been created from land once claimed by Spain.

The Presidents before Jackson had all come from wealthy families from either Massachusetts or Virginia. They also had all been well educated. Jackson had a different background. He had been born on the frontier

President Andrew Jackson

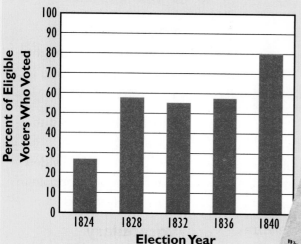

Voter Participation, 1824–1840

Percent of Eligible Voters Who Voted

| 100 |
| 90 |
| 80 |
| 70 |
| 60 |
| 50 |
| 40 |
| 30 |
| 20 |
| 10 |
| 0 |

Election Year: 1824, 1828, 1832, 1836, 1840

LEARNING FROM GRAPHS This graph shows the percent of eligible voters who voted between 1824 and 1840. The poster (right) helped persuade people to vote for Andrew Jackson.

■ *About what percent of eligible voters voted in the election of 1828?*

of South Carolina to a poor family living in a log cabin. Tough and stubborn, he taught himself law and became a judge. As a soldier he earned the nickname Old Hickory, hickory being a very hard wood. "He's tough," said his soldiers. "Tough as hickory." As a general he had become a hero during the War of 1812.

The election that made Jackson President was the first in which all white American men could vote. Before that time, voting had been only for men who owned property. The change came about partly because of the new western states. There the vote was given to all white men, not just property owners. By the election of 1828, the eastern states were following this example. Many of the new voters chose Jackson because they felt he was a "common man," like them.

REVIEW *What change in voting helped Andrew Jackson become President?*

Regional Disagreements

As President, Andrew Jackson went right on being both tough and stubborn. He vetoed a bank bill that would have helped the rich factory owners in the North. Government should not help the rich get richer, he said. Government should instead "shower its favors alike on the high and the low, the rich and the poor."

Many of President Jackson's decisions were based on his background of living on the western frontier. People from the North and the South were just as interested in helping their own section, or region, rather than the country as a whole. This regional loyalty is called **sectionalism**.

Sectionalism became a problem in 1828, when Congress set a high tariff on imports. The tariff was supposed to help northern factory owners sell their manufactured goods because it made European goods cost more. However, the tariff also raised the prices southerners had to pay for goods they could get only from Europe.

Jackson's Vice President, John C. Calhoun of South Carolina, was loyal to the South. He argued against the tariff. Calhoun believed in **states' rights**, or the idea that the states have final authority over the national government. No one knew how President Jackson felt about states' rights until he spoke at a dinner in honor of the

Vice President John C. Calhoun believed that the states should have authority over the national government.

late Thomas Jefferson. Jackson looked straight at Calhoun and said,

> 66 Our Union—It must be preserved [kept]. 99

Calhoun answered, "The Union—next to our liberty most dear." Calhoun also believed that the Union was important. But he still felt that the rights of individual states were more important than the Union. This was the beginning of a deep split between Jackson and Calhoun. Calhoun soon resigned as Jackson's Vice President.

The debate over states' rights went on. In 1832 Congress passed another tariff. South Carolina said it would **secede**, or leave the Union, because of it. President Jackson warned South Carolina's leaders that leaving the Union was treason. South Carolina's leaders backed down, but sectionalism only grew stronger in the years to come.

REVIEW *What leader spoke out for states' rights? Who spoke against it?*

Indian Removal

Pathfinders had reported that the plains west of the Mississippi were of no use to the settlers. At that time people believed that soil was good only where trees grew. They began to think that the Indians should move west to those treeless lands. Jackson put the idea into action.

In 1830 Congress passed the Indian Removal Act. This act said that all Indians east of the Mississippi must leave their lands and move west. Once this bill became a law, President Jackson ordered the Choctaws, Creeks, Seminoles, Chickasaws, Cherokees, and other tribes to live in the Indian Territory, which is today the state of Oklahoma.

Many tribes fought against removal. The Seminoles of Florida, led by Chief Osceola, were among those who struggled to keep their lands. Many runaway slaves helped the Seminoles in their fight. Chief Osceola was captured, and most of the Seminoles, like other tribes, were either killed or forced to leave their homes.

The 15,000 Cherokees made up one of the richest tribes in the United States. They had many towns and villages throughout

New Echota, Georgia

By the 1830s New Echota, the capital of the Cherokee republic, was a city like any other city in the United States. It had churches, businesses, and schools. It also had its own newspaper, the *Cherokee Phoenix*, which was printed in both English and Cherokee. Although spoken for hundreds of years, the Cherokee language was not written until 1821. In that year a Cherokee leader named Sequoyah (sih•KWOY•uh) created an alphabet and a writing system for it.

0 50 100 Miles	
0 50 100 Kilometers	
Albers Equal-Area Projection	

TENNESSEE

NORTH CAROLINA

Brainerd •   • Red Clay

Spring Place •

• Dahlonega

Chattooga Village •   ■ **NEW ECHOTA**

Gunter's Landing

Turkey Town •   **CHEROKEE NATION**

GEORGIA

ALABAMA

N W E S

This picture of Sequoyah shows the Cherokee alphabet he invented.

the Southeast. Many Cherokees owned small farms, and a few had large plantations where Africans were enslaved. The Cherokees had their own government, a republic with a constitution and elected leaders who met at their capital of New Echota (ih•KOHT•uh) in Georgia.

In 1791 the United States government had agreed to the independence of the Cherokee nation by signing a treaty. However, in 1828, lawmakers in Georgia said that Cherokee laws were no longer in effect. In 1829, when gold was discovered on Cherokee lands, settlers poured in to stake their claims.

The Cherokee nation, led by Chief John Ross, fought back in the United States courts, and their case went all the way to the Supreme Court. In 1832 the Chief Justice of the United States Supreme Court, John Marshall, gave the Court's **ruling**, or decision. He said the United States should protect the Cherokees and their lands in Georgia. Yet, instead of supporting the court ruling, President Jackson ignored it.

By late 1838, soldiers had forced the last large group of Cherokees to leave their lands. They traveled from North Carolina and Georgia

This painting, called *The Choctaw Removal*, was created by the Choctaw artist Valjean Hessing. The Choctaw were one of the many Indian tribes that were forced to leave their homes. What feelings does the artist show in the painting?

through Tennessee, Kentucky, Illinois, Missouri, and Arkansas—more than 800 miles (1,287 km)—to the Indian Territory. The Cherokees called their long, painful journey "Trail Where They Cried." It later became known as the Trail of Tears. It

ended on March 26, 1839. More than 4,000 Cherokees had died of cold, disease, and lack of food during the 116-day journey. John G. Burnett, a soldier who was there, said, "The trail was a trail of death." **REVIEW** *What was the Trail of Tears?*

LESSON 2 REVIEW

1825 — 1830 — 1835 — 1840

1829
• Andrew Jackson becomes the President of the United States

1830
• Congress passes the Indian Removal Act

1838
• The last large group of Cherokees are forced from their lands

Check Understanding
1 Remember the Facts Who helped Andrew Jackson win the election of 1828?

2 Recall the Main Idea What problems divided the American people in the early 1800s?

Think Critically
3 Explore Viewpoints How would the Cherokees have viewed the Indian Removal Act? How would Georgia's settlers have viewed it?

4 Think More About It How do you think life on the frontier encouraged the growth of democracy?

Show What You Know

Writing Activity Make a list of the qualities that helped Andrew Jackson get elected President. Then write phrases that he might have used as campaign slogans for his elections in 1828 and 1832. Copy your slogans onto large sheets of paper and display them in the classroom.

FOCUS

How might a country today expand its territory?

Main Idea   Read to learn how the United States expanded its territory in the 1800s.

Vocabulary

manifest destiny
dictator
forty-niner

Westward Ho!

In the early 1800s Americans began to move beyond their country's borders in search of more land. They looked to the Spanish colony of Texas, the Oregon Country in the Pacific Northwest, and other western lands with the rallying cry "Westward Ho!" The idea of the lands in the West being set aside for Indian peoples was soon forgotten. In 1845 the words *manifest destiny* were heard for the first time. The **manifest destiny** was the belief shared by many Americans that it was the certain future of the United States to stretch from the Atlantic Ocean to the Pacific Ocean.

Americans in Texas

Since the earliest years of European settlement, Spain had built missions and presidios all over Texas. Yet, few settlers lived on this open borderland. In 1820 Moses Austin, a Missouri banker, asked Spanish leaders if he might start a colony of Americans in Texas. The Spanish agreed, but Austin died before he could carry out his plan.

Stephen F. Austin, Moses Austin's son, took up his father's work and started the colony. He chose land in southeastern Texas between the Brazos and Colorado rivers. In 1821 the first colonists began to settle there. That same year, Mexico won its independence from Spain. Texas now belonged to Mexico.

Austin and the American settlers worked hard, and they soon did well in raising cotton, corn, and cattle. Encouraged by their success, the Mexican government decided to let more people settle in Texas. At first the Mexican government left the Americans in Texas alone. But in time Mexico's leaders became worried about the growing number of Americans on their land.

Stephen F. Austin began a settlement in Texas. Present-day Austin, Texas, was named for him.

At the Alamo fewer than 200 Texans faced more than 2,000 Mexican soldiers. In this painting Davy Crockett swings his rifle at the enemy after having run out of ammunition. The Alamo was one of the most well-known battles of the Texas revolution.

In 1830 the Mexican government passed a law that said no more American settlers could come to Texas. The Mexican government also said that settlers already in Texas had to obey Mexico's laws and pay more taxes. These changes angered Texans.

Then, in 1834, another change took place. General Antonio López de Santa Anna took over the Mexican government and made himself **dictator**, a leader who has total authority. When Santa Anna sent soldiers to Texas to enforce Mexican laws, fighting broke out.

REVIEW *Why did Americans first come to Texas?*

The Texas Revolution

Working together, a force of Americans and Mexicans living in Texas attacked the town of San Antonio on December 5, 1835. After four days of fighting, Mexican troops were driven from the center of the town. They surrendered on December 11. The defeat angered General Santa Anna. He marched on San Antonio with thousands of soldiers, planning to take back the city.

Church bells rang out a warning as the huge Mexican army came close to the city in February 1836. Texas rebels in San Antonio

Chapter 12 • **445**

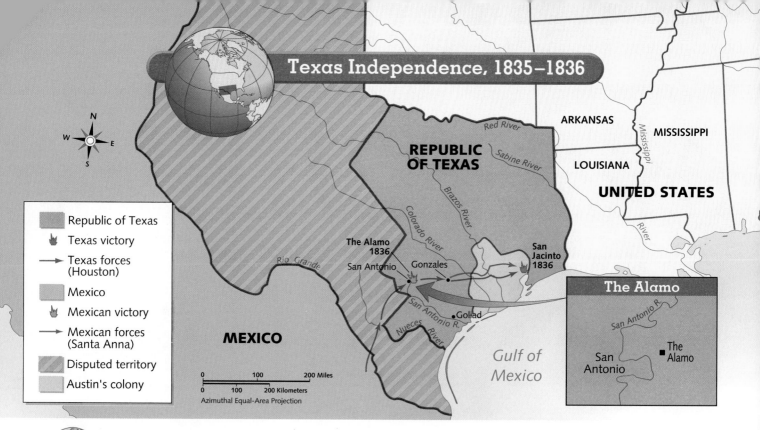

Texas Independence, 1835–1836

ARKANSAS

MISSISSIPPI

REPUBLIC OF TEXAS

LOUISIANA

Red River

Sabine River

UNITED STATES

Brazos River

Colorado River

Rio Grande

The Alamo 1836
San Antonio

Gonzales

San Jacinto 1836

MEXICO

San Antonio R.

Goliad

Nueces River

Gulf of Mexico

The Alamo

San Antonio R.

San Antonio

The Alamo

Legend:
- Republic of Texas
- Texas victory
- Texas forces (Houston)
- Mexico
- Mexican victory
- Mexican forces (Santa Anna)
- Disputed territory
- Austin's colony

0   100   200 Miles
0   100   200 Kilometers
Azimuthal Equal-Area Projection

Place This map shows Austin's original colony and the battles for Texas independence fought with Mexico from 1835 to 1836.
■ *Which battle did the Texans win during their fight for independence?*

---

took shelter behind the walls of the Alamo, an old Spanish mission church. Among them were American volunteers willing to help the Texans in their fight for freedom. They included James Bowie, Davy Crockett, and their commander, William B. Travis. Juan Seguín (say•GEEN) and several other Texans also arrived to help.

For 13 days the Mexican soldiers attacked the Alamo. The defenders fought to the end. Finally, on March 6, 1836, the Alamo fell. The force of about 189 Texans had been killed. Santa Anna spared the lives of the women and children. He sent a survivor named Susanna Dickenson to tell the Texas leaders that the Alamo had fallen.

During the attack at the Alamo, Texas leaders met. On March 2, 1836, they declared independence from Mexico and set up the Republic of Texas. They chose David

G. Burnet as president and Sam Houston as commander of the army.

After the fall of the Alamo, Santa Anna moved quickly to put down the Texas revolution. On March 27 he ordered more than 300 prisoners killed at Goliad. But other Texans fought on, yelling "Remember the Alamo!" and "Remember Goliad!"

On April 21 Houston's army took the Mexicans by surprise at the Battle of San Jacinto (jah•SIN•toh) and captured Santa Anna. Houston offered to let Santa Anna live in return for Texas's independence. Santa Anna agreed. Texas remained an independent republic until it became a state of the United States in 1845. Sam Houston served twice as president of the republic and later as governor of the state of Texas.

REVIEW *When did Texas become a republic?*

The Oregon Country

American pioneers continued to push west. In 1834, Christian missionaries journeyed to the Oregon Country. This region was made up of present-day Oregon, Washington, and Idaho, and parts of Montana and Wyoming. In 1836 Marcus and Narcissa Whitman and Henry and Eliza Spalding set up missions near the Walla Walla Valley. They hoped to teach Christianity to the Indians.

The missionaries' letters to people back East told of the green valleys, wooded hills, and fertile soil of the Oregon Country—a place many began to dream of. In 1842 the first large group of pioneers headed for Oregon. Thousands more followed. The route they took came to be called the Oregon Trail. The Oregon Trail led northwest more than 2,000 miles (3,219 km) from Independence, Missouri, to the Platte River. The pioneers then traveled across the Continental Divide, an imaginary line that runs north and south along the highest points of the Rocky Mountains. The trail continued to the Snake and Columbia rivers and ended at the Willamette (wuh•LA•muht) Valley of Oregon.

The journey lasted as long as six months. What a hard trip it was! Fresh water was scarce, but sudden storms soaked the travelers. Wagons broke down. Rivers had to be crossed. Many people died along the way. Yet,

This quilt was signed by people traveling together in a wagon train.

many reached Oregon, and the settlements there grew quickly.

To protect its settlements, the United States wanted a clear dividing line between its Oregon territory and nearby British land. In 1846 President James K. Polk signed a treaty with Britain fixing the 49th parallel of latitude as the boundary between the United States and the British territory in Canada. The treaty gave the United States the lands of what are now Oregon, Washington, Idaho, western Montana, and Wyoming.

REVIEW *How did people in the East learn about the Oregon Country?*

The Mormons in Utah

In the 1840s the Mormons, or members of the Church of Jesus Christ of Latter-day Saints, joined the pioneers moving west. Under their leader, Joseph Smith, the Mormons had settled in Illinois in the town of Nauvoo (naw•VOO). But their beliefs caused problems with other settlers, and in 1844 an angry crowd killed Joseph Smith.

When Brigham Young became the new leader of the Mormons, he decided that they should move to a place where no one would bother them. In 1846 Young and the first group of Mormons to head west set out for the Rocky Mountains.

In July 1847 the Mormons reached the Great Salt Lake valley in the Great Basin. Young chose this harsh land to settle in because he thought that no other settlers would want it. He used words from the Bible to tell his followers,

❝ We will make this desert blossom as the rose. ❞

One of the first things the Mormons did was build irrigation canals. The canals brought water from the mountains to turn the dry land into farmland.

The Mormons did make the land blossom with crops of grain, fruit, and vegetables. The region grew rapidly, and soon became known as the Utah Territory. Brigham Young became its first governor.

REVIEW *Why did the Mormons move to present-day Utah?*

Mormon pioneers get ready to move out from what is today Omaha, Nebraska. They stayed there for the winter before completing their journey westward.

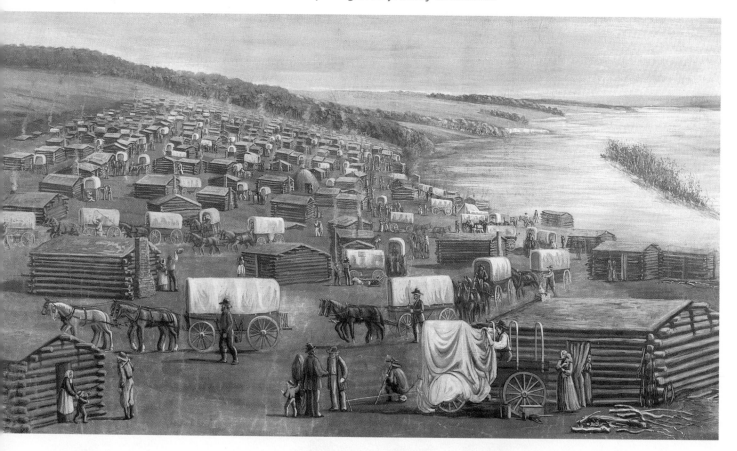

The Growth of the United States

RUSSIA

ALASKA PURCHASE 1867

CANADA

0 200 400 Miles
0 400 Kilometers

PACIFIC OCEAN

CANADA

—— Present-day border

TREATY WITH BRITAIN 1842

OREGON TERRITORY 1846

TREATY WITH BRITAIN 1818

Lake Superior

Lake Michigan
Lake Huron
Lake Ontario
Lake Erie

0 200 400 Miles
0 200 400 Kilometers
Albers Equal-Area Projection

40°N

LOUISIANA PURCHASE 1803

40°N

70°W

MEXICAN CESSION 1848

UNITED STATES 1783

PACIFIC OCEAN

ATLANTIC OCEAN

30°N

GADSDEN PURCHASE 1853

TEXAS ANNEXATION 1845

1810

N
E
W
S

120°W

1812

1813

FLORIDA 1819

HAWAII ANNEXATION 1898

PACIFIC OCEAN

0 100 Miles
0 100 Kilometers

MEXICO

Gulf of Mexico

90°W

80°W

Regions By 1898 the United States had gained the land for what would become the present-day 50 states.

MAP THEME

■ **When did the United States first gain land on the Pacific coast?**

War with Mexico

The land the Mormons settled in the Great Basin belonged to Mexico. In 1848, only a few months later, that land became part of the United States.

James K. Polk was now President. He believed in the manifest destiny and wanted to see the United States reach the Pacific Ocean. He thought that all the lands west of Texas should be part of the United States.

In January 1846 President Polk sent American soldiers into lands in southern

Texas that were disputed between the United States and Mexico. In April, Mexican troops crossed the Rio Grande and attacked an American patrol. Polk then asked Congress to declare war on Mexico.

In 1847 the United States invaded Mexico by sea. American soldiers led by General Winfield Scott marched from Veracruz to Mexico City. After a year of fighting, the war was over. In 1848 Mexico and the United States signed the Treaty of Guadalupe Hidalgo (gwah•dah•LOO•pay ee•DAHL•goh). After the treaty ended the war, the United States purchased California and the land that now makes up Utah and Nevada and parts of Arizona, New Mexico, Colorado, and Wyoming for $15 million. Then in 1853, the United States purchased more land from Mexico in the Gadsden Purchase. This brought the part of the country between Canada and Mexico to its present size. This area, made up of 48 states, is known as the Continental United States.

REVIEW *What did the United States gain in its war with Mexico?*

The California Gold Rush

Not long before the treaty with Mexico was signed, gold was found in California. In January 1848 James Marshall and his workers were building a waterwheel for John Sutter's new sawmill near Sacramento. Something in the water glittered. Marshall picked it up. He held a shiny stone that was half the size of a pea. Then he and his workers saw more. News soon reached the eastern states. Gold had been discovered!

Less than a year later, more than 80,000 gold seekers came to California. They were called **forty-niners** because they arrived in the year 1849. Most had made their way west on the Oregon Trail, cutting south across the Nevada desert to California. The longer but easier way was to travel around Cape Horn, the southern tip of South America, by clipper ship. Clipper ships were the fastest ships to sail the oceans. For gold seekers in a hurry to reach California and willing to pay extra to get there fast, the journey around Cape Horn took from three to four months.

These forty-niners are trying to find gold among stones in a riverbed. Looking for gold was hard work, and the chances of finding any were slim.

The gold rush quickly filled California with new people. They came from Europe and Asia as well as from the United States. In 1850, only two years after Marshall's discovery at Sutter's Mill, California became a state.

REVIEW *Why did thousands of people travel to California in 1849?*

THE WAY THEY GO TO CALIFORNIA.

The cartoon (left) uses humor to show that some people would do anything to get to California during the gold rush. This guide (above) to the California gold fields was printed in Boston in 1849.

LESSON 3 REVIEW

1820	1840	1860

1821
• Colonists settle Texas

1836
• Texas declares independence from Mexico

1848
• Gold is found in California

1853
• The Continental United States is formed

Check Understanding

1 Remember the Facts Why did American settlers move west into Texas, Oregon, Utah, and California?

2 Recall the Main Idea How did the United States expand its territory in the 1800s?

Think Critically

3 Personally Speaking What qualities do you think a pioneer needed? Why would those qualities be important?

4 Past to Present Are there still pioneers and frontiers today? Explain your answer.

Show What You Know

Art Activity Make a picture map of the growth of the western United States. On your map, show the Alamo, the Whitman and Spalding missions, travelers on the Oregon Trail, Mormon settlers, and forty-niners. Share your map with family members.

Use Relief and

1. Why Learn This Skill?

Early pioneers had to travel long distances, cross steep mountains, and wade across wide rivers. Relief maps and elevation maps can help you better understand their difficult journeys. Both types of maps show how high or how low the land is.

2. Relief and Elevation

A relief map helps you picture the physical features of the land. **Relief** (rih•LEEF),

or the differences in height of an area of land, is often shown by shading. Heavily shaded areas on a relief map show high relief, or sharp rises and drops in the land. Lightly shaded areas show low relief, where the land gently rises or falls. Areas with no shading show land that is mostly flat.

Look at the relief map showing trails to the West. There is heavy shading in the western lands—showing areas of high relief, such as the Rocky Mountains and the Cascade Range. In the eastern lands, there is

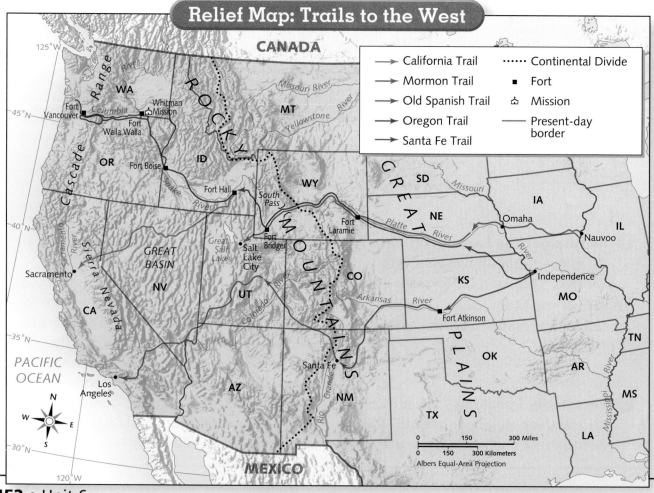

Relief Map: Trails to the West

→ California Trail
→ Mormon Trail
→ Old Spanish Trail
→ Oregon Trail
→ Santa Fe Trail
••••• Continental Divide
■ Fort
⌂ Mission
— Present-day border

Albers Equal-Area Projection

Elevation Maps

little shading—showing land that has low relief, such as the Great Plains.

Although a relief map shows you where mountains, hills, and plains are located, it does not tell you the elevation (eh•luh•VAY•shuhn) of the land. **Elevation** is the height of the land. Land that is level with the surface of the ocean is said to be at sea level. Its elevation is zero. The elevation of all other land is measured from sea level, up or down, in feet or meters. To find the elevation of a place, you must look at an elevation map.

Most elevation maps use color to show elevation. Look at the elevation map showing the end of the Oregon Trail. The map key tells you which colors are used to show different elevations. Green is used for the lowest land shown on this map, which is between sea level and 655 feet (200 m). Purple is used for the highest land, which is above 13,120 feet (4,000 m).

3. Understand the Process

Use the questions that follow as a guide for learning how to use relief maps and elevation maps.

1. What is the difference between a relief map and an elevation map?

2. To find the elevation at Fort Walla Walla, should you use a relief map or an elevation map?

3. Will a relief map tell you whether western Oregon is flat or mountainous?

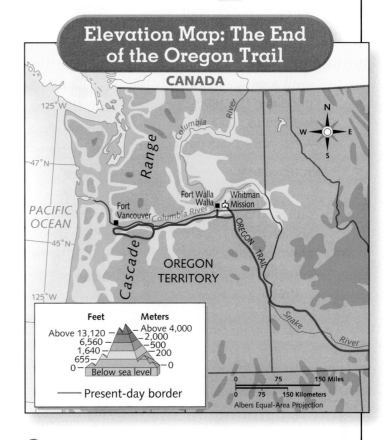

Elevation Map: The End of the Oregon Trail

4. How high are the highest areas in Oregon?

5. Where are the lowest areas in Oregon?

6. What is the elevation of the land at Fort Vancouver?

4. Think and Apply

Imagine that you are a pioneer on the Oregon Trail. On the relief map, use your finger to trace the route of the trail from Independence to Fort Vancouver. Describe the landforms you pass along the way. Once you reach Oregon, use the elevation map to describe the end of your journey.

FOCUS

How do people today work to make things better in their school, community, or country?

Main Idea As you read, look for ways people in the 1800s worked to make American society better.

Vocabulary

reform
public school
abolish
abolitionist
equality
suffrage

An Age of Reform

| 1845 | 1850 | 1855 |

T he fast growth of the United States in the first half of the 1800s made many Americans hopeful. They saw how the nation's growth in manufacturing and in size helped many people. But they also saw the need to **reform**, or change for the better, many parts of American life.

America's growth caused some problems, too. So many Americans were concerned about these problems that the 1830s through the 1850s became an age of reform. During this time many Americans worked to improve life for others.

Better Schools

Young Horace Mann was excited to see the red leaves falling from the oak and maple trees in Massachusetts. He knew that when winter put an end to farm work, he would be able to go to school. Horace's school had only one room and one teacher for children of all ages. And there were very few books.

When Horace Mann grew up, he became a reformer in education. In 1837 Mann was made secretary of the Massachusetts Board of Education. He worked to improve the state's **public schools**, the schools paid for by taxes and open to all children.

Horace Mann wanted more specific laws requiring children to go to school. He called for special schools to train teachers. In Mann's day

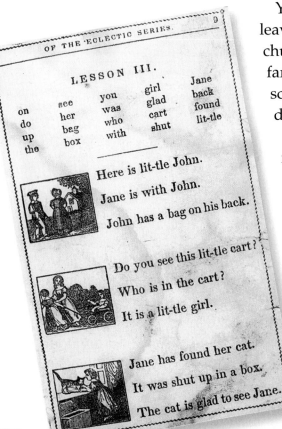

This spelling book was used in some schools during the early 1800s. How is this similar to spelling books used today?

most teachers worked only part-time. They were often students in law or in the clergy. Mann wanted full-time, well-trained teachers. He also wanted new schools built. Before this time most public-school classes were held in stores or in people's homes.

By 1850 many of Horace Mann's ideas were being used in the North and the West. Most white children received an elementary education and sometimes a high-school education. Free African children, however, had to go to separate schools. In the South, most boys who were white went to private schools. Girls had few chances for education. Enslaved children had none.

REVIEW *What reforms in education did Horace Mann try to bring about?*

The Fight Against Slavery

While Horace Mann worked to improve education during the age of reform, other reformers worked to **abolish**, or end, slavery. Since the early days of the country's history, some Americans had been deeply troubled by slavery. Soon they started working together to help enslaved people

FREE LECTURE!
SOJOURNER TRUTH,

Who has been a slave in the State of New York, and who has been a Lecturer for the last twenty-three years, whose characteristics have been so vividly portrayed by Mrs. Harriet Beecher Stowe, as the African Sybil, will deliver a lecture upon the present issues of the day,

At   On

And will give her experience as a Slave mother and religious woman. She comes highly recommended as a public speaker, having the approval of many thousands who have heard her earnest appeals, among whom are Wendell Phillips, Wm. Lloyd Garrison, and other distinguished men of the nation.

☞ At the close of her discourse she will offer for sale her photograph and a few of her choice songs.

Large crowds came to hear Sojourner Truth. She spoke against slavery and in favor of women's rights.

gain their freedom. Among the first to speak out were members of a religious group called the Quakers. In 1775 the Quakers formed the first group to work against slavery —an antislavery society.

People who wanted to abolish slavery were called **abolitionists** (a•buh•LIH•shuhn•ists). Some abolitionists used the written word to spread their message. In 1827 Samuel Cornish and John Russwurm started a newspaper that called for **equality**, or the same rights, for all Americans. The newspaper, *Freedom's Journal*, was the first to be owned and written by Africans in the United States. "Too long," Cornish and Russwurm wrote, "have others spoken for us."

A few years later another abolitionist, William Lloyd Garrison, founded a newspaper called *The Liberator*. In it he called for a complete end to slavery at once.

66 On this subject I do not wish to think, or speak, or write with moderation. I am in earnest . . . I will not excuse. I will not retreat a single inch—AND I WILL BE HEARD. 99

In 1852 a novel by abolitionist Harriet Beecher Stowe turned many people against slavery. The book, called *Uncle Tom's Cabin*, told the heartbreaking story of slaves being mistreated by a cruel slave owner. The book quickly became a best-seller and was made into a play.

While some abolitionists were writing, others were giving speeches. One of the speakers was Frederick Douglass, a runaway slave. William Lloyd Garrison asked him to speak at an abolitionist meeting. Douglass slowly rose and walked up to the stage. He shared from his heart how it felt to be free. And he told his listeners the story of his escape from slavery.

When Douglass finished speaking, everyone cheered. Before long, he had become the leading abolitionist speaker. His speeches made many people agree that slavery had to be stopped.

Like Douglass, Sojourner Truth traveled the country speaking out against slavery.

Sojourner Truth was a former slave named Isabella. She believed that God had called her to "travel up and down the land" to preach. She decided to change her name to *Sojourner*, which means "traveler." She chose *Truth* as a last name.

Sojourner Truth believed that slavery could be ended peacefully. Frederick Douglass argued in his speeches that only rebellion would end it.

In the end, Douglass was proved right. The nation that grew large and strong in the 1800s would soon be divided by civil war.

REVIEW *How did abolitionists work to end slavery?*

Millions of people around the world read about the cruel conditions of slavery in the novel *Uncle Tom's Cabin* (above). The Webb family (left) read the novel to audiences in the North.

Seneca Falls, New York

Seneca Falls is a small town in the middle of New York State, between Rochester and Syracuse. Seneca Falls was the home of Elizabeth Cady Stanton. With Lucretia Mott, she planned the first women's rights convention in the summer of 1848. Those attending the Seneca Falls Convention called for women to work together to win their rights as citizens. Today Seneca Falls has a Women's Hall of Fame.

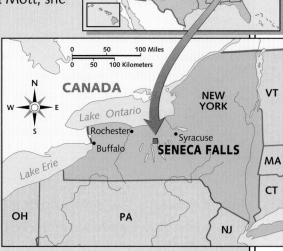

Elizabeth Cady Stanton spoke at the first women's rights convention and wrote a document called the Declaration of Sentiments. It describes women's rights by using words from the Declaration of Independence. But Stanton added some words, as in "all men *and* women are created equal."

Rights for Women

In 1840 Elizabeth Cady Stanton and Lucretia Mott went to a convention of abolitionists in London, Britain. However, they were not allowed to speak because they were women. Stanton and Mott were so angry that they decided to hold their own convention—for women's rights.

The first women's rights convention met on July 19 and 20, 1848, at Seneca Falls, New York. Those who attended wanted women to have the same political, social, and economic rights as men. They wrote a statement saying women should have "all the rights and privileges which belong to them as citizens of the United States." The statement called for women to be able to own property, to keep wages they earned, and to be given **suffrage**, or the right to vote.

The reformers began to get some support. In 1850 Susan B. Anthony of New York worked for women teachers to have the same pay as men and for women to have the same property rights as men. She later became a leader of the women's suffrage movement.

Sojourner Truth used her speaking skills to help. In 1851 she was at a women's rights convention in Ohio when a man said, "Women are weak." She stood up quickly and answered the man.

66 The man over there says women need to be helped into carriages and lifted over ditches and puddles, and have the best place everywhere. Nobody helps me into carriages and over puddles, or gives me the best place—and ain't I a woman?

Look at my arm! I have plowed and planted and gathered into barns, and no man could beat me— and ain't I a woman? 99

Susan Brownell Anthony, 1820–1906

For most of her life, Susan B. Anthony worked to get women the right to vote. She was once arrested and fined $100 for breaking the law by voting in an election for President. Anthony also started a weekly newspaper and wrote books to spread her message. Susan B. Anthony died 14 years before the Nineteenth Amendment to the Constitution became law. From 1979 to 1981, the United States government honored her work for women's rights by minting one-dollar coins with her picture on them. Susan B. Anthony was the first woman to have her picture on a coin in the United States.

Women won a few rights during this time. A few states gave women control of the money they earned and of the property they owned. Some places, like Wyoming Territory, allowed women to vote. This was the first place in the United States and in the world to grant women suffrage. However, it would not be until 1920 that the Nineteenth Amendment gave all women in the United States this right.

REVIEW *What reforms did Elizabeth Cady Stanton and others work for?*

LESSON 4 REVIEW

1845	1850	1855

1848
• The first women's rights convention is held

1852
• *Uncle Tom's Cabin* is published

Check Understanding

1 **Remember the Facts**   What did reformers want to change about American society?

2 **Recall the Main Idea**   How did reformers in the 1800s work to improve American society?

Think Critically

3 **Cause and Effect**   How might public schools today be different if Horace Mann had not worked to change them?

4 **Personally Speaking**   Why do you think so many people wanted to hear Frederick Douglass tell his story?

Show What You Know

Writing Activity   Imagine that you are a reformer in the 1800s. Write a letter in which you try to persuade a member of the school board to make a change in the public schools. Be sure to give the reason the change is needed. Collect the letters in a binder for classroom display.

Use a Double-Bar Graph

1. Why Learn This Skill?

People often make comparisons and look at how things have changed over time. A good way to compare information is by making a double-bar graph. A double-bar graph allows you to compare information quickly and to see changes over time.

2. Understand the Process

Between 1790 and 1850 both the urban and rural populations of the United States grew at a steady pace. The double-bar graph on this page shows the differences in urban and rural populations for these years. It also shows how urban and rural populations have changed over time.

1. Notice that the years are listed along the bottom, and the numbers of people are listed along the left-hand side.

2. The information on this graph is shown only for every tenth year from 1790 to 1850.

3. Blue and red are used to show the urban population and the rural population.

4. Read the graph by running your finger up to the top of each bar and then left to the population number. If the top of the bar is between numbered lines, estimate the population by selecting a number between those two numbers.

5. Compare the heights of the blue bars. How did the urban population change over time?

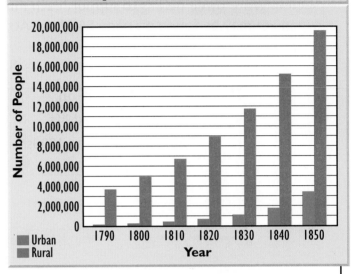

Urban and Rural Population, 1790–1850

6. How did the rural population change over time?

7. Compare the heights of the blue bar and the red bar for each year shown. This allows you to compare urban growth with rural growth over time. How does this graph help you understand how the population of the United States grew between 1790 and 1850?

3. Think and Apply

Make a double-bar graph of your test scores in social studies and in another subject. Label the bottom of your graph by grading periods. Along the left-hand side of your graph, list possible test scores. Each period, make a bar to represent your test scores for each subject. Remember to use a different color for each subject.

REVIEW

1829
• Andrew Jackson becomes the President of the United States

1830
• Steam locomotives

CONNECT MAIN IDEAS

Use this organizer to show how the chapter's main ideas are connected. Write three details to support each main idea. A copy of the organizer may be found on page 84 of the Activity Book.

The Industrial Revolution
New technology changed life in the United States in the 1800s.
1. _____
2. _____
3. _____

The Age of Jackson
Problems divided the American people in the early 1800s.
1. _____
2. _____
3. _____

The Way West   W—✦—E   N ... S

Westward Ho!
The United States expanded its territory in the 1800s.
1. _____
2. _____
3. _____

An Age of Reform
People in the 1800s worked to make American society better.
1. _____
2. _____
3. _____

WRITE MORE ABOUT IT

Write a Conversation Write a conversation that could have taken place between Eli Whitney and a factory owner. Whitney and the factory owner should discuss how mass production will affect Americans.

Write a Letter Imagine that you witnessed the race between the *Tom Thumb* locomotive and the railroad car pulled by a horse. Write a letter to a friend describing the excitement of the event.

1840	1850	1860

1838
• Cherokees are forced
  from their land

1848
• Gold is found
  in California

1853
• Continental United States
  is formed

USE VOCABULARY

Write a term from this list to complete each of the sentences that follow.

equality   secede

manifest destiny   transport

1 Factories needed to _____ their products to their customers.

2 South Carolina threatened to _____ in 1832 because Congress passed another tariff.

3 In 1845 the term _____ was first used to describe the idea that the United States would one day stretch from the Atlantic Ocean to the Pacific Ocean.

4 Some reformers called for _____, or the same rights, for all Americans.

CHECK UNDERSTANDING

5 How was Francis Cabot Lowell's textile mill different from earlier ones?

6 How was the National Road important to the country's growth?

7 What change in voting helped Andrew Jackson become President?

8 What was the Trail of Tears?

9 What group settled the Utah Territory? Why did they go there?

10 What lands did the United States gain from the war with Mexico?

11 Who were Frederick Douglass and Sojourner Truth? How did they spread their messages?

12 Why was the first women's rights convention held?

THINK CRITICALLY

13 **Explore Viewpoints** How did Vice President Calhoun's view of states' rights differ from the one held by President Jackson?

14 **Cause and Effect** What effect did the California gold rush have on the growth of the United States?

APPLY SKILLS

Use Relief and Elevation Maps
Use the maps on pages 452 and 453 to answer these questions.

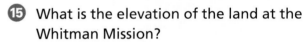

15 What is the elevation of the land at the Whitman Mission?

16 How would you describe the land near Fort Laramie?

Use a Double-Bar Graph Make a double-bar graph showing the high and low temperatures over the next five days. Each day, make bars for the high and low temperatures. Use different colors for the two temperatures.

READ MORE ABOUT IT

Erie Canal: Canoeing America's Great Waterway by Peter Lourie. Boyds Mills Press. Enjoy a historical canoe tour of the Erie Canal.

Visit the Internet at
http://www.hbschool.com
for additional resources.

TODAY'S PATHFINDERS

The space suit (below) allows a space explorer to breathe while in space where there is no air. The special suit for exploring the ocean (right) protects the wearer from the crushing pressures of the deep ocean waters.

Two hundred years ago much of North America was still unknown to people living in the United States. It lay beyond the frontier—the edge of settled regions. Today most places on the continent have been explored, and those that can be lived in have been settled. People today are exploring new kinds of frontiers.

Two of today's new frontiers are space and the deep ocean. Instead of traveling by horse or by wagon, present-day pathfinders explore in special vehicles that can travel great distances above the Earth or deep within the ocean waters. Instead of clothes made from animal furs to protect them from cold weather, today's explorers wear special suits to protect them from the harsh environments of space or the ocean floor.

Like those of the past, today's pathfinders are leading the way for others who will follow. Space stations and underwater laboratories already have been built where pathfinders can live and work for a period of time. Their success may lead to the building of permanent settlements in the future. One day people may live their whole lives in space or in the ocean waters.

The *Deepstar 4000* (bottom left) was one of the first vehicles used to explore the deep ocean. The *Nautile* (below) was used to explore the sunken ship *Titanic* that lies 12,300 feet (3,750 m) below the ocean's surface. Space explorers (bottom right) perform tasks outside the space shuttle far above the Earth.

Think and Apply

BUILDING CITIZENSHIP

Think about ways the work of present-day pathfinders could change the way people live. Create a poster that shows what life might be like in the future because of the exploration taking place today. Share your poster with classmates.

HARCOURT BRACE

Visit the Internet at **http://www.hbschool.com** for additional resources.

CNN
Turner Le@rning

Check your media center or classroom video library for the Making Social Studies Relevant videotape of this feature.

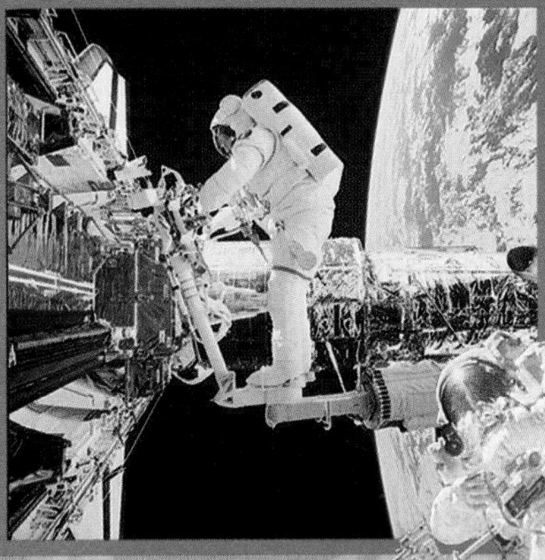

VISUAL SUMMARY

Summarize the Main Ideas
Study the pictures and captions to help you review the events you read about in Unit 6.

Create a Visual Summary
Choose a topic that is discussed in this unit. Then create your own visual summary about that topic. Draw simple pictures, and label each one. Remember to add a title.

1 The Industrial Revolution brought great changes to the United States. The nation's first factory was built in 1790.

4 In 1811 work began on the National Road. It became the main land route between the East and the West.

6 By the mid-1800s, the nation had gained Texas, the Oregon Country, and other western lands. At the Alamo in 1836, Texans had fought for independence from Mexico.

2 In 1803 the Louisiana Purchase doubled the nation's size. Lewis and Clark explored the new territory with help from Sacagawea.

3 In the early 1800s, steamboats made travel by river much faster.

5 The first locomotive in the nation was built in 1830. Railroads grew quickly after that.

7 The Indian Removal Act of 1830 forced American Indians to leave their homes and make difficult journeys to the West.

ABOLISH SLAVERY

8 Many Americans saw the need for reform. People such as Sojourner Truth spoke out against slavery.

USE VOCABULARY

Use each term in a sentence that will help explain its meaning.

1. purchase
2. doctrine
3. Industrial Revolution
4. textile mill
5. canal
6. forty-niners
7. reform
8. abolitionist

CHECK UNDERSTANDING

9. How was the Cumberland Gap important to Daniel Boone and the Wilderness Road?

10. How did Thomas Jefferson help double the size of the United States?

11. What was the purpose of the Lewis and Clark expedition?

12. What is mass production? Who first put this idea for producing goods into practice?

13. Why was the Erie Canal built?

14. What was the result of the Indian Removal Act of 1830?

15. What physical features first attracted pioneers to the Oregon Country?

THINK CRITICALLY

16. **Past to Present** Technology changed life for Americans in the 1800s. How does technology change life for Americans today?

17. **Personally Speaking** If you had been alive in 1849, would you have gone to California in search of gold? Explain your answer.

18. **Think More About It** What do you think helped make Frederick Douglass such an effective abolitionist speaker?

APPLY SKILLS

Use Relief and Elevation Maps
Use the map below to answer the questions.

19. Where did the Trail of Tears lead to?

20. Which part of the Trail of Tears passed through mountains? How do you know?

21. What is the elevation of the land near Murfreesboro? near Springfield?

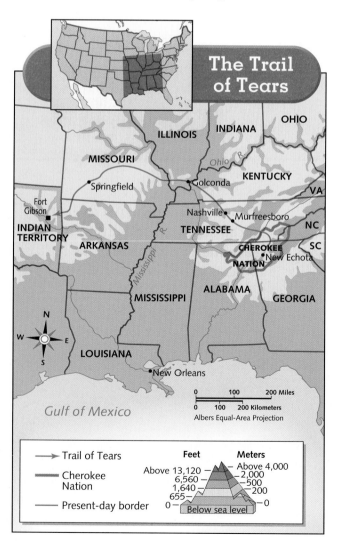

The Trail of Tears

OHIO
ILLINOIS INDIANA
MISSOURI
Ohio
Springfield KENTUCKY
Golconda VA
Fort Gibson Nashville Murfreesboro
INDIAN TERRITORY TENNESSEE NC
ARKANSAS CHEROKEE SC
NATION New Echota
Mississippi
ALABAMA
MISSISSIPPI GEORGIA
N
W E
S
LOUISIANA
New Orleans
Gulf of Mexico

0   100   200 Miles
0 100   200 Kilometers
Albers Equal-Area Projection

→ Trail of Tears
— Cherokee Nation
— Present-day border

Feet   Meters
Above 13,120 — — Above 4,000
6,560 — — 2,000
1,640 — — 500
655 — — 200
0 — Below sea level — 0

REMEMBER

- Share your ideas.
- Cooperate with others to plan your work.
- Take responsibility for your work.
- Help one another.
- Show your group's work to the class.
- Discuss what you learned by working together.

ACTIVITY

Write and Perform a Scene for a Play

Work with members of a group to write a scene for a play about a typical workday at an early textile mill. The scene should tell something about the workers and the working conditions at the mill. Decide who the characters in the scene will be, and write dialogue for them. Then choose roles, practice the scene, and perform it for your class.

ACTIVITY

Draw a Map

Work together to draw a map showing how the United States grew in the first half of the 1800s. Maps in your textbook and in atlases can help you. First, draw an outline map of the country, and label major landforms and bodies of water. Then, color the boundaries of the United States in 1783, following the American Revolution. Use different colors to show the Louisiana Purchase, Florida, Texas, the Oregon Country, and the land that the United States gained following its war with Mexico. Add a map key to your map.

ACTIVITY

Make a Time Line

Work in a group to draw a time line on a large sheet of paper. Show the years from 1770 to 1850, using ten-year periods. Then label the time line with events from this unit. Draw pictures to illustrate the events.

Unit Project Wrap-Up

Make a Diorama Finish the Unit Project from page 395. Then work in groups to discuss the scenes shown in each diorama. Discuss how important it was for the pioneers to cooperate with each other if they were to survive. Work together to write descriptions for each scene shown. Be sure to include examples of how pioneers helped one another. Share your dioramas and descriptions with the class.

WAR DIVIDES THE NATION

468

During the early 1800s the United States grew and changed. New towns sprang up across the land. Many Americans moved west to explore and settle distant places.

Yet all was not well in the young country. Problems divided the people of the United States. In 1861 the problems dividing Americans led to war. The war split the country in two, with people living in the North fighting people living in the South.

The United States was not the same after this terrible war. The war brought some good changes, but it left bitter feelings among the country's people for many years to come.

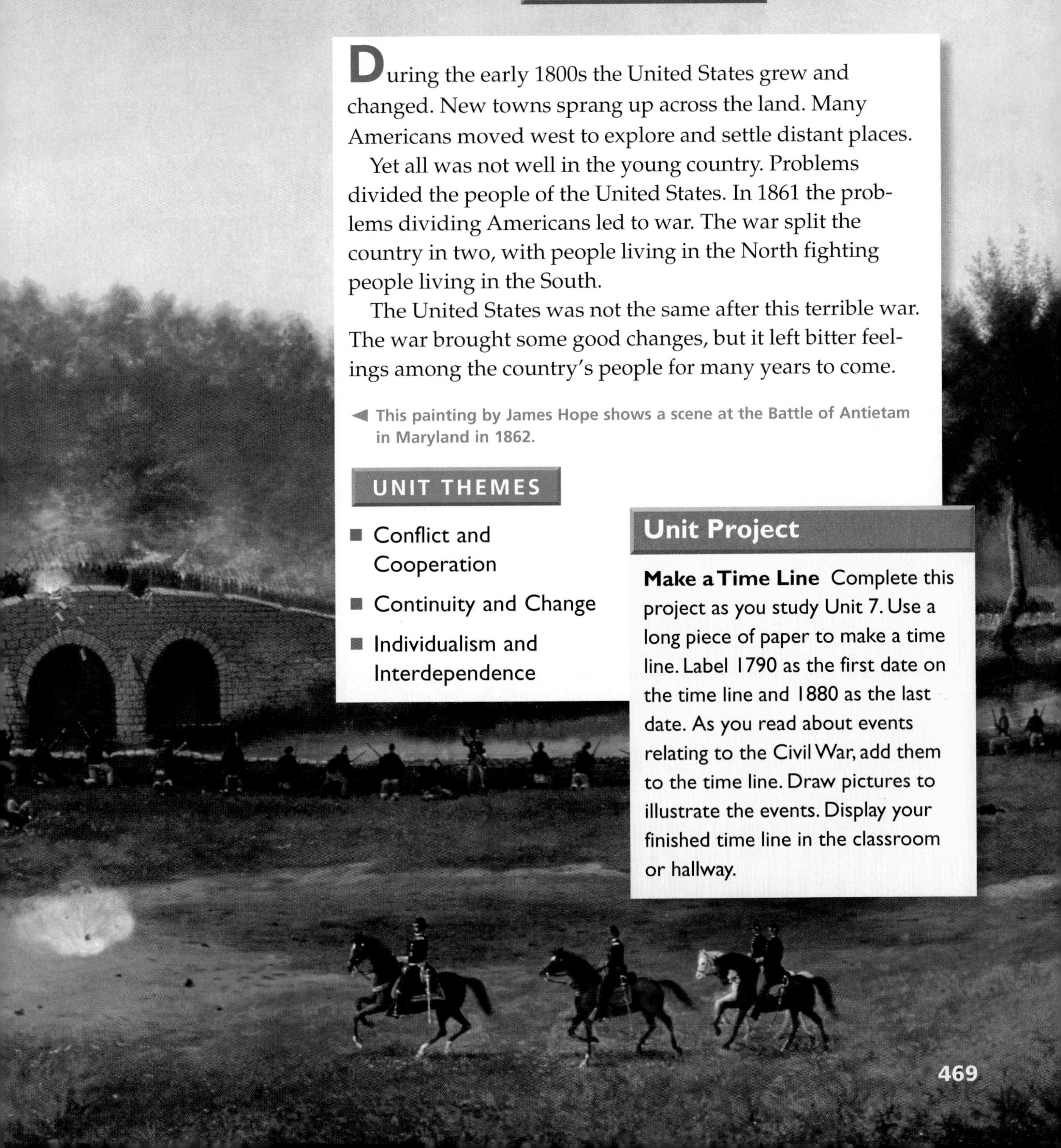

◀ This painting by James Hope shows a scene at the Battle of Antietam in Maryland in 1862.

UNIT THEMES

- Conflict and Cooperation
- Continuity and Change
- Individualism and Interdependence

Unit Project

Make a Time Line Complete this project as you study Unit 7. Use a long piece of paper to make a time line. Label 1790 as the first date on the time line and 1880 as the last date. As you read about events relating to the Civil War, add them to the time line. Draw pictures to illustrate the events. Display your finished time line in the classroom or hallway.

469

CANADA

WASHINGTON
TERRITORY

ROCKY

Columbia

Missouri *River*

GREAT

OREGON

DAKOTA
TERRITORY

PLAINS

PACIFIC
OCEAN

Snake

River

NEVADA
TERRITORY

Great
Salt
Lake

NEBRASKA
TERRITORY

Platte River

*GREAT
BASIN*

UTAH
TERRITORY

M
O
U
N

COLORADO
TERRITORY

Sacramento

Arkansas

KANSAS

River

San Francisco

T

CALIFORNIA

River

A

N

Colorado

*Mojave
Desert*

I

N

NEW MEXICO
TERRITORY

Santa Fe

S

N
W   E
S

Los Angeles

TEXAS

San Diego

El Paso

| 0 | 200 | 400 Miles |
| 0 | 200 | 400 Kilometers |

Albers Equal-Area Projection

Rio Grande

MEXICO

1860   1862   1864

1860
Lincoln Is Elected
President
PAGE 496

1861
Civil War Begins
PAGE 497

The Nation Divided, 1861

MINNESOTA

CANADA

MAINE

Lake Superior

MICHIGAN

Lake Huron

WISCONSIN

Lake Michigan

Mississippi River

Milwaukee

Detroit

Lake Ontario

Lake Erie

VT
NH
• Portland

Troy
Albany •

MA

Boston •
Providence •

NEW YORK

CT

RI

Cedar
Rapids •

Chicago •

Cleveland •

Buffalo

New York City •

IOWA

Pittsburgh •

PA

Gettysburg •

NEW JERSEY

Philadelphia •

ILLINOIS

INDIANA

OHIO

Cincinnati •

River

MD

Baltimore •
Annapolis •

DE

Missouri River

St. Louis •

Louisville •
Perryville •

Ohio River

WEST
VIRGINIA
(1863)

Washington, D.C. •

VIRGINIA

Richmond •

APPALACHIAN MOUNTAINS

Norfolk •

ATLANTIC
OCEAN

MISSOURI

KENTUCKY

Appomattox •

Paducah •

Nashville •

Tennessee River

NORTH
CAROLINA

Raleigh •

INDIAN
TERRITORY

Memphis •

TENNESSEE

Wilmington •

Mississippi River

ARKANSAS

ALABAMA

SOUTH
CAROLINA

Atlanta •

Charleston •

MISSISSIPPI

GEORGIA

Dallas •

Vicksburg •

Jackson •

Montgomery •

Savannah •

LOUISIANA

Mobile •

Pensacola •

Jacksonville •
St. Augustine •

Port
Hudson •

New Orleans •

Gulf of Mexico

FLORIDA

	Union state
	Border state
	Confederate state
	Territory
●	Major city

1866

1865
Lee Surrenders

PAGE 526

1865
Freedmen's Bureau

PAGE 532

STONEWALL

by Jean Fritz

Confederate General Thomas Jackson earned the name "Stonewall" during the Civil War.

In towns and cities across the country, thousands of excited young men signed up to join the army. It was 1861, and the country was at war. Northerners and Southerners alike signed up, but not to fight on the same side. They signed up to fight each other.

Most people said that it would be a quick and easy war. It would be over, they said, after only one or two battles.

Most people also said that their side would win.

Read now about the war's first major battle, which took place near the small Virginia town of Manassas Junction, not far from Washington, D.C. Imagine Northern soldiers, called Yankees, lining up for the first time against Southern soldiers, called Confederates or Rebels, as crowds looked on.

This building, known as the "Stone House," was used as a hospital by Confederate and Union soldiers during the Battle of Bull Run.

As the participants gathered at Manassas, excitement mounted. At last! This was it! The war was starting! Victory was in the air as if nothing else could possibly exist. The Confederates, obviously outnumbered, were lined up in a defensive position beside a small stream known as Bull Run, but if they worried, they didn't show it. Hadn't they always believed that one rebel could beat five Yankees? As for the Yankees, they straggled down to Manassas, stopping to pick blackberries—in no hurry, for hadn't they been told that the Rebs would run once they saw how bold the Yanks were? Even the civilians in Washington, high-ranking officials and their wives, were so sure of a Union victory that they planned to picnic on the outskirts of Manassas on the Big Day. They would drink champagne and toast the army and cry "Bravo! Bravo!" What could be nicer?

Although there had been several days of initial skirmishing, the Big Day turned out to be Sunday, July 21st. A beautiful sunny day—perfect for a picnic. Carriages were drawn up on a hill overlooking Bull Run; ladies rustled under parasols; gentlemen adjusted field glasses; couriers galloped up with the latest news. Good news, all of it. Yankee advances. Confederate confusion. So it went for the first six hours.

Yet not all the Confederates had been heard from. The Army of the Shenandoah that was supposed to be held in the hills by the Union watchdog forces had eluded their enemy on July 18th and had left for Manassas. At first they'd been slow. The men didn't know where they were going or why and saw no reason to rush just because their officers told them to. Finally General Thomas Jackson, whose brigade led the march, stopped them and read an official statement. "Our gallant army under General Beauregard is now attacked by overwhelming numbers," Jackson read. He asked the troops if they would not "step out like men and make a forced march to save the country."

A battle! The men yelled their approval—a special rebel yell. . . . It was a fierce sound that a Yankee soldier once said sent a corkscrew sensation down the spine. Woh-who-ey. The yell rose to a pitch on the *who* and held there, trembling and drawn out, then fell with a thud on the *ey*. The men quickened their pace. Woh-who-ey. For eighteen hours they marched until at last, having waded waist deep through the green Shenandoah River, they dropped, exhausted. They marched and they rode a train for a few hours, and then they marched again. But they were there now. The question was: Were they in time?

By noon on the 21st it was clear that Beauregard had positioned the major part of his army in the wrong place. While the enemy was concentrating its forces on the left, the Confederates were wasting their time on the right. In the general scramble to change positions, Jackson and his brigade found themselves in the thick of the activity. Union men were in the distance but steadily advancing; the Confederates were retreating. As one officer passed Jackson, he shook his head. "The day is going against us," he said.

"If you think so, sir," Jackson replied, "don't say anything about it."

Jackson did not plunge forward to meet the enemy, as his men might have expected. Looking over the field, he saw a plateau which he recognized as the best possible position for making a stand. Here he placed his men and artillery and when the enemy fire closed in, Jackson stood before his brigade, his blue eyes blazing, the old battle fever upon him. Walking back and forth, indifferent to bullets, he was lifted out of himself, possessed with a power he'd known only once before, in Mexico. He understood exactly how to get the most out of every man and every gun and he *willed* victory into the day. "The fight," as one officer put it, "was just then hot enough to make [Jackson] feel well." Shot in the hand as he held it up, Jackson wrapped a handkerchief around the wound and went on as if nothing had happened.

In another part of the field, General Bee, a West Point classmate of Jackson's, was desperately trying to stop a retreat. "Look yonder!" he cried to his men. "There's Jackson standing like a stone wall."

General Bee was killed almost as soon as he'd finished speaking, but retreating Confederates did see how well Jackson's line was holding and gradually they began to rally around it. The last reinforcements from Shenandoah army, which had just arrived, were rushed to the scene. And the tide of the battle began to turn.

Men were supposed to be at least 18 years old to join the army, but some boys much younger—like the two shown here—still signed up. Most boys were not allowed to fight. Instead they tended horses, drove wagons, or served as drummer boys.

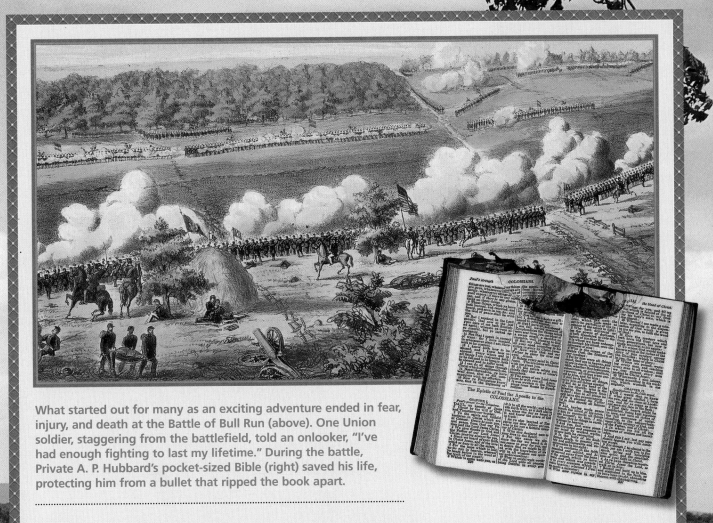

What started out for many as an exciting adventure ended in fear, injury, and death at the Battle of Bull Run (above). One Union soldier, staggering from the battlefield, told an onlooker, "I've had enough fighting to last my lifetime." During the battle, Private A. P. Hubbard's pocket-sized Bible (right) saved his life, protecting him from a bullet that ripped the book apart.

When the center of the Union line was in plain sight, General Beauregard ordered a charge. Jackson relayed the order.

"Reserve your fire till they come within fifty yards," he shouted, "then fire and give them the bayonet. And when you charge, yell like furies."

The orders were carried out precisely.

Woh-who-ey!

Woh-who-ey!

Suddenly the entire Union army was falling back, then turning around and hurrying off the field. A huge, confused mob mixed with panic-stricken picnickers headed pell-mell back to Washington.

The battle was over and with it some of the innocent glory was gone. For the fields were strewn with bodies—young men who only the day before had been laughing and making jokes. Two thousand Confederates killed or wounded; three thousand Union men. Stopped right in the midst of doing something. In the middle of a sentence perhaps, in mid-step, in the act of raising a rifle, at the beginning of a smile. Struck down, blown apart as if they weren't *people*. As if they weren't *young*. How could inexperienced men have imagined what death would be like on a battlefield?

In one day soldiers on both sides became veterans, but of course the victors felt better than the losers. If they could win a battle, southerners said, they could win a war.

BACKGROUND TO THE CONFLICT

"I appear this evening as a thief and robber. I stole this head, these limbs, this body from my master, and ran off with them."

Frederick Douglass, a runaway slave and abolitionist, about 1842

This photograph of Frederick Douglass was taken in 1856.

476

Differences Divide
North and South

FOCUS
What might cause people living in different regions to disagree today?

Main Idea As you read, look for the reasons that caused people in the North and the South to disagree during the mid-1800s.

Vocabulary
cotton gin

Differences among Americans help make the United States strong. Sometimes, however, differences come between people. In the mid-1800s differences became disagreements between Americans living in two regions—the North and the South. These disagreements threatened to tear the country apart.

Regional Differences

Many of the differences between the North and the South developed over time, as people in each region found different ways of making a living. In the mid-1800s most Americans still lived and worked on farms. For many people, however, life was changing.

In the North, factories seemed to be springing up everywhere, making all kinds of goods. Many people were moving from farms to towns and cities, where they hoped to work in the factories. People even came from other countries to find jobs.

Life in the South was not changing as quickly. Factories were being built and cities were growing, yet farming remained the most common way to earn a living. The biggest farms were huge plantations along the Coastal Plain and near the Mississippi River, where the soil was rich and the weather was warm. Planters there raised acres and acres of cash crops, such as cotton, rice, tobacco, and sugarcane, to sell at market.

Wealthy plantation owners were among the South's leaders. Many white Southerners

Cotton was an important cash crop in the South. Many Southerners depended on cotton to make a living.

477

Many people in the North were moving to cities to find work. This painting (top) shows a busy street scene in New York City. In the South farming continued to be the center of life. This scene (below) shows a cotton plantation along the Mississippi River.

copied the ways of these planters and dreamed about owning their own plantations someday. Yet few ever did. Most lived on small farms, where they raised cattle, cut lumber, and grew only enough food to feed their families.

Partly because of the differences in work opportunities between the two regions,

many more people lived in the North than in the South. By 1860 the population of the North had grown to more than 19 million. Only 11 million people lived in the South. Of those 11 million people, nearly 4 million were Africans held as slaves.

REVIEW *How was the North different from the South?*

The Slave Economy

Slavery had been a part of American life since colonial days. In many places, however, slavery did not last. Some people thought that slavery was wrong. Others could not make money using enslaved workers. The cost of feeding, clothing, and housing slaves was too great.

Yet slavery continued in the South, where owners had come to depend on the work of enslaved people. Slaves were made to work as miners, carpenters, factory workers, and house servants. Most, however, were taken to large plantations. There they worked in the fields, raising cash crops for the planters to sell.

Not every white Southerner owned slaves. In fact, most did not. By 1860 only one white Southern family in four owned

slaves. Many of these families lived on small farms with one or two slaves. Only a few wealthy slaveholders lived on large plantations with many slaves. These planters together owned more than half the slaves in the South.

REVIEW *Why was slavery important in the Southern states?*

"King Cotton"

In the early years of settlement in the South, few planters grew cotton—the plant from which soft, cool cotton cloth is made. Cotton was in great demand. But before it could be sold, workers had to separate the small seeds from the white cotton fibers. This was a slow, tiring job that took too many people too much time. Inventor Eli Whitney changed this.

In 1793 Whitney invented a machine called the cotton gin, or engine. The cotton gin removed the seeds from the cotton fibers much faster than workers could. This one change in technology led to many other changes.

With the cotton gin, cotton could be cleaned and prepared for market in less time. Planters could then sell more cotton and make more money. They sold the cotton to textile mills in the North and in Europe.

Worldwide demand for cotton made both Southern planters and Northern textile-mill owners rich. It also created a demand for more slaves. Planters needed slaves to plant the seeds, weed the fields, pick the cotton, and run the cotton gins. "Cotton is King," said Senator James Henry Hammond of South Carolina, "and the African must be a slave, or there's an end of all things, and soon."

REVIEW *How did the cotton gin help speed up cotton production?*

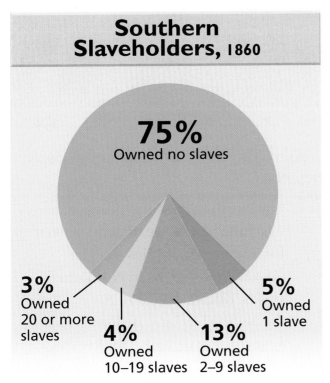

Southern Slaveholders, 1860

75% Owned no slaves

3% Owned 20 or more slaves

4% Owned 10–19 slaves

13% Owned 2–9 slaves

5% Owned 1 slave

LEARNING FROM GRAPHS Most Northerners once thought that all Southerners owned slaves. Look at the circle graph to tell if this is true.
■ *What percent of Southerners owned no slaves at all in 1860? What percent did own slaves?*

Eli Whitney
1765–1825

Eli Whitney taught school and studied law. He also liked to fix things. While visiting a friend's Georgia plantation, he learned how hard it was to remove the seeds from cotton.

Whitney invented a machine that could take care of the problem. Soon so many people wanted cotton gins that he could not make enough to keep up with the demand. Other people began to make and sell copies of his invention. Whitney had to pay lawyers to stop others from copying his work. This used up most of the money he made from inventing the cotton gin.

North and South Disagree

The biggest disagreement between the North and the South was over states' rights and slavery. Northerners and Southerners had argued since colonial days about whether states should allow slavery. By the mid-1800s some Southerners also had developed bad feelings over the growth in the North. They did not like the way industry was booming there. Tariffs on imports were still causing Southerners to buy most of the manufactured goods they needed from the North.

As a writer for one Alabama newspaper described it,

66 The North fattens and grows rich upon the South. We depend upon it for our entire supplies. . . . The slaveholder dresses in Northern goods, rides in a Northern saddle. . . . His land is cleared with a Northern axe, and a Yankee clock sits upon his mantel-piece; his floor is swept by a Northern broom, and is covered with a Northern carpet . . . and he is furnished with Northern inventions. 99

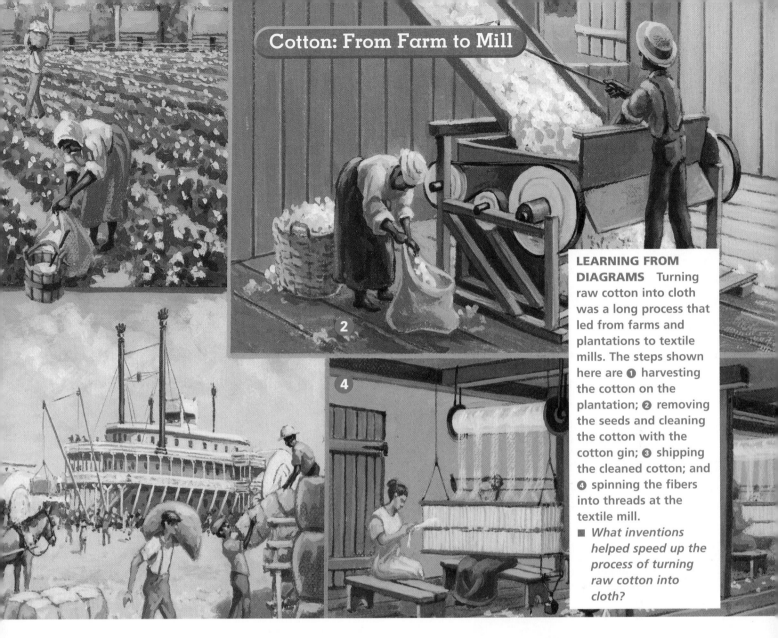

Cotton: From Farm to Mill

LEARNING FROM DIAGRAMS Turning raw cotton into cloth was a long process that led from farms and plantations to textile mills. The steps shown here are ❶ harvesting the cotton on the plantation; ❷ removing the seeds and cleaning the cotton with the cotton gin; ❸ shipping the cleaned cotton; and ❹ spinning the fibers into threads at the textile mill.

■ *What inventions helped speed up the process of turning raw cotton into cloth?*

The disagreement over slavery flared up again with the rapid settlement of the western frontier. Over the years American pioneers and soldiers had pushed many of the Indian peoples off their lands. This made it possible for more settlers to move west into territories such as Illinois, Iowa, Missouri, and Arkansas. The settlers took with them their own ways of life. For settlers from the North, this meant a way of life without slaves. For some settlers from the South, however, this meant taking their enslaved workers with them.

It was not long before the question of the spread of slavery to the frontier became one of the most argued issues in the country. Most white Northerners thought that slavery should go no farther than where it already was—in the South. Most white Southerners believed that slave owners had the right to take their slaves wherever they wanted, including to the west.

The disagreement over slavery led to fierce arguments. Even so, the number of people held as slaves in the South continued to grow. So did the number of enslaved people who were taken west.

REVIEW *Why did the settlement of the western frontier bring about new arguments over slavery?*

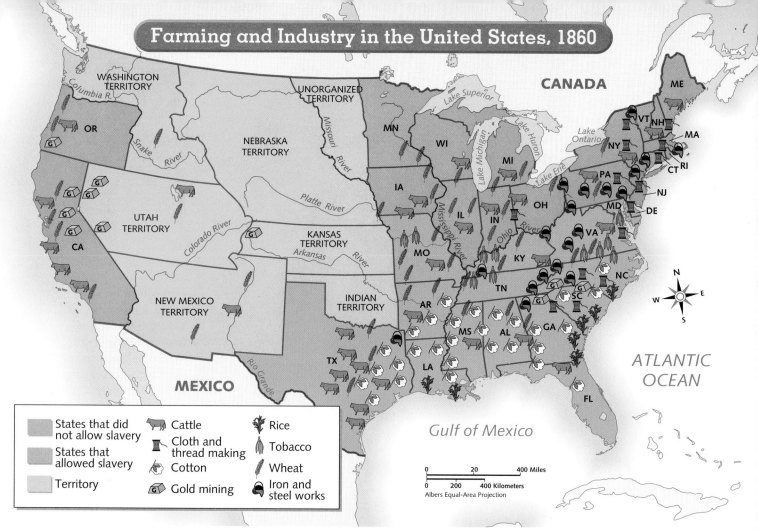

Farming and Industry in the United States, 1860

WASHINGTON TERRITORY

Columbia R.

OR

Snake River

CA

UTAH TERRITORY

NEW MEXICO TERRITORY

Colorado River

Rio Grande

MEXICO

NEBRASKA TERRITORY

Platte River

KANSAS TERRITORY

Arkansas River

INDIAN TERRITORY

TX

LA

UNORGANIZED TERRITORY

Missouri River

MN

WI

IA

MO

AR

MS

AL

Lake Superior

Lake Michigan

Lake Huron

MI

IL

IN

KY

TN

GA

FL

CANADA

ME

Lake Ontario

Lake Erie

NY

PA

OH

VA

NC

SC

VT NH

MA

CT RI

NJ

MD

DE

Mississippi River

Ohio River

ATLANTIC OCEAN

Gulf of Mexico

Legend

- States that did not allow slavery
- States that allowed slavery
- Territory
- Cattle
- Cloth and thread making
- Cotton
- Gold mining
- Rice
- Tobacco
- Wheat
- Iron and steel works

0   20   400 Miles
0   200   400 Kilometers
Albers Equal-Area Projection

Human-Environment Interactions   This map shows where there was farming and industry in the Northern and Southern states.

■ *Which industry in the North depended on a crop in the South?*

LESSON 1 REVIEW

Check Understanding

1 Remember the Facts   In what ways were the North and the South different?

2 Recall the Main Idea   What caused people living in the North and the South to disagree during the mid-1800s?

Think Critically

3 Think More About It   How did the differences between the North and the South affect the ways of life in the two regions?

4 Cause and Effect   How did the invention of the cotton gin affect Southern planters? How did it affect Northern textile-mill owners?

Show What You Know

Art Activity   Think about how the cotton gin changed life in the 1800s. Create an advertisement for the people of that time that explains how the cotton gin affects those who make and buy cotton and cotton products. Then present your advertisement to a group of your classmates.

Use Graphs to Identify Trends

1. Why Learn This Skill?

Some graphs show information that can help you see patterns of change over time. These patterns are called **trends**. Graphs can show trends that go upward, go downward, or hold steady. Some graphs show trends that change. For example, a graph could show a downward trend for a time and then an upward trend.

2. Understand the Process

Follow the numbered steps to identify the trends shown by the two graphs on this page. The first is a line graph that shows the amount of cotton produced in the United States from 1800 to 1860. The second is a bar graph that shows the number of people enslaved in the United States from 1800 to 1860.

1 Look at the line graph. About how much cotton was produced in 1800? in 1830? in 1860? You can see that the amount of cotton produced from 1800 to 1860 went up. The trend, then, was for cotton production to go up during this period of time.

2 Look at the bar graph. About how many people were enslaved in 1800? in 1830? in 1860? What trend does the bar graph show?

3. Think and Apply

Think about the trends shown in these graphs. Write a paragraph that describes what the trends tell you about the connection between cotton production and slavery between 1800 and 1860. Share your paragraph with a classmate.

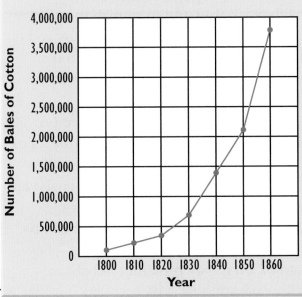

Cotton Production, 1800–1860

Number of Bales of Cotton / Year

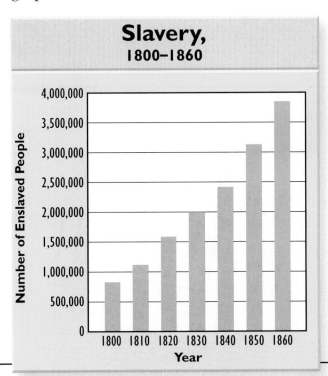

Slavery, 1800–1860

Number of Enslaved People / Year

483

FOCUS

In what ways do people today protest against unfair treatment?

Main Idea As you read, look for ways enslaved people protested against being held in slavery.

Vocabulary

slave code
overseer
spiritual
resist
Underground Railroad

Many slaves had to wear identification badges (above). This poster (below) called for an end to slavery.

Africans in Slavery and Freedom

In 1800 there were nearly 900,000 slaves in the United States. By 1860 there were nearly 4 million. Some Africans—both in the North and in the South—were free. In fact, by 1860 nearly 500,000 free Africans were living in the United States. Yet they did not have the rights of full citizenship. Despite the hardships, most Africans found ways to survive. Some also found ways to fight back.

Life Under Slavery

Most Southern states had laws that shaped the day-to-day lives of enslaved people. These laws were called **slave codes**. Under these codes slaves were not allowed to leave their owners' land, to meet in groups, or to buy or sell goods. Most were not allowed to learn to read and write. They were treated as property, and few were given any special privileges.

Some slave owners hired people called **overseers** to watch the slaves as they worked and to punish them if they fell behind. Some slave owners broke up families by selling husbands without their wives, and children without their parents. They punished enslaved people harshly for disobeying.

"No day ever dawns for the slave, nor is it looked for," one African of the time wrote. "For the slave it is all night—all night, forever."

To help themselves survive, many enslaved people formed close-knit communities. Families, friends, and neighbors helped one another, giving comfort and support. They talked of what they remembered about

Enslaved people were sold, usually one at a time, at auctions. Families were often separated because relatives could be bought by different slave owners.

Africa or what they had heard about it from others. They tried to keep their traditions alive.

Religious beliefs gave many enslaved people the strength they needed to handle the hardships of life under slavery. Some slaves expressed their beliefs by singing spirituals. **Spirituals** (SPIR•ih•chuh•wuhlz) are religious songs based on Bible stories. One spiritual told the deepest feelings of those who were enslaved.

> 66 If I had my way,
> If I had my way,
> If I had my way,
> I'd tear this building down. 99

REVIEW *How did people in slave communities help one another?*

Fighting Back

Most enslaved Africans did whatever they could to **resist**, or act against, slavery. Some resisted in quiet ways, secretly damaging the plantation. They broke tools, making the damage look like an accident. They left gates open so that farm animals could escape. They let boats drift away. They hid household goods.

Such actions were dangerous, and slaves had to be very careful to escape punishment. Some acted as if they did not understand what they had been told. They said they were sorry and would try to do better. "Got one mind for the boss to see," one slave song went. "Got another mind for what I know is me."

Other slaves chose a more violent way to resist—they rebelled. One rebellion took place in Southampton County, Virginia, on a hot August night in 1831. An enslaved African named Nat Turner led an attack that killed 57 people, among them Turner's owner and the owner's family. Slave owners who were trying to end the rebellion killed more than 100 slaves. Turner and the other leaders were caught, put on trial, and hanged.

Despite the dangers, other people who were against slavery rebelled. On the night of October 16, 1859, a white abolitionist named John Brown and a group of followers seized a government storehouse in Harpers Ferry, in what is now West Virginia. The storehouse was filled with guns. Brown planned to give the guns to slaves so they could fight for their freedom. Like Turner, Brown was caught, put on trial, and hanged.

Such rebellions frightened many white Southerners. As one visitor to the South reported, "I have known times here when not a single planter had a calm night's rest. They never lie down to sleep without . . . loaded pistols at their sides."

REVIEW *In what ways did enslaved people resist slavery?*

Running Away

Over the years, thousands of slaves chose another way to resist slavery. They tried to gain their freedom by running away.

Some slaves ran away alone. Others tried to escape with their families or friends. Some planned their escape carefully, slowly gathering what they would need. Others saw a sudden chance and decided quickly—they ran.

Once away from their owners' land, runaways had to find safe places to hide. Many were helped along the way by other slaves. Some were taken in by Indian peoples. Others hid in forests, swamps, or mountains—sometimes for years. One former slave from Virginia remembered,

66 Father got beat up so much that after a while he ran away and lived in the woods. Mama used to send John, my oldest brother, out to the woods with food for Father. . . . Father wasn't the only one hiding in the woods. There was his cousin, Gabriel, that was hiding and a man named Charlie. 99

This scene shows Nat Turner (leaning on a walking stick) planning his rebellion with other enslaved Africans.

$150 REWARD

RANAWAY from the subscriber, on the night of the 2d instant, a negro man, who calls himself *Henry May*, about 22 years old, 5 feet 6 or 8 inches high, ordinary color, rather chunky built, bushy head, and has it divided mostly on one side, and keeps it very nicely combed; has been raised in the house, and is a first rate dining-room servant, and was in a tavern in Louisville for 18 months. I expect he is now in Louisville trying to make his escape to a free state, (in all probability to Cincinnati, Ohio.) Perhaps he may try to get employment on a steamboat. He is a good cook, and is handy in any capacity as a house servant. Had on when he left, a dark cassinett coatee, and dark striped cassinett pantaloons, new—he had other clothing. I will give $50 reward if taken in Louisville; 100 dollars if taken out of this State, and 150 dollars if taken out of this State, and delivered to me, or secured in any jail so that I can get him again.

Hardstown, Ky., September 3d, 1838. WILLIAM BURKE.

Slave owners often sent out posters (above) offering rewards for the return of runaway slaves. This painting by Eastman Johnson (left) shows one family's escape.

Some runaways stayed in hiding, but others went on with their journey until they reached free land in the Northern states or in Canada or Mexico. They traveled for weeks or months, some guided only by the North Star. Others found helping hands to lead the way—the brave men and women of the Underground Railroad.

The Underground Railroad was not under the ground, and it was not a real railroad. The **Underground Railroad** was a system of escape routes leading to freedom. Most routes led from the South to the Northern states and to Canada. Some led to Mexico and to the Caribbean islands.

Members of the Underground Railroad were called conductors. Working at night, the conductors led runaways from one hiding place to the next along the routes. These hiding places—barns, attics, secret rooms—were called stations. There the runaway slaves could rest and eat, preparing for the next night's journey to the next station on the route.

Most conductors were free Africans, white Northerners who opposed slavery, and some church leaders. Harriet Tubman, who had escaped from slavery herself, was one of the best-known conductors of the Underground Railroad. During the 1850s Tubman returned to the South 20 times and guided about 300 people to freedom. She proudly claimed, "I never lost a single passenger."

REVIEW *How did the Underground Railroad help slaves escape?*

Free Africans

Not all Africans of the time were enslaved. By 1860 nearly half a million free Africans lived in the United States. A few were members of families that had been free since colonial times, or at least since the American Revolution. Some were former slaves who had been freed by their owners. Others had bought their freedom or had become free by running away.

The Underground Railroad

0   150   300 Miles
0   150   300 Kilometers
Azimuthal Equal-Area Projection

UNORGANIZED
TERRITORY

CANADA

Lake Superior

Lake Michigan

Lake Huron

Lake Ontario

Lake Erie

MN

WI

MI

ME

VT

NH

MA

NY

CT   RI

PA

NJ

MD   DE

40° N

NEBRASKA
TERRITORY

IA

Missouri River

Mississippi River

IL

IN

OH

Ohio River

VA

APPALACHIAN MOUNTAINS

70° W

KANSAS
TERRITORY

MO

KY

NC

80° W

INDIAN
TERRITORY

Arkansas River

AR

TN

Tennessee River

SC

N
E
W
S

TX

MS

AL

GA

LA

Mississippi River

FL

30° N

ATLANTIC
OCEAN

Free state
Slave state

Major routes of
the Underground
Railroad

90° W   Gulf of Mexico

Movement This map of the
Underground Railroad shows the major
routes leading to free land.

■ *Which rivers may have been used as water routes
to free land?*

Harriet Tubman (far left) used the routes of the
Underground Railroad to help this group of Africans
escape from slavery.

Many free Africans lived in cities, where they had a better chance of finding a job. They worked in many different professions. Some were carpenters, tailors, blacksmiths, and shopkeepers. Others became ministers, doctors, nurses, and teachers.

Some free Africans became quite wealthy. Jehu Jones, for example, owned and ran one of South Carolina's best hotels. Thomy Lafon made a fortune from his businesses in New Orleans. James Forten ran a busy sail factory in Philadelphia, where many ships were built. Forten had invented a new sail that made it easier for people to steer ships. The new sail made Forten's business very successful.

For most Africans, however, life was very hard no matter where they lived. They were unwelcome in many places and often were treated unfairly. State laws in both the North and the South gave them little freedom. Most were not allowed to vote or to meet in groups. They could not attend certain schools or hold certain jobs. Some free Africans were wrongly accused of being runaway slaves. Others were taken

and sold into slavery. The danger that free Africans could lose what little freedom they had was very real.

REVIEW *What was life like for most free Africans in the early 1800s?*

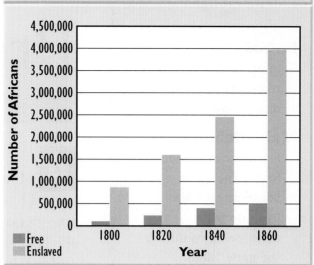

Africans in the United States, 1800–1860

Number of Africans (y-axis: 0 to 4,500,000)
Year (x-axis: 1800, 1820, 1840, 1860)

■ Free
■ Enslaved

LEARNING FROM GRAPHS This graph shows the numbers of free and enslaved Africans in the United States from 1800 to 1860.
■ *What trends does the graph show?*

LESSON 2 REVIEW

Check Understanding
1 Remember the Facts What was the Underground Railroad?

2 Recall the Main Idea In what ways did enslaved people protest against being held in slavery?

Think Critically
3 Personally Speaking Why do you think many enslaved people were willing to risk their lives to resist being held as slaves? Explain your answer.

4 Past to Present In what ways do people today protest if they are denied freedom?

Show What You Know
Poster Activity Think about some symbols of freedom. Look through magazines and newspapers for pictures that express the meaning of freedom. Cut out the pictures, and use them to create a poster that shows the idea of freedom. Add your poster to a class display titled *Freedom*.

FOCUS

In what ways do people today try to settle disagreements?

Main Idea Read to learn about the ways Northerners and Southerners tried to settle their disagreements during the early 1800s.

Vocabulary

free state
slave state

Henry Clay became known as the Great Compromiser because of his work to help settle the differences between the North and the South.

Facing a National Problem

1820	1840	1860

As time passed, more and more Northerners wanted an end to slavery, while more and more slave owners grew angry and bitter. Americans began to understand that slavery was not just a problem between the people of two regions. It had become a problem for the whole country.

New Compromises

One leader who worked hard to help settle the differences dividing the country was Henry Clay of Kentucky. As a member of Congress, Clay often found himself in the middle of heated arguments about slavery.

The worst arguments broke out over the spread of slavery to the West. Each time groups of settlers asked to join the Union as a new state, the same question arose. Would the new state be a free state or a slave state? A **free state** did not allow slavery. A **slave state** did.

For a time there were as many free states as slave states. This kept a balance between the North and the South. Then, in 1819, settlers in the Missouri Territory, a part of the Louisiana Purchase, asked to join the Union as a slave state. If this happened, slave states would outnumber free states.

The Missouri question became a heated debate that dragged on for months. Henry Clay worked day and night to help solve the problem. Clay himself owned slaves. But he did not want to see the question of slavery tear the country apart. Finally, in 1820, he persuaded Congress to agree to a compromise—the Missouri Compromise.

Under this plan Missouri would be allowed to join the Union as a slave state. Maine would join as a free state. This would keep the balance between free states and slave states. Then an imaginary line would be drawn through the rest of

This scene shows Henry Clay (center) telling Congress about his plan that became known as the Compromise of 1850.

the lands gained in the Louisiana Purchase. Slavery would be allowed south of the line. Places north of the line would be free.

The Missouri Compromise kept the peace for nearly 30 years. During this time six new states joined the Union, but the number of free states and slave states remained equal.

Then, in 1848, the United States gained new lands after winning the war with Mexico. Settlers in California, a part of these new lands, soon asked to join the Union as a free state.

Henry Clay once again found himself in the middle of an argument in Congress over slavery. Once again he worked toward a compromise. This plan became known as the Compromise of 1850.

Under this compromise California joined the Union as a free state. The rest of the lands won from Mexico were divided into two territories—New Mexico and Utah. The people there would decide for their territory whether or not to allow slavery.

The Compromise of 1850 also had a new law dealing with runaway slaves. Under

Regions
The Missouri Compromise line divided lands that could join the Union as free states from lands that could join as slave states.

■ *Which two states were admitted to the Union as part of the compromise? Were they admitted as free states or as slave states?*

The Missouri Compromise, 1820

Free state
Free territory
Admitted as a free state
Slave state
Slave territory
Admitted as a slave state
Missouri Compromise line

0   200   400 Miles
0   200   400 Kilometers
Albers Equal-Area Projection

491

Compromise of 1850

Free state
Free territory
Slave state
Indian territory
Decision on slavery left to territory

Regions
Henry Clay's Compromise of 1850 divided lands gained from Mexico into two new territories. It also brought California into the Union as a free state.

■ *What states were later formed from the Utah territory?*

the Fugitive Slave Law, anyone caught helping slaves to escape would be punished. People who found runaway slaves—even runaways who had reached the North—had to return them to the South.

Henry Clay, who became known as the Great Compromiser, died in 1852. He never gave up hope that the country would find a peaceful way to settle its differences. On a marker by his grave in Lexington, Kentucky, are the words *I know no North—no South—no East—no West.*

REVIEW *What two compromises on the spread of slavery did Congress reach?*

Hopes for Peace Fade

Even with the compromises, bad feelings grew between the North and the South. In 1854 harsh words turned to violence.

The problem began when Congress passed the Kansas–Nebraska Act. This new law changed the rules of the Missouri Compromise. Under the compromise,

slavery would not have been allowed in the territories of Kansas and Nebraska. Under the Kansas–Nebraska Act, people living in those lands were now given the chance to decide for themselves whether to allow slavery. They would decide by voting.

Kansas quickly became the center of attention. People for and against slavery rushed into the territory, hoping to help decide the vote. It was not long before fighting broke out between the two sides. More than 200 people were killed in the dispute that came to be known as Bleeding Kansas.

While fighting went on in Kansas, those against slavery suffered another defeat. In 1857 the Supreme Court decided the case of an enslaved African named Dred Scott. Scott had asked the Court for his freedom. The Court said no.

Scott argued that he should be free because he had once lived on free land. Scott's owner had often moved from place to place. When he moved, Scott went with him. For a time they lived in Illinois, a free state. Then they lived in the Wisconsin

In 1857 the Supreme Court decided that Dred Scott (far left) should not be given his freedom. Chief Justice Roger Taney (left) spoke for the Court.

Territory, a free territory under the Missouri Compromise.

After Scott's owner died, Scott took his case to court. The case moved from judge to judge until it landed in the Supreme Court. There Scott lost his fight for freedom. Chief Justice Roger B. Taney (TAW•nee) said that Scott had "none of the rights and privileges" of American citizens. He was a slave, Taney said. Living on free land did not change that.

Taney had more to say. He declared that Congress had no right to outlaw slavery in the Wisconsin Territory to begin with. The Constitution protects people's right to own property. Slaves, he said, were property. He believed that the Missouri Compromise was keeping people in some places from owning property. This, he said, went against the Constitution.

Many people had hoped that the Dred Scott decision would settle the battle over slavery once and for all. Instead, it made the problem worse.

REVIEW *Why did the Supreme Court deny freedom to Dred Scott?*

Regions
The Kansas–Nebraska Act allowed people in the Kansas and Nebraska territories to decide by voting whether they would be free or slave territories.

■ *How many territories could now decide for themselves whether to allow slavery?*

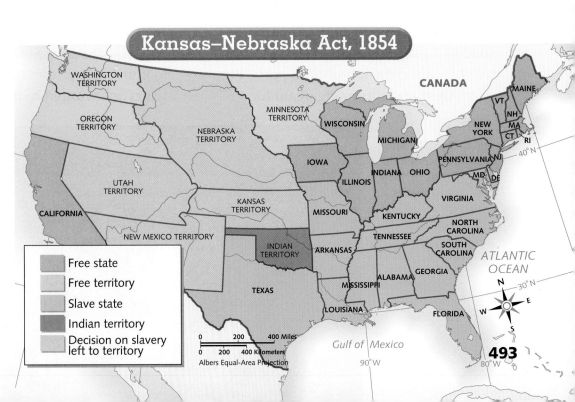

Kansas–Nebraska Act, 1854

Free state
Free territory
Slave state
Indian territory
Decision on slavery left to territory

Abraham Lincoln Works for Change

The Kansas–Nebraska Act and the Dred Scott decision caused violence and anger that caught the attention of Americans across the country. Soon new leaders began to speak out. One of these leaders was Abraham Lincoln.

Abraham Lincoln had grown up on the frontier in Kentucky and Indiana. Like other pioneers, he had had a hard life. He worked so many hours on the family farm that he often could not go to school. But he borrowed books and read all he could.

When Lincoln was a young man, he moved with his family to Illinois. There he held several jobs before serving in the state legislature. He studied law, and in time he became a lawyer. In the late 1840s he served a term in Congress. During these years the matter of the spread of slavery to the West became an important question.

Lincoln was against the spread of slavery. He did not think the government had the right to end all slavery in the country. But he hoped that if slavery were not allowed to spread, it would one day die out.

Lincoln joined a new political party formed to fight the spread of slavery. This party was called the Republican party. He even thought about running again for government office. The Kansas–Nebraska Act and the Dred Scott decision helped him make up his mind. In 1858 Lincoln entered a race for the United States Senate. He ran against Stephen A. Douglas, who had written the Kansas–Nebraska Act.

REVIEW *Why did Abraham Lincoln join the Republican party?*

The Lincoln–Douglas Debates

Few people could have been more different from each other than Lincoln and Douglas. Abraham Lincoln was a tall, thin man from the frontier. He wore plain, dark clothes that were a bit rumpled. He was not well known around the country. In fact, few people outside of Illinois had heard of him.

Stephen Douglas was heavy and a full foot shorter than Lincoln. He was well educated and wore fine clothes—a ruffled shirt, tailored suit, and polished boots. He was already serving in the Senate, and many Americans across the country knew of him.

In one way, though, Lincoln and Douglas were very much alike. They were both powerful public speakers. In the summer of 1858, the two men traveled around Illinois and debated questions that were important to voters. Huge crowds turned out to listen. Everyone wanted to hear Lincoln and

Stephen Douglas and Abraham Lincoln held seven debates in 1858. This painting shows Lincoln (standing) and Douglas (to Lincoln's right) debating in Charleston, Illinois.

This ticket was to a fair held in 1858 where money was raised to fight slavery.

Douglas debate about whether slavery should be allowed in the West.

Stephen Douglas argued that each new state should decide the slavery question for itself. That was what the country's founders had allowed, he said, and that was what the new Kansas–Nebraska Act allowed.

Abraham Lincoln disagreed. He said that "the framers of the Constitution intended and expected" slavery to end. The problem, Lincoln pointed out, was more than a question of what each state wanted. It was a question of right and wrong. Slavery should not spread to the West, he said, because slavery was wrong. Lincoln said,

66 That is the real issue. That is the issue that will continue in this country when these poor tongues of Judge Douglas and myself shall be silent. It is the eternal struggle between these two principles—right and wrong— throughout the world. 99

Stephen Douglas won the race for the Senate. But people around the country now knew who Abraham Lincoln was.

REVIEW *How did Lincoln's views differ from those of Douglas?*

LESSON 3 REVIEW

1820	1840	1860
1820 • The Missouri Compromise	1850 • The Compromise of 1850	1858 • The Lincoln–Douglas debates

Check Understanding

1 Remember the Facts What events led Abraham Lincoln to speak out against slavery?

2 Recall the Main Idea In what ways did the Northerners and the Southerners try to settle their disagreements during the early 1800s?

Think Critically

3 Think More About It How was the Missouri Compromise changed by the Kansas–Nebraska Act and the Dred Scott decision?

4 Past to Present Do you think it is still important for leaders today to hold debates before elections? Explain your answer.

Show What You Know

Simulation Activity
Imagine that you have been asked to interview Henry Clay, Dred Scott, Stephen Douglas, or Abraham Lincoln. Write the questions you would ask and the answers the person might give. With a friend, role-play your interview. Present your interview to the class.

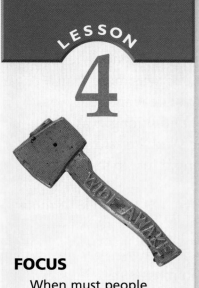

LESSON 4

FOCUS

When must people today make difficult decisions in their lives?

Main Idea Read to learn about the difficult decisions Americans had to make in 1860 and 1861.

Vocabulary

Confederacy

The gold ax (above) was a campaign pin worn by Lincoln's supporters. The "WIDE AWAKE" on the handle meant that his supporters were "wide awake" to dangers to the Union. A supporter of Stephen Douglas wore this campaign button (below) during the election of 1860.

A Time for Hard Decisions

| 1860 | 1861 | 1862 |

In 1860 Americans prepared to choose a new President. They listened to speeches. They read newspapers. They watched parades. They also worried. Anger and bitterness were driving the North and the South farther apart than ever. Could a new President hold the country together?

The Election of 1860

The question of the spread of slavery to the West seemed to be all that people talked about during the election of 1860. Stephen Douglas ran as a member of the Democratic party. He argued that western settlers should decide for themselves whether to allow slavery. However, many Democrats in the South backed another leader—John Breckinridge of Kentucky. Breckinridge thought that the government should allow slavery everywhere in the West.

Abraham Lincoln ran as a member of the Republican party. He spoke out strongly against the spread of slavery. He promised not to stop slavery in the South, where it was already practiced. But he said that he hoped it would one day end there, too.

Many white Southerners worried about what would happen if Lincoln became President. They thought that the problem was far greater than the question of slavery. They believed that their whole way of life was being attacked. Some said that their states would secede from the Union if Lincoln was elected.

On Election Day, November 6, 1860, Lincoln won the Presidency. Southern leaders did not wait long before carrying out their threat.

STEPHEN A. DOUGLAS.

496 • Unit 7

This poster urged people to vote for Lincoln and his running mate, Hannibal Hamlin.

On December 20, South Carolina's leaders declared that

> 66 . . . the United States of America is hereby dissolved. 99

With these words the state seceded from the Union.

There were six other states—Mississippi, Florida, Alabama, Georgia, Louisiana, and Texas—that soon followed South Carolina's example. Together these seven states formed a new country. They called the new country the Confederate States of America, or the **Confederacy** (kuhn•FEH•duh•ruh•see). They elected a Mississippi senator, Jefferson Davis, as president. The United States was now split in two.

REVIEW *What did seven Southern states decide to do after Lincoln was elected President?*

Fort Sumter

Lincoln had little time to celebrate winning the election. He wanted to save the Union—to keep the country together. Yet seven states had said that they were no longer part of the Union. What would he do about those states?

Some people told Lincoln to let the Southern states go. Others said that he should give in on the slavery question and hope that the Southern states would return. Still others felt that Lincoln should use the army to end the revolt.

Lincoln thought a great deal about his choices. He hoped to prevent a war. "We are not enemies, but friends," Lincoln told Southerners after taking the oath of office as President of the United States on March 4, 1861. "We must not be enemies." The very next day, however, Lincoln received an important message. When he read it, he knew that time was running out. The message was from Major Robert Anderson. Anderson was the commander of Fort Sumter.

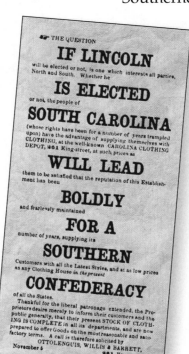

THE QUESTION

IF LINCOLN
will be elected or not, is one which interests all parties, North and South. Whether he

IS ELECTED
or not, the people of

SOUTH CAROLINA
(whose rights have been for a number of years trampled upon) have the advantage of supplying themselves with CLOTHING, at the well-known CAROLINA CLOTHING DEPOT, 261 King-street, at such prices as

WILL LEAD
them to be satisfied that the reputation of this Establishment has been

BOLDLY
and fearlessly maintained

FOR A
number of years, supplying its

SOUTHERN
Customers with all the Latest Styles, and at as low prices as any Clothing House in the present

CONFEDERACY
of all the States.

Thankful for the liberal patronage extended, the Proprietors desire merely to inform their customers and the public generally, that their present STOCK OF CLOTHING IS COMPLETE in all its departments, and are now prepared to offer Goods on the most reasonable and satisfactory terms. A call is therefore solicited by
OTTOLENGUIS, WILLIS & BARRETT,
November 6   261 King-street.

A clothing store in South Carolina had this poster made to support South Carolina's decision to secede from the Union if Lincoln was elected.

When the Southern states seceded, they had taken over post offices, forts, and other federal government property. Fort Sumter, which was located on an island off the coast of South Carolina, near Charleston, was one of the few forts in the South that remained in Union hands. The message from Major Anderson said that supplies at the fort were almost gone. If new supplies were not sent soon, Anderson would have to surrender the fort to the Confederacy.

Lincoln knew that he had an important decision to make. His goal was to keep Fort Sumter under Union control. But several problems stood in the way. The most important problem was that the fort was running out of supplies.

Lincoln thought carefully about his choices. Each had its own possible consequence. He could send supplies to the fort. If he did, the Southerners might attack. He could send troops to the fort. If he did, the Southerners would surely attack. He could choose to do nothing at all. By doing nothing, he would really be giving the fort to the Confederacy because Major Anderson would have to surrender.

Finally, Lincoln made the choice he thought was the best. He decided that he should send supply ships to the fort. Then he waited to see how the Southerners would react.

Now Confederate president Jefferson Davis had to make a decision. His goal was

This scene (right) shows the Confederate attack on Fort Sumter. The photo (above) shows the Confederate flag flying over Fort Sumter after the Union forces surrendered.

to take control of Fort Sumter for the Confederacy. His problem was that Union troops held the fort. Lincoln was now sending supplies to help those troops.

Like Lincoln, Davis thought carefully about his choices and their possible consequences. Then he made what he thought was the best choice, even though he knew that one possible result was war. Davis decided to take over the fort before the supply ships arrived. On April 12, 1861, Confederate leaders demanded that the Union forces surrender Fort Sumter. But Major Anderson refused. The Confederate troops then fired on the fort. The next day Major Anderson and his men ran out of ammunition and had to give up.

GEOGRAPHY

Fort Sumter

Fort Sumter was one of several forts built to protect American coastlines following the War of 1812. Building the fort was a long, difficult job. Workers first had to build the island on which the fort would stand. Then they built the fort itself, with walls 5 to 10 feet (1.5–3 m) thick and nearly 40 feet (12 m) high. Today Fort Sumter is part of the national park system.

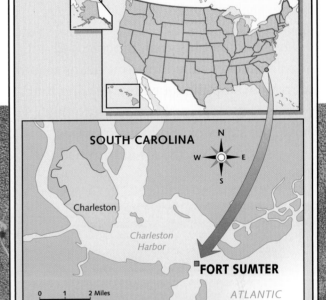

SOUTH CAROLINA

N W E S

Charleston

Charleston Harbor

FORT SUMTER

ATLANTIC OCEAN

0   1   2 Miles
0   1   2 Kilometers

THE UNION BREAKS APART

November 1860	December 1860	January 1861	February 1861	March 1861	April 1861	May 1861
• Lincoln is elected President	• South Carolina secedes	• Mississippi, Florida, Alabama, Georgia, and Louisiana secede	• Texas secedes	• Lincoln is inaugurated President	• Southern troops attack Fort Sumter • Virginia secedes	• Arkansas, Tennessee, and North Carolina secede

LEARNING FROM TIME LINES This time line shows when each of 11 Southern states seceded from the Union.

■ *Which state was the first to secede from the Union? Which states were the last to secede?*

Davis had met his goal. Lincoln had not. Lincoln quickly called for Americans to join an army to stop the rebellion. Fearing that Northern armies would march into the South, the states of Virginia, Arkansas, Tennessee, and North Carolina joined the seven already in the Confederacy. Now the country was even more divided. The Civil War had begun.

REVIEW *What did Davis decide to do when Lincoln said he would send supplies to Fort Sumter?*

LESSON 4 REVIEW

1860	1861	1862
1860 • Abraham Lincoln is elected President	**1861** • Confederate soldiers attack Fort Sumter	

Check Understanding

1 Remember the Facts What event led South Carolina's leaders to secede from the Union?

2 Recall the Main Idea What difficult decisions did Americans make in 1860 and 1861?

Think Critically

3 Personally Speaking Do you think Lincoln made the right decision when he decided to send supplies to Fort Sumter? Explain your answer.

4 Think More About It Why was Fort Sumter important to both Abraham Lincoln and Jefferson Davis?

Show What You Know

Writing Activity The attack on Fort Sumter marked the beginning of the Civil War. Write two headlines that could have appeared in newspapers after the attack. The first should be a headline for a newspaper in the North. The second should be for a newspaper in the South.

Make a Thoughtful Decision

1. Why Learn This Skill?

You make many decisions every day. Some decisions are easy. Other decisions are more difficult. The difficult ones may require more thought because your choices may have lasting consequences.

2. Understand the Process

You have read about the difficult decisions Abraham Lincoln and Jefferson Davis had to make as supplies ran out at Fort Sumter in South Carolina. The ways in which these leaders came to their decisions show how a thoughtful decision can be made. Think again about what happened.

1 What goal did each leader have?

2 What steps did each leader follow in making a decision?

3 What choice did each leader make?

4 What were the consequences of Lincoln's choice? of Davis's choice?

You can use similar steps to help make a thoughtful decision.

- Identify your goal.
- Think about problems that may keep you from reaching your goal.
- Identify actions you could take to reach your goal.
- Think about the possible consequences of each action.
- List your choices for action. Begin with those that might have the best results, and end with those that might have the worst results.
- Make the choice that seems best.
- Put your choice into action.
- Think about whether your choice helped you reach your goal.

3. Think and Apply

Think about a decision you made at school. What steps did you follow? What choice did you make? What were the consequences? Do you think you made a thoughtful decision? Explain your answer.

Abraham Lincoln
(far left)
Jefferson Davis
(left)

Union or Secession?

The Union flag as it looked in 1861

An early Confederate flag

At the news of Abraham Lincoln's election as President, Americans in both the North and the South got ready for what some called the Revolution of 1860. Some hoped that the South would not carry out its threat to secede. Lincoln himself said, "The people of the South have too much sense to attempt the ruin of the government." But he and others did not understand how badly many Southerners wanted their independence.

Not all Southerners agreed about seceding, though. Some were against it. Others thought that the South should first give Lincoln a chance. They would be willing to secede only if nothing else worked. Still others wanted to secede right away.

Two Southerners who made their feelings clear were Edmund Ruffin of Virginia and Sam Houston, the governor of Texas. The words of the two men show how they felt about secession, or seceding from the Union.

Edmund Ruffin

❝I will be out of Virginia before Lincoln's inauguration, and so . . . avoid being, as a Virginian, under his government even for an hour. I, at least, will become a citizen of the seceded Confederate States, and will not again reside in my native state, nor enter it except to make visits to my children, until Virginia shall also secede. . . . This result . . . cannot be delayed long.

The bloodshed of South Carolinians defending their soil and their rights, or maintaining the possession of their harbor . . . will stir doubly fast the sluggish blood of the more backward Southern States into secession.❞

Sam Houston

❝Let me tell you what is coming. . . . Your fathers and husbands, your sons and brothers, will be herded at the point of the bayonet. . . . You may, after the sacrifice of countless millions of treasure and hundreds of thousands of lives, as a bare possibility, win Southern independence. . . . But I doubt it. I tell you that, while I believe with you in the doctrine of States' Rights, the North is determined to preserve this Union. They are not a fiery, impulsive people as you are, for they live in colder climates. But when they begin to move in a given direction . . . they move with the steady momentum and perseverance of a mighty avalanche.❞

Compare Viewpoints

1. What viewpoint about seceding did Ruffin hold? How do you know?

2. What viewpoint about seceding did Houston hold? How do you know?

3. What other viewpoints might Southerners have held on the matter of secession? Governor Thomas H. Hicks of Maryland said, "The only safety of Maryland lies in preserving a neutral position between our brethren of the North and of the South." What view did the governor hold?

Think and Apply

You have read that three Southerners—Ruffin, Houston, and Hicks—each had a different view about secession. At what other times in history have people from the same region held different views about something?

1820   **1830**

1820
• The Missouri
  Compromise

1831
• Nat Turner's
  rebellion

CONNECT MAIN IDEAS

Use this organizer to show how the chapter's main ideas are connected. Write three details to support each main idea. A copy of the organizer may be found on page 91 of the Activity Book.

Differences Divide North and South
People in the North and the South disagreed during the mid-1800s.

1. _____
2. _____
3. _____

Africans in Slavery and Freedom
Enslaved people protested against being held in slavery.

1. _____
2. _____
3. _____

Background to the Conflict

Facing a National Problem
Northerners and Southerners tried to settle disagreements during the 1800s.

1. _____
2. _____
3. _____

A Time for Hard Decisions
Americans had to make important decisions in 1860 and 1861.

1. _____
2. _____
3. _____

WRITE MORE ABOUT IT

Write Your Opinion Tell whether or not you think agreeing to a compromise is always a good way to settle differences. Explain your answer.

Compare Viewpoints Write a paragraph that compares Stephen Douglas's and Abraham Lincoln's points of view on how the slavery question should be settled.

1850
• The Compromise of 1850

1861
• Confederate soldiers attack Fort Sumter

USE VOCABULARY

For each pair of terms, write a sentence or two that explains how the terms are related.

1. slave code, overseer
2. resist, spiritual
3. free state, slave state

CHECK UNDERSTANDING

4. How was life in the North changing in the mid-1800s?
5. How did the invention of the cotton gin affect cotton production?
6. How did the settlement of the West add to the argument over slavery?
7. What kinds of laws affected the everyday lives of slaves?
8. What role did religion play in the lives of many enslaved people?
9. Why was the North Star important to some runaway slaves?
10. How did the Compromise of 1850 help satisfy the demands of slaveholders?
11. Why did the Kansas–Nebraska Act lead to fighting?
12. What major decisions led to the start of the Civil War?

THINK CRITICALLY

13. **Personally Speaking** What kind of person do you think a conductor on the Underground Railroad needed to be?

14. **Cause and Effect** Why did compromises fail to settle disagreements over the issue of slavery?
15. **Explore Viewpoints** How do you think Henry Clay would have felt about the Dred Scott decision?
16. **Think More About It** How did the Lincoln–Douglas debates affect Lincoln's political career?

APPLY SKILLS

Use Graphs to Identify Trends Look in newspapers or magazines for a bar graph or a line graph that shows a trend. Cut out the graph and tape it to a sheet of paper. Below the graph, identify the trend shown. How does the trend change over time?

Make a Thoughtful Decision Imagine that a friend has asked you to allow your home to be used as a station on the Underground Railroad. What steps might you follow to come to a decision?

READ MORE ABOUT IT

Lincoln: In His Own Words by Milton Meltzer. Harcourt Brace. In this book, read about Lincoln's life, thoughts, and actions through his own words.

Visit the Internet at
http://www.hbschool.com
for additional resources.

CIVIL WAR
AND
RECONSTRUCTION

"I put in many hours of weary work and soon thought myself quite a soldier. . . . I was elected First Sergeant, much to my surprise. Just what a First Sergeant's duties might be, I had no idea."

Elisha Rhodes,
Pawtucket,
Rhode Island, 1861

Confederate private Edwin Jennison, killed at the Seven Days' Battles in 1862

The Fighting Begins

When Confederate soldiers fired on Fort Sumter, hopes for peace between the North and the South ended. Now Americans had to make some hard decisions about going to war.

Taking Sides

In the weeks following the attack on Fort Sumter, many people thought that the war would be short and easy. For most, the choice of which side to support was clear.

Most Northerners supported the Union. They believed that it was wrong that the Southern states had broken away from the Union. They were willing to go to war to save their flag and all that it stood for. "If it is necessary that I should fall on the battlefield for my country," wrote a soldier from New England, "I am ready. . . . I am willing—perfectly willing—to lay down all my joys in this life, to help maintain this government."

Most white Southerners supported the Confederacy. They were willing to go to war to win their independence. Whether they owned slaves or not, many felt that the North was trying to change the South. They thought that the government was taking away their rights. The only way to get those rights back, they believed, was to leave the Union.

The need to defend their land also led many Southerners to join the fight. One young soldier, caught early in the war by Union troops, told his captors, "I'm fighting because you're down here."

For some Americans, however, the choice between the

This Confederate bugle (above) was used to lead soldiers into battle. This Union officer's mess kit (below) carried supplies for eating and drinking.

507

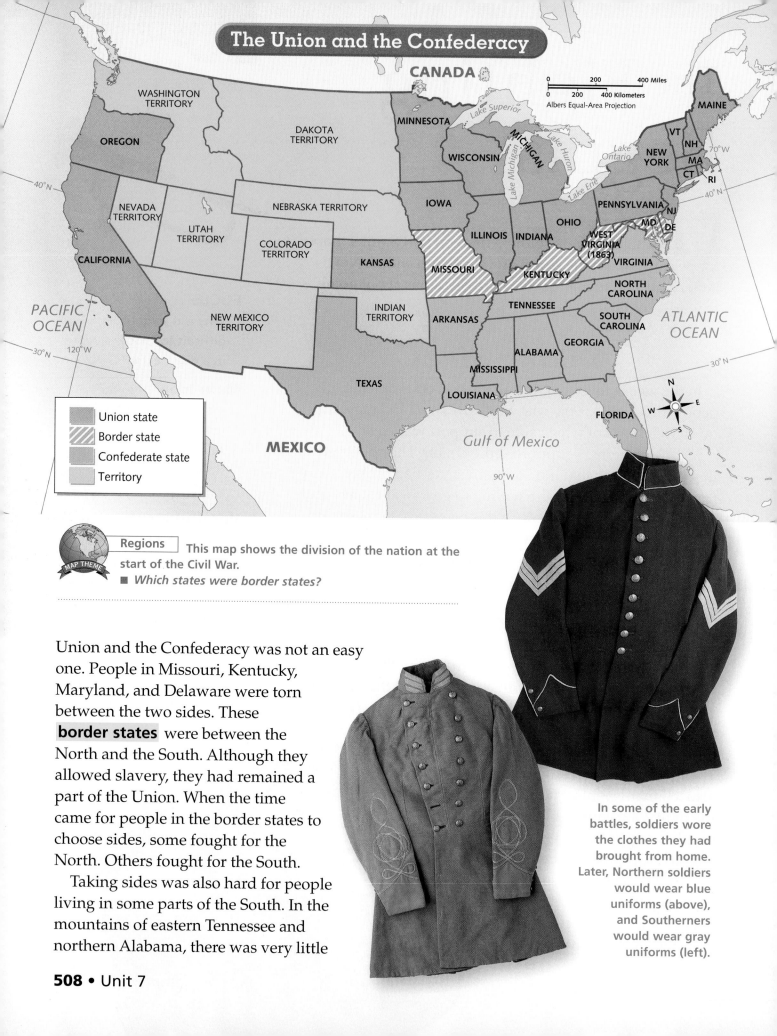

The Union and the Confederacy

CANADA

WASHINGTON TERRITORY

OREGON

MINNESOTA

WISCONSIN

MICHIGAN

MAINE

VT

NH

NEW YORK

MA

CT

RI

DAKOTA TERRITORY

Lake Superior

Lake Michigan

Lake Huron

Lake Ontario

Lake Erie

70°W

40°N

NEVADA TERRITORY

UTAH TERRITORY

NEBRASKA TERRITORY

IOWA

PENNSYLVANIA

NJ

OHIO

MD

DE

40°N

CALIFORNIA

COLORADO TERRITORY

KANSAS

ILLINOIS

INDIANA

WEST VIRGINIA (1863)

VIRGINIA

MISSOURI

KENTUCKY

NORTH CAROLINA

PACIFIC OCEAN

30°N

120°W

NEW MEXICO TERRITORY

INDIAN TERRITORY

ARKANSAS

TENNESSEE

SOUTH CAROLINA

ATLANTIC OCEAN

GEORGIA

ALABAMA

30°N

MISSISSIPPI

TEXAS

LOUISIANA

FLORIDA

N

W   E

S

MEXICO

Gulf of Mexico

90°W

0   200   400 Miles

0   200   400 Kilometers

Albers Equal-Area Projection

Legend:
- Union state
- Border state
- Confederate state
- Territory

Regions This map shows the division of the nation at the start of the Civil War.

■ *Which states were border states?*

Union and the Confederacy was not an easy one. People in Missouri, Kentucky, Maryland, and Delaware were torn between the two sides. These **border states** were between the North and the South. Although they allowed slavery, they had remained a part of the Union. When the time came for people in the border states to choose sides, some fought for the North. Others fought for the South.

Taking sides was also hard for people living in some parts of the South. In the mountains of eastern Tennessee and northern Alabama, there was very little

In some of the early battles, soldiers wore the clothes they had brought from home. Later, Northern soldiers would wear blue uniforms (above), and Southerners would wear gray uniforms (left).

slavery. Many people there sided with the North. In western Virginia, feelings for the Union were so strong that the people voted to break away from Virginia and form a new state. West Virginia joined the Union in 1863.

Taking sides was also hard for many in the Indian nations. By the time of the war, the Cherokee, Creek, Seminole, Choctaw, and Chickasaw peoples had been driven from their lands to the Indian Territory, which is today Oklahoma. When it came time to choose sides, most people in these five tribes had little reason to like either the North or the South. In the end the Choctaws and the Chickasaws fought for the South. The Creeks, Seminoles, and Cherokees were divided between the Union and the Confederacy.

The decisions people had to make in these early days of the war divided families and friends. When war finally came, four of Henry Clay's grandsons decided to join the Confederacy. Three others fought for the Union. Even President Lincoln's own family was divided. Mary Todd Lincoln, his wife, had been born in Kentucky. Four of her brothers fought for the South.

REVIEW *Why was taking sides hard for people in the border states?*

Lee Joins the Confederacy

On April 19, 1861—a week after the attack on Fort Sumter—Robert E. Lee paced his bedroom floor. It was nearly midnight. Lee was a United States Army colonel. The day before, President Lincoln had asked him to take command of a Union

Robert E. Lee (above) led the Confederate troops throughout the war. These gloves (left) protected Lee's hands when he was in battle.

army. Just hours later Lee had learned that his home state of Virginia had seceded. Lee loved his country. He was a graduate of the United States Military Academy at West Point, New York. He had fought in the war with Mexico and had served his country for 32 years. Yet Lee also loved

LEARNING FROM GRAPHS This graph compares the resources of the North and the South at the beginning of the Civil War. The photograph above shows Union soldiers building a bridge across a river in northern Virginia. The bridge made it easier to carry supplies to Union troops in the area.

■ *Which side had more resources?*

Resources of the North and South, 1860

North
South
Slave population

Resources: Population, Factories, Farms, Railroads, Bank deposits

Virginia. Could he lead an army that would fight his family and neighbors?

The next morning Lee told Mary, his wife, what he had decided. He turned down Lincoln's offer and quit the Union army. A few days later he took command of Virginia's troops. Lee knew he would be fighting old friends who were fighting for the Union. Even so, he decided to serve Virginia. "I cannot raise my hand against my birthplace, my home, my children," he said.

REVIEW *Why was it difficult for Robert E. Lee to choose sides in the war?*

Battle Plans

Three months after the attack on Fort Sumter, two armies of eager young men prepared for the first major battle of the war. The battle took place at Bull Run, a stream near the town of Manassas Junction, Virginia.

After hours of fighting, the South won the battle. The defeat shocked the Union.

Northerners had entered the war feeling very strong. The North had nearly twice as many people as the South. It had more factories to make weapons and supplies. It had more railroads to get those supplies to the troops.

But the South had proved more powerful than most Northerners had expected. Southerners fighting to defend their own land had a very strong will to win. Stories were already being told about the bravery of officers such as "Stonewall" Jackson.

Lincoln quickly began to look for new officers of his own. He called for more soldiers. He also called for new battle plans.

An early Northern plan to win the war had to do with trade. The South depended on trade with the North and with other countries to buy such goods as cloth, shoes, and guns. The North hoped to cut off trade by setting up a blockade. Northern warships would stop trading ships from leaving or entering Southern ports. Without trade, the South would slowly become weaker.

Not everyone in the North liked the idea of a blockade. Some made fun of it, calling it the Anaconda (a•nuh•KAHN•duh) Plan. An anaconda is a large snake that squeezes its prey to death. Although this plan would slowly weaken the South, many people in the North wanted quicker action. They said the government should send the army to enter the South by force—to invade. "On to Richmond!" they cried. Richmond, Virginia, had become the capital of the Confederacy.

At first the most important fighting plan of the Confederate leaders was simply to protect their lands. Some Southerners compared their situation with the way things were for George Washington and the Patriots during the Revolutionary War. Southerners hoped to defend their homes against invaders and slowly wear down their enemy, just as the Patriots had worn down the British.

But many Southerners, just like many Northerners, were impatient. Cries of "On to Washington!" were soon answered with plans to invade the North.

Southerners also hoped that some countries in Europe would help them win the war. Britain and France depended on cotton to keep their textile mills running. Many thought that these countries would help the South as soon as their supplies of cotton ran low.

REVIEW *What were the strengths of the North? of the South?*

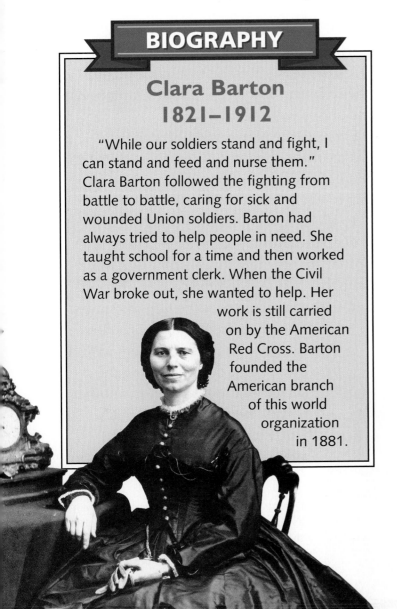

BIOGRAPHY

Clara Barton
1821–1912

"While our soldiers stand and fight, I can stand and feed and nurse them." Clara Barton followed the fighting from battle to battle, caring for sick and wounded Union soldiers. Barton had always tried to help people in need. She taught school for a time and then worked as a government clerk. When the Civil War broke out, she wanted to help. Her work is still carried on by the American Red Cross. Barton founded the American branch of this world organization in 1881.

Life on the Home Front

Life on the home front during the Civil War was difficult for people in both the North and the South. The **home front** describes the places where civilians are active when their country is at war. **Civilians** are people who are not in the military. The war affected these people in different ways. Many civilians did what they could to help support the soldiers on their side. The fear that friends and loved ones who went off to war might be injured or killed in battle made each day difficult for many people on the home front.

Because the Union and the Confederacy both did not allow women to join their armies, most civilians during the Civil War were women. But women found many ways to help. They took over factory, business, and farm jobs that men left behind. Some even took on the responsibility of running businesses or plantations while their husbands were at war. Others sent food to the troops, made clothing and bandages, and collected supplies. "I do not know when I have seen a woman without knitting in her hand. Socks for the soldiers is the cry," Mary Chesnut, a Southerner, wrote in her diary.

Many women, such as Clara Barton and Sally Tompkins, worked as nurses. Before the Civil War, most nurses were men. Tompkins eventually ran her own private hospital in Richmond. Some women left the home front to serve as spies in the war. A few even dressed as men, joined the army, and fought in battles.

REVIEW *In what ways did women on the home front help the soldiers who went off to war?*

The War and Slavery

As the fighting dragged on into 1862, Northern plans seemed to be working. The blockade brought trade to a halt, and supplies ran very low in the South. Plantations and shops were destroyed.

Even so, the North had not won yet. Thousands of Union soldiers were dying in battle. President Lincoln knew he had to find a way to push the North to victory.

To Lincoln, the purpose of the war was to keep the country together—to save the Union. Yet he knew that slavery was the issue that had divided the country. He realized that writing an order to free the slaves would greatly help the North. The loss of millions of enslaved workers would be a blow to the South. Freeing the slaves would also help in another way. It would turn the British, who needed cotton but were against slavery, toward the Union.

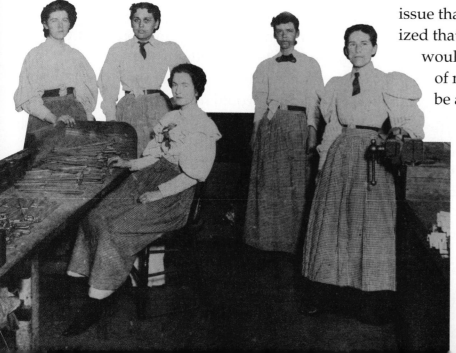

During the Civil War, many women, such as these factory workers, took over jobs that once belonged to men only.

This photograph shows runaway slaves in Virginia heading to the North with Union soldiers in 1862. Some enslaved people decided to escape from slavery without the help of an Emancipation Proclamation.

Lincoln held back on declaring an **Emancipation Proclamation**, an order freeing the slaves. He feared that such a step might turn people in the border states, as well as some states in the North, against the Union. Lincoln's waiting made the abolitionists angry. William Lloyd Garrison wrote that Lincoln was "nothing better than a wet rag."

As the war went on, Lincoln thought more and more about the question of slavery. Had the time come to write an Emancipation Proclamation? What would be the consequences if he made such a decision?

REVIEW *Why did Lincoln think that an Emancipation Proclamation would help the North?*

LESSON I REVIEW

Check Understanding

1. **Remember the Facts** What were the battle plans of the North and the South?

2. **Recall the Main Idea** Why was it difficult for many Americans to choose sides during the Civil War?

Think Critically

3. **Explore Viewpoints** Why might a person in a border state have joined the Union army or the Confederate army?

4. **Past to Present** During the war many people told President Lincoln how they felt about slavery. How do government leaders learn about people's opinions today?

Show What You Know

Writing Activity Imagine that you are living in the South during the Civil War. Write a diary entry describing how the Union's blockade is changing your life.

LESSON 2 LEARN HISTORY *through* Literature

The Signature That Changed America

by Harold Holzer

In 1862 Abraham Lincoln faced one of his hardest decisions as President. He wanted to save the Union, but the fighting seemed to go on and on between Union and Confederate troops. Lincoln knew that an order to free the slaves could help the North. Abolitionists wanted him to sign such an order. But Lincoln also knew that an Emancipation Proclamation would make some people in both the North and the South angry.

Read now about the days when Lincoln made a decision about slavery and took action. As you read, think about why it is important for leaders to consider many points of view before making a decision.

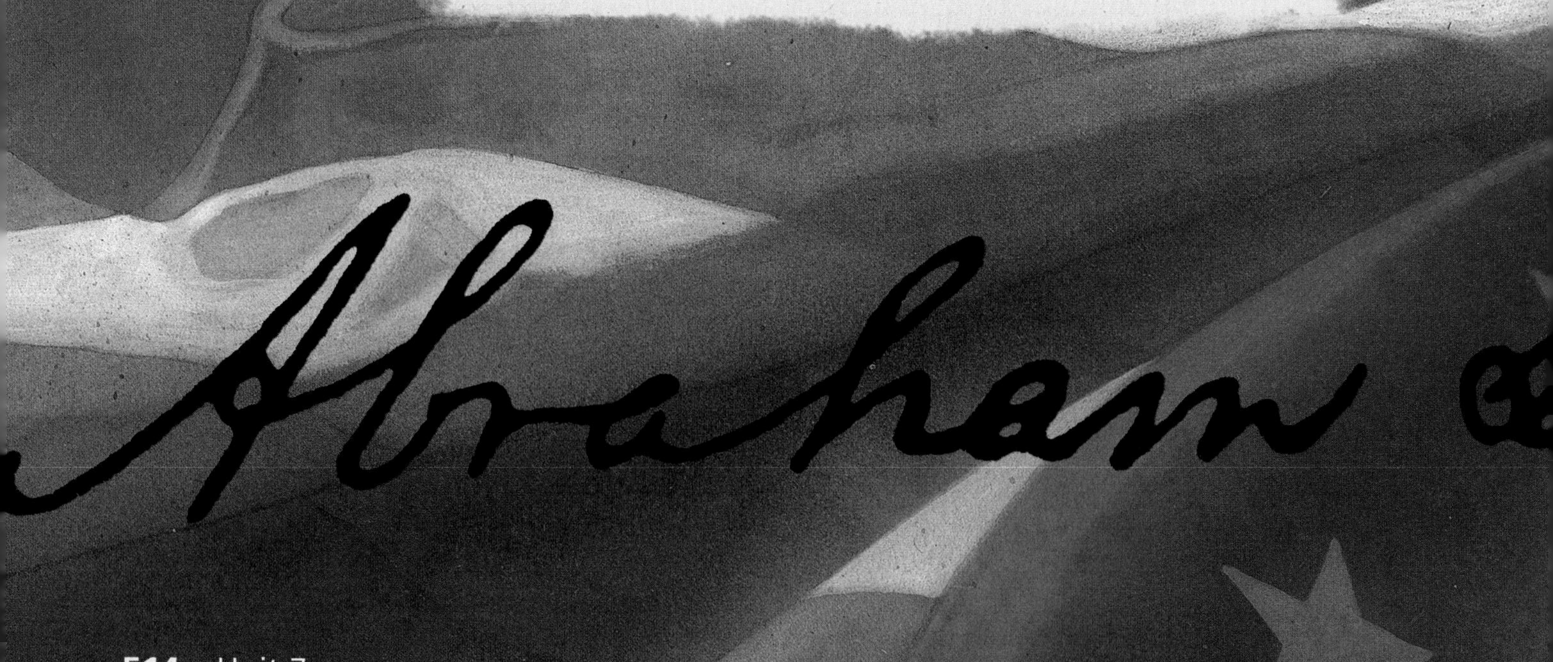

It was January 1, 1863. The Civil War was still raging, but in Washington, D.C., this was a day of celebration. At the White House, President and Mrs. Abraham Lincoln welcomed the new year by hosting a party. For hours they greeted hundreds of visitors, just as Presidents and First Ladies had done for years.

But this was no ordinary New Year's Day at the White House. Today history would be made.

In mid-afternoon the President quietly left the party and walked upstairs to his office on the second floor. Waiting for him there were Secretary of State William H. Seward and members of Lincoln's staff. On a large table in the center of the room sat an official-looking document, written out in beautiful handwriting by a professional "engrosser." Lincoln sat down at the table, the document spread out before him. The moment was at hand. Now, at last, the President would sign the Emancipation Proclamation.

Abraham Lincoln took pen in hand, dipped it in ink, and then, unexpectedly, paused and put the pen down. To his surprise—and to everyone else's—Lincoln's hand was trembling.

It was not, Lincoln later said, "because of any uncertainty or hesitation on my part." As he put it, "I never in my life felt more certain that I am doing right than I do in signing this paper."

But greeting so many guests had taken a toll. "I have been shaking hands since 9 o'clock this morning, and my hand is almost paralyzed," Lincoln explained. "If my name ever goes into history it will be for this act, and my whole soul is in it. If my hand trembles when I sign the proclamation, all who examine the document hereafter will say, 'He hesitated.'"

After a few moments Lincoln again took pen in hand. The room was quiet except for the muffled sounds of laughter and music drifting upstairs from the party below. Slowly but firmly he wrote "Abraham Lincoln" at the bottom of the document that declared all slaves in the Confederacy "forever free."

With that, Lincoln glanced at his signature, looked up, smiled, and modestly said, "That will do."

What Lincoln's proclamation did—and did not do—has been debated ever since. Some argue that the Emancipation Proclamation did little. After all, it ordered slaves freed only in the states of the Confederacy—the states where Lincoln had no authority. But in the words of one contemporary, the document struck like a second Declaration of Independence. In truth, nothing so revolutionary had happened since the Revolutionary War itself. Perhaps that is why Lincoln worried so long before finally doing what some thought he should have done the moment he became President.

Lincoln had been against slavery all his life. Seeing slaves in chains for the first time in New Orleans, he vowed: "If I ever get a chance to hit this thing, I'll hit it hard." As a young legislator in Illinois, he had been one of the few lawmakers to sign a resolution against slavery. Years later he spoke angrily against the idea that slavery should be allowed to spread to the western territories.

Abraham Lincoln (right) wrote this draft (below) of the Emancipation Proclamation.

True, Lincoln did not then believe in equality for Africans living in the United States. He did not yet think they should be permitted to vote or sit on juries. But he differed with most citizens of the day by declaring, "In the right to eat the bread which his own hands earn," a black man "is my equal and . . . the equal of every living man."

When Lincoln was elected President in 1860, he promised to do nothing to interfere with slavery in the slave states. He still believed that slavery was wrong, but he felt that personal belief did not give him the right to act. After a year of war, however, Lincoln decided that the only way to put the Union back together was to fight not only against Confederate armies but also against slavery itself. "We must free the slaves," he confided, "or ourselves be subdued."

Then why did he not order slaves freed immediately? Lincoln believed that the country was simply not ready for it. "It is my conviction," he said, "that had the proclamation been issued even six months earlier than it was, public sentiment would not have sustained it." The President worried that if he acted against slavery too soon, he would lose support in the important border states, which he wanted so much to keep in the Union. Lincoln could not afford to lose the slave state of Maryland, for example. If Maryland seceded, then Washington, D.C., would become a capital city inside an enemy country! Lincoln worried, too, that Northern voters might turn against Republicans and elect a new Congress unwilling to continue the war. So he waited.

Not until July 1862 did Lincoln finally decide that he could safely act. "Things had gone on from bad to worse," he said, "until I felt that we had reached the end of our rope . . . that we had about played our last card and must change our tactics, or lose the game."

On July 22, a blisteringly hot summer day, Lincoln called a meeting of the Cabinet and told the members he had an important decision to announce. He warned them that he would listen to no arguments. He had already made up his mind. Then he unfolded some papers and slowly read aloud his first draft of the proclamation. No one present dared speak against it, but Secretary of State Seward expressed a reasonable concern. With the war going so badly, wouldn't the announcement be taken by most Americans as "a cry for help— our last shriek on the retreat?" Seward wanted the President to postpone the proclamation until the Union could win a victory on the battlefield. Lincoln agreed.

Over the next two months, emancipation was the best-kept secret in America. Then, on September 17, 1862, Union troops finally gave Lincoln a victory. The North defeated the South at the Battle of Antietam in Maryland. Five days later Abraham Lincoln announced the Emancipation Proclamation.

Just as Lincoln had feared, the emancipation was immediately and bitterly attacked. Some newspapers warned that it would set off riots. Union soldiers began deserting in greater

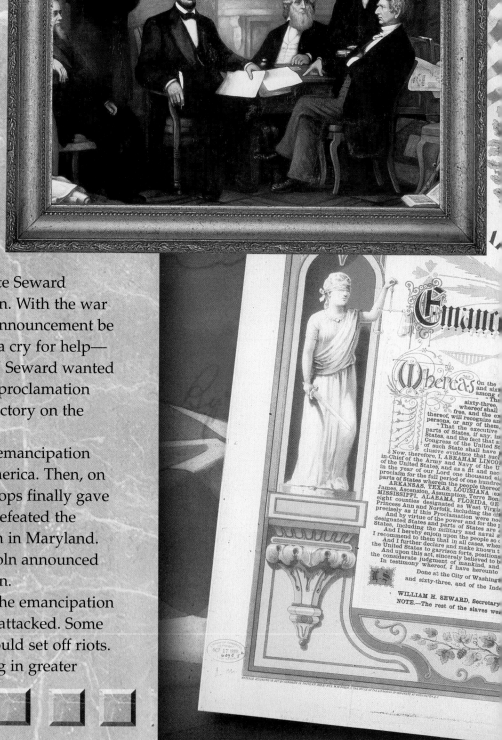

Abraham Lincoln meets with members of his cabinet to discuss the Emancipation Proclamation (left). William H. Seward is sitting across from Lincoln. To celebrate the Emancipation Proclamation, the document was reprinted on this poster (below).

numbers than ever. That fall, Lincoln's Republican party suffered losses in elections for Congress.

But Lincoln did not back down. On January 1—with his trembling hand steadied—he signed the final proclamation. He even added his hope that former slaves would now join Union armies to fight for the freedom the emancipation promised. Everyone knew that, for all its good intentions, the Emancipation Proclamation would do nothing unless Union armies could win victories in Rebel states. That is exactly what happened. The Emancipation Proclamation freed 200,000 slaves as Union troops marched farther and farther into the Confederacy.

By the stroke of his pen, Lincoln had launched a second American Revolution. He not only had helped end the shame of human bondage in America but had guaranteed the survival of American democracy. As he put it, "By giving freedom to the slave, we assure freedom to the free."

LITERATURE REVIEW

1. Why was it important for Lincoln to think about all points of view before deciding to write the Emancipation Proclamation?

2. Why did some people think the Emancipation Proclamation did very little?

3. Lincoln said, "By giving freedom to the slave, we assure freedom to the free." Rewrite Lincoln's words in your own words to show classmates what you think he meant.

FOCUS

What actions might help bring a difficult conflict to an end?

Main Idea As you read, think about the events that helped bring the Civil War to an end.

Vocabulary

Gettysburg Address
assassination

The Long Road to a Union Victory

1862	1864	1866

The Emancipation Proclamation did not give enslaved people instant freedom. The order was only for the states that had left the Union—not the four border states. And until Union troops were sent to the Confederate states to see that the proclamation was carried out, many people there remained enslaved. Still, it gave new hope to Africans and new spirit to the North.

In the months that followed, the North seemed to be winning the war. Yet terrible battles lay ahead, and many more soldiers would die before the war's end.

African Regiments

Africans had fought to defend the United States since the Revolutionary War. Over the years, however, many had been kept from joining the army. By the start of the Civil War, they were not allowed to serve in the army.

As the war went on, many Africans decided to form their own regiments to fight for the Union. While they trained, their leaders asked Congress to let them enlist. Finally, in 1862, with no end to the war in sight and fewer white soldiers joining the army, Congress agreed. More than 186,000 Africans signed up. They formed 166 regiments of artillery, cavalry, infantry, and engineers.

At first African soldiers were not paid as much as white soldiers. They were given poor equipment, and they often ran out of supplies. To make things worse, Confederate soldiers

Crackers like the one above were sometimes the only source of food for soldiers. This African soldier (left) fought for the Union.

African troops played a key role in support of the Union. This photograph shows members of an artillery unit completing cannon drills.

said that they would enslave or kill any African soldiers they captured.

Even with the hardships and the dangers, African soldiers soon proved themselves in battle. They led raids behind Confederate lines and served as spies and scouts. They fought in almost every battle, facing some of the worst fighting of the war. More than 38,000 African soldiers lost their lives defending the Union.

REVIEW *How did African regiments help the Union war effort?*

Grant Leads the Union

Another boost for the North came when President Lincoln finally found a general as good as Confederate general Robert E. Lee. His name was Ulysses S. Grant.

Like Lee, Grant had been educated at West Point and had fought in the war with Mexico. When the Civil War began, Grant offered his services to the Union army. His quick decisions in battles soon led to Union victories. After one battle, when the Confederates asked for the terms of surrender, Grant replied, "No terms except an unconditional and immediate surrender can be accepted." After that, Northerners liked to say that Grant's initials, *U. S.,* stood for *Unconditional Surrender.*

One of Grant's most important battles began in May 1863 at Vicksburg, Mississippi. After two attacks Grant decided to surround and lay siege to the city. For weeks Union guns pounded Vicksburg. Grant and his soldiers cut off all supplies to the city. The trapped Confederates, both soldiers and townspeople, soon ran out of food. They had to tear down houses for firewood and dig caves in hillsides for shelter. Finally, on the Fourth of July, the starving people of Vicksburg gave in.

Vicksburg proved to be a key victory. It gave the Union control of the Mississippi River. This, in turn, helped weaken the Confederacy by cutting it into two parts.

As one Union soldier wrote from Vicksburg, "This was the most glorious Fourth I ever spent." President Lincoln was overjoyed when he heard about the victory. Before long he gave Grant command of all Union troops.

REVIEW *Why was Grant's victory at Vicksburg important?*

Gettysburg

At about the same time that Grant won Vicksburg, other Union troops were facing the invading army of Robert E. Lee in the small town of Gettysburg, Pennsylvania. The Battle of Gettysburg ended in one of the most important Union victories of the war. But more than 3,000 Union soldiers and nearly 4,000 Confederates were killed. More than 20,000 on each side were wounded or reported missing.

The fate of the Fourteenth Tennessee Regiment tells the story. When the battle began, there were 365 men in the unit. When the battle ended, there were only 3.

On November 19, 1863, President Lincoln went to Gettysburg to dedicate a cemetery for those who had died there. A crowd of nearly 6,000 people gathered for the ceremony.

Lincoln gave a short speech that day. In fact, he spoke for less than three minutes. A photographer who was there hoped to take a picture of the President as he gave his

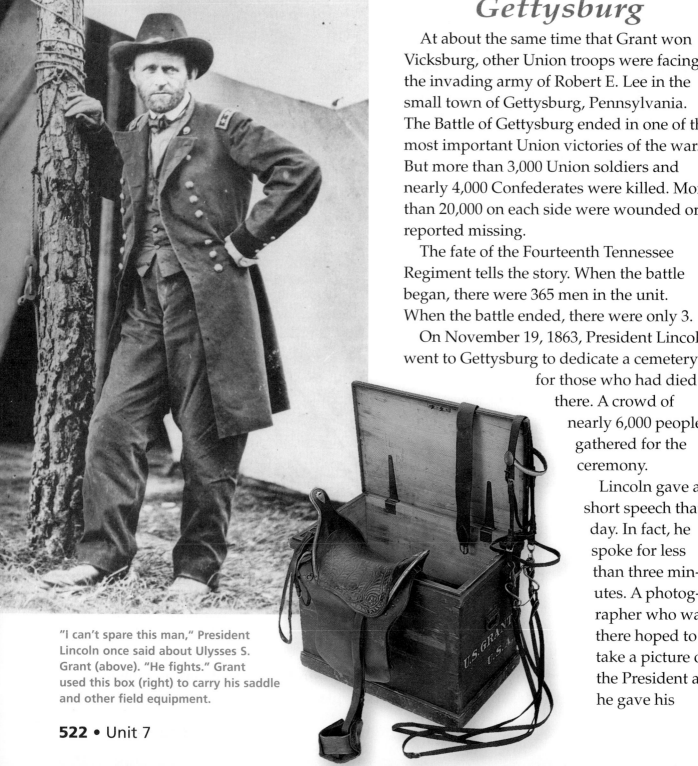

"I can't spare this man," President Lincoln once said about Ulysses S. Grant (above). "He fights." Grant used this box (right) to carry his saddle and other field equipment.

THE GETTYSBURG ADDRESS

Four score and seven years ago our fathers brought forth on this continent, a new nation, conceived in Liberty, and dedicated to the proposition that all men are created equal.

Now we are engaged in a great civil war, testing whether that nation, or any nation so conceived and so dedicated, can long endure. We are met on a great battlefield of that war. We have come to dedicate a portion of that field, as a final resting place for those who here gave their lives that that nation might live. It is altogether fitting and proper that we should do this.

But, in a larger sense, we can not dedicate—we can not consecrate—we can not hallow—this ground. The brave men, living and dead, who struggled here, have consecrated it, far above our poor power to add or detract. The world will little note, nor long remember what we say here, but it can never forget what they did here. It is for us the living, rather, to be dedicated here to the unfinished work which they who fought here have thus far so nobly advanced. It is rather for us to be here dedicated to the great task remaining before us—that from these honored dead we take increased devotion to that cause for which they gave the last full measure of devotion—that we here highly resolve that these dead shall not have died in vain—that this nation, under God, shall have a new birth of freedom—and that government of the people, by the people, for the people, shall not perish from the earth.

speech. But by the time the photographer had set up his heavy camera, Lincoln had already sat down!

Lincoln's speech at Gettysburg was so short that many people in the crowd were disappointed. Lincoln himself called it "a flat failure." But people soon realized that this short speech, later known as the **Gettysburg Address**, was one of the most inspiring ever given by an American leader.

In the Gettysburg Address, Lincoln spoke to the heart of the war-weary North. He spoke of the ideals of liberty and equality on which the country had been founded. He honored the soldiers who had died defending those ideals. And he called on Americans to try even harder to win the struggle those soldiers had died for—to save the "government of the people, by the people, for the people" so that the Union would be preserved.

REVIEW *What did President Lincoln ask Americans to do in his speech at Gettysburg?*

This photograph shows a home that was damaged in Atlanta, Georgia, during the Union army's March to the Sea.

The March to the Sea

More Union victories followed those at Vicksburg and Gettysburg. Then came one of the worst times for the South—the invasion of Georgia.

In 1864 Union General William Tecumseh Sherman led his army south from Tennessee into Georgia. Through heavy fighting Sherman pushed to Atlanta, the railroad center of the South. As he took the city, much of it burned to the ground.

From Atlanta, Sherman's troops headed toward Savannah, on the Atlantic coast. Their march has become known as the March to the Sea. The goal of this terrible march was to destroy everything that could help the South in the war. Sherman hoped that this would break the South's will to fight. "We cannot change the hearts of those people of the South," Sherman said, "but we can make war so terrible . . . make them so sick of war that generations would pass away before they would again appeal to it." Cutting a path of destruction 60 miles (97 km) wide and 300 miles (483 km) long, Union troops burned homes and stores, destroyed crops, wrecked bridges, and tore up railroad tracks.

On December 22, 1864, Savannah fell to Union troops. That night Sherman sent a message to President Lincoln. "I beg to present you as a Christmas gift the city of Savannah." Sherman then turned north and marched through South Carolina, destroying even more than he had in Georgia.

REVIEW *What was the purpose of Sherman's March to the Sea?*

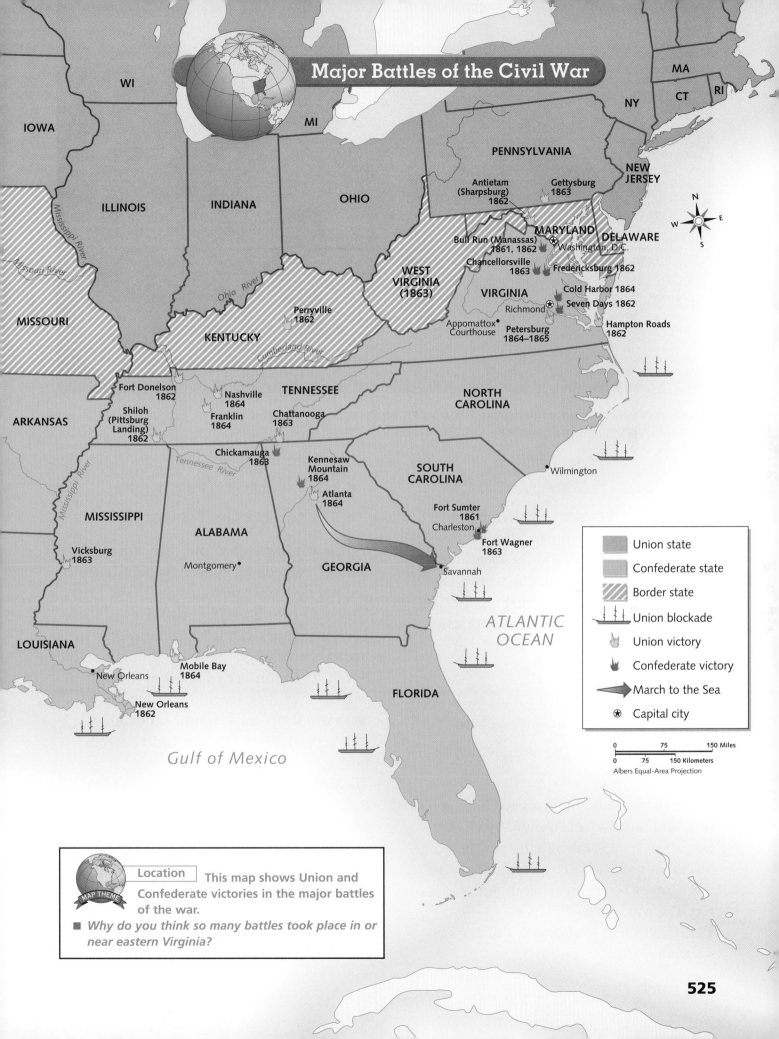

Major Battles of the Civil War

WI

IOWA

ILLINOIS

INDIANA

OHIO

MI

MA

RI

CT

NY

PENNSYLVANIA

NEW JERSEY

MISSOURI

KENTUCKY

Perryville 1862

WEST VIRGINIA (1863)

Antietam (Sharpsburg) 1862

Gettysburg 1863

MARYLAND

DELAWARE

Bull Run (Manassas) 1861, 1862

Washington, D.C.

Chancellorsville 1863

Fredericksburg 1862

VIRGINIA

Cold Harbor 1864

Richmond

Seven Days 1862

Appomattox Courthouse

Petersburg 1864–1865

Hampton Roads 1862

ARKANSAS

Fort Donelson 1862

Nashville 1864

TENNESSEE

NORTH CAROLINA

Shiloh (Pittsburg Landing) 1862

Franklin 1864

Chattanooga 1863

Chickamauga 1863

Kennesaw Mountain 1864

SOUTH CAROLINA

Wilmington

MISSISSIPPI

ALABAMA

Atlanta 1864

GEORGIA

Fort Sumter 1861

Charleston

Vicksburg 1863

Montgomery

Fort Wagner 1863

Savannah

ATLANTIC OCEAN

LOUISIANA

New Orleans

Mobile Bay 1864

FLORIDA

New Orleans 1862

Gulf of Mexico

Mississippi River

Missouri River

Ohio River

Cumberland River

Tennessee River

Mississippi River

Legend

- Union state
- Confederate state
- Border state
- Union blockade
- Union victory
- Confederate victory
- March to the Sea
- Capital city

0   75   150 Miles
0   75   150 Kilometers
Albers Equal-Area Projection

Location This map shows Union and Confederate victories in the major battles of the war.

■ *Why do you think so many battles took place in or near eastern Virginia?*

Robert E. Lee (seated at left) surrendered to Ulysses S. Grant (seated at right) at the home of Wilmer McLean in Appomattox Courthouse.

Lee Surrenders

In April 1865 Grant's Union army met Lee's Confederate army in Virginia. Lee's troops were starving, and their clothes were in rags. Grant's soldiers, who were well armed and well fed, kept pushing the Confederate troops. Finally, Lee was trapped. He could neither fight nor retreat. He decided to surrender. Lee said,

❝ There is nothing left for me to do but to go and see General Grant, and I would rather die a thousand deaths. ❞

Lee surrendered his army to Grant at the tiny Virginia town of Appomattox Courthouse on April 9, 1865. In the next few weeks, as word of Lee's surrender reached them, other Southern generals surrendered, too. The war was finally over.

REVIEW *What problems led to Lee's surrender?*

One More Tragic Death

The war had ended, but there was still another tragedy to come. Abraham Lincoln did not live to see peace return to the Union. On April 14, 1865, just five days after Lee's surrender, Lincoln was murdered by a man who thought he was helping the South. The murder of a political leader such as President Lincoln is called an **assassination** (uh•sa•suhn•AY•shuhn).

The President and Mary Todd Lincoln, his wife, had been watching a play at Ford's Theater in Washington, D.C. It was there that an actor named John Wilkes Booth shot the President and ran. Booth died later, during his escape.

Lincoln's assassination shocked both the North and the South. Northerners had lost the leader who had guided the Union to victory. Many gathered in the streets when they heard the news. Some cried openly.

Others marched silently. People hung black cloth everywhere—on buildings, fences, and trees.

Many Southerners were also saddened by the death of the President. Lincoln had said he would treat the South fairly in defeat. He had promised to bring the country together again "with malice toward none, with charity for all." What would happen now that the President was dead?

Mary Chesnut feared the worst. When she learned of the assassination, Chesnut wrote in her diary, "Lincoln—old Abe Lincoln—killed . . . I know this foul murder will bring down worse miseries on us."

REVIEW *Why was Lincoln's death a shock to both the North and the South?*

HERITAGE

Memorial Day

On May 5, 1866, people in Waterloo, New York, honored those who died in the Civil War. The people closed businesses for the day and decorated soldiers' graves with flowers. This was the beginning of the holiday known as Memorial Day, or Decoration Day. On this day Americans remember those who gave their lives for their country. At the Arlington National Cemetery, a wreath is placed on the Tomb of the Unknowns. Three unknown American soldiers who were killed in war are buried there. Today most states observe Memorial Day on the last Monday in May.

The Tomb of the Unknowns

LESSON 3 REVIEW

1862	1864	1866

1862
• Congress allows Africans to enlist in the Union army

1863
• Abraham Lincoln delivers the Gettysburg Address

1865
• Robert E. Lee surrenders to Ulysses S. Grant
• Abraham Lincoln is assassinated

Check Understanding

1 Remember the Facts What is the Gettysburg Address?

2 Recall the Main Idea What events helped bring the Civil War to an end?

Think Critically

3 Think More About It In what ways did individual Americans make a difference during the war?

4 Past to Present Why do you think people today still find meaning in the words of Lincoln's Gettysburg Address?

5 Explore Viewpoints If you had lived in the North during the Civil War, how might you have felt about the March to the Sea? How might you have felt if you had lived in the South?

Show What You Know

Diorama Activity Make a diorama of one of the events described in this lesson. Your diorama should show either conflict or cooperation. Share your diorama with your classmates.

Compare Maps with

1. Why Learn This Skill?

A map scale compares a distance on a map to a distance in the real world. It helps you find the real distance between places. Map scales are different depending on how much area is shown. Knowing about different map scales can help you choose the best map for gathering the information you need.

2. Understand the Process

Look at the map below and the map on page 529. They show the same area around Gettysburg, Pennsylvania, but with different scales. On Map A, Gettysburg looks smaller. For that reason the scale is said to be smaller. On Map B, Gettysburg appears larger, and the scale is said to be larger.

When the map scale is larger, more details can be shown. Also note that Map B is the larger map. It takes a larger piece of paper to show a place on a map with a large scale than to show it on a map with a smaller scale.

On July 2, 1863, the Union line stretched from Spangler's Spring north to Culp's Hill, on to Cemetery Hill, south along Cemetery Ridge to the hill called Little Round Top, and beyond. What was the real distance in miles between Cemetery Hill and Little Round Top? To find out, follow the steps below:

1 On Map A, use a ruler to measure the exact length of the scale, or use a pencil to mark off the length on a sheet of paper. How long is the line that stands for one mile?

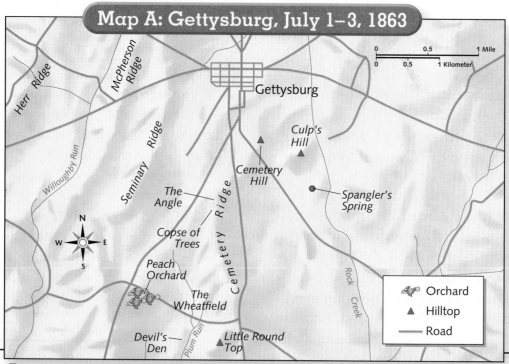

Map A: Gettysburg, July 1–3, 1863

Different Scales

2 Still using Map A, find Cemetery Hill and Little Round Top. Using the ruler or the sheet of paper you marked, measure the distance between these two hills. How many times can you fit the scale length end to end between the hills? Multiply the number of scale lengths between the hills by the distance that the scale length represents. What is the real distance between Cemetery Hill and Little Round Top?

3 Now go through the same steps for Map B. How long is the scale length that stands for one mile? Use that scale length to measure the distance between Cemetery Hill and Little Round Top.

Are the real distances you found on the two maps the same? You should see that even when map scales are different, the real distances shown on the maps are the same.

3. Think and Apply

Find two road maps with different scales—perhaps a road map of your state and a road map of a large city within your state. Compare the real distances between two places that are on both maps. Are the distances the same on both maps? When would it be more helpful to use the state map? When would it be more helpful to use the city map?

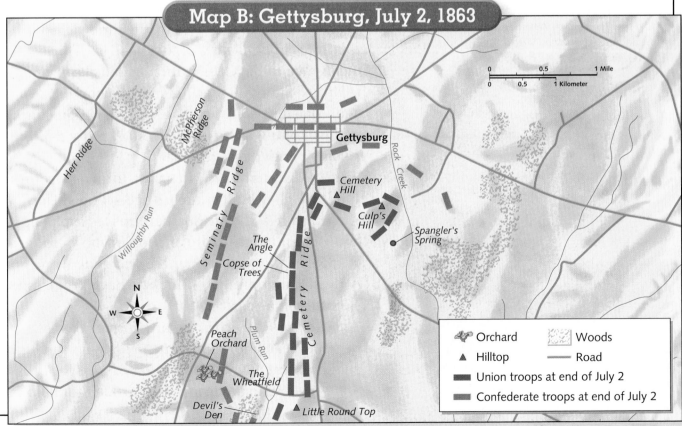

Map B: Gettysburg, July 2, 1863

Gettysburg

McPherson Ridge
Herr Ridge
Seminary Ridge
Willoughby Run
Cemetery Hill
Culp's Hill
Rock Creek
Spangler's Spring
The Angle
Copse of Trees
Cemetery Ridge
Peach Orchard
Plum Run
The Wheatfield
Devil's Den
Little Round Top

0   0.5   1 Mile
0   0.5   1 Kilometer

N W E S

🌳 Orchard   🌲 Woods
▲ Hilltop   — Road
▬ Union troops at end of July 2
▬ Confederate troops at end of July 2

FOCUS

How can new laws affect the lives of citizens?

Main Idea Read to learn about how new laws affected the lives of Americans in the years following the Civil War.

Vocabulary

sharecropping
Reconstruction
scalawag
carpetbagger
segregation

Life After the War

| 1865 | 1870 | 1875 | 1880 |

When the Civil War finally ended, it was clear that peace had not come easily. More than 600,000 soldiers had died. Many others had returned home wounded. Much of the South was destroyed. And now the President was dead. As one Southerner remembered, "All the talk was of burning homes, houses knocked to pieces . . . famine, murder, desolation."

The years following the war were hard ones. However, the end of the war brought new hope to at least one group of people—the former slaves.

A Free People

With the Union victory, 4 million enslaved people were freed. Most slaves were already free by the time the Civil War ended in 1865. In December of that year, the Thirteenth Amendment to the Constitution ended slavery in the United States forever. "I felt like a bird out of a cage," one former slave remembered, looking back on the day he was set free. "I could hardly ask to feel any better than I did that day."

Free Africans quickly began to form new communities. They built churches and schools. They opened stores. They formed groups to help people find jobs and to take care of people who were sick. In 1866, only one year after the war ended, one African leader proudly said, "We have progressed a century in a year."

As soon as they could, many former slaves began to search for family members who had been sold and sent away under slavery. Newspapers were filled with advertisements asking for help in

By making slavery against the law, the Thirteenth Amendment ended slavery in the United States forever.

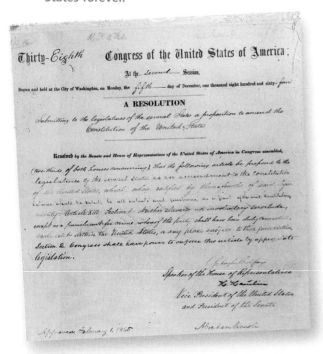

In this painting a preacher (far left) visits a family of former slaves. Many African families had been split up because of slavery.

finding loved ones. This ad appeared in a newspaper in Nashville, Tennessee.

66 During the year 1849, Thomas Sample carried away from this city, as his slaves, our daughter, Polly, and son, George. . . . We will give $100 each for them to any person who will assist them, or . . . get word to us of their whereabouts. 99

Many families never found their missing loved ones. But for those that did, it was a time of great joy. "I wish you could see this people as they step from slavery into freedom," one Union soldier wrote to his wife. "Families which had been for a long time broken up are united and oh! such happiness."

Former slaves worked hard to build new lives. Yet life remained difficult. Often it was hard just to find food, clothing, and shelter. Many began to look to the United States government for help.

REVIEW *How did free Africans help one another after the war?*

HERITAGE

Juneteenth

Abraham Lincoln signed the Emancipation Proclamation on January 1, 1863. But because Union troops did not control Texas at the time, the order had little effect there. On June 19, 1865, Union soldiers landed at Galveston, Texas. On that day Union General Gordon Granger read an order declaring that all slaves in Texas were free. Today people in Texas and across the country celebrate June 19, or Juneteenth, as a day of freedom. It is a holiday marked by picnics, parades, and family gatherings.

This photograph shows people going to a Juneteenth celebration.

Many former slaves, like those shown outside this Freedmen's Bureau school, were eager to learn to read and write.

The Freedmen's Bureau

In 1865 Congress set up an organization to help former slaves. This group was called the Bureau of Refugees, Freedmen, and Abandoned Lands—or the Freedmen's Bureau.

The Freedmen's Bureau gave food and other supplies to freed slaves. It also helped some white farmers rebuild their farms. The most important work of the Freedmen's Bureau, however, was education. Newly freed slaves were eager to learn to read and write. To help meet this need, the Freedmen's Bureau built more than 4,000 schools and hired thousands of teachers.

The Freedmen's Bureau also wanted to help former slaves earn a living by giving them land to farm. This plan, however, did not work out. The land was to have come from the plantations taken during the war. But the government decided to give the plantations back to their original owners. In the end, most former slaves were not given land. Without money to buy land of their own, many had to work for other people.

REVIEW *What was the purpose of the Freedmen's Bureau?*

Sharecropping

In their search for jobs, some former slaves went back to work on plantations. Many planters welcomed them. Fields needed to be plowed, and crops needed to be planted. Now, however, planters had to pay Africans for their work.

In the days following the war, there was not much money. Instead of paying workers in cash, many landowners paid them in shares. Under this system, known as **sharecropping**, a landowner gave a worker a cabin, mules, tools, and seed. The worker then farmed the land. At harvesttime the landowner took part of the crops, plus enough to cover the cost of the worker's rent and supplies. What was left was the worker's share.

As sharecroppers, former slaves were paid for their work. But sharecropping was a hard way to make a living, and it put many families in debt.

Sharecropping gave landowners the help they needed to work the fields. It also gave former slaves work for pay. Yet few people got ahead through sharecropping. When crops failed, both landowners and workers suffered. Even in good times, most workers' shares were very little, if anything at all.

REVIEW *Why did landowners pay workers in shares rather than in cash?*

A New President

As Americans were getting used to their new lives after the war, government leaders began making plans for bringing the country back together. This time of rebuilding was called **Reconstruction**.

After Lincoln's death the Vice President, Andrew Johnson, became the new President. Johnson tried to carry out Lincoln's promise to be fair to the South in defeat. He pardoned most Confederates who promised loyalty to the United States. They were then given back the rights of citizenship and were allowed to vote. Their states held elections, and state governments went back to work.

Johnson also said that the Confederate states must abolish slavery. This requirement was met when the Thirteenth Amendment was passed late in 1865. Johnson then said that the last of the Confederate states could return to the Union.

Such easy terms, however, made some people angry. Many Northerners felt that the Confederates were not being punished at all. White Southerners were being elected to office and taking over state governments just as they always had. Yet no one talked about the rights of former slaves. What would happen to them?

It was not long before laws were passed in the South that limited the rights of former slaves. These laws were called black codes. The black codes differed from state to state. In most states Africans were not allowed to vote. In some they were not allowed to travel freely. They could not own certain kinds of property or work in certain businesses. They could be made to work in the fields without pay if they could not find another job.

Many, however, faced an even worse problem. Shortly after the war ended, secret groups formed in the South that tried to keep Africans from having their rights as free persons. Most of those who joined these groups were upset about their war losses and angry about the new rights of former slaves.

President Andrew Johnson tried his best to carry out Lincoln's promise to be fair to the South after the war. But his disagreements with Congress took away his strength as a leader.

One such group was the Ku Klux Klan, or the KKK. Dressed in white robes and hoods, its members delivered nighttime messages of hate. Klan members broke into homes and attacked and killed Africans. They burned African schools and churches. They punished anyone who helped former slaves. It was a time of terror for many people.

REVIEW *What did Andrew Johnson try to carry out when he became President?*

Congress Takes Action

Many leaders of Congress were alarmed about the way former slaves in some Southern states were being treated. They believed that President Johnson's Reconstruction plan was not working. So they voted to change to a plan of their own—a plan that was much tougher on white Southerners.

First, Congress did away with the new state governments and put the Southern states under the army's rule. Union soldiers kept order, and army officers were made governors. Before each Southern state could reestablish its government, it had to write a new state constitution giving all men, both black and white, the right to vote. To return to the Union, a state also had to pass the Fourteenth Amendment. This amendment gave citizenship to all people born in the United States—including former slaves.

Johnson was very angry about this plan and about other laws that Congress passed to cut back his authority. Believing that these laws were unconstitutional, Johnson refused to carry them out. Then, in 1868, the House of Representatives voted to impeach

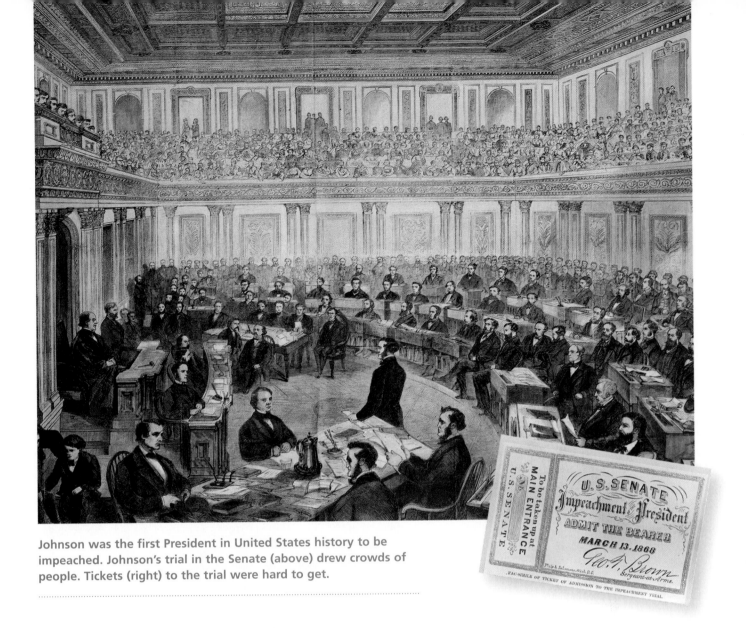

Johnson was the first President in United States history to be impeached. Johnson's trial in the Senate (above) drew crowds of people. Tickets (right) to the trial were hard to get.

the President, or charge him with a crime. He was put on trial in the Senate. There, in a very close vote, he was found not guilty. Although he stayed in office, Johnson was no longer a strong leader.

The Southern states began to write new state constitutions and pass the Fourteenth Amendment. State elections were held once again. For the first time, African Americans from the South were elected to Congress. They also served in state governments that took over the job of rebuilding the South.

REVIEW *Why did Congress vote to change Johnson's Reconstruction plan?*

Reconstruction Ends

The new state governments made many important changes. They did away with the black codes. They approved the Fifteenth Amendment, which said that no citizen could be kept from voting because of race. They built hospitals and schools and repaired roads, bridges, and railroads.

Yet the work of the state governments did not make everyone happy. To pay for their Reconstruction projects, state leaders placed high taxes on land. These taxes hurt landowners, who were trying to get their farms and plantations working again. Some were forced to sell their land because they could not pay the taxes.

Many white Southerners soon grew angry with their state leaders. They did not like the fact that African Americans were voting and taking part in government. They did not like the white Southerners who supported the government. They called them **scalawags** (SKA•lih•wagz)—people who support something for their own gain. They also did not like being told what to do by Northerners. Under military rule Northern soldiers guarded their streets. Other Northerners went to the South to try to help with Reconstruction or to make money buying land or opening businesses. White Southerners called them **carpetbaggers**

This poster (right) celebrates the passing of the Fifteenth Amendment that gave African Americans the right to vote. The first African Americans to serve in the United States Congress (below) were elected during Reconstruction.

because many of them arrived carrying their belongings in suitcases made of carpet pieces.

Some white Southerners tried again to take authority from their state leaders. One way they did this was to control the way people voted. Groups such as the Ku Klux Klan used violence to keep African Americans from voting or to make sure they voted as they were told. Sometimes the votes of African Americans simply were not counted.

In time white Southerners once again took control of

This suitcase belonged to a carpetbagger who came to the South during Reconstruction.

their state governments. New state laws were passed that made it very hard, if not impossible, for African Americans to vote. African Americans had to go to separate schools and churches and sit in separate railroad cars. Such laws led to the **segregation**, or separation, of black people and white people.

Reconstruction was over by 1877. In that year the last of the Union troops left the South. The rights and freedoms African Americans had just won were again taken away in the South.

REVIEW *How did white Southerners take authority back from their state leaders as Reconstruction ended?*

LESSON 4 REVIEW

1865 — 1870 — 1875 — 1880

1865
• The Civil War ends
• The Thirteenth Amendment is passed

1877
• Reconstruction ends

Check Understanding

1 Remember the Facts In what ways did the government try to help former slaves?

2 Recall the Main Idea How did new laws affect the lives of Americans in the years following the Civil War?

Think Critically

3 Think More About It In what ways did life change for former slaves who became sharecroppers?

4 Explore Viewpoints Why do you think Lincoln wanted to be fair to the South in defeat?

5 Cause and Effect Why were many white Southerners angry with the state governments that were set up during military rule?

Show What You Know

Writing Activity Imagine that you are a news reporter writing a story about Reconstruction. Write an interview with a former slave, a Southern white landowner, a Union soldier stationed in the South, or a carpetbagger. Give both your questions and the person's answers. Present your interview to the class.

1860 ● 1865

1863
- The Emancipation Proclamation is signed
- Abraham Lincoln delivers the Gettysburg Address

1865
- The Civil War ends
- Abraham Lincoln is assassinated

CONNECT MAIN IDEAS

Use this organizer to show how the chapter's main ideas are connected. Write a sentence or two telling how each event or idea affected the lives of Americans during the Civil War and Reconstruction. A copy of the organizer may be found on page 97 of the Activity Book.

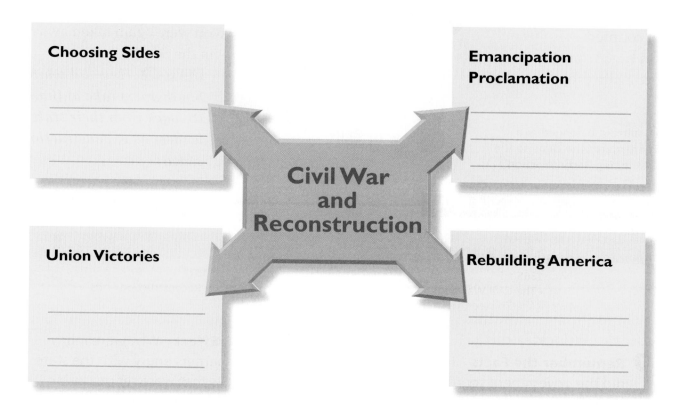

Choosing Sides

Emancipation Proclamation

Civil War and Reconstruction

Union Victories

Rebuilding America

WRITE MORE ABOUT IT

Write a Diary Entry Imagine that you are living in one of the border states at the beginning of the Civil War. Write a diary entry in which you tell why you think some members of your family have chosen to fight for the North while others have chosen to fight for the South.

Write a News Story Imagine that you are a newspaper reporter covering the White House in 1863. Write an article for your newspaper in which you tell readers what the Emancipation Proclamation will do, why President Lincoln has decided to issue it, and how it will affect the war.

USE VOCABULARY

Use each term in a complete sentence that will help explain its meaning.

1 border state

2 Emancipation Proclamation

3 assassination

4 sharecropping

5 carpetbagger

6 segregation

CHECK UNDERSTANDING

7 Why did the Confederacy hope to receive help from Britain and France?

8 Why did Lincoln finally decide to issue the Emancipation Proclamation?

9 How did African soldiers help the North?

10 Why were some Southerners sad about Lincoln's death?

11 What was the purpose of the Freedmen's Bureau?

12 How did the black codes help bring about the end of President Johnson's Reconstruction plan?

THINK CRITICALLY

13 **Personally Speaking** If you had been in Robert E. Lee's place, would you have made the decision to join the Confederacy? Why or why not?

14 **Explore Viewpoints** Mary Chesnut wrote, "I know this foul murder will bring down worse miseries on us." What do you think she meant? Explain your answer.

15 **Think More About It** The most important work of the Freedmen's Bureau was education. Why is education important to people in a free country?

16 **Past to Present** Government leaders raised taxes to pay for rebuilding the South. Today government leaders sometimes increase taxes to help pay for new projects. How can taxes both help and hurt people?

APPLY SKILLS

Compare Maps with Different Scales The maps of Gettysburg on pages 528 and 529 show the sites of many battles. You can visit these battle sites today at the Gettysburg National Military Park in Pennsylvania. Use either map to answer the questions.

17 How far would you have to walk to go from the battle sites of Devil's Den to the Wheatfield?

18 Which map did you use to answer this question? Why did you choose that map?

READ MORE ABOUT IT

A House Divided: The Lives of Ulysses S. Grant and Robert E. Lee by Jules Archer. Scholastic. This book tells about two well-known military leaders in the Civil War.

HARCOURT BRACE

Visit the Internet at **http://www.hbschool.com** for additional resources.

Chapter 14 • **539**

The Fight For FREEDOM Goes On

The Civil War changed forever the way most Americans thought about one another. People who had been friends had fought as enemies. People who had been enslaved were now free. Those who had been thought of as property were now citizens of the United States.

Yet the rights that African Americans had fought so long for were still kept out of reach. In the years following the Civil War, many African Americans were kept from voting and holding office. They were made to live their lives apart from other citizens, in separate neighborhoods and schools. It would be 100 years after the Civil War before African Americans would gain the full rights of United States citizenship.

In the 1950s and 1960s, Americans across the country began to take part in the Civil Rights movement. This was a movement to gain the rights promised to all people in the Constitution. One of the greatest leaders of the Civil Rights movement was Dr. Martin Luther King, Jr. In 1963 King gave a speech about his hopes for the future. He said that he dreamed of a time when all the unfair ways of the past would end. He dreamed of a day when "the sons of former slaves and the sons of former slave owners will be able to sit down together at the table of brotherhood." On that day, King said, all Americans will finally be able to sing together the words of an old spiritual,

> " Free at last!
> Free at last!
> Thank God Almighty,
> We are free at last! "

Think and Apply

Think about people today who are working for equal rights. Identify an individual or a group working to protect people's rights and freedoms. Gather information about the person or group, and prepare a report for the class.

HARCOURT BRACE

Visit the Internet at **http://www.hbschool.com** for additional resources.

CNN Turner Le@rning

Check your media center or classroom video library for the Making Social Studies Relevant videotape of this feature.

UNIT 7
REVIEW

Summarize the Main Ideas
Study the pictures and captions to help you review the events you read about in Unit 7.

Dramatize the Story
Choose any of the people shown in this visual summary, and invent a conversation they might have with us today describing their experiences. Act out the conversation with a classmate.

1 As slavery continued in the South, more and more enslaved people tried to escape by running away.

3 During the Civil War thousands of people in both the North and the South joined the war effort.

6 During Reconstruction the Freedmen's Bureau opened schools for former slaves.

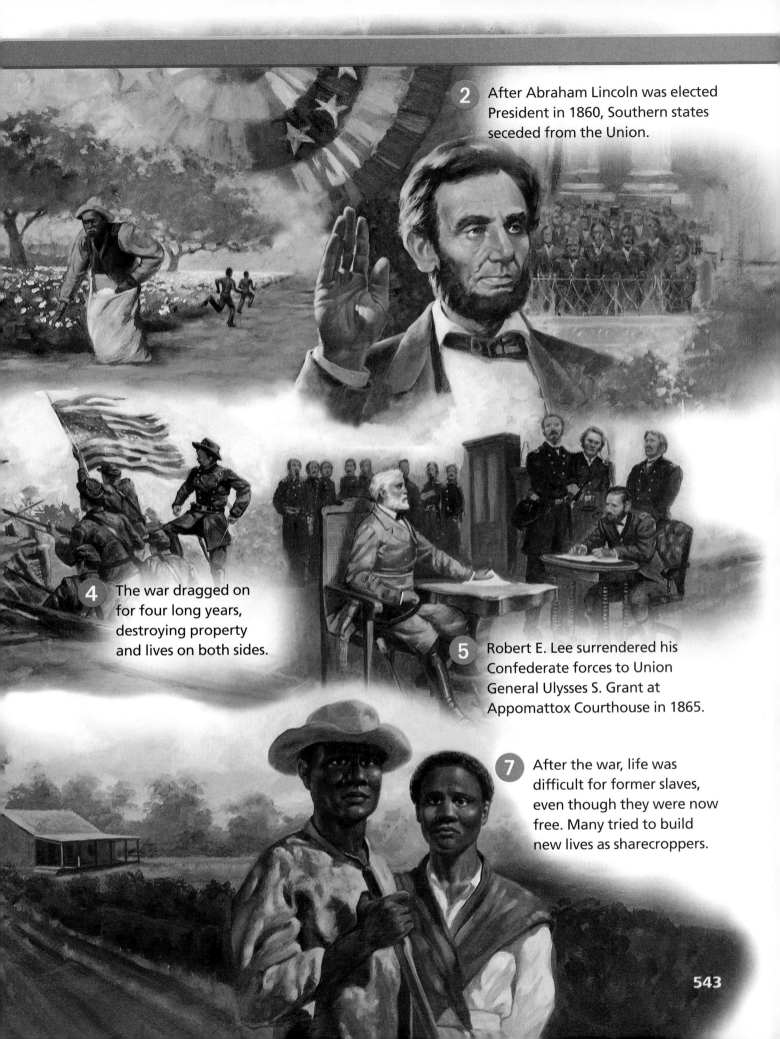

2 After Abraham Lincoln was elected President in 1860, Southern states seceded from the Union.

4 The war dragged on for four long years, destroying property and lives on both sides.

5 Robert E. Lee surrendered his Confederate forces to Union General Ulysses S. Grant at Appomattox Courthouse in 1865.

7 After the war, life was difficult for former slaves, even though they were now free. Many tried to build new lives as sharecroppers.

USE VOCABULARY

Write the term that correctly matches each definition. Then use each term in a complete sentence.

Confederacy   **Reconstruction**

Gettysburg Address   **spiritual**

1 a religious song based on a Bible story

2 the new country formed by the Southern states after they seceded from the Union

3 a famous speech given by Abraham Lincoln

4 a time of rebuilding

CHECK UNDERSTANDING

5 In what ways had the South come to depend on the work of enslaved people?

6 How did the Underground Railroad help enslaved Africans?

7 What was the Missouri Compromise? What was the Kansas–Nebraska Act?

8 How did the Emancipation Proclamation affect the war?

9 What problems led Congress to change President Andrew Johnson's Reconstruction plan?

THINK CRITICALLY

10 **Explore Viewpoints** Lincoln once was called "the miserable tool of traitors and rebels." Today he is thought of as a great leader. Why might someone at the time have been so critical of him?

11 **Past to Present** Why is it important for Presidents today to consider different viewpoints before making a decision?

APPLY SKILLS

Compare Maps with Different Scales The Battle of Gettysburg ended on July 3, 1863, when Pickett's Charge—led by Confederate General George Pickett—was stopped at the Angle and the Copse of Trees. Use the map below to answer the question.

12 Compare the map on this page to Map A on page 528. Which would more clearly show Pickett's Charge or other troop movements over small distances? Explain your answer.

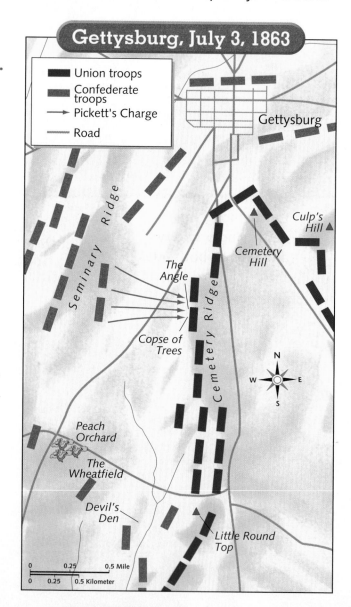

Gettysburg, July 3, 1863

- Union troops
- Confederate troops
- → Pickett's Charge
- Road

Gettysburg

Seminary Ridge

Culp's Hill

Cemetery Hill

The Angle

Cemetery Ridge

Copse of Trees

Peach Orchard

The Wheatfield

Devil's Den

Little Round Top

0   0.25   0.5 Mile
0   0.25   0.5 Kilometer

REMEMBER

- Share your ideas.
- Cooperate with others to plan your work.
- Take responsibility for your work.
- Help one another.
- Show your group's work to the class.
- Discuss what you learned by working together.

ACTIVITY

Publish a Class Magazine

You and your classmates have decided to put together a magazine about the Civil War. First, plan your magazine by preparing a table of contents. Decide what articles and illustrations you would like to include. Give your magazine a title. Then form several small groups, with each group working on a different part of the magazine. Once all the groups have finished, put the parts together. Ask permission to display the magazine in the school library.

ACTIVITY

Draw a Map

Work together to draw a map of the United States at the time of the Civil War. Use different colors for the states of the Union and the states of the Confederacy. Write the date on which each Southern state seceded. Draw diagonal lines on the border states. Label the capitals of the North and the South and the key battle sites. Use your map to tell your classmates about one event of the Civil War.

ACTIVITY

Honor Your Hero

Choose someone you admire from the Civil War as the subject of a poster for a display called *Heroes of the Civil War*. Work together to find or draw a picture of the person or a picture of a scene showing the person in action. Then add words or phrases around the picture that tell what made that person a hero. Present your poster to the class.

Unit Project Wrap-Up

Make a Time Line Work with a partner to finish the Unit Project that was described on page 469. First, make a list of the major events of the Civil War. Then exchange lists with your partner to make sure that you have included the most important events on your time line. Write captions describing any illustrations that you have drawn for the time line. Share your time lines with the class.

545

AMERICANS, THEN AND NOW

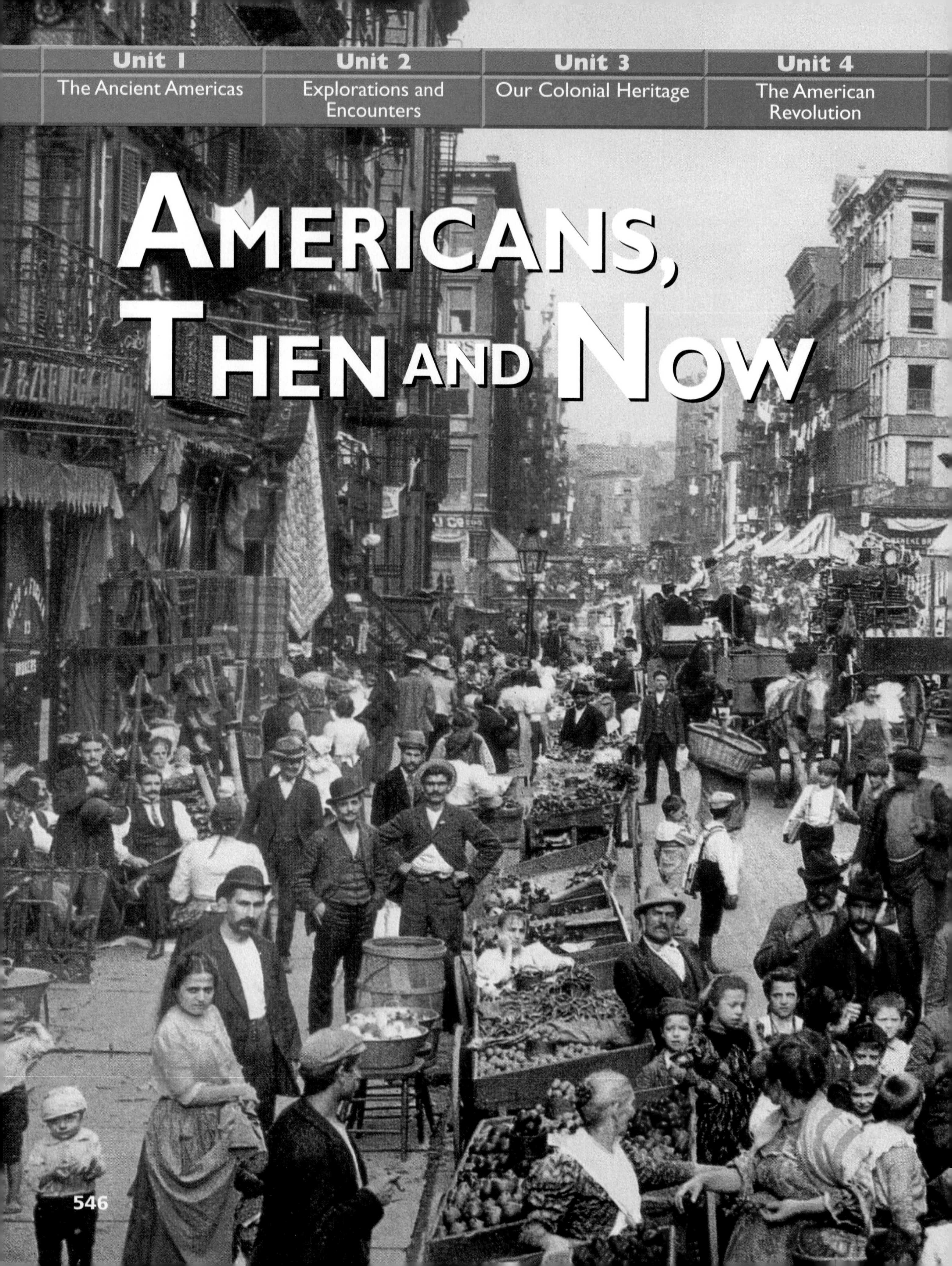

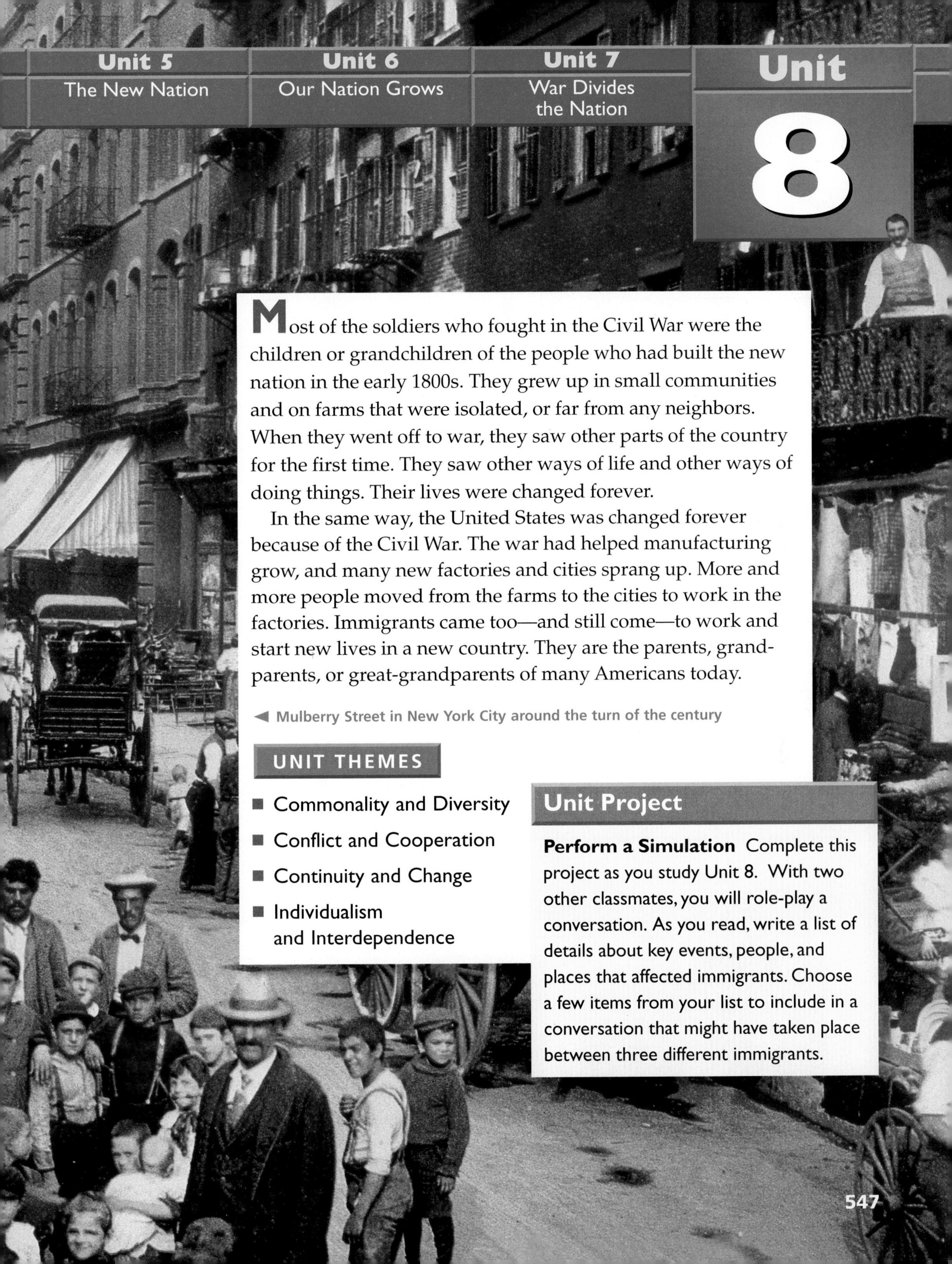

Most of the soldiers who fought in the Civil War were the children or grandchildren of the people who had built the new nation in the early 1800s. They grew up in small communities and on farms that were isolated, or far from any neighbors. When they went off to war, they saw other parts of the country for the first time. They saw other ways of life and other ways of doing things. Their lives were changed forever.

In the same way, the United States was changed forever because of the Civil War. The war had helped manufacturing grow, and many new factories and cities sprang up. More and more people moved from the farms to the cities to work in the factories. Immigrants came too—and still come—to work and start new lives in a new country. They are the parents, grand-parents, or great-grandparents of many Americans today.

◀ Mulberry Street in New York City around the turn of the century

UNIT THEMES

■ Commonality and Diversity

■ Conflict and Cooperation

■ Continuity and Change

■ Individualism and Interdependence

Unit Project

Perform a Simulation Complete this project as you study Unit 8. With two other classmates, you will role-play a conversation. As you read, write a list of details about key events, people, and places that affected immigrants. Choose a few items from your list to include in a conversation that might have taken place between three different immigrants.

547

RUSSIA

ARCTIC OCEAN

ALASKA
1959

CANADA

Anchorage

Bering Sea

Aleutian Islands

PACIFIC OCEAN

0   200   400 Miles
0   200   400 Kilometers

PACIFIC OCEAN

0   250   500 Miles
0   250   500 Kilometers
Albers Equal-Area Projection

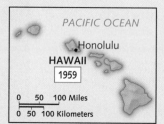

PACIFIC OCEAN

Honolulu

HAWAII
1959

0   50   100 Miles
0   50   100 Kilometers

Seattle
WA
1889

Portland

Columbia River

ROCKY

Helena

ID
1890

Boise

Snake River

OR
1859

San Francisco

NV
1864

Salt Lake City

UT
1896

CA
1850

Las Vegas

Colorado River

Los Angeles

San Diego

AZ
1912

Phoenix

Tucson

	Settled by 1850
	Settled by 1870
	Settled by 1890
	Settled after 1890
1787	Year of statehood
——	Present-day border

1850

1900

LATE **1800s**
New Inventions
PAGE 562

LATE **1800s**
New Immigrants
PAGE 583

EARLY **1900s**
African American Migration
PAGE 592

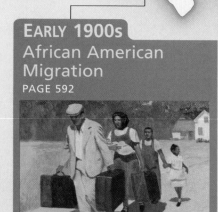

Settlement of the United States, 1850–Present

CANADA

ATLANTIC OCEAN

MEXICO

Gulf of Mexico

State	Year
MT	1889
ND	1889
SD	1889
WY	1890
NE	1867
MN	1858
WI	1848
MI	1837
IA	1846
KS	1861
CO	1876
IL	1818
IN	1816
OH	1803
MO	1821
KY	1792
TN	1796
AR	1836
OK	1907
NM	1912
TX	1845
LA	1812
MS	1817
AL	1819
GA	1788
SC	1788
NC	1789
VA	1788
WV	1863
PA	1787
NY	1788
NJ	1787
DE	1787
MD	1788
ME	1820
VT	1791
NH	1788
MA	1788
RI	1790
CT	1788
FL	1845

Missouri River, Great Plains, Rocky Mountains, Lake Superior, Lake Huron, Lake Michigan, Lake Ontario, Lake Erie, Appalachian Mountains, Platte River, Arkansas River, Missouri River, Mississippi River, Ohio River, Tennessee River, Rio Grande

Fargo, St. Paul, Minneapolis, Sioux Falls, Cheyenne, Omaha, Des Moines, Milwaukee, Chicago, Detroit, Cleveland, Columbus, Pittsburgh, Denver, Topeka, Kansas City, St. Louis, Indianapolis, Cincinnati, Louisville, Charleston, Richmond, Norfolk, Santa Fe, Oklahoma City, Little Rock, Memphis, Charlotte, Dallas, Jackson, Birmingham, Atlanta, Charleston, Savannah, San Antonio, Houston, New Orleans, Jacksonville, Miami, Buffalo, Hartford, Newark, New York, Philadelphia, Baltimore, Washington, D.C., Burlington, Portland, Manchester, Boston, Providence

N E W S

1950 ——————————————— Present

1960s
Civil Rights Movement

PAGE 598

THE PRESENT
Sharing Responsibilities

PAGE 608

549

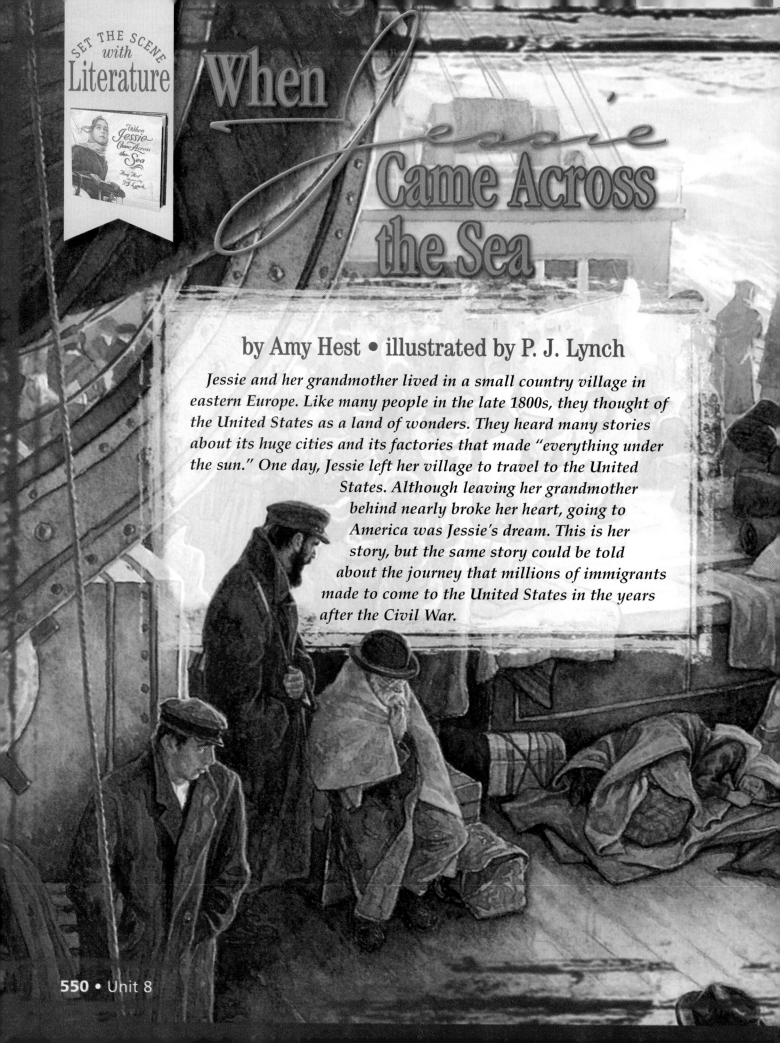

When Jessie Came Across the Sea

by Amy Hest • illustrated by P. J. Lynch

Jessie and her grandmother lived in a small country village in eastern Europe. Like many people in the late 1800s, they thought of the United States as a land of wonders. They heard many stories about its huge cities and its factories that made "everything under the sun." One day, Jessie left her village to travel to the United States. Although leaving her grandmother behind nearly broke her heart, going to America was Jessie's dream. This is her story, but the same story could be told about the journey that millions of immigrants made to come to the United States in the years after the Civil War.

The morning the ship was to sail, it rained so hard there was no telling where the sky met the sea. "America! Good things await you there," Grandmother had promised.

Jessie stood at the rail, holding her hat against the wind and the rain. At her feet was a small trunk, packed with a few simple clothes and layers of lace. In Jessie's pocket was the tiny silver box with a tiny lace lining, but her mother's wedding band was not inside.

"Keep it safe for me, Grandmother," she had whispered as they kissed good-bye.

"Grandmother!" she called. But the boat slipped away from the dock, then into the channel and on toward the sea. Umbrellas faded in the mist. Rain pelted Jessie's face. It slid down the back of her collar.

Later, she sat on her trunk and cried. Passengers pitied the girl with the auburn hair and ginger-colored

freckles. But what could they do? Crammed together and fearful, speaking strange languages, huddling close to keep warm, what could they do for Jessie?

The ship sailed west for many days.

At first it was stormy. Jessie lay curled on a mat, too ill to eat, too ill to sleep. She thought about Grandmother in the hut with the slanting roof, eating her soup alone.

On the fourth morning the sun came up and the passengers dried out. They played cards and sang, and sometimes they argued. But mostly they talked, swapping stories and dreams.

Dreams of America, where the streets were paved with gold. America, land of plenty.

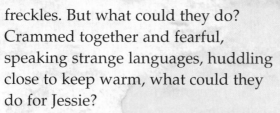

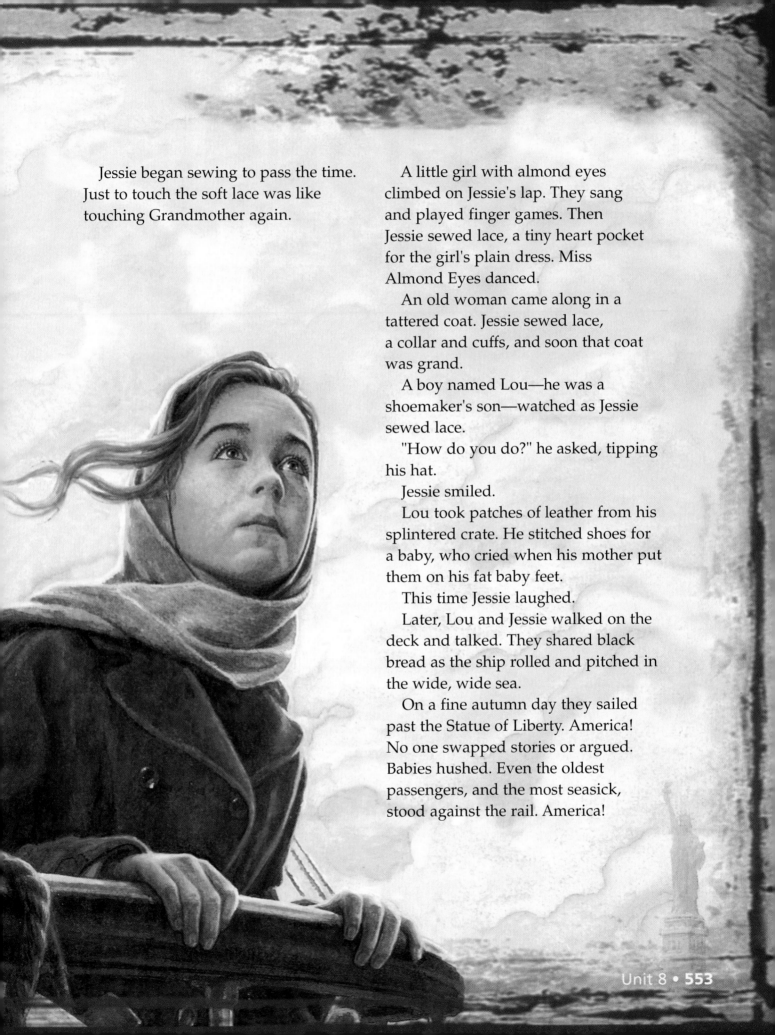

Jessie began sewing to pass the time. Just to touch the soft lace was like touching Grandmother again.

A little girl with almond eyes climbed on Jessie's lap. They sang and played finger games. Then Jessie sewed lace, a tiny heart pocket for the girl's plain dress. Miss Almond Eyes danced.

An old woman came along in a tattered coat. Jessie sewed lace, a collar and cuffs, and soon that coat was grand.

A boy named Lou—he was a shoemaker's son—watched as Jessie sewed lace.

"How do you do?" he asked, tipping his hat.

Jessie smiled.

Lou took patches of leather from his splintered crate. He stitched shoes for a baby, who cried when his mother put them on his fat baby feet.

This time Jessie laughed.

Later, Lou and Jessie walked on the deck and talked. They shared black bread as the ship rolled and pitched in the wide, wide sea.

On a fine autumn day they sailed past the Statue of Liberty. America! No one swapped stories or argued. Babies hushed. Even the oldest passengers, and the most seasick, stood against the rail. America!

A CHANGING AMERICA

"The conditions of human life have not only been changed, but revolutionized, within the past few hundred years."

Andrew Carnegie in an article titled "Wealth," June 1889, describing how life in America had changed

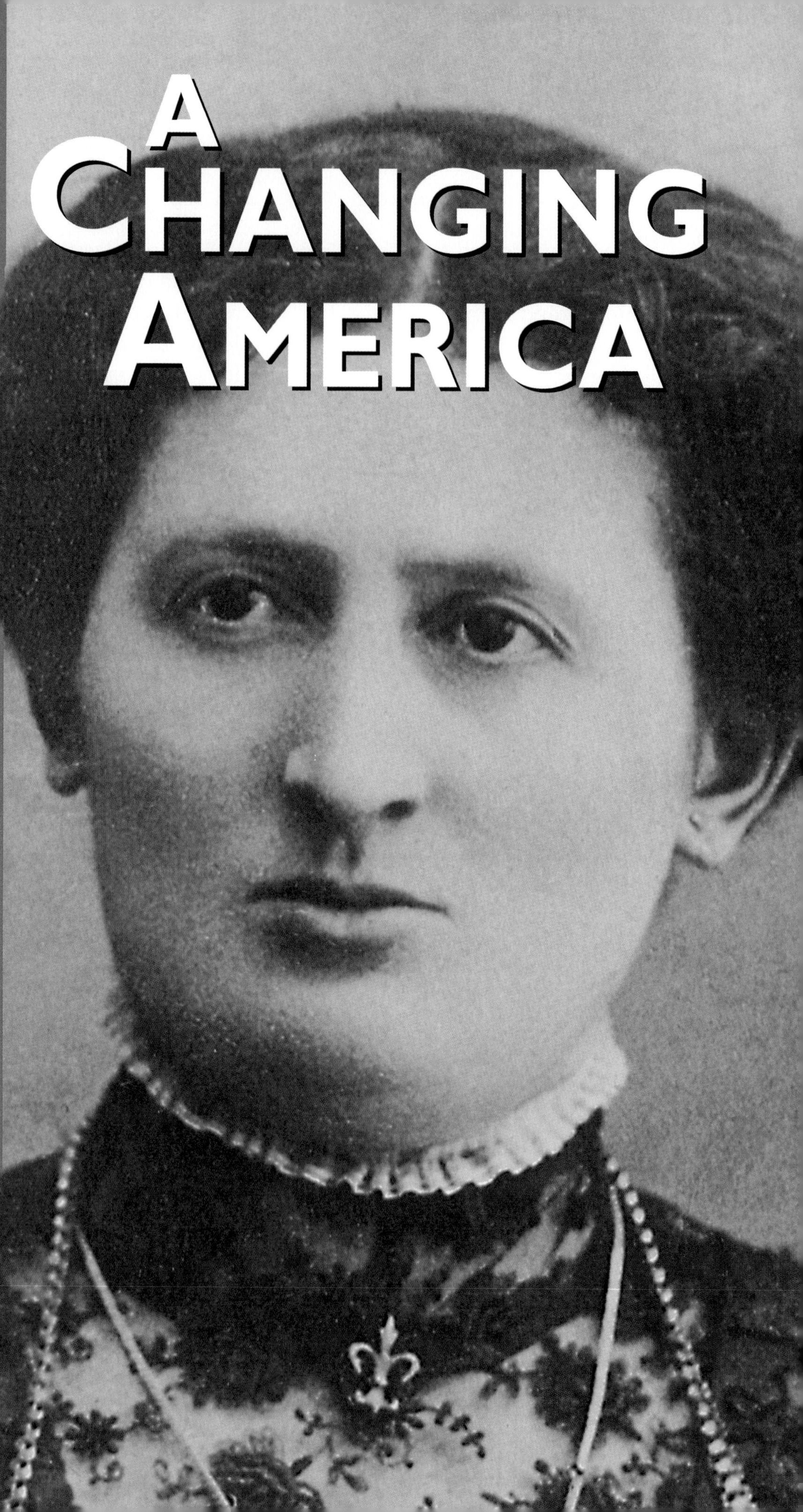

Bella Schonbach, an early immigrant worker

Big Business and Industrial Cities

1860	1875	1890

The Industrial Revolution came to the United States in the early 1800s. During this time, machines took the place of hand tools, and factories took the place of workshops. After the Civil War even greater changes happened in American industry. Inventors developed new technologies, and business owners had more freedom to run their businesses in new ways. It was an important time for **free enterprise**—an economic system in which people are able to start and run their own businesses with little control by the government.

New Technology, New Industries

When Abraham Lincoln ran for President in 1860, the Republican party promised that it would build a **transcontinental railroad**. This railroad would cross the continent, linking the Atlantic and Pacific coasts. When Lincoln was elected, he kept his party's promise. In 1862 Congress gave two companies the right to build the railroad. The government gave them land and loaned them money. Railroads had already been built from the Atlantic coast west to Nebraska. The Union Pacific built its railroad west from Omaha, Nebraska. The Central Pacific built east from Sacramento, California. On May 10, 1869, the two railroads met at Promontory, Utah.

The Union Pacific-Central Pacific was not the only railroad across the West for long. By the 1890s a total

FOCUS

How has new technology helped new industries grow today?

Main Idea   As you read, look for ways new technology helped new industries grow in the United States in the years after the Civil War.

Vocabulary

free enterprise
transcontinental
   railroad
entrepreneur
refinery

After a golden spike (above) was used to complete the first transcontinental railroad, the two railroad companies celebrated (below).

555

of four more railroads had been built from midwestern cities to the Pacific coast. Railroads in the East added to their systems, too. In 1860 the United States had just over 30,000 miles (48,000 km) of track. By 1900 it had more than 193,000 miles (311,000 km) of track.

One reason for the growth of railroads was the development of new inventions that improved rail transportation. George Westinghouse's air brake made trains safer by stopping the locomotive and all the cars at the same time. Inventor Granville T. Woods improved the air brake and developed a telegraph system that let trains and stations communicate with one another.

The early growth of railroads depended on iron tracks. As locomotives got bigger and heavier, however, iron tracks were no longer strong enough. They lasted only about three years. Steel tracks were harder and lasted longer, but steel cost a great deal to make. Steel is made from iron with small amounts of other metals added. Because of its cost, steel was used only for small items, such as knives and swords.

By the 1850s inventors in both Britain and the United States had developed a way to make steel more cheaply and easily. British inventor Henry Bessemer's process melted iron ore and other metals together in a new kind of "blast furnace." The higher heat of this furnace made the steel stronger.

In the early 1870s an American entrepreneur (ahn•truh•pruh•NER) named Andrew Carnegie visited Britain and saw the Bessemer process for the first time. An **entrepreneur** is a person who sets up a new business, taking a chance on making or losing money. After returning to the United States, Carnegie looked for investors to help him build a small steel mill near Pittsburgh,

---

LEARNING FROM DIAGRAMS The steps of the Bessemer process of making steel are ❶ air is heated in stove ❷ iron ore and carbon are poured into blast furnace ❸ heated air in furnace melts iron ore and carbon ❹ waste product pours out ❺ melted mixture, called pig iron, is collected ❻ pig iron is poured into Bessemer converter ❼ oxygen blown over pig iron, turning mixture into steel ❽ melted steel is poured into containers ❾ melted steel is poured into molds
■ *How does pig iron become steel?*

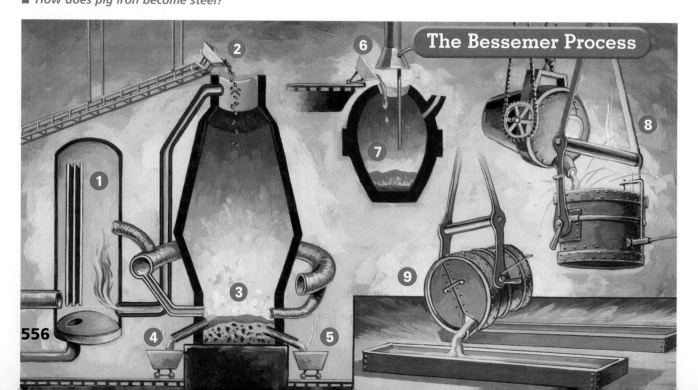

The Bessemer Process

The Telegraph

Just as railroad tracks carried people and goods across the country, the telegraph began carrying messages. An American inventor, Samuel F. B. Morse, experimented with sending electricity along iron wires during the 1830s. To send messages along the wires, Morse invented a code system in which dots and dashes stood for letters of the alphabet. The railroads saw how useful Morse code and the telegraph would be, and telegraph lines were soon strung from pole to pole along railroad tracks. The telegraph helped railroads run their trains safely and on time. It also carried news to every part of the country in minutes. News could now travel faster than people.

By tapping out messages on the telegraph people could communicate over long distances.

Pennsylvania. By the mid-1870s Carnegie was doing well in the steel industry. With his profits he built more steel mills and made even larger profits. Carnegie became one of the richest people in the world.

John D. Rockefeller saw that he also could become rich in business. Rockefeller was 24 years old in 1863 when he set up an oil refinery near Cleveland, Ohio. A **refinery** is a factory where crude, or raw, oil is made

LEARNING FROM GRAPHS Andrew Carnegie (left) helped the steel industry grow in the United States.
- *Between which years did steel production increase the most?*

LEARNING FROM GRAPHS John D. Rockefeller (right) controlled most of the oil business in the United States.
- *About how many barrels of oil were produced in 1890?*

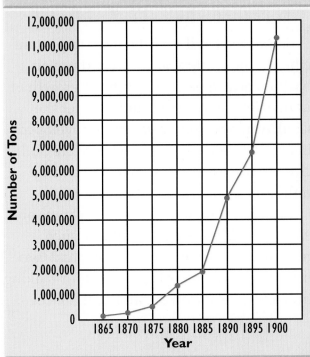

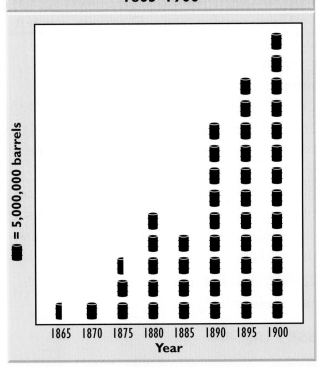

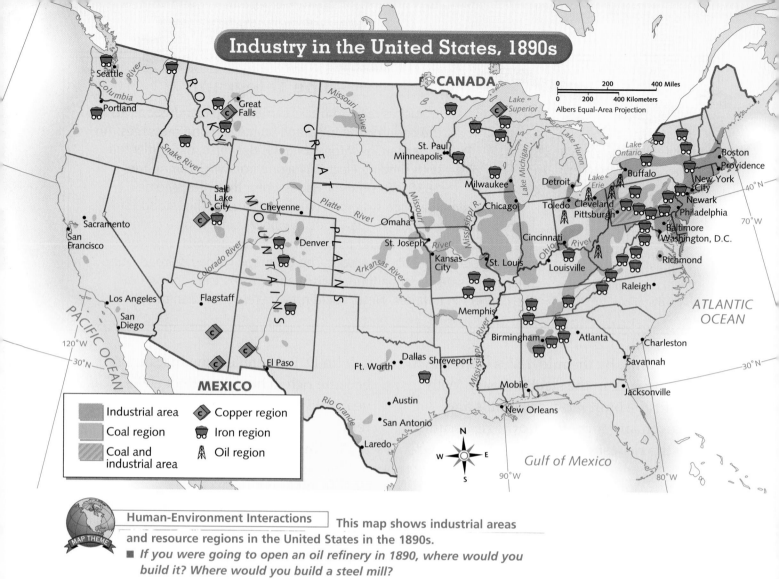

Industry in the United States, 1890s

Industrial area
Coal region
Coal and industrial area
Copper region
Iron region
Oil region

Human-Environment Interactions This map shows industrial areas and resource regions in the United States in the 1890s.

■ *If you were going to open an oil refinery in 1890, where would you build it? Where would you build a steel mill?*

into usable products. The first products made by Rockefeller's refinery were grease and kerosene for lamps. Electricity was not yet in use.

Many business people were building refineries because oil had been found in Ohio, Pennsylvania, and West Virginia. By 1870 Rockefeller had bought most of the other refineries in the Cleveland area. He joined them into one business, called the Standard Oil Company. After the invention of the gasoline engine, when automobiles came into use, the company produced gasoline and engine oil.

REVIEW *What new inventions helped the railroads grow?*

The New Industrial Cities

Before the Civil War the most important cities in the United States were those on harbors near the ocean. With the growth of industries such as steel and oil after the Civil War, new industrial cities developed inland, far from the coast. They were built close to the natural resources needed by mills and factories.

The region west of the Appalachians and east of the Mississippi had many such resources. Western Pennsylvania had two important raw materials needed for making iron and steel—iron ore and coal. Places such as Pittsburgh were among the first iron-and-steel centers in the North. Birmingham, Alabama, in the South, was close to iron and coal deposits, and also became an iron-and-steel center.

Iron ore deposits also were found in the hills of the Mesabi Range near Lake Superior. The ore was taken by barge across Lake Superior and on to Chicago and other cities on the Great Lakes. Trains brought coal from the Appalachian region to the same cities. With these resources, Chicago, Illinois; Gary, Indiana; Cleveland, Ohio; and Detroit, Michigan, became industrial centers.

Businesses that used iron and steel to make their products built factories near iron-and-steel centers. They depended on the railroads to bring in raw materials and to carry out finished products. Because of

Most of the new industrial cities were not on harbors. They depended on trains to bring in raw materials and to carry out finished products.

this, cities such as Chicago; Pittsburgh; St. Louis, Missouri; and Atlanta, Georgia, became railroad centers.

REVIEW *Why did inland cities become important in the late 1800s?*

LESSON 1 REVIEW

1860	•	•	1875	•	1890

1863
• Rockefeller sets up an oil refinery

1869
• The transcontinental railroad is completed

Early 1870s
• Carnegie sees the Bessemer process for the first time

Late 1800s
• New industrial cities develop inland

Check Understanding

1 **Remember the Facts**   Who were the important business leaders in the steel and oil industries?

2 **Recall the Main Idea**   How did new technology help new industries grow in the United States in the years after the Civil War?

Think Critically

3 **Past to Present**   What kinds of industries do you think are the most important in the United States today?

4 **Cause and Effect**   How did the location of natural resources affect the development of the new industrial cities?

Show What You Know

Mapping Activity   Draw a map of the United States. Using an atlas, label the cities that were connected by the western part of the transcontinental railroad. To get an idea of the path the railroad followed, draw a line to connect these cities.

Use a Time

1. Why Learn This Skill?

People have always used sun time, basing the time of day on the sun's position. Telling time by the sun was not a problem until people began to travel long distances. When railroads began to cross North America, no one knew what times to put on train schedules. So a new time system was developed. Knowing how to use this system is just as important today as it was during the late 1800s.

2. Time Zones

As the railroad industry grew, managers set schedules of times that trains would arrive at and depart from places along their routes. This was difficult to do because of the many time differences from place to place. No one knew whose time to use. Most railroads set their own time, called "railroad time." By the 1880s there were about 100 different railroad times. This was very confusing.

Finally, two men thought of a way to solve the problem. Charles Dowd of the United States and Sandford Fleming of Canada divided the world into time zones. A **time zone** is a region in which a single time is used.

A new time zone begins at every fifteenth meridian, starting at the prime meridian and moving west. In each new zone to the west, the time is one hour earlier than in the zone before it. All parts of a time zone use the same time. In the 1880s the railroads began to use this system. Today most of the countries in the world follow it.

The United States has six time zones. From east to west, they are the eastern, central, mountain, Pacific, Alaska, and Hawaii-Aleutian time zones.

3. Understand the Process

How can you figure out what time it is in different time zones? Following the steps in these examples can help you.

An accurate pocket watch (far right) was important to the engineer on a train (right). Time zones solved the problem of how to set the watch.

1834

Zone Map

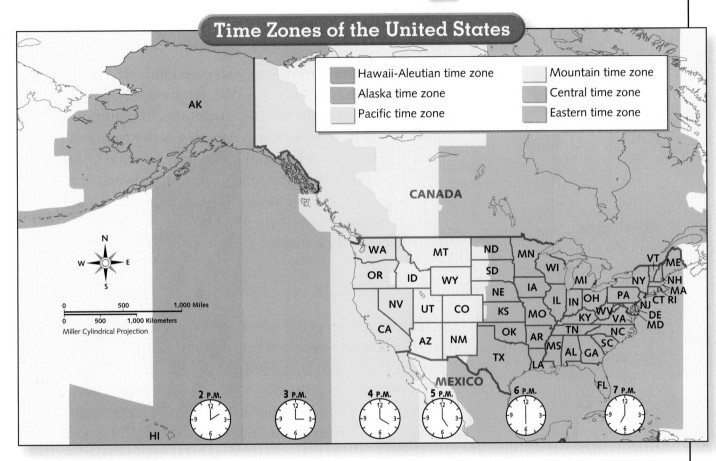

Time Zones of the United States

Hawaii-Aleutian time zone | Mountain time zone
Alaska time zone | Central time zone
Pacific time zone | Eastern time zone

AK

CANADA

N
W — E
S

0   500   1,000 Miles
0   500   1,000 Kilometers
Miller Cylindrical Projection

WA, MT, ND, MN, WI, VT, ME
OR, ID, WY, SD, MI, NY, NH, MA
NV, UT, CO, NE, IA, IL, IN, OH, PA, CT, RI
CA, AZ, NM, KS, MO, KY, WV, VA, NJ, DE, MD
OK, AR, TN, NC, SC
TX, MS, AL, GA
LA, FL

MEXICO

HI

2 P.M.   3 P.M.   4 P.M.   5 P.M.   6 P.M.   7 P.M.

1. Find Pennsylvania on the map in the eastern time zone. Now find California in the Pacific time zone. The time there is three hours earlier than in the eastern time zone. To find the time in California, subtract three hours from the time in Pennsylvania. When it is 7:00 P.M. in Pennsylvania, what time is it in California?

2. Locate Minnesota in the central time zone. The time there is four hours later than in the Hawaii-Aleutian time zone. To find the time in Minnesota, add four hours to the time in Hawaii. When it is 9:00 A.M. in Hawaii, what time is it in Minnesota?

4. Think and Apply

Find a world time zone map in an almanac or atlas. Suppose it is 9:00 A.M. where you live. Find the time in Tokyo, Japan, and in Cairo, Egypt. Describe how you figured out the time for each of these cities. Explain to your class when it would be helpful to know the time in different places.

MAP SKILLS

LESSON

2

FOCUS

How have new inventions changed your life?

Main Idea Read to learn how new inventions changed daily life in the United States in the years after the Civil War.

Vocabulary

assembly line
aviation
jazz

Thomas Edison (right) listens to his new invention, the talking machine. Edison also invented the first electric light bulb (above).

Inventions
Change Daily Life

1875	1890	1905

New inventions not only changed industry in the United States after the Civil War. They also changed the everyday lives of the people. Inventions that improved industry helped make life in America easier for many. Work that was once done by hand could now be done faster and with less difficulty using machinery. Faster ways of travel and new ways of communication saved people valuable time. New inventions helped many people have more free time to enjoy their lives.

New Inventions

The invention of the telephone by Alexander Graham Bell in 1876 started a revolution in communications. For the first time people could communicate over long distances using their own voices. This was a great improvement over the telegraph. In 1877 Thomas Edison carried the revolution even further with his invention of a talking machine. Edison's first phonograph, or machine that can record and play back sound, looked very different from the stereo systems that people use today.

This photograph shows one of Edison's early power stations in New York City. Power stations brought electricity to many homes and factories for the first time. They helped change the way people lived and worked.

It used a rotating metal cylinder to record sound. In the first recording, Edison recited "Mary Had a Little Lamb."

Edison's most important invention by far was the electric light bulb. Today it is hard to imagine our world without electric lights. The first electric light bulbs were called filament bulbs because of the way they worked. Electricity flowed through a thin piece of carbon—the filament—inside a glass bulb. The filament became so hot that it glowed with white light. Edison demonstrated the electric light bulb to the public for the first time in 1879 at his workshop in Menlo Park, New Jersey.

Edison next worked on making electric light available to more people. In 1881 he built the first power station in New York City. The power station could produce electricity and transport it by way of thick wires called power lines. Soon electricity was brought to many factories and homes. As Edison had more power stations built,

people depended less and less on lanterns and candlelight to see in the dark. Edison's power stations also made it easier for people to use other inventions that were powered by electricity.

In the mid-1800s many machines had been invented that helped people with housework. Treadle, or foot-powered, sewing machines reduced the time needed to make clothes. Washing machines that worked by turning a crank made washday easier. By the early 1900s, some people were using sewing machines and washing machines that were powered by electricity in their homes.

In September 1899 the Italian inventor Guglielmo Marconi (goo•LYEL•moh mar•KOH•nee) tried out a new invention to report on a sailing race while he was at sea. His reports of the race were the first use of radio in America. Twenty years later the first radio stations began broadcasting in Detroit and in Pittsburgh.

In the late 1800s the first automobiles came into use. The way people traveled on the ground changed forever. On July 4, 1894, Indiana inventor Elwood Haynes test-drove the first gasoline-powered automobile. By the 1920s United States automobile makers were making more than 3 million automobiles a year.

Leading the automobile industry was a Michigan man named Henry Ford. Ford had found a way to produce cars less expensively. His system of mass production used a moving **assembly line**. Instead of being built one at a time, Ford's cars were assembled, or put together, as they were moved past a line of workers. The assembly line cut the amount of time it took to make a car to less than 2 hours!

Soon traveling by air was made possible by brothers Orville and Wilbur Wright. They made the first flight in 1903 at Kitty Hawk, North Carolina. By the 1920s the first scheduled airlines were flying people from place to place. **Aviation**, or air transportation, became an important industry.

In 1927 Charles Lindbergh, an airmail pilot, became the first person to fly alone across the Atlantic Ocean. He flew from New York to Paris, France, in his plane named the *Spirit of St. Louis*. Lindbergh's flight helped make people more interested in air travel. Between 1926 and 1930 alone, the number of people traveling by airplane grew from about 6,000 to about 400,000.

REVIEW *How did Edison make electricity available to more people?*

Automobile Sales, 1920–1929

Year	
1920	🚗🚗🚗🚗
1921	🚗🚗🚗
1922	🚗🚗🚗🚗
1923	🚗🚗🚗🚗🚗🚗🚗
1924	🚗🚗🚗🚗🚗🚗
1925	🚗🚗🚗🚗🚗🚗🚗
1926	🚗🚗🚗🚗🚗🚗🚗
1927	🚗🚗🚗🚗🚗🚗
1928	🚗🚗🚗🚗🚗🚗🚗
1929	🚗🚗🚗🚗🚗🚗🚗🚗

🚗 = 500,000 automobiles

LEARNING FROM GRAPHS This graph shows the number of automobiles that were sold each year from 1920 to 1929.
■ *About how many automobiles were sold in 1920? in 1929? Why do you think automobile sales increased over the years?*

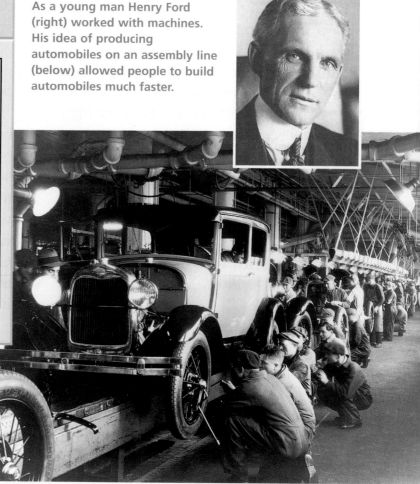

As a young man Henry Ford (right) worked with machines. His idea of producing automobiles on an assembly line (below) allowed people to build automobiles much faster.

Aviation

Aviation developed quickly after Charles Lindbergh's famous flight. By 1935 there were four major airlines making flights in the United States. One airline began to make regular flights to places outside the United States. Soon people all over the world were traveling by plane. By the late 1950s, airlines began using planes with jet engines that could fly much faster than propeller planes. In 1962 American Air Force Major Robert H. White flew a rocket plane that had a very powerful jet engine. He flew so high above the Earth that he became the first person to fly into space. Soon the United States and the Soviet Union were sending people up in rockets to explore space. In this country these people became known as astronauts. In 1969 astronauts from the United States took a rocket into space and landed on the moon for the first time. In the 1980s the United States started using space shuttles to send people up in space. Today American astronauts take space shuttles into space to explore and conduct experiments.

The Wright brothers' Flyer (left) takes off on the first airplane flight. The space shuttle (right) launches like a rocket but lands like an airplane.

Entertainment

In the late 1800s, improvements on Edison's phonograph helped start a new kind of entertainment. In 1887 a German immigrant named Emile Berliner (uh•MEEL BER•luhn•er) invented a phonograph that played flat discs, or records. Berliner's records reproduced better sound than Edison's cylinders. He also invented a practical way of manufacturing these records. By the late 1890s, several companies began mass-producing records that had recordings of popular music. By 1918 playing records at home became a popular form of entertainment. Phonographs allowed people to hear music that was being performed in other parts of the country and around the world.

The invention of the radio also helped bring entertainment into the homes of many Americans. Radio made

Louis Armstrong (seated at the piano) made records with his group, the Hot Five. His music helped jazz become popular. People could play his records on a phonograph or hear his music on the radio.

possible an audience of millions of people at one time. By 1929 more than 800 radio stations were reaching about 10 million families.

Listening to the radio, Americans could follow sports around the country. They could also hear a new kind of music called jazz. **Jazz** grew out of the African American musical heritage. This heritage was music brought from West Africa and spirituals sung by enslaved people in the United States. Jazz became so popular with Americans of all different backgrounds that some

have called the 1920s the Jazz Age. Popular performers of the time were trumpeter Louis Armstrong and bandleader Duke Ellington.

The development of the motion-picture camera in the 1890s by several inventors helped start the movie business. Most early movies re-created news events of the day to show the public what was happening in the world. In 1903 Thomas Edison's movie company made one of the

Records played on phonographs allowed people to hear music and other recordings from all over the world without leaving their homes.

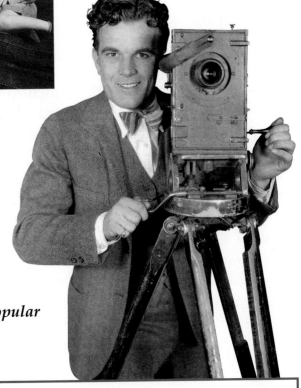

In the 1920s many families would gather around a radio (left) to hear music and other forms of entertainment. Nick Stuart (below), an actor in silent movies, poses with an early motion-picture camera.

first movies that told a story. It was a silent movie called *The Great Train Robbery*. By the 1920s silent movies made in Hollywood, California, became popular all over the world. By the late 1920s, many companies were making movies with sound. Several inventors were developing the television around this time. But it was not until the early 1950s that television started to become a popular form of home entertainment.

REVIEW *What kinds of entertainment became popular in the 1920s?*

LESSON 2 REVIEW

1875		1890	1905

1879
• Edison demonstrates the first light bulb

1899
• Marconi tests the first radio

1903
• The Wright brothers make the first flight

Check Understanding

1 Remember the Facts What new inventions brought about faster ways of communication?

2 Recall the Main Idea How did new inventions change daily life in the United States in the years after the Civil War?

Think Critically

3 Explore Viewpoints How do you think an inventor felt when an invention changed the way people lived?

4 Past to Present What kinds of entertainment do people still enjoy today as a result of inventions created in the late 1800s?

Show What You Know

Table Activity Make a table listing information about the inventors and inventions described in this lesson. Be sure to include information about how each invention changed daily life. Share your table with a classmate.

FOCUS

How do people today improve their working conditions?

Main Idea   Read to find out how people fought for better working conditions in the late 1800s and early 1900s.

Vocabulary

strike
labor union
federation
regulate

Growing Pains

1880	1890	1900

The growth of industry caused a need for more workers. People were needed to build railroads, mine coal, fire furnaces in steel mills, refine oil, and make machines and other products. Thousands of workers—many of them immigrants—moved to the industrial cities to fill these jobs.

Work in the Factories

Because there were so many people looking for work, factory owners were able to hire people willing to work for little pay, or low wages. As the years passed, the number of workers went up and wages went down. Soon many factory workers could no longer support their families on the low wages. They needed more money just to buy food and pay rent. To bring in the money they needed, many parents sent their children to work.

Between 1890 and 1910 the number of working children between the ages of 10 and 15 went from 1.5 million to 2 million. By 1910, almost one-fifth of the workers in the United States were children.

Many children no longer had time for school. They worked in factories all day, or in some cases all night. In

This photo shows men and women working in a clothing shop in New York City. People often had to work long hours for little pay.

1906 John Spargo, a reporter, described what he saw in one glassmaking factory.

66 The hours of labor for the 'night shift' were from 5:30 P.M. to 3:30 A.M. . . . Then began the work of . . . the 'carrying-in boys,' sometimes called 'carrier pigeons,' [who] took the red-hot bottles from the benches, three or four at a time. . . . The work of these 'carrying-in boys,' several of whom were less than twelve years old, was by far the hardest of all. They were kept on a slow run all the time from the benches to the annealing [finishing] oven . . . [the trip] was one hundred feet, and the boys made seventy-two trips per hour, making the distance traveled in eight hours nearly twenty-two miles. Over half of this distance the boys were carrying their hot loads to the oven. The pay of these boys varies from sixty cents to a dollar for eight hours' work. 99

Workers of all ages had another problem, too—machines that were unsafe. Hundreds of workers were killed each year in factory accidents, and thousands more were badly hurt.

REVIEW *What problems did working children face?*

These boys worked in a coal mine. Young mine workers were often sent to parts of the mine that were too small for adults to crawl through.

Some employers saved money by hiring children, because they could be paid much less than adults. The children shown in this photograph are working in a textile mill.

Owners Against Workers

Some workers complained about their working conditions. Others went on **strike**, or stopped work, as a way to get the factory owners to listen to them. Few factory owners did. They just fired the people who complained and then hired new workers. Plenty of people were still looking for jobs.

As conditions grew worse, some workers got together to form labor unions. A **labor union** is a group of workers who take action to improve their working conditions.

One early labor union leader was Samuel Gompers.

When Gompers was 13 years old, he went to work in a cigarmakers' shop. The cigarmakers worked from dawn until sunset. Most were paid only pennies an hour. Gompers joined a cigarmakers' union, and soon he was the union leader in his shop. In 1877 Gompers helped bring all of the cigarmakers' unions together to form one large union. Members of the union went on strike because they wanted a shorter workday and better wages. The strike failed. The people who owned the cigarmakers' shops also owned many of the apartment buildings where workers lived. They fired the striking workers and put them out of their apartments.

Samuel Gompers, a British immigrant of Dutch and Jewish heritage, helped form the American Federation of Labor.

After this experience Gompers decided that cigarmakers needed the support of other workers to make the labor union stronger. So he asked other workers to join his union. He believed that only skilled workers should be in this group. If skilled workers went on strike, it would be hard to replace them. A strike might then have a better chance of success. Gompers and other leaders organized groups of carpenters, plumbers, and bricklayers to join with the cigarmakers in one large federation. A **federation** is an organization made up of many related groups.

In 1886 Samuel Gompers helped form the American Federation of Labor, or AFL. As the AFL got larger, business leaders began to listen to its representatives. The AFL asked for higher wages and a shorter workday. Workers sang,

> 66 Eight hours for work,
> eight hours for rest,
> eight hours for what we will. 99

The AFL also wanted better working conditions, accident insurance, and an end to child labor. The insurance would pay the wages and medical bills for workers who were hurt on the job.

REVIEW *What were the goals of the American Federation of Labor?*

Labor Unions and Strikes

Going on strike became the labor unions' most important way to be heard by the factory owners. Sometimes, however, strikes became violent. Violence did not help the unions. In fact, some labor unions lost their power as a result.

One of the demands of these New York City clothing workers was an eight-hour workday. Many of the workers in this photograph were immigrants and carried signs in their own languages, including Italian, Yiddish, and Russian.

In 1886 workers belonging to a labor union known as the Knights of Labor went on strike against the McCormick Harvesting Machine Company. The union demanded higher wages and an eight-hour workday. During one protest meeting, strikers fought with police at Haymarket Square in Chicago. When someone threw a bomb, seven police officers were killed and many other people were hurt. Police did not find out who threw the bomb, but people blamed the labor union. The Knights of Labor lost many of its members.

One of the most violent strikes during this time took place in 1892 at a Carnegie steel mill in the town of Homestead, Pennsylvania, near Pittsburgh. While Andrew Carnegie was in Scotland, one of his managers, Henry Clay Frick, announced a pay cut. In June the workers went on strike. Frick fought back. He shut down the mill and hired private police from the Pinkerton National Detective Agency to protect it.

When 300 Pinkertons, as Pinkerton agents were called, arrived in Homestead, they were met by hundreds of angry union workers. A fight broke out, and 7 Pinkertons and 9 strikers were killed. The governor of Pennsylvania sent in soldiers from the National Guard to keep order.

The Homestead strike went on for more than four months. Finally the union gave up. Frick won, but many people began to think that factory owners should listen to labor unions' demands.

REVIEW *What caused the Homestead strike?*

Professional workers like bookkeepers and court stenographers also joined unions. These women are marching for fair treatment in their workplaces.

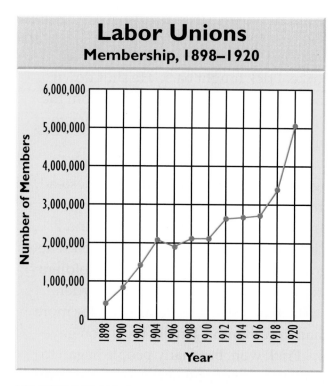

Labor Unions
Membership, 1898–1920

Number of Members / Year

LEARNING FROM GRAPHS This graph shows the number of workers who joined unions from 1898 to 1920.

■ *How did union membership change during this time?*

Government and Business

Workers went on strike in the hope of making their lives and working conditions better. But pay was still low, and many children still had to work. More and more workers were hurt in accidents every year. Workers hoped that the government would help, but many government leaders took the side of the factory owners.

Government leaders believed that business people helped make the country's economy strong by producing goods and creating new jobs. The leaders felt that the government should leave factory owners and their businesses alone. For industry to grow, they said, businesses had to be free to produce goods in the ways that were best for them.

Labor Day

In New York City on September 5, 1882, Americans held the first Labor Day parade. Matthew Maguire, a machine worker, and Peter McGuire, a carpenter and a founder of an early labor union, came up with the idea of Labor Day. It is a day intended to honor working people and to recognize their importance to the United States. In 1894 Congress made Labor Day a legal holiday. Today the United States and Canada celebrate Labor Day on the first Monday in September. Many other countries also have a special day to honor workers.

A Labor Day parade in the early 1900s

Business leaders also felt that the government should leave their companies alone. They did not want the government telling them how to run their own businesses. They feared that the government would then **regulate** their businesses, or control them with laws. Business owners wanted to be controlled by as few laws as possible. They wanted the government to have limited authority.

REVIEW *Why did the government choose to leave business owners alone?*

LESSON 3 REVIEW

1880	1890	1900

1886
• Gompers helps form the AFL
• The Knights of Labor go on strike

1892
• The Homestead steel mill workers go on strike

Check Understanding

1 Remember the Facts What were conditions like for factory workers during the late 1800s and early 1900s?

2 Recall the Main Idea How did people fight for better working conditions in the late 1800s and early 1900s?

Think Critically

3 Explore Viewpoints How do you think workers in the late 1800s felt about going on strike? How do you think business owners felt about strikes?

4 Personally Speaking Suppose you had been one of the young workers in the glassmaking factory that the reporter John Spargo described. How do you think you might have felt about your job?

Show What You Know

Art Activity Think about the problems factory workers faced in the late 1800s. Draw a poster that a labor union might have used to get people to join. Display your poster in the classroom.

FOCUS

What problems do people face in cities today?

Main Idea Read to learn about the problems people faced as cities grew larger, and how some people worked to solve them.

Vocabulary

tenement
settlement house
skyscraper

The Growth of Cities

1870	1880	1890

By the beginning of the twentieth century, cities in the United States were growing fast. Some people thought they were growing too fast. No one had expected it, and no one had planned for it. Millions of people were moving to American cities from farms, and millions more were coming from other countries. There were just too many people in one place. As cities grew, so did their problems.

City Problems

One city problem was that of overcrowded tenements. **Tenements** were poorly built apartment houses. When one person in a tenement became ill, disease spread through the tenement quickly. In one overcrowded Chicago tenement, three out of every five children born in 1900 died before they were three years old. A newspaper reporter named Jacob Riis (REES) described the same kind of poor living conditions in New York City tenements.

Riis saw that when someone died in a tenement, a ribbon tied into a bow was hung on the tenement door—black for an adult and white for a child. Riis wrote,

> 66 Listen! that short hacking cough, that tiny, helpless wail—what do they mean? They mean that the soiled bow of white you saw on the door downstairs will have another story to tell—Oh! a sadly familiar story—before the day is at an end. The child is dying with measles. With half a chance it might have lived; but it had none. 99

Insects and rats in the garbage spread the germs of illness. With so many people in the cities, garbage piled

Jacob Riis was a Danish immigrant whose photographs and newspaper articles helped improve living conditions in the cities.

This photograph of a family living in a crowded tenement apartment was taken by Jessie Tarbox Beals, the first woman to work as a news photographer.

up. At this time there was no regular garbage collection. Even in the largest cities, garbage was eaten by pigs in the streets.

The danger of fire became greater as new buildings went up. Most were made partly of wood. Terrible fires burned down whole city blocks. The Great Chicago Fire of 1871 was one of the worst. It burned for 24 hours, killing at least 300 people and leaving more than 90,000 people homeless. Few cities at that time had full-time fire departments.

Crime was another problem in cities. Because of the crowds, it was hard for the police to find lawbreakers. Sometimes a gang would take over an entire city neighborhood, and even the police would be afraid to go into it.

REVIEW *What problems faced many people who were living in cities?*

Help for the Cities' Poor

Some people who lived in cities tried to solve the problems they saw around them. Jane Addams was one of these people. Addams came from a wealthy family and had gone to college, something few women at that time were able to do. She worried about the growing problems of the tenements in Chicago.

While traveling in Britain, Addams had visited a place called Toynbee Hall. It was a **settlement house**, a community center where people could learn new

Crime became a problem in many places as cities grew. This police badge is from the city of Paterson, New Jersey.

Chapter 15 • **575**

Children in this New York City settlement house are attending a class. Settlement houses offered help for many people living in cities.

skills. Addams took the idea back to Chicago.

> ❝ It is hard to tell just when the very simple plan . . . began to form itself in my mind. . . . But I gradually became convinced that it would be a good thing to rent a house in a part of the city where many . . . needs are found. ❞

In 1889 Jane Addams started Hull House in Chicago with a friend, Ellen Gates Starr. The workers in the settlement house ran a kindergarten for children whose mothers worked. They taught classes in sewing, cooking, and the English language. Later they did other things to help people living in cities. They worked to improve living conditions in tenements and health and safety conditions in the mills and factories. They also tried to get laws passed to regulate child labor.

Hull House became a model for other community centers. In 1890 African American teacher Janie Porter Barrett founded a settlement house in Hampton,

Virginia. Three years later, Lillian Wald started the Henry Street Settlement in New York City. By 1900 almost 100 settlement houses had opened in American cities.

REVIEW *Why were settlement houses important to the cities?*

The Changing City

Even with their many problems, cities came to stand for much that was good in industrial America. Besides factories, stores, and tenements, cities had parks, theaters, and zoos that people could enjoy when they had free time. Cities also had schools, railroad stations, and tall office buildings.

Before this time buildings could not be taller than four or five stories because their walls were made only of bricks. The bricks on the bottom had to hold up the weight of all the bricks above them. In the 1880s an engineer named William Jenney found a way to build taller buildings. Jenney used steel frames to hold up a building the way a skeleton holds up a body. In 1885 Jenney finished building the ten-story Home Insurance Company Building in Chicago. It was the world's first tall steel-frame building, or **skyscraper**.

As buildings were made taller and taller—20 stories, then 50 stories, then 100 stories—fast, safe elevators were needed. The first electric elevator was put into a skyscraper in New York City in 1889.

As cities grew upward, they also grew outward. When the first cities were built in the United States, people walked to and from work. As people began moving away from the center of the city, transportation was needed to help them get to their jobs.

In 1865 most cities had streetcars pulled by horses. Horses could go only about

6 miles (9.7 km) an hour on flat ground, and each horse cost about $200—about the price of a car in today's money. In San Francisco the horses had to pull the cars up very steep hills. This was hard for the horses and slow for the passengers. An inventor named Andrew S. Hallidie worked on the

problem. In 1871 he invented the cable car. Cable cars ran on tracks and were attached to a steam-powered cable, or strong wire, that ran in a slot in the street. The cable pulled the cars at about 9 miles (14.5 km) an hour up and down steep hills. Fifteen cities put in cable cars. Chicago had 710 cable cars!

A Skyscraper

This photograph shows New York City's Flatiron Building in 1901.

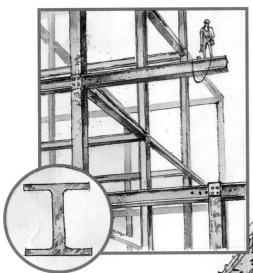

I-beams help make a skyscraper's steel frame very strong.

LEARNING FROM DIAGRAMS
This diagram shows an early skyscraper being built. Electric elevators like the one below were first put into skyscrapers.
■ *Why do you think skyscrapers need elevators?*

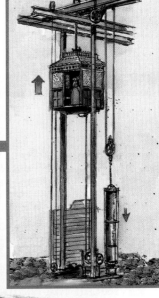

Streetcars were an important form of transportation in many cities. This streetcar had open sides that made it easy to board.

Then, in the late 1880s, Frank Sprague built an electric streetcar that was first used in Richmond, Virginia. His streetcar also ran on tracks, but it was powered by electricity rather than by steam. A small wheel on a trolley pole on top of the car rode along an overhead electric wire. The new streetcar was called a trolley car. By 1890 more than

50 cities in the United States had trolley transportation systems.

As more tracks were laid, people moved farther from the center of the city. They could ride the trolley cars to work in the city and live away from the inner city's problems. **REVIEW** *What inventions helped cities grow during the late 1800s?*

LESSON 4 REVIEW

1870	1880	1890
1871 • Hallidie invents the cable car	**1885** • Jenney builds the first skyscraper	**1889** • Jane Addams starts Hull House

Check Understanding

1 **Remember the Facts**   How did cities change in the late 1800s?

2 **Recall the Main Idea**   What problems did people face as cities grew larger, and how did some people work to solve them?

Think Critically

3 **Think More About It**   In what ways do you think Jane Addams was like the labor union leader Samuel Gompers? How were they different?

4 **Cause and Effect**   How did the inventions you read about in this lesson affect the way people lived in cities?

Show What You Know

TV Program Activity   With several classmates, prepare an outline for a TV program on life in the cities in the late 1800s. Write down topics for your program. Then list ideas for interviews, pictures, maps, charts, and graphs. Present your outline to your classmates.

Solve a Problem

1. Why Learn This Skill?

People everywhere face problems. Think about a problem you have faced. Were you able to solve it? Did you wish you could have found a better way to solve the problem? Knowing how to solve problems is a skill that you will use all your life.

2. Understand the Process

You have read about the many problems that made city life difficult in the late 1800s and early 1900s. Overcrowding, disease, fire, and crime were among the problems that people faced. Jane Addams was one person who tried to help. Think again about the problems Addams saw and the way she tried to solve them.

1 What problems did Jane Addams see in Chicago?

2 What solution did Addams learn about when she visited Toynbee Hall?

3 What did Addams decide was one of the best ways to solve the problems in Chicago?

4 How did Addams carry out her solution?

5 How did Addams's solution help solve the problems of city life?

You can use similar steps to help you solve problems.

- Identify the problem.
- Think of possible solutions.
- Compare the solutions, and choose the best one.
- Plan how to carry out the solution.
- Try your solution, and think about how well it solved the problem.

Jane Addams started Hull House (below) to help Chicago's immigrants. Addams (right, with a child at Hull House) was one of the country's best-known reformers.

3. Think and Apply

Identify a problem in your community or school. Write a plan for solving the problem. What solution did you choose? Do you think your solution will solve the problem? Explain your answer.

1865   1875

1869
• The transcontinental railroad is completed

CONNECT MAIN IDEAS

Use this organizer to show how the chapter's main ideas are connected. Complete the organizer by writing two or three sentences that summarize the main idea of each lesson. A copy of the organizer may be found on page 105 of the Activity Book.

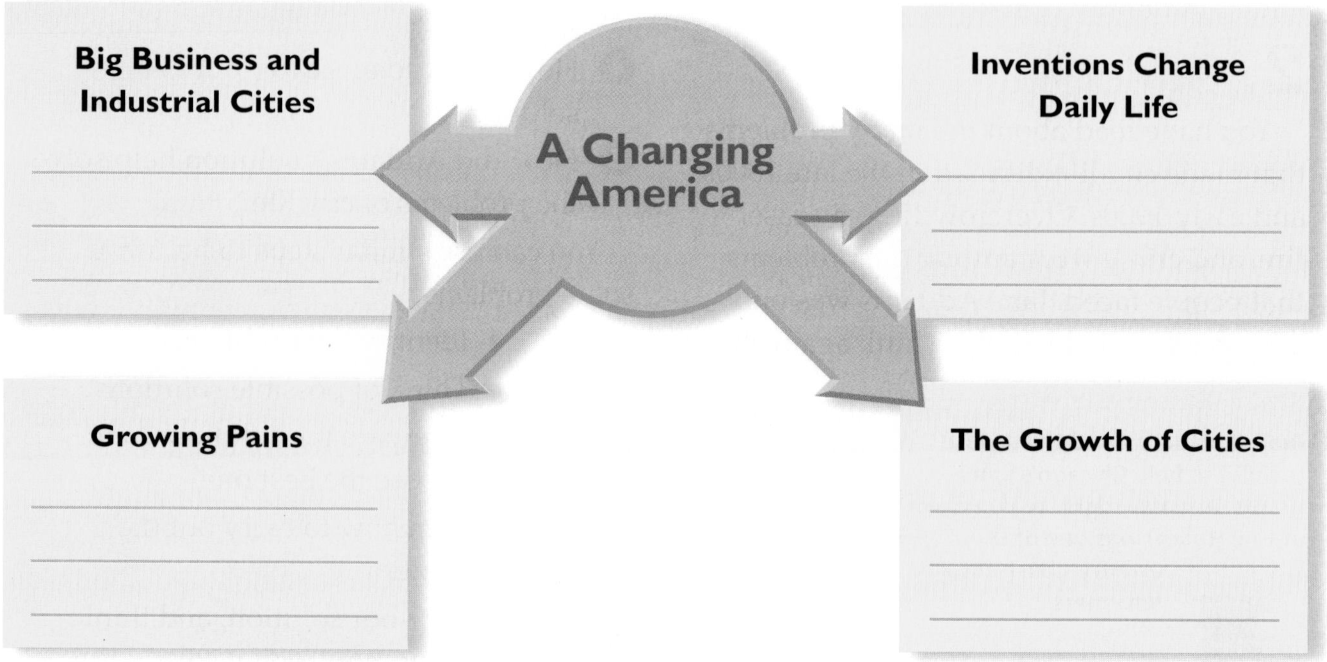

Big Business and Industrial Cities

_____

_____

_____

A Changing America

Inventions Change Daily Life

_____

_____

_____

Growing Pains

_____

_____

_____

The Growth of Cities

_____

_____

_____

WRITE MORE ABOUT IT

Write a Description Imagine that you have been asked to write a book about working conditions in the United States in the early 1900s. Describe what you see as you visit several factories.

Write a Letter Imagine that you are living in the early 1900s and have just moved from a farm to a city. Write a letter to a friend. Describe how life in the city is different from life on the farm.

1879
• Edison demonstrates the first light bulb

1886
• Samuel Gompers helps form the AFL

1889
• Jane Addams starts Hull House

1903
• The Wright brothers make the first flight

USE VOCABULARY

For each group of underlined words in the sentences, write the term from the list below that has the same meaning.

aviation   refinery

free enterprise   settlement house

labor union   skyscraper

1 The years after the Civil War were an important time for <u>an economic system in which people are able to start and run their own businesses with little control by the government</u>.

2 John D. Rockefeller was only 24 years old when he set up a <u>factory where crude, or raw, oil is made into usable products</u>.

3 By the 1920s <u>air transportation</u> became an important industry.

4 Some workers joined a <u>group of workers who take action to improve their working conditions</u>.

5 Poor people living in cities could get help at a <u>community center where people could learn new skills</u>.

6 William Jenney built the first <u>tall steel-frame building</u>.

CHECK UNDERSTANDING

7 What was the transcontinental railroad?

8 What is an entrepreneur?

9 What inventions brought new kinds of entertainment into people's homes?

10 Why did Samuel Gompers help form the AFL?

THINK CRITICALLY

11 **Personally Speaking** How would your life be different if the electric light bulb had never been invented?

12 **Explore Viewpoints** How do you think workers' views of labor unions might have differed from the views held by factory owners?

APPLY SKILLS

Use a Time Zone Map Use the time zone map on page 561 to answer these questions.

13 When it is 10:00 A.M. in Illinois, what time is it in Ohio?

14 If it is 5:00 P.M. in Maryland, what is the time in New Mexico?

Solve a Problem Identify a problem that a person you read about in this chapter faced. Use the steps listed on page 579 to write a plan that you think might help solve the problem.

READ MORE ABOUT IT

Flying to the Moon: An Astronaut's Story by Michael Collins. Farrar, Straus & Giroux. In this book, learn about space exploration from an astronaut's point of view.

HARCOURT BRACE

Visit the Internet at **http://www.hbschool.com** for additional resources.

Chapter 15 • **581**

CHAPTER

16 THE PROMISE OF AMERICA

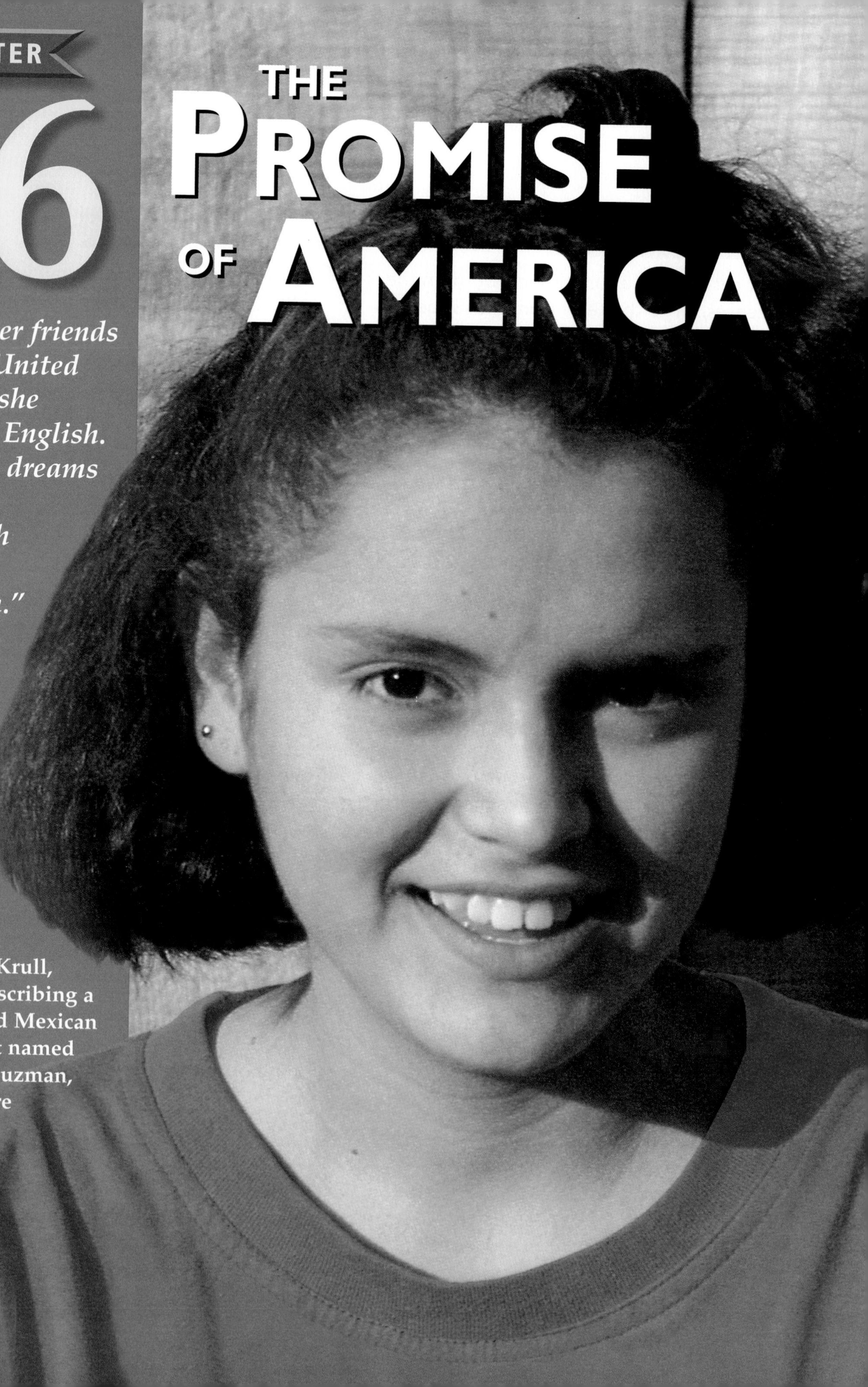

"With her friends in the United States she speaks English. . . . She dreams in both Spanish and English."

Kathleen Krull, author, describing a 12-year-old Mexican immigrant named Cinthya Guzman, shown here

New Immigrants

1850	1875	1900

FOCUS
What problems do immigrants to the United States face today?

Main Idea Read to learn about some of the problems that immigrants to the United States faced in the past.

Vocabulary
prejudice
barrio
naturalization

About three of every four workers in the Carnegie steel mills had been born outside the United States. Carnegie himself had been born in Scotland. When he was 12 years old, he had moved to the United States with his father. Between 1860 and 1910, about 23 million immigrants arrived in the United States. Those from Europe settled mostly in the cities in the East and in the growing industrial cities of the Middle West. Those from Asia and Latin America settled mostly in the West and Southwest. Latin America is made up of all the countries in the Americas south of the United States. Immigrants from all over the world played an important part in the growth of industry and agriculture in the United States.

European Immigrants

European immigrants were by far the largest group to come to the United States. Between 1890 and 1920, nearly 16 million immigrants arrived from countries in Europe.

Before 1890 most European immigrants had come from northern and western Europe. They had come from countries such as Britain, Ireland, Scotland, Germany, Norway, and Sweden. These were the immigrants who had helped build the Erie Canal and who had taken part in the great westward movement.

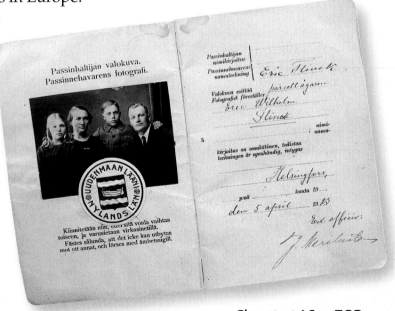

In the early 1900s, many countries required travelers to carry passports. This passport belonged to the Flinck family who immigrated to the United States from Sweden in 1923.

Most immigrants, like the members of this family, brought few belongings with them. They came to the United States hoping to find a better life.

Around 1890 a new period of immigration began. Some people still came from the countries of northern and western Europe, but now others also came from countries in southern and eastern Europe. They came from Italy, Greece, Poland, Austria, Hungary, Turkey, Armenia, and Russia. Many of these people were poor and unhappy in their homelands. Often they did not have enough to eat. They came to the United States hoping for a better life.

Most of the ships that brought European immigrants to the United States landed at Ellis Island in New York Bay. Many immigrants stayed in New York City. After a while some moved to the new industrial cities, where they hoped to find factory jobs. Many immigrants had lived on small farms in Europe, and they had hoped to buy land in the United States. But few had enough money to do that. Most lived with relatives or friends. Many lived in crowded tenements. Wages were so low that everyone in the family, even young children, had to work just to earn enough money for food.

Like other immigrants, the Europeans often met with prejudice. **Prejudice** is a negative feeling some people have against others because of their race or culture. Posters about jobs sometimes said things like "Irish need not apply." Some newcomers were even treated badly by immigrants who had arrived earlier. Immigrants who were already living and working in the United States worried that the new immigrants would take away their jobs.

REVIEW *From what parts of Europe did many immigrants come after 1890?*

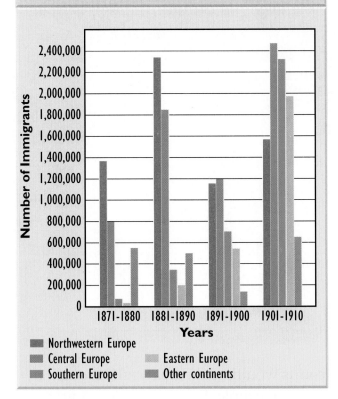

Immigration
to the United States, 1871–1910

Number of Immigrants

2,400,000
2,200,000
2,000,000
1,800,000
1,600,000
1,400,000
1,200,000
1,000,000
800,000
600,000
400,000
200,000
0

1871–1880   1881–1890   1891–1900   1901–1910

Years

- Northwestern Europe
- Central Europe
- Southern Europe
- Eastern Europe
- Other continents

LEARNING FROM GRAPHS The number of immigrants to the United States is shown on this graph for four different periods of time.
- *When were there more immigrants from eastern Europe than from northwestern Europe?*

Many Chinese immigrants, like those in this photograph, came to the United States after the California gold rush. When gold became hard to find, some found work in mining towns.

Asian Immigrants

Chinese people came to the United States in great numbers after the California gold rush of 1849. By 1852 about 25,000 Chinese had arrived in San Francisco and were working in the goldfields. Like other immigrant groups, the Chinese faced prejudice from some Americans. The Chinese had to pay a tax to pan for gold that no one else had to pay. Some Americans tried to force the Chinese out of the goldfields.

As less and less gold was found in the goldfields, the Chinese looked for other work. Because they wanted to stay in the United States, they worked for low wages. Some Chinese immigrants worked in mining and agriculture. Thousands worked for the Central Pacific Railroad to build the transcontinental railroad.

By the 1870s many Americans wanted to stop the Chinese from coming to the United States. They also wanted Chinese people who were already in the United States to go back to China. The Americans worried that the immigrants would take their jobs. California and other western states passed laws that made life harder for the Chinese. Chinese people could not get state jobs, and they had to pay higher state taxes. State

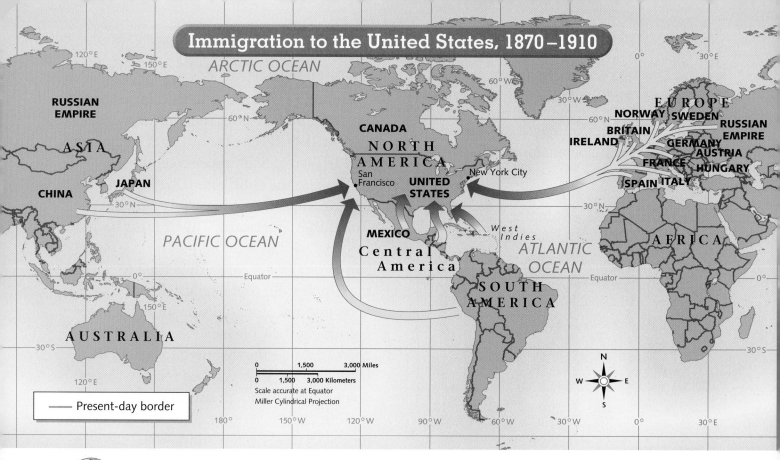

Immigration to the United States, 1870–1910

ARCTIC OCEAN

RUSSIAN EMPIRE

ASIA

JAPAN

CHINA

PACIFIC OCEAN

Equator

AUSTRALIA

CANADA

NORTH AMERICA

San Francisco

UNITED STATES

New York City

MEXICO

Central America

West Indies

SOUTH AMERICA

ATLANTIC OCEAN

Equator

EUROPE

NORWAY SWEDEN

BRITAIN RUSSIAN EMPIRE

IRELAND GERMANY AUSTRIA

FRANCE HUNGARY

SPAIN ITALY

AFRICA

Present-day border

0   1,500   3,000 Miles
0   1,500   3,000 Kilometers
Scale accurate at Equator
Miller Cylindrical Projection

N W E S

Regions This map shows the areas of the world where most immigrants to the United States were coming from between 1870 and 1910.

■ *From which countries did most Asian immigrants come to the United States?*

Many Asian immigrants, like these Japanese rice farmers, ran their own farms in California and in the Southwest.

courts would not hear lawsuits brought by Chinese people. Finally, in 1882, Congress passed a law that stopped all immigration by Chinese people for ten years. By this time there were about 75,000 Chinese immigrants living in the United States.

Japanese and other Asian people were still allowed to come to the United States. Most found jobs in agriculture. Many bought small farms in California and parts of the Southwest. Others helped build new railroads in California. Some people from India and the Philippine Islands came to get an education at American colleges and universities. In time Asian immigrants were again meeting with prejudice. By the early 1900s many Americans were calling for a stop to all immigration from Asia. But instead of putting a stop to it, the United States government passed laws to limit the number of immigrants from Asia.

REVIEW *Why did many Americans want to stop Asian immigration?*

Latin American Immigrants

During the late 1800s, immigrants from Latin America moved to many places in the United States to find jobs. By 1900 about 80,000 Mexicans had come to Texas, New Mexico, Arizona, and southern California. Immigrants from Cuba also came to the United States around this time. Some came to escape from the Spanish who were at war with Cuba in the late 1800s. Others came to find work in cigarmakers' shops. During the 1860s people from Chile and Peru settled in the western United States to mine for gold and silver. By 1900 more than 14,000 people from Central and South America had settled in the United States. Mexicans made up the largest group of immigrants that came from Latin America at this time.

Some Mexicans had lived in the southwestern part of the United States for years. Many lived in places that had been part of Mexico before the Treaty of Guadalupe Hidalgo, which ended the war between the United States and Mexico in 1848.

Like most other new immigrants to the United States, few Mexicans spoke English or knew people in the United States. Imagine how these immigrants must have felt when they met people from their homeland already living in the United States. Just to be able to talk with people in their own language made them feel more at home.

Soon barrios sprang up in most cities in the Southwest. A **barrio** is a neighborhood of Spanish-speaking people. People in the barrios helped one another. The immigrants who had been there longer helped the newcomers find homes and jobs. Many immigrants found jobs on farms. They spent up to 14 hours a day planting, weeding, and picking lettuce, tomatoes, and grapes. Others found factory jobs in the cities.

Like other immigrants, those from Mexico met with prejudice. Some people tried to make them go back to Mexico. In 1910 a writer for a Mexican newspaper wondered what made "our workingmen, so attached to the land, . . . abandon the country [Mexico], even at the risk of the Yankee contempt [lack of respect] with which they are treated on the other side of the Bravo [Rio Grande]."

REVIEW *How did living in the barrios help immigrants from Mexico?*

Some Mexican American families had lived in the United States for many years. This photograph shows five generations of the Aguilar family in Texas in 1902.

Becoming a Citizen

No matter how hard their lives were, many immigrants felt that becoming an American citizen was very important. Being a citizen meant taking part in the government, voting, and serving on juries. To many immigrants, these rights were something new.

Immigrants could become citizens through a process called **naturalization**. They had to live in the United States for five years and then pass a test. The test asked questions about the government and history of the United States, such as *Who makes the laws in the United States?* and *Who was the first President?*

The questions on the test had to be answered in English. Thousands of immigrants went to school after work so they could learn English to take the test. Those who passed the test pledged allegiance, or loyalty, to the United States.

> ❝ I pledge allegiance to the Flag of the United States of America, and to the Republic for which it stands, one Nation under God, indivisible, with liberty and justice for all. ❞

REVIEW *How did an immigrant become a citizen of the United States?*

Immigrant children came from many different cultures. This diversity is shown by these children (left) who were living in Gary, Indiana. The immigrants below are being sworn in as citizens of the United States.

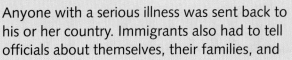

Angel Island and Ellis Island

In the late 1800s and early 1900s, Angel Island in San Francisco Bay and Ellis Island in New York Bay were the places where ships carrying immigrants landed in the United States. At the immigration stations on both islands, immigrants were checked for health problems.

Anyone with a serious illness was sent back to his or her country. Immigrants also had to tell officials about themselves, their families, and their job skills. Sometimes the names of immigrants were changed by mistake because the workers filling out their papers could not understand their languages.

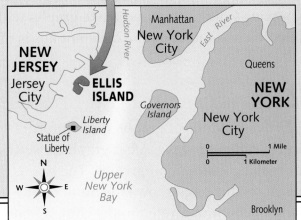

1850	1875	1900
1850s • Many Chinese immigrants come to the United States	**Late 1800s** • Many Latin Americans come to the United States	**1890s** • New immigrants from Europe come to the United States

Check Understanding

1 Remember the Facts   Why did immigrants come to the United States?

2 Recall the Main Idea   What problems did immigrants to the United States face in the past?

Think Critically

3 Personally Speaking   How might you feel if someone showed prejudice toward you?

4 Think More About It   Why was becoming an American citizen important to many immigrants?

Show What You Know

Writing Activity   Imagine that it is the late 1800s and you are an immigrant who has just arrived in the United States. You are looking for a job. Write a journal entry about what you might see and do.

Compare Information

1. Why Learn This Skill?

Suppose you want to prepare a report on immigration today. You want to show a lot of information in a brief, clear way. One way you might do this is by making graphs. Knowing how to read and make graphs will help you see and compare different kinds of information more easily.

2. Understand the Process

Different kinds of graphs show information in different ways. A bar graph is useful for making quick comparisons. The bar graph on this page shows the number of people who immigrated to the United States in 1996 from ten different countries around the world.

A circle graph compares amounts and makes it easy to see how much each part is of the whole. The circle graph on the next page compares the numbers of people who immigrated to the United States in 1996 from different regions of the world.

A line graph is used to show trends. The line graph on page 591 shows how the number of people immigrating to the United States has changed between the years 1900 and 1996.

Compare and contrast the information in the bar, circle, and line graphs by answering the following questions. As you do, think

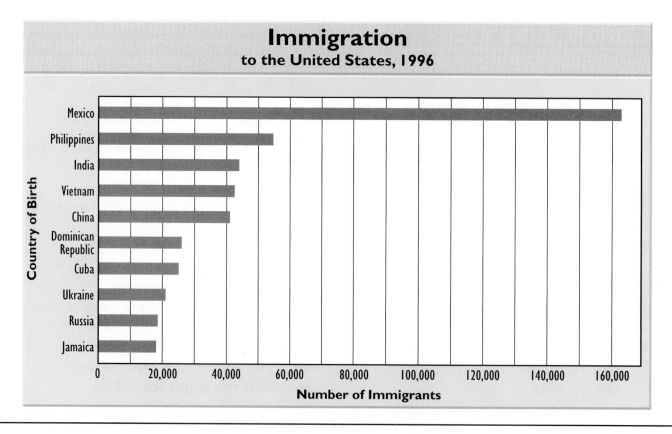

Immigration
to the United States, 1996

Country of Birth: Mexico, Philippines, India, Vietnam, China, Dominican Republic, Cuba, Ukraine, Russia, Jamaica

Number of Immigrants: 0, 20,000, 40,000, 60,000, 80,000, 100,000, 120,000, 140,000, 160,000

on Graphs

about why some graphs work better than others to show certain kinds of information.

1 Which graph or graphs would you use to find out how much the number of immigrants who came to the United States changed between 1920 and 1940? Explain your choice.

2 Which graph or graphs would you use to find out how many immigrants came from the Philippines in 1996? Explain your choice.

3 Which graph or graphs would you use to compare the numbers of people who immigrated from Latin America and Africa in 1996? Explain your choice.

4 Which graph or graphs would you use to find the years in which more than 250,000 people immigrated to the United States? Explain your choice.

5 Do you think that the information on the line graph could be better shown on a bar graph? Explain your answer.

6 Do you think that the information on the bar graph could be better shown on a circle graph? Explain your answer.

3. Think and Apply

Write a paragraph summarizing the information that the graphs show about immigration to the United States. Share your paragraph with a classmate, and compare your summaries.

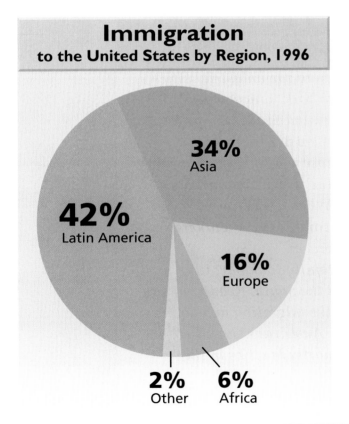

**Immigration
to the United States by Region, 1996**

- **34%** Asia
- **42%** Latin America
- **16%** Europe
- **2%** Other
- **6%** Africa

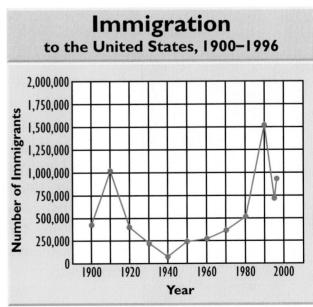

**Immigration
to the United States, 1900–1996**

THE GREAT MIGRATION

AN AMERICAN STORY

*story and paintings
by Jacob Lawrence*

Even as immigrants were moving to the United States from other countries, people within the United States were moving from place to place. This was true of many different groups of Americans, including African Americans.

After the Civil War, most African Americans in the South found jobs as workers on farms or as sharecroppers on plantations. Few moved into the cities. But between 1916 and 1919, many decided to move to the industrial cities in the North—to New York, Chicago, Detroit, Pittsburgh, Cleveland, and St. Louis. During these years workers were needed to take over the factory jobs of those who had left to fight in a war in Europe. The war would later be called World War I. When African Americans left their farms to become factory workers, their lives changed forever.

Jacob Lawrence's family took part in this great migration from the South. Read his story to learn more about the migration and about the problems African Americans shared with other newcomers to northern cities in the early 1900s.

Around the time I was born, many African-Americans from the South left home and traveled to cities in the North in search of a better life. My family was part of this great migration.

There was a shortage of workers in northern factories because many had left their jobs to fight in the First World War.

The factory owners had to find new workers to replace those who were marching off to war.

Northern industries offered southern blacks jobs as workers and lent them money, to be repaid later, for their railroad tickets. The northbound trains were packed with recruits.

Nature had ravaged the South. Floods ruined farms. The boll weevil destroyed cotton crops.

The war had doubled the cost of food, making life even harder for the poor.

Railroad stations were so crowded with migrants that guards were called in to keep order.

The flood of migrants northward left crops back home to dry and spoil.

For African-Americans the South was barren in many ways. There was no justice for them in the courts, and their lives were often in danger.

Although slavery had long been abolished, white landowners treated the black tenant farmers harshly and unfairly.

And so the migration grew.

Segregation divided the South.

The black newspapers told of better housing and jobs in the North.

Families would arrive very early at railroad stations to make sure they could get on the northbound trains.

Early arrival was not easy, because African-Americans found on the streets could be arrested for no reason.

And the migrants kept coming.

In the South there was little opportunity for education, and children labored in the fields. These were more reasons for people to move north, leaving some communities deserted.

There was much excitement and discussion about the great migration.

Agents from northern factories flocked into southern counties and towns, looking for laborers.

Families often gathered to discuss whether to go north or to stay south. The promise of better housing in the North could not be ignored.

The railroad stations were crowded with migrants.

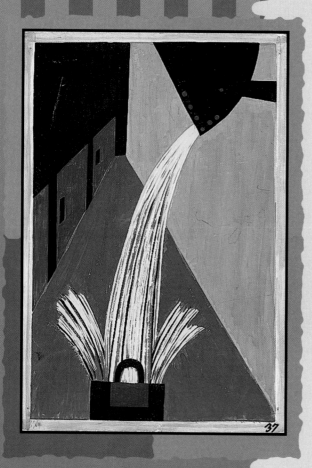

Letters from relatives in the North and articles in the black press portrayed a better life outside the South.

Many migrants arrived in Chicago.

In Chicago and other cities they labored in the steel mills . . . and on the railroads.

And the migrants kept coming.

Southern landowners, stripped of cheap labor, tried to stop the migration by jailing the labor agents and the migrants. Sometimes the agents disguised themselves to avoid arrest, but the migrants were often taken from railroad stations and jailed until the trains departed.

Black and white southern leaders met to discuss ways to improve conditions to stop the flow of workers north.

Although life in the North was better, it was not ideal.

Many migrants moved to Pittsburgh, which was a great industrial center at the time.

Although they were promised better housing in the North, some families were forced to live in overcrowded and unhealthy quarters.

The migrants soon learned that segregation was not confined to the South.

Many northern workers were angry because they had to compete with the migrants for housing and jobs. There were riots.

Longtime African-American residents living in the North did not welcome the newcomers from the South and often treated them with disdain.

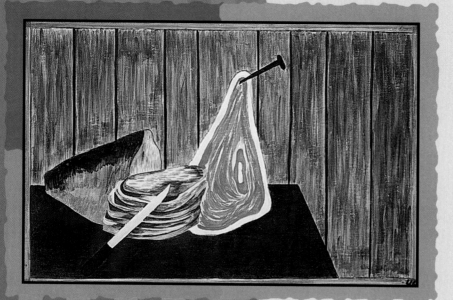

The migrants had to rely on each other. The storefront church was a welcoming place and the center of their lives, in joy and in sorrow.

Black professionals, such as doctors and lawyers, soon followed their patients and clients north. Female workers were among the last to leave.

Life in the North brought many challenges, but the migrants' lives had changed for the better. The children were able to go to school, and their parents gained the freedom to vote.

And the migrants kept coming.

Theirs is a story of African-American strength and courage. I share it now as my parents told it to me, because their struggles and triumphs ring true today. People all over the world are still on the move, trying to build better lives for themselves and for their families.

LITERATURE REVIEW

1. What events and problems caused Jacob Lawrence's family to move to the North?

2. What problems did African Americans share with other newcomers to northern cities in the early 1900s?

3. Imagine that you are an African American who has moved to the North during the time of World War I. Write a letter to Jacob Lawrence's family describing how life in the North is different from life in the South.

FOCUS
How do individuals today work to improve life in the United States?

Main Idea As you read, look for ways individuals worked to improve life in the United States in the twentieth century.

Vocabulary
civil rights
nonviolence
integration

The Struggle for Equal Rights

| 1900 | 1925 | 1950 | 1975 |

All over the United States, African Americans faced the same problems of prejudice and economic hardship that the immigrants did. Most African Americans earned low wages. They were not hired for some kinds of jobs. In some places they were not allowed to go to the same parks, theaters, and schools that other Americans went to. In time a struggle to change these unfair ways began. It became known as the Civil Rights movement. **Civil rights** are the rights guaranteed to all citizens by the Constitution.

Washington and Du Bois

Two of the best-known African American leaders in the early 1900s were Booker T. Washington and W. E. B. Du Bois (doo•BOYS). Each worked in a different way to solve the problems of prejudice and economic hardship that African Americans faced.

Booker T. Washington was born into slavery. During Reconstruction, he saw for himself how hard it was for people to fight prejudice. He believed that African Americans could get fair treatment only by becoming skilled workers. With training, they could earn more money and improve their lives. To provide that training, Washington founded Tuskegee Institute, a trade school for African Americans, in Alabama.

William Edward Burghardt Du Bois, known as W. E. B. Du Bois, was a teacher and a writer. He believed that the problems of prejudice and economic hardship would not be solved until African

Booker T. Washington improved the lives of many African Americans by providing them with training that helped them find better jobs.

African American scientist George Washington Carver (above, standing at center) taught science skills to students at Tuskegee Institute. W. E. B. Du Bois (left, standing at far right) is shown here in the office of *Crisis*, the NAACP magazine that he helped write and publish.

Americans were given their full civil rights. In 1909 Du Bois and other African American leaders formed the National Association for the Advancement of Colored People (NAACP). Members of the NAACP worked to change state laws that did not give full civil rights to African Americans.

Another group that worked for civil rights for African Americans was founded in 1910. This was the National Urban League, which worked to find jobs and homes for African Americans living in cities.

REVIEW *How did Washington and Du Bois help fight prejudice against African Americans in the early 1900s?*

A Court Ruling

For years the NAACP and the National Urban League continued their struggle to improve the lives of African Americans. By the 1950s the NAACP had won several court cases that helped change state laws and helped protect civil rights for African Americans. One case that turned out well was about an incident that took place in the state of Kansas.

Seven-year-old Linda Brown of Topeka wanted to go to school with the other children in her neighborhood. She did not understand why African Americans and other Americans had to go to separate schools. Federal laws said this segregation, or separation of the races, was all right as long as the separate schools were equal. Most often, however, they were not.

Thirteen African American families, among them Linda Brown's, decided to try to get these laws changed. The NAACP agreed to help them. One of its lawyers, Thurgood Marshall, presented the case before the United States Supreme Court. Marshall argued that separate schools did not provide equal education.

In 1954 the Supreme Court made a very important decision that supported what Thurgood Marshall had said. Chief Justice Earl Warren said, "In the field of education the doctrine [idea] of 'separate but equal' has no place." The Court ordered an end to segregation in public schools. However, many states were slow to obey that order. Their schools and other public places remained segregated.

REVIEW *What did the Supreme Court say about segregation in public schools?*

The Montgomery Bus Boycott

On December 1, 1955, Rosa Parks of Montgomery, Alabama, got on a city bus and sat in the middle section. Under Alabama law, African Americans had to sit in the back. They could sit in the middle section only if the seats were not needed for white passengers.

As the bus filled up, the bus driver told Rosa Parks to give up her seat to a white

These lawyers (left)—(left to right) George Hayes, Thurgood Marshall, and James Nabrit—argued against school segregation. They are standing outside the Supreme Court Building just after the Court's decision to end segregation in public schools. Because of the Court's decision, the African American child in this public school in Virginia (above) no longer had to go to a separate school for African Americans.

Rosa Parks (left) is fingerprinted after her arrest for not moving to the back of the bus. During the 1956 bus boycott in Montgomery, a bus (below) is almost empty.

man. She refused. The bus driver called the police, and Parks was arrested and taken to jail.

Many African Americans were angry when they heard what had happened. They held a meeting and decided to show the bus company's owners how they felt. They knew the company needed the money from African Americans' bus fares. So they passed the word—"Don't take the bus on Monday." A bus boycott began.

One of the leaders of the protest was Martin Luther King, Jr., a young minister in Montgomery. For more than a year, King and other African Americans boycotted the buses. King said that by working together they could bring about change peacefully. At last the United States Supreme Court ruled that all public transportation companies had to end segregation.

King believed in using **nonviolence**, or peaceful ways, to bring change. He said that nonviolence would change people's minds

and hearts, while violence would only make matters worse. So, many African Americans protested segregation in other public places—lunch counters, bus stations, schools, and other public buildings—in nonviolent ways.

The protesters often used songs to tell their goals. They sang,

> 66 We shall overcome,
> We shall overcome,
> We shall overcome someday.
> Oh, deep in my heart, I do believe,
> We shall overcome someday. 99

REVIEW *What did the protesters hope the Montgomery bus boycott would do?*

Civil Rights Marches

Many African Americans looked to Martin Luther King, Jr., as their leader in the fight against segregation and for civil rights. In April 1963 King led marches in Birmingham, Alabama. The marchers wanted an end to all segregation. They called for **integration**, or the bringing together of people of all races in education, jobs, and housing.

For eight days there were marches. Many of the marchers were arrested, and King was one of those taken to jail. While he was

in jail, he wrote, "We know through painful experience that freedom is never voluntarily given. . . . It must be demanded."

Later that year a crowd of about 250,000, including many white people, gathered for a march in Washington, D.C. The marchers were showing their support for a new civil rights law that President Kennedy had asked the United States Congress to pass. As the marchers assembled in front of the Lincoln Memorial, Martin Luther King, Jr., spoke to them of his hopes. He said,

> 66 I have a dream that my four little children will one day live in a nation where they will not be judged by the color of their skin but by the content of their character. 99

In 1964 Congress passed the new civil rights law. The Civil Rights Act of 1964 made segregation in public places illegal. It also said that people of all races should have equal job opportunities.

REVIEW *What was the importance of the Civil Rights Act of 1964?*

Working for Change

In 1964 Martin Luther King, Jr., received the Nobel Peace Prize. He won the award for his use of nonviolent ways to bring about change. Not all African American leaders shared King's belief in nonviolent protest, however. One of them, Malcolm X, wanted change to happen faster.

Malcolm X was named Malcolm Little when he was born. He changed his last name to X to stand for the unknown African name his family had lost through slavery.

Malcolm X was a member of the Nation of Islam, or the Black Muslims. In his early

---

HERITAGE

Martin Luther King, Jr. Federal Holiday

Dr. Martin Luther King, Jr., was born on January 15, 1929, in Atlanta, Georgia. With the Montgomery bus boycott, he became a leader of the Civil Rights movement. He worked tirelessly for racial justice, despite many arrests and many threats on his life. On April 4, 1968, King was assassinated. Just four days later, people in Congress began working to make his birthday a federal holiday. But it was 1983 before a law was signed making the third Monday in January Martin Luther King, Jr., Day. The holiday was first held on January 20, 1986. Today people celebrate the day with parades and other events. The special activities help them think about how they can keep alive King's dream of equality, justice, and peace.

Proud of his African heritage, Malcolm X visited Egypt in 1964.

speeches he called for a complete separation between white people and black people. Only in this way, he said, could African Americans truly be free. Malcolm X believed that freedom should be brought about "by any means necessary." Later, after a trip to the Islamic holy city of Mecca in April 1964, he talked less about separation and more about cooperation among groups.

Malcolm X had little time to act on his ideas. In February 1965 he was assassinated.

Then, in April 1968, Martin Luther King, Jr., also was assassinated.

Even though they had lost two important leaders, African Americans continued to work for change. Civil rights workers helped African Americans register to vote so they could bring about change that way. By 1968 more than half of those African Americans who were old enough to vote were registered voters.

REVIEW *How did Malcolm X's views change later in his life?*

Native Americans and Farm Workers Claim Their Rights

Following the lead of the African American Civil Rights movement, other groups of Americans began to work for change. They, too, wanted equal rights under the law.

In the late 1960s, many civil rights workers helped African Americans register to vote.

César Chávez (center) became a leader of labor organizations for farm workers. Chávez was still fighting for the rights of farm workers when he died in 1993.

were allowed to run businesses and health and education programs.

In the 1960s César Chávez organized a group that would become the United Farm Workers. Its members were mostly Mexican Americans. Like Martin Luther King, Jr., Chávez called for nonviolent action. In 1965 he called a strike of California grape pickers and started a boycott of grapes across the country. His goal was to get better wages for workers and to improve working conditions. In 1970 Chávez reached agreement with the growers and helped the workers gain more rights.

REVIEW *What did other groups of Americans such as the American Indian Movement want to achieve?*

American Indians formed groups to claim the rights that they had been guaranteed in earlier treaties with the federal government. Although the government had promised these rights, in many cases the treaties had not been honored. Groups such as the National Congress of American Indians, the National Tribal Chairman's Association, and the American Indian Movement (AIM) began to work for Indian rights. In 1975 the Indian Self-Determination and Educational Assistance Act was signed into law. For the first time Indian tribes

Betty Friedan (far right) marches with members of NOW.

The Women's Rights Movement

Although the Civil Rights Act of 1964 said that all people should have equal job opportunities, many jobs still were not open to women. When men and women did have the same kind of job, women were often paid less than men. In 1966 writer Betty

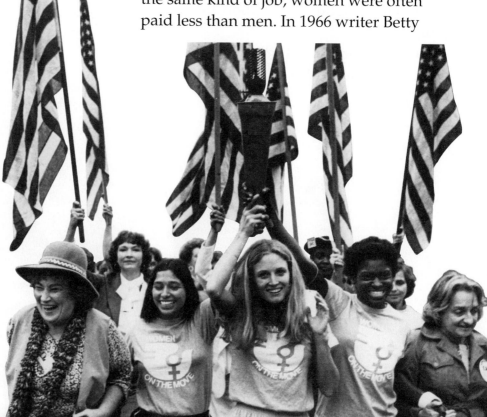

Friedan and others started the National Organization for Women, or NOW.

NOW and other women's rights groups helped elect many women to public office. They believed that these women would be able to get unfair laws changed.

By the 1970s new laws had been passed saying that employers must treat men and women equally. No job could be open to men only or women only. More women began careers in law, medicine, and business. Some became astronauts, construction workers, and firefighters. Others won elections and became members of Congress and mayors of cities. In 1981 Sandra Day O'Connor became the first woman to be appointed to the United States Supreme Court. In 1984 Geraldine Ferraro became the first woman to be nominated for Vice President by a major political party.

REVIEW *What rights had women gained by the 1970s?*

Women in the Labor Force, 1960–1990

(Graph: Number of Employed Women vs. Year. Y-axis ranges from 0 to 60,000,000 in increments of 10,000,000. X-axis years: 1960, 1970, 1980, 1990. Values rise from about 23,000,000 in 1960 to about 57,000,000 in 1990.)

LEARNING FROM GRAPHS This graph shows how the number of women who worked outside the home increased from 1960 to 1990.

■ *About how many more women were employed in 1990 than in 1960? About how many times as many were employed in 1990 than in 1960?*

LESSON 3 REVIEW

Timeline:
1900 — 1925 — 1950 — 1975

Early 1900s
• Washington and Du Bois work to improve African Americans' lives

1954
• The Supreme Court orders an end to segregation in public schools

1966
• Betty Friedan and others start NOW

Check Understanding

1 Remember the Facts Who were the main civil rights leaders in the United States during the twentieth century?

2 Recall the Main Idea How did individuals work to improve life in the United States in the twentieth century?

Think Critically

3 Think More About It Why is it important for everyone to be treated equally?

4 Past to Present What rights do people have today as a result of the struggles in the 1950s and 1960s?

Show What You Know

Simulation Activity
Imagine that it is 1963, and you are listening to Martin Luther King, Jr., speak in Washington, D.C. With a partner, role-play a conversation between you and another marcher. Discuss how you feel about King's speech.

Act as a Responsible Citizen

1. Why Learn This Skill?

Countries with governments that are democracies need responsible citizens. Citizens must know what is happening in their country, choose wise leaders, and take part in their government. When a country faces problems, its citizens may need to take action to solve those problems.

2. Understand the Process

You have read about the struggle for civil rights in the United States during the 1950s and 1960s. Many citizens took part in the Civil Rights movement, which won important rights for African Americans. Martin Luther King, Jr., was a leader of this movement. The peaceful protests he led caught the attention of people around the world. Many other citizens were also important in the Civil Rights movement. Hundreds of ordinary citizens took part. Many risked their lives as they worked to gain civil rights for all.

Acting as a responsible citizen is not always as difficult as it was for those who struggled for civil rights. It can be as simple as listening to the news or voting. It does, however, take both thought and action.

Civil rights workers followed these five steps to act as responsible citizens:

- They learned about the problems of prejudice and economic hardship in their country.
- They thought about what could be done to bring about change.

- They decided on the plans that would be good for the whole country.
- Each person decided how he or she could help best.
- People worked as individuals or with others to bring about change.

3. Think and Apply

Some acts of citizenship, such as voting, can be done only by adults. Other acts can be done by citizens of almost any age. The steps above can help anyone know how to act as a responsible citizen. Use the five steps as you decide on ways you and your classmates can act as responsible citizens of your community. Share your ideas with the class.

Many citizens marched with Martin Luther King, Jr., in the Civil Rights movement.

Americans Today

FOCUS

How do citizens in your community use their talents and skills to improve life in our nation today?

Main Idea   Read to learn how citizens of the United States contribute to their communities and our nation as a whole.

Vocabulary

descendant
volunteer

People have been coming to America since before history was recorded. Ancestors of Native American peoples may have been the first immigrants to come to what is now the United States. The next group of immigrants was the European settlers who came to America in the early days of exploration. Since that time many people have come—and still come—to the United States from every part of the world. Over the years the United States has become a country of many cultures.

Americans All

Today the population of the United States is more than 267 million people. About 195 million Americans are of European background. Over 32 million are African Americans, and more than 29 million are Hispanics. More than 9 million are of Asian background, and over 2 million are Native Americans. Over the years people from each culture have contributed to American life. Each group has made contributions in many different fields such as science, medicine, politics, and the arts.

Most people in the United States are either immigrants or descendants (di•SEN•duhnts) of immigrants. **Descendants** are children or grandchildren of an ancestor. Some people's families have been living in America for many years. Others have come to live in this country only recently. Some people who have immigrated to this country still speak the language of the country in which they were born. So do some of the descendants of immigrants. Some may still dress in the style of their homeland or take part in

Americans take pride in their diversity. The children in this photograph come from different cultures, but they are all Americans.

607

The American's Creed

The American's Creed, or set of beliefs, was written by William Tyler Page of Maryland. The American's Creed won a national writing contest in 1917. It names some of the responsibilities that American citizens must share to help protect the United States and keep the country running smoothly.

I believe in the United States of America as a government of the people, by the people, for the people; whose just powers are derived from the consent of the governed; a democracy in a Republic; a sovereign Nation of many sovereign States; a perfect Union, one and inseparable; established upon those principles of freedom, equality, justice, and humanity for which American patriots sacrificed their lives and fortunes.

I therefore believe it is my duty to my country to love it; to support its Constitution; to obey its laws; to respect its flag; and to defend it against all enemies.

The motto *e pluribus unum* can be found on all coins made in the United States.

customs or holidays that are unique to their culture.

We as people are alike in many ways. There are also many differences from person to person. The same is true for the different cultures that make up our nation. The motto *e pluribus unum*, which is Latin for "out of many, one," appears on all coins made in the United States. It helps define the American people and our nation as a whole. It has been used as a motto by the United States for over 200 years. Today we can relate the motto to the many people from different cultures in our nation that live together as one people.

REVIEW *How does the motto* **e pluribus unum** *describe the United States today?*

Sharing Rights and Responsibilities

Americans are a diverse group of people, but they also share many things. They live under the same laws, and they have the same national government and leaders. All citizens of the United States are guaranteed the rights listed in the Constitution. But with these rights come many responsibilities. With the right to vote comes the responsibility to vote. It is important that each citizen takes part in choosing our leaders and deciding on laws. With freedom of speech and freedom of the press comes the responsibility to know what is happening in the country. With all of these rights comes the responsibility to respect the rights of others.

Some responsibilities are stated in laws. Federal and state laws say that it is a citizen's responsibility to pay taxes, obey laws, and be loyal. Some people, however, also take on additional responsibilities that help make their communities better places to live. **Volunteers** (vah•luhn•TEERZ), or people who work without pay, help out in places such as schools, hospitals, senior citizen centers, and shelters for homeless people. Some volunteers take part in community cleanup projects. Volunteering to help a neighbor with yard work is a simple way to help make your community a better place to live.

REVIEW *What are some of the major responsibilities that citizens of the United States share?*

A teacher and students have volunteered to make their school grounds look more beautiful. They are planting flowers.

LESSON 4 REVIEW

Check Understanding

1 **Remember the Facts** What are some of the rights that citizens of the United States share?

2 **Recall the Main Idea** How do citizens of the United States contribute to their communities and our nation as a whole?

Think Critically

3 **Past to Present** What hopes do you think immigrants today share with immigrants of the past?

4 **Think More About It** Why do rights come with responsibilities?

5 **Personally Speaking** What are some things you can do to help improve your community?

Show What You Know

Research Activity The American's Creed on page 608 uses words and phrases from some of the nation's most important documents—the Declaration of Independence, the Preamble to the Constitution, and the Gettysburg Address. Read the American's Creed alongside the documents listed above and find out which phrases come from each document.

Late 1800s
• New immigrants from Europe, Asia, and Latin America come to the United States

Early 1900s
• Washington and Du Bois work to improve the lives of African Americans

CONNECT MAIN IDEAS

Use this organizer to show how the chapter's main ideas are connected. Write three details to support each main idea. A copy of the organizer may be found on page 112 of the Activity Book.

Immigrants in the United States faced problems.

1._____
2._____
3._____

The Promise of America

African Americans shared problems with other newcomers to cities.

1._____
2._____
3._____

Individuals worked to improve life in the United States in the twentieth century.

1._____
2._____
3._____

Citizens of the United States contribute to their communities and our nation as a whole.

1._____
2._____
3._____

WRITE MORE ABOUT IT

Write an Explanation Suppose that you are an immigrant who plans to become a citizen through naturalization. What would you tell someone who asks why you want to become a citizen? Write your response.

Write an Interview Imagine that you have been chosen to interview the President of the United States. Write a list of the questions you would ask about what citizens can do to improve their communities and the nation.

1925	1950	1975	Present

1954
• The Supreme Court orders an end to segregation in public schools

1970s
• New laws are passed saying that employers must treat men and women equally

1975
• The Indian Self-Determination and Educational Assistance Act is signed into law

USE VOCABULARY

Write a term from this list to complete each of the sentences that follow.

barrio	nonviolence
integration	prejudice
naturalization	volunteers

1 Immigrants often faced ____.

2 A ____ is a neighborhood of Spanish-speaking people.

3 Immigrants could become citizens through a process called ____.

4 Working for change using ____ was important to Martin Luther King, Jr.

5 The bringing together of all races in education, jobs, and housing is called ____.

6 ____ work without pay to make their communities a better place.

CHECK UNDERSTANDING

7 What regions of the world did new immigrants come from?

8 How were Angel Island and Ellis Island important to immigrants?

9 Why did many African Americans migrate to industrial cities in the North?

10 How did a Supreme Court decision in 1954 change public schools?

11 How did Martin Luther King, Jr., work to bring about change?

12 What is the American's Creed?

13 What responsibilities do some Americans take on to improve their communities?

THINK CRITICALLY

14 **Think More About It** Why do you think immigrants often moved to neighborhoods made up of other immigrants from their homeland?

15 **Explore Viewpoints** How were the views of Malcolm X different from the views of Martin Luther King, Jr.?

APPLY SKILLS

Compare Information on Graphs Use the graphs on pages 590–591 to answer this question.

16 Which graph or graphs would you use to compare the numbers of people that immigrated from India and Vietnam in 1996?

Act as a Responsible Citizen
Identify a person who you think acts like a responsible citizen. Write a paragraph telling why you think that person is acting responsibly.

READ MORE ABOUT IT

Sarah, Also Known As Hannah by Lillian Hammer Ross. Albert Whitman & Co. This is a true story about a young girl who immigrates to America from the Ukraine.

HARCOURT BRACE

Visit the Internet at **http://www.hbschool.com** for additional resources.

Chapter 16 • **611**

"Give me your tired, your poor, Your huddled masses yearning to breathe free..."

Coming to the United States Today

Since colonial times, people from all over the world have come to the Americas, many of them to the United States. Some chose to come to start new lives, sometimes because of hard times in their homelands.

In 1883 an American named Emma Lazarus wrote "The New Colossus," a poem that helped welcome the hundreds of thousands of people who were immigrating to the United States each year. The poem is written on the base of the Statue of Liberty, which stands in New York Bay. Part of it says

66 Give me your tired, your poor,
Your huddled masses yearning to
breathe free . . . 99

The Statue of Liberty and Lazarus's words continue to welcome the large numbers of immigrants who come to the United States today. The United States still attracts people from all over the world who hope to find better lives and greater freedom. The Statue of Liberty has become a well-known symbol of this freedom.

Think and Apply

Think about why people come to the United States today. Collect magazine and newspaper articles about present-day immigrants. Compare their reasons for moving with those of immigrants of the early twentieth century. Report your findings to the class.

BUILDING CITIZENSHIP

HARCOURT BRACE
Visit the Internet at
http://www.hbschool.com
for additional resources.

CNN Turner Le@rning
Check your media center or classroom video library for the Making Social Studies Relevant videotape of this feature.

UNIT 8 REVIEW

Summarize the Main Ideas
Study the pictures and captions to help you review the events you read about in Unit 8.

Write a Newspaper Article
Imagine that you are a newspaper reporter covering one of the events in this visual summary. Write an article describing the event.

1 After the Civil War, American industry grew and changed. The first transcontinental railroad was completed in 1869.

3 During the late 1800s and early 1900s, millions of immigrants came to the United States hoping to find better lives.

5 In 1963 Martin Luther King, Jr., spoke for civil rights to a large gathering of people in Washington, D.C.

2 Inventions helped industry grow. Some inventions, such as the light bulb, changed daily life.

4 Between 1916 and 1919, many African Americans in the South migrated to industrial cities in the North to find jobs in factories.

6 American citizens come from many different backgrounds. They all share the rights guaranteed in the Constitution, and the responsibilities that go with them.

USE VOCABULARY

Write the term that correctly matches each definition.

civil rights   jazz

entrepreneur   naturalization

1 a person who sets up a new business, taking a chance on making or losing money

2 a kind of music that grew out of the African American musical heritage

3 the process by which immigrants become American citizens

4 the rights guaranteed to all citizens by the Constitution

CHECK UNDERSTANDING

5 Why did Edison build power stations?

6 How did workers try to improve their working conditions in the late 1800s?

7 Why did many Latin American immigrants come to the United States during the late 1800s?

THINK CRITICALLY

8 **Past to Present** How do new inventions change the lives of people today like they did in the late 1800s?

9 **Personally Speaking** How do you think aviation has changed people's lives?

10 **Think More About It** In what ways has the women's rights movement changed the United States?

APPLY SKILLS

Use a Time Zone Map Suppose you live in Nevada and you have a friend in Utah. Use the map below to answer the questions.

11 When you are getting ready for school at 7:00 A.M., what time is it in Utah?

12 If your friend gets home from school at 3:00 P.M. in Utah, what time is it in Nevada?

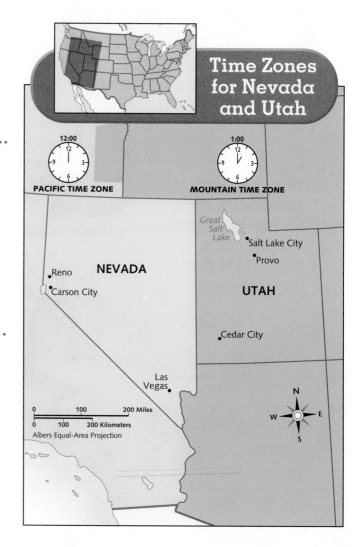

Time Zones for Nevada and Utah

12:00 — PACIFIC TIME ZONE

1:00 — MOUNTAIN TIME ZONE

Great Salt Lake

Salt Lake City
Provo

Reno   NEVADA

Carson City

UTAH

Cedar City

Las Vegas

0   100   200 Miles
0   100   200 Kilometers
Albers Equal-Area Projection

N W E S

REMEMBER

- Share your ideas.
- Cooperate with others to plan your work.
- Take responsibility for your work.
- Help one another.
- Show your group's work to the class.
- Discuss what you learned by working together.

 ACTIVITY

Hold a
Debate

Hold a debate that might have taken place between workers and business owners during the late 1800s. The topic should be whether labor unions are needed. To prepare for the debate, work in a group. Each group should research the concerns of business owners and the problems and working conditions of workers. Then the class should decide which groups will represent workers and which groups will represent business owners. During the debate, group members should take turns speaking.

 ACTIVITY

Create a
Hall of Fame

People from different ethnic groups and cultures have worked to bring about change in the United States. Your class should list 25 of these people to include in a Hall of Fame. They may be people that you read about in this unit or earlier units. The 25 names on the list should then be divided among small groups. Each group should make a poster for each person assigned to the group. The poster should include a drawing and words or phrases that describe the person. Display all the posters together on a classroom wall or in a hallway.

Unit Project Wrap-Up

Perform a Simulation Work with two of your classmates to complete the Unit Project on page 547. Write a conversation that might have taken place between three different immigrants. From your lists, you and your partners should decide on which details to include in your conversation. You should also decide which country each member of your group will represent. Write the conversation with your partners and perform it for your classmates. While role-playing the conversation, each member of your group should hold the flag from the country he or she is representing.

For
Your
Reference

Contents

How to Gather and Report Information

To write a report, make a poster, or do many other social studies projects, you may need information that is not in your textbook. You would need to gather this information from reference books, electronic references, or community resources. The following guide can help you in gathering information from many sources and in reporting what you find.

HOW TO USE REFERENCE TOOLS

Reference works are collections of facts. They include books and electronic resources, such as almanacs, atlases, dictionaries, and encyclopedias. In a library a reference book has *R* or *REF*—for *reference*—on its spine along with the call number. Most reference books are for use only in the library. Many libraries also have electronic references on CD-ROM and on the Internet.

▶ WHEN TO USE AN ENCYCLOPEDIA

An encyclopedia is a good place to begin to look for information. An encyclopedia has articles on nearly every subject. The articles are in alphabetical order. Each gives basic facts about people, places, and events. Some electronic encyclopedias allow you to hear music and speeches and see short movies.

▶ WHEN TO USE A DICTIONARY

A dictionary can give you information about words. Dictionaries explain word meanings and show the pronunciations of words. A dictionary is a good place to check the spelling of a word. Some dictionaries also include the origins of words and lists of foreign words, abbreviations, well-known people, and place names.

▶ WHEN TO USE AN ATLAS

You can find information about places in an atlas. An atlas is a book of maps. Some atlases have road maps. Others have maps of countries around the world. There are atlases with maps that show crops, population, products, and many other things. Ask a librarian to help you find the kind of atlas you need.

▶ WHEN TO USE AN ALMANAC

An almanac is a book or electronic resource of facts and figures. It shows information in tables and charts. However, the subjects are not in alphabetical order. You will need to use the index, which does list the subjects in alphabetical order. Most almanacs are brought up to date every year. So an almanac can give you the latest information.

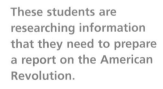

These students are researching information that they need to prepare a report on the American Revolution.

A card file can help you find the nonfiction book you want.

▶ HOW TO FIND NONFICTION BOOKS

Nonfiction books give facts about real people and things. In a library, all nonfiction books are numbered and placed in order on the shelves. To find the nonfiction book you want, you need to know its call number. You can find this number by using a card file or a computer catalog, but you will need to know the book's title, author, or subject. Here are some sample entries for a book on American Indians.

Subject Card

INDIANS OF NORTH AMERICA.

970.004   America's fascinating Indian heritage /
REA   [editor, James A. Maxwell]. -- Pleasantville,
           N.Y. : Reader's Digest Association, c1978.

           416 p. : ill. ; 29 cm.

           ISBN 0-89577-019-9

E77.A56

Author Card

Maxwell, James A., 1912-

970.004   America's fascinating Indian heritage /
REA   [editor, James A. Maxwell]. -- Pleasantville,
           N.Y. : Reader's Digest Association, c1978.

           416 p. : ill. ; 29 cm.

E77.A56   ISBN 0-89577-019-9

970.004   America's fascinating Indian heritage /
REA   [editor, James A. Maxwell]. -- Pleasantville,
           N.Y. : Reader's Digest Association, c1978.

           416 p. : ill. ; 29 cm.

E77.A56   At head of title: Reader's digest.
           Includes index.
           ISBN 0-89577-019-9

           1. Indians of North America.   I. Maxwell,
           James A., 1912- II. Title: Reader's digest.

Title Card

E77.A56   970'.004
                                                  78-55614

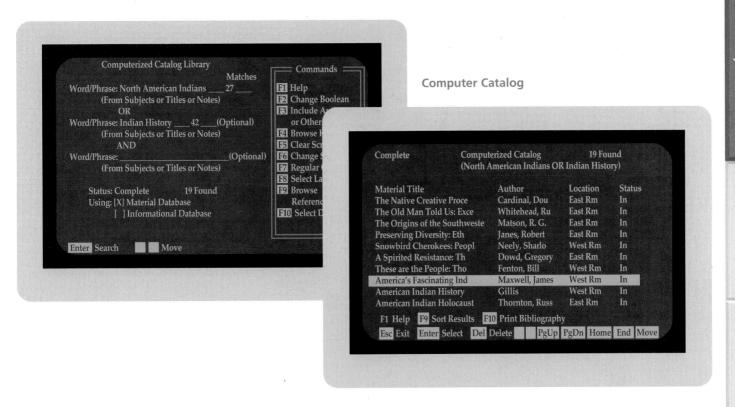

Computer Catalog

▶ HOW TO FIND PERIODICALS

Libraries have special sections for periodicals—newspapers and magazines. Periodicals are good sources for the latest information and for topics not covered in books. New issues of periodicals are usually displayed on a rack. Older issues are stored away, sometimes on film. Most libraries have an index or guide that lists magazine articles by subject. The most widely used guides are the *Children's Magazine Guide* and the *Readers' Guide to Periodical Literature*.

The entries in these guides are usually in alphabetical order by subject, author, or title. Abbreviations may be used for many parts of an entry, such as the name of the magazine and the date of the issue. Here is a sample entry for an article on the Civil War.

Heading
The general topic you are researching

Title
The title of the article

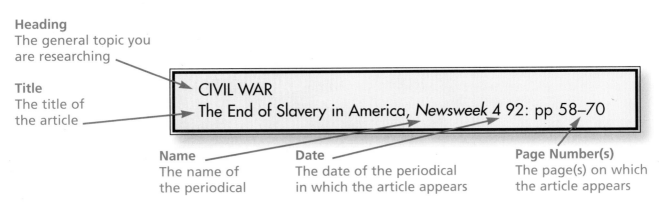

CIVIL WAR
The End of Slavery in America, *Newsweek* 4 92: pp 58–70

Name
The name of the periodical

Date
The date of the periodical in which the article appears

Page Number(s)
The page(s) on which the article appears

How to Find Internet Resources

The World Wide Web, part of the Internet, is a rich resource for information. You can use the World Wide Web to read documents, see photographs and artworks, and examine other primary sources. You can also use it to listen to music, read electronic books, take a "tour" of a museum, or get the latest news.

Information on the World Wide Web changes all the time. What you find today may not be there tomorrow, and new information is always being added. Much of the information you find may be useful, but remember that some of it may not be accurate.

▶ Plan Your Search

1. Make a list of your research questions.
2. Think about possible sources for finding your answers.
3. Identify key words to describe your research topic.
4. Consider synonyms and variations of those terms.
5. Decide exactly how you will go about finding what you need.

▶ Search by Subject

To search for topics, or subjects, choose a search engine. You can get a list of available search engines by clicking the SEARCH or NET SEARCH button at the top of your screen.

If you want to find Web sites for baseball, for example, enter "baseball" in the search engine field. Then click SEARCH or GO on the screen. You will see a list of sites all over the World Wide Web having to do with baseball. Because not all search engines list the same sites, you may need to use more than one search engine.

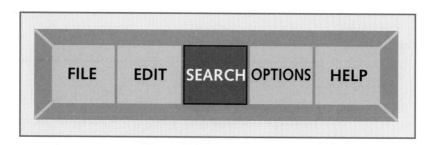

FILE   EDIT   SEARCH   OPTIONS   HELP

▶ SEARCH BY USING ADDRESSES

Each site on the World Wide Web has an address called a Uniform Resource Locator, or URL for short. A typical URL is shown in the box below.

To find URL listings, look in manuals, books, newspapers, magazines, and television and radio credits. To use a URL to go to a Web site, type the URL in the LOCATION/GO TO or NETSITE box in the upper left corner of the screen.

> Go To   http://www.hbschool.com

▶ BOOKMARK YOUR RESOURCES

Once you have found a site that you think will be helpful, you can bookmark it. Bookmarking makes a copy of a URL and keeps a record of it so you can easily go back to the site later.

While you are at the site you want to bookmark, click BOOKMARKS at the top of your screen and choose ADD BOOKMARK. Your list of bookmarks might look like this:

BOOKMARKS

- Harcourt Brace School Publishers: The Learning Site

- Library of Congress Home Page

- The Smithsonian Institution Home Page

- National Archives Online Exhibit Hall

Knowing how to use the Internet can help you find a wide range of information on a topic quickly and easily.

Skills Handbook • **R7**

Conducting an interview can be a good way to gather firsthand information about a topic.

HOW TO CONDUCT AN INTERVIEW

Conducting interviews, or asking people questions, is a good way to get facts and points of view.

▶ PLANNING AN INTERVIEW

1. Make a list of people to interview.
2. Call or write to each person to request an interview. When you contact the person, identify yourself and let the person know what you want to talk about.
3. Ask the person you will interview to set a time and place to meet.

▶ BEFORE THE INTERVIEW

1. Read more about your topic, and, if possible, about the person. That way, you will be better able to talk with the person about your topic.
2. Make a list of questions to ask.

▶ DURING THE INTERVIEW

1. Listen carefully. Do not interrupt or argue with the person.
2. Take notes, and write down the person's exact words.
3. If you want to use a tape recorder, first ask the person if you may do so.

▶ AFTER THE INTERVIEW

1. Before you leave, thank the person you interviewed.
2. Follow up by writing a thank-you note.

HOW TO CONDUCT A SURVEY

A good way to get information about the views of people in your community is to conduct a survey.

1. Identify your topic, and make a list of questions. Write them so that they can be answered with "yes" or "no" or with "for" or "against." You may also want to give a "no opinion" or "not sure" choice.
2. Make a tally sheet for recording the responses.
3. Decide how many people you will ask and where you will conduct your survey.
4. During the survey, record the responses carefully on the tally sheet.
5. When you have finished your survey, count the responses and write a summary statement or conclusion that your survey supports.

HOW TO WRITE FOR INFORMATION

People in places far away can also give you information. You can write a letter to ask for information about a certain topic. When you write, be sure to do these things:

- Write neatly or use a computer.
- Say who you are and why you are writing.
- Make your request specific and reasonable.
- Provide a self-addressed, stamped envelope for the answer.

HOW TO WRITE A REPORT

You may be asked to write a report on the information you have gathered. Most reports are 300 to 500 words long.

▶ GATHER AND ORGANIZE YOUR INFORMATION

Gather information about your topic from reference books, electronic references, or community resources. Then organize the information you have gathered.

- Take notes as you find information for your report.
- Review your notes to make sure that you have all the information you need.
- Outline your information.
- Make sure the information is in the right order.

▶ DRAFT YOUR REPORT

- Review your information. Decide whether you need more.
- Remember that the purpose of your report is to share information about your topic.
- Write a draft of your report. Put all your ideas on paper.

▶ REVISE

- Check that you have followed the order of your outline. Move sentences that seem out of place.
- Add any information that seems needed.
- Add quotations that show people's exact words.
- Reword sentences if too many follow the same pattern.

▶ PROOFREAD AND PUBLISH

- Check for errors.
- Make sure nothing has been left out.
- Write a clean copy of your report, or use a computer.

A good report is well-organized and full of important information about a topic.

Almanac

FACTS ABOUT THE STATES

State Flag	State	Year of Statehood	Population*	Area (sq. mi.)	Capital	Origin of State Name
	Alabama	1819	4,319,000	51,609	Montgomery	Choctaw, *alba ayamule,* "one who clears land and gathers food from it"
	Alaska	1959	609,000	586,412	Juneau	Aleut, *alayeska,* "great land"
	Arizona	1912	4,555,000	113,909	Phoenix	Papago, *arizonac,* "place of the small spring"
	Arkansas	1836	2,523,000	53,104	Little Rock	Quapaw, "the downstream people"
	California	1850	32,268,000	158,693	Sacramento	Spanish, a fictional island
	Colorado	1876	3,893,000	104,247	Denver	Spanish, "red land" or "red earth"
	Connecticut	1788	3,270,000	5,009	Hartford	Mohican, *quinnitukqut,* "at the long tidal river"
	Delaware	1787	732,000	2,057	Dover	Named for Lord de la Warr
	Florida	1845	14,654,000	58,560	Tallahassee	Spanish, "filled with flowers"
	Georgia	1788	7,486,000	58,876	Atlanta	Named for King George II of England
	Hawaii	1959	1,187,000	6,450	Honolulu	Polynesian, *hawaiki* or *owykee,* "homeland"
	Idaho	1890	1,210,000	83,557	Boise	Shoshone, "light on the mountains"

State Flag	State	Year of Statehood	Population*	Area (sq. mi.)	Capital	Origin of State Name
	Illinois	1818	11,896,000	56,400	Springfield	Algonquian, *iliniwek*, "men" or "warriors"
	Indiana	1816	5,864,000	36,291	Indianapolis	*Indian + a*, "land of the Indians"
	Iowa	1846	2,852,000	56,290	Des Moines	Dakota, *ayuba*, "beautiful land"
	Kansas	1861	2,595,000	82,264	Topeka	Sioux, "land of the south wind people"
	Kentucky	1792	3,908,000	40,395	Frankfort	Cherokee, *kentake*, "meadowland"
	Louisiana	1812	4,352,000	48,523	Baton Rouge	Named for King Louis XIV of France
	Maine	1820	1,242,000	33,215	Augusta	Named after a French province
	Maryland	1788	5,094,000	10,577	Annapolis	Named for Henrietta Maria, Queen Consort of Charles I of England
	Massachusetts	1788	6,118,000	8,257	Boston	Algonquian, "at the big hill" or "place of the big hill"
	Michigan	1837	9,774,000	58,216	Lansing	Chippewa, *mica gama*, "big water"
	Minnesota	1858	4,686,000	84,068	St. Paul	Dakota Sioux, "sky-blue water"
	Mississippi	1817	2,731,000	47,716	Jackson	Chippewa, *mici sibi*, "big river"
	Missouri	1821	5,402,000	69,686	Jefferson City	Algonquian, "muddy water"or "people of the big canoes"

*These population figures are from the most recent available statistics.

FACTS ABOUT THE STATES

Almanac

State Flag	State	Year of Statehood	Population*	Area (sq. mi.)	Capital	Origin of State Name
	Montana	1889	879,000	147,138	Helena	Spanish, "mountainous"
	Nebraska	1867	1,657,000	77,227	Lincoln	Omaha, *ni-bthaska*, "river in the flatness"
	Nevada	1864	1,677,000	110,540	Carson City	Spanish, "snowy" or "snowed upon"
	New Hampshire	1788	1,173,000	9,304	Concord	Named for Hampshire County, England
	New Jersey	1787	8,053,000	7,836	Trenton	Named for the Isle of Jersey
	New Mexico	1912	1,730,000	121,666	Santa Fe	Named by Spanish explorers from Mexico
	New York	1788	18,137,000	49,576	Albany	Named after the Duke of York
	North Carolina	1789	7,425,000	52,586	Raleigh	Named after King Charles II of England
	North Dakota	1889	641,000	70,665	Bismarck	Sioux, *dakota*, "friend" or "ally"
	Ohio	1803	11,186,000	41,222	Columbus	Iroquois, *oheo*, "beautiful, beautiful water"
	Oklahoma	1907	3,317,000	69,919	Oklahoma City	Choctaw, "red people"
	Oregon	1859	3,243,000	96,981	Salem	Algonquian, *wauregan*, "beautiful water"
	Pennsylvania	1787	12,020,000	45,333	Harrisburg	*Penn + sylvania*, meaning "Penn's woods"

State Flag	State	Year of Statehood	Population*	Area (sq. mi.)	Capital	Origin of State Name
	Rhode Island	1790	987,000	1,214	Providence	Dutch, "red-clay island"
	South Carolina	1788	3,760,000	31,055	Columbia	Named after King Charles II of England
	South Dakota	1889	738,000	77,047	Pierre	Sioux, *dakota,* "friend" or "ally"
	Tennessee	1796	5,368,000	42,244	Nashville	Name of a Cherokee village
	Texas	1845	19,439,000	267,338	Austin	Native American, *tejas,* "friend" or "ally"
	Utah	1896	2,059,000	84,916	Salt Lake City	Ute, "land of the Ute"
	Vermont	1791	589,000	9,609	Montpelier	French, *vert,* "green," and *mont,* "mountain"
	Virginia	1788	6,734,000	40,817	Richmond	Named after Queen Elizabeth I of England
	Washington	1889	5,610,000	68,192	Olympia	Named for George Washington
	West Virginia	1863	1,816,000	24,181	Charleston	From the English-named state of Virginia
	Wisconsin	1848	5,170,000	56,154	Madison	Possibly Algonquian, "grassy place" or "place of the beaver"
	Wyoming	1890	480,000	97,914	Cheyenne	Algonquian, *mache-weaming,* "at the big flats"
	District of Columbia		529,000	67		Named after Christopher Columbus

*These population figures are from the most recent available statistics.

Country	Population*	Area (sq. mi.)	Capital	Origin of Country Name
North America				
Antigua and Barbuda	66,000	171	St. Johns	Named for the Church of Santa María la Antigua in Seville, Spain
Bahamas	262,000	5,382	Nassau	Spanish, *bajamar,* "shallow water"
Barbados	258,000	166	Bridgetown	Means "bearded"—probably referring to the beardlike vines early explorers found on its trees
Belize	225,000	8,867	Belmopan	Mayan, "muddy water"
Canada	29,123,000	3,849,674	Ottawa	Huron-Iroquois, *kanata,* "village" or "community"
Costa Rica	3,534,000	19,730	San José	Spanish, "rich coast"
Cuba	10,999,000	42,804	Havana	Origin unknown
Dominica	83,000	290	Roseau	Latin, *dies dominica,* "Day of the Lord"
Dominican Republic	8,228,000	18,704	Santo Domingo	Named after the capital city
El Salvador	5,662,000	8,124	San Salvador	Spanish, "the Savior"
Grenada	96,000	133	St. George's	Origin unknown
Guatemala	11,558,000	42,042	Guatemala City	Indian, "land of trees"
Haiti	6,611,000	10,695	Port-au-Prince	Indian, "land of mountains"
Honduras	5,751,000	43,277	Tegucigalpa	Spanish, "profundities"—probably referring to the depth of offshore waters
Jamaica	2,616,000	4,244	Kingston	Arawak, *xamayca,* "land of wood and water"
Mexico	97,563,000	756,066	Mexico City	Aztec, *mexliapan,* "lake of the moon"
Nicaragua	4,386,000	50,880	Managua	From *Nicarao,* the name of an Indian Chief
Panama	2,693,000	29,157	Panama City	From an Indian village's name

Almanac

Country	Population*	Area (sq. mi.)	Capital	Origin of Country Name
St. Kitts-Nevis	42,000	104	Basseterre	Named by Christopher Columbus—Kitts for St. Christopher, a Catholic saint; Nevis, for a cloud-topped peak that looked like las nieves, "the snows"
St. Lucia	160,000	238	Castries	Named by Christopher Columbus for a Catholic saint
St. Vincent and the Grenadines	119,000	150	Kingstown	May have been named by Christopher Columbus for a Catholic saint
Trinidad and Tobago	1,273,000	1,980	Port-of-Spain	Trinidad, from the Spanish word for "trinity"; Tobago, named for tobacco because the island has the shape of an Indian smoking pipe
United States of America	267,636,000	3,787,318	Washington, D.C.	Named after the explorer Amerigo Vespucci

South America

Country	Population*	Area (sq. mi.)	Capital	Origin of Country Name
Argentina	35,798,000	1,073,518	Buenos Aires	Latin, *argentum,* "silver"
Bolivia	7,670,000	424,164	La Paz/Sucre	Named after Simón Bolívar, the famed liberator
Brazil	164,511,000	3,286,470	Brasília	Named after a native tree that the Portuguese called "bresel wood"
Chile	14,508,000	292,135	Santiago	Indian, *chilli,* "where the land ends"
Colombia	37,418,000	440,831	Bogotá	Named after Christopher Columbus
Ecuador	11,691,000	105,037	Quito	From the Spanish word for *equator,* referring to the country's location
Guyana	706,000	83,044	Georgetown	Indian, "land of waters"
Paraguay	5,652,000	157,048	Asunción	named after the Paraguay River, which flows through it
Peru	24,950,000	496,255	Lima	Quechua, "land of abundance"
Suriname	443,000	63,251	Paramaribo	From an Indian word, *surinen*
Uruguay	3,262,000	68,037	Montevideo	Named after the Uruguay River, which flows through it
Venezuela	22,396,000	352,144	Caracas	Spanish, "Little Venice"

*These population figures are from the most recent available statistics.

FACTS ABOUT THE
Presidents

1 ## George Washington

Birthplace:
  *Westmoreland County,
  VA*
Home State: *VA*
Political Party: *None*
Age at Inauguration: *57*
Served: *1789–1797*
Vice President:
  John Adams
1732–1799

2 ## John Adams

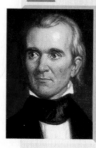

Birthplace: *Braintree,
  MA*
Home State: *MA*
Political Party: *Federalist*
Age at Inauguration: *61*
Served: *1797–1801*
Vice President:
  Thomas Jefferson
1735–1826

3 ## Thomas Jefferson

Birthplace: *Albemarle
  County, VA*
Home State: *VA*
Political Party:
  Democratic-Republican
Age at Inauguration: *57*
Served: *1801–1809*
Vice Presidents: *Aaron
  Burr, George Clinton*
1743–1826

4 ## James Madison

Birthplace: *Port Conway,
  VA*
Home State: *VA*
Political Party:
  Democratic-Republican
Age at Inauguration: *57*
Served: *1809–1817*
Vice Presidents:
  *George Clinton,
  Elbridge Gerry*
1751–1836

5 ## James Monroe

Birthplace:
  *Westmoreland County,
  VA*
Home State: *VA*
Political Party:
  Democratic-Republican
Age at Inauguration: *58*
Served: *1817–1825*
Vice President:
  Daniel D. Tompkins
1758–1831

6 ## John Quincy Adams

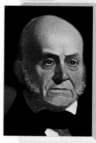

Birthplace: *Braintree,
  MA*
Home State: *MA*
Political Party:
  Democratic-Republican
Age at Inauguration: *57*
Served: *1825–1829*
Vice President:
  John C. Calhoun
1767–1848

7 ## Andrew Jackson

Birthplace: *Waxhaw
  settlement, SC*
Home State: *TN*
Political Party:
  Democratic
Age at Inauguration: *61*
Served: *1829–1837*
Vice Presidents:
  *John C. Calhoun,
  Martin Van Buren*
1767–1845

8 ## Martin Van Buren

Birthplace: *Kinderhook,
  NY*
Home State: *NY*
Political Party:
  Democratic
Age at Inauguration: *54*
Served: *1837–1841*
Vice President:
  Richard M. Johnson
1782–1862

9 ## William H. Harrison

Birthplace: *Berkeley, VA*
Home State: *OH*
Political Party: *Whig*
Age at Inauguration: *68*
Served: *1841*
Vice President:
  John Tyler
1773–1841

10 ## John Tyler

Birthplace: *Greenway,
  VA*
Home State: *VA*
Political Party: *Whig*
Age at Inauguration: *51*
Served: *1841–1845*
Vice President: *none*
1790–1862

11 ## James K. Polk

Birthplace: *near
  Pineville, NC*
Home State: *TN*
Political Party:
  Democratic
Age at Inauguration: *49*
Served: *1845–1849*
Vice President:
  George M. Dallas
1795–1849

12 ## Zachary Taylor

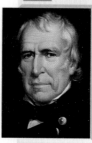

Birthplace: *Orange
  County, VA*
Home State: *LA*
Political Party: *Whig*
Age at Inauguration: *64*
Served: *1849–1850*
Vice President:
  Millard Fillmore
1784–1850

Home state refers to the state of residence when elected.

13 Millard Fillmore

Birthplace: *Locke, NY*
Home State: *NY*
Political Party: *Whig*
Age at Inauguration: *50*
Served: *1850–1853*
Vice President: *none*

1800–1874

14 Franklin Pierce

Birthplace: *Hillsboro, NH*
Home State: *NH*
Political Party: *Democratic*
Age at Inauguration: *48*
Served: *1853–1857*
Vice President: *William R. King*

1804–1869

15 James Buchanan

Birthplace: *near Mercersburg, PA*
Home State: *PA*
Political Party: *Democratic*
Age at Inauguration: *65*
Served: *1857–1861*
Vice President: *John C. Breckinridge*

1791–1868

16 Abraham Lincoln

Birthplace: *near Hodgenville, KY*
Home State: *IL*
Political Party: *Republican*
Age at Inauguration: *52*
Served: *1861–1865*
Vice Presidents: *Hannibal Hamlin, Andrew Johnson*

1809–1865

17 Andrew Johnson

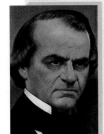

Birthplace: *Raleigh, NC*
Home State: *TN*
Political Party: *National Union*
Age at Inauguration: *56*
Served: *1865–1869*
Vice President: *none*

1808–1875

18 Ulysses S. Grant

Birthplace: *Point Pleasant, OH*
Home State: *IL*
Political Party: *Republican*
Age at Inauguration: *46*
Served: *1869–1877*
Vice Presidents: *Schuyler Colfax, Henry Wilson*

1822–1885

19 Rutherford B. Hayes

Birthplace: *near Delaware, OH*
Home State: *OH*
Political Party: *Republican*
Age at Inauguration: *54*
Served: *1877–1881*
Vice President: *William A. Wheeler*

1822–1893

20 James A. Garfield

Birthplace: *Orange, OH*
Home State: *OH*
Political Party: *Republican*
Age at Inauguration: *49*
Served: *1881*
Vice President: *Chester A. Arthur*

1831–1881

21 Chester A. Arthur

Birthplace: *Fairfield, VT*
Home State: *NY*
Political Party: *Republican*
Age at Inauguration: *51*
Served: *1881–1885*
Vice President: *none*

1829–1886

22 Grover Cleveland

Birthplace: *Caldwell, NJ*
Home State: *NY*
Political Party: *Democratic*
Age at Inauguration: *47*
Served: *1885–1889*
Vice President: *Thomas A. Hendricks*

1837–1908

23 Benjamin Harrison

Birthplace: *North Bend, OH*
Home State: *IN*
Political Party: *Republican*
Age at Inauguration: *55*
Served: *1889–1893*
Vice President: *Levi P. Morton*

1833–1901

24 Grover Cleveland

Birthplace: *Caldwell, NJ*
Home State: *NY*
Political Party: *Democratic*
Age at Inauguration: *55*
Served: *1893–1897*
Vice President: *Adlai E. Stevenson*

1837–1908

25 William McKinley

Birthplace: *Niles, OH*
Home State: *OH*
Political Party: *Republican*
Age at Inauguration: *54*
Served: *1897–1901*
Vice Presidents: *Garret A. Hobart, Theodore Roosevelt*

1843–1901

26 Theodore Roosevelt

Birthplace: *New York, NY*
Home State: *NY*
Political Party: *Republican*
Age at Inauguration: *42*
Served: *1901–1909*
Vice President: *Charles W. Fairbanks*

1858–1919

27 William H. Taft

Birthplace: *Cincinnati, OH*
Home State: *OH*
Political Party: *Republican*
Age at Inauguration: *51*
Served: *1909–1913*
Vice President: *James S. Sherman*

1857–1930

28 Woodrow Wilson

Birthplace: *Staunton, VA*
Home State: *NJ*
Political Party: *Democratic*
Age at Inauguration: *56*
Served: *1913–1921*
Vice President: *Thomas R. Marshall*

1856–1924

29 Warren G. Harding

Birthplace: *near Blooming Grove, OH*
Home State: *OH*
Political Party: *Republican*
Age at Inauguration: *55*
Served: *1921–1923*
Vice President: *Calvin Coolidge*

1865–1923

30 Calvin Coolidge

Birthplace: *Plymouth Notch, VT*
Home State: *MA*
Political Party: *Republican*
Age at Inauguration: *51*
Served: *1923–1929*
Vice President: *Charles G. Dawes*

1872–1933

31 Herbert Hoover

Birthplace: *West Branch, IA*
Home State: *CA*
Political Party: *Republican*
Age at Inauguration: *54*
Served: *1929–1933*
Vice President: *Charles Curtis*

1874–1964

32 Franklin D. Roosevelt

Birthplace: *Hyde Park, NY*
Home State: *NY*
Political Party: *Democratic*
Age at Inauguration: *51*
Served: *1933–1945*
Vice Presidents: *John N. Garner, Henry A. Wallace, Harry S. Truman*

1882–1945

33 Harry S. Truman

Birthplace: *Lamar, MO*
Home State: *MO*
Political Party: *Democratic*
Age at Inauguration: *60*
Served: *1945–1953*
Vice President: *Alben W. Barkley*

1884–1972

34 Dwight D. Eisenhower

Birthplace: *Denison, TX*
Home State: *NY*
Political Party: *Republican*
Age at Inauguration: *62*
Served: *1953–1961*
Vice President: *Richard M. Nixon*

1890–1969

35 John F. Kennedy

Birthplace: *Brookline, MA*
Home State: *MA*
Political Party: *Democratic*
Age at Inauguration: *43*
Served: *1961–1963*
Vice President: *Lyndon B. Johnson*

1917–1963

36 Lyndon B. Johnson

Birthplace: *near Stonewall, TX*
Home State: *TX*
Political Party: *Democratic*
Age at Inauguration: *55*
Served: *1963–1969*
Vice President: *Hubert H. Humphrey*

1908–1973

37 Richard M. Nixon

Birthplace: *Yorba Linda, CA*
Home State: *NY*
Political Party: *Republican*
Age at Inauguration: *56*
Served: *1969–1974*
Vice Presidents: *Spiro T. Agnew, Gerald R. Ford,*

1913–1994

38 Gerald R. Ford

Birthplace: *Omaha, NE*
Home State: *MI*
Political Party: *Republican*
Age at Inauguration: *61*
Served: *1974–1977*
Vice President: *Nelson A. Rockefeller*

1913–

39 Jimmy Carter

Birthplace: *Plains, GA*
Home State: *GA*
Political Party: *Democratic*
Age at Inauguration: *52*
Served: *1977–1981*
Vice President: *Walter F. Mondale*

1924–

40 Ronald W. Reagan

Birthplace: *Tampico, IL*
Home State: *CA*
Political Party: *Republican*
Age at Inauguration: *69*
Served: *1981–1989*
Vice President: *George H. W. Bush*

1911–

41 George H. W. Bush

Birthplace: *Milton, MA*
Home State: *TX*
Political Party: *Republican*
Age at Inauguration: *64*
Served: *1989–1993*
Vice President: *Dan Quayle*

1924–

42 William Clinton

Birthplace: *Hope, AR*
Home State: *AR*
Political Party: *Democratic*
Age at Inauguration: *46*
Served: *1993–*
Vice President: *Albert Gore*

1946–

Home state refers to the state of residence when elected.

American Documents

THE DECLARATION OF INDEPENDENCE

**In Congress, July 4, 1776.
The unanimous Declaration of the
thirteen United States of America,**

When in the Course of human events it becomes necessary for one people to dissolve the political bands which have connected them with another, and to assume among the powers of the earth, the separate and equal station to which the Laws of Nature and of Nature's God entitle them, a decent respect to the opinions of mankind requires that they should declare the causes which impel them to the separation.

We hold these truths to be self-evident, that all men are created equal, that they are endowed by their Creator with certain unalienable Rights, that among these are Life, Liberty and the pursuit of Happiness.
That to secure these rights, Governments are instituted among Men, deriving their just powers from the consent of the governed,
That whenever any Form of Government becomes destructive of these ends, it is the Right of the People to alter or to abolish it, and to institute new Government, laying its foundation on such principles and organizing its powers in such form, as to them shall seem most likely to effect their Safety and Happiness. Prudence, indeed, will dictate that Governments long established should not be changed for light and transient causes; and accordingly all experience hath shown, that mankind are more disposed to suffer, while evils are sufferable, than to right themselves by abolishing the forms to which they are accustomed. But when a long train of abuses and usurpations, pursuing invariably the same Object evinces a design to reduce them under absolute Despotism, it is their right, it is their duty, to throw off such Government, and to provide new Guards for their future security.

Such has been the patient sufferance of these Colonies; and such is now the necessity which constrains them to alter their former Systems of Government. The history of the present King of Great Britain is a history of repeated injuries and usurpations, all having in direct object the establishment of an absolute Tyranny over these States. To prove this, let Facts be submitted to a candid world.

He has refused his Assent to Laws, the most wholesome and necessary for the public good.
He has forbidden his Governors to pass Laws of immediate and pressing importance, unless suspended in their operation till his Assent should be obtained; and when so suspended, he has utterly neglected to attend to them.

PREAMBLE
The Preamble tells why the Declaration was written. It states that the members of the Continental Congress believed the colonies had the right to break away from Britain and become a free nation.

STATEMENT OF RIGHTS
The opening part of the Declaration tells what rights the members of the Continental Congress believed that all people have. All people are equal and have the rights to life, liberty, and the pursuit of happiness. These rights cannot be taken away. When a government tries to take these rights away from the people, the people have the right to change the government or do away with it. The people can then form a new government that gives them these rights.

CHARGES AGAINST THE KING
The Declaration lists more than 25 charges against the king. He was mistreating the colonists, the Declaration says, in order to gain total control over the colonies.

The king rejected many laws passed by colonial legislatures.

He has refused to pass other Laws for the accommodation of large districts of people, unless those people would relinquish the right of Representation in the Legislature, a right inestimable to them and formidable to tyrants only.

He has called together legislative bodies at places unusual, uncomfortable, and distant from the depository of their public Records, for the sole purpose of fatiguing them into compliance with his measures.

The king made the colonial legislatures meet at unusual times and places.

He has dissolved Representative Houses repeatedly, for opposing with manly firmness his invasions on the rights of the people.

He has refused for a long time, after such dissolutions, to cause others to be elected; whereby the Legislative powers, incapable of Annihilation, have returned to the People at large for their exercise; the State remaining in the mean time exposed to all the dangers of invasion from without, and convulsions within.

The king and the king's governors often dissolved colonial legislatures for disobeying their orders.

He has endeavored to prevent the population of these States; for that purpose obstructing the Laws for Naturalization of Foreigners; refusing to pass others to encourage their migrations hither, and raising the conditions of new Appropriations of Lands.

The king stopped people from moving to the colonies and into the western lands.

He has obstructed the Administration of Justice, by refusing his Assent to Laws for establishing Judiciary powers.

He has made Judges dependent on his Will alone, for the tenure of their offices, and the amount and payment of their salaries.

The king prevented the colonists from choosing their own judges. The king chose the judges, and they served only as long as the king was satisfied with them.

He has erected a multitude of New Offices, and sent hither swarms of Officers to harrass our people, and eat out their substance.

The king hired people to help collect taxes in the colonies.

He has kept among us, in times of peace, Standing Armies without the Consent of our legislatures.

He has affected to render the Military independent of and superior to the Civil power.

He has combined with others to subject us to a jurisdiction foreign to our constitution, and unacknowledged by our laws; giving his Assent to their Acts of pretended Legislation:

The king appointed General Thomas Gage, commander of Britain's military forces in the Americas, as governor of Massachusetts.

For quartering large bodies of armed troops among us:

For protecting them, by a mock Trial, from punishment for any Murders which they should commit on the Inhabitants of these States:

For cutting off our Trade with all parts of the world:

For imposing Taxes on us without our Consent:

The king expected the colonists to provide housing and supplies for the British soldiers in the colonies.

The king and Parliament demanded that colonists pay many taxes, even though the colonists did not agree to pay them.

For depriving us in many cases, of the benefits of Trial by Jury:

Colonists were tried by British naval courts, which had no juries.

For transporting us beyond Seas to be tried for pretended offences:

For abolishing the free System of English Laws in a neighboring Province, establishing therein an Arbitrary government, and enlarging its Boundaries so as to render it at once an example and fit instrument for introducing the same absolute rule into these Colonies:

Colonists accused of treason were sent to Britain to be tried.

For taking away our Charters, abolishing our most valuable Laws, and altering fundamentally the Forms of our Governments:

For suspending our own Legislatures, and declaring themselves invested with power to legislate for us in all cases whatsoever.

He has abdicated Government here, by declaring us out of his Protection and waging War against us.

He has plundered our seas, ravaged our Coasts, burnt our towns, and destroyed the lives of our people.

He is at this time transporting large Armies of foreign Mercenaries to complete the works of death, desolation and tyranny, already begun with circumstances of Cruelty & perfidy scarcely paralleled in the most barbarous ages, and totally unworthy the Head of a civilized nation.

He has constrained our fellow Citizens taken Captive on the high Seas to bear Arms against their Country, to become the executioners of their friends and Brethren, or to fall themselves by their Hands.

He has excited domestic insurrections amongst us, and has endeavored to bring on the inhabitants of our frontiers, the merciless Indian Savages, whose known rule of warfare, is an undistinguished destruction of all ages, sexes and conditions.

In every stage of these Oppressions We have Petitioned for Redress in the most humble terms: Our repeated Petitions have been answered only by repeated injury. A Prince, whose character is thus marked by every act which may define a Tyrant, is unfit to be the ruler of a free people.

Nor have We been wanting in attentions to our British brethren. We have warned them from time to time of attempts by their legislature to extend an unwarrantable jurisdiction over us. We have reminded them of the circumstances of our emigration and settlement here. We have appealed to their native justice and magnanimity, and we have conjured them by the ties of our common kindred to disavow these usurpations, which, would inevitably interrupt our connections and correspondence. They too have been deaf to the voice of justice and of consanguinity. We must, therefore, acquiesce in the necessity, which denounces our Separation, and hold them, as we hold the rest of mankind, Enemies in War, in Peace Friends.

We, therefore, the Representatives of the united States of America, in General Congress, Assembled, appealing to the Supreme Judge of the world for the rectitude of our intentions, do, in the Name, and by Authority of the good People of these Colonies, solemnly publish and declare, That these United Colonies are, and of Right ought to be Free and Independent States; that they are Absolved from all Allegiance to the British Crown, and that all political connection between them and the State of Great Britain, is and ought to be totally dissolved; and that as Free and Independent States, they have full Power to levy War, conclude Peace, contract Alliances, establish Commerce, and to do all other Acts and Things which Independent States may of right do.

The king allowed General Gage to take military action to enforce British laws in the colonies.

The king hired Hessian mercenaries and sent them to fight the colonists.

The king's governor in Virginia promised freedom to all enslaved people who joined the British forces. The British also planned to use Indians to fight the colonists.

The Declaration explained the efforts of the colonists to avoid separation from Britain. But the colonists said that the king had ignored their protests. Because of the many charges against the king, the writers of the Declaration concluded that he was not fit to rule free people.

A STATEMENT OF INDEPENDENCE The writers declared that the colonies were now free and independent states. All ties with Britain were broken. As free and independent states, they had the right to make war and peace, to trade, and to do all the things free countries could do.

To support the Declaration, the signers promised one another their lives, their fortunes, and their honor.

And for the support of this Declaration, with a firm reliance on the protection of divine Providence, we mutually pledge to each other our Lives, our Fortunes and our sacred Honor.

John Hancock

NEW HAMPSHIRE
Josiah Bartlett
William Whipple
Matthew Thornton

MASSACHUSETTS
John Adams
Samuel Adams
Robert Treat Paine
Elbridge Gerry

NEW YORK
William Floyd
Philip Livingston
Francis Lewis
Lewis Morris

RHODE ISLAND
Stephen Hopkins
William Ellery

NEW JERSEY
Richard Stockton
John Witherspoon
Francis Hopkinson
John Hart
Abraham Clark

PENNSYLVANIA
Robert Morris
Benjamin Rush
Benjamin Franklin
John Morton
George Clymer
James Smith
George Taylor
James Wilson
George Ross

DELAWARE
Caesar Rodney
George Read
Thomas McKean

MARYLAND
Samuel Chase
William Paca
Thomas Stone
Charles Carroll of Carrollton

NORTH CAROLINA
William Hopper
Joseph Hewes
John Penn

VIRGINIA
George Wythe
Richard Henry Lee
Thomas Jefferson
Benjamin Harrison
Thomas Nelson, Jr.
Francis Lightfoot Lee
Carter Braxton

SOUTH CAROLINA
Edward Rutledge
Thomas Heyward, Jr.
Thomas Lynch, Jr.
Arthur Middleton

CONNECTICUT
Roger Sherman
Samuel Huntington
William Williams
Oliver Wolcott

GEORGIA
Button Gwinnett
Lyman Hall
George Walton

Members of the Continental Congress stated that copies of the Declaration should be sent to all Committees of Correspondence and to commanders of the troops and that it should be read in every state.

Resolved, That copies of the Declaration be sent to the several assemblies, conventions, and committees, or councils of safety, and to the several commanding officers of the continental troops; that it be proclaimed in each of the United States, at the head of the army.

THE CONSTITUTION OF
THE UNITED STATES OF AMERICA

Preamble*

We the people of the United States, in order to form a more perfect Union, establish justice, insure domestic tranquillity, provide for the common defense, promote the general welfare, and secure the blessings of liberty to ourselves and our posterity, do ordain and establish this Constitution for the United States of America.

ARTICLE I
THE LEGISLATIVE BRANCH

SECTION 1. CONGRESS

All legislative powers herein granted shall be vested in a Congress of the United States, which shall consist of a Senate and House of Representatives.

SECTION 2. THE HOUSE OF REPRESENTATIVES

(1) The House of Representatives shall be composed of members chosen every second year by the people of the several states, and the electors in each state shall have the qualifications requisite for electors of the most numerous branch of the state legislature.

(2) No person shall be a Representative who shall not have attained to the age of twenty-five years, and been seven years a citizen of the United States, and who shall not, when elected, be an inhabitant of that state in which he shall be chosen.

(3) Representatives [*and direct taxes*]** shall be apportioned among the several states which may be included within this Union, according to their respective numbers [*which shall be determined by adding to the whole number of free persons, including those bound to service for a term of years, and excluding Indians not taxed, three-fifths of all other persons*]. The actual enumeration shall be made within three years after the first meeting of the Congress of the United States, and within every subsequent term of ten years, in such manner as they shall by law direct. The number of Representatives shall not exceed one for every 30,000, but each state shall have at least one Representative [*; and until such enumeration shall be made, the State of New Hampshire shall be entitled to choose three; Massachusetts eight; Rhode Island and Providence Plantations one; Connecticut five; New York six; New Jersey four; Pennsylvania eight; Delaware one; Maryland six; Virginia ten; North Carolina five; South Carolina five; and Georgia three*].

*Titles have been added to make the Constitution easier to read. They did not appear in the original document.

**The parts of the Constitution that no longer apply are printed in italics within brackets [ ]. These portions have been changed or set aside by later amendments.

PREAMBLE
The introduction to the Constitution states the purposes and principles for writing it. The writers wanted to set up a fairer form of government and to secure peace and freedom for themselves and for future generations.

CONGRESS
Congress has the authority to make laws. Congress is made up of two groups of lawmakers: the Senate and the House of Representatives.

(1) ELECTION AND TERM OF MEMBERS
Qualified voters are to elect members of the House of Representatives every two years. Each member of the House of Representatives must meet certain requirements.

(2) QUALIFICATIONS
Members of the House of Representatives must be at least 25 years old. They must have been citizens of the United States for at least seven years. They must live in the state that they will represent.

(3) DETERMINING APPORTIONMENT
The number of representatives a state may have depends on the number of people living in each state. Every ten years the federal government must take a census, or count, of the population in every state. Every state will have at least one representative.

(4) FILLING VACANCIES
If there is a vacancy in representation in Congress, the governor of the state involved must call a special election to fill it.

(5) SPECIAL AUTHORITY
The House of Representatives chooses a Speaker as its presiding officer. It also chooses other officers as appropriate. The House is the only government branch that may impeach, or charge, an official in the executive branch or a judge of the federal courts for failing to carry out his or her duties. These cases are tried in the Senate.

(1) NUMBER, TERM, AND SELECTION OF MEMBERS
Each state is represented by two senators. Until Amendment 17 was passed, state legislatures chose the senators for their states. Each senator serves a six-year term and has one vote in Congress.

(2) OVERLAPPING TERMS AND FILLING VACANCIES
One-third of the senators are elected every two years for a six-year term. This grouping allows at least two-thirds of the experienced senators to remain in the Senate after each election. Amendment 17 permits state governors to appoint a replacement to fill a vacancy until the next election is held.

(3) QUALIFICATIONS
Senators must be at least 30 years old. They must have been citizens of the United States for at least nine years. They must live in the state that they will represent.

(4) PRESIDENT OF THE SENATE
The Vice President acts as chief officer of the Senate but does not vote unless there is a tie.

(5) OTHER OFFICERS
The Senate chooses its other officers and a president pro tempore, who serves if the Vice President is not present or if the Vice President becomes President. *Pro tempore* is a Latin term meaning "for the time being."

(4) When vacancies happen in the representation from any state, the executive authority thereof shall issue writs of election to fill such vacancies.

(5) The House of Representatives shall choose their Speaker and other officers; and shall have the sole power of impeachment.

SECTION 3. THE SENATE

(1) The Senate of the United States shall be composed of two Senators from each state [*chosen by the legislature thereof*], for six years, and each Senator shall have one vote.

(2) [*Immediately after they shall be assembled in consequence of the first election, they shall be divided as equally as may be into three classes. The seats of the Senators of the first class shall be vacated at the expiration of the second year, of the second class at the expiration of the fourth year, and of the third class at the expiration of the sixth year, so that one-third may be chosen every second year; and if vacancies happen by resignation, or otherwise, during the recess of the legislature of any state, the executive thereof may make temporary appointments until the next meeting of the legislature, which shall then fill such vacancies.*]

(3) No person shall be a Senator who shall not have attained to the age of thirty years, and been nine years a citizen of the United States, and who shall not, when elected, be an inhabitant of that state for which he shall be chosen.

(4) The Vice President of the United States shall be President of the Senate, but shall have no vote, unless they be equally divided.

(5) The Senate shall choose their other officers, and also a President *pro tempore*, in the absence of the Vice President, or when he shall exercise the office of the President of the United States.

(6) The Senate shall have the sole power to try all impeachments. When sitting for that purpose, they shall be on oath or affirmation. When the President of the United States is tried, the Chief Justice shall preside; and no person shall be convicted without the concurrence of two-thirds of the members present.

(7) Judgment in cases of impeachment shall not extend further than to removal from office, and disqualification to hold and enjoy any office of honor, trust, or profit under the United States; but the party convicted shall nevertheless be liable and subject to indictment, trial, judgment and punishment, according to law.

SECTION 4. ELECTIONS AND MEETINGS

(1) The times, places, and manner of holding elections for Senators and Representatives shall be prescribed in each state by the legislature thereof; but the Congress may at any time by law make or alter such regulations, [*except as to the places of choosing Senators*].

(2) The Congress shall assemble at least once in every year, [*and such meeting shall be on the first Monday in December, unless they shall by law appoint a different day*].

SECTION 5. RULES OF PROCEDURE

(1) Each house shall be the judge of the elections, returns and qualifications of its own members, and a majority of each shall constitute a quorum to do business; but a smaller number may adjourn from day to day, and may be authorized to compel the attendance of absent members, in such manner and under such penalties as each house may provide.

(2) Each house may determine the rules of its proceedings, punish its members for disorderly behavior, and, with the concurrence of two-thirds, expel a member.

(3) Each house shall keep a journal of its proceedings, and from time to time publish the same, excepting such parts as may in their judgment require secrecy; and the yeas and nays of the members of either house on any question shall, at the desire of one-fifth of those present, be entered on the journal.

(6) IMPEACHMENT TRIALS
If the House of Representatives votes articles of impeachment, the Senate holds a trial. A two-thirds vote is required to convict a person who has been impeached.

(7) PENALTY FOR CONVICTION
If convicted in an impeachment case, an official is removed from office and may never hold office in the United States government again. The convicted person may also be tried in a regular court of law for any crimes.

(1) HOLDING ELECTIONS
Each state makes its own rules about electing senators and representatives. However, Congress may change these rules at any time. Today congressional elections are held on the Tuesday after the first Monday in November, in even-numbered years.

(2) MEETINGS
The Constitution requires Congress to meet at least once a year. That day is the first Monday in December, unless Congress sets a different day. Amendment 20 changed this date to January 3.

(1) ORGANIZATION
Each house of Congress may decide if its members have been elected fairly and are able to hold office. Each house may do business only when a quorum—a majority of its members—is present. By less than a majority vote, each house may compel absent members to attend.

(2) RULES
Each house may decide its own rules for doing business, punish its members, and expel a member from office if two-thirds of the members agree.

(3) JOURNAL
The Constitution requires each house to keep records of its activities and to publish these records from time to time. The House Journal and the Senate Journal are published at the end of each session. How each member voted must be recorded if one-fifth of the members ask for this to be done.

(4) ADJOURNMENT

When Congress is in session, neither house may take a recess for more than three days without the consent of the other.

(1) PAY AND PRIVILEGES

Members of Congress set their own salaries, which are to be paid by the federal government. Members cannot be arrested or sued for anything they say while Congress is in session. This privilege is called congressional immunity. Members of Congress may be arrested while Congress is in session only if they commit a crime.

(2) RESTRICTIONS

Members of Congress may not hold any other federal office while serving in Congress. A member may not resign from office and then take a government position created during that member's term of office or for which the pay has been increased during that member's term of office.

(1) MONEY-RAISING BILLS

All money-raising bills must be introduced first in the House of Representatives, but the Senate may suggest changes.

(2) HOW A BILL BECOMES A LAW

After a bill has been passed by both the House of Representatives and the Senate, it must be sent to the President. If the President approves and signs the bill, it becomes law. The President can also veto, or refuse to sign, the bill. Congress can override a veto by passing the bill again by a two-thirds majority. If the President does not act within ten days, two things may happen. If Congress is still in session, the bill becomes a law. If Congress ends its session within that same ten-day period, the bill does not become a law.

(3) ORDERS AND RESOLUTIONS

Congress can pass orders and resolutions, some of which have the same effect as a law. Congress may decide on its own when to end the session. Other such acts must be signed or vetoed by the President.

(4) Neither house, during the session of Congress, shall, without the consent of the other, adjourn for more than three days, nor to any other place than that in which the two houses shall be sitting.

SECTION 6. PRIVILEGES AND RESTRICTIONS

(1) The Senators and Representatives shall receive a compensation for their services, to be ascertained by law and paid out of the Treasury of the United States. They shall in all cases, except treason, felony, and breach of the peace, be privileged from arrest during their attendance at the session of their respective houses, and in going to and returning from the same; and for any speech or debate in either house, they shall not be questioned in any other place.

(2) No Senator or Representative shall, during the time for which he was elected, be appointed to any civil office under the authority of the United States, which shall have been created, or the emoluments whereof shall have been increased, during such time; and no person holding any office under the United States shall be a member of either house during his continuance in office.

SECTION 7. MAKING LAWS

(1) All bills for raising revenue shall originate in the House of Representatives; but the Senate may propose or concur with amendments as on other bills.

(2) Every bill which shall have passed the House of Representatives and the Senate shall, before it become a law, be presented to the President of the United States; if he approve, he shall sign it, but if not, he shall return it, with his objections, to that house in which it shall have originated, who shall enter the objections at large on their journal, and proceed to reconsider it. If after such reconsideration two-thirds of that house shall agree to pass the bill, it shall be sent, together with the objections, to the other house, by which it shall likewise be reconsidered, and, if approved by two-thirds of that house, it shall become a law. But in all such cases the votes of both houses shall be determined by yeas and nays, and the names of the persons voting for and against the bill shall be entered on the journal of each house respectively. If any bill shall not be returned by the President within ten days (Sundays excepted) after it shall have been presented to him, the same bill shall be a law, in like manner as if he had signed it, unless the Congress by their adjournment prevent its return, in which case it shall not be a law.

(3) Every order, resolution, or vote to which the concurrence of the Senate and House of Representatives may be necessary (except on a question of adjournment) shall be presented to the President of the United States; and before the same shall take effect, shall be approved by him, or being disapproved by him, shall be repassed by two-thirds of the Senate and House of Representatives, according to the rules and limitations prescribed in the case of a bill.

SECTION 8. POWERS DELEGATED TO CONGRESS

The Congress shall have power

(1) To lay and collect taxes, duties, imposts and excises, to pay the debts and provide for the common defense and general welfare of the United States; but all duties, imposts and excises shall be uniform throughout the United States;

(2) To borrow money on the credit of the United States;

(3) To regulate commerce with foreign nations, and among the several states [and with the Indian tribes];

(4) To establish a uniform rule of naturalization, and uniform laws on the subject of bankruptcies throughout the United States;

(5) To coin money, regulate the value thereof, and of foreign coin, and fix the standard of weights and measures;

(6) To provide for the punishment of counterfeiting the securities and current coin of the United States;

(7) To establish post offices and post roads;

(8) To promote the progress of science and useful arts by securing for limited times to authors and inventors the exclusive right to their respective writings and discoveries;

(9) To constitute tribunals inferior to the Supreme Court;

(10) To define and punish piracies and felonies committed on the high seas and offenses against the law of nations;

(1) TAXATION
Only Congress has the authority to raise money to pay debts, defend the United States, and provide services for its people by collecting taxes or tariffs on foreign goods. All taxes must be applied equally in all states.

(2) BORROWING MONEY
Congress may borrow money for national use. This is usually done by selling government bonds.

(3) COMMERCE
Congress can control trade with other countries and between states.

(4) NATURALIZATION AND BANKRUPTCY
Congress decides what requirements people from other countries must meet to become United States citizens. Congress can also pass laws to protect people who are bankrupt, or cannot pay their debts.

(5) COINS, WEIGHTS, AND MEASURES
Congress can print and coin money and decide its value. Congress also decides on the system of weights and measures to be used throughout the nation.

(6) COUNTERFEITING
Congress may pass laws to punish people who make fake money, bonds, or stamps.

(7) POSTAL SERVICE
Congress can build post offices and make rules about the postal system and the roads used for mail delivery.

(8) COPYRIGHTS AND PATENTS
Congress can issue patents and copyrights to inventors and authors to protect the ownership of their works.

(9) FEDERAL COURTS
Congress can establish a system of federal courts under the Supreme Court.

(10) CRIMES AT SEA
Congress can pass laws to punish people for crimes committed at sea. Congress may also punish United States citizens for breaking international law.

(11) DECLARING WAR
Only Congress can declare war.

(12) THE ARMY
Congress can establish an army, but it cannot vote enough money to support it for more than two years. This part of the Constitution was written to keep the army under civilian control.

(13) THE NAVY
Congress can establish a navy and vote enough money to support it for as long as necessary. No time limit was set because people thought the navy was less of a threat to people's liberty than the army was.

(14) MILITARY REGULATIONS
Congress makes the rules that guide and govern all the armed forces.

(15) THE MILITIA
Each state has its own militia, now known as the National Guard. The National Guard can be called into federal service by the President, as authorized by Congress, to enforce laws, to stop uprisings against the government, or to protect the people in case of floods, earthquakes, and other disasters.

(16) CONTROL OF THE MILITIA
Congress helps each state support the National Guard. Each state may appoint its own officers and train its own guard according to rules set by Congress.

(17) NATIONAL CAPITAL AND OTHER PROPERTY
Congress may pass laws to govern the nation's capital (Washington, D.C.) and any land owned by the government.

(18) OTHER NECESSARY LAWS
The Constitution allows Congress to make laws that are necessary to enforce the powers listed in Article I. This clause allows Congress to stretch its authority when new situations arise.

(11) To declare war, [*grant letters of marque and reprisal,*] and make rules concerning captures on land and water;

(12) To raise and support armies, but no appropriation of money to that use shall be for a longer term than two years;

(13) To provide and maintain a navy;

(14) To make rules for the government and regulation of the land and naval forces;

(15) To provide for calling forth the militia to execute the laws of the Union, suppress insurrections and repel invasions;

(16) To provide for organizing, arming, and disciplining the militia, and for governing such part of them as may be employed in the service of the United States, reserving to the states, respectively, the appointment of the officers, and the authority of training the militia according to the discipline prescribed by Congress;

(17) To exercise exclusive legislation in all cases whatsoever, over such district (not exceeding ten miles square) as may, by cession of particular states, and the acceptance of Congress, become the seat of government of the United States, and to exercise like authority over all places purchased by the consent of the legislature of the state in which the same shall be, for the erection of forts, magazines, arsenals, dock-yards, and other needful buildings; —and

(18) To make all laws which shall be necessary and proper for carrying into execution the foregoing powers, and all other powers vested by this Constitution in the government of the United States, or in any department or officer thereof.

SECTION 9. POWERS DENIED TO CONGRESS

(1) [*The migration or importation of such persons as any of the states now existing shall think proper to admit shall not be prohibited by the Congress prior to the year 1808; but a tax or duty may be imposed on such importation, not exceeding 10 dollars for each person.*]

(2) The privilege of the writ of habeas corpus shall not be suspended, unless when in cases of rebellion or invasion the public safety may require it.

(3) No bill of attainder or ex post facto law shall be passed.

(4) [*No capitation or other direct tax shall be laid, unless in proportion to the census or enumeration herein before directed to be taken.*]

(5) No tax or duty shall be laid on articles exported from any state.

(6) No preference shall be given by any regulation of commerce or revenue to the ports of one state over those of another; nor shall vessels bound to, or from, one state, be obliged to enter, clear, or pay duties in another.

(7) No money shall be drawn from the Treasury, but in consequence of appropriations made by law; and a regular statement and account of the receipts and expenditures of all public money shall be published from time to time.

(1) SLAVE TRADE
Some authority is not given to Congress. Congress could not prevent the slave trade until 1808, but it could put a tax of ten dollars on each slave brought into the United States. After 1808, when a law was passed to stop slaves from being brought into the United States, this section no longer applied.

(2) HABEAS CORPUS
A writ of habeas corpus is a privilege that entitles a person to a hearing before a judge. The judge must then decide if there is good reason for that person to have been arrested. If not, that person must be released. The government is not allowed to take this privilege away except during a national emergency, such as an invasion or a rebellion.

(3) SPECIAL LAWS
Congress cannot pass laws that impose punishment on a named individual or group, except in cases of treason. Article III sets limits to punishments for treason. Congress also cannot pass laws that punish a person for an action that was legal when it was done.

(4) DIRECT TAXES
Congress cannot set a direct tax on people, unless it is in proportion to the total population. Amendment 16, which provides for the income tax, is an exception.

(5) EXPORT TAXES
Congress cannot tax goods sent from one state to another or from a state to another country.

(6) PORTS
When making trade laws, Congress cannot favor one state over another. Congress cannot require ships from one state to pay a duty to enter another state.

(7) PUBLIC MONEY
The government cannot spend money from the treasury unless Congress passes a law allowing it to do so. A written record must be kept of all money spent by the government.

(8) TITLES OF NOBILITY AND GIFTS
The United States government cannot grant titles of nobility. Government officials cannot accept gifts from other countries without the permission of Congress. This clause was intended to prevent government officials from being bribed by other nations.

(1) COMPLETE RESTRICTIONS
The Constitution does not allow states to act as if they were individual countries. No state government may make a treaty with other countries. No state can print its own money.

(2) PARTIAL RESTRICTIONS
No state government can tax imported goods or exported goods without the consent of Congress. States may charge a fee to inspect these goods, but profits must be given to the United States Treasury.

(3) OTHER RESTRICTIONS
No state government may tax ships entering its ports unless Congress approves. No state may keep an army or navy during times of peace other than the National Guard. No state can enter into agreements called compacts with other states without the consent of Congress.

(1) TERM OF OFFICE
The President has the authority to carry out our nation's laws. The term of office for both the President and the Vice President is four years.

(2) THE ELECTORAL COLLEGE
This group of people is to be chosen by the voters of each state to elect the President and Vice President. The number of electors in each state is equal to the number of senators and representatives that state has in Congress.

(3) ELECTION PROCESS
This clause describes in detail how the electors were to choose the President and Vice President. In 1804 Amendment 12 changed the process for electing the President and the Vice President.

(8) No title of nobility shall be granted by the United States; and no person holding any office of profit or trust under them, shall, without the consent of the Congress, accept of any present, emolument, office, or title, of any kind whatever, from any king, prince, or foreign state.

SECTION 10. POWERS DENIED TO THE STATES
(1) No state shall enter into any treaty, alliance, or confederation; grant letters of marque and reprisal; coin money; emit bills of credit; make anything but gold and silver coin a tender in payment of debts; pass any bill of attainder, ex post facto law, or law impairing the obligation of contracts, or grant any title of nobility.

(2) No state shall, without the consent of the Congress, lay any imposts or duties on imports or exports, except what may be absolutely necessary for executing its inspection laws; and the net produce of all duties and imposts, laid by any state on imports or exports, shall be for the use of the Treasury of the United States; and all such laws shall be subject to the revision and control of the Congress.

(3) No state shall, without the consent of Congress, lay any duty of tonnage, keep troops, or ships of war in time of peace, enter into any agreement or compact with another state, or with a foreign power, or engage in war, unless actually invaded, or in such imminent danger as will not admit of delay.

ARTICLE II
THE EXECUTIVE BRANCH

SECTION 1. PRESIDENT AND VICE PRESIDENT
(1) The executive power shall be vested in a President of the United States of America. He shall hold his office during the term of four years, and together with the Vice President, chosen for the same term, be elected as follows:

(2) Each state shall appoint, in such manner as the legislature thereof may direct, a number of electors, equal to the whole number of Senators and Representatives to which the state may be entitled in the Congress; but no Senator or Representative, or person holding an office of trust or profit under the United States, shall be appointed an elector.

(3) [*The electors shall meet in their respective states, and vote by ballot for two persons, of whom one at least shall not be an inhabitant of the same state with themselves. And they shall make a list of all the persons voted for, and of the number of votes for each; which list they shall sign and certify, and transmit sealed to the seat of the government of the United States, directed to the president of the Senate. The president of the Senate shall, in the presence of the Senate and House of Representatives, open all the certificates, and the votes shall then be counted. The person having the greatest number of votes shall be the President, if such number be a majority of the whole number of electors appointed; and if*

there be more than one who have such majority, and have an equal number of votes, then the House of Representatives shall immediately choose by ballot one of them for President; and if no person have a majority, then from the five highest on the list the said House shall in like manner choose the President. But in choosing the President the votes shall be taken by states, the representation from each state having one vote: A quorum for this purpose shall consist of a member or members from two-thirds of the states, and a majority of all the states shall be necessary to a choice. In every case, after the choice of the President, the person having the greatest number of votes of the electors shall be the Vice President. But if there should remain two or more who have equal votes, the Senate shall choose from them by ballot the Vice President.]

(4) The Congress may determine the time of choosing the electors, and the day on which they shall give their votes; which day shall be the same throughout the United States.

(5) No person except a natural-born citizen [*or a citizen of the United States, at the time of the adoption of this Constitution,*] shall be eligible to the office of the President; neither shall any person be eligible to that office who shall not have attained to the age of thirty-five years, and been fourteen years a resident within the United States.

(6) [*In case of the removal of the President from office, or of his death, resignation, or inability to discharge the powers and duties of the said office, the same shall devolve on the Vice President, and the Congress may by law provide for the case of removal, death, resignation or inability, both of the President and Vice President, declaring what officer shall then act as President, and such officer shall act accordingly, until the disability be removed, or a President shall be elected.*]

(7) The President shall, at stated times, receive for his services, a compensation, which shall neither be increased nor diminished during the period for which he shall have been elected, and he shall not receive within that period any other emolument from the United States, or any of them.

(8) Before he enter on the execution of his office, he shall take the following oath or affirmation:—"I do solemnly swear (or affirm) that I will faithfully execute the office of President of the United States, and will to the best of my ability, preserve, protect, and defend the Constitution of the United States."

SECTION 2. POWERS OF THE PRESIDENT
(1) The President shall be Commander in Chief of the Army and Navy of the United States, and of the militia of the several states, when called into the actual service of the United States; he may require the opinion, in writing, of the principal officer in each of the executive departments, upon any subject relating to the duties of their respective offices, and he shall have power to grant reprieves and pardons for offenses against the United States, except in cases of impeachment.

(4) TIME OF ELECTIONS
Congress decides the day the electors are to be elected and the day they are to vote.

(5) QUALIFICATIONS
The President must be at least 35 years old, be a citizen of the United States by birth, and have been living in the United States for 14 years or more.

(6) VACANCIES
If the President dies, resigns, or is removed from office, the Vice President becomes President.

(7) SALARY
The President receives a salary that cannot be raised or lowered during a term of office. The President may not be paid any additional salary by the federal government or any state or local government. Today the President's salary is $200,000 a year, plus expenses for things such as housing, travel, and entertainment.

(8) OATH OF OFFICE
Before taking office, the President must promise to perform the duties faithfully and to protect the country's form of government. Usually the Chief Justice of the Supreme Court administers the oath of office.

(1) THE PRESIDENT'S LEADERSHIP
The President is the commander of the nation's armed forces and of the National Guard when it is in service of the nation. All government officials of the executive branch must report their actions to the President when asked. The President can excuse people from punishment for crimes committed.

(2) TREATIES AND APPOINTMENTS
The President has the authority to make treaties, but they must be approved by a two-thirds vote of the Senate. The President appoints justices to the Supreme Court, ambassadors to other countries, and other federal officials with the Senate's approval.

(3) FILLING VACANCIES
If a government official's position becomes vacant when Congress is not in session, the President can make a temporary appointment.

DUTIES
The President must report to Congress on the condition of the country. This report is now presented in the annual State of the Union message.

IMPEACHMENT
The President, the Vice President, or any government official will be removed from office if impeached, or accused, and then found guilty of treason, bribery, or other serious crimes. The Constitution protects government officials from being impeached for unimportant reasons.

FEDERAL COURTS
The authority to decide legal cases is granted to a Supreme Court and to a system of lower courts established by Congress. The Supreme Court is the highest court in the land. Justices and judges are in their offices for life, subject to good behavior.

(1) GENERAL AUTHORITY
Federal courts have the authority to decide cases that arise under the Constitution, laws, and treaties of the United States. They also have the authority to settle disagreements among states and among citizens of different states.

(2) SUPREME COURT
The Supreme Court can decide certain cases being tried for the first time. It can review cases that have already been tried in a lower court if the decision has been appealed, or questioned, by one side.

---

(2) He shall have power, by and with the advice and consent of the Senate, to make treaties, provided two-thirds of the senators present concur; and he shall nominate, and by and with the advice and consent of the Senate, shall appoint ambassadors, other public ministers and consuls, judges of the Supreme Court, and all other officers of the United States, whose appointments are not herein otherwise provided for, and which shall be established by law; but the Congress may by law vest the appointment of such inferior officers, as they think proper, in the President alone, in the courts of law, or in the heads of departments.

(3) The President shall have power to fill up all vacancies that may happen during the recess of the Senate, by granting commissions which shall expire at the end of their next session.

SECTION 3. DUTIES OF THE PRESIDENT
He shall from time to time give to the Congress information of the state of the Union, and recommend to their consideration such measures as he shall judge necessary and expedient; he may, on extraordinary occasions, convene both houses, or either of them, and in case of disagreement between them, with respect to the time of adjournment, he may adjourn them to such time as he shall think proper; he shall receive ambassadors and other public ministers; he shall take care that the laws be faithfully executed, and shall commission all the officers of the United States.

SECTION 4. IMPEACHMENT
The President, Vice President and all civil officers of the United States, shall be removed from office on impeachment for, and conviction of, treason, bribery, or other high crimes and misdemeanors.

ARTICLE III
THE JUDICIAL BRANCH

SECTION 1. FEDERAL COURTS
The judicial power of the United States shall be vested in one Supreme Court, and in such inferior courts as the Congress may from time to time ordain and establish. The judges, both of the supreme and inferior courts, shall hold their offices during good behavior, and shall, at stated times, receive for their services a compensation, which shall not be diminished during their continuance in office.

SECTION 2. AUTHORITY OF THE FEDERAL COURTS
(1) The judicial power shall extend to all cases, in law and equity, arising under this Constitution, the laws of the United States, and treaties made or which shall be made, under their authority; to all cases affecting ambassadors, other public ministers and consuls; to all cases of admiralty and maritime jurisdiction; to controversies to which the United States shall be a party; to controversies between two or more states; [*between a state and citizens of another state;*] between citizens of different states; —between citizens of the same state claiming lands under grants of different states, [*and between a state or the citizens thereof, and foreign states, citizens, or subjects.*]

(2) In all cases affecting ambassadors, other public ministers and consuls, and those in which a state shall be party, the Supreme Court shall have original jurisdiction. In all the other cases before mentioned, the Supreme Court shall have appellate jurisdiction, both as to law and fact, with such exceptions, and under such regulations as the Congress shall make.

(3) The trial of all crimes, except in cases of impeachment, shall be by jury; and such trial shall be held in the state where the said crimes shall have been committed; but when not committed within any state, the trial shall be at such place or places as the Congress may by law have directed.

SECTION 3. TREASON

(1) Treason against the United States shall consist only in levying war against them, or in adhering to their enemies, giving them aid and comfort. No person shall be convicted of treason unless on the testimony of two witnesses to the same overt act, or on confession in open court.

(2) The Congress shall have power to declare the punishment of treason, but no attainder of treason shall work corruption of blood, or forfeiture except during the life of the person attainted.

ARTICLE IV
RELATIONS AMONG STATES

SECTION 1. OFFICIAL RECORDS

Full faith and credit shall be given in each state to the public acts, records, and judicial proceedings of every other state. And the Congress may by general laws prescribe the manner in which such acts, records, and proceedings shall be proved, and the effect thereof.

SECTION 2. PRIVILEGES OF THE CITIZENS

(1) The citizens of each state shall be entitled to all privileges and immunities of citizens in the several states.

(2) A person charged in any state with treason, felony, or other crime, who shall flee from justice, and be found in another state, shall on demand of the executive authority of the state from which he fled, be delivered up, to be removed to the state having jurisdiction of the crime.

(3) [*No person held to service or labor in one state, under the laws thereof, escaping into another, shall in consequence of any law or regulation therein, be discharged from such service or labor, but shall be delivered up on claim of the party to whom such service or labor may be due.*]

(1) ADMISSION OF NEW STATES
Congress has the authority to admit new states to the Union. All new states have the same rights as existing states.

(2) FEDERAL PROPERTY
The Constitution allows Congress to make or change laws governing federal property. This applies to territories and federally owned land within states, such as national parks.

GUARANTEES TO THE STATES
The federal government guarantees that every state have a republican form of government. The United States must also protect the states against invasion and help the states deal with rebellion or local violence.

AMENDING THE CONSTITUTION
Changes to the Constitution may be proposed by a two-thirds vote of both the House of Representatives and the Senate or by a national convention called by Congress when asked by two-thirds of the states. For an amendment to become law, the legislatures or conventions in three-fourths of the states must approve it.

(1) PUBLIC DEBT
Any debt owed by the United States before the Constitution went into effect was to be honored.

(2) FEDERAL SUPREMACY
This clause declares that the Constitution and federal laws are the highest in the nation. Whenever a state law and a federal law are found to disagree, the federal law must be obeyed so long as it is Constitutional.

(3) OATHS OF OFFICE
All federal and state officials must promise to follow and enforce the Constitution. These officials, however, cannot be required to follow a particular religion or satisfy any religious test.

SECTION 3. NEW STATES AND TERRITORIES

(1) New states may be admitted by the Congress into this Union; but no new state shall be formed or erected within the jurisdiction of any other state; nor any state be formed by the junction of two or more states, or parts of states, without the consent of the legislatures of the states concerned as well as of the Congress.

(2) The Congress shall have power to dispose of and make all needful rules and regulations respecting the territory or other property belonging to the United States; and nothing in this Constitution shall be so construed as to prejudice any claims of the United States, or of any particular state.

SECTION 4. GUARANTEES TO THE STATES

The United States shall guarantee to every state in this Union a republican form of government, and shall protect each of them against invasion; and on application of the legislature, or of the executive (when the legislature cannot be convened) against domestic violence.

ARTICLE V
AMENDING THE CONSTITUTION

The Congress, whenever two-thirds of both houses shall deem it necessary, shall propose amendments to this Constitution, or, on the application of the legislatures of two-thirds of the several states, shall call a convention for proposing amendments, which, in either case, shall be valid to all intents and purposes, as part of this Constitution, when ratified by the legislatures of three-fourths of the several states, or by conventions in three-fourths thereof, as the one or the other mode of ratification may be proposed by the Congress; provided that [*no amendment which may be made prior to the year 1808 shall in any manner affect the first and fourth clauses in the Ninth Section of the First Article; and that*] no state, without its consent, shall be deprived of its equal suffrage in the Senate.

ARTICLE VI
GENERAL PROVISIONS

(1) All debts contracted and engagements entered into, before the adoption of this Constitution, shall be as valid against the United States under this Constitution, as under the Confederation.

(2) This Constitution, and the laws of the United States which shall be made in pursuance thereof, and all treaties made, or which shall be made, under the authority of the United States, shall be the supreme law of the land; and the judges in every state shall be bound thereby, anything in the Constitution or laws of any state to the contrary notwithstanding.

(3) The Senators and Representatives before mentioned, and the members of the several state legislatures, and all executive and judicial officers, both of the United States and of the several states, shall be bound by oath or affirmation, to support this Constitution; but no religious test shall ever be required as a qualification to any office or public trust under the United States.

ARTICLE VII
RATIFICATION

The ratification of the conventions of nine states, shall be sufficient for the establishment of this Constitution between the states so ratifying the same.

Done in convention by the unanimous consent of the states present the seventeenth day of September in the year of our Lord one thousand seven hundred and eighty seven and of the independence of the United States of America the Twelfth. In witness whereof we have hereunto subscribed our names.
George Washington—President and deputy from Virginia

DELAWARE
George Read
Gunning Bedford, Jr.
John Dickinson
Richard Bassett
Jacob Broom

MARYLAND
James McHenry
Daniel of St. Thomas Jenifer
Daniel Carroll

VIRGINIA
John Blair
James Madison, Jr.

NORTH CAROLINA
William Blount
Richard Dobbs Spaight
Hugh Williamson

SOUTH CAROLINA
John Rutledge
Charles Cotesworth Pinckney
Charles Pinckney
Pierce Butler

GEORGIA
William Few
Abraham Baldwin

NEW HAMPSHIRE
John Langdon
Nicholas Gilman

MASSACHUSETTS
Nathaniel Gorham
Rufus King

CONNECTICUT
William Samuel Johnson
Roger Sherman

NEW YORK
Alexander Hamilton

NEW JERSEY
William Livingston
David Brearley
William Paterson
Jonathan Dayton

PENNSYLVANIA
Benjamin Franklin
Thomas Mifflin
Robert Morris
George Clymer
Thomas FitzSimons
Jared Ingersoll
James Wilson
Gouverneur Morris

ATTEST: William Jackson, secretary

RATIFICATION
In order for the Constitution to become law, 9 of the 13 states had to approve it. Special conventions were held for this purpose. The process took 9 months to complete.

BASIC FREEDOMS

The Constitution guarantees our five basic freedoms of expression. It provides for the freedoms of religion, speech, the press, peaceable assembly, and petition for redress of grievances.

WEAPONS AND THE MILITIA

This amendment was included to prevent the federal government from taking away guns used by state militias.

HOUSING SOLDIERS

The federal government cannot force people to house soldiers in their homes during peacetime. However, Congress may pass laws allowing this during wartime.

SEARCHES AND SEIZURES

This amendment protects people's privacy and safety. Subject to certain exceptions, a law officer cannot search a person or a person's home and belongings unless a judge has issued a valid search warrant. There must be good reason for the search. The warrant must describe the place to be searched and the people or things to be seized, or taken.

RIGHTS OF ACCUSED PERSONS

If a person is accused of a crime that is punishable by death or of any other crime that is very serious, a grand jury must decide if there is enough evidence to hold a trial. People cannot be tried twice for the same crime, nor can they be forced to testify against themselves. No person shall be fined, jailed, or executed by the government unless the person has been given a fair trial. The government cannot take a person's property for public use unless fair payment is made.

American Documents

AMENDMENT 1 (1791)***
BASIC FREEDOMS

Congress shall make no law respecting an establishment of religion, or prohibiting the free exercise thereof; or abridging the freedom of speech, or of the press; or the right of the people peaceably to assemble, and to petition the government for a redress of grievances.

AMENDMENT 2 (1791)
WEAPONS AND THE MILITIA

A well-regulated militia, being necessary to the security of a free state, the right of the people to keep and bear arms shall not be infringed.

AMENDMENT 3 (1791)
HOUSING SOLDIERS

No soldier shall, in time of peace, be quartered in any house, without the consent of the owner; nor in time of war, but in a manner to be prescribed by law.

AMENDMENT 4 (1791)
SEARCHES AND SEIZURES

The right of the people to be secure in their persons, houses, papers, and effects, against unreasonable searches and seizures, shall not be violated; and no warrants shall issue but upon probable cause, supported by oath or affirmation, and particularly describing the place to be searched, and the persons or things to be seized.

AMENDMENT 5 (1791)
RIGHTS OF ACCUSED PERSONS

No person shall be held to answer for a capital, or otherwise infamous crime, unless on a presentment or indictment of a grand jury, except in cases arising in the land or naval forces, or in the militia, when in actual service in time of war or public danger; nor shall any person be subject for the same offense to be twice put in jeopardy of life or limb; nor shall be compelled in any criminal case to be a witness against himself; nor be deprived of life, liberty, or property, without due process of law; nor shall private property be taken for public use without just compensation.

*** The date beside each amendment is the year that the amendment was ratified and became part of the Constitution.

AMENDMENT 6 (1791)
RIGHT TO A FAIR TRIAL

In all criminal prosecutions, the accused shall enjoy the right to a speedy and public trial, by an impartial jury of the state and district wherein the crime shall have been committed, which district shall have been previously ascertained by law, and to be informed of the nature and cause of the accusation; to be confronted with the witnesses against him; to have compulsory process for obtaining witnesses in his favor, and to have the assistance of counsel for his defense.

AMENDMENT 7 (1791)
JURY TRIAL IN CIVIL CASES

In suits at common law, where the value in controversy shall exceed 20 dollars, the right of trial by jury shall be preserved, and no fact tried by a jury shall be otherwise re-examined in any court of the United States, than according to the rules of the common law.

AMENDMENT 8 (1791)
BAIL AND PUNISHMENT

Excessive bail shall not be required, nor excessive fines imposed, nor cruel and unusual punishments inflicted.

AMENDMENT 9 (1791)
RIGHTS OF THE PEOPLE

The enumeration in the Constitution, of certain rights, shall not be construed to deny or disparage others retained by the people.

AMENDMENT 10 (1791)
POWERS OF THE STATES AND THE PEOPLE

The powers not delegated to the United States by the Constitution, nor prohibited by it to the states, are reserved to the states respectively, or to the people.

AMENDMENT 11 (1798)
SUITS AGAINST STATES

The judicial power of the United States shall not be construed to extend to any suit in law or equity, commenced or prosecuted against one of the United States or citizens of another state, or by citizens or subjects of any foreign state.

RIGHT TO A FAIR TRIAL
A person accused of a crime has the right to a public trial by an impartial jury, locally chosen. The trial must be held within a reasonable amount of time. The accused person must be told of all charges and has the right to see, hear, and question any witnesses. The federal government must provide a lawyer free of charge to a person who is accused of a serious crime and who is unable to pay for legal services.

JURY TRIAL IN CIVIL CASES
In most federal civil cases involving more than 20 dollars, a jury trial is guaranteed. Civil cases are those disputes between two or more people over money, property, personal injury, or legal rights. Usually civil cases are not tried in federal courts unless much larger sums of money are involved or unless federal courts are given the authority to decide a certain type of case.

BAIL AND PUNISHMENT
Courts cannot treat harshly people accused of crimes or punish them in unusual or cruel ways. Bail is money put up as a guarantee that an accused person will appear for trial. In certain cases bail can be denied altogether.

RIGHTS OF THE PEOPLE
The federal government must respect all natural rights, whether or not they are listed in the Constitution.

POWERS OF THE STATES AND THE PEOPLE
Any rights not clearly given to the federal government or denied to the states belong to the states or to the people.

SUITS AGAINST STATES
A citizen of one state cannot sue another state in federal court.

ELECTION OF PRESIDENT
AND VICE PRESIDENT
This amendment replaces the part
of Article II, Section 1, that originally explained the process of
electing the President and Vice
President. Amendment 12 was an
important step in the development
of the two-party system. It allows a
party to nominate its own candidates for both President and Vice
President.

END OF SLAVERY
People cannot be forced to work
against their will unless they have
been tried for and convicted of a
crime for which this means of punishment is ordered. Congress may
enforce this by law.

CITIZENSHIP
All persons born or naturalized in
the United States are citizens of the
United States and of the state in
which they live. State governments
may not deny any citizen the full
rights of citizenship. This amendment also guarantees due process
of law. According to due process of
law, no state may take away the
rights of a citizen. All citizens must
be protected equally under law.

AMENDMENT 12 (1804)
ELECTION OF PRESIDENT AND VICE PRESIDENT

The electors shall meet in their respective states, and vote by ballot for President
and Vice President, one of whom, at least, shall not be an inhabitant of the same
state with themselves; they shall name in their ballots the person voted for as
President, and in distinct ballots the person voted for as Vice President, and they
shall make distinct lists of all persons voted for as President, and of all persons
voted for as Vice President, and of the number of votes for each, which lists they
shall sign and certify, and transmit, sealed, to the seat of government of the United
States, directed to the President of the Senate; the President of the Senate shall, in
the presence of the Senate and House of Representatives, open all the certificates,
and the votes shall then be counted; the person having the greatest number of votes
for President shall be the President, if such a number be a majority of the whole
number of electors appointed; and if no person have such majority; then from the
persons having the highest numbers not exceeding three on the list of those voted
for as President, the House of Representatives shall choose immediately, by ballot,
the President. But in choosing the President, the votes shall be taken by states, the
representation from each state having one vote; a quorum for this purpose shall
consist of a member or members from two thirds of the states, and a majority of all
the states shall be necessary to a choice. [*And if the House of Representatives shall not
choose a President whenever the right of choice shall devolve upon them, before the fourth
day of March next following, then the Vice President shall act as President, as in the case of
the death or other constitutional disability of the President.*] The person having the
greatest number of votes as Vice President, shall be the Vice President, if such number be a majority of the whole number of electors appointed, and if no person have
a majority, then, from the two highest numbers on the list the Senate shall choose
the Vice President; a quorum for the purpose shall consist of two thirds of the
whole number of Senators, and a majority of the whole number shall be necessary
to a choice. But no person constitutionally ineligible to the office of President shall
be eligible to that of Vice President of the United States.

AMENDMENT 13 (1865)
END OF SLAVERY

SECTION 1. ABOLITION
Neither slavery nor involuntary servitude, except as a punishment for crime
whereof the party shall have been duly convicted, shall exist within the United
States, or any place subject to their jurisdiction.

SECTION 2. ENFORCEMENT
Congress shall have power to enforce this article by appropriate legislation.

AMENDMENT 14 (1868)
RIGHTS OF CITIZENS

SECTION 1. CITIZENSHIP
All persons born or naturalized in the United States and subject to the jurisdiction thereof, are citizens of the United States and of the state wherein they reside.
No state shall make or enforce any law which shall abridge the privileges or immunities of citizens of the United States, nor shall any state deprive any person of life,
liberty, or property, without due process of law; nor deny to any person within its
jurisdiction the equal protection of the laws.

SECTION 2. NUMBER OF REPRESENTATIVES

Representatives shall be apportioned among the several states according to their respective numbers, counting the whole number of persons in each state, [*excluding Indians not taxed*]. But when the right to vote at any election for the choice of electors for President and Vice President of the United States, representatives in Congress, the executive and judicial officers of a state, or the members of the legislature thereof, is denied to any of the [*male*] inhabitants of such state, being [*twenty-one years of age and*] citizens of the United States, or in any way abridged, except for participation in rebellion or other crime, the basis of representation therein shall be reduced in the proportion which the number of such [*male*] citizens shall bear to the whole number of [*male*] citizens [*twenty-one years of age*] in such state.

SECTION 3. PENALTY FOR REBELLION

No person shall be a Senator or Representative in Congress, or elector of President and Vice President, or hold any office, civil or military, under the United States, or under any state, who, having previously taken an oath, as a member of Congress, or as an officer of the United States, or as a member of any state legislature, or as an executive or judicial officer of any state, to support the Constitution of the United States, shall have engaged in insurrection or rebellion against the same, or given aid or comfort to the enemies thereof. But Congress may, by a vote of two thirds of each house, remove such disability.

SECTION 4. GOVERNMENT DEBT

The validity of the public debt of the United States, authorized by law, including debts incurred for payment of pensions and bounties for services in suppressing insurrection or rebellion, shall not be questioned. But neither the United States nor any state shall assume or pay any debt or obligation incurred in aid of insurrection or rebellion against the United States, [*or any claim for the loss or emancipation of any slave;*] but all such debts, obligations, and claims shall be held illegal and void.

SECTION 5. ENFORCEMENT

The Congress shall have power to enforce, by appropriate legislation, the provisions of this article.

AMENDMENT 15 (1870)
VOTING RIGHTS

SECTION 1. RIGHT TO VOTE

The right of citizens of the United States to vote shall not be denied or abridged by the United States or by any state on account of race, color, or previous condition of servitude.

SECTION 2. ENFORCEMENT

The Congress shall have power to enforce this article by appropriate legislation.

AMENDMENT 16 (1913)
INCOME TAX

The Congress shall have power to lay and collect taxes on incomes, from whatever source derived, without apportionment among the several states, and without regard to any census or enumeration.

NUMBER OF REPRESENTATIVES
Each state's representation in Congress is based on its total population. Any state denying eligible citizens the right to vote will have its representation in Congress decreased. This clause abolished the Three-fifths Compromise in Article 1, Section 2. Later amendments granted women the right to vote and lowered the voting age to 18.

PENALTY FOR REBELLION
No person who has rebelled against the United States may hold federal office. This clause was originally added to punish the leaders of the Confederacy for failing to support the Constitution of the United States.

GOVERNMENT DEBT
The federal government is responsible for all public debts. It is not responsible, however, for Confederate debts or for debts that result from any rebellion against the United States.

ENFORCEMENT
Congress may enforce these provisions by law.

RIGHT TO VOTE
No state may prevent a citizen from voting simply because of race or color or condition of previous servitude. This amendment was designed to extend voting rights to enforce this by law.

INCOME TAX
Congress has the power to collect taxes on its citizens, based on their personal incomes rather than on the number of people living in a state.

DIRECT ELECTION OF SENATORS
Originally, state legislatures elected senators. This amendment allows the people of each state to elect their own senators directly. The idea is to make senators more responsible to the people they represent.

PROHIBITION
This amendment made it illegal to make, sell, or transport liquor within the United States or to transport it out of the United States or its territories. Amendment 18 was the first to include a time limit for approval. If not ratified within seven years, it would be repealed, or canceled. Many later amendments have included similar time limits.

WOMEN'S VOTING RIGHTS
This amendment granted women the right to vote.

TERMS OF OFFICE
The terms of the President and the Vice President begin on January 20, in the year following their election. Members of Congress take office on January 3. Before this amendment newly elected members of Congress did not begin their terms until March 4. This meant that those who had run for reelection and been defeated remained in office for four months.

AMENDMENT 17 (1913)
DIRECT ELECTION OF SENATORS

SECTION 1. METHOD OF ELECTION
The Senate of the United States shall be composed of two Senators from each state, elected by the people thereof, for six years; and each Senator shall have one vote. The electors in each state shall have the qualifications requisite for electors of the most numerous branch of the state legislatures.

SECTION 2. VACANCIES
When vacancies happen in the representation of any state in the Senate, the executive authority of such state shall issue writs of election to fill such vacancies: *Provided,* that the legislature of any state may empower the executive thereof to make temporary appointments until the people fill the vacancies by election as the legislature may direct.

SECTION 3. EXCEPTION
[*This amendment shall not be so construed as to affect the election or term of any Senator chosen before it becomes valid as part of the Constitution.*]

AMENDMENT 18 (1919)
BAN ON ALCOHOLIC DRINKS

SECTION 1. PROHIBITION
[*After one year from the ratification of this article the manufacture, sale, or transportation of intoxicating liquors within, the importation thereof into, or the exportation thereof from the United States and all territory subject to the jurisdiction thereof for beverage purposes is hereby prohibited.*]

SECTION 2. ENFORCEMENT
[*The Congress and the several states shall have concurrent power to enforce this article by appropriate legislation.*]

SECTION 3. RATIFICATION
[*This article shall be inoperative unless it shall have been ratified as an amendment to the Constitution by the legislatures of the several states as provided in the Constitution, within seven years from the date of the submission hereof to the states by the Congress.*]

AMENDMENT 19 (1920)
WOMEN'S VOTING RIGHTS

SECTION 1. RIGHT TO VOTE
The right of citizens of the United States to vote shall not be denied or abridged by the United States or by any state on account of sex.

SECTION 2. ENFORCEMENT
Congress shall have power to enforce this article by appropriate legislation.

AMENDMENT 20 (1933)
TERMS OF OFFICE

SECTION 1. BEGINNING OF TERMS
The terms of the President and Vice President shall end at noon on the 20th day of January, and the terms of Senators and Representatives at noon on the 3rd day of January, of the years in which such terms would have ended if this article had not been ratified; and the terms of their successors shall then begin.

SECTION 2. SESSIONS OF CONGRESS

The Congress shall assemble at least once in every year, and such meeting shall begin at noon on the 3rd day of January, unless they shall by law appoint a different day.

SECTION 3. PRESIDENTIAL SUCCESSION

If, at the time fixed for the beginning of the term of the President, the President-elect shall have died, the Vice President-elect shall become President. If a President shall not have been chosen before the time fixed for the beginning of his term, or if the President-elect shall have failed to qualify, then the Vice President-elect shall act as President until a President shall have qualified; and the Congress may by law provide for the case wherein neither a President-elect nor a Vice President-elect shall have qualified, declaring who shall then act as President, or the manner in which one who is to act shall be selected and such person shall act accordingly until a President or Vice President shall be qualified.

SECTION 4. ELECTIONS DECIDED BY CONGRESS

The Congress may by law provide for the case of the death of any of the persons from whom the House of Representatives may choose a President whenever the right of choice shall have devolved upon them, and for the case of the death of any of the persons from whom the Senate may choose a Vice President whenever the right of choice shall have devolved upon them.

SECTION 5. EFFECTIVE DATE

[*Sections 1 and 2 shall take effect on the 15th day of October following the ratification of this article.*]

SECTION 6. RATIFICATION

[*This article shall be inoperative unless it shall have been ratified as an amendment to the Constitution by the legislatures of three fourths of the several states within seven years from the date of its submission.*]

AMENDMENT 21 (1933)
END OF PROHIBITION

SECTION 1. REPEAL OF AMENDMENT 18

The eighteenth article of amendment to the Constitution of the United States is hereby repealed.

SECTION 2. STATE LAWS

The transportation or importation into any state, territory, or possession of the United States for delivery or use therein of intoxicating liquors, in violation of the laws thereof, is hereby prohibited.

SECTION 3. RATIFICATION

[*This article shall be inoperative unless it shall have been ratified as an amendment to the Constitution by conventions in the several states, as provided in the Constitution within seven years from the date of the submission hereof to the states by Congress.*]

SESSIONS OF CONGRESS
Congress meets at least once a year, beginning at noon on January 3. Congress had previously met at least once a year beginning on the first Monday of December.

PRESIDENTIAL SUCCESSION
If the newly elected President dies before January 20, the newly elected Vice President becomes President on that date. If a President has not been chosen by January 20 or does not meet the requirements for being President, the newly elected Vice President becomes President. If neither the newly elected President nor the newly elected Vice President meets the requirements for office, Congress decides who will serve as President until a qualified President or Vice President is chosen.

END OF PROHIBITION
This amendment repealed Amendment 18. This is the only amendment to be ratified by state conventions instead of by state legislatures. Congress felt that this would give people's opinions about prohibition a better chance to be heard.

AMENDMENT 22 (1951)
TWO-TERM LIMIT FOR PRESIDENTS

SECTION 1. TWO-TERM LIMIT

No person shall be elected to the office of the President more than twice, and no person who has held the office of President, or acted as President, for more than two years of a term to which some other person was elected President shall be elected to the office of the President more than once. [*But this article shall not apply to any person holding the office of President when this article was proposed by the Congress, and shall not prevent any person who may be holding the office of President, or acting as President, during the term within which this article becomes operative from holding the office of President, or acting as President, during the remainder of such term.*]

SECTION 2. RATIFICATION

[*This article shall be inoperative unless it shall have been ratified as an amendment to the Constitution by the legislatures of three-fourths of the several states within seven years from the date of its submission to the states by the Congress.*]

AMENDMENT 23 (1961)
PRESIDENTIAL ELECTORS FOR DISTRICT OF COLUMBIA

SECTION 1. NUMBER OF ELECTORS

The District constituting the seat of Government of the United States shall appoint in such manner as Congress may direct:

A number of electors of President and Vice President equal to the whole number of Senators and Representatives in Congress to which the District would be entitled if it were a state, but in no event more than the least populous state; they shall be in addition to those appointed by the states, but they shall be considered, for the purposes of the election of President and Vice President, to be electors appointed by a state, and they shall meet in the District and perform such duties as provided by the twelfth article of amendment.

SECTION 2. ENFORCEMENT

The Congress shall have power to enforce this article by appropriate legislation.

AMENDMENT 24 (1964)
BAN ON POLL TAXES

SECTION 1. POLL TAX ILLEGAL

The right of citizens of the United States to vote in any primary or other election for President or Vice President, for electors for President or Vice President, or for Senator or Representative in Congress, shall not be denied or abridged by the United States or any state by reason of failure to pay any poll tax or other tax.

SECTION 2. ENFORCEMENT

The Congress shall have power to enforce this article by appropriate legislation.

AMENDMENT 25 (1967)
PRESIDENTIAL SUCCESSION

SECTION 1. PRESIDENTIAL VACANCY

In case of the removal of the President from office or of his death or resignation, the Vice President shall become President.

SECTION 2. VICE PRESIDENTIAL VACANCY

Whenever there is a vacancy in the office of the Vice President, the President shall nominate a Vice President who shall take the office upon confirmation by a majority vote of both houses of Congress.

SECTION 3. PRESIDENTIAL DISABILITY

Whenever the President transmits to the President pro tempore of the Senate and the Speaker of the House of Representatives his written declaration that he is unable to discharge the powers and duties of his office, and until he transmits to them a written declaration to the contrary, such powers and duties shall be discharged by the Vice President as Acting President.

SECTION 4. DETERMINING PRESIDENTIAL DISABILITY

Whenever the Vice President and a majority of either the principal officers of the executive departments or of such other body as Congress may by law provide, transmit to the President pro tempore of the Senate and the Speaker of the House of Representatives their written declaration that the President is unable to discharge the powers and duties of his office, the Vice President shall immediately assume the powers and duties of the office as Acting President.

Thereafter, when the President transmits to the President pro tempore of the Senate and the Speaker of the House of Representatives his written declaration that no inability exists, he shall resume the powers and duties of his office unless the Vice President and a majority of either the principal officers of the executive department or of such other body as Congress may by law provide, transmit within four days to the President pro tempore of the Senate and the Speaker of the House of Representatives their written declaration that the President is unable to discharge the powers and duties of his office. Thereupon Congress shall decide the issue, assembling within 48 hours for that purpose if not in session. If the Congress, within 21 days after receipt of the latter written declaration, or, if Congress is not in session, within 21 days after Congress is required to assemble, determines by two-thirds vote of both houses that the President is unable to discharge the powers and duties of his office, the Vice President shall continue to discharge the same as Acting President; otherwise the President shall resume the powers and duties of his office.

AMENDMENT 26 (1971)
VOTING AGE

SECTION 1. RIGHT TO VOTE

The right of citizens of the United States, who are 18 years of age or older, to vote shall not be denied or abridged by the United States or any state on account of age.

SECTION 2. ENFORCEMENT

The Congress shall have the power to enforce this article by appropriate legislation.

AMENDMENT 27 (1992)
CONGRESSIONAL PAY

No law, varying the compensation for the services of the Senators and Representatives, shall take effect, until an election of Representatives shall have intervened.

VICE PRESIDENTIAL VACANCY
If the office of the Vice President becomes open, the President names someone to assume that office and that person becomes Vice President if both houses of Congress approve by a majority vote.

PRESIDENTIAL DISABILITY
This section explains in detail what happens if the President cannot continue in office because of sickness or any other reason. The Vice President takes over as acting President until the President is able to resume office.

DETERMINING PRESIDENTIAL DISABILITY
If the Vice President and a majority of the Cabinet inform the Speaker of the House and the president pro tempore of the Senate that the President cannot carry out his or her duties, the Vice President then serves as acting President. To regain the office, the President has to inform the Speaker and the president pro tempore in writing that he or she is again able to serve. But, if the Vice President and a majority of the Cabinet disagree with the President and inform the Speaker and the president pro tempore that the President is still unable to serve, then Congress decides who will hold the office of President.

VOTING AGE
All citizens 18 years or older have the right to vote. Formerly, the voting age was 21.

CONGRESSIONAL PAY
A law raising or lowering the salaries for members of Congress cannot be passed for that session of Congress.

THE NATIONAL ANTHEM

The Star-Spangled Banner

"The Star-Spangled Banner" was written by Francis Scott Key in September 1814 and adopted as the national anthem in March 1931. The army and navy had recognized it as such long before Congress approved it.

During the War of 1812, Francis Scott Key spent a night aboard a British warship in the Chesapeake Bay while trying to arrange for the release of an American prisoner. The battle raged throughout the night, while the Americans were held on the ship. The next morning, when the smoke from the cannons finally cleared, Francis Scott Key was thrilled to see the American flag still waving proudly above Fort McHenry. It symbolized the victory of the Americans.

There are four verses to the national anthem. In these four verses, Key wrote about how he felt when he saw the flag still waving over Fort McHenry. He wrote that the flag was a symbol of the freedom for which the people had fought so hard. Key also told about the pride he had in his country and the great hopes he had for the future of the United States.

(1)

Oh, say can you see by the dawn's early light
What so proudly we hail'd at the twilight's last gleaming,
Whose broad stripes and bright stars through the perilous fight
O'er the ramparts we watch'd were so gallantly streaming?
And the rockets' red glare, the bombs bursting in air,
Gave proof through the night that our flag was still there.
Oh, say does that star-spangled banner yet wave
O'er the land of the free and the home of the brave?

(2)

On the shore dimly seen through the mists of the deep,
Where the foe's haughty host in dread silence reposes,
What is that which the breeze, o'er the towering steep,
As it fitfully blows, half conceals, half discloses?
Now it catches the gleam of the morning's first beam,
In full glory reflected now shines in the stream.
'Tis the star-spangled banner, oh, long may it wave
O'er the land of the free and the home of the brave!

(3)

And where is that band who so vauntingly swore
That the havoc of war and the battle's confusion
A home and a country should leave us no more?
Their blood has wash'd out their foul footstep's pollution.
No refuge could save the hireling and slave
From the terror of flight or the gloom of the grave,
And the star-spangled banner in triumph doth wave
O'er the land of the free and the home of the brave.

(4)

Oh, thus be it ever when freemen shall stand
Between their lov'd home and the war's desolation!
Blest with vict'ry and peace may the heav'n-rescued land
Praise the power that hath made and preserv'd us a nation!
Then conquer we must, when our cause it is just,
And this be our motto, "In God is our Trust,"
And the star-spangled banner in triumph shall wave
O'er the land of the free and the home of the brave.

THE PLEDGE OF ALLEGIANCE

I pledge allegiance to the Flag

of the United States of America,

and to the Republic

for which it stands,

one Nation under God, indivisible,

with liberty and justice for all.

The flag is a symbol of the United States of America. The Pledge of Allegiance says that the people of the United States promise to stand up for the flag, their country, and the basic beliefs of freedom and fairness upon which the country was established.

Biographical Dictionary

The Biographical Dictionary lists many of the important people introduced in this book. The page number tells where the main discussion of each person starts. See the Index for other page references.

A

Adams, Abigail *1744–1818* Patriot who wrote about women's rights in letters to John Adams, her husband. pp. 303, 332

Adams, John *1735–1826* 2nd U.S. President and one writer of the Declaration of Independence. pp. 262, 289

Adams, Samuel *1722–1803* American Revolutionary leader who set up a Committee of Correspondence in Boston and helped form the Sons of Liberty. p. 279

Addams, Jane *1860–1935* American reformer who brought the idea of settlement houses from Britain to the United States. With Ellen Gates Starr, she founded Hull House in Chicago. pp. 575–576

Alexander VI (al•ig•ZAN•der) *1431–1503* Pope who in 1493 divided the lands in the Americas between Spain and Portugal. p. 156

Allen, Ethan *1738–1789* Leader of the Green Mountain Boys, who won one of the first American victories in the Revolutionary War. p. 313

Anderson, Robert *1805–1871* Union commander of Fort Sumter who was forced to surrender to the Confederacy. p. 497

Anthony, Susan B. *1820–1906* Women's suffrage leader who worked to enable women to have the same rights as men. p. 457

Anza, Juan Bautista de (AHN•sah) *1735–1788?* Spanish explorer who founded San Francisco. p. 194

Armstrong, Louis *1901–1971* Noted jazz trumpeter who helped make jazz popular in the 1920s. p. 566

Arnold, Benedict *1741–1801* Continental army officer who became a traitor and worked for the British army. p. 314

Atahuallpa (ah•tah•WAHL•pah) *1502?–1533* Inca ruler who was killed in the Spanish conquest of the Incas. p. 152

Attucks, Crispus *1723?–1770* Patriot and former slave who was killed during the Boston Massacre. p. 278

Austin, Moses *1761–1821* American pioneer who wanted to start an American colony in Texas. p. 444

Austin, Stephen F. *1793–1836* Moses Austin's son. He carried out his father's dream of starting an American colony in Texas. p. 444

B

Balboa, Vasco Núñez de (bahl•BOH•ah, NOON•yes day) *1475–1519* Explorer who in 1513 became the first European to reach the western coast of the Americas—proving to Europeans that the Americas were separate from Asia. p. 141

Banneker, Benjamin *1731–1806* African who helped survey the land for the new capital of the United States. p. 382

Barker, Penelope One of the first politically active women in the American colonies, she led the women of Edenton, North Carolina, in a "tea party" of their own to boycott British tea. p. 280

Barrett, Janie Porter *1865–1948* African American teacher who founded a settlement house in Hampton, Virginia. p. 576

Barton, Clara *1821–1912* Civil War nurse and founder of the American Red Cross. p. 511

Beauregard, Pierre Gustave (BOH•ruh•gard) *1818–1893* Confederate army officer. p. 473

Bee, Barnard Elliott *1824–1861* Confederate army officer. p. 474

Behaim, Martin (BAY•hym) *1436?–1507* German geographer who in 1492 made the first world globe in Europe. p. 121

Bell, Alexander Graham *1847–1922* American who invented the telephone. p. 562

Berliner, Emile (BER•luhn•er, uh•MEEL) *1851–1929* German immigrant who, in 1887, invented a phonograph that played flat discs, or records. p. 565

Bessemer, Henry *1813–1898* British inventor of a way to make steel more easily and cheaply than before. p. 556

Bienville, Jean Baptiste Le Moyne, Sieur de (byan•VEEL, ZHAHN ba•TEEST luh MWAHN) *1680–1747* French explorer who—with his brother, Pierre Le Moyne, Sieur d'Iberville—started an early settlement at the mouth of the Mississippi River. p. 204

Bonaparte, Napoleon (BOH•nuh•part, nuh•POH•lee•uhn) *1769–1821* French leader who sold all of the Louisiana region to the United States. p. 409

Boone, Daniel *1734–1820* American pioneer who was one of the first to cross the Appalachians. pp. 242, 403

Booth, John Wilkes *1838–1865* Actor who assassinated President Abraham Lincoln. p. 526

Bowie, James *1796–1836* American soldier killed at the Alamo. p. 446

Bradford, William *1590–1657* Governor of Plymouth Colony. p. 176

Breckinridge, John *1821–1875* Democrat from Kentucky who ran against Abraham Lincoln in the 1860 presidential election. p. 496

Brendan *485?–578* Irish monk said to have sailed to an unknown land between Europe and Asia. p. 119

Brown, John *1800–1859* American abolitionist who seized a weapons storehouse to help slaves rebel. He was caught and hanged. p. 486

Brown, Linda *1943–* African American student whose family was among a group that challenged public-school segregation. p. 599

Biographical Dictionary

Brown, Moses *1738–1836* Textile pioneer who built the first textile mill in the United States, using Samuel Slater's plans. p. 431

Burgoyne, John (ber•GOYN) *1722–1792* British general who lost a battle to the Continental army on October 17, 1777, at Saratoga, New York. p. 312

Burnet, David G. *1788–1870* 1st president of the Republic of Texas, when it was formed in 1836. p. 446

Byrd, William, II *1674–1744* Early Virginia planter who kept a diary of his daily life. p. 239

C

Cabeza de Vaca, Álvar Núñez (kah•BAY•sah day VAH•kuh) *1490?–1560?* Spanish explorer who went to Mexico City and told stories of the Seven Cities of Gold. p. 155

Caboto, Giovanni *1450?–1499?* Italian explorer who in 1497 sailed from England and landed in what is now Newfoundland, though he thought he had landed in Asia. The English called him John Cabot. p. 138

Cabral, Pedro (kah•BRAHL) *1467?–1520* Portuguese explorer who claimed Brazil for Portugal when his fleet accidentally sailed there in 1500. p. 156

Calhoun, John C. *1782–1850* Vice President under John Quincy Adams and Andrew Jackson. He was a strong believer in states' rights. p. 440

Calvert, Cecilius *1605–1675* First proprietor of the Maryland colony. p. 220

Cameahwait (kah•MEE•ah•wayt) *1800s* Chief of the Shoshones during the Lewis and Clark expedition. He was Sacagawea's brother. p. 410

Carnegie, Andrew *1835–1919* Entrepreneur who helped the steel industry grow in the United States. p. 556

Cartier, Jacques (kar•TYAY, ZHAHK) *1491–1557* French explorer who sailed up the St. Lawrence River and began a fur-trading business with the Hurons. p. 167

Carver, George Washington *1864–1943* African American scientist who developed new ways of farming in the South. p. 599

Cavelier, René-Robert (ka•vuhl•YAY) *See* La Salle.

Champlain, Samuel de (sham•PLAYN) *1567?–1635* French explorer who founded the first settlement at Quebec. p. 168

Charles I *1500–1558* King of Spain. p. 160

Charles I *1600–1649* British king who chartered the colonies of Massachusetts and Maryland. pp. 206, 220

Charles II *1630–1685* British king who granted a charter for the Carolina colony. Son of Charles I and Henrietta Maria. p. 221

Chávez, César *1927–1993* Labor leader and organizer of the United Farm Workers. p. 604

Clark, George Rogers *1752–1818* Revolutionary War leader who helped protect the Ohio River valley against the British. He was brother of William Clark. p. 313

Clark, William *1770–1838* American explorer who aided Meriwether Lewis in an expedition through the Louisiana Purchase. p. 410

Clay, Henry *1777–1852* Representative from Kentucky who worked for compromises on the slavery issue. p. 490

Clinton, George *1739–1812* American politician who helped form the Democratic-Republican party. p. 368

Columbus, Christopher *1451–1506* Italian-born Spanish explorer who in 1492 sailed west from Spain and thought he had reached Asia but had actually reached islands near the Americas, lands that were unknown to Europeans. p. 119

Cooper, Peter *1791–1883* American manufacturer who built *Tom Thumb*, one of the first locomotives made in the United States. p. 437

Cornish, Samuel *1795–1858* African who in 1827 helped John Russwurm found an abolitionist newspaper called *Freedom's Journal*. p. 455

Cornwallis, Charles *1738–1805* British general who surrendered at the Battle of Yorktown, resulting in victory for the Americans in the Revolutionary War. p. 315

Coronado, Francisco Vásquez de (kawr•oh•NAH•doh) *1510?–1554* Spanish explorer who led an expedition from Mexico City into what is now the southwestern United States in search of the Seven Cities of Gold. p. 155

Cortés, Hernando (kawr•TEZ) *1485–1547* Spanish conquistador who conquered the Aztec Empire. p. 150

Crockett, Davy *1786–1836* American pioneer who was killed at the Alamo. p. 446

D

da Gama, Vasco (dah GAH•muh) *1460?–1524* Portuguese navigator who sailed from Europe, around the southern tip of Africa, and on to Asia between 1497 and 1499. p. 129

Dare, Virginia *1587–?* First child born of English parents in America. She vanished with the other settlers of the Lost Colony. p. 172

Davis, Jefferson *1808–1889* United States senator from Mississippi who became president of the Confederacy. p. 497

Dawes, William *1745–1799* American who, along with Paul Revere, warned the Patriots that the British were marching toward Concord. p. 283

de Soto, Hernando (day SOH•toh) *1496?–1542* Spanish explorer who led an expedition into what is today the southeastern United States. p. 157

de Triana, Rodrigo Sailor on the *Pinta* during Columbus's first voyage; he was the first to sight land. p. 133

Dekanawida (deh•kahn•uh•WIH•duh) *1500s* Legendary Iroquois holy man who called for an end to the fighting among the Iroquois, a view that led to the formation of the Iroquois League. p. 93

Dias, Bartholomeu (DEE•ahsh) *1450?–1500* Portuguese navigator who in 1488 became the first European to sail around the southern tip of Africa. p. 129

Dickenson, Susanna Survivor of the Alamo who was sent by Santa Anna to tell Texas leaders that the Alamo had fallen. p. 446

Dickinson, John *1732–1808* Member of the Continental Congress who wrote most of the Articles of Confederation, adopted in 1781. p. 333

Douglas, Stephen A. *1813–1861* American legislator who wrote the Kansas–Nebraska Act and debated Lincoln in a race for a Senate seat from Illinois. p. 494

Douglass, Frederick *1817–1895* Abolitionist speaker and writer who had escaped from slavery. pp. 456, 476

Drake, Francis *1543–1596* English explorer who sailed around the world. p. 171

Du Bois, W. E. B. (doo•BOYS) *1868–1963* African American leader who helped form the National Association for the Advancement of Colored People (NAACP). pp. 598–599

Edison, Thomas *1847–1931* American who invented a talking machine and the electric light bulb; he also built the first power station to supply electricity to New York City. p. 562

Elizabeth I *1533–1603* Queen of England during the middle to late 1500s. p. 171

Ellicott, Andrew *1754–1820* American surveyor who helped survey land for the new United States capital. p. 382

Ellington, Edward Kennedy (Duke) *1899–1974* Band leader who became well-known playing jazz during the 1920s. p. 566

Emerson, Ralph Waldo *1803–1882* American poet. p. 284

Endecott, John *1588–1665* Colonist who led the first group of Puritans in building a settlement he named Salem. p. 206

Equiano, Olaudah (ek•wee•AHN•oh, OHL•uh•dah) *1750–1797* African who was kidnapped from his village and sold into slavery. He later wrote a book describing his experiences. p. 238

Eriksson, Leif (AIR•ik•suhn, LAYV) *?–1020?* Viking explorer who sailed from Greenland to North America in the A.D. 1000s. p. 120

Eriksson, Thorvald (AIR•ik•suhn, TUR•val) *1000s* Brother of Leif Eriksson. He led one trip to Vinland. p. 120

Estéban (ehs•TAY•bahn) *1500–1539* African explorer who went with Cabeza de Vaca to Mexico City and told stories of the Seven Cities of Gold. Estéban was killed on a later expedition, the purpose of which was to find out whether the stories were true. p. 155

Farragut, Jorge (FAIR•uh•guht, HAWR•hay) *1755–1817* Spanish-born man who fought in the Continental army and the navy. p. 312

Ferdinand II *1452–1516* King of Spain who—with Queen Isabella, his wife—sent Christopher Columbus on his voyage to find a western route to Asia. p. 131

Ferraro, Geraldine *1935–* First woman to be nominated as a major party's candidate for Vice President of the United States. p. 605

Finley, John Fur trader who helped Daniel Boone find the way across the Appalachian Mountains to Kentucky. p. 403

Ford, Henry *1863–1947* American automobile manufacturer who mass-produced cars at low cost by using assembly lines. p. 564

Forten, James *1766–1842* Free African in Philadelphia who ran a busy sail factory and became wealthy. p. 489

Franklin, Benjamin *1706–1790* American leader who was sent to Britain to ask Parliament for representation. He was a writer of the Declaration of Independence, a delegate to the Constitutional Convention, and a respected scientist and business leader. pp. 215, 276

Frémont, John *1813–1890* Surveyor who led an early expedition to make maps of the West. His careful descriptions helped thousands of settlers. p. 447

Frick, Henry Clay *1849–1919* Manager of a steel mill in Homestead, Pennsylvania. His announcement of a pay cut led to a violent strike. p. 571

Friedan, Betty *1921–* Writer who helped set up the National Organization for Women to work for women's rights. pp. 604–605

Frontenac, Louis de Buade, Count de (FRAHN•tuh•nak) *1622–1698* French leader who was appointed governor-general of New France by King Louis XIV. p. 202

Fulton, Robert *1765–1815* American inventor who built one of the earliest steamboats. p. 436

Gage, Thomas *1721–1787* Head of the British army in North America and colonial governor of Massachusetts. p. 280

Gálvez, Bernardo de (GAHL•ves) *1746–1786* Spanish governor of Louisiana who sent supplies to the Patriots in the Revolutionary War and led his own soldiers in taking a British fort in Florida. p. 312

Garrison, William Lloyd *1805–1879* American abolitionist who started a newspaper called *The Liberator*. p. 455

Gates, Horatio *1728–1806* American general who defeated the British in 1777, at Saratoga, New York. p. 312

George II *1683–1760* British king who chartered the Georgia colony. p. 222

George III *1738–1820* King of England during the Revolutionary War. p. 266

Gerry, Elbridge *1744–1814* Massachusetts delegate to the Constitutional Convention. p. 361

Gompers, Samuel *1850–1924* Early labor union leader who formed the American Federation of Labor. pp. 569–570

Gorham, Nathaniel *1738–1796* Massachusetts delegate to the Constitutional Convention. p. 362

Granger, Gordon Union general who read the order declaring all slaves in Texas to be free. p. 531

Grant, Ulysses S. *1822–1885* 18th U.S. President and, earlier, commander of the Union army in the Civil War. p. 521

Greene, Nathanael *1742–1786* Commander of the Continental army in the southern colonies. p. 313

Grenville, George *1712–1770* British prime minister who passed the Stamp Act in 1765. p. 271

Hale, Nathan *1755–1776* Patriot hero who was captured and executed by the British. p. 313

Hallidie, Andrew S. *1836–1900* American who invented the cable car. p. 577

Hamilton, Alexander *1755–1804* American leader in calling for the Constitutional Convention and winning support for it. He favored a strong national government. pp. 339, 379

Hammond, James Henry *1807–1864* Senator from South Carolina. p. 479

Hancock, John *1737–1793* Leader of the Sons of Liberty in the Massachusetts colony. p. 283

Harrison, William Henry *1773–1841* 9th U.S. President. Earlier he directed U.S. forces against the Indians at the Battle of Tippecanoe and was a commander in the War of 1812. p. 415

Hart, Nancy *1747?–1840?* A woman from Georgia who served as a spy for the Patriots during the Revolutionary War. p. 303

Harvard, John *1607–1638* American colonial pastor for whom Harvard University is named. When the new school was founded, he gave it more than 400 books. p. 208

Haynes, Elwood *1857–1925* Indiana inventor who developed the first gasoline-powered automobile, in 1894. p. 564

Hays, Mary Ludwig *1754?–1832* Known as Molly Pitcher, she carried water to American soldiers during the Battle of Monmouth; when her husband fell during the battle, she began firing his cannon. p. 303

Henrietta Maria *1609–1669* Queen of Charles I of England. The Maryland colony was named in her honor. p. 220

Henry *1394–1460* Henry the Navigator, prince of Portugal, who set up the first European school for training sailors in navigation. p. 127

Henry, Patrick *1736–1799* American colonist who spoke out in the Virginia legislature against paying British taxes. His views became widely known, and Loyalists accused him of treason. p. 274

Henry IV *1553–1610* King of France. p. 168

Hiawatha (hy•uh•WAH•thuh) *1500s* Onondaga chief who persuaded other Iroquois tribes to form the Iroquois League. p. 93

Hooker, Thomas *1586?–1647* Minister who helped form the Connecticut colony. His democratic ideas were adopted in the Fundamental Orders. p. 208

Houston, Sam *1793–1863* President of the Republic of Texas and, later, governor of the state of Texas. p. 446

Huascar (WAHS•kar) Brother of Atahuallpa, who killed him to become the last Inca king of Peru. p. 152

Hudson, Henry *?–1611* Explorer who sailed up the Hudson River, giving the Dutch a claim to the area. p. 169

Huishen *500s* Chinese Buddhist monk said to have sailed to an unknown land between Europe and Asia. p. 119

Hutchinson, Anne Marbury *1591–1643* English-born woman who left Massachusetts because of her religious beliefs. She settled near Providence, which joined with other settlements to form the Rhode Island colony. p. 209

Iberville, Pierre Le Moyne, Sieur d' (ee•ber•VEEL) *1661–1706* French explorer who—with his brother, Jean Baptiste Le Moyne, Sieur de Bienville—started an early settlement at the mouth of the Mississippi River. p. 204

Idrisi, al- (uhl•ih•DREE•see) *1100–1165* Arab geographer and cartographer. p. 122

Isabella I *1451–1504* Queen of Spain who—with King Ferdinand, her husband—sent Columbus on his voyage to find a western route to Asia. p. 131

Jackson, Andrew *1767–1845* 7th U.S. President and, earlier, commander who won the final battle in the War of 1812. As President he favored a strong Union and ordered the removal of Native Americans from their lands. pp. 418, 439

Jackson, Thomas (Stonewall) *1824–1863* Confederate general. p. 472

James I *1566–1625* King of England in the early 1600s. The James River and Jamestown were named after him. p. 173

Jay, John *1745–1829* American leader who wrote letters to newspapers, defending the Constitution. He became the first chief justice of the Supreme Court. pp. 370

Jefferson, Thomas *1743–1826* 3rd U.S. President and the main writer of the Declaration of Independence. p. 296

Jenney, William *1832–1907* American engineer who developed the use of steel frames to build tall buildings. p. 576

John I *1357–1433* King of Portugal during a time of great exploration. Father of Prince Henry, who set up a school of navigation. p. 127

Johnson, Andrew *1808–1875* 17th U.S. President. Differences with Congress about Reconstruction led to his being impeached, though he was found not guilty. p. 533

Joliet, Louis (zhohl•YAY, loo•EE) *1645–1700* French fur trader who explored lakes and rivers for France, with Marquette and five others. p. 203

Jones, Jehu Free African who owned one of South Carolina's best hotels before the Civil War. p. 489

Jones, John Paul *1747–1792* Patriot naval commander. p. 313

Kalb, Johann, Baron de *1721–1780* German soldier who helped the Patriots in the Revolutionary War. p. 310

Kennedy, John F. *1917–1963* 35th U.S. President. He helped pass the Civil Rights Act of 1964. p. 602

Key, Francis Scott *1779–1843* American lawyer and poet who wrote the words to "The Star-Spangled Banner." p. 423

King, Martin Luther, Jr. *1929–1968* African American civil rights leader who worked for integration in nonviolent ways. He won the Nobel Peace Prize in 1964. pp. 540, 601

King, Rufus *1755–1827* Massachusetts delegate to the Constitutional Convention. p. 362

Knox, Henry *1750–1806* Secretary of war in the first government under the Constitution. p. 379

Kosciuszko, Thaddeus (kawsh•CHUSH•koh) *1746–1817* Polish officer who helped the Patriots in the Revolutionary War. He later returned to Poland and led a revolution there. p. 310

Kublai Khan (KOO•bluh KAHN) *1215–1294* Ruler of China who was visited by Marco Polo. p. 124

La Salle, René-Robert Cavelier, Sieur de (luh•SAL) *1643–1687* French explorer who found the mouth of the Mississippi River and claimed the whole Mississippi Valley for France. p. 203

Lafayette, Marquis de (lah•fee•ET) *1757–1834* French noble who fought alongside the Americans in the Revolutionary War. p. 310

Lafon, Thomy *1810–1893* Free African who made a fortune from businesses in New Orleans. p. 489

Las Casas, Bartolomé de (lahs KAH•suhs, bar•toh•luh•MAY day) *1474–1566* Spanish missionary who spent much of his life trying to help native peoples in the Americas. p. 160

Law, John *1671–1729* Scottish banker who was appointed proprietor of the Louisiana region in 1717. p. 205

Lazarus, Emma *1849–1887* Poet who wrote, in 1883, the poem now on the base of the Statue of Liberty. p. 612

Le Moyne, Jean-Baptiste (luh•MWAHN, ZHAHN ba•TEEST) *See* Bienville.

Le Moyne, Pierre *See* Iberville.

Lee, Charles *1731–1782* American officer during the Revolutionary War. p. 289

Lee, Richard Henry *1732–1794* American Revolutionary leader who said to the Continental Congress that the colonies should become independent from Britain. p. 295

Lee, Robert E. *1807–1870* United States army colonel who gave up his post and became commander of the Confederate army in the Civil War. p. 509

L'Enfant, Pierre Charles *1754–1825* French-born American engineer who planned the buildings and streets of the new capital of the United States. p. 382

Lewis, Meriwether *1774–1809* American explorer chosen by Thomas Jefferson to be a pathfinder in the territory of the Louisiana Purchase. p. 410

Lincoln, Abraham *1809–1865* 16th U.S. President, leader of the Union in the Civil War, and signer of the Emancipation Proclamation. pp. 494, 496

Lincoln, Benjamin *1733–1810* Continental army general. p. 315

Lincoln, Mary Todd *1818–1882* Wife of Abraham Lincoln. p. 509

Lindbergh, Charles *1902–1974* Airplane pilot who was the first to fly solo between the United States and Europe. p. 564

Livingston, Robert R. *1746–1813* One of the writers of the Declaration of Independence. p. 296

Louis XIV *1638–1715* King of France. p. 201

Lowell, Francis Cabot *1775–1817* Textile pioneer who set up an American mill in which several processes were completed under one roof. p. 433

Lucas, Eliza *1722?–1793* South Carolina settler who experimented with indigo plants. She gave away seeds, and indigo then became an important cash crop. p. 221

Madison, Dolley *1768–1849* James Madison's wife and First Lady during the War of 1812. p. 418

Madison, James *1751–1836* 4th U.S. President. He was a leader in calling for the Constitutional Convention, writing the Constitution, and winning support for it. p. 338

Magellan, Ferdinand (muh•JEH•luhn) *1480?–1521* Portuguese explorer who in 1519 led a fleet of ships from Spain westward to Asia. He died on the voyage, but one of the ships made it back to Spain, completing the first trip around the world. p. 142

Malcolm X *1925–1965* African American leader who disagreed with the views of Martin Luther King, Jr., on nonviolence and integration. pp. 602–603

Malintzin (mah•LINT•suhn) *1501?–1550* Aztec princess who interpreted for Hernando Cortés and helped him in other ways to conquer Mexico. p. 150

Mann, Horace *1796–1859* American school reformer in the first half of the 1800s. p. 454

Marconi, Guglielmo (mar•KOH•nee, goo•LYEL•moh) *1874–1937* Italian who invented the radio. p. 563

Marion, Francis *1732?–1795* Known as the Swamp Fox, he led Continental soldiers through the swamps of South Carolina on daring raids against the British. p. 313

Marquette, Jacques (mar•KET, ZHAHK) *1637–1675* Catholic missionary who knew several Indian languages. With Joliet, he explored lakes and rivers for France. p. 202

Marshall, James *1810–1885* Carpenter who found gold at John Sutter's sawmill near Sacramento, California, leading to the California gold rush of 1849. p. 450

Marshall, John *1755–1835* Chief Justice of the Supreme Court in 1832; he ruled that the United States should protect the Cherokees and their lands in Georgia. p. 442

Marshall, Thurgood *1908–1993* NAACP lawyer who argued the school segregation case that the Supreme Court ruled on in 1954 and, later, was the first African American to serve on the Supreme Court. p. 599

Mason, George *1725–1792* Virginia delegate to the Constitutional Convention who argued for an end to the slave trade. p. 350

Massasoit (ma•suh•SOYT) *?–1661* Chief of the Wampanoags, who lived in peace with the Pilgrims. p. 177

Menéndez de Avilés, Pedro (meh•NEN•des day ah•vee•LAYS) *1519–1574* Spanish leader of settlers in St. Augustine, Florida, the first permanent European settlement in what is now the United States. p. 195

Metacomet *1639?–1676* Chief of the Wampanoags, son of Massasoit, he was known by the colonists as King Philip. He made war on the colonists. p. 210

Mongoulacha (mahn•goo•LAY•chah) *1700s* Indian leader who helped Bienville and Iberville. p. 204

Monroe, James *1758–1831* 5th U.S. President. He established the Monroe Doctrine, which said that the United States would stop any European nation from expanding its American empire. p. 419

Morris, Gouverneur (guh•vuh•NIR) *1752–1816* American leader who was in charge of the final wording of the United States Constitution. p. 342

Morse, Samuel F. B. *1791–1872* American who invented the telegraph and the Morse code. p. 557

Motecuhzoma (maw•tay•kwah•SOH•mah) *1466–1520* Emperor of the Aztecs when they were conquered by the Spanish. He is also known as Montezuma. p. 149

Mott, Lucretia *1793–1880* American reformer who, with Elizabeth Cady Stanton, organized the first convention for women's rights. p. 457

Muhlenberg, Peter *1746–1807* Young minister, son of the colonies' Lutheran leader, who became a Patriot militia officer. p. 301

Murray, John *1732–1809* Royal governor of Virginia during the Revolutionary War. He promised enslaved Africans their freedom if they would fight for the British government. p. 305

Niza, Marcos de (day NEE•sah) *1495–1558* Spanish priest who was sent with Estéban to confirm stories of the Seven Cities of Gold. When he returned to Mexico City, he said he had seen a golden city. p. 155

North, Lord Frederick *1732–1792* Prime minister of Britain in 1773. His laws concerning tea led to the Boston Tea Party. p. 280

O'Connor, Sandra Day *1930–* First woman to be appointed to the United States Supreme Court. p. 605

Oglethorpe, James *1696–1785* English settler who was given a charter to settle Georgia. He wanted to bring in debtors from England to help settle it. p. 222

Osceola *1804–1838* Leader of the Seminoles in Florida. p. 441

Oswald, Richard *1705–1784* British merchant who met with Benjamin Franklin to negotiate terms between America and Britain at the end of the Revolutionary War. p. 316

Otis, James *1725–1783* Massachusetts colonist who spoke out against British taxes and called for "no taxation without representation." p. 272

Page, William Tyler Wrote "The American's Creed," which won a national writing contest in 1917. p. 608

Paine, Thomas *1737–1809* Author of a widely read pamphlet called *Common Sense*, in which he attacked King George III and called for a revolution to make the colonies independent. p. 295

Parks, Rosa *1913–* African American woman whose refusal to give up her seat on a Montgomery, Alabama, bus started a year-long bus boycott. pp. 600–601

Paterson, William *1745–1806* Constitutional delegate from New Jersey who submitted the New Jersey Plan, under which each state would have one vote, regardless of population. p. 348

Penn, William *1644–1718* Proprietor of Pennsylvania under a charter from King Charles II of Britain. Penn was a Quaker who made Pennsylvania a refuge for settlers who wanted religious freedom. p. 215

Perry, Oliver Hazard *1785–1819* American naval commander who won an important battle in the War of 1812. p. 416

Pigafetta, Antonio (pee•gah•FET•ah) *1500s* A sailor who kept a journal during his travels with Magellan. p. 143

Pike, Zebulon *1779–1813* American who led an expedition down the Arkansas River to explore the southwestern part of the Louisiana Purchase. p. 412

Pinzón, Martín Captain of the *Pinta*. Brother of Vincente Pinzón. p. 133

Pinzón, Vincente Captain of the *Niña*. Brother of Martín Pinzón. p. 133

Pizarro, Francisco (pee•ZAR•oh) *1475?–1541* Spanish conquistador who conquered the Inca Empire in 1533. p. 151

Pocahontas (poh•kuh•HAHN•tuhs) *1595–1617* Indian chief Powhatan's daughter. p. 174

Polk, James K. *1795–1849* 11th U.S. President. He gained land for the United States by setting a northern boundary in 1846 and winning a war with Mexico in 1848. p. 447

Polo, Maffeo Trader from Venice; uncle of Marco Polo. p. 124

Polo, Marco *1254–1324* Explorer from Venice who spent many years in Asia in the late 1200s. He wrote a book about his travels that gave Europeans information about Asia. p. 124

Polo, Niccolò Trader from Venice; father of Marco Polo. p. 124

Ponce de León, Juan (PAHN•say day lay•OHN) *1460–1521* Spanish explorer who landed on the North American mainland in 1513, in what is now Florida. p. 154

Powhatan (pow•uh•TAN) *1550?–1618* Chief of a federation of Indian tribes that lived in the Virginia territory. Pocahontas was his daughter. p. 174

Ptolemy, Claudius (TAH•luh•mee) *100s* Astronomer in ancient Egypt. p. 139

Pulaski, Casimir (puh•LAS•kee) *1747–1779* Polish noble who came to the British colonies to help the Patriots in the Revolutionary War. p. 310

Raleigh, Sir Walter (RAH•lee) *1554–1618* English explorer who used his own money to set up England's first colony in North America, on Roanoke Island near North Carolina. p. 171

Randolph, Edmund *1753–1813* Virginia delegate to the Constitutional Convention who thought the number of representatives a state would have in Congress should be based on the population of the state. p. 347

Read, George *1733–1798* Delaware delegate to the Constitutional Convention who thought the states should be done away with in favor of a strong national government. p. 346

Revere, Paul *1735–1818* American who warned the Patriots that the British were marching toward Concord, where Patriot weapons were stored. p. 283

Riis, Jacob (REES) *1849–1914* Reformer and writer who described the living conditions of the poor in New York City. p. 574

Rockefeller, John D. *1839–1937* American oil entrepreneur who joined many refineries into one business, called the Standard Oil Company. p. 557

Rolfe, John *1585–1622* Jamestown settler who brought tobacco plants from the Caribbean region to the colony. He later married Pocahontas. p. 218

Ross, John *1790–1866* Chief of the Cherokee nation. He fought in United States courts to prevent the loss of the Cherokees' lands in Georgia. Though he won the legal battle, he still had to lead his people along the Trail of Tears to what is now Oklahoma. p. 442

Ruffin, Edmund *1794–1865* Agriculturist from Virginia. He fired the first shot on Fort Sumter. p. 503

Russwurm, John *1799–1851* Helped Samuel Cornish found an abolitionist newspaper called *Freedom's Journal* in 1827. p. 455

Rutledge, John *1739–1800* Delegate to the Constitutional Convention, South Carolina governor, and Supreme Court Justice. p. 350

Sacagawea (sak•uh•juh•WEE•uh) *1786?–1812?* Shoshone woman who acted as an interpreter for the Lewis and Clark expedition. p. 410

Salem, Peter *1750?–1816* African who fought with the Minutemen at Concord and at the Battle of Bunker Hill. p. 305

Samoset *1590?–1653?* Native American chief who spoke English and who helped the settlers at Plymouth. p. 176

Santa Anna, Antonio López de *1794–1876* Dictator of Mexico; defeated Texans at the Alamo. p. 445

Scott, Dred *1795?–1858* Enslaved African who took his case for freedom to the Supreme Court and lost. p. 492

Scott, Winfield *1786–1866* American general in the war with Mexico. p. 449

Seguín, Juan (say•GEEN) Defender of the Alamo, where he was killed. p. 446

Sequoyah (sih•KWOY•uh) *1765?–1843* Cherokee leader who in 1921 created a writing system for the Cherokee language. p. 442

Serra, Junípero *1713–1784* Spanish missionary who helped build a string of missions in California. p. 198

Seward, William H. *1801–1872* Secretary of State in the cabinet of Abraham Lincoln. p. 515

Shays, Daniel *1747?–1825* Leader of Shays's Rebellion, which showed the weakness of the government under the Articles of Confederation. p. 335

Shen Tong Student from Beijing University in China who compared the Tiananmen Square massacre with the Boston Massacre. p. 320

Sherman, Roger *1721–1793* One of the writers of the Declaration of Independence. Connecticut delegate to the Constitutional Convention who worked out the compromise in which Congress would have two houses—one based on state population and one with two members from each state. pp. 296, 348

Sherman, William Tecumseh *1820–1891* Union general who, after defeating Confederate forces in Atlanta, led the March to the Sea, on which his troops caused great destruction. p. 524

Slater, Samuel *1768–1835* Textile pioneer who helped bring the Industrial Revolution to the United States by providing plans for a new spinning machine. p. 431

Slocumb, Mary *1700s* North Carolina colonist who fought in the Revolutionary War. p. 303

Smith, John *1580–1631* English explorer who, as leader of the Jamestown settlement, saved its people from starvation. p. 174

Smith, Joseph *1805–1844* Mormon leader who settled his people in Illinois and was killed there. p. 448

Spalding, Eliza *1807–1851* American missionary and pioneer in the Oregon Country. p. 447

Spalding, Henry *1801–1874* American missionary and pioneer in the Oregon Country. p. 447

Sprague, Frank *1857–1934* American inventor who built the trolley car, an electric streetcar. p. 578

Squanto *See* Tisquantum.

Stanton, Elizabeth Cady *1815–1902* American reformer who, with Lucretia Mott, organized the first convention for women's rights. p. 457

Starr, Ellen Gates *1860–1940* Reformer who, with Jane Addams, founded Hull House in Chicago. p. 576

Steuben, Friedrich, Baron von (vahn SHTOY•buhn) *1730–1794* German soldier who helped train Patriot troops in the Revolutionary War. p. 310

Stowe, Harriet Beecher *1811–1896* American abolitionist who in 1852 wrote the book *Uncle Tom's Cabin*. p. 455

Stuyvesant, Peter (STY•vuh•suhnt) *1610?–1672* Last governor of the Dutch colony of New Netherland. p. 211

Sutter, John *1803–1880* American pioneer who owned the sawmill where gold was discovered, leading to the California gold rush. p. 450

Taney, Roger B. (TAW•nee) *1777–1864* Supreme Court Chief Justice who wrote the ruling against Dred Scott. p. 493

Tascalusa (tuhs•kah•LOO•sah) *1500s* Leader of the Mobile people when they battled with Spanish troops led by Hernando de Soto. p. 157

Tecumseh (tuh•KUHM•suh) *1768–1813* Shawnee leader of Indians in the Northwest Territory. He wanted to form a strong Indian confederation. p. 414

Tenskwatawa (ten•SKWAHT•uh•wah) *1768–1834* Shawnee leader known as the Prophet. He worked with his brother Tecumseh and led the Indians at the Battle of Tippecanoe in 1811. p. 414

Tisquantum *1585?–1622* Native American who spoke English and who helped the Plymouth colony. p. 176

Tompkins, Sally *1833–1916* Civil War nurse who eventually ran her own private hospital in Richmond, Virginia. She was a captain in the Confederate army, the only woman to achieve such an honor. p. 512

Tonti, Henri de (TOHN•tee, ahn•REE duh) *1650–1704* French explorer with La Salle. p. 204

Toussaint-Louverture, Pierre (TOO•san LOO•ver•tur) *1743–1803* Haitian revolutionary and general who took over the government of St. Domingue from France and became the ruler of Haiti. p. 410

Travis, William B. *1809–1836* Commander of the Texas force at the Alamo, where he was killed. p. 446

Truth, Sojourner *1797?–1883* Abolitionist and former slave who became a leading preacher against slavery. p. 456

Tubman, Harriet *1820–1913* Abolitionist and former slave who became a conductor on the Underground Railroad. She led about 300 slaves to freedom. p. 487

Turner, Nat *1800–1831* Enslaved African who led a rebellion against slavery. More than 100 slaves were killed, and Turner was caught and hanged. p. 486

Vespucci, Amerigo (veh•SPOO•chee, uh•MAIR•ih•goh) *1454–1512* Italian explorer who made several voyages from Europe to what many people thought was Asia. He determined that he had landed on another continent, which was later called America in his honor. p. 138

Wald, Lillian *1867–1940* Reformer who started the Henry Street Settlement in New York City. p. 576

Waldseemüller, Martin (VAHLT•zay•mool•er) *1470–1518?* German cartographer who published a map in 1507 that first showed a continent named America. p. 139

Ward, Artemas *1727–1800* American commander during the Revolutionary War. p. 289

Warren, Earl *1891–1974* Chief Justice of the Supreme Court who wrote the 1954 decision against school segregation. p. 600

Warren, Mercy Otis *1728–1814* Massachusetts colonist who spoke out against new British taxes on goods. p. 272

Washington, Booker T. *1856–1915* African American who founded Tuskegee Institute in Alabama. p. 598

Washington, George *1732–1799* 1st U.S. President, leader of the Continental army during the Revolutionary War, and president of the Constitutional Convention. pp. 265, 340

Westinghouse, George *1846–1914* American inventor who designed an air brake for stopping trains. p. 556

Wheatley, John Boston slave owner who bought a young African girl to be maidservant to his wife; the family educated the girl and freed her. She became one of the earliest American poets, Phillis Wheatley. p. 304

Wheatley, Phillis *1753?–1784* American poet who wrote poems that praised the Revolution. p. 303

White, John *?–1593?* English painter and cartographer who led the second group that settled on Roanoke Island. p. 172

Whitman, Marcus *1802–1847* American missionary and pioneer in the Oregon Country. p. 447

Whitman, Narcissa *1808–1847* American missionary and pioneer in the Oregon Country. p. 447

Whitney, Eli *1765–1825* American inventor most famous for his invention of the cotton gin and his idea of interchangeable parts, which made mass production possible. pp. 432, 479

Williams, Roger *1603?–1683* Founder of Providence in what is now Rhode Island. He had been forced to leave Massachusetts because of his views. p. 209

Wilson, James *1742–1798* Pennsylvania delegate to the Constitutional Convention who argued for a single chief executive elected by an electoral college. pp. 354–355

Winthrop, John *1588–1649* First governor of Massachusetts Bay colony. p. 206

Woods, Granville T. *1856–1910* African American who improved the air brake and developed a telegraph system for trains. p. 556

Wright, Orville *1871–1948* Pioneer in American aviation who—with his brother, Wilbur—made and flew the first successful airplane, at Kitty Hawk, North Carolina. p. 564

Wright, Wilbur *1867–1912* Pioneer in American aviation who—with his brother, Orville—made and flew the first successful airplane, at Kitty Hawk, North Carolina. p. 564

York *1800s* Enslaved African whose hunting and fishing skills contributed to the Lewis and Clark expedition. p. 410

Young, Brigham *1801–1877* Mormon leader who came after Joseph Smith. He moved his people west to the Great Salt Lake valley. p. 448

Gazetteer

The Gazetteer is a geographical dictionary that will help you locate places discussed in this book. The page number tells where each place appears on a map.

A

Acadia Original name of Nova Scotia, Canada; once a part of New France. p. 191

Adena (uh•DEE•nuh) An ancient settlement of the Mound Builders; located in present-day southern Ohio. (40°N, 81°W) p. 68

Adirondack Mountains (a•duh•RAHN•dak) A mountain range in northeastern New York. p. 93

Alamo A mission in San Antonio, Texas; located in the southeastern part of the state; used as a fort during the Texas Revolution. (29°N, 98°W) p. 446

Alaska Range A mountain range in south central Alaska. p. 40

Albany The capital of New York; located in the eastern part of the state, on the Hudson River; once known as Beverwyck. (43°N, 74°W) p. 34

Albemarle Sound (AL•buh•marl) An inlet of the Atlantic Ocean; located in northeastern North Carolina. p. 172

Alcatraz Island (AL•kuh•traz) A rocky island in San Francisco Bay, California; formerly a U.S. penitentiary, closed in 1963. (38°N, 123°W) p. 589

Aleutian Islands (uh•LOO•shuhn) A chain of volcanic islands; located between the North Pacific and the Bering Sea, extending west from the Alaska Peninsula. (52°N, 177°W) p. 40

Alexandria (Egypt) (a•lig•ZAN•dree•uh) A port city on the Mediterranean Sea; located on the northern coast of Egypt. (31°N, 30°E) p. 115

Alexandria (VA) A city in northern Virginia; located on the Potomac River. (39°N, 77°W) p. 392

Allegheny River (a•luh•GAY•nee) A river in the north-eastern United States; flows southwest to join the Monongahela River in Pennsylvania, forming the Ohio River. p. 93

Altamaha River (AWL•tuh•muh•haw) A river that begins in southeastern Georgia and flows into the Atlantic Ocean. p. 219

Amazon River The longest river in South America, flowing from the Andes Mountains across Brazil and into the Atlantic Ocean. p. 151

Anastasia Island (an•uh•STAY•zhuh) An island in northeastern Florida; located south of St. Augustine, off the coast of St. Johns County. (30°N, 81°W) p. 196

Andes Mountains (AN•deez) The longest chain of mountains in the world; located along the entire western coast of South America. p. 151

Angel Island An island in San Francisco Bay, California. (38°N, 123°W) p. 589

Annapolis (uh•NA•puh•luhs) The capital of Maryland; located on Chesapeake Bay; home of the United States Naval Academy. (39°N, 76°W) p. 340

Antietam (an•TEE•tuhm) A creek near Sharpsburg in north central Maryland; site of a Civil War battle in 1862. (39°N, 78°W) p. 525

Antioch A city in western California; located near the mouth of the Sacramento River. (38°N, 122°W) p. 36

Appalachian Mountains (a•puh•LAY•chuhn) A mountain system of eastern North America; extends from southeastern Quebec, Canada, to central Alabama. p. 41

Appomattox (a•puh•MA•tuhks) A village in central Virginia; site of the battle that ended the Civil War in 1865; once known as Appomattox Courthouse. (37°N, 79°W) p. 525

Arkansas River A tributary of the Mississippi River, beginning in central Colorado and ending in southeastern Arkansas. p. 40

Astoria A port city in northwestern Oregon; located at the mouth of the Columbia River. (46°N, 124°W) p. 76

Athabasca River A southern tributary of the Mackenzie River in Alberta, west central Canada; flows northeast and then north into Lake Athabasca. p. 190

Atlanta Georgia's capital and largest city; located in the northwest central part of the state; site of a Civil War battle in 1864. (33°N, 84°W) p. 34

Augusta A city in eastern Georgia; located on the Savannah River. (33°N, 82°W) p. 219

Austin The capital of Texas; located in the central part of the state on the Colorado River. (30°N, 98°W) p. 34

B

Baffin Bay A large inlet of the Atlantic Ocean between western Greenland and the Northwest Territories, Canada. p. 41

Baffin Island The largest and easternmost island in the Canadian Arctic Islands; once known as Helluland. p. 41

Bahamas An island group in the North Atlantic; located southeast of Florida and north of Cuba. p. 41

Baja California A peninsula in northwestern Mexico extending south-southeast between the Pacific Ocean and the Gulf of California. (32°N, 115°W) p. 40

Bakersfield A city in southern California; located in the San Joaquin Valley. (35°N, 119°W) p. 36

Balboa (bal•BOH•ah) A port town at the southeastern part of the Panama Canal area. (9°N, 80°W) p. 142

Baltimore A major seaport in Maryland; located on the upper end of the Chesapeake Bay. (39°N, 77°W) p. 219

Beaufort Sea (BOH•fert) That part of the Arctic Ocean between northeastern Alaska and the Canadian Arctic Islands. p. 40

Beijing (BAY•JING) The capital of China; located on a large plain in northeastern China; once known as Khanbalik. (40°N, 116°E) p. 320

Benin (buh•NEEN) A former kingdom in West Africa; located along the Gulf of Guinea; present-day southern Nigeria. p. 162

Bennington A town in the southwestern corner of Vermont; site of a major Revolutionary War battle in 1777. (43°N, 73°W) p. 311

Bering Strait A narrow strip of water; separates Asia from North America. p. 49

Beringia (buh•RIN•gee•uh) An ancient land bridge that once connected Asia and North America. p. 49

Berkeley A city in western California; located on the San Francisco Bay. (38°N, 122°W) p. 36

Birmingham A city in north central Alabama. (34°N, 87°W) p. 397

Bismarck The capital of North Dakota; located in the south central part of the state, on the Missouri River. (47°N, 101°W) p. 34

Black Sea A large inland sea between Europe and Asia. p. 125

Boise (BOY•zee) Idaho's capital and largest city; located in the southwestern part of the state. (44°N, 116°W) p. 34

Bonampak An ancient settlement of the Mayan civilization; located in present-day southeastern Mexico. (16°N, 91°W) p. 100

Boone's Trail Daniel Boone's trail that began in North Carolina and ended in Tennessee. p. 404

Boonesborough (BOONZ•ber•oh) A village in eastern central Kentucky; site of a fort founded by Daniel Boone; present-day Boonesboro. (38°N, 84°W) p. 404

Boston The capital and largest city of Massachusetts; a port city located on the Massachusetts Bay. (42°N, 71°W) p. 34

Brainerd A town in southeastern Tennessee; once part of the Cherokee Nation. (35°N, 85°W) p. 442

Brandywine A battlefield on Brandywine Creek in southeastern Pennsylvania; site of a major Revolutionary War battle in 1777. (40°N, 76°W) p. 311

Brazos River (BRA•zuhs) A river in central Texas; flows southeast into the Gulf of Mexico. p. 155

Brooklyn A borough of New York City, New York; located on the western end of Long Island. (41°N, 74°W) p. 589

Brooks Island An island off the coast of California, in San Francisco Bay. (39°N, 122°W) p. 589

Brooks Range A mountain range crossing northern Alaska; forms the northwestern end of the Rocky Mountains. p. 40

Buffalo A city in western New York; located on the northeastern point of Lake Erie. (43°N, 79°W) p. 397

Bull Run A stream in northeastern Virginia; flows toward the Potomac River; site of a Civil War battle in 1861 and in 1862. (39°N, 77°W) p. 525

Cahokia (kuh•HOH•kee•uh) A village in southwestern Illinois; site of an ancient settlement of the Mound Builders. (39°N, 90°W) p. 68

Cajamarca (kah•hah•MAR•kah) A town in northern Peru; located on the Cajamarca River, northwest of Lima. (7°S, 79°W) p. 151

Calicut (KA•lih•kuht) A city in southwestern India; located on the Malabar Coast. (11°N, 76°E) p. 115

Camden A city in north central South Carolina, near the Wateree River; site of a major Revolutionary War battle in 1780. (34°N, 81°W) p. 311

Canary Islands An island group in the Atlantic Ocean off the northwestern coast of Africa. (28°N, 16°W) p. 137

Canton A port city in southeastern China; located on the Canton River; known in China as Guangzhou. (23°N, 113°E) p. 115

Cape Cod A peninsula of southeastern Massachusetts, extending into the Atlantic Ocean and enclosing Cape Cod Bay. (42°N, 70°W) p. 207

Cape Fear A cape at the southern end of Smith Island; located off the coast of North Carolina, at the mouth of the Cape Fear River. (34°N, 78°W) p. 219

Cape Fear River A river in central and southeastern North Carolina; formed by the Deep and Haw rivers; flows southeast into the Atlantic Ocean. p. 219

Cape Hatteras (HA•tuh•ruhs) A cape on southeastern Hatteras Island; located off the coast of North Carolina. (35°N, 75°W) p. 219

Cape of Good Hope A cape located on the southernmost tip of Africa. (34°S, 18°E) p. 129

Cape Verde Islands (VERD) A group of volcanic islands off the western coast of Africa. (16°N, 24°W) p. 129

Caribbean Sea A part of the Atlantic Ocean between the West Indies and Central and South America. p. 41

Carson City The capital of Nevada; located in the western part of the state, near the Carson River. (39°N, 120°W) p. 34

Cascade Range A mountain range in the western United States; a continuation of the Sierra Nevada; extends north from California to Washington. p. 40

Chachapoyas (chah•chah•POH•yahs) A town in northern Peru. (6°S, 78°W) p. 151

Chaco Canyon (CHAH•koh) An ancient settlement of the Anasazi; located in present-day northwestern New Mexico. (37°N, 108°W) p. 68

Chancellorsville (CHAN•suh•lerz•vil) A location in northeastern Virginia, just west of Fredericksburg; site of a Civil War battle in 1863. (38°N, 78°W) p. 525

Chapultepec (chah•POOL•teh•pek) An ancient settlement of the Aztec civilization; located in present-day south central Mexico. (32°N, 116°W) p. 100

Charleston A city in southeastern South Carolina; a major port on the Atlantic Ocean; once known as Charles Towne. (33°N, 80°W) p. 191

Charleston Harbor An inlet of the Atlantic Ocean in eastern South Carolina; located near Charleston. (33°N, 80°W) p. 499

Gazetteer

Charlotte The largest city in North Carolina; located in the south central part of the state. (35°N, 81°W) p. 311

Chattanooga (cha•tuh•NOO•guh) A city in southeastern Tennessee; located on the Tennessee River; site of a Civil War battle in 1863. (35°N, 85°W) p. 525

Chattooga Village A town in northwestern Georgia; once part of the Cherokee Nation. (35°N, 85°W) p. 442

Cherokee Nation (CHAIR•uh•kee) A Native American nation located in present-day northern Georgia, eastern Alabama, southern Tennessee, and western North Carolina. p. 442

Chesapeake Bay An inlet of the Atlantic Ocean; surrounded by Virginia and Maryland. p. 177

Cheyenne (shy•AN) The capital of Wyoming; located in the southeastern part of the state. (41°N, 105°W) p. 34

Chicago A city in northeastern Illinois; located on Lake Michigan; the third-largest city in the United States. (42°N, 88°W) p. 397

Chickamauga (chik•uh•MAW•guh) A city in northwestern Georgia; site of a Civil War battle in 1863. (35°N, 85°W) p. 525

Cholula (choh•LOO•lah) An ancient settlement of the Aztec civilization, located in present-day southern central Mexico. (19°N, 98°W) p. 100

Cincinnati (sin•suh•NA•tee) A large city in southwestern Ohio; located on the Ohio River. (39°N, 84°W) p. 437

Cleveland The largest city in Ohio; located in the northern part of the state; at the mouth of the Cuyahoga River on Lake Erie. (41°N, 82°W) p. 396

Coast Mountains A mountain range in western British Columbia and southern Alaska; a continuation of the Cascade Range. p. 40

Coast Ranges Mountains along the Pacific coast of North America, extending from Alaska to Lower California. p. 40

Cold Harbor A location in east central Virginia, north of the Chickahominy River; site of a Civil War battle in 1862 and in 1864. (38°N, 77°W) p. 525

Colorado River A river in the southwestern United States; its basin extends from the Rocky Mountains to the Sierra Nevada; flows into the Gulf of California. p. 40

Columbia River A river that begins in the Rocky Mountains in southwestern Canada, forms the Washington–Oregon border, and empties into the Pacific Ocean below Portland; supplies much of that area's hydroelectricity. p. 76

Columbus The capital of Ohio; located in the central part of the state, on the Scioto River. (40°N, 83°W) p. 34

Compostela (kahm•poh•STEH•lah) A city in west central Mexico. (21°N, 105°W) p. 155

Concord A town in northeastern Massachusetts, near Boston; site of a major Revolutionary War battle in 1775. (42°N, 71°W) p. 311

Connecticut River The longest river in New England; begins in New Hampshire, flows south, and empties into Long Island Sound, New York. p. 207

Constantinople (kahn•stant•uhn•OH•puhl) A port city in northwestern Turkey. (41°N, 29°E) p. 115

Copán (koh•PAHN) An ancient settlement of the Mayan civilization; located in present-day Honduras, in northern Central America. (15°N, 89°W) p. 100

Cowpens A town in northwestern South Carolina; located near the site of a major Revolutionary War battle in 1781. (35°N, 82°W) p. 311

Coxcatlán (kohs•kaht•LAHN) An ancient settlement of the Aztec civilization; located in present-day south central Mexico. p. 100

Cozumel (koh•soo•MEL) An island in the Caribbean Sea; located east of the Yucatán Peninsula; part of present-day Mexico. (21°N, 87°W) p. 100

Crab Orchard An ancient settlement of the Mound Builders; located in present-day southern Illinois. (38°N, 89°W) p. 68

Cuba An island country in the Caribbean; the largest island of the West Indies. (22°N, 79°W) p. 41

Cumberland Gap A pass through the Appalachian Mountains; located in northeastern Tennessee. p. 404

Cumberland River A river in southern Kentucky and northern Tennessee; flows west to the Ohio River. p. 311

Cuzco (KOOS•koh) The ancient capital of the Inca empire; a city located in present-day Peru, in western South America. (14°S, 72°W) p. 114

Dahlonega (duh•LAHN•uh•guh) A city in northern Georgia; once part of the Cherokee Nation. (35°N, 85°W) p. 442

Dallas A city in northeastern Texas; located on the Trinity River. (33°N, 97°W) p. 397

Deerfield A town in northwestern Massachusetts. (43°N, 73°W) p. 207

Delaware Bay An inlet of the Atlantic Ocean; located between southern New Jersey and Delaware. p. 213

Delaware River A river in the northeastern United States; begins in southern New York and flows into the Atlantic Ocean at Delaware Bay. p. 93

Detroit The largest city in Michigan; located in the southeastern part of the state, on the Detroit River. (42°N, 83°W) p. 191

Dickson An ancient settlement of the Mound Builders; located in present-day central Illinois. p. 68

Dover (DE) The capital of Delaware; located in the central part of the state. (39°N, 76°W) p. 34

Dover (NH) A city in southeastern New Hampshire. (43°N, 71°W) p. 207

East River A strait located in New York; connects Long Island Sound and New York Bay. p. 589

Edenton (EE·duhn·tuhn) A town in northeastern North Carolina; located on Albemarle Sound, near the mouth of the Chowan River. (36°N, 77°W) p. 219

El Paso A city at the western tip of Texas; located on the Rio Grande. (32°N, 106°W) p. 396

Ellesmere Island (ELZ·mir) An island located in the northeastern part of the Northwest Territories; the northernmost point of Canada. p. 40

Ellis Island An island in Upper New York Bay; located southwest of Manhattan. (40°N, 74°W) p. 589

Emerald Mound An ancient settlement of the Mound Builders; located in present-day southwestern Mississippi. (32°N, 91°W) p. 68

Erie Canal The longest canal in the world; located in New York; connects Buffalo (on Lake Erie) with Troy (on the Hudson River). p. 434

Falmouth (FAL·muhth) A town in southwestern Maine. (44°N, 70°W) p. 207

Fargo A city in eastern North Dakota; located on the Red River. (47°N, 97°W) p. 549

Flagstaff A city in northern Arizona. (35°N, 112°W) p. 558

Fort Atkinson A fort in southern Kansas; located on the Sante Fe Trail. (43°N, 89°W) p. 452

Fort Boise (BOY·zee) A fort in eastern Oregon, located on the Snake River and on the Oregon Trail. p. 452

Fort Bridger A present-day village in southwestern Wyoming; once an important station on the Oregon Trail. (41°N, 110°W) p. 452

Fort Christina A Swedish settlement in northern Delaware; present-day Wilmington. (40°N, 76°W) p. 212

Fort Crevecoeur (KREEV·KER) A fort in central Illinois; located on the Illinois River; built by La Salle in 1680. (41°N, 90°W) p. 203

Fort Crown Point A French fort; located in northeastern New York, on the shore of Lake Champlain. p. 265

Fort Cumberland A British fort located in northeastern West Virginia, on its border with Maryland. p. 265

Fort Dearborn A fort in northeastern Illinois; built in 1803; eventually became part of Chicago; site of a major battle in the War of 1812. (42°N, 88°W) p. 417

Fort Donelson A fort located in northwestern Tennessee; site of a major Civil War battle in 1862. p. 525

Fort Duquesne (doo·KAYN) A French fort in present-day Pittsburgh, southwestern Pennsylvania; captured and renamed Fort Pitt in 1758. (40°N, 80°W) p. 265

Fort Edward A British fort in eastern New York, on the Hudson River; a present-day village. (43°N, 74°W) p. 265

Fort Frontenac (FRAHNT·uhn·ak) A French fort once located on the site of present-day Kingston, Ontario, in southeastern Canada; destroyed by the British in 1758. (44°N, 76°W) p. 203

Fort Gibson A fort in eastern Oklahoma; end of the Trail of Tears. (36°N, 95°W) p. 466

Fort Hall A fort in southeastern Idaho; located on the Snake River, at a junction on the Oregon Trail. p. 452

Fort Laramie A fort in southeastern Wyoming; located on the Oregon Trail. (42°N, 105°W) p. 452

Fort Le Boeuf (luh·BUHF) A French fort in northwestern Pennsylvania, just south of Lake Erie; located in present-day Waterford. (42°N, 80°W) p. 265

Fort Ligonier (lig·uh·NIR) A British fort located in southern Pennsylvania near the Ohio River. p. 265

Fort Louisbourg (LOO·is·berg) A French fort; located in eastern Canada on the Atlantic coast. (46°N, 60°W) p. 265

Fort Mackinac (MA·kuh·naw) A fort located on the tip of present-day northern Michigan; site of a major battle in the War of 1812. (46°N, 85°W) p. 417

Fort Mandan A fort in present-day central North Dakota, on the Missouri River; site of a winter camp for the Lewis and Clark Expedition. (48°N, 104°W) p. 409

Fort McHenry A fort in central Maryland; located on the harbor in Baltimore; site of a major battle in the War of 1812. (39°N, 77°W) p. 417

Fort Miamis A French fort located on the southern shore of Lake Michigan, in present-day southwestern Michigan. p. 203

Fort Necessity A British fort in southwestern Pennsylvania; located in present-day Great Meadows. (38°N, 80°W) p. 265

Fort Niagara A fort located in western New York, at the mouth of the Niagara River. (43°N, 79°W) p. 265

Fort Oswego A British fort in western New York, on the coast of Lake Ontario. (43°N, 77°W) p. 265

Fort Sumter A fort on a human-made island, off the coast of South Carolina, in Charleston Harbor; site of the first Civil War battle in 1861. (33°N, 80°W) p. 499

Fort Ticonderoga (ty·kahn·der·OH·gah) A historic French fort on Lake Champlain, in northeastern New York. (44°N, 73°W) p. 265

Fort Vancouver A fort in southwestern Washington, on the Columbia River; the western end of the Oregon Trail; present-day city of Vancouver. (45°N, 123°W) p. 452

Fort Wagner A fort in southeastern South Carolina, on Morris Island in Charleston Harbor; site of a major Civil War battle in 1863. p. 525

Fort Walla Walla A fort in southeastern Washington; located on the Oregon Trail. (46°N, 118°W) p. 452

Fort William Henry A British fort located in eastern New York. (43°N, 74°W) p. 265

Fort Worth A city in northern Texas; located on the Trinity River. (33°N, 97°W) p. 558

Fox River Located in southeast central Wisconsin; flows southwest toward the Wisconsin River, and then flows northeast and empties into Green Bay. p. 203

Franklin (MO) A city in central Missouri, on the Missouri River. (39°N, 93°W) p. 437

Franklin (TN) A city in central Tennessee; site of a major Civil War battle in 1864. (36°N, 87°W) p. 525

Fredericksburg A city in northeastern Virginia; located on the Rappahannock River; site of a Civil War battle in 1862. (38°N, 77°W) p. 219

Fremont A city in west central California, east of San Francisco Bay. (38°N, 122°W) p. 36

Frenchtown A town in present-day eastern Michigan; site of a major battle in the War of 1812. (42°N, 83°W) p. 417

Fresno A city in California; located southeast of San Francisco, in the San Joaquin Valley. (37°N, 120°W) p. 36

Gatun Lake (gah•TOON) A lake in Panama; part of the Panama Canal system. p. 142

Germantown A residential section of present-day Philadelphia, on Wissahickon Creek, in southeastern Pennsylvania; site of a major Revolutionary War battle in 1777. (40°N, 75°W) p. 311

Gettysburg A town in southern Pennsylvania; site of a Civil War battle in 1863. (40°N, 77°W) p. 471

Golconda (gahl•KAHN•duh) A city in the southeastern corner of Illinois; a point on the Trail of Tears. (37°N, 88°W) p. 466

Gonzales (gohn•ZAH•lays) A city in south central Texas; site of the first battle of the Texas Revolution. (30°N, 97°W) p. 446

Governors Island An island in New York Bay; located near the mouth of the East River. (41°N, 74°W) p. 589

Great Basin One of the driest parts of the United States; located in Nevada, Utah, California, Idaho, Wyoming, and Oregon; includes the Great Salt Lake Desert, the Mojave Desert, and Death Valley. p. 40

Great Bear Lake A lake located in northwest central Mackenzie district, Northwest Territories, Canada. p. 40

Great Lakes A chain of five lakes; located in central North America; the largest group of freshwater lakes in the world. p. 68

Great Plains A continental slope in western North America; borders the eastern base of the Rocky Mountains from Canada to New Mexico and Texas. p. 40

Great Salt Lake The largest lake in the Great Basin; located in northwestern Utah. p. 40

Great Slave Lake A lake in the south central mainland part of the Northwest Territories, Canada. p. 40

Greenland The largest island on Earth; located in the northern Atlantic Ocean, east of Canada. p. 41

Groton (GRAH•tuhn) A town in southeastern Connecticut; located on Long Island Sound at the mouth of the Thames River. (41°N, 72°W) p. 207

Guilford Courthouse (GIL•ferd) A location in north central North Carolina, near Greensboro; site of a major Revolutionary War battle in 1781. (36°N, 80°W) p. 311

Gulf of Alaska A northern inlet of the Pacific Ocean; located between the Alaska Peninsula and the southwestern coast of Canada. p. 40

Gulf of California An inlet of the Pacific Ocean located between Baja California and the northwestern coast of Mexico. p. 40

Gulf of Mexico An inlet of the Atlantic Ocean; located on the southeastern coast of North America; surrounded by the United States, Cuba, and Mexico. p. 40

Gulf of Panama A large inlet of the Pacific Ocean; located on the southern coast of Panama. p. 142

Gulf of St. Lawrence A deep gulf of the Atlantic Ocean, located on the eastern coast of Canada, between Newfoundland and the Canadian mainland. p. 167

Hampton Roads A channel in southeastern Virginia that flows into the Chesapeake Bay; site of a Civil War naval battle in 1862 between two iron-clad ships, the *Monitor* and the *Merrimack*. p. 525

Harrodsburg A city in central Kentucky; located at an end of the Wilderness Road. (38°N, 85°W) p. 404

Havana The capital of Cuba; located on the northwestern coast of the country. (23°N, 82°W) p. 155

Hawikuh (hah•wee•KOO) A city in southwestern North America; located on the route of the Spanish explorer Coronado; present-day northwestern New Mexico. p. 155

Hispaniola (ees•pah•NYOH•lah) An island in the West Indies made up of Haiti and the Dominican Republic; located in the Caribbean Sea between Cuba and Puerto Rico. p. 41

Hopewell An ancient settlement of the Mound Builders; located in present-day southern Ohio. (39°N, 83°W) p. 68

Horseshoe Bend A location in eastern Alabama; site of a battle in the War of 1812; a present-day national military park. p. 417

Houston A city in southeastern Texas; third-largest port in the United States; leading industrial center in Texas. (30°N, 95°W) p. 397

Hudson Bay An inland sea in east central Canada surrounded by the Northwest Territories, Manitoba, Ontario, and Quebec. p. 41

Hudson River A river in the northeastern United States beginning in upper New York and flowing into the Atlantic Ocean; named for the explorer Henry Hudson. p. 220

Illinois River A river in western and central Illinois; flows southwest into the Mississippi River. p. 203

Independence A city in western Missouri; the starting point of the Oregon Trail. (39°N, 94°W) p. 452

Isthmus of Panama (IHS•muhs) A narrow strip of land that connects North America and South America. p. 143

Jackson The capital of Mississippi; located in the southwest central part of the state, on the Pearl River. (32°N, 90°W) p. 34

Jacksonville A city in northeastern Florida; located near the mouth of the St. Johns River. (30°N, 82°W) p. 397

Jamaica (juh•MAY•kuh) An island country in the West Indies, located south of Cuba. p. 137

James River A river in central Virginia; begins where the Jackson and Cowpasture rivers join; flows east into the Chesapeake Bay. p. 177

Jamestown The first permanent English settlement in the Americas; located in eastern Virginia, on the shore of the James River. (37°N, 76°W) p. 177

Jerusalem The capital of Israel; located in the central part of the country. (32°N, 35°E) p. 115

Juneau (JOO•noh) The capital of Alaska; located in the southeastern part of the state. (58°N, 134°W) p. 34

Kansas City The largest city in Missouri; located in the west central part of the state, on the Missouri River. (39°N, 95°W) p. 549

Kaskaskia (ka•SKAS•kee•uh) A village in southwestern Illinois; site of a major Revolutionary War battle in 1778. (38°N, 90°W) p. 311

Kennebec River (KEN•uh•bek) A river in west central and southern Maine; flows south from Moosehead Lake to the Atlantic Ocean. p. 207

Kennesaw Mountain (KEN•uh•saw) An isolated peak in northwestern Georgia, near Atlanta; site of a Civil War battle in 1864. p. 525

Kentucky River A river in north central Kentucky; flows northwest into the Ohio River. p. 404

Kings Mountain A ridge in northern South Carolina and southern North Carolina; site of a Revolutionary War battle in 1780. p. 311

La Venta An ancient settlement of the Olmecs; located in present-day southern Mexico, on an island near the Tonalá River. (18°N, 94°W) p. 68

Labrador A peninsula in northeastern North America; once known as Markland. p. 41

Labrador Sea Located south of Greenland and northeast of North America. p. 41

Lake Champlain (sham•PLAYN) A lake between New York and Vermont. p. 93

Lake Erie The fourth-largest of the Great Lakes; borders Canada and the United States. p. 41

Lake Huron The second-largest of the Great Lakes; borders Canada and the United States. p. 41

Lake Michigan The third-largest of the Great Lakes; borders Michigan, Illinois, Indiana, and Wisconsin. p. 41

Lake Ontario The smallest of the Great Lakes; borders Canada and the United States. p. 41

Lake Superior The largest of the Great Lakes; borders Canada and the United States. p. 41

Lake Texcoco (tes•KOH•koh) A dry lake in present-day Mexico City; site of the ancient Aztec capital city of Tenochtitlán. p. 103

Lake Titicaca (tih•tih•KAH•kah) The highest navigable lake in the world; located on the border between Peru and Bolivia. p. 151

Lake Winnipeg A lake located in south central Manitoba, Canada. p. 40

Lancaster A city in southeastern Pennsylvania. (40°N, 76°W) p. 213

Lansing The capital of Michigan; located in the south central part of the state. (43°N, 84°W) p. 34

Laredo A city and port of entry in present-day southern Texas; located on the Rio Grande River. (28°N, 100°W) p. 328

Las Vegas (lahs VAY•guhs) A city in the southeastern corner of Nevada. (36°N, 115°W) p. 548

Lexington A town in northeastern Massachusetts; site of the first battle of the Revolutionary War in 1775. (42°N, 71°W) p. 311

Liberty Island A small island in Upper New York Bay; the Statue of Liberty is located there; once known as Bedloe's Island. p. 589

Lincoln The capital of Nebraska; located in the southeastern part of the state. (41°N, 97°W) p. 34

Lisbon The capital of Portugal; a port city located in the western part of the country. (39°N, 9°W) p. 115

Little Rock The capital of Arkansas; a city located in the central part of the state, on the south bank of the Arkansas River. (35°N, 92°W) p. 34

London A city located in the southern part of England; capital of present-day Britain. (52°N, 0°) p. 115

Long Beach A city in southwestern California; located on San Pedro Bay. (34°N, 118°W) p. 36

Long Island An island located east of New York City and south of Connecticut; lies between Long Island Sound and the Atlantic Ocean. p. 213

Los Adaes Site of a mission of New Spain; located in present-day eastern Texas. p. 199

Los Angeles The largest city in California; second-largest city in the United States; located in the southern part of the state. (34°N, 118°W) p. 36

Louisiana Purchase A territory in the west central United States purchased from France in 1803; extended from the Mississippi River to the Rocky Mountains, and from the Gulf of Mexico to Canada. p. 409

Louisville (LOO•ih•vil) The largest city in Kentucky; located in the north central part of the state, on the Ohio River. (38°N, 86°W) p. 397

Machu Picchu (mah•choo PEEK•choo) The site of an ancient Inca city on a mountain in the Andes, northwest of Cuzco, Peru. (13°S, 73°W) p. 151

Mackenzie River A river located in western Mackenzie district, Northwest Territories, Canada; flows north-northwest into Mackenzie Bay; second longest river in North America. p. 40

Macon (MAY•kuhn) A city in central Georgia; located on the Ocmulgee River. (33°N, 84°W) p. 437

Madeira (mah•DAIR•uh) An island group in the eastern Atlantic Ocean, off the coast of Morocco. p. 137

Madison The capital of Wisconsin; located in the southern part of the state. (43°N, 89°W) p. 34

Manchester A city in southern New Hampshire; located on the Merrimack River. (43°N, 71°W) p. 548

Manhattan An island in southeastern New York; located at the mouth of the Hudson River. (41°N, 74°W) p. 589

Massachusetts Bay An inlet of the Atlantic Ocean on the east coast of Massachusetts; extends from Cape Ann to Cape Cod. p. 207

Maumee River (maw•MEE) A river located in Indiana and Ohio; formed by the junction of the St. Joseph and St. Marys rivers in northeastern Indiana; flows east and then northeast into Lake Erie. p. 311

Mediterranean Sea (meh•duh•tuh•RAY•nee•uhn) An inland sea, enclosed by Europe on the west and north, Asia on the east, and Africa on the south. p. 125

Memphis A city in the southwestern corner of Tennessee; located on the Mississippi River. (35°N, 90°W) p. 437

Merrimack River A river in southern New Hampshire and northeastern Massachusetts; formed by the junction of the Pemigewasset and Winnipesaukee rivers; empties into the Atlantic. p. 207

Mesa Verde (MAY•suh VAIR•day) An ancient settlement of the Anasazi; located in present-day southwestern Colorado. (37°N, 108°W) p. 68

Mexico City A city on the southern edge of the Central Plateau; the present-day capital of Mexico. (19°N, 99°W) p. 190

Miami A city in southeastern Florida, located on Biscayne Bay. (26°N, 80°W) p. 549

Milwaukee (mil•WAW•kee) The largest city in Wisconsin; located in the southeastern part of the state, on Lake Michigan. (43°N, 88°W) p. 397

Minneapolis The largest city in Minnesota; located in the southeast central part of the state, on the Mississippi River; twin city with St. Paul. (45°N, 93°W) p. 549

Mississippi River The longest river in the United States; located centrally, its source is Lake Itasca in Minnesota; flows south into the Gulf of Mexico. p. 40

Missouri River A tributary of the Mississippi River, located centrally, beginning in Montana and ending at St. Louis, Missouri. p. 40

Mobile (moh•BEEL) The only seaport city in southern Alabama; located at the mouth of the Mobile River. (31°N, 88°W) p. 471

Mobile Bay An inlet of the Gulf of Mexico; located off the coast of southern Alabama; the site of a Civil War naval battle in 1864. p. 525

Mohawk River A river in central New York, flowing east to the Hudson River. p. 93

Monte Albán (MAHN•tay ahl•BAHN) An ancient settlement of the Aztec civilization; located in present-day south central Mexico. (17°N, 97°W) p. 100

Monterey A city in western California; located at the southern end of Monterey Bay. (37°N, 122°W) p. 36

Montgomery The capital of Alabama; located in the southeast central part of the state. (32°N, 86°W) p. 34

Montreal The largest city in present-day Canada; located in southern Quebec, on Montreal Island at the north bank of the St. Lawrence River. (46°N, 73°W) p. 167

Morristown A town in northern New Jersey, located west-northwest of Newark. (41°N, 74°W) p. 213

Moscow The capital and largest city of Russia; located in the western part of the country. (56°N, 38°E) p. 115

Moundville An ancient settlement of the Mound Builders; located in present-day central Alabama. (33°N, 88°W) p. 68

Mount Vernon The home and burial place of George Washington; located in Fairfax County, Virginia, on the Potomac River, below Washington, D.C. (39°N, 77°W) p. 382

Murfreesboro A city in central Tennessee; located on the west fork of the Stones River; a site on the Trail of Tears. (36°N, 86°W) p. 466

Narragansett Bay An inlet of the Atlantic Ocean in southeastern Rhode Island. (41°N, 71°W) p. 207

Natchez A city in southwestern Mississippi; located on the Mississippi River. (32°N, 91°W) p. 328

Natchitoches (NAH•kuh•tahsh) The first settlement in present-day Louisiana; located in the northwest central part of the state. (32°N, 93°W) p. 409

Nauvoo (naw•VOO) A city in western Illinois, located on the Mississippi River; beginning of the Mormon Trail. (41°N, 91°W) p. 452

Nazca (NAHS•kah) Site of an Indian civilization; located on the west central coast of Peru. (15°S, 75°W) p. 151

New Amsterdam A Dutch city on Manhattan Island that later became New York City. (41°N, 74°W) p. 177

New Bern A city and port in southeastern North Carolina. (35°N, 77°W) p. 219

New Echota (ih•KOHT•uh) An Indian town in northwestern Georgia; chosen as the capital of the Cherokee Nation in 1819. (35°N, 85°W) p. 442

New France The possessions of France in North America from 1534 to 1763; included Canada, the Great Lakes region, and Louisiana. p. 204

New Haven A city in southern Connecticut; located on New Haven Harbor. (41°N, 73°W) p. 207

New London A city in southeastern Connecticut; located on Long Island Sound at the mouth of the Thames River. (41°N, 72°W) p. 246

New Netherland A Dutch colony in North America from 1613 to 1664; located along the Hudson River in parts of present-day New York and New Jersey. p. 212

New Orleans The largest city in Louisiana; a major port located between the Mississippi River and Lake Pontchartrain. (30°N, 90°W) p. 191

New River A river in southwestern Virginia and southern West Virginia; flows north across Virginia, into south central West Virginia. p. 404

New Spain The former Spanish possessions from 1535 to 1821; included the southwestern United States, Mexico, Central America north of Panama, the West Indies, and the Philippines. p. 190

New Sweden A Swedish colony in North America, founded in 1638; located near the mouth of the Delaware River, in parts of present-day Delaware, Pennsylvania, and New Jersey. p. 212

Gazetteer

New York City The largest city in the United States; located in southeastern New York at the mouth of the Hudson River. Once known as New Amsterdam. (41°N, 74°W) p. 191

Newark A port in northeastern New Jersey; located on the Passaic River and Newark Bay. (41°N, 74°W) p. 213

Newfoundland (NOO•fuhn•luhnd) One of Canada's ten provinces; among the earliest Viking settlements in North America; once known as Vinland. p. 41

Newport A city on the southern end of Rhode Island; located at the mouth of Narragansett Bay. (41°N, 71°W) p. 207

Norfolk (NAWR•fawk) A city in southeastern Virginia; located on the Elizabeth River. (37°N, 76°W) p. 219

North Pole The northernmost point on the Earth. p. 56

Norwich A city located in east central Vermont. p. 344

Nova Scotia (NOH•vuh SKOH•shuh) A province of Canada; located in the eastern part of the country, on a peninsula. p. 167

Nueces River (noo•AY•says) A river in southern Texas; flows into Nueces Bay, which is at the head of Corpus Christi Bay. p. 446

Oakland A city in western California; located on the eastern side of San Francisco Bay. (38°N, 122°W) p. 36

Ocmulgee (ohk•MUHL•gee) An ancient settlement of the Mound Builders; located in central Georgia. (32°N, 83°W) p. 68

Ocmulgee River A river in central Georgia; formed by the junction of the Yellow and South rivers; flows south to join the Altamaha River. p. 219

Ohio River A tributary of the Mississippi River, beginning in Pittsburgh, Pennsylvania, and ending at Cairo, Illinois. p. 41

Oklahoma City Oklahoma's capital and largest city; located in the central part of the state. (35°N, 98°W) p. 34

Omaha (OH•muh•hah) The largest city in Nebraska; located in the eastern part of the state, on the Missouri River. (41°N, 96°W) p. 452

Oregon Country A former region in western North America; located between the Pacific coast and the Rocky Mountains, from the northern border of California to Alaska. p. 328

Oregon Trail A former route to the Oregon Country; extending from the Missouri River northwest to the Columbia River in Oregon. p. 452

Outer Banks A chain of narrow peninsulas and islands off the coast of North Carolina. p. 172

Palenque (pah•LENG•kay) An ancient settlement of the Mayan civilization; located in present-day Chiapas, in southern Mexico. (18°N, 92°W) p. 100

Palm Springs A city in southeastern California; located in the Coachella Valley. (34°N, 117°W) p. 36

Panama Canal A canal across the Isthmus of Panama; extends from the Caribbean Sea to the Gulf of Panama. p. 142

Panama City The capital of Panama; located in Central America. (9°N, 80°W) p. 142

Pee Dee River A river in North Carolina and South Carolina; forms where the Yadkin and Uharie rivers meet; empties into Winyah Bay. p. 219

Perryville A city in east central Kentucky; site of a major Civil War battle in 1862. (38°N, 90°W) p. 471

Perth Amboy A port city in central New Jersey; located on Raritan Bay. (40°N, 74°W) p. 213

Petersburg A port city in southeastern Virginia, located on the Appomattox River; site of a series of Civil War battles from 1864 to 1865. (37°N, 77°W) p. 525

Philadelphia A city in southeastern Pennsylvania, on the Delaware River; a major United States port; once known as Fort New Gothenburg. (40°N, 75°W) p. 290

Philippine Islands A group of more than 7,000 islands off the coast of southeastern Asia, making up the country of the Philippines. p. 143

Pikes Peak A mountain in east central Colorado; part of the Rocky Mountains. p. 409

Pittsburgh The second-largest city in Pennsylvania; located in the southwestern part of the state, on the Ohio River. (40°N, 80°W) p. 328

Platte River (PLAT) A river in central Nebraska; flows east into the Missouri River below Omaha. p. 190

Plattsburg A city in the northeastern corner of New York; located on the western shore of Lake Champlain; site of a major battle in the War of 1812. (45°N, 73°W) p. 417

Plymouth A town in southeastern Massachusetts, on Plymouth Bay; site of the first settlement built by the Pilgrims, who sailed on the *Mayflower*. (42°N, 71°W) p. 177

Port Royal A town in western Nova Scotia, Canada; name changed to Annapolis Royal in honor of Queen Anne; capital city until 1749. (45°N, 66°W) p. 167

Portland (ME) A port city in southwestern Maine; located on the Casco Bay. (44°N, 70°W) p. 397

Portland (OR) Oregon's largest city and principal port; located in the northwestern part of the state on the Willamette River. (46°N, 123°W) p. 548

Portsmouth (NH) (PAWRT•smuhth) A port city in southeastern New Hampshire; located at the mouth of the Piscataqua River. (43°N, 71°W) p. 207

Portsmouth (RI) A town in southeastern Rhode Island; located on the Sakonnet River. (42°N, 71°W) p. 207

Potomac River (puh•TOH•muhk) A river on the Coastal Plain of the United States; begins in West Virginia and flows into Chesapeake Bay; Washington, D.C., is located on this river. p. 219

Potosí (poh•toh•SEE) One of the highest cities in the world; located in present-day south central Bolivia. (20°S, 66°W) p. 151

Princeton A borough in west central New Jersey; site of a major Revolutionary War battle in 1777. (40°N, 75°W) p. 311

Providence Rhode Island's capital and largest city; located in the northern part of the state, at the head of the Providence River. (42°N, 71°W) p. 34

Provo A city in north central Utah; located on the Provo River. (40°N, 112°W) p. 616

Puerto Rico An island of the West Indies, located southeast of Florida; a commonwealth of the United States. p. 40

Put-in-Bay A bay on South Bass Island, north of Ohio in Lake Erie; site of a major battle in the War of 1812. (42°N, 83°W) p. 417

Quebec (kwih•BEK) The capital of the province of Quebec, Canada; located on the northern side of the St. Lawrence River; the first successful French settlement in the Americas; established in 1608. (47°N, 71°W) p. 167

Queens A borough of New York City; located on the western end of Long Island. (41°N, 74°W) p. 589

Quito (KEE•toh) A city in northwestern South America, located near the equator; present-day capital of Ecuador. (0°, 79°W) p. 151

Raleigh (RAW•lee) The capital of North Carolina; located in the east central part of the state. (36°N, 79°W) p. 34

Red Clay A town located in southeastern Tennessee; once part of the Cherokee Nation. p. 442

Red River A tributary of the Mississippi River; rises in eastern New Mexico, flows across Louisiana and into the Mississippi River; forms much of the Texas-Oklahoma border. p. 409

Richmond The capital of Virginia; a port city located in the east central part of the state, on the James River. (38°N, 77°W) p. 34

Rio Balsas (BAHL•sahs) A river in southern Mexico. p. 40

Rio Grande A river in southwestern North America; it begins in Colorado and flows into the Gulf of Mexico; forms the border between Texas and Mexico. p. 40

Rio Usumacinta (oo•sooh•mah•SIN•tah) A river located in southern Mexico; forms part of the border between Mexico and Guatemala. p. 100

Roanoke Island (ROH•uh•nohk) An island near the coast of North Carolina; the site of the lost colony. (36°N, 76°W) p. 172

Roanoke River (ROH•uh•nohk) A river in southern Virginia and northeastern North Carolina; flows east and southeast across the North Carolina border and into Albemarle Sound. p. 219

Rochester (RAH•chuh•ster) A port city located in western New York. (43°N, 78°W) p. 434

Rocky Mountains A range of mountains in the western United States and Canada, extending from Alaska to New Mexico; these mountains divide rivers that flow east from those that flow west. p. 40

Sabine River (suh•BEEN) A river in eastern Texas and western Louisiana; flows southeast to the Gulf of Mexico. p. 446

Sacramento The capital of California; located in the north central part of the state, on the Sacramento River. (39°N, 121°W) p. 34

Sacramento River A river in northwestern California; rises near Mt. Shasta and flows south into Suisun Bay. p. 452

Salem A city on the northeastern coast of Massachusetts. (43°N, 71°W) p. 207

Salisbury (SAWLZ•bair•ee) A city in central North Carolina; the beginning of Boone's Trail. (36°N, 80°W) p. 344

Salt Lake City Utah's capital and largest city; located in the northern part of the state, on the Jordan River. (41°N, 112°W) p. 34

San Antonio A city in south central Texas; located on the San Antonio River; site of the Alamo. (29°N, 98°W) p. 328

San Antonio River A river in southern Texas; flows southeast and empties into San Antonio Bay. p. 446

San Diego A large port city in southern California; located on San Diego Bay. (33°N, 117°W) p. 36

San Francisco The second-largest city in California; located in the northern part of the state, on San Francisco Bay. (38°N, 123°W) p. 36

San Francisco Bay An inlet of the Pacific Ocean, located in west central California. p. 36

San Jacinto (jah•SIN•toh) A location in southeastern Texas; site of a battle in the Texas Revolution in 1836. (31°N, 95°W) p. 446

San Jose A city in western California; located southeast of San Francisco Bay. (37°N, 122°W) p. 36

San Lorenzo An ancient settlement of the Olmecs; located in present-day southern Mexico. (29°N, 113°W) p. 68

San Pablo Bay A northern extension of San Francisco Bay; located in west central California. p. 36

San Salvador One of the islands in the southern Bahamas; Christopher Columbus landed there in 1492. p. 137

Santa Fe (SAN•tah FAY) The capital of New Mexico; located in the north central part of the state. (36°N, 106°W) p. 34

Santa Fe Trail A former commercial route to the western United States; extended from western Missouri to Santa Fe, in central New Mexico. p. 452

Santee River A river in southeast central South Carolina; formed by the junction of the Congaree and Wateree rivers; flows southeast into the Atlantic Ocean. p. 219

Saratoga A village on the western bank of the Hudson River in eastern New York; site of a major Revolutionary War battle in 1777; present-day Schuylerville. (43°N, 74°W) p. 311

Gazetteer

Savannah The oldest city and a principal seaport in Georgia; located in the southeastern part of the state, at the mouth of the Savannah River. (32°N, 81°W) p. 191

Savannah River A river that forms the border between Georgia and South Carolina; flows into the Atlantic Ocean at Savannah, Georgia. p. 219

Schenectady (skuh•NEK•tuh•dee) A city in eastern New York; located on the Mohawk River. (43°N, 74°W) p. 213

Seattle The largest city in Washington; a port city located in the west central part of the state, on Puget Sound. (48°N, 122°W) p. 548

Seneca Falls (SEN•uh•kuh) A town located in west central New York on the Seneca River. (43°N, 77°W) p. 457

Serpent Mound An ancient settlement of the Mound Builders; located in present-day southern Ohio. (39°N, 83°W) p. 68

Shiloh (SHY•loh) A location in southwestern Tennessee; site of a major Civil War battle in 1862; also known as Pittsburg Landing. (35°N, 88°W) p. 525

Shreveport A city in northwestern Louisiana; located on the Red River. (33°N, 94°W) p. 558

Siberia A region in north central Asia, mostly in Russia. p. 49

Sierra Madre Occidental (see•AIR•ah MAH•dray ahk•sih•den•TAHL) A mountain range in western Mexico, running parallel to the Pacific coast. p. 40

Sierra Madre Oriental (awr•ee•en•TAHL) A mountain range in eastern Mexico, running parallel to the coast along the Gulf of Mexico. p. 40

Sierra Nevada A mountain range in eastern California that runs parallel to the Coast Ranges. p. 40

Sioux Falls (SOO) A city in southeastern South Dakota; located on the Big Sioux River. (44°N, 97°W) p. 549

Snake River A river that begins in the Rocky Mountains and flows west into the Pacific Ocean; part of the Oregon Trail ran along this river. p. 190

Sonoran Desert An arid region in western North America; includes southwestern Arizona and southeastern California; in Mexico includes western Sonora and northern Baja California. p. 40

South Pole The southernmost point on the Earth. p. 136

Spiro An ancient settlement of the Mound Builders; located in eastern Oklahoma. (35°N, 95°W) p. 68

Spring Place A town in northwestern Georgia; once part of the Cherokee Nation. (35°N, 85°W) p. 442

Springfield (IL) The capital of Illinois; located in the central part of the state. (40°N, 90°W) p. 34

Springfield (MA) A city in southwestern Massachusetts; located on the Connecticut River. (42°N, 73°W) p. 207

Springfield (MO) A city in southwestern Missouri. (37°N, 93°W) p. 466

St. Augustine (AW•guh•steen) A city on the coast of northeastern Florida; the oldest city founded by Europeans in the United States. (30°N, 81°W) p. 196

St. Croix (KROY) A city in Maine; located west of Port Royal. (45°N, 67°W) p. 167

St. Ignace (IG•nuhs) A city in Michigan, located on the southeastern side of Michigan's upper peninsula. (46°N, 85°W) p. 203

St. Joseph A city in northwestern Missouri on the Missouri River. (40°N, 95°W) p. 558

St. Lawrence River A river in northeastern North America; begins at Lake Ontario and flows into the Atlantic Ocean; forms part of the border between the United States and Canada. p. 41

St. Louis A major port city in east central Missouri; known as the Gateway to the West. (38°N, 90°W) p. 204

St. Marys A village in southern Maryland; the capital until 1694; present-day St. Marys City. (38°N, 76°W) p. 221

St. Paul The capital of Minnesota; located in the eastern part of the state, on the Mississippi River. (45°N, 93°W) p. 34

Strait of Magellan (muh•JEH•luhn) The narrow waterway between the southern tip of South America and Tierra del Fuego; links the Atlantic Ocean with the Pacific Ocean. p. 143

Sunnyvale A city in western California. (37°N, 122°W) p. 36

Susquehanna River (suhs•kwuh•HA•nuh) A river in Maryland, Pennsylvania, and central New York; rises in Otsego Lake, New York, and empties into the northern Chesapeake Bay. p. 93

Syracuse A city in central New York; located south of the western end of the Oneida Lake. (43°N, 76°W) p. 434

Tennessee River A tributary of the Mississippi River; begins in eastern Tennessee and flows into the Ohio River in Kentucky. p. 311

Tenochtitlán (tay•nohch•teet•LAHN) The ancient capital of the Aztec Empire, on the islands of Lake Texcoco; located in present-day Mexico City, southern Mexico. (19°N, 99°W) p. 103

Thames, The (TEMZ) A location near the north central shore of Lake Erie, in present-day Canada; site of a major battle in the War of 1812. p. 417

Tiahuanaco (tee•ah•wah•NAH•koh) A site of prehistoric ruins, located in western South America, in present-day Bolivia. (17°S, 69°W) p. 151

Tikal (tih•KAHL) An ancient settlement of the Mayan civilization; located in present-day southern Central America. (17°N, 89°W) p. 100

Timbuktu A town in Mali; located in western Africa, near the Niger River. (17°N, 3°W) p. 115

Toledo (tuh•LEE•doh) A port city, located in northwestern Ohio, at the southwestern corner of Lake Erie. (42°N, 84°W) p. 437

Trail of Tears A trail that was the result of the Indian Removal Act of 1830; extended from the Cherokee Nation to Fort Gibson, in the Indian Territory. p. 466

Treasure Island An artificial island in San Francisco Bay, California; present-day naval base. (38°N, 122°W) p. 589

Trenton The capital of New Jersey; located in the west central part of the state; site of a major Revolutionary War battle in 1776. (40°N, 75°W) p. 34

Tres Zapotes (TRAYS sah•POH•tays) An ancient settlement of the Olmecs; located in southern Mexico. (18°N, 95°W) p. 68

Troy A city in eastern New York; located on the eastern bank of the Hudson River. (43°N, 74°W) p. 397

Tucson (TOO•sahn) A city in southern Arizona; located on the Santa Cruz River. (32°N, 111°W) p. 190

Tula An ancient settlement of the Aztec civilization; located in present-day central Mexico, north of Tenochtitlán. (23°N, 100°W) p. 100

Tumbes (TOOM•bays) A town in northwestern Peru; located on the Tumbes River, near the Peru-Ecuador border. (4°S, 80°W) p. 151

Turkey Town A town in eastern Alabama; once part of the Cherokee Nation. (34°N, 86°W) p. 442

Turtle Mound An ancient settlement of the Mound Builders; located on the present-day east central coast of Florida. (29°N, 81°W) p. 68

Uxmal (oosh•MAHL) An ancient settlement of the Mayan civilization; located in the northern Yucatán Peninsula. (20°N, 90°W) p. 100

Vallejo (vuh•LAY•oh) A city in central California; located on the San Pablo Bay. (38°N, 122°W) p. 36

Valley Forge A location in southeastern Pennsylvania, on the Schuylkill River; site of General George Washington's winter headquarters during the Revolutionary War. (40°N, 77°W) p. 311

Vancouver Island An island off the southwestern coast of British Columbia, Canada. p. 40

Vandalia (van•DAYL•yuh) A city in south central Illinois. (39°N, 89°W) p. 437

Venice A port city in northeastern Italy; located on 118 islands in the Lagoon of Venice. (45°N, 12°E) p. 115

Veracruz (veh•rah•KROOZ) A seaport in Veracruz, Mexico; located in the eastern part of the country, on the Gulf of Mexico. (19°N, 96°W) p. 150

Vicksburg A city in western Mississippi; located on the Mississippi River; site of a major Civil War battle in 1863. (32°N, 91°W) p. 471

Victoria Island The third-largest of Canada's Arctic Islands; located north of the central mainland part of the Northwest Territories. p. 40

Vincennes (vihn•SENZ) A town in southwestern Indiana; oldest town in Indiana. (39°N, 88°W) p. 191

Wabash River (WAW•bash) A river in western Ohio and Indiana; flows west and south to the Ohio River, to form part of the Indiana–Illinois border. p. 311

Warrior's Path A Native American path that began in North Carolina and crossed the Appalachian Mountains to Kentucky and Ohio. p. 404

Washington, D.C. The capital of the United States; located between Maryland and Virginia, on the Potomac River in a special district that is not part of any state. (39°N, 77°W) p. 382

West Indies The islands stretching from Florida in North America to Venezuela in South America. p. 232

West Point A United States military post since the Revolutionary War; located in southeastern New York on the western bank of the Hudson River p. 311

Whitman Mission Site of a Native American mission, established in 1836 by Marcus Whitman and his wife; located in present-day southeastern Washington. p. 452

Wilderness Road A pioneer road that began in Tennessee and crossed the Appalachian Mountains into Kentucky. p. 404

Williamsburg A city in southeastern Virginia; located on a peninsula between the James and York rivers. (37°N, 77°W) p. 190

Wilmington (DE) A city in northern Delaware; located where the Delaware and Christina rivers meet Brandywine Creek; once known as Fort Christina. (40°N, 76°W) p. 213

Wilmington (NC) A city in southeastern North Carolina; located on the Cape Fear River. (34°N, 78°W) p. 191

Winchester A city in northern Virginia, located in the Shenandoah Valley. (39°N, 78°W) p. 344

Wisconsin River A river in central Wisconsin that flows south and southeast to the Mississippi River. p. 203

Yadkin River The upper course of the Pee Dee River; flows south across North Carolina. p. 404

Yagul An ancient settlement of the Aztec civilization; located in present-day southern Mexico. p. 100

Yellowstone River A river in northwestern Wyoming, southeastern Montana, and northwestern North Dakota; flows northwest to the Missouri River. p. 409

Yorktown A small town in southeastern Virginia; located on Chesapeake Bay; site of the last major Revolutionary War battle in 1781. (37°N, 76°W) p. 311

Yucatán Peninsula (yoo•kah•TAN) A peninsula in southeastern Mexico and northeastern Central America; separated from Cuba by the Yucatán Channel. p. 41

Yukon River A river that begins in the southwestern part of the Yukon Territory, Canada; flows through Alaska, and empties into the Bering Sea. p. 40

Gazetteer

Glossary

The Glossary contains important social studies words and their definitions. Each word is respelled as it would be in a dictionary. When you see this mark (′) after a syllable, pronounce that syllable with more force than the other syllables. The page number at the end of the definition tells where to find the word in your book.

add, āce, câre, pälm; end, ēqual; it, īce; odd, ōpen, ôrder; tŏŏk, pōōl; up, bûrn; yōō as *u* in *fuse*; oil; pout; ə as *a* in *above*, *e* in *sicken*, *i* in *possible*, *o* in *melon*, *u* in *circus*; check; ring; thin; this; zh as in *vision*

abolish (ə·bä′lish) To end. p. 455

abolitionist (a·bə·li′shən·ist) A person who wanted to abolish slavery. p. 455

absolute location (ab′sə·lōōt lō·kā′shən) Exact location on the Earth. p. 31

adobe (ä·dō′bä) A mixture of sand and straw that is dried into bricks. p. 70

agent (ā′jənt) A person who does business for other people. p. 168

agriculture (a′grə·kul·chər) Farming. p. 62

allegiance (ə·lē′jənts) Loyalty. p. 296

ally (a′lī) A friend, especially in time of war. p. 264

ambassador (am·ba′sə·dər) A representative from one country to another. p. 334

amendment (ə·mend′mənt) An addition or change to the Constitution. p. 374

analyze (a′nəl·īz) To break something into its parts and look closely at how those parts connect with one another. p. 29

annex (ə·neks′) To add on. p. 419

Anti-Federalist (an′tī·fe′də·rə·list) A citizen who was against ratification of the Constitution. p. 370

apprentice (ə·pren′təs) A person who learns a trade by living with the family of a skilled worker and working for several years. p. 233

archaeologist (är·kē·o′lə·jist) A scientist who studies the cultures of people of long ago. p. 50

arid (âr′əd) Very dry. p. 81

armada (är·mä′dä) A fleet of warships. p. 172

artifact (är′tə·fakt) An object that early people had made. p. 51

assassination (ə·sa·sən·ā′shən) The murder of a political leader such as a President. p. 526

assembly line (ə·sem′blē līn) A system of mass production in which parts of a product, such as a car, are put together as they move past a line of workers. p. 564

auction (ôk′shən) A public sale. p. 238

authority (ə·thär′ə·tē) Control over someone or something. p. 267

aviation (ā·vē·ā′shən) Air transportation. p. 564

backcountry (bak′kən·trē) An area beyond settled lands. p. 241

band (band) A small group of people who work together to do activities. p. 48

barrio (bär′ē·ō) A neighborhood of Spanish-speaking people. p. 587

barter (bär′tər) To exchange goods with other people. p. 78

bill (bil) An idea for a new law. p. 348

Bill of Rights (bil uv rīts) A list of freedoms added to the Constitution as the first ten amendments. p. 374

blockade (blä·kād′) To use warships to prevent other ships from entering or leaving a harbor. p. 280

border state (bôr′dər stāt) During the Civil War, a state between the North and the South that allowed slavery but did not secede from the Union. p. 508

borderlands (bôr′dər·landz) Areas of land on or near the borders between countries, colonies, or regions. p. 195

boycott (boi′kät) A refusal to buy goods or services. p. 275

broker (brō′kər) A person who is paid to buy and sell for someone else. p. 236

buffer (bu′fər) An area of land that serves as a barrier. p. 195

Cabinet (kab′nit) A group of the President's most important advisers. p. 379

campaign (kam·pān′) A race for office. p. 384

canal (kə·nal′) A human-made waterway. p. 434

cardinal direction (kär′də·nəl də·rek′shən) One of the main directions: north, south, east, or west. p. 35

carpetbagger (kär′pət·ba·gər) A Northerner who went to the South after the Civil War to try to help with Reconstruction or to make money buying land or opening a business. p. 536

cartographer (kär·tä′grə·fər) A person who makes maps. p. 122

cash crop (kash krop) A crop that people raise to sell rather than to use themselves. p. 218

cause (côz) Any action that makes something happen. p. 29

census (sen'səs) A population count. p. 353

century (sen'chə·rē) A period of 100 years. p. 64

ceremony (ser'ə·mō·nē) A service performed for a special purpose, such as for a religion. p. 82

charter (chär'tər) A document giving a person or group official approval to take a certain action. p. 206

checks and balances (cheks and ba'lən·səz) A system that gives each branch of government different powers so that each branch can check the authority of the others. p. 357

chronology (krə·nä'lə·jē) Time order. p. 29

citizen (si'tə·zən) A member of a town or city, state, or country. p. 19

city-state (si'tē·stāt) A city that has its own ruler and government. p. 98

civil rights (si'vəl rīts) The rights guaranteed to all citizens by the Constitution. p. 598

civil war (si'vəl wôr) A war between people of the same country. p. 152

civilian (sə·vil'yən) A person who is not in the military. p. 512

civilization (si·və·lə·zā'shən) A culture that has developed forms of government, religion, and learning. p. 66

claim (klām) To declare that you or your country owns something. p. 156

clan (klan) A group of families that are related to one another. p. 78

class (klas) A group of people treated with the amount of respect that is given to the group's place in society. p. 98

classify (kla'sə·fī) To sort. p. 225

colonist (kä'lə·nist) A person who lives in a colony. p. 159

colony (kä'lə·nē) A settlement ruled by another country. p. 159

Columbian Exchange (kə·lum'bē·ən iks·chānj') The movement of plants, animals, and people from one continent to another. It is named for Christopher Columbus, one of the first explorers to transfer items across the Atlantic Ocean. p. 164

Committee of Correspondence (kə·mi'tē əv kôr·ə·spän'dəns) A group set up in each of the colonies to quickly share information about taxes and other issues by writing letters to groups in the other colonies. p. 279

common (kä'mən) An open area where sheep and cattle grazed. p. 229

compact (käm'pakt) An agreement. p. 175

compass (kəm'pəs) An instrument used to find direction. It has a needle that always points north. p. 127

compass rose (kəm'pəs rōz) A direction marker on a map. p. 35

compromise (käm'prə·mīz) To give up some of what you want in order to reach an agreement. p. 346

conclusion (kən·klōō'zhən) A decision or an idea reached by thoughtful study. p. 139

Conestoga (kä·nə·stō'gə) A large covered wagon used by farmers to carry their produce to market towns. p. 231

Confederacy (kən·fe'də·rə·sē) The Confederate States of America, a new country that was formed by Southern states that seceded from the Union after Abraham Lincoln was elected President in 1860. p. 497

confederation (kən·fe·də·rā'shən) A loosely united group of governments. p. 94

congress (kän'grəs) A meeting of representatives who have the authority to make decisions. p. 277

conquistador (kän·kēs'tə·dôr) Any of the Spanish conquerors in the Americas during the early 1500s. p. 151

consequence (kän'sə·kwens) The result of an action. p. 280

constitution (kän·stə·tōō'shən) A plan of government. p. 333

Continental (kän·tən·en'təl) A soldier in the first colonial army, which was headed by George Washington. p. 291

Continental Congress (kän·tən·en'təl kän'grəs) A meeting of representatives of the British colonies. p. 281

convention (kən·ven'shən) An important meeting. p. 339

cotton gin (kä'tən jin) A machine that removes the seeds from cotton fibers. p. 479

council (koun'səl) A group that makes laws. p. 94

county (koun'tē) A large part of a colony. Today, it is a part of a state. A county has its own local government. p. 231

county seat (koun'tē sēt) The main town for a large part of a colony. Today, it is the city where a county government is located. p. 231

coureur de bois (kōō·rûr'də bwä) A French word meaning "runner of the woods." This was a person who traded with American Indians for furs. p. 245

cultural diffusion (kul'chə·rəl di·fyōō'zhən) The spread of a culture from one place to another. p. 67

cultural region (kul'chə·rəl rē'jən) An area where peoples share some ways of life. p. 75

culture (kul'chər) A way of life. pp. 21, 50

debate (di·bāt') To argue opposite sides of an issue. p. 349

debtor (de'tər) A person who had been in prison for owing money. p. 223

decade (de'kād) A period of ten years. p. 64

declaration (de·klə·rā'shən) An official statement. p. 296

delegate (de'li·gət) A representative. p. 339

democracy (di•mä′krə•sē) A government in which the people take part. p. 263

descendants (di•sen′dənts) The children or grandchildren of an ancestor. p. 607

desertion (di•zûr′shən) Running away from duties, such as military service. p. 157

dictator (dik′tā•tər) A leader who has total authority. p. 445

distortion (di•stôr′shən) An area that is not accurate on a map. p. 56

diversity (də•vûr′sə•tē) Differences, such as those among different peoples. p. 75

doctrine (däk′trən) A government plan of action. p. 420

drought (drout) A long dry spell. p. 71

due process of law (dōō prä′ses uv lô) A process that guarantees the right to a fair public trial. p. 375

dugout (dəg′out) A boat made from a large, hollowed-out log. p. 76

earthwork (ərth′wərk) A mound, or hill of earth, that people built. p. 67

economy (i•kä′nə•mē) The way people use resources to meet their needs. p. 37

effect (i•fekt′) What happens because of an action. p. 29

electoral college (i•lek′tə•rəl kä′lij) A group of electors chosen by citizens to vote for the President. p. 355

elevation (e•lə•vā′shən) The height of the land. p. 453

Emancipation Proclamation (i•man•sə•pā′shən prä•klə•mā′shən) The Presidential order of 1863 that freed enslaved people in the Confederate states. p. 513

emperor (em′pər•ər) The ruler of an empire. p. 101

empire (em′pīr) A conquered land of many people and places governed by one ruler. p. 101

encounter (in•koun′tər) A meeting, such as one between peoples who have never met before. p. 120

encroach (in•krōch′) To move onto without asking permission. p. 304

enlist (in•list′) To join. p. 292

entrepreneur (än•trə•prə•nûr′) A person who sets up a new business, taking a chance on making or losing money. p. 556

equality (i•kwä′lə•tē) The same rights for all people. p. 455

evidence (e′və•dəns) Proof. p. 51

executive branch (ig•ze′kyə•tiv branch) The branch of government that carries out the laws. p. 353

expedition (ek•spə•di′shən) A journey made for a special reason. p. 142

exploration (ek•splə•rā′shən) Searching the unknown. p. 121

export (ek′spôrt) A good sent from one country to another to be sold. p. 232

extinct (ik•stingkt′) No longer living, like a kind of animal that has died out. p. 60

fact (fakt) A statement that can be proved true. p. 145

fall line (fol līn) A place where the land drops sharply, causing the rivers to form waterfalls. p. 241

farm produce (färm prō′dōos) Grains, fruits, and vegetables that farmers can trade for goods and services or sell for money. p. 231

federal system (fe′də•rəl sis′təm) A governing system in which the states share authority with the national government. p. 346

Federalist (fe′də•rə•list) A citizen who was in favor of ratifying the Constitution. p. 370

federation (fe•də•rā′shən) An organization made up of many related groups. p. 570

forty-niner (fôr′tē•nī′nər) A gold seeker who arrived in California in the year 1849. p. 450

free enterprise (frē en′tər•prīz) An economic system in which people are able to start and run their own businesses with little control by the government. p. 555

free state (frē stāt) A state that did not allow slavery. p. 490

frontier (frən•tir′) The land beyond a settlement. p. 216

Fundamental Orders (fən•də•men′təl ôr′dərz) The first written system of government in North America. It was adopted in Connecticut. p. 208

generalization (jen•rə•lə•zā′shən) A statement that summarizes facts and shows how they are related. p. 246

geographer (jē•ä′grə•fər) A person whose work is to study geography. p. 31

Gettysburg Address (ge′tēz•bûrg ə•dres′) A short speech given by Abraham Lincoln in 1863 at the dedication of a cemetery at Gettysburg, Pennsylvania. p. 523

glacier (glā′shər) A huge sheet of ice. p. 48

grant (grant) A gift of money to be used for a special purpose. p. 154

grid (grid) On a map, the north-south and east-west lines that cross each other to form a pattern of squares. p. 36

grievance (grē′vəns) A complaint. p. 298

hacienda (ä•sē•en′dä) A large estate. p. 197

hatch lines (hach līnz) A pattern of lines often used on historical maps to indicate land that was claimed by two or more countries. p. 269

heritage (her′ə•tij) Culture that has come from the past and continues today. p. 37

Glossary

historical empathy (hi·stôr'i·kəl em'pə·thē) Understanding the actions and feelings of people from other times and other places. p. 28

hogan (hō'gän) A cone-shaped house built by covering a log frame with mud or grass. p. 84

home front (hōm frunt) The places where civilians are active when their country is at war. p. 512

House of Burgesses (hous əv bûr'jə·səz) An assembly that met in the colony of Virginia to make laws. p. 218

human features (hyoo'mən fē'chərz) The buildings, bridges, farms, roads, and people themselves that are found in a place. p. 32

human rights (hyoo'mən rīts) Freedoms that all people should have. p. 376

immigrant (i'mi·grənt) A person who comes to live in a country from his or her home country. p. 216

impeach (im·pēch') To accuse a government official, such as the President, of wrongdoing. p. 355

import (im'pôrt) A good brought into a country from another country, to be sold. p. 231

impressment (im·pres'mənt) Forcing people into military service. p. 416

indentured servant (in·den'shərd sər'vənt) A person who agrees to work for another person without pay for a certain length of time. p. 236

independence (in·də·pen'dəns) Freedom to govern on one's own. p. 295

indigo (in'di·gō) A plant from which a blue dye is made. p. 221

Industrial Revolution (in·dus'trē·əl re·və·loo'shən) A time during the late 1700s and early 1800s when new inventions changed the way people lived, worked, and traveled. p. 431

inflation (in·flā'shən) An economic condition in which it takes more and more money to buy the same goods. p. 335

influence (in'floo·əns) The ability people or things have to affect other people or things. p. 214

inset map (in'set map) A small map within a larger map. p. 36

integration (in·tə·grā'shən) The bringing together of people of all races in education, jobs, and housing. p. 602

interchangeable parts (in·tər·chān'jə·bəl pärts) Identical copies of parts made by machines so that if one part breaks, an identical one can be installed. p. 432

intermediate direction (in·tər·mē'dē·it də·rek'shən) One of the in-between directions: northeast, northwest, southeast, or southwest. p. 35

interpreter (in·tûr'prə·tər) A person who translates from one language to another. p. 176

Iroquois League (ir'ə·kwoi lēg) A group of Iroquois tribes that worked together for peace. p. 94

isthmus (is'məs) A narrow strip of land that connects two larger land areas. p. 141

jazz (jaz) A kind of music that grew out of the African American musical heritage. p. 566

judicial branch (joo·di'shəl branch) The branch of government that settles differences about the meaning of the laws. p. 353

jury (jûr'ē) A group of citizens who decide a case in court. p. 376

justice (jus'təs) A judge who serves on the Supreme Court. p. 355

kachina (kə·chē'nə) One of the spirits that are important in the religion of the Hopis and other Pueblo peoples. p. 82

kiva (kē'və) A special underground room where the Anasazi held religious services. p. 71

knoll (nōl) A small, round hill. p. 120

labor union (lā'bər yoon'yən) A group of workers who take action to improve their working conditions. p. 569

legend (le'jənd) A story handed down over time, often to explain the past. p. 93

legislative branch (le'jəs·lā·tiv branch) The branch of government that makes the laws. p. 353

legislature (le'jəs·lā·chər) The lawmaking branch of a colony, a state government, or the national government. p. 264

liberty (li'bər·tē) Freedom. p. 275

lines of latitude (līnz uv la'tə·tood) *See* parallels

lines of longitude (līnz uv lon'jə·tood) *See* meridians

locator (lō'kā·tər) A small map or picture of a globe. It shows where the area shown on the main map is located in a state, in a country, on a continent, or in the world. p. 35

locomotive (lō·kə·mō'tiv) A railroad engine. p. 437

lodge (läj) A circular house built over a shallow pit and covered with sod. p. 86

loft (loft) The part of a house between the ceiling and the roof. p. 243

longhouse (lông'hous) A long wooden building in which several Indian families lived together. p. 94

Loyalist (loi'ə·list) A colonist who supported the British monarch and laws. p. 273

mainland (mān′land) The main part of a continent, rather than an island near the continent. p. 154

maize (māz) Corn. p. 62

majority (mə·jôr′ə·tē) The greater part of a whole. p. 353

manifest destiny (ma′nə·fest des′tə·nē) The belief shared by many Americans that it was the certain future of the United States to stretch from the Atlantic Ocean to the Pacific Ocean. p. 444

map key (map kē) A part of a map that explains what the symbols on the map stand for. Also called a legend. p. 35

map scale (map skāl) A part of a map that compares a distance on the map to a distance in the real world. p. 35

map title (map tī′təl) Words on a map that describe the subject of the map. p. 35

mass production (mas prə·duk′shən) A way of manufacturing that produces large amounts of goods at one time. p. 432

massacre (ma′si·kər) The killing of people who cannot defend themselves. p. 278

Mayflower Compact (mā′flou·ər käm′pakt) An agreement by those on the *Mayflower* to make and obey laws for their colony. This was the first example of self-rule by American colonists. p. 175

mercenary (mûr′sən·âr·ē) A hired soldier. p. 292

meridians (mə·ri′dē·ənz) North-south lines on a map or globe that run from pole to pole. Also called lines of longitude. pp. 36, 136

mesa (mā′sä) A high, flat-topped hill. p. 70

migration (mī·grā′shən) A voluntary or forced movement of people from one place to another. p. 47

militia (mə·li′shə) A volunteer army. p. 229

millennium (mə·le′nē·əm) A period of 1,000 years. p. 64

Minuteman (mi′nət·man) A member of the Massachusetts colony militia who could quickly be ready to fight the British. p. 283

mission (mi′shən) A small religious community. p. 198

missionary (mi′shə·ner·ē) A person who teaches his or her religion to others. p. 159

monarch (mä′närk) A king or queen. p. 126

movement (mo͞ov′mənt) An effort by many people. p. 302

nationalism (na′shə·nəl·i·zəm) Pride in a country. p. 419

naturalization (na·chə·rə·lə·zā′shən) The process of becoming an American citizen by living in the country for five years and then passing a test. p. 588

naval stores (nā′vəl stôrz) Products made from pine tar that were used in building and repairing ships. p. 221

navigation (na·və·gā′shən) The study or act of planning and controlling the course of a ship. p. 127

negotiate (ni·gō′shē·āt) To talk with one another to work out an agreement. p. 316

neutral (no͞o′trəl) Not taking a side in a conflict. p. 301

noble (nō′bəl) A person from an important family. p. 99

nomad (nō′mad) A wanderer who has no settled home. p. 48

nonviolence (nän·vī′ə·ləns) The use of peaceful ways to bring about change. p. 601

Northwest Passage (nôrth·west′ pa′sij) A water route that explorers wanted to find so that traders could cut through North America to Asia. p. 167

olive branch (ä′liv branch) A symbol of peace. p. 289

opinion (ə·pin′yən) A statement that tells what a person believes. p. 145

opportunity cost (ä·pər·to͞o′nə·tē kôst) The cost of giving up one thing to get another. p. 285

oral history (ôr′əl his′tə·rē) Accounts that tell the experiences of people who did not have a written language or who did not write down what happened. p. 27

ordinance (ôr′dən·əns) A law or a set of laws. p. 337

origin story (ôr′ə·jən stōr′ē) A story that tells of a people's beliefs about the world and their place in it. p. 52

override (ō′və·rīd) To cancel. p. 357

overseer (ō′vər·sē·ər) A person who was hired to watch slaves to see that they did their work. p. 484

P

pacifist (pa′sə·fist) A believer in a peaceful settlement of differences p. 302

parallels (par′ə·lelz) East-west lines on a map or globe that are always the same distance apart. Also called lines of latitude. pp. 36, 136

Parliament (pär′lə·mənt) The part of the British government in which members make laws for the British people. p. 263

pathfinder (path′fīn·dər) Someone who finds a way through an unknown region. p. 410

Patriot (pā′trē·ət) A colonist who was against British rule. p. 283

patriotism (pā′trē·ə·ti·zəm) Love of one's country. p. 377

permanent (pər′mə·nənt) Long-lasting. p. 195

perspective (pər·spek′tiv) Point of view. p. 28

petition (pə·ti′shən) A request for action signed by many people. p. 275

physical features (fi′zi•kəl fē′chərz) The landforms, bodies of water, climate, soil, plant and animal life, and other natural resources that are found in a place. p. 32

pilgrim (pil′grəm) A person who makes a journey for a religious reason. p. 175

pioneer (pī•ə•nir′) A person who first settles a new place. p. 403

pit house (pit hous) A house built partly over a hole dug in the earth so that some of its rooms are under the ground. p. 78

plantation (plan•tā′shən) A huge farm. p. 159

political cartoon (pə•li′ti•kəl kär•tōōn′) A cartoon that expresses opinions about politics or about government. p. 294

political party (pə•li′ti•kəl pär′tē) A group of people involved in government who try to get others to agree with their ideas and who choose leaders who share the group's points of view. p. 381

portage (pôr′tij) The carrying of canoes and supplies around waterfalls and rapids or overland between rivers. p. 202

potlatch (pät′lach) A special Native American gathering at which the host gives away valuable gifts. p. 79

Preamble (prē′am•bəl) The introduction to the Constitution. p. 342

prediction (pri•dik′•shən) A telling beforehand of what will most likely happen next, based on what has happened before. p. 421

prejudice (pre′jə•dəs) A negative feeling some people have against others because of their race or culture. p. 584

presidio (prā•sē′dē•ō) A fort. p. 195

primary source (prī′mer•ē sôrs) A record made by people who saw or took part in an event. p. 26

prime meridian (prīm mə•ri′dē•ən) The meridian marked 0°. It runs north and south through Greenwich, Britain. p. 136

profit (prä′fət) In a business, money left over after everything has been paid for. p. 173

projection (prə•jek′•shən) One of many different views showing the round Earth on flat paper. p. 56

proprietary colony (prə•prī′ə•ter•ē kä′lə•nē) A colony that was owned and ruled by one person who was chosen by a king or queen. p. 205

proprietor (prə•prī′ə•tər) An owner. p. 205

public opinion (pu′blik ə•pin′yən) What the people of a community think. p. 274

public school (pu′blik skōōl) A school paid for by taxes and open to all children. p. 454

pueblo (pwe′blō) A group of adobe houses that the Anasazi and other Pueblo peoples lived in. p. 70

purchase (pûr′chəs) To buy. p. 409

Puritan (pyûr′ə•tən) A member of the Church of England who settled in North America to follow Christian beliefs in a more "pure" way. p. 206

pyramid (pir′ə•mid) A building with three or more triangle-shaped sides that slant toward a point at the top. p. 66

quarter (kwôr′tər) To provide or pay for housing. p. 280

ratify (ra′tə•fī) To agree to something and so make it a law. p. 367

Reconstruction (rē•kən•strək′shən) A time of rebuilding the country after the Civil War. p. 533

refinery (ri•fī′nə•rē) A factory where crude, or raw, oil is made into usable products. p. 557

reform (ri•fôrm′) A change for the better. p. 454

refuge (re′fyōōj) A safe place. p. 215

regiment (re′jə•mənt) A troop of soldiers. p. 305

region (rē′jən) An area on the Earth with features that make it different from other areas. p. 33

regulate (reg′yə•lāt) To control with laws. p. 573

relative location (re′lə•tiv lō•kā′shən) The location of a place in relation to what it is near. p. 32

relief (ri•lēf′) Differences in height of an area of land. p. 452

religion (ri•li′jən) Beliefs about God or gods. p. 63

Renaissance (re′nə•sänts) A French word meaning "rebirth," used to name a time of advances in thought, learning, art, and science. p. 126

repeal (ri•pēl′) To undo a law or tax. p. 277

representation (re•pri•zen•tā′shən) Acting or speaking on behalf of someone or something. p. 273

republic (ri•pu′blik) A form of government in which people elect representatives to run a country. p. 334

resist (ri•zist′) To act against. p. 485

revolution (re•və•lōō′shən) A sudden, complete change of government. p. 295

right (rīt) A freedom. p. 281

royal colony (roi′əl kä′lə•nē) A colony controlled by a king or queen. p. 201

ruling (rōō′ling) A decision. p. 442

rumor (rōō′mər) A story that has been told but has not been proved. p. 155

saga (sä′gə) An adventure story about the brave deeds of people long ago. p. 119

scalawag (ska′li•wag) A person who supports something for his or her own gain. p. 536

scarce (skers) Not plentiful. p. 197

scurvy (skûr′vē) A sickness caused by not getting enough vitamin C, which is found in fruit and vegetables. p. 143

secede (si•sēd′) To leave the Union. p. 441

secondary source (se′kən•der•ē sôrs) A record of an event, written by someone who was not there at the time. p. 27

Glossary

sectionalism (sek′shə•nəl•i•zəm) Regional loyalty. p. 440

segregation (se•gri•gā′shən) Separation. p. 537

self-government (self•gu′vərn•mənt) A system of government in which people make their own laws. p. 263

self-sufficient (self•sə•fi′shənt) Self-supporting. p. 197

separation of powers (se•pə•rā′shən əv pou′erz) The division of the national government into three branches instead of having one all-powerful branch. p. 353

settlement house (se′təl•mənt hous) A community center where people can learn new skills. p. 575

shaman (shä′mən) A religious leader and healer. p. 85

sharecropping (sher′krä•ping) A system of working the land, in which the worker was paid with a "share" of the crop. p. 533

siege (sēj) A long-lasting attack. p. 312

skyscraper (skī′skrā•pər) A tall steel-frame building. p. 576

slave code (slāv kōd) A law that shaped the day-to-day lives of enslaved people. p. 484

slave state (slāv stāt) A state that allowed slavery. p. 490

slavery (slā′və•rē) The practice of holding people against their will and making them carry out orders. p. 99

society (sə•sī′ə•tē) A human group. p. 37

sod (sod) Earth cut into blocks or mats that are held together by grass and its roots. p. 86

specialize (spe′shə•līz) To work mostly on one job that could be done well. p. 63

spiritual (spir′i•chə•wəl) A religious song based on Bible stories. p. 485

states' rights (stāts rīts) The idea that individual states have final authority over the national government. p. 440

strike (strīk) To stop work in protest of working conditions. p. 569

suffrage (su′frij) The right to vote. p. 457

surplus (sûr′pləs) More than is needed. p. 63

tariff (tar′əf) A tax on goods brought into a country. p. 272

tax (taks) Money that is paid by people to run the country. p. 266

technology (tek•nä′lə•jē) The use of scientific knowledge or tools to make or do something. p. 60

temple (tem′pəl) A place of worship. p. 66

tenement (te′nə•mənt) A poorly built apartment house. p. 574

tepee (tē′pē) A cone-shaped tent made of poles covered with animal skins. p. 90

territory (ter′ə•tôr•ē) Land that belongs to a national government but is not a state. p. 337

textile mill (tek′stīl mil) A factory where fibers such as cotton and wool are woven into cloth. p. 431

theory (thē′ə•rē) A possible explanation for something. p. 50

time line (tīm līn) A diagram that shows the events that took place during a certain period of time. p. 64

time zone (tīm zōn) A region in which a single time is used. p. 560

totem pole (tō′təm pōl) A wooden post that is carved with shapes of people and animals. p. 80

town meeting (toun mē′ting) An assembly in the New England colonies in which male landowners could take part in government. p. 229

township (toun′ship) A square of land in the Northwest Territory that measured 6 miles per side. p. 337

trade network (trād net′wərk) A system in which trade takes place between certain groups of people. p. 168

trade-off (trād′ôf) What you have to give up buying or doing in order to buy or do something else. p. 285

transcontinental railroad (trans•kän•tən•en′təl rāl′rōd) A railroad that crosses a continent, such as one that links the Atlantic and Pacific coasts of the United States. p. 555

transport (trans•pōrt′) To carry. p. 434

travois (trə•voi′) A kind of carrier made up of two poles fastened to the harness of an animal. p. 91

treason (trē′zən) Working against one's own government. p. 274

treaty (trē′tē) An agreement between countries. p. 316

trend (trend) A pattern of change over time. p. 483

triangular trade route (trī•ang′gyə•lər trād rōot) A shipping route that included Britain, the British colonies, and Africa. p. 232

tribe (trīb) A group made up of many bands of people with a shared culture and land. p. 63

tributary (tri′byə•ter•ē) A branch of a river or stream. p. 203

tribute (tri′byōot) Payments a ruler demands from his or her people. p. 101

unconstitutional (un•kän•stə•tōo′shə•nəl) Going against the Constitution. p. 357

Underground Railroad (un′dər•ground rāl′rōd) A system of escape routes for enslaved people, leading to freedom. p. 487

Union (yōon′yən) The United States of America. p. 351

veto (vē′tō) A power the President has to reject a bill passed by Congress. p. 355

volunteer (vä•lən•tir′) A person who works without pay to help make the community a better place to live. p. 609

Glossary

Index

Page references for illustrations are set in italic type. An italic *m* indicates a map. Page references set in boldface type indicate the pages on which vocabulary terms are defined.

Index

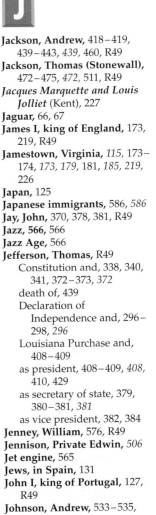

National Palace, Mexico City, D.F., Mexico. Schalkwijk/Art Resource; 106 (bc) First Light; 106 (br) Paul Grebliunas/Tony Stone Images; 106 (tc) Steve Dunwell/The Image Bank; 107 (cl) David Young Wolff/Tony Stone Images; 107 (bl) Harald Sund/The Image Bank; 107 (bc) Peter Hendrie Photo/The Image Bank; 107 (c) Art Brewer/Tony Stone Images; 107 (tr) First Light.

UNIT 2

HARCOURT BRACE & COMPANY

116 (tl) Victoria Bowen; 126 (t) Sheri O'Neal; 130 (tl) Harcourt Brace & Company; 164 (bc) Rich Franco; 164 (l) Weronica Ankarorn; 181 (br) Victoria Bowen; 187 (b) Harcourt Brace & Company.

OTHER

112–113 Rijksmuseum Amsterdam; 118 Scala/Art Resource, NY; 119 (br) Werner Forman/Art Resource NY; 119 (tr) Giraudon/Art Resource; 120 (br) Werner Forman/Art Resource NY; 121 (t) World Book Publishing; 122 (bl) The Granger Collection; 122 (t) New York Public Library; 123 (tc) Giraudon/Art Resource, NY; 124 (bl) Giraudon/Art Resource NY; 124 (tl) Biblioteque National, Paris; 125 (tc) Collection of the National Palace Museum, Taipei, Taiwan, Republic of China; 127 (bc) Michael Holford; 127 (r) National Maritime Museum Picture Library; 128 (cl) Bibliotheque Nationale, Paris; 128 (br) Bibliotheque Nationale, Paris; 130 (c) National Museum of American Art, Washington/Art Resource, NY; 130 (br) Institut Amatller D'Art Hispanic; 131 (tc) Rebecca E. Marvil/Light Sources Stock; 132 (t) The Granger Collection, New York; 133 (tc) Museo Naval; 133 (bc) Museo Naval; 134 (bl) Museo Navale di Pegli, Genoa, Italy/Scala/Art Resource, NY; 134 (t) National Graphics, Inc.; 135 (tr) Scala/Art Resource, NY; 138 (bl) ZIN41924 Selection of Arab and European Astrolabes from the 14th to 16th century, copper, Museum of the History of Science, Oxford/Bridgeman Art Library, London; 139 (t) The New York Public Library, Map Division; 142 (cl) Will & Deni McIntyre/Photo Researchers; 144 (tc) Scala/Art Resource; 144 (tl) Richard Hurley/John Carter Brown Library; 145 (bl) The Bettman Archive; 148 E. T. Archive; 149 (tr) Courtesy of the Hispanic Society of America; 149 (bc) Scala/Art Resource; 150 (b) American Museum of Natural History; 151 (bc) Werner Forman Archive, Museum fur Volkerkunde, Berlin/Art Resource; 152 (cr) Loren McIntyre; 152 (br) ET Archive; 153 (tc) Werner Forman/Art Resource; 154 (bl) Courtesy of the Oakland Museum of California; 156 (cr) The Pierpoint Morgan Library/Art Resource, NY; 157 (insert) Jeffery M. Mitchem; 157 (b) Library of Congress; 159 (br) Culver Pictures, Inc.; 159 (tr) © 1986 Mel Fisher/Maritime Heritage Society, Key West, FL. Photo by Scott Nierling; 160 (cr) Archivo Fotographico Sevillo; 160 (bl) Courtesy of The Hispanic Society of America, New York; 162 (br) Werner Forman, Art Resource, NY; 163 (tr) The Granger Collection, New York; 163 (insert) Stock Montage; 166 (insert) The Granger Collection, New York; 166–167 (b) Dotte Larsen/Bruce Coleman, Inc.; 168 (tc) The Granger Collection, New York; 169 (b) "The Surveyor: Portrait of Captian John Henry Lefroy", Paul Kane, Glenbow Collection, Calgary, Alberta, Canada; 169 (cr) From the Collection of the Minnesota Historical Society; 170 (tr) The Minnesota Historical Society, #67.230.177; 170 (tl) The Granger Collection, New York; 171 (b) BAL1648 Elizabeth 1, Armada portrait by Anonymous Private Collection/Bridgeman Art Library, London; 172 (tl) The British Museum; 173 A. H. Robins, photo by Don Eiler; 174 (br) The Granger Collection, New York; 174 (tl) The Library of Virginia; 176 (c) Courtesy of The Pilgrim Society, Plymouth, Massachusetts; 182–183 (bg) Jeff Brice, Represented by Kola Baker.

UNIT 3

HARCOURT BRACE & COMPANY

227 (br) Victoria Bowen; 249 (br) Victoria Bowen; 255 (b) Weronica Ankarorn.

OTHER

188–189 Print Collection. Miriam and Ira Wallach Division of Art, Prints and Photographs. The New York Public Library. Astor, Lenox, and Tilden Foundation; 192 (tl) Rare Books & Manuscripts Division, The New York Public Library; 192 (bl) Courtesy of The Pilgrim Society; 193 (br) Courtesy Peabody Essex Museum, Salem, MA; (; 193) 193 (tc) Courtesy of The Pilgrim Society, Plymouth, Massachusetts; 193 (tr) Walter Meayers Edwards/National Geographic Image Collection; 193 (bl) The Pilgrim Society; 194 Courtesy Museum of New Mexico, Neg. No. 50828; 195 (tr) David Barnes/Tony Stone; 195 (bc) Florida Museum of Natural History; 196 (b) St. Augustine National Park Service; 197 (t) California Historical Society, gift of Mr. and Mrs. Reginald Walker; 200 (tc) George H. H. Huey; 201 (br) Corbis-Bettmann; 202–203 (b) Kevin Magee/Tom Stack & Associates; 202 (tc) Courtesy of The Adirondack Museum, Photo by James Swedberg; 205 (tr) The Historic New Orleans Collection, Accession No. 1991.60; 206 (tl) The Granger Collection; 206 (bl) The Commonwealth of Massachusetts, Archives Division; 207 (bl) "Courtesy of the Pilgrim Society, Plymouth, Massachusetts."; 208 (b) The Granger Collection, New York; 209 (bc) The Bettmann Archive; 209 (tr) Worcester Art Museum, Worcester, Massachusetts Gift of Mr. and Mrs. Albert Rice; 210 (tc) Corbis-Bettmann; 211 (br) Culver Pictures, Inc.; 212 (bl) Culver Pictures, Inc.; 213 (b) Collection of the Albany Institute of History and Art, Bequest of Ledyard Cogswell, Jr.; 215 (tr) Historical Society of Pennsylvania; 215 (bl) The Granger Collection, New York; 216 (b) Giraudon/Art Resource, NY; 217 (tr) The Historical Society of Pennsylvania; 218 (tl) Science and Technology Section Science, Industry & Business Library. The New York Public Library, Astor, Lenox and Tilden Foundations; 219 (b) Courtesy of the Jamestown-Yorktown Educational Trust; 222–223 (t) The Granger Collection, New York; 223 (bl) Archives and History Center of the United Methodist Church, Madison, New Jersey; 223 (br) Courtesy of Oglethorp University; 224 (tc) Archive Photos; 228 Founders Society Purchase, Gibbs-Williams Fund, The Detroit Institute of Arts; 229 (br) New York Public Library Picture Collection; 231 (tr) Smithsonian Institution, Division of Transportation; 233 (t) Colonial Williamsburg Foundation; 235 (br) Arthur C. Smith, III/Grant Heilman Photography; 238 (bl) Chicago Historical Society; 238 (br) EX 17082 Negro Portrait: Olaudah Equiano by English School, (18th century) Royal Albert Memorial Museum, Exeter/Bridgeman Art Library, London; 238 (tc) Courtesy, American Antiquarian Society; 239 (t) The Metropolitan Museum of Art, Gift of Edgar William and Bernice Chrysler Garbisch, 1963. (63.201.3) Photograph © 1984 The Metropolitan Museum of Art.; 240 (tc) Smithsonian Institution; 241 (tr) Smithsonian Institution, Domestic Life Division, Neg # LIA-83–30016–9; 241 (br) National Geographic Image Collection; 244 (tr) Smithsonian Institution, Division of Agriculture, Neg # 34769; 245 (c) "American Beaver" by J. J. Audobon (detail). Taken from Plate XLVI Vivb., Quadrupeds of North America. Missouri Historical Society, St. Louis.; 250–251 (bg) Chip Henderson/Tony Stone Images; 250 (bl) Mark E. Gibson; 251 (bc) Louis Grandadam/Tony Stone Images; 251 (br) Henley & Savage/The Stock Market.

UNIT 4

HARCOURT BRACE & COMPANY

260 (tl) Victoria Bowen; 263 (tr) Weronica Ankarorn; 279 (br) Weronica Ankarorn; 287 (br) Victoria Bowen; 306 (tl) Victoria Bowen; 319 (br) Victoria Bowen; 325 (br) Harcourt Brace & Company.

OTHER

256–257 Historical Society of Pennsylvania; 262 Library of the Boston Athenaeum; 265 (br) Washington/Custis/Lee Collection, Washington and Lee University, Lexington, Va.; 266 (t) Dan McCoy/Rainbow; 267 (tc) Library of Congress; 268 (b) Yale University Library; 270 (b) The Granger Collection, New York; 271 (b) By courtesy of the National Portrait Gallery, London; 272 (bl) Peabody Essex Museum, Salem, MA. Photo by Mark Sexton; 272 (tl) Nawrocki Stock Photo; 273 (c) Fraunces Tavern Museum, New York; 273 (bl) Massachusetts Historical Society; 273 (lc) Massachusetts Historical Society; 273 (cr) Corbis Media; 274 (b) Virginia Historical Society; 275 (cr) Christie's Images; 276 (cr) Ed Eckstein for The Franklin Institute Science Museum; 276 (bl) Historical Society of Pennsylvania; 277 (tl) Courtesy, Peabody Essex Museum, Salem, Mass.; 277 (tr) © Collection of The New York Historical Society; 278 (tl) The Granger Collection, New York; 278 (cr) Library Company of Philadelphia; 278 (tc) Stock Montage, Inc.; 279 (tr) Daughters of The American Revolution Museum, Washington, D.C.; 280 (tl) Deposited by the City of Boston. Courtesy, Museum of Fine Arts, Boston; 281 (t) The Bridgeman Art Library International Ltd.; 284 (tl) Gift of Joseph W. Revere, William B. Revere, and Edward H. R. Revere. Courtesy, Museum of Fine Arts, Boston; 285 (tr) Archive Photos; 288 Bequest of Winslow Warren/Courtesy, Museum of Fine Arts, Boston; 289 (br) The New York Public Library/Harcourt Brace & Company; 290 (tl) Historical Society of Pennsylvania; 291 (bl) Library of Congress; 291 (cr) Yale University Art Gallery, Gift of the Associates; in Fine Arts and Mrs. Henry B. Loomis in Memory of Henry Bradford Loomis, B. A. 1875; 292 (t) Delaware Art Museum, Howard Pyle Collection; 293 (t) Corbis-Bettmann; 294 (bl) The Granger Collection, New York; 295 (br) Chicago Historical Society; 296 (cr) Corbis-Bettmann; 296 (bl) Library of Congress; 297 (b) Smithsonian Institution; 298 (t) Yale University Art Gallery, Trumbull Collection; 299 (tc) Sisse Brimberg/Woodfin Camp & Associates; 300 (b) John McRae/Kennedy Galleries, Inc.; 301 (br) Ted Spiegel; 302 (tl) The Granger Collection, New York; 303 (tr) Louis S. Glanzman/National Geographic Society; 304 (tl) The Granger Collection, New York; 305 (tc) Yale University Art Gallery, Trumbull Collection; 310 (tl) The Bettmann Archive; 310 (bl) Ted Spiegel/National Geographic Society; 312 (b) Pennsylvania Capital Preservation Committee/Photo by Brian D. Hunt; 313 (t) Amon Carter Museum, Fort Worth, Texas; 315 (c) A detail, John Trumbull "The Surrender of Lord Cornwallis at Yorktown, 19 October 1781", Yale University Art Gallery, Trumbull Collection.; 316 (bl) Ken McVey/Tony Stone Images; 320–321 Reuters/Bettmann.

UNIT 5

HARCOURT BRACE & COMPANY

330 (tl) Victoria Bowen; 342 (ct) Harcourt Brace & Company; 352 (bl) Harcourt Brace; 358 (tl) Victoria Bowen; 365 (br) Victoria Bowen; 371 (tr) Weronica Ankarorn; 387 (br) Victoria Bowen; 393 (br) Weronica Ankarorn.

OTHER

326–327 Architect of The Capital/National Graphics Center; 332 New York Historical Association, Cooperstown, Photo by Richard Walker; 333 (br) Historical Society of Pennsylvania; 334 (c) Cranbrook Institute of Science; 335 (tr) Corbis-Bettmann; 335 (tl) Courtesy, American Antiquarian Society; 337 (tc) Smithsonian Institution, Division of Political History, Neg. #81–5397; 338 (bl) Courtesy Commonwealth of Massachusetts. Photo by Douglas Christian; 339 (tr) The Granger Collection, New York; 339 (tl) Library of Congress; 340 (tl) The Granger Collection, New York; 341 (c) Joseph Nettis/Tony Stony Images; 342 (b) Independence National Historical Park; 343 (tr) North Wind Picture Archives; 346 (bl) The Granger Collection, New York; 346 (cl) Courtesy of The National Archives; 348 (cr) Emmet Collection, Rare Books and Manuscripts Division, The New York Public Library, Astor, Lenox and Tilden Foundations; 348 (tc) The Library of Virginia; 349 (tl) New York Public Library; 349 (tc) The Art Museum, Princeton University; 350 (bl) Continental Insurance Co./Photo by Larry Phillips Photo; 351 (t) 'Residences and Slave Quarters of Mulbery Plantation' by Thomas Coram, The Gibbes Museum of Art, Charleston, SC; 352 (bl) Ralph Earl Roger Sherman (1721–1793) M. A. (Hon.) 1786 Yale University Art Gallery. Gift of Roger Sherman White, B.A. 1899, L.L.B 1902; 353 (br) U. S. Senate Collection; 354, 356 (cl, tc) James Foote/Photo Researchers; 354, 356 (tl, tcl, bl, b) Dale E. Boyer/Photo Researchers; 356 (br) Joe Sohm/Photo Researchers; 357 (t) Library of Congress #39543; 360 (t) Michael Bryant/Woodfin Camp; 361 (c) National Portrait Gallery, Smithsonian Institution/Art Resource, NY; 362 (c) Superstock; 363 (c) Tom McHugh/Photo Researchers; 366 Corcoran Gallery of Art/Corbis; 367 (br) Independence National Historical Park; 368 (br) The Granger Collection, New York; 368 (tc) Michael Byrant/Woodfin Camp; 368 (tl) Michael Bryant/Woodfin Camp; 370 (bl) The Granger Collection, New York; 370 (br) Collection of The New York Historical Society; 372 (cl) Archive Photos; 372 (cr) Archive Photos; 372 (tl) Colonial Williamsburg Foundation; 372 (tr) The White House Historical Association; 374 (tl) Larry Stevens/Nawrocki Stock Photo; 374 (bl) © 1998 North Wind Pictures; 375 (tl) The New York Historical Society; 375 (tr) Franklin Institute of Philadelphia; 376 (tl) Superstock; 377 (c) Dover Publications; 378 (bl) Smithsonian Institution; 378 (tl), 380 (br) Sally Andersen-Bruce; 379 (t) Mr & Mrs. John Harney; 380 (tr) Courtesy of the John Carter Brown Library at Brown University; 381 (tc) Independence National Historical Park Collection; 381 (tr) Independence National Historical Park Collection; 382 (tl) Maryland Historical Society; 384 (tc) Jack Zehrt/FPG International; 385 (b) American Numismatic Association; 388–389 Museum of Political Life, University of Hartford.

UNIT 6

HARCOURT BRACE & COMPANY

398 (tl); 422 (tl),429 (br) Victoria Bowen; 461 (br) Victoria Bowen.

OTHER

394–395 The National Cowboy Hall of Fame and Western Heritage Center, Oklahoma City, Oklahoma; 402 Colorado Historical Society; 403 (tr) William Strode; 403 (br) Hulton Getty Picture Collection/Tony Stone Images; 404 (t) George Calieb Bingham, Daniel Boone Escorting Settlers Through The Cumberland Gap, 1851–52, detail. Oil on Canvas, 35 1/2 x 50 1/4'. Washington University Gallery of Art, St. Louis; 406 (b) Reynolda House, Museum of American Art, Photography by Jackson Smith; 407 (tr) America Hurrah Archive, NYC; 408 (tl) Smithsonian Institution; 408 (bl) Collection of The New York Historical Society; 409 (cl) Erich Lessing/Art Resource; 410 (tl) The Bettmann Archive; 411 (bc) North Wind Picture Archives; 411 (t) Amon Carter Museum, Fort Worth, TX; 412–413 (b) Bob Thomason/Tony Stone Images; 412 (cl) Courtesy of The Montana Historical Society; 414 (bl) National Portrait Gallery, Smithsonian Institution/Art Resource, NY; 415 (b) Prophetstown used courtesy of Pathway Productions, Inc. All rights reserved. Copyright 1994; 415 (cr) The Field Museum Neg # A93851c; 418 (b) U. S. Naval Academy Museum; 419 (t) The Granger Collection, New York; 419 (cr) Collection of the New York Historical; 420 (t) The Bettmann Archive; 421 (b) Emanuel G. Leutze, "Westward the Course of Empire Takes Its Way", ca. 1861, Oil on Canvas. 0126.1615 From the Collection of Gilcrease Museum, Tulsa; 427 (bl) Library of Congress; 430 Oregon Historical Society; 431 (tr) Cooper-Hewitt, National Design Museum, Smithsonian Institute/Art Resource, NY; 431 (br) North Wind Picture Archives; 432 (cr) Smithsonian Institution, Division of Engineering, Neg #86–9625; 432 (t) Smithsonian Institution; 433 (br) Museum of American Textile History; 433 (bl) Progress for cotton-No.4 Carding, detail, Yale University Art Gallery, Mabel Brady Garvin Collection; 436 PNI; 436 (t) Maryland Historical Society; 436 (b) The Granger Collection, New York; 438 (t) B&O Railroad Museum; 439 (br) The Granger Collection, New York; 440 Collection of The New York Historical Society; 441 The Granger Collection, New York; 442 (bc) National Portrait Gallery, Smithsonian Institution/ Art Resource, New York; 443 (t) Craig Smith/Philbrook Museum of Art, Tulsa, OK; 444 (bl) Archives Division—Texas State Library; 445 (t) Friends of the Governor's Mansion, Austin, Texas; 447 (bc) San Joaquin County Historical Society; 447 (tr) National Portrait Gallery; 448 (b) David W. Hawkinson/ Brigham Young University Museum of Art; 450 (b) California State Library; 451 (tr) Stock Montage, Inc.; 451 (lc) Corbis-Bettmann; 454 (bl) The Bettmann Archive; 455 (tc) State Achives of Michigan; 456 (cr) Book cover slide of *Uncle Tom's Cabin* by Harriet Beecher Stowe. Courtesy of the Charles L. Blockson Afro-American Collection, Temple University; 456 (bl) Harriet Beecher Stowe Center, Hartford, CT; 457 (tl) The Bettman Archives; 458 (tr) The Bettman Archives; 462 (br) Charles Nicklin/Al Giddings' Images, Inc.; 62 (bl) Picture Perfect; 463 (tl) Ron Church/Photo Researchers, Inc.; 463 (bl) Photo Researchers, Inc.; 463 (br) World Perspectives/Tony Stone Images; 463 (tc) World Perspectives/Tony Stone Images.

UNIT 7

HARCOURT BRACE & COMPANY

472 (tl) Victoria Bowen; 505 (br) Victoria Bowen; 545 (br) Weronica Ankarorn.

OTHER

468–469 High Impact Photography; 472 (bc) Brown Brothers; 472–473 (bg) Peter Gridley/FPG International; 473 (t) Peter Gridley/FPG International; 474 (bl) Valentine Museum, Richmond, Virginia; 474 (br) The Bettmann Archive; 474–475(bg) Ellis-Sawyer/FPG International; 475 (t) Anne S. K. Brown Military Collection, Brown University Library; 475 (insert) Eleanor S. Brockenbrough Library/The Museum of the Confederacy, Richmond, Virginia photograph by Katherine Wetzel; 476 National Portrait Gallery, Smithsonian Institution/Art Resource, NY; 477 (br) James H. Karales/Peter Arnold, Inc.; 478 (tc) Superstock; 478 (c) The Library of Congress; 480 (tl) The Granger Collection, New York; 481 (tl) The Charleston Museum; 484 (bl) The Bettmann Archive; 485 (t) "Last Sale of Slaves on the Courthouse Steps" by Thomas Satterwhite Noble, 1860. Oil on canvas. Missouri Historical Society, St. Louis, MO #1939.003.0001; 486 (b) The Granger Collection, New York; 487 (tl) The Brooklyn Museum; 487 (tr) The Bettmann Archive; 488 (bl) The Library of Congress; 490 (bl) The Metropolitan Museum of Art, Gift of I. N. Phelps Stokes, Edward S. Hawes, Alice Mary Hawes, Marion Augusta Hawes, 1937; 491 (t) Corbis-Bettmann; 493 (tr) Library of Congress; 493 (tl) Missouri Historical Society, St. Louis; 494 (br) Courtesy of the Illinois State Historical Library; 495 (tl) Sophia Smith Collection, Smith College, Northampton, MA; 496 (bl) Museum of Political Life, University of Hartford; 496 (tl) Museum of American Political Life, University of Hartford, West Hartford, CT; 497 (bc) Corbis-Bettmann; 497 (tl) Stock Montage; 498–499 (b) Library of Congress; 498 (cl) National Archives; 501 (bl) The Granger Collection, New York; 501 (br) National Portrait Gallery, Smithsonian Institute/Art Resource, NY; 503 (tc) Photri, Inc.; 503 (bc) The Granger Collection, New York; 506 Library of Congress; 507 (br) Superstock; 507 (tr) High Impact Photography; 508 (cr) The Museum of the Confederacy, Richmond, VA. Photo by Larry Sherer. TLB 2713: from *Echoes of Glory: Arms & Equipment of the Confederacy* (c)1991 Time-Life Books, Inc.; 508 (bc) NMAH, Smithsonian, TLB 2717 from *Echoes of Glory: Arms & Equipment of the Union*, Photographed by Larry Sherer (c)1991 Time-Life Books, Inc.; 509 (tr) Library of Congress #LC-US2623794; 509 (c) High Impact Photography; 510 (t) Chicago Historical Society; 511 (bl) National Archives; 512 (bl) The Connecticut Historical Society, Hartford; 513 (t) The Granger Collection, New York; 514 (b) The Granger Collection, New York; 516 Granger Collection, New York; 517 (tl) The Bettmann Archive; 518–519 (c) Library of Congress; 518 (tr) National Portrait Gallery, Smithsonian Institution, Washington, D.C.; 520 (tl) Chicago Historical Society; 520 (bl) Peter Newark; 521 (t) Chicago Historical Society; 522 (cl) Corbis-Bettmann; 522 (cb) Salamander Books; 524 (t) The National Archives/Corbis; 526 (t) Tom Lovell © National Geographic Society; 527 (c) Jeffrey Sylvester/FPG International; 530 (bl) National Archives; 531 (t) In the Collection of The Corcoran Gallery of Art, Museum Purchase, Gallery Fund.; 531 (br) Courtesy Houston Metropolitan Research Center, Houston Public Library; 532 (t) Library of Congress; 533 (bl) The Metropolitan Museum of Art, Morris K. Jesup Fund, 1940.; 534 (bl) Library of Congress; 535 (cr) Library of Congress; 535 (t) The Granger Collection, New York; 536 (b) The Granger Collection, New York; 536 (c) Library of Congress; 537 (c) Breton Littlehales/National Geographic Image Collection; 540–541 UPI/Bettmann.

UNIT 8

HARCOURT BRACE & COMPANY

550 (tl) Victoria Bowen; 581 (br) Victoria Bowen; 588 (b) Ellis Island National Memorial Park; 592 (tl) Victoria Bowen; 607 (br) Weronica Ankarorn; 608 (c) Carroll Morgan; 609 (tr) Weronica Ankarorn; 611 (br) Victoria Bowen; 617 (cb) Weronica Ankarorn/ Harcourt Brace and Company

OTHER

546–547 Library of Congress; 554 Wendy Lewis; 555 (br) Corbis-Bettmann; 555 (tr) Stanford University Museum of Art/AAA Gift of David Hewes; 557 (cl) The Bettmann Archive; 557 (cr) Corbis-Bettmann; 559 (tr) The Granger Collection, New York; 560 (br) The Granger Collection, New York; 560 (bl) Culver Pictures; 562 (tl) Michael Freeman; 562 (b) From the Collections of Henry Ford Museum & Greenfield Village; 563 (tl) Brown Brothers; 564 (cr) Culver Pictures; 564 (b) From the Collections of Henry Ford Museum & Greenfield Village; 565 (tr) Photri/The Stock Market; 565 (cl) The Granger Collection, New York; 566 (t) Corbis-Bettmann; 566 (insert) Blank Archives/ Archive Photos; 566 (b) Superstock; 567 (cr) The Granger Collection, New York; 567 (tl) Ewing Galloway/Index Stock; 568 (b) Brown Brothers; 569 (bl) The Library of Congress; 569 (tr) Corbis-Bettmann; 570 (bl) The George Meany Memorial Archives; 571 (t) Brown Brothers; 572 (t) Brown Brothers; 573 (tr) Library of Congress/Corbis; 574 (bl) Library of Congress/Corbis; 575 (t) The Jacob A. Riis Collection, Museum of the City of New York; 575 (c) Steven Mays/*The Encyclopedia of Collectibles*, for Time-Life Books, courtesy of Rebus, Inc., New York, NY; 576 (tl) Brown Brothers; 577 (cl) The Bettmann Archive; 578 (t) Detail "Trolley Car, Brooklyn Trolley Car Strike, 1899"/The Museum of the City of New York, The Byron Collection; 579 (bl) Stock Montage; 579 (c) University of Illinois at Chicago/The University Library/Jane Addams Memorial Collection; 582 David Hautzig; 583 (br) "By Courtesy of the Statue of Liberty National Monument"; 584 (t) Brown Brothers; 585 (b) California State Library/Neg. #912; 586 (bl) Brown Brothers; 587 (b) The Institute of Texan Cultures, San Antonio, Texas; 588 (cl) Calumet Regional Archives, Indiana University Northwest; 588 (b) Ellis Island National Memorial Park; 592 (tl) The Phillips Collection, Washington, D. C.; 593 (t) The Phillips Collection, Washington, D. C.; 594 (t) "They also worked on the railroads." Panel No. 38 from The Migration Series by Jacob Lawrence. (1940–41; text and title revised by the artist, 1993). Tempera on gesso on composition board, 12 x 18" (30.5 x 45.7 cm.) The Museum of Modern Art, New York. Gift of Mrs. David M. Levy. Photograph © 1999 The Museum of Modern Art; 594 (b) "The migrants arrived in great numbers." Panel No. 40 from The Migration Series by Jacob Lawrence. (1940–41; text and title revised by the artist, 1993). Tempera on gesso on composition board, 12x18" (30.5 x 45.7 cm) The Museum of Modern Art, New York. Gift of Mrs. David M. Levy. Photograph © 1999 The Museum of Modern Art; 595 (br) Panel No. 18 "The migration gained in momentum." from The Migration Series by Jacob Lawrence (1940–41; text and title revised by the artist, 1993). Tempera on gesso on compostion board, 12 x 18" (30.5 x 45.7 cm.)The Museum of Modern Art, New York. Gift of Mrs. David M. Levy. Photograph © 1999 The Museum of Modern Art; 596 (bl) "But living conditions were better in the North." Panel No. 44 from The Migration Series by Jacob Lawrence (1940–41; text and title revised by the artist, 1993). Tempera on gesso on compostion board, 12 x 18" (30.5 x 45.7 cm.) The Museum of Modern Art, New York. Gift of Mrs. David M. Levy. Photograph © 1999 The Museum of Modern Art; 596 (tl) The Phillips Collection, Washington, D. C.; 597 (t) "In the North the African American had more educational opportunities." Panel No. 58 from The Migration Series by Jacob Lawrence. (1940–41; text and title revised by the artist, 1993) Tempera on gesso on composition board, 12 x 18" (30.5x45.7cm.) The Museum of Modern Art, New York. Gift of Mrs. David M. Levy. Photograph © 1999 The Museum of Modern Art; 598 (bl) Brown Brothers; 599 (t) Corbis-Bettmann; 599 (insert) The Bettmann Archive; 600 (c) UPI/Corbis-Bettmann; 600 (bl) UPI/Corbis-Bettmann; 601 (tl) AP/Wide World Photos; 601 (cr) Dan Weiner, Courtesy of Sandra Weiner; 602 (cl) UPI/Corbis-Bettmann; 603 (br) Matt Herron/Black Star; 603 (tl) John Lounois/Black Star; 604 (tl) Bob Fitch/Black Star; 604 (br) Diana Mara Henry; 606 (br) UPI/Corbis-Bettmann; 612–613 (bg) Ken Biggs/Tony Stone Images; 613 (r) Jon Ortner/Tony Stone Images; 613 (c) Joseph Pobereskin/Tony Stone Images.

REFERENCE

facing R1 Dennis Hallinan/FPG International; R1 (tl) Comstock; R1, (bl) Hartman-Dewit/Comstock; R2-R3 (b) Harcourt Brace & Company; R4 (t) P & F Communications; R7 (br) Weronica Ankarorn; R9 (br) Harcourt Brace & Company; R16 Row 1, (l) National Portrait Gallery; (c) National Portrait Gallery; (r) Bettman; Row 2, (l) National Portrait Gallery; (c) National Portrait Gallery; (r) National Portrait Gallery; Row 3, (l) The Granger Collection, New York; (c) National Portrait Gallery; (r) National Portrait Gallery; Row 4, (l) National Portrait Gallery; (c) National Portrait Gallery; (r) The Granger Collection, New York; R17 Row 1, (l) The Granger Collection, New York; (c) Bettmann; (r) National Portrait Gallery; Row 2, (l) The New York Historical Society; (c) The Granger Collection, New York; (r) The Granger Collection, New York; Row 3, (l) National Portrait Gallery; (c) National Portrait Gallery; (r) National Portrait Gallery; Row 4, (l,c & r) Harcourt Brace & Company Row 5, (l) National Portrait Gallery; (c) The Granger Collection, New York; (r) The Bettmann Archive; R18 Row 1, (l) National Portrait Gallery; (c) National Portrait Gallery; (r) The Granger Collection, New York; Row 2, (l) The Granger Collection, New York; (c) The Granger Collection, New York; (r) National Portrait Gallery; Row 3, (l) Eisenhower Library; (c) The Granger Collection, New York; (r) Wide World Photos; Row 4, (l) The Granger Collection, New York; (c) National Portrait Gallery; (r) White House Historical Association; Row 5, (l) Wide World Photos; (c) David Valdez/The White House Historical Society; (r) The White House Historical Society.